BAPTISM ON ACCOUNT OF THE DEAD
(1 COR 15:29)

Society of Biblical Literature

Academia Biblica

Steven L. McKenzie,
Hebrew Bible/Old Testament Editor

Mark Allan Powell,
New Testament Editor

Number 22

BAPTISM ON ACCOUNT OF THE DEAD
(1 COR 15:29)
An Act of Faith in the Resurrection

BAPTISM ON ACCOUNT OF THE DEAD
(1 COR 15:29)
An Act of Faith in the Resurrection

Michael F. Hull

Society of Biblical Literature
Atlanta

BAPTISM ON ACCOUNT OF THE DEAD
(1 COR 15:29)
An Act of Faith in the Resurrection

Copyright © 2005 by the Society of Biblical Literature

All rights reserved. No part of this work may be reproduced or transmitted in any form or by any means, electronic or mechanical, including photocopying and recording, or by means of any information storage or retrieval system, except as may be expressly permitted by the 1976 Copyright Act or in writing from the publisher. Requests for permission should be addressed in writing to the Rights and Permissions Office, Society of Biblical Literature, 825 Houston Mill Road, Atlanta, GA 30329, USA.

Library of Congress Cataloging-in-Publication Data

Hull, Michael F.
  Baptism on account of the dead (1 Cor 15:29) : an act of faith in the resurrection / by Michael F. Hull.
    p. cm. — (Society of Biblical Literature Academia Biblica, ISSN 1570-1980 ; no. 22)
  Includes bibliographical references and index.
  ISBN-13: 978-1-58983-177-3 (alk. paper)
  ISBN-10: 1-58983-177-2 (alk. paper)
  1. Bible. N.T. Corinthians, 1st, XV, 29—Criticism, interpretation, etc. 2. Baptism for the dead—Biblical teaching. I. Title. II. Series : Academia Biblica (Series) (Brill Academic Publishers) ; no. 22.

BS2675.6.B36H85 2005
227'.206—dc22

                                                2005014694

Printed in the United States of America
on acid-free paper

Contents

Acknowledgements vii

Abbreviations and Sigla ix
   Primary Literature ix
   Secondary Literature x

Introduction 1

I. Contemporary Readings of 1 Corinthians 15:29 7

   Vicarious Baptism 10
      The Majority Reading 12
      The Majority Reading and Syncretism 17
   Ordinary Baptism 21
      Emendations and Variations of the Text 21
      Ordinary Baptism with Ὑπέρ in the Final Sense 29
      Ordinary Baptism with Ὑπέρ in the Causal Sense 31
   An Assessment of the Contemporary Readings 36
      A Scrutiny of the Readings 37
      The *Status Quæstionis* 47

II. Reading 1 Corinthians 15:29 in Literary Context 51

   The Genre and Integrity of 1 Corinthians 51
      The Genre of 1 Corinthians 52
      The Integrity of 1 Corinthians 71
   The Structure of 1 Corinthians 15 84
      1 Corinthians 15 84
      1 Corinthians 15:29–34 90
   The Morphology and Syntax of 1 Corinthians 15:29 95
      The Morphology of 1 Corinthians 15:29 95
      The Syntax of 1 Corinthians 15:29 102
   The Literary Context of 1 Corinthians 15:29 108

III. Reading 1 Corinthians 15:29 in Historical Context 113

    St. Paul the Apostle 114
        Pre-Christian Paul 118
        Christian Paul 137
        Paul and Readings of 1 Corinthians 15:29 148
    Greco-Roman Corinth 150
        The City of Corinth 150
        Ancient Religion in Corinth 156
        Ancient Corinth and Readings of 1 Corinthians 15:29 165
    Corinthian Christianity and Its Early Crises 168
        Factionalism (1 Corinthians 1–4) 172
        Ethical Issues (1 Corinthians 5–11) 183
        Spiritual Issues (1 Corinthians 12–14) 197
        The Resurrection of the Dead (1 Corinthians 15) 204
        Christian Corinth and Readings of 1 Corinthians 15:29 218
    The Historical Contex of 1 Corinthians 15:29 222

IV. Rereading 1 Corinthians 15:29 229

    A New Reading of 1 Corinthians 15:29 229
        Reading 1 Corinthians 15:29 Anew 230
        1 Corinthians 15:29 and the Resurrection of the Dead 236
    Baptism in the Theology of St. Paul 240
        Romans 6:1–14 241
        Galatians 3:26–29 244
        Baptism in the Pauline Literature 247
        1 Corinthians 15:29 and Baptism in St. Paul 250
    Baptism and Resurrection 255

Bibliography 257
    Primary Sources and Principal Reference Works 257
    Secondary Literature Consulted 260

Index of Biblical Literature 303
Index of Ancient Literature and Apocrypha 311
Index of Modern Authors 315
Index of Subjects 323

Acknowledgements

Baptism "on account of the Dead" (1 Cor 15:29): An Act of Faith in the Resurrection is a revised version of my doctoral dissertation by the same title, which I defended successfully at the Pontifical Gregorian University in December 2003.

During the long course of writing the dissertation and preparing it for publication, many persons were of help to me—too many, in fact, to mention here. Yet, I must single out those to whom I owe a special debt of gratitude.

I would like to thank the Archbishops of New York under whom I have had the privilege to serve: the late John Cardinal O'Connor, who assigned me to study in Rome and later appointed me a professor at St. Joseph's Seminary, Dunwoodie, N.Y.; and Edward Cardinal Egan, who had me continue teaching and, additionally, appointed me Dean of St. John Neumann Hall.

I would like to thank the Society of Jesus under whose auspices I received a superb graduate education at the Gregorian. In particular, I would like to thank the Reverend Professors Ugo Vanni, S.J., and Scott Brodeur, S.J. Father Vanni, despite a very hectic schedule, not only readily agreed to serve as mentor, but also allowed me considerable leeway in research and writing. His many kindnesses have been a considerable source of encouragement. Father Brodeur, ever available in Rome and Boston, brought this work to its conclusion by his personal support. I am deeply indebted to Scott for his attention to detail, diligent scholarship, and priestly example.

I would like to thank my brother priests at Dunwoodie and the Casa Santa Maria for their fraternity and scholarly example.

I would like to offer special thanks to Dr. Mary M. Bolan, M.D., who painstakingly read through all the drafts of this book. Mary's many corrections and expert advice on style and usage proved invaluable in bringing this work to press. In addition, Mary prepared each of the indices, a task of immense effort for which I am most appreciative. Any mistakes or oversights remain my own.

Finally, I would like to thank Dr. Mark Allan Powell, Ph.D., and the reviewers of the Society of Biblical Literature for accepting my work in the excellent Academia Biblica series.

Abbreviations and Sigla

Unless otherwise noted, all biblical citations are from the *Novum Testamentum Graece* (27th ed.; Stuttgart: Deutsche Bibelgesellschaft, 1993), the *Biblia Hebraica Stuttgartensia* (4th ed.; Stuttgart: Deutsche Bibelgesellschaft, 1990), the *Septuaginta* (2 vols. in 1; Stuttgart: Deutsche Bibelgesellschaft, 1979), and the Revised Standard Version of the Bible, 1973.

Abbreviations, sigla, and citation style follow the format of the "Instructions for Contributors" (*JBL* 107 [1988] 579–96). The following abbreviations and sigla are offered for the convenience of the reader.

PRIMARY LITERATURE

A.J.	Josephus, *Antiquities judaicae*
Abr.	Philo, *De Abrahamo*
Act. Jn.	*Acta Johannis*
Act. Paul. et Thec.	*Acta Pauli et Theclae*
Adv. haer.	Irenaeus, *Adversus haereses*
Adv. Marc.	Tertullian, *Adversus Marcionem*
Ant.	Plutarch, *Antonius*
Apoc. Paul.	*Apocalypsis Pauli*
Ars rhet.	Aristotle, *Ars rhetorica*
Att.	Cicero, *Epistulae ad Atticum*
B.J.	Josephus, *Bellum judaicum*
C. Ap.	Josephus, *Contra Apionem*
Claud.	Suetonius, *Divus Claudius*
Com. 1 Cor.	Ambrosiaster, *Commentarius in I ad Corinthios*
De chor.	Pomponius Mela, *De chorographia*
De doc. chr.	Augustine, *De doctrina christiana*
De res. carn.	Tertullian, *De resurrectione carnis*
Deipn.	Athenaeus, *Deipnnosophistae*
Descr.	Pausanias, *Graeciae description*
En. in Ps.	Augustine, *Enarrationes in Psalmos*
Ep. Phil.	Polycarp, *Epistola ad Phillippenses*
Ep. Tra.	Pliny the Younger, *Epistulae ad Trajanum*

Ep.	Horace, *Epistulae*
Fr. 1 Cor.	Origen, *Fragmenta ex commentariis in epistulam I ad Corinthios*
Fr.	Aristophanes, *Fragmenta*
Geogr.	Strabo, *Geographica*
Hist. adv. pag.	Orosius, *Historiae adversum paganos*
Hist. eccl.	Eusebius, *Historia ecclesiastica*
Hist. rom.	Appian, *Historia romana*
Hist. roma.	Dio Cassius, *Historia romana*
Hist.	Herodotus, *Historiae*
Hom. in 1 Cor.	John Chrysostom, *Homiliae in 1 ad Corinthios*
Il.	Homer, *Ilias*
In Matt. Hom.	Origen, *Homiliae in Matthaeum*
Inst.	Gaius, *Institutiones*
Leg. man.	Cicero, *Pro Lege manilia (De imperio Cn. Pompeii)*
Legat.	Philo, *Legatio ad Gaium*
Med.	Marcus Aurelius, *Meditationes*
Metam.	Apuleius, *Metamorphoses*
Mor.	Plutarch, *Moralia*
Od.	Homer, *Odyssea*
Opif.	Philo, *De opificio mundi*
Or.	Dio Chrysostom, *Orationes*
P. Oxy.	*Oxyrhynchus Papyri*
Pan.	Epiphanius, *Panarion (Adversus haereses)*
Pass. Perp. et Fel.	*Passio Perpetuae et Felicitatis*
Pomp.	Plutarch, *Pompeius*
Resp.	Plato, *Respublica*
Sim.	Shepherd of Hermas, *Similtudes*
Smyrn.	Ignatius of Antioch, *Epistula ad Smyrnaeos*
Strom.	Clement of Alexandria, *Stromata*
T. Meg.	*Tosefta Megillah*
Vir. ill.	Jerome, *De viris illustribus*
Vit. Apoll.	Philostratus, *Vita Apollonii*

SECONDARY LITERATURE

AASF	Annales Academiae scientiarum fennicae
AB	Anchor Bible
ABD	D. N. Freedman et al. (eds.), *The Anchor Bible Dictionary*
ABRL	Anchor Bible Reference Library
ACLSLHR	American Council of Learned Societies Lectures on the History of Religions
ACNT	Augsburg Commentaries on the New Testament
AGRL	Aspects of Greek and Roman Life
AJA	*American Journal of Archeology*
AnBib	Analecta biblica
AnGreg	Analecta gregoriana

ANRW	*Aufstieg und Niedergang der römischen Welt*
ANTF	Arbeiten zur neutestamentlichen Textforschung
ATANT	Abhandlungen zur Theologie des Alten und Neuen Testaments
ATJ	*Ashland Theological Journal*
AusBR	*Australian Biblical Review*
AW	The Ancient World
BA	*Biblical Archeologist*
BAGD	W. Bauer, W. F. Arndt, F. W. Gingrich, and F. W. Danker, *A Greek-English Lexicon of the New Testament and Other Early Christian Literature*
BAR	*Biblical Archeology Review*
BDF	F. Blass, A. Debrunner, and R. W. Funk, *A Greek Grammar of the New Testament and Other Early Christian Literature*
BETL	Bibliotheca ephemeridum theologicarum lovaniensium
Bib	*Biblica*
BJRL	*Bulletin of the John Rylands University Library of Manchester*
BJS	Brown Judaic Studies
BL	Bible and Literature
BLG	Biblical Languages: Greek
BNTC	Black's New Testament Commentaries
BolS	Bollingen Series
BR	*Biblical Research*
BS	Biblical Series
BSac	*Bibliotheca Sacra*
BSem	Biblical Seminar
BT	*Bible Translator*
BTB	*Biblical Theology Bulletin*
BWANT	Beiträge zur Wissenschaft vom Alten und Neuen Testament
BZ	*Biblische Zeitschrift*
BZNW	Beihefte zur Zeitschrift für die neutestamentliche Wissenshaft
CB	Clarendon Bible
CBET	Contributions to Biblical Exegesis and Theology
CBNTS	Coniectanea Biblica—New Testament Series
CBQ	*Catholic Biblical Quarterly*
CCC	*Catechism of the Catholic Church*
CCC	Crossway Classic Commentaries
CFTL	Clark's Foreign Theological Library
CGTSC	Cambridge Greek Testament for Schools and Colleges
CivC	*La Civiltà Cattolica*
CNT	Commentaire du Nouveau Testament
Con	Concilium
CSHJ	Chicago Studies in the History of Judaism
CSJLCS	Critical Studies in Jewish Literature, Culture, and Society
CToday	*Christianity Today*
DACL	F. Cabrol and H. Leclercq (eds.), *Dictionnaire d'archéologie chrétienne et de liturgie*
DRev	*Downside Review*

DS	H. Denzinger and A. Schönmetzer, *Enchiridion symbolorum: Definitionum et declarationum de rebus fidei et morum*
DunRev	*Dunwoodie Review*
EBib	Études biblique
EC	Epworth Commentaries
ED	*Euntes docente*
EDNT	H. Balz and G. Schneider (eds.), *Exegetical Dictionary of the New Testament*
EGT	Expositor's Greek Testament
ESEC	Emory Studies in Early Christianity
ETL	*Ephemerides theologicae lovanienses*
EV	Évangile et vie
EvQ	*Evangelical Quarterly*
EWNT	H. Balz and G. Schneider (eds.), *Exegetisches Wörterbuch zum Neuen Testament*
ExpTim	*Expository Times*
FFNT	Foundations and Facets, New Testament
FRC	The Family, Religion, and Culture
FRLANT	Forschungen zur Religion und Literatur des Alten und Neuen Testaments
GBS	Guides to Biblical Scholarship
GBSNTS	Guides to Biblical Scholarship—New Testament Series
GGNT	A. T. Robertson, *A Grammar of the Greek New Testament in the Light of Historical Research.*
GNS	Good News Studies
GNT^4	Aland, B., K. Aland, M. Black, J. Karavidopoulos, C. M. Martini, and B. M. Metzger (eds.), *The Greek New Testament*
Greg	*Gregorianum*
GTA	Göttinger theologischer Arbeiten
GTJ	*Grace Theological Journal*
HCS	Hellenistic Culture and Society
HNTC	Harper's New Testament Commentaries
HTR	*Harvard Theological Review*
HTS	Harvard Theological Studies
HUT	Hermeneutische Untersuchungen zur Theologie
IBO	Interpretare la Bibbia oggi
IBS	*Irish Biblical Studies*
IBT	Interpreting Biblical Texts
ICC	International Critical Commentary
IDB	G. A. Buttrick (ed.), *Interpreter's Dictionary of the Bible*
IDBSup	Supplementary Volume to *IDB*
IE	*Improvement Era*
Int	*Interpretation*
JAAR	*Journal of the American Academy of Religion*
JAARSup	*Journal of the American Academy of Religion Supplement*
JBC	R. E. Brown, J. A. Fitzmyer, and R. E. Murphy (eds.), *The Jerome Biblical Commentary*

JBL	*Journal of Biblical Literature*
JRelS	*Journal of Religious Studies*
JRH	*Journal of Religious History*
JSJ	*Journal for the Study of Judaism*
JSJSup	Journal for the Study of Judaism, Supplements
JSNT	*Journal for the Study of the New Testament*
JSNTSup	Journal for the Study of the New Testament—Supplement Series
JTS	*Journal of Theological Studies*
KTAH	Key Themes in Ancient History
LCD	Lutherans and Catholics in Dialogue
LEC	Library of Early Christianity
LPGL	G. W. H. Lampe (ed.), *Patristic Greek Lexicon*
LPS	Library of Pauline Studies
LS	*Louvain Studies*
LSJ	Liddell-Scott-Jones, *Greek-English Lexicon*
MeyerK	H. A. W. Meyer (ed.), *Kritisch-exegetischer Kommentar über das Neue Testament*
MFC	Message of the Fathers of the Church
MH	Magic in History
MKA	Monographien zur klassischen Altertumswissenschaft
MNTC	Moffatt New Testament Commentary
MNTS	McMaster New Testament Studies
MTS	Münchener theologische Studien
N-A^{27}	Nestle, E., B. and K. Aland, J. Karavidopoulos, C. M. Martini, and B. M. Metzger (eds.), *Novum Testamentum Graece*
NCBC	New Century Bible Commentary
Neot	*Neotestamentica*
NFTL	New Foundations Theological Library
NICNT	New International Commentary on the New Testament
NIDNTT	C. Brown (ed.) *New International Dictionary of New Testament Theology*
NIGTC	New International Greek Testament Commentary
NJBC	R. E. Brown, J. A. Fitzmyer, and R. E. Murphy (eds.), *The New Jerome Biblical Commentary*
NovT	*Novum Testamentum*
NovTSup	Novum Testamentum, Supplements
NTAbh	Neutestamentliche Abhandlungen
NTC	New Testament Commentary
NTG	New Testament Guides
NTL	New Testament Library
NTM	New Testament Message
NTOA	Novum Testamentum et Orbis Antiquus
NTS	*New Testament Studies*
NTSR	New Testament for Spiritual Reading
NTT	New Testament Theology
OBS	Oxford Bible Series

OCD	N. G. L. Hammond and H. H. Scullard (eds.), *The Oxford Classical Dictionary*
OCT	Outstanding Christian Thinkers
OSHT	Oxford Studies in Historical Theology
PC	Proclamation Commentaries
PG	J.-P. Minge (ed.), *Patrologia graeca*
PHC	*Problèmes d'histoire du christianisme*
PL	J.-P. Minge (ed.), *Patrologia latina*
PP	*Priests and People*
PRSt	*Perspectives in Religious Studies*
PTMS	Pittsburgh Theological Monograph Series
QJS	*Quarterly Journal of Speech*
RB	*Revue biblique*
RelSRev	*Religious Studies Review*
RevExp	*Review and Expositor*
RFCC	Religion in the First Christian Centuries
RHAW	Routledge History of the Ancient World
RLC	Roman Literature and Its Contexts
RSB	*Religious Studies Bulletin*
SacPag	Sacra Pagina Series
SAE	Southern Academic Editions
SBLDS	Society of Biblical Literature Dissertation Series
SBLRBS	Society of Biblical Literature Resources for Biblical Study
SBLSBS	Society of Biblical Literature Sources for Biblical Study
SBLSP	*Society of Biblical Literature Seminar Papers*
SBT	Studies in Biblical Theology
ScEs	*Science et esprit*
ScrC	*Scripture in Church*
SD	Studies and Documents
SJLA	Studies in Judaism in Late Antiquity
SJT	*Scottish Journal of Theology*
SMB	Série Mongraphique de "Benedictina"
SNTSMS	Society for New Testament Studies Monograph Series
SNTW	Studies of the New Testament and Its World
SPIB	Scripta Pontificii Instituti Biblici
SPNT	Studies on Personalities of the New Testament
SpT	*Spirituality Today*
SOC	Scritti delle origini cristiane
SR	Studies in Religion
StCl	Studies in Classics
StLit	*Studia Liturgica*
StPB	Studia post-Biblica
SWE	Scripture for Worship and Education
TBST	The Bible Speaks Today
TBT	*The Bible Today*
TCGNT	B. M. Metzger, *Textual Commentary on the Greek NewTestament*

TDNT	G. Kittel and G. Friedrich (eds.), *Theological Dictionary of the New Testament*
TDOT	G. J. Botterweck and H. Ringgren (eds.), *Theological Dictionary of the Old Testament*
TGST	Tesi Gregoriana—Serie teologia
ThH	Théologie historique
TNTC	Tyndale New Testament Commentaries
TS	*Theological Studies*
TSK	*Theologische Studien und Kritiken*
TST	Toronto Studies in Theology
TU	Texte und Untersuchungen
TWAT	G. J. Botterweck and H. Ringgren (eds.), *Theologisches Wörterbuch zum Alten Testament*
TWNT	G. Kittel and G. Friedrich (eds.), *Theologisches Wörterbuch zum Neuen Testament*
TynBul	*Tyndale Bulletin*
TZ	*Theologische Zeitschrift*
TZT	*Tübingen Zeitschrift für Theologie*
VC	*Vigiliae christianae*
VoxT	*Vox theological*
WBC	Word Biblical Commentary
WC	Westminster Commentaries
WJT	*Westminster Theological Journal*
WUNT	Wissenschaftliche Untersuchungen zum Neuen Testament
ZM	*Zeitschrift für Mission*
ZNW	Zeitschrift für die neutestamentliche Wissenschaft

Introduction

"What do you ask of God's Church?" "Eternal life." So begins the Catholic baptismal rite. From the earliest days of the Church, baptism has been inextricably linked with eternal life, with resurrection from death to new life. Baptism has everything to do with eternal life. Were it not for faith in the Lord's promise thereof, baptism (and the New Testament itself) should be accounted as nothing more than the heirloom of an ancient Jewish sectarian movement. Yet, the aforementioned quotation is recited daily throughout the world as countless numbers of men and women assert their faith in Jesus Christ and his promise to raise them up on the last day (John 6:40). It is fitting that Christians would be unremittingly interested in any reference to baptism in their nascent Church and Sacred Scripture, for such is the nature of the *fides quærens intellectum*. One such reference is the object of this study: St. Paul's mention of baptism "on account of the dead." In 1 Cor 15:29, Paul asks: "Otherwise what are they to do, who have themselves baptized on account of the dead? If the dead are not really raised, why are they baptized on account of them?"[1]

1 Cor 15:29 has received a vast amount of attention from Christian scholars for two predominant reasons. First, 1 Cor 15:29 is a *crux interpretum*. 1 Corinthians is the earliest letter of Paul to mention baptism, and baptism is more frequently mentioned in 1 Corinthians than in any other of Paul's letters. By any and all accounts, 1 Cor 15:29 is a strange turn of phrase. At first glance, one could read it to mean that vicarious baptism had been practiced, at least at some point in time, by Corinthian Christians. But, also at first glance, one could read it as a reference, albeit an extraordinary one, to ordinary baptism, even if Paul's point in mentioning it is unclear. While all Christians acknowledge the importance of baptism, there is much division among them as to what precisely baptism is or represents. If 1 Cor 15:29 has something to say about baptism— and all Christians believe that it certainly does—then its interpretation is critical. Still and all, there is little consensus as to what it means. Second, the Church of Jesus Christ of Latter-Day Saints (Mormons) practice ordinary baptism *and* vicarious (or proxy) baptism. In the practice of vicarious baptism, Mormons

---

[1] This is our own translation of 1 Cor 15:29: Ἐπεὶ τί ποιήσουσιν οἱ βαπτιζόμενοι ὑπὲρ τῶν νεκρῶν; εἰ ὅλως νεκροὶ οὐκ ἐγείρονται, τί καὶ βαπτίζονται ὑπὲρ αὐτῶν; [?]

stand alone.² As we shall see, the (non-Mormon) biblical scholars,³ who concede that some form of vicarious baptism was practiced in first-century Corinth, believe that such a practice was at best an anomaly and at worst an aberration. Hence, what 1 Cor 15:29 has to say about vicarious baptism, if anything at all, is of momentous importance to Christians and Mormons in their common deliberations.

As a *crux interpretum*, 1 Cor 15:29 remains one of the most contested and controversial verses in the NT. Since its earliest extant interpretation by Tertullian until the present day, it has confounded exegetes; and the proliferation of learned articles—past and present—manifest the ongoing interest in and importance of this verse. Despite the multitude of readings presented throughout the centuries, none has achieved anything even resembling a consensus. No *apologia* need be made for offering yet another reading of this verse. Thus, our study aspires to enter the fray of scholarly debate and offer another reading. Such a reading, it is hoped, will advance our understanding of 1 Corinthians, Paul, and the sacrament of baptism.

In addition, it is hoped that our study will serve in some small way as an aid to ecumenical dialogue among Catholics, Protestants, and Mormons. The Mormon theology of baptism is one of the more exacerbating of contemporary concerns between Mormons and other Christians. On the one hand, Catholics question the validity of ordinary Mormon baptism because of the Catholic understanding of the nature of the Trinity.⁴ Catholics have rejected vicarious baptism as an heretical practice since the second century A.D. On the other hand, Protestants are vehemently opposed to vicarious baptism because of the radical efficaciousness it betokens for baptism in general. Yet for Mormons, vicarious baptism is a revealed and charitable practice. According to the revelations given to Joseph Smith, Mormons hold that Christ continues to offer salvation to the

---

[2] It is beyond the pale of this study to consider the Mormon rationale for vicarious baptism. Suffice it to say that Mormons extend God's scriptural revelation beyond the Bible to include *The Book of Mormon* (1830) and *The Book of Doctrine and Covenants* (1935). Proxy baptism (for the dead) is not mentioned in the former, but it is found in the latter (sections 107:10–12; 109:57; and 110:1, 12, 16, 17, 18), wherein 1 Cor 15:29 is specifically invoked as a biblical example. For a succinct introduction to Mormon theology, see S. M. McMurrin, *The Theological Foundations of the Mormon Religion* (1965; rpt. Salt Lake City: University of Utah Press, 1977); for a succinct introduction to Mormon history, see J. Shipps, *Mormonism: The Story of a New Religious Tradition* (Urbana and Chicago: University of Illinois Press, 1985); and for terms and definitions, see D. H. Ludlow, ed. *Encyclopedia of Mormonism* (5 vols.; New York: Macmillan, 1992).

[3] It is also beyond the pale of this study to consider the Mormon biblical scholarship, since Mormons profess belief in revealed texts other than the Bible. See P. L. Barlow, "The Mormon Response to Higher Criticism" (chap. 4), in *Mormons and the Bible: The Place of the Latter-Day Saints in American Religion* (Oxford: Oxford University Press, 1991) 103–47.

[4] See, e.g., P. M. Brankin, "Are Mormons Christians?" *Extension* 82 (March-April) 1988; the editorial "I mormoni chi sono? In che cosa credono?" *CivC* 3 (July 16, 1994) 107–20; and O. F. Cummings, "Is Mormon Baptism Valid?" *Worship* 71 (1997) 146–53.

dead.[5] And, although they believe that the practice of vicarious baptism is warranted by the latter-day revelations to Smith, they look to the Bible for support. If baptism is necessary for salvation (John 3:3–5), God desires that all be saved (1 Tim 2:4), and Christ preaches to the dead (1 Pet 3:18–30; 4:6), then there must be some means by which the dead, who no longer have bodies to be baptized, can receive the necessary baptism, i.e., vicarious baptism. Pious Mormons have themselves baptized again and again as proxies for those dead in need of baptismal unction, to help those who cannot help themselves, as they claim the Corinthian Christians once did. To be sure, the confessional differences of Catholics, Protestants, and Mormons extend well beyond baptism (ordinary or vicarious) and 1 Cor 15:29. Thus, should our interpretation of the verse fail to gain acceptance, we hope that our efforts will at least demonstrate an intention to explore honestly and openly the common conundrum of 1 Cor 15:29 and, thereby, to succor our mutual understanding.

What have we to say about 1 Cor 15:29? Our thesis is simple: 1 Cor 15:29 is a dual rhetorical question in which Paul holds up one group within the Corinthian community as a laudable example for the entire community. The βαπτιζόμενοι are those who are undergoing the rite of baptism. Their motivation for so doing is their steadfast faith in the resurrection of Christ and, concomitantly, of Christians. They believe that the νεκροί are to be raised as Christ has been raised. They undergo the rite of baptism "on account of the dead"—on account of the fact that the dead are destined for life, having died hoping in the Lord's promise of salvation—on account of their faith in the fact that "if there is no resurrection from the dead, then Christ has not been raised" (1 Cor 15:13). By committing themselves to baptism, the βαπτιζόμενοι shame the arrogance and ignorance of those among the Corinthians who deny the resurrection (1 Cor 15:12). The example of the βαπτιζόμενοι, along with that of Paul himself (1 Cor 15:30–32), serves as a source of edification for the entire community. 1 Cor 15:29–32 is the crown of chapter 15 in terms of the personal examples given by Paul. After his long theoretical defense of the resurrection in 1 Cor 15:1–28, Paul is able to turn to two practical examples: the βαπτιζόμενοι and himself. Therewith, he is able to warn the Corinthians that they should not be deceived, to tell them that he defends the resurrection to their shame (1 Cor 15:33–34), and to continue his defensive discourse by explaining how, in fact, the dead are raised (1 Cor 15:35–58).

In order to defend this thesis, our study proceeds in four chapters. In Chapter I, the readings of 1 Cor 15:29 in contemporary biblical scholarship are summarily presented. An exposition of these various and sundry interpretations is deemed essential to their assessment. Consequently, we first elucidate the contemporary readings. Thereupon, we are suitably prepared to undertake their assessment, to scrutinize and appraise them by means of comparison and con-

---

[5] See *Doctrine and Covenants*, 138.

trast. In so doing, we are able to establish the parameters of the *status quæstionis* of 1 Cor 15:29 and contrive our findings in such a fashion that the *status quæstionis* itself might serve as the framework for a rereading of the verse. Therefore, Chapter I concludes in its appraisal of the contemporary readings that a reexamination of the verse's literary and historical contexts is requisite, if the baptismal insight that Paul offered in 1 Cor 15:29 to his first-century interlocutors—and offers to us today—is to be grasped.

Chapter II of our study outlines the literary context of 1 Cor 15:29. It closely examines the literary genre and integrity of 1 Corinthians in order to build a foundation for a close examination of 1 Corinthians 15 and, particularly, 1 Cor 15:29's place and function therein. After investigating the pertinent literary and structural issues surrounding 1 Corinthians and chapter 15 in particular, we address the function of 1 Cor 15:29 therein. Here, we perceive the importance of vv. 29–34, which lie dead center between the *cruces* of chapter 15, viz., that the dead are raised (vv. 12–28) and how the dead are raised (vv. 35–58). This brings us to an extensive examination of the morphology and syntax of 1 Cor 15:29. The principal terms of the verse (and the most contested term, ὑπέρ) are assessed and examined anew. This leads to a survey of the verse's syntax. 1 Cor 15:29 is a question. Specifically, it is a rhetorical question. Like all questions, it seeks an answer; like all rhetorical questions, it bespeaks a statement. However, a close examination of the literary context reveals that the verse, when taken alone and out of any historical context, may be read as a reference to ordinary or vicarious baptism. Therefore, this chapter prepares us, albeit only partially, for the new reading of 1 Cor 15:29 to be found in Chapter IV, a reading that is only possible after passing through the crucible of the Corinthian historical context.

Chapter III looks to the historical context that surrounds 1 Cor 15:29—to Paul, Corinth, and Corinthian Christianity. While another reference to ordinary baptism in 1 Corinthians presents certain challenges to Pauline baptismal theology, a reading of vicarious baptism is a total departure from Paul's baptismal norms. Vicarious baptism, without precedent in the NT or the early Church, cannot be claimed as a workable reading of 1 Cor 15:29 on the basis of the literary context alone; there must be some historical underpinning. Chapter III, our longest chapter, proceeds along a *via negativa*. In vain we search for "a needle in the haystack," i.e., for the vicarious baptism that so many commentators claim to find—even as an anomaly or abberation—in 1 Corinthians. During the mid-30s, Saul of Tarsus encountered the risen Jesus on the road to Damascus, and his life changed radically. Years later, Paul the Apostle preached that same Christ to the people of Corinth. Corinth, an originally Greek city, populated as early as the fifth millennium B.C., prospered as a trade city until its destruction by Metellus and Lucius Mummius in 146 B.C. However, the strategically located city would not lay dormant for long. History attributes the establishment of a Roman colony—Roman in government, but not necessarily in culture or religion, for its new settlers were mostly freed slaves from a plethora of backgrounds—to Julius Caesar ca. 44 B.C. Corinth was a crossroads in the Roman empire. It was within this multicultural and multicreedal society that Paul converted many to Christ. There he established a "church of God" (1 Cor 1:2) within a particular and peculiar sliver of Greco-Roman society, which eventually underwent a number of crises in faith, at least in Paul's estimation. This chapter looks to those crises within the Corinthian community. While their exact nature may never be known with certitude, it is possible to glean from the Corinthian correspondence what Paul perceived them to be. Although he addresses a number of crises (e.g., 1 Corinthians 1, 5, and 7–14), the most important, and the one to which Paul lends more attention than any other, is the crisis of faith in the resurrection of the dead (1 Corinthians 15). Some among the Corinthians denied the resurrection. Paul made it his business in 1 Corinthians 15 to prove them wrong. Herein, we test the text of 1 Cor 15:29, and we seek to see how it fits, not merely cogently as a rhetorical question in 1 Cor 15:29–34, but as a crucial link in Paul's lengthy demonstration on behalf of the resurrection's reality in chapter 15, which would have made sense to Christian converts in first-century Greco-Roman Corinth. We conclude that vicarious baptism is *not* a viable option for interpreting 1 Cor 15:29. Without any semblance of precedence in Paul, Greco-Roman Corinth, or Corinthian Christianity, reading 1 Cor 15:29 as a reference to vicarious baptism is unfeasible.

At this point, the stage is set for a rereading of 1 Cor 15:29. With the literary and historical contexts established, Chapter IV presents that rereading. In our rereading, we see that 1 Cor 15:29 is a reference to ordinary baptism, extraordinary circumstances notwithstanding. Baptism "on account of the dead" is baptism into eternal life; it is a rite for the living, and undergoing it expresses faith in the resurrection of Christ and of Christians. 1 Cor 15:29 has a distinct place within 1 Corinthians and particular poignancy for the Corinthian community. When 1 Cor 15:29 is read as we maintain it ought to be read, significant baptismal insights and theological implications arise. 1 Cor 15:29 is illustrative of baptism as Paul understood it. For Paul, baptism is the means by which one is incorporated into Christ and into his Church. The importance of baptism and the importance of Paul's understanding thereof cannot be overstated. Paul believed that submission to the baptismal rite was *the* act of faith in the resurrection of Jesus Christ and of his dead by which one secured the opportunity for eternal life. Therefore, in an atmosphere of denial of resurrection, to accept baptism "on account of the dead," that is, with a faith in the resurrection of once baptized and now dead Christians, is, to say the least, laudable in Paul's estimation. Without the resurrection, his and their faith is in vain (1 Cor 15:12–14) and his struggles useless (1 Cor 15:30–34). Finally, a right reading of 1 Cor 15:29 compels us to rethink Paul's baptism, to challenge some of the established thinking and to offer prospects for future consideration. In the sacrament of baptism, we are buried into Christ's death so that we might share in his resurrection (Rom 6:4), and baptism "on account of the dead" is a testimony to that sacrament as a sign and seal of faith in Christ's promise and the Apostle's preaching of everlasting life. "For the trumpet shall sound, and the dead shall be raised incorruptible, and we shall be changed" (1 Cor 15:52).

I. Contemporary Readings of 1 Corinthians 15:29

The oblique reference to baptism in 1 Cor 15:29 has piqued Christian curiosity for centuries.[1] Given the significance of baptism in the Church, any reference thereto in Sacred Scripture is certainly noteworthy; the importance of baptism among Christians needs no explanation. Unfortunately, Christians are divided in their understanding as to the precise nature of baptism and its effects, and they use the term "baptism" to mean different things. To be sure, it is outside the pale of our study to probe the debate among Christians as to the precise nature of baptism, especially since there are as many variations on the theme as there are Christian denominations. For the sake of clarity and consistency, one definition of the term must be operative throughout our work. In our study, "baptism" is used in its classical Roman Catholic sacramental sense. The sacrament of baptism is an efficacious rite, "for it signifies and actually brings about the birth of water and the Spirit without which no one 'can enter the kingdom of God' (Titus 3:5; John 3:5)."[2] Initiation and incorporation into Christ and into the Church take place at the rite itself, along with the cleansing from original sin and the gift of the Holy Spirit. That is, baptism effects what it signifies. As such, our use of the term is at odds with the classical Protestant understanding wherein baptism is a sign or recognition of something already accomplished. In such an understanding, a person becomes a "Christian" by means of an act of faith within the heart concomitant with the acceptance of the gospel. Thus, a rite of baptism is merely the symbolic act of a reality already present. Christians, then, undergo the rite of baptism as an external manifestation of an internal conversion. However, in the Catholic position, a person is not a "Christian" until he or she has undergone the normative baptismal rite.[3] The differences of understanding among Christians about the nature of baptism and the ferocity with which Christians hold to their particular positions illustrate a common ecumenical theme: the momentous importance of baptism to all Christians.

---

[1] Hereafter, 1 Cor 15:29 is simply "15:29."

[2] *CCC*, no. 1215.

[3] The normative baptismal rite is, of course, immersion in water and the Trinitarian formula. Exceptions to the rite, viz., the baptisms of desire and of blood, are just that—exceptions—wherein the effects of the baptismal rite are conferred without the rite itself because of extraordinary circumstances.

This momentous importance lends urgency to the task of seeking to understand the nature of the baptism referred to in 15:29. Without doubt, a reference to baptism in one of Christianity's earliest letters and canonical texts, 1 Corinthians, by one of Christianity's earliest authors and apologists, Paul of Tarsus, is of monumental significance.[4] It comes as no surprise that throughout the centuries over forty readings have been offered to explain 15:29. A glance at the commentaries on 1 Corinthians shows that it is not uncommon for some exegetes to speak of two hundred readings or more, but a careful examination of the many readings they delineate reveals that, minor variations notwithstanding, there are really about forty general hypotheses.[5] In contemporary biblical studies, this reflects an enormous variation in exegetical opinion. Despite the surfeit of alternatives, no single reading of 15:29 has yet marshaled scholarly consensus. In fact many scholars, even after considering an array of alternatives and expressing their dissatisfaction therewith, simply shake their heads in frustration and admit ignorance as to how 15:29 ought to be read.[6]

The forty or so general readings of 15:29 and the legion of slight variations thereupon have themselves become an object of study. The most impressive efforts to systematize the various hypotheses rendered to explain this somewhat vexing verse are Bernard M. Foschini's *"Those Who Are Baptized for the Dead" I Cor. 15:29: An Exegetical Historical Dissertation* and Mathis Rissi's

---

[4] We accept the prevailing scholarly opinion that only seven of the thirteen letters in the NT attributed to Paul were composed by the Apostle himself (Romans, 1 and 2 Corinthians, Galatians, Philippians, 1 Thessalonians, and Philemon) and that the other six letters attributed to him (Ephesians, Colossians, 2 Thessalonians, 1 and 2 Timothy, and Titus) are most likely the products of his disciples, of a "Pauline school." In this study, we refer to the former as the "Pauline letters" and to the latter as the "Pauline pseudepigrapha." When spoken of collectively, we refer to the Pauline letters and the Pauline pseudepigrapha as the "Pauline literature."

[5] Cf. H. Conzelmann, *1 Corinthians: A Commentary on the First Epistle to the Corinthians* (trans. J. W. Leitch; Hermeneia; Philadelphia: Fortress, 1975) 276 n. 120; and K. C. Thompson, "I Corinthians 15, 29 and Baptism for the Dead," in *Studia Evangelica* (ed. F. L. Cross; TU 87; Berlin: Akademie Verlag, 1964) 2.1:647 n. 2.

[6] For example, W. G. Simon: "We have no clue to the meaning of this obscure and difficult verse" (*The First Epistle to the Corinthians* [London: SCM, 1959] 147); W. A. Meeks: "What *are* they doing [in 15:29]? The Corinthians presumably knew, but we do not, despite interesting speculations without end" (*The First Urban Christians: The Social World of the Apostle Paul* [New Haven and London: Yale University Press, 1983] 162); G. D. Fee: "The best one can do in terms of particulars is to point out what appear to be the more viable options, but finally to admit ignorance" (*The First Epistle to the Corinthians* [NICNT; Grand Rapids, MI: Eerdmans, 1987] 763); S. J. Kistemaker: "In all humility I confess that the sense of this text escapes me; verse 29 remains a mystery" (*I Corinthians* [NTC; Grand Rapids, MI: Baker, 1993] 560); R. P. Carlson: "Despite dozens of proposed solutions, the reference itself is simply so obscure and our knowledge so limited that we cannot discern just what this rite actually involved or meant" ("The Role of Baptism in Paul's Thought," *Int* 47 [1993] 261); and C. Hodge: "The darkness that rests on this passage can never be entirely cleared away, because the reference is to a custom of which no account is extant" (*1 Corinthians* [CCC; Wheaton, IL: Good News {Crossway}, 1995] 293).

Die Taufe für die Toten: Ein Beitrag zur paulinischen Tauflehre.[7] Their respective accounts of the verse's interpretation and criticisms thereof are invaluable. Both accounts are startling in their demonstrations of the disparate readings held by scholars and commentators. And both accounts lend some credence to J. Daniel Joyce's wry observation that, given the multiplicity of interpretations for 15:29, "no one could catalogue them in their entirety,"[8] for both Foschini and Rissi go to great pains to sort through all of the readings. Rarely in the history of biblical interpretation has a single verse elicited so much attention and so little concert. Nevertheless, there remains an abiding interest in the verse on account of its locus in 1 Corinthians, and new interpretations continue to appear in scholarly journals.[9] That 1 Corinthians 15 is a key both to understanding 1 Corinthians and, consequently, Paul's theorization of the resurrection is sure. Richard E. DeMaris sums it up best:

> Modern biblical scholarship has paid considerable attention to baptism for the dead not because of its own merits but because of how and where Paul made use of it. It is no overstatement to say that Paul's understanding of the resurrection was central to his theology, that chapter 15 of 1 Corinthians is key to interpreting the entire letter, and that 1 Corinthians has been crucial for NT scholarship's reconstruction of what the earliest Christian communities were like. Consequently, Paul's inclusion of baptism for the dead among his arguments for the resurrection in 1 Corinthians 15 has elevated the practice to prominence.[10]

Hence, Paul's allusion to "baptism on account of the dead" in 15:29 compels our attention.

We commence our investigation by looking to recent renderings of 15:29. However, our study does not proffer a history of the verse's interpretation, as that task has been admirably accomplished by Foschini and Rissi. In 1962, just prior to the publication of Rissi's *Die Taufe für die Toten*, George R. Beasley-

---

[7] B. M. Foschini, *"Those Who Are Baptized for the Dead" 1 Cor. 15:29: An Exegetical Historical Dissertation* (Worchester, MA: Heffernan, 1951); and M. Rissi, *Die Taufe für die Toten: Ein Beitrag zur paulinischen Tauflehre* (ATANT 42; Zurich: Zwingli, 1962). Note that Foschini's work appears in two other forms: "'Those Who Are Baptized for the Dead' 1 Cor. 15:29: An Exegetical Historical Dissertation" (S.T.D. diss., Pontificium Athenaeum Antonianum, 1948) and a series of five articles under the same title in the *CBQ* 12 (1950) 260–76, 379–88 and 13 (1951) 46–78, 172–98, 276–83. Citations in our study are taken from the book.

[8] J. D. Joyce, "Baptism on behalf of the Dead: An Interpretation of I Corinthians 15:29–34," *Encounter* 26 (1965) 269.

[9] For example, J. D. Reaume, "Another Look at 1 Corinthians 15:29, 'Baptized for the Dead,'" *BSac* 152 (1995) 457–66; and J. R. White, "'Baptized on account of the Dead': The Meaning of 1 Corinthians 15:29 in Its Context," *JBL* 116 (1997) 488–92. Both provide admirably clear and brief summaries of the contemporary readings as well as interpretive proposals. In addition, though not an interpretation in the strict sense, is R. E. DeMaris, "Corinthian Religion and Baptism for the Dead (1 Corinthians 15:29): Insights from Archeology and Anthropology," *JBL* 114 (1995) 661–82.

[10] DeMaris, "Corinthian Religion and Baptism for the Dead," 677–78.

Murray, commenting on the diversity of readings for 15:29, said: "What kind of a publication would be required at this stage in history to collate the interpretations of the saying and pass a judgment on them may be left to the reader's imagination."[11] Rissi's work was certainly an attempt to fill the void noticed by Beasley-Murray, but like Foschini's efforts, no consensus was forthcoming. Another systematization of all the readings of the verse throughout the ages would most likely prove fruitless at this point in time. On the one hand, it would be a mere duplication, which scarcely could hope to supersede its predecessors; on the other hand, it would be forced to recount those numerous readings of 15:29 now obsolete. Nineteenth- and twentieth-century advances in biblical scholarship, classical studies, and archeology have made dozens of the verse's readings *passé*. In the twenty-first century, a far smaller number of readings vie for scholarly assent. Therefore, our study considers only those readings of 15:29 that are postulated or held in contemporary biblical literature. Even if they should prove to be of only minimal assistance in actually interpreting the verse,[12] they are the readings to be examined and assessed in order to delineate the parameters of the *status quæstionis* of 15:29 and clarify the steps necessary for a rereading of 15:29. As we see below in our examination of the contemporary readings of 15:29, scholarly opinions fall into one of two camps: vicarious or ordinary baptism.

Thus, we proceed under the headings of vicarious baptism and ordinary baptism in order to present the contemporary readings of 15:29 and summarize the salient issues and scholarly opinions therein. Then, we assess them in order to establish the *status quæstionis*, so that we might be prepared to read this troublesome verse anew.

VICARIOUS BAPTISM

With reference to our verse, the designation "vicarious baptism" is simple: living persons, whether previously baptized solely for themselves or baptized simultaneously for themselves and others, were baptized in the place of dead unbaptized persons. The *raison d'être* for this seemingly aberrant custom? To secure the (presumed) benefits of baptism for those who died without baptism. Since it is widely held that "none of the attempts to escape a theory of vicarious baptism in primitive Christianity seems to be wholly successful,"[13] the vast majority of exegetes and commentators hold that 15:29 is a reference to some

---

[11] G. R. Beasley-Murray, *Baptism in the New Testament* (Grand Rapids, MI: Eerdmans, 1962) 185.

[12] At the beginning of the last century, P. Dürselen ("'Die Taufe für die Toten': I Kor. 15,29," *TSK* {no vol.} [1903] 291–98) examined the history of 15:29's interpretation in the second century onward and found it to be of little help.

[13] H. Riesenfeld, "ὑπέρ," *TDNT* 8:512–13.

form of vicarious baptism[14]—even those who reject such a reading acknowledge its preponderance[15]—and it is aptly labeled the "majority reading." Because 15:29 "is one of the most difficult passages in the NT,"[16] anyone who holds to the majority reading is led to address the naturally ensuing questions: What of the paucity of historical attestation in Corinth and the early Church to vicarious

---

[14] For example, J. Weiss, *Der erste Korintherbrief* (MeyerK 5; Göttingen: Vandenhoeck and Ruprecht, 1910) 362–64; A. Carr, "Baptism for the Dead (1 Corinthians XV.19 [sic])," *Expositor* 9 (1901) 375; H. Preisker, "Die Vikariatstaufe I Cor 15:29—ein eschatologischer, nicht sakramentaler Brauch," *ZNW* 23 (1924) 298–99; R. St. J. Parry, *The First Epistle of Paul the Apostle to the Corinthians* (2nd ed.; CGTSC; Cambridge: Cambridge University Press, 1926) 228; F. Pratt, *The Theology of Saint Paul* (trans. J. L. Stoddard; 2 vols.; Westminster, MD: Newman Bookshop, 1927) 1.136–37; J. Moffatt, *The First Epistle to the Corinthians* (MNTC; London: Hodder and Stoughton, 1938) 252–53; R. Bultmann, *Theology of the New Testament* (trans. K. Grobel; 2 vols.; London: SCM, 1952–55) 1:135–36; H. V. Martin, "Baptism for the Dead," *ExpTim* 54 (1942–43) 192–93; E.-B. Allo, *Saint Paul: Première épître aux Corinthiens* (EBib; Paris: Gabalda, 1956) 410–11; Rissi, *Die Taufe für die Toten*, 57; G. Wagner, *Das religionsgeschichtliche Problem von Römer 6,1–11* (ATANT 39; Zurich: Zwingli, 1962) 284–85; Joyce, "Baptism on behalf of the Dead," 273; C. K. Barrett, *A Commentary on the First Epistle to the Corinthians* (2nd ed.; BNTC; London: A&C Black, 1971) 363–64; Conzelmann, *1 Corinthians*, 276–77; H. Ridderbos, *Paul: An Outline of His Theology* (trans. J. R. de Witt; Grand Rapids, MI: Eerdmans, 1975) 24–26, 411, 540; W. F. Orr and J. A. Walther, *I Corinthians* (AB 32; Garden City, NY: Doubleday, 1976) 754; C. Senft, *La première épître de saint-Paul aux Corinthiens* (CNT 7; Neuchâtel/Paris: Delachaux and Niestlé, 1979) 201; G. L. Borchet, "The Resurrection: 1 Corinthians 15," *RevExp* 80 (1983) 401–15; R. A. Harrisville, *I Corinthians* (ACNT; Minneapolis: Augsburg, 1987) 269; J. Downey, "1 Cor 15:29 and the Theology of Baptism," *ED* 38 (1985) 23; G. Sellin, *Der Streit um die Auferstehung der Toten: Eine religionsgeschichtliche und exegetische Untersuchung von 1. Korinther 15* (FRLANT 138; Göttingen: Vandenhoeck and Ruprecht, 1986) 279–84; B. Witherington III, *Conflict and Community in Corinth: A Socio-Rhetorical Commentary on 1 and 2 Corinthians* (Grand Rapids, MI: Eerdmans, 1994) 294; G. Barbaglio, *La prima lettera ai Corinzi: Introduzione, versione, commento* (SOC 16; Bologna: Dohoniane, 1995) 832–33; DeMaris, "Corinthian Religion and Baptism for the Dead," 662; P. de Surgy and M. Carrez, *Les épîtres de Paul—1 Corinthiens: Commentaire pastoral* (EV; Paris: Bayard, 1996) 126; L. Hartman, *"Into the Name of the Lord Jesus": Baptism in the Early Church* (SNTW; Edinburgh: T&T Clark, 1997) 90–91; J. D. G. Dunn, *The Theology of Paul the Apostle* (Edinburgh: T&T Clark, 1998) 449; S. Agersnap, *Baptism and New Life: A Study of Romans 6.1–14* (trans. C. and F. Crowley; Aarhus, Den.: Aarhus University Press, 1999) 175–78; and R. F. Collins, *First Corinthians* (SacPag 7; Collegeville, MN: Liturgical [Glazier], 1999) 559. It is also the earlier opinion of R. Schnackenburg (*Das Heilsgeschehen bei der Taufe noch dem Apostel Paulus: Eine Studie zur paulinischen Theologie* [MTS 1; Munick: Zink, 1950] 90–92) who changed his position in favor of ordinary baptism in *Baptism in the Thought of St. Paul: A Study in Pauline Theology* (trans. G. R. Beasley-Murray; Oxford: Basil Blackwell, 1964) 95.

[15] For example, Foschini, *Baptized for the Dead*, 31–32; M. Raeder, "Vikariatstaufe in 1 Cor 15:29?" *ZNW* 46 (1955) 258; Schnackenburg, *Baptism in the Thought of St. Paul*, 95; J. C. O'Neill, "1 Corinthians 15:29," *ExpTim* 91 (1979) 310; J. Murphy-O'Connor, "'Baptized for the Dead' (I Cor., XV, 29): A Corinthian Slogan?" *RB* 88 (1981) 532; Fee, *First Corinthians*, 766; Kistemaker, *I Corinthians*, 560; Reaume, "Another Look at 1 Corinthians 15:29," 458; and A. C. Thiselton, *The First Epistle to the Corinthians: A Commentary on the Greek Text* (NIGTC; Grand Rapids, MI; Eerdmans, 2000) 1242–49.

[16] F. W. Grosheide, *Commentary on the First Epistle to the Corinthians* (NICNT; Grand Rapids, MI: Eerdmans, 1953) 371.

baptism? What of its seeming incongruence with Paul's (baptismal) theology? For the moment, we leave these questions and their varied answers aside in order to accentuate the reading of vicarious baptism as such. Although "no one has succeeded in giving an interpretation which is generally accepted,"[17] vicarious baptism is the theme upon which the vast majority of interpretations are variants. As we turn to the individual readings of those who subscribe to the majority reading, for the sake of clarity and brevity we also leave aside a consideration of the patristic readings of 15:29—mentioned by almost every commentator—and entertain such questions below in our assessment of the contemporary readings.

The Majority Reading

Readings of vicarious baptism are based on the plain sense of the verse's words: Ἐπεὶ τί ποιήσουσιν οἱ βαπτιζόμενοι ὑπὲρ τῶν νεκρῶν; εἰ ὅλως νεκροὶ οὐκ ἐγείρονται, τί καὶ βαπτίζονται ὑπὲρ αὐτῶν; [?] Arguments in support of a reading for vicarious baptism in 15:29 are legion. Reginald St. John Parry argues that vicarious baptism cannot be refuted, for to do so would be to refute "the plain and necessary sense of the words."[18] Søren Agersnap claims that "it cannot be denied that Paul is here speaking of vicarious baptism: one is baptized for the dead to ensure for them a share in the effect of baptism, and this must relate to a post-mortal life."[19] And Albrecht Oepke even goes so far as to suggest that any and all interpretations of 15:29 which circumvent a reading of vicarious baptism are misleading.[20] These opinions are representative of the tenacity of the majority reading in contemporary biblical scholarship. But how do they explain such a seemingly aberrant practice, even if it were anomalous? As we see below, the oddity of vicarious baptism elicits various and creative explanations. For the most part, those who hold for a reading of vicarious baptism presume that it was practiced either on behalf of deceased family members and friends or deceased "catechumens."[21] These specifications are not mutually inclusive among exegetes: opinions range from those who hold that deceased relatives or friends, who had no intention to be baptized, were baptized vicariously by their living relatives and friends, to those who hold that vicarious baptism was reserved to catechumens alone. Now, we turn to Arthur Carr, Herbert Preisker, James Moffatt, Mathis Rissi, C. K. Barrett, H. V. Martin, and a few others for specific examples of the majority reading.

---

[17] Ibid.

[18] Parry, *First Corinthians*, 228.

[19] Agersnap, *Baptism and the New Life*, 175.

[20] A. Oepke, "βάπτω, βαπτίζω, βαπτισμός, βάπτισμα, βαπτιστής," *TDNT* 1:542 n. 63. Beasley-Murray (*Baptism in the New Testament*, 187) is just one of the many who follow Oepke in this assertion.

[21] For the purposes of our study, the anachronistic term "catechumen" is used simply to describe one who intends to undergo the baptismal rite but has not yet done so.

Arthur Carr, writing at the beginning of the twentieth century, takes vicarious baptism for granted as the only way to read 15:29. Though Carr considers a few alternatives and dismisses them, his interest is not in explaining the origin or the practice of vicarious baptism. Carr wishes to explain what the practice meant to the Corinthians and Paul.[22] According to Carr, it is most likely that the earliest Christian community in Corinth was composed of Jews who awaited the consolation of Israel and "God-fearers."[23] Overjoyed that their hopes for a Messiah had been fulfilled in Jesus, believing that baptism was the means by which one was incorporated into the resurrection, and expecting the imminent return of the Messiah, these early Christians began to wonder about their friends, who would also have accepted baptism had they lived long enough to hear the gospel preached in Corinth. Given the limited means at their disposal, since they comprised a nascent community of limited theological means, they developed a practice of vicarious baptism.[24] Paul, who would have frowned on such a custom, did not condemn it because he wished to deal gently with his new converts. Paul's only reason for mentioning the practice of vicarious baptism in 15:29 was to show the incongruity within the community wherein some practice vicarious baptism, an indication of great (though exotic) faith in the resurrection, and others deny that same resurrection vis-à-vis 1 Cor 15:12. As time passed and the faith of the community matured, the absurdity of such a custom manifested itself to the Corinthian Christians, and vicarious baptism fell out of practice and memory.[25]

Cognizant of the possibility that some might read 15:29 to be an instance of "high sacramentalism" among the Corinthians (and even Paul), Herbert Preisker claims that 15:29 is not to be read in such a fashion; rather 15:29 should be read in terms of a heightened eschatological concern in Corinth, a concern that is especially indicated by 1 Cor 15:28.[26] Preisker maintains, basing his argument on various apocalyptic texts including 2 Esdr 4:35; Rev 7:4; *1 Enoch* 47:5; and Shepherd of Hermas, *Sim.* 6.5–6, that the Corinthians expected an imminent parousia to commence at the moment the number of the elect was filled. Preisker holds that the necessity of baptism for inclusion in the Christian community is a later development (e.g., Acts 18:23–28) from the original means of inclusion in the community: faith. Relatively early on, a slight corruption among the Corinthians baptismal understanding replaced faith as a means of entrance into the number of the elect with the baptismal rite. Since many early Christians remained and died unbaptized, Preisker sees 15:29 to be an attempt on the part of some Corinthians to fill the number of the elect, and therefore to hasten the

---

[22] Carr, "Baptism for the Dead," 371–74.
[23] But this categorization is tenuous; see T. M. Finn, "The God-Fearers Reconsidered," *CBQ* 47 (1985) 75–84.
[24] Carr, "Baptism for the Dead," 374–76.
[25] Ibid., 376–78.
[26] Preisker, "Die Vikariatstaufe I Cor 15:29," 299, 304.

parousia, while at the same time guaranteeing salvation for those deceased among their number who had died without the baptismal rite.[27] Even so, Preisker concludes that vicarious baptism is less the result of a baptismal misunderstanding (though it is certainly that too) than it is the result of an eschatological urgency.[28] Thus, for Preisker, vicarious baptism was merely a momentary aberration brought about by misconceptions in the early Church regarding the efficacy of baptism and the time of the parousia.

Unlike Preisker, James Moffatt holds the baptismal rite to be efficacious. Moffatt contends that the βαπτιζόμενοι of 15:29 are Christians, who were vicariously baptized on behalf of loved ones who were catechumens, who died before they received baptism. Without baptism, the catechumens had no hope of sharing in Christ's resurrection. Because the Corinthian Christians had an intense interest in the resurrection along the lines of 2 Macc 12:39–45, with a concept of solidarity among the Christian community as mentioned in 1 Cor 7:14, they inaugurated a practice of a baptism by proxy wherein "evidently some [Corinthian Christians] believed so firmly in the resurrection that they underwent a vicarious baptism for their dead who had not been more than catechumens before they died."[29] In other words, Moffatt sees a particular and peculiar form of the baptism of desire being acted out ritually for those catechumens who died before their expected baptismal initiation into the Christian community.[30]

A reading of 15:29 similar to that of Moffatt's is held by Mathis Rissi. But Rissi extends vicarious baptism beyond familial and friendly catechumens. Rissi sees the meaning of 15:29's Greek as self-evident: the living are baptized for the dead.[31] Because he, like Preisker, rejects the presence of any high sacramentalism in Corinth, he speculates that the only possible explanation for the vicarious baptism practiced in Corinth must be a rare existential anomaly, e.g., an epidemic or an accident, which occasioned an anomalous response: vicarious baptism. Hence, the emergence of this peculiarity was limited to special circumstances in Corinth. According to Rissi, vicarious baptism was not intended to

---

[27] Ibid., 301–2. Preisker's theory is supported by G. W. H. Lampe as "plausible," in regard to filling the number of the elect, though he doubts that baptism was ever an "'option extra'" (*The Seal of the Spirit: A Study in the Doctrine of Baptism and Confirmation in the New Testament and the Fathers* [2nd ed.; London: SPCK, 1967] 94). A. Schweitzer accepts the idea of vicarious baptism along Preisker's lines only if it is taken as a means by living Christians to assist their relatives on the basis of 1 Cor 7:14 (*Die Mystik des Apostels Paulus* [Tübingen: Mohr {Siebeck}, 1930] 276–78).

[28] Preisker, "Die Vikariatstaufe I Cor 15:29," 304.

[29] Moffatt, *First Corinthians*, 252–53, quotation 253. This is also the opinion of Pratt, *Theology of Saint Paul*, 1:136–37; and Senft, *La première épître aux Corinthiens*, 201.

[30] J. A. Trumbower (*Rescue for the Dead: The Posthumous Salvation of Non-Christians in Early Christianity* [Oxford: Oxford University Press, 2001] 36–37) adopts a position very similar to Moffatt's, although Trumbower does not mention Moffatt but largely follows Mathis Rissi (see below). For Trumbower, vicarious baptism was an efficacious rite, which "set a posthumous seal onto a faith that was already present in life" (36).

[31] Rissi, "Die Taufe für die Toten," 57.

produce any benefits for the living or the dead, and it effected nothing. The Corinthians (and Paul) understood it merely as an act of proclamation, i.e., an act demonstrative of their prior belief in the resurrection of particular dead persons. Paul mentions it in order to show the incongruity of those among the Corinthians who would deny the resurrection while suborning such a practice.[32] Again, like Carr and Preisker, Rissi sees vicarious baptism in Corinth as an odd curiosity based on a conflation of misconceptions mentioned by Paul only to clarify inexplicable inconsistencies in the Corinthian understanding of the resurrection.[33]

Following Rissi, C. K. Barrett also claims that 15:29 refers to those within the Corinthian community who died before a desire to be baptized was fulfilled. However, Barrett focuses on the use of the definite article in 15:29 (οἱ βαπτιζόμενοι) as the indication that Paul is referring to a particular group within the Corinthian community and not the whole of the community.[34] For Barrett, common sense and the temperament of Paul show that he could hardly have used a practice he disapproved of in defense of the resurrection, so he must have seen some benefit in the Corinthian practice. The sense of the verse is clear: the βαπτιζόμενοι were vicariously baptized for others who died before their anticipated baptism. Yet, those who were the supposed beneficiaries of the rite, i.e., those who had died before baptism, were already Christians through their faith and needful of nothing according to Barrett. Adamant in denying any efficacy to a baptismal rite (vicarious or otherwise), the only explanation for vicarious baptism at Corinth is that "baptism was a powerful proclamation of death and resurrection, and in this [highly sacramental] setting it is not impossible to conceive of a rite—practiced, it may be, only once—which Paul, though he evidently took no steps to establish it as normal Christian usage, need not actively have disapproved."[35] Thus, the meaning of the verse is clear only insofar as we recall that there is no efficacy to be attached to baptism and that Paul might have tacitly approved of any affirmation of the resurrection.

---

[32] Ibid., 89 et passim.

[33] Conzelmann (*1 Corinthians*, 277 with n. 123) follows Rissi's general reading in that Paul is attempting to show a discrepancy between action and belief in his defense of the resurrection. Yet, Conzelmann is reluctant to press a precise interpretation of 15:29, because he maintains that Paul is stringing together a number of somewhat unrelated arguments in vv. 29–34 to buttress his argument in 1 Corinthians 15. Note that, for Conzelmann, the custom of vicarious baptism *is* evidence of a high sacramentalism at Corinth, and it is this mistaken notion of sacramentalism that leads to problems like vicarious baptism (276–77). Likewise, Trumbower (*Rescue for the Dead*, 36–37 with n. 7) agrees with Rissi in that vicarious baptism, a practice of which Paul approved, was performed on behalf of those who died while preparing for ordinary baptism, especially given an hiatus between conversion and baptism vis-à-vis 1 Cor 1:14–17. However, Trumbower disagrees with Rissi on vicarious baptism's efficacy; Trumbower notes that "the participants probably thought the vicarious baptism effected a real change in the fate of the dead person, or else why carry it out?" (36 n. 7).

[34] Barrett, *First Corinthians*, 362.

[35] Ibid., 363–64, quotation 364.

A somewhat enigmatic reading of 15:29 is proffered by H. V. Martin. Martin maintains that 15:29 is an example of "kataleptic" baptism. With reference to Rom 6:4–5, he suggests that baptism in the apostolic age was viewed not so much as entrance into the Church as entrance into the kingdom of God. St. John the Baptist's baptism was a "proleptic" baptism, i.e., anticipatory entrance into the kingdom of God about to be proclaimed by the Messiah (cf. Mark 1:8; Acts 19:1–6). Thus, Martin asks, "If proleptic baptism is possible, then why not kataleptic baptism under the reverse circumstances?"[36] Citing 1 Cor 6:16 and 7:14 to demonstrate the spiritual unity of the family in Paul's mind, he maintains that the new believers were probably of the same mind and would naturally have been concerned about their deceased relatives who had never heard the gospel. In this, Martin's position is almost identical to Carr's (though Martin does not seem to be aware of Carr's work). Despite their common starting point (concern for those who did not hear the gospel), their notions of the Corinthian understanding of vicarious baptism are different in that Martin sees the principal effect of baptism as a means to resurrection rather than incorporation into the Church. Martin claims that living family members were baptized vicariously on behalf of departed ones in order to incorporate the latter into the kingdom of God and, therefore, into the resurrection. The factor of time, as with John's baptism, was secondary to the primary importance of membership in the kingdom. Such an interpretation of 15:29 elucidates why Paul would have used such a practice, a practice which he approved of, as an example in his defense of the resurrection in 1 Corinthians 15.[37]

Finally, there are numerous commentators who would permit a reading of vicarious baptism, but who shy away from any specific definition or explanation of the practice *per se*. For example, Archibald Robertson and Alfred Plummer consider 15:29 "a reference to some abnormal baptismal rite known to the Corinthians, which would be meaningless without a belief in the resurrection. This hypothesis, when left quite indefinite, is admissible."[38] J. Daniel Joyce contends that no other reading than that of some form of vicarious baptism is possible and that Paul's reference thereto is too vague for us to determine precisely what the Corinthians were doing.[39] Paul sought to use the practice (an affirmation of the resurrection) as a foil against those who denied the resurrection (1 Cor 15:12–19). Paul is not interested in condoning or condemning this aberrant rite but only in continuing the argument he had begun in v. 12 in favor of the resurrection.[40]

---

[36] Martin, "Baptism for the Dead," 193. Our study precludes a detailed examination of Martin's somewhat singular understanding of things kataleptic, proleptic, and eschatological. For more on these issues, see idem, "Proleptic Eschatology," *ExpTim* 51 (1939–40) 88–90; and idem, "The Messianic Age," *ExpTim* 52 (1940–41) 270–75.

[37] Martin, "Baptism for the Dead," 193.

[38] A. Robertson and A. Plummer, *A Critical and Exegetical Commentary on the First Epistle of St. Paul to the Corinthians* (2nd ed.; ICC; Edinburgh: T&T Clark, 1914) 359.

[39] Joyce, "Baptism on behalf of the Dead," 273–74.

[40] Ibid., 269, 275.

A similar opinion is proffered by Guiseppe Barbaglio, though he maintains that Paul seeks to discredit this practice. According to Barbaglio, 15:29 is addressed to the entire community, not just to those who deny the resurrection, in an attempt to demonstrate to all that vicarious baptism, lacking any rationality, is a misguided affirmation of the resurrection.[41] Or, as William F. Orr and James A. Walther claim, vicarious baptism "must be considered a curious anomaly, which apparently dropped out of view until revived by some second- and third-century sectarians."[42] Whether or not an interpretation of 15:29 as vicarious baptism is linked to later sectarian practices of baptizing corpses is considered below in our treatment of the patristic references to 15:29.

Up to this point, the majority readings of vicarious baptism hinge upon one or another misunderstanding of Christianity in Corinth (at least insofar as Paul preached it) without emphasis on the historical conditions within which the Corinthian community found itself. This leaves an obvious lacuna. Is it possible, presuming that 15:29 is a reference to vicarious baptism, that the root of the allusion is to be found not in Christian misconception but in some non-Christian religious practice? Could it be that vicarious baptism was borrowed by the Corinthian Christians from their pagan neighbors?

The Majority Reading and Syncretism

James Downey and Richard E. DeMaris both presume a reading of vicarious baptism for 15:29 on a simple reading of the Greek text. Consequently, neither of the two attempts a detailed exegesis of the verse; each takes the majority reading as a given. On that basis, both of them attempt to explain the why and wherefore of vicarious baptism within the historical context of Greco-Roman Corinth. Neither Downey nor DeMaris employs the word "syncretism," and each may loathe to find his work under such a heading. Yet, given their respective emphases on the strong influence of cosmic powers and local pagan funerary rites, it seems that their interpretations lend themselves, at the very least, to a mild form of syncretism within the Corinthian community.[43]

James Downey accepts the words of 15:29 at "face value," i.e., as a reference to vicarious baptism, and he recognizes the difficulty entailed in interpreting such a seemingly bizarre phrase. Not unlike Martin, whose article he does not seem to know, Downey begins his explanation by looking to the efficacy of baptism. He seeks to draft an understanding of the verse from the

---

[41] Barbaglio, *La prima lettura ai Corinzi*, 833. "In realtà, come si è detto, egli si rivolge alla comunità, non ai negatori che praticavano un battesimo vicario, per mostrarle, basandosi sulla sua prospettiva della risurrezione quale unica via alla salvezza, come quello che essi fanno è privo di senso. Non intende addebitare loro una contraddizione interna, ma una prassi che ai suoi occhi risulta priva di ragionevolezza" (ibid.).

[42] Orr and Walther, *I Corinthians*, 337.

[43] J. R. White ("Baptized on account of the Dead," 490, esp. n. 15) makes the same point with reference to DeMaris. White's own interpretation of 15:29 is considered below.

perspective of the polyvalent purpose of baptism and intertestamental cosmology and eschatology. He highlights that aspect of baptism, often stressed by Paul, wherein the baptized share in Christ's victory over death rather than baptism as a forgiveness of sin and rite of incorporation (in parallel fashion to Martin's emphasis on membership in the kingdom over membership in the Church). Jews and Greeks alike believed in extrahuman powers that were operative in this life and the life hereafter. Downey holds for a particular reading of vicarious baptism, i.e., baptism as "protection against the principalities and powers in the afterlife ... protection against and deliverance from the superior powers both in this world and the next."[44] He claims that this cosmic power of baptism is also indicated in Col 2:10–15; 1 Pet 3:19–22; and 1 Cor 8:6.[45] According to Downey, Christ's death, resurrection, and "descent/ascent" were viewed in the early Church as having had the effect of destroying the power of sin and death as well as subjugating "super-human" powers as indicated in 1 Cor 15:24–28.[46] A neglect of first-century belief in cosmic powers is, for Downey, a neglect of the first-century context in which we find Paul, Corinth, and 15:29.

Downey argues that the practice of and the reasons for baptism were hardly uniform in the early Church. He notes that baptism as a means of the forgiveness of sins and entrance into the Church were not the only reasons it was administered and that undue emphasis on these motivations for the reception of baptism have obscured other motivations, especially the "cosmic" motivation. Moreover, Downey argues that baptism was not a condition for membership in the early Church.[47] Vicarious baptism arose in Corinth as the unique response of a community that was unduly influenced by gnosticism and bewildered by the delay of the parousia. The advent of the death of members of the community coupled with the prevalent gnosticism of the day made such an impact on the Corinthians that they began to see baptism, rather than an imminent parousia, as the means to subjugate such powers. Vicarious baptism arose as some within the Corinthian community began to fear that friends or relatives who died unbaptized might fall prey to cosmic powers in the afterlife. On that account, they were baptized on behalf of these dead ones. Downey accepts a high sacramentalism among the Corinthians, a sacramentalism which would have allowed for a vicarious or "representational" baptism, i.e., a baptism that certainly did not imply a conversion after death or "magic" (as we use the term today). Instead, strong gnostic influences and fear of cosmic powers in first-century Corinth led to a practice—now abandoned in a world which no longer fears such powers—that

---

[44] Downey, "1 Cor 15:29," 23–24.

[45] Ibid.

[46] Ibid., 25. For further elaboration of Downey's thought on Christ's "descent/ascent," see idem, "Der Christus der jüdischen Christen: Ein pluralistisches Modell für afrikanische Theologie," *ZM* 1 (1975) 197–214.

[47] Downey, "1 Cor 15:29," 26–34.

Paul did not see fit to condemn.[48] Furthermore, Downey hints that Paul himself might have sanctioned vicarious baptism. He writes: "It is sometimes objected that, if 1 Cor 15:29 refers to vicarious baptism, Paul would have condemned it. This again represents a failure to see Paul in the context of his time."[49]

Like Downey, Richard E. DeMaris is interested in the Corinthians' historical context. For DeMaris, vicarious baptism in Corinth arose out of the Corinthians' baptismal enthusiasm (1 Cor 10:1–13) coupled with an ardent and local (pagan) interest in and concern for their dead. The result was a practice peculiar to Corinth: vicarious baptism. Since it was the dead who were to profit thereby, DeMaris focuses on the treatment of the dead in Greco-Roman Corinth. He carefully traces the archaeological and anthropological evidence which indicates the rise of the Palaimon cult in Roman times and an increased fascination in first-century Corinth with the chthonic and the world of the dead as well as an overshadowing of the earlier Demeter cult.[50] The evidence also suggests a divergence in burial customs between Greeks (inhumation) and Romans (cremation) which heightened concern over all aspects of death and burial. Those Corinthians who became Christians would have shared the concern of their fellow Corinthians in regard to death, funerary rites, passage to the next world, and especially one's needs in the afterlife. According to DeMaris, "the Corinthian Christians would not have instituted baptism on behalf of the dead if Corinthian religion of the Roman era had not been preoccupied with the realm of the dead."[51]

---

[48] Ibid., 33–34.

[49] Ibid., 34 n. 31. This position is remarkably close to Bultmann's: "When people have themselves baptized for the dead, as they did in Corinth—i.e., when their intention is to have the supranatural powers that the sacrament bestows made effective for the dead—then no distinction is made between the sacrament and a magical act ... Paul mentions the custom without any criticism whatever; for the mode of thought behind it is precisely his own, too, as it was for earliest Christian thought in general (with the exception of John)" (*Theology of the New Testament*, 1:136). Cf. Beasley-Murray: "If the baptism for the dead refers to a practice of baptizing living persons for dead persons, then we have a sub-Christian use of the sacrament, presumably adapted from pagan customs, introduced into a Pauline church within a few years of its founding" (*Baptism in the New Testament*, 353–54). Cf. also Dunn who proffers a similar opinion of baptism as "quasi-mystical event" (*Theology of Paul*, 613).

[50] DeMaris, "Corinthian Religion and Baptism for the Dead," 662–66. The Palaimon cult is significant because of Paul's reference to the Isthmian games in 1 Cor 9:24–25. On the Palaimon cult (variously Melicertes Palaemon and Melikertes Palaimon), see H. Koester, "Melikertes at Isthmia: A Roman Mystery Cult," in *Greeks, Romans, and Christians: Essays in Honor of Abraham J. Malherbe* (ed. D. L. Balch, E. Ferguson and W. A. Meeks; Minneapolis: Fortress, 1990) 355–66. On the Demeter cult, see R. E. DeMaris, "Demeter in Roman Corinth: Local Development in a Mediterranean Religion," *Numen* 42 (1995) 105–17. (Note that the genesis of DeMaris' "Corinthian Religion and Baptism for the Dead" is found in his "Demeter in Roman Corinth," 114 with n. 44.) See also O. T. Broneer, "Paul and the Pagan Cults at Isthmia," *HTR* 64 (1971) 169–187, and the various headings in the *OCD* for more.

[51] DeMaris, "Corinthian Religion and Baptism for the Dead," 666–671, quotation 671–72.

Although questions about the dead arose elsewhere (e.g., 1 Thess 4:13–18; Shepherd of Hermas, *Sim.* 9.16.5–6; Eusebius, *Hist. Eccl.* 6.44.2–6), DeMaris contends that the singular local environment in which the Corinthian community found itself is the key to understanding the rise of the vicarious baptismal rite.[52] To be sure, he concedes that funerary practices at Corinth were not the sole influence on the Corinthian Christians' understanding of the passage from life to death. Noting the "meager context" in which we find 15:29, the pervasive belief in the first century of the arduous journey from this world to the next (even in Christian circles, e.g., *Pass. Perp. et Fel.* 4; *Act. Jn.* 114; *Apoc. Paul.* 13–14), and the baptismal language of Paul in 1 Corinthians and Romans, DeMaris concludes that baptism of the dead may have functioned not only as a rite of incorporation but also as a rite of passage.[53] For DeMaris, "baptism normally functioned as a ritual of initiation into the Christian community, but it could have served equally well as a rite of passage between life and death. Understood as such, the Corinthians would have considered it ideally suited to assist the deceased community member to leave the world of the living and to enter the world of the dead."[54]

Next, DeMaris turns to the wider implications for Pauline theology. Certainly, Paul had a reason for referring to this practice within his argument on behalf of the resurrection, i.e., a practice that connoted a belief in the resurrection that some were denying in Corinth. Paul's approval or disapproval is not the issue in his mentioning this unusual practice at the conclusion of 1 Corinthians 15. Rather, according to DeMaris, Paul utilized a circumstance at his disposal in order to further his message and to show the indubitable contradiction between baptizing for the dead and denying the resurrection.[55] DeMaris specifically rejects any interpretation other than that of vicarious baptism for the benefit of the dead. Other interpretations, he claims, "even if they are textually possible, deserve criticism because they are unmindful of the religious orientation of first-century Corinth."[56]

---

[52] Ibid., 672.

[53] Ibid., 673–77.

[54] Ibid., 677. DeMaris explores his understanding of ritual theory in "Funerals and Baptisms, Ordinary and Otherwise: Ritual Criticism and Corinthian Rites," *BTB* 29 (1999) 23–34. However, since this later article presumes his reading of 15:29 in "Corinthian Religion and Baptism for the Dead," it is of little help here.

[55] DeMaris, "Corinthian Religion and Baptism for the Dead," 677–82. DeMaris also suggests that one reason for Paul's reluctance to criticize the practice was part of an effort to appease the Corinthian women, since women primarily were responsible for funerary rituals in the Greco-Roman world (680–81). On women in Corinth, see A. C. Wire, *The Corinthian Women Prophets: A Reconstruction through Paul's Rhetoric* (Minneapolis: Fortress, 1990).

[56] DeMaris, "Corinthian Religion and Baptism for the Dead," 674.

ORDINARY BAPTISM

By now it is evident that the majority of contemporary scholars read 15:29 as a reference to one form or another of vicarious baptism. However, given the gravity of baptism in Christian theology, the atypical character of vicarious baptism, and the lack of any parallel to 15:29, any reading of the verse in terms of vicarious baptism is bound to evoke serious challenges. This is especially so when we find a scholar such as DeMaris holding for vicarious baptism while at the same time implying that the text of 15:29 itself might admit of other interpretations. The most obvious of these other interpretations is that 15:29 refers to some form of ordinary baptism, and many challenges are offered against vicarious baptism on behalf of ordinary baptism. Generally speaking, such challenges maintain that, whatever Paul is speaking of in 15:29, he is not speaking of any form of vicarious baptism: either Paul is speaking about something else in the verse (heretofore misunderstood) or the verse is a reference to some (albeit extraordinary) form of ordinary, traditional baptism. It is not surprising that such a difficult verse as 15:29 should elicit suggestions of textual inaccuracy or mistranslation. It is less surprising to find that many read 15:29 to be an example of ordinary baptism. First, we look to those who would amend or suggest a variance of 15:29, then to those who read the verse as a citation of ordinary baptism.

Emendations and Variations of the Text

Although they do not agree on the particulars, Paul Dürselen, Bernard M. Foschini, and K. C. Thompson presume that 15:29 is best read with textual emendations in punctuation. They consider the present punctuation of 15:29 to be askew, and they think that the key to the interpretation of the verse lies in the adjustment thereof. While suggestions of variant punctuation to solve the riddle of 15:29 are hardly new,[57] theirs are the ones given credence in contemporary biblical literature. Foschini bases his reading of 15:29 on the work of Dürselen, whom Foschini claims violated the very principles Dürselen himself formed for the interpretation of the verse. Thompson, cognizant of both their works and unswayed by Dürselen's principles, configures his own reading. J. C. O'Neill goes one step farther than Dürselen, Foschini, and Thompson. O'Neill finds the very words of 15:29 inaccurate and opts for a rare textual variant as well as a subtle understanding of νεκρός and ὅλως. Finally, Jerome Murphy-O'Connor, who agrees with O'Neill as to the usage of νεκρός and ὅλως, offers a most original rendition of the verse as a gibe.

Given the abstruse nature of 15:29, Paul Dürselen begins his investigation by excluding the prospect of easily dismissing 15:29 as an interpolation; difficult as it is, 15:29 is part of 1 Corinthians. Next, Dürselen traces the verse's

---

[57] See Thompson ("I Corinthians 15, 29," 648–50) for a succinct history of such emendations in nineteenth-century biblical criticism.

history through the Fathers and other commentators, whom he concludes, are of very little help in interpreting the verse.[58] Then, with a careful eye on 1 Corinthians, and especially on chapter 15, Dürselen lays down four general norms for his inquiry: (1) that v. 29 parallels v. 30 as a proof of the resurrection; (2) that the practice referred to in 15:29 was established and did not demand explanation; (3) that Paul's opponents, to whom the argument is directed for instruction, understood it; and (4) that these opponents were members of the community as shown in 1 Cor 15:12.[59]

Using these norms, Dürselen finds that ὑπὲρ τῶν νεκρῶν modifies neither τί ποιήσουσιν nor οἱ βαπτιζόμενοι, but that it stands alone as a separate question.[60] Thus, there should be an additional question mark placed after βαπτιζόμενοι in 15:29a. Also, Dürselen contends that the final two words of 15:29b, ὑπὲρ αὐτῶν, ought to be read with v. 30 as its beginning.[61] Accordingly, he renders vv. 29–30: "Ἐπεὶ τί ποιήσουσιν οἱ βαπτιζόμενοι; ὑπὲρ τῶν νεκρῶν; εἰ ὅλως νεκροὶ οὐκ ἐγείρονται, τί καὶ βαπτίζονται; ὑπὲρ αὐτῶν τί καὶ ἡμεῖς κινδυνεύομεν πᾶσαν ὥραν;"[62] Or, "Otherwise what will they do who are being baptized? Do they do so for the dead? If the dead are not to rise, why are people baptized? For them, are we in danger every hour?"[63] In other words, Paul's question is the opposite of vicarious baptism. Paul is simply asking a short series of rhetorical questions within chapter 15, his great treatise on the resurrection, to mark the absurdity of those who would accept baptism while not believing in the resurrection of the dead.[64]

Bernard Foschini presents his own solution on the basis of Dürselen's norms. However, Foschini accuses Dürselen of violating his own strictures in his solution because Dürselen's rendering of the text negates a parallel between vv. 29 and 30 by identifying them.[65] Yet like Dürselen, Foschini would also add two more question marks to the text: the first after βαπτίζονται and the second after ὑπὲρ αὐτῶν. Thus he punctuates the verse: "*Epei ti poiesousin hoi baptizomenoi; hyper ton nekron; ei holos nekroi ouk egeirontai, ti kai baptizontai;*

---

[58] Dürselen, "Die Taufe für die Toten," 291–98.

[59] Ibid., 302–3. Cf. Foschini (*Baptized for the Dead*, 91), who as we see below, uses Dürselen's norms in his own investigation of 15:29.

[60] Dürselen writes: "Die Worte [ὑπὲρ τῶν νεκρῶν] gehören grammatische weder zu τί ποιήσουσιν noch zu οἱ βαπτιζόμενοι, sondern sind einfach selbstständig. Sie sind eine aus der Lebhaftigkeit der Beweisführung, die sum Dialoge gewoden ist, geborene Gegenfrage" ("Die Taufe für die Toten," 305).

[61] Ibid., 305. Note that Dürselen considers βαπτίζω to refer to ordinary baptism and νεκρός to refer to non-Christian dead since no form of ἀνάστασις is present (304–7).

[62] Ibid., 308.

[63] See Ibid.

[64] See Thompson ("I Corinthians 15, 29," 560) who notes that Dürselen's position on the punctuation of 15:29 was once so favorably regarded that it was included as an option in E. Nestle and K. Aland's revision of the Greek New Testament in 1960.

[65] Foschini, *Baptized for the Dead*, 92.

hyper auton;"⁶⁶ Foschini asserts that this punctuation is consistent with the general patterns of paleographical and stichometric studies of textual variations in the NT.⁶⁷ So for him, 15:29b is a parallel repetition of 15:29a, and 15:29 would be rendered: "'Otherwise what shall they do who are baptized? for the dead? (that is, are they baptized to belong to, to be numbered among the dead, who are never to rise again)? Indeed, if the dead do not rise at all, why are people baptized? For them? (that is, are they baptized to be numbered among the dead who are never to rise again)?'"⁶⁸

Foschini accepts βαπτίζω in its ordinary usage, but he places the emphasis of its use in Paul's letters on its aspect of incorporation. Also on the basis of Pauline usage of βαπτίζω, he equates ὑπέρ with εἰς, and considers the phrases οἱ βαπτιζόμενοι ὑπὲρ τῶν νεκρῶν and οἱ βαπτιζόμενοι εἰς τῶν νεκρῶν to mean the same thing. He speculates that Paul used the former (ὑπέρ), the more unusual preposition of the two, in order to stress the absurdity of those who would deny the resurrection, rather than degrade his habitual common usage of εἰς with βαπτίζω, which Paul is wont to use in reference to baptism into Christ.⁶⁹ Indeed, Foschini further speculates that Paul knew there was no such thing as baptism of the dead and fabricated it as a means of argumentation. On νεκρός, Foschini is a bit vague: "We interpret the phrase *ton nekron* in the same sense in which *nekros* is used throughout the whole of chapter 15; namely, the actually dead, those who have departed this life. The use of the article *ton* does not specify any particular dead; rather it rushes from the Apostle's excited mind and gives power to his words."⁷⁰

For Foschini, 15:29 is probably not a reference to any custom, aberrant or not, but the opening of part of a continuing argument on behalf of the resurrection. Foschini's reading is scarcely different in substance from Dürselen's; and we wonder whether or not Foschini himself is violating Dürselen's second norm, viz., that such a practice was established. Again, like Dürselen, Foschini sees little meaning in 15:29 as such, i.e., it is neither a reference to vicarious baptism nor to some strange form or invocation of ordinary baptism. On the contrary, 15:29 is a rhetorical device that has been grossly misunderstood and exaggerated.

Like Dürselen and Foschini, both of whose works he cites liberally and favorably, K. C. Thompson sees the key to understanding 15:29 in a change of punctuation. Thompson claims to have arrived at his own idea independently of Ernest Evans who published the same idea thirty years earlier.⁷¹ Although he

---

⁶⁶ Ibid.
⁶⁷ Ibid., 93.
⁶⁸ Ibid.
⁶⁹ Ibid., 94–96.
⁷⁰ Ibid., 97.
⁷¹ Thompson, "I Corinthians 15, 29," 647. For a detailed chronology of Thompson's thought from 1928 until his article's publication in 1964, see 647–48, wherein Thompson traces the sugges-

ponders another solution which he considers acceptable,[72] Thompson prefers to read 15:29 with a comma after βαπτιζόμενοι and a question mark after ἐγείρονται. The Greek would then read: "'Ἐπεὶ τί ποιήσουσιν οἱ βαπτιζόμενοι, ὑρέρ τῶν νεκρῶν; εἰ ὅλως νεκροὶ οὐκ ἐγείρονται τί καὶ βαπτίζονται ὑπὲρ αὐτῶν;"[73] Against an anticipated accusation that the Greek may be too "choppy," Thompson cites Rom 3:27.[74] Thompson translates 15:29 as "'Else what will they achieve who are baptized—merely for the benefit of their dead bodies, if dead bodies never rise again? And why do people get baptized merely for them.'"[75] This would fit much better with Paul's argument in v. 30: "'And why then (i.e., if our only future is as dead corpses) do we risk our lives (for the gospel) every hour?'"[76]

Next, Thompson turns to Origen, Tertullian, and St. John Chrysostom in support of his reading. Origen quotes only the latter half of 15:29 (*In Matt. Hom.* 17.29); thus, the words οἱ βαπτιζόμενοι ὑπὲρ τῶν νεκρῶν do not occur. However, in his comments about the Lord's dispute with the Sadducees over the resurrection, Origen maintains that the Lord's example did not account for the separation of body and soul because his interlocutors were incapable of envisaging such a distinction. In a digression thereon, Origen indicates that the same may be said of Paul and his example in 15:29. Thompson believes Origen's remark to be in concord with his own rendering of νεκρός. Thompson's examination of the usage of νεκρός shows that it is always used in reference to a dead body. Even so, arguing from the distinction between the Jewish and Platonic milieux of resurrection, Thompson concludes that ὑπὲρ τῶν νεκρῶν primarily refers to corpses and, secondarily, "to their souls as somehow entangled with their bodies.... To be 'baptized for them (i.e. their dead bodies)' therefore meant 'to be baptized with only Sheol in view as their final destiny,' with no hope of a joyful life hereafter for body or for soul."[77] Thus, according to Thompson, Origen quotes 15:29 to illustrate the same point. "Origen quotes the final part only, because (as properly phrased) only that part expresses the complete idea. And it is only as so phrased, i.e. with our punctuation, that it illustrates this argument. Origen therefore supports our emendation."[78]

---

tion even farther back through Foschini, Dürselen, A. L. C. Heydenreich to J. S. Semler. Though, by his own admission, the idea is not original to Thompson, he presents the more lucid reasoning on its behalf. Cf. E. Evans, *The Epistles of Paul the Apostle to the Corinthians* (CB; Oxford: Clarendon, 1930) 136–40.

[72] Thompson, "I Corinthians 15, 29," 651. For Thompson's earlier (unpublished) position of 1928, which he still considers acceptable, see 647, 650–51, 659.

[73] Ibid., 651, 659.
[74] Ibid., 649–50, 658.
[75] Ibid., 651, 659.
[76] Ibid., 651.
[77] Ibid., 652–53, quotation 653.
[78] Ibid., 654.

Tertullian also comments on 15:29 in *De res. carn.* 48.11 and *Adv. Marc.* 5.10. Although Thompson acknowledges that Tertullian shows familiarity with what Thompson would hold to be an incorrect phrasing of the Greek, that Tertullian's (faulty) Latin translation has been a catalyst for such an incorrect phrasing, and that Thompson's own translation of Tertullian's Latin differs from others', he manages to determine that Tertullian interpreted 15:29 in a manner which significantly coincides with the sense given by his own emended version. Furthermore, Thompson believes his emendation to be supported by St. John Chrysostom (*Hom. in 1 Cor.* 40) almost two hundred years later.[79] Again, against an anticipated accusation that this is so because Chrysostom was merely following Tertullian, Thompson concludes that Chrysostom was not following Tertullian at all; instead, both were—independently—using a source no longer extant.[80] Finally, attempting to go much farther than Foschini in adding external support to his argument from the manuscript evidence, Thompson turns to the Codex Vaticanus and Codex Sinaiticus. These fourth-century uncials, he claims, "both contrive to end the line with the crucial word βαπτιζόμενοι. In other words they make the break just where we want it, where we wish to insert our new punctuation mark. Can this be just a coincidence? Perhaps; but I hardly think it so."[81] Paul's intent in 15:29 is to show, and therefore confirm against any latent incomplete understanding among the Corinthians, that baptism is meaningless if one does not believe that the soul and the body rise again in the resurrection of the dead.

Cognizant that most exegetes read 15:29 as a reference to vicarious baptism, J. C. O'Neill rejects that reading. Along with many others, he stresses the lack of historical evidence for such a practice in the early Church. He prefers a variant textual reading and a nuanced understanding of the use of νεκρός in 15:29. O'Neill proposes that the variant reading found in the Leicester codex 69, αυτων των νεκρων, is the original ending of 15:29.[82] Despite the weight of manuscript evidence against such a reading, he maintains that the unusual word order of codex 69 belies its originality rather than the conflation of a scribe. O'Neill contends that if a scribe were conflating, "he could easily have put *huper tōn nekrōn autōn*, but since he did not do that, it is more likely that his reading was the original form of the verse, which all the other manuscripts have

---

[79] Ibid., 654–55.

[80] Ibid., 655. Here, Thompson, ibid., n. 2, cites Foschini (*Baptized for the Dead*, 64 n. 227) in support of his assertion. Yet, Foschini only says that the use of a lost, though common source, for Tertullian and Chrysostom is "probable." On Tertullian and Chrysostom, see Thompson's Appendix I ("I Corinthians 15, 29," 656–57).

[81] Thompson, "I Corinthians 15, 29," 652. Thompson provides a detailed simulation of these manuscripts in his Appendix II (see 658–59).

[82] O'Neill, "1 Corinthians 15:29," 310.

'improved.'"[83] And he cites Mark 7:6 (περὶ ὑμῶν τῶν ὑποκριτῶν) as an example of such a construction.[84]

O'Neill's reading hinges on his rendering of νεκρός. He says that at its first and third occurrences (in the variant reading) νεκρός means "corpses." In support of this, he notes "the well-known fact that Hellenistic Greek formed more than one plural noun from the adjective *nekros*; there was an expression *ta nekra*, corpses (Plutarch, *Moralia*, 773 d; Marcus Aurelius, 12.33), as well as the more common expression *hoi nekroi*, the dying or the dead."[85] The two uses of νεκρός governed by ὑπέρ refer to corpses, dead bodies. That is, ὑπὲρ τῶν νεκρῶν should be read as meaning ὑπὲρ τῶν νεκρῶν σωμάτων. Such a reading, according to O'Neill, is supported by the Greek Fathers.[86] Furthermore, he contends that the adverb ὅλως ought to be taken—not with the verb ἐγείρονται as most exegetes would have it—but with the noun, νεκροί. To wit, O'Neill translates ὅλος νεκροί as the "completely" or "already" dead;[87] these are the dying, those about to die. O'Neill sees another such usage in 1 Cor 6:7, wherein he claims ὅλως modifies the noun ἥττημα.[88] For O'Neill, νεκρός has two different meanings within the same verse, i.e., it refers twice to corpses and once to the dying.[89] For O'Neill, baptism is accepted for the preservation of the body after death. "The bodily rite of baptism was used by people who expected the body soon to die and decay, because they expected the rite to ensure eternal life

---

[83] Ibid.

[84] Ibid.

[85] Ibid.

[86] Ibid. To support this assertion, O'Neill cites only Chrysostom. Yet, as we see below, the Greek Fathers are hardly consistent on this point. For now, see K. Staab, "1 Kor 15,29 im Lichte der Exegese der griechischen Kirche," in *Studiorum Paulinorum Congressus Internationalis Catholicus 1961* (2 vols.; AnBib 17–18; Rome: Pontificium Institutum Biblicum, 1963) 1:443–50.

[87] O'Neill, "1 Corinthians 15:29," 310, 311. Cf. Reaume ("Another Look at 1 Corinthians 15:29," 469–70) who considers O'Neill's position on this and rejects it. Reaume's own position is considered below.

[88] O'Neill, "1 Corinthians 15:29," 310–311. Although we do not wish to get ahead of ourselves by criticizing a reading of 15:29 before we come to our assessment of all the readings (below), we should clarify a few things at this point. There is no support for O'Neill's reading of 1 Cor 6:7 (never mind 15:29). O'Neill, who appeals to Barrett's *First Corinthians* (without proper citation) as supportive of this translation of ὅλως, omits to mention two crucial details. First, ὅλως is an adverb in the Greek, and in his rendering into English, Barrett merely fits the Greek to an English idiom; Barrett makes no statement about ὅλως' precise meaning and usage or its role in 1 Cor 6:7 (see *First Corinthians*, 138). Second, Barrett does not take ὅλως to modify the νεκρός in 15:29, the verse in question (see 362–64).

[89] Once again, we do not wish to get ahead of ourselves, but two problems immediately present themselves for clarification. First, ὅλως notwithstanding, it is rare to find a word used equivocally in the same sentence. Second, O'Neill never mentions the other ten occurrences of νεκρός in 1 Corinthians or its numerous occurrences in Paul's other letters. This is noteworthy here, because as we see below, Murphy-O'Connor ("Baptized for the Dead," 540, 543 n. 23) makes a similar argument with reference to O'Neill's positions.

at the resurrection of the body."[90] O'Neill paraphrases the verse: "'Otherwise what do those hope to achieve who are baptized for their dying bodies? If the completely dead are not raised, why then are they baptized for them?'"[91]

Jerome Murphy-O'Connor's reading of 15:29 as a gibe is *sui generis*. Building on his previous research of "Corinthian slogans," he fits 15:29 into the same category.[92] Murphy-O'Connor begins with the context. Verse 29 is linked to vv. 31–32 with v. 30 as a transitional phrase. A reading of vicarious baptism must be dismissed because such a reading isolates v. 29 from its immediate context. For Murphy-O'Connor, 15:29 is a "general statement" followed by an example: Paul's apostolic labor. This forms a parallel with the preceding verses. The apogee of the discussion in vv. 20–28 (the mission of Christ) elicited in Paul's mind an "association of ideas." The example of Christ, as an argument in favor of the resurrection, is naturally followed by the example of apostolic labors.[93] Thus, unless v. 29 is to be taken apart from its context, it is the context that reveals its meaning. For Murphy-O'Connor, such a context forces us "to exclude the literal sense of *baptizein*, be it understood in a sacramental or non-sacramental sense, and to opt for the metaphorical sense of the verb."[94] He is quick to admit that "Paul never uses *baptizein* in a metaphorical sense; in every other instance he intends a reference to the sacrament of baptism,"[95] but he appeals to similar usage in Mark 10:38 and Luke 12:50, and thinks it justifiable to translate 15:29's βαπτιζόμενοι as "those being destroyed,"[96] following the translation of Frederick Godet.[97]

Like O'Neill, Murphy-O'Connor does not take νεκρός as referring exclusively to physical death, i.e., he agrees with O'Neill on the exceptional use of ὅλως in 15:29.[98] Therewith, Murphy-O'Connor gives a brief account of O'Neill's work, which he discovered after his own article was submitted for publication, but before it went to press. Murphy-O'Connor notes that he and O'Neill both agree on the interpretation of ὅλως and ὑπὲρ τῶν νεκρῶν (i.e., ὑπὲρ αὐτῶν). However, conceding that O'Neill's interpretation is "possible," Murphy-O'Connor considers his own "most probable" because of his close

---

[90] O'Neill, "1 Corinthians 15:29," 311.

[91] Ibid. Note that O'Neill's general hypothesis is accepted by J. Moiser ("1 Corinthians 15," *IBS* 14 (1992) 14, 17), but Moiser translates 1 Cor 15:29 as "What, may I ask, is the point of baptism, if Christians are to be eternally dead? If the dead are not raised, why bother to be baptised?"

[92] See J. Murphy-O'Connor, "Corinthian Slogans in 1 Cor 6:12–20," *CBQ* 40 (1978) 391–96.

[93] Murphy-O'Connor, "Baptized for the Dead," 532–34.

[94] Ibid., 534. In support of his position, he cites Oepke, "βάπτω," 530.

[95] Murphy-O'Connor, "Baptized for the Dead," 536.

[96] Ibid., 534.

[97] F. Godet, *Commentary on St. Paul's First Epistle to the Corinthians* (trans. A. Cusin; 2 vols.; CFTL 30; Edinburgh: T&T Clark, 1898) 2:389. Godet translates βαπτιζόμενοι in the sense of physical destruction of the body, i.e., martyrdom, specifically on the basis of Mark 10:38 and Luke 12:50.

[98] Murphy-O'Connor, "Baptized for the Dead," 539–40.

attention to the literary context of 15:29.⁹⁹ Apropos to that context, Murphy-O'Connor cites extensively from Philo and the research of Richard A. Horsley, who posits the existence of a spiritually elitist group that denied the resurrection among the Corinthians.¹⁰⁰ Murphy-O'Connor holds that Paul is using νεκρός in the spiritual sense and that the spiritually elite among the Corinthians would have understood it so. In order to speak of the physically dead, the really dead, Paul used ὅλως to qualify νεκρός in 15:29b. Murphy-O'Connor's case for reading ὅλως with νεκρός rather than ἐγείρονται is stronger than O'Neill's. Murphy-O'Connor cites 1 Cor 5:1; 6:7; Matt 5:34, as well as Josephus.¹⁰¹ For Murphy-O'Connor, the reading of ὑπὲρ τῶν νεκρῶν is the key to the verse. He reads ὑπέρ as "for, because of, by reason of, on account of."¹⁰² He precludes an ellipsis in this phrase that would have νεκρός refer to the resurrected dead for the same reason as Robertson and Plummer: "If St. Paul had wanted to abbreviate ὑπὲρ τῆς ἀναστάσεως τῶν νεκρῶν, he would have left out τῶν νεκρῶν, not τῆς ἀναστάσεως."¹⁰³

Therefore, 15:29 is an effort on Paul's part to point out the incongruity of those Corinthians who deny the resurrection by means of a rhetorical question that has its origin in the spiritual elite's (supposed) depreciation of his apostolic labors. Murphy-O'Connor paraphrases v. 29 thus: "Supposing that there is no resurrection from the dead, will they continue to work, those who are being destroyed on account of an inferior class of believers who are dead to true Wisdom? [29a] . . . If those who are really dead are not raised, why indeed are they baptized on their account? [29b]."¹⁰⁴ Paul is offering a polemic against the Corinthian spiritual elite in order to show that his apostolic efforts (and those of others) are far from futile. Paul intends to imply that his apostolic labors would be useless if the dead are not raised; so too, if that were the case, all labors based upon hope in the resurrection would be in vain vis-à-vis 1 Cor 15:14. With his firm faith in the resurrection, Paul is able to turn their assumptions against them and to give them a gibe.¹⁰⁵ Oddly enough, then, we see that for Murphy-O'Connor, 15:29 has little to do with baptism in itself, ordinary or otherwise.

---

⁹⁹ Ibid., 543 n. 23.

¹⁰⁰ For Murphy-O'Connor's extensive treatment of Philo, see ibid., 537–38. See also R. A. Horsley, "Pneumatikos vs. Psychikos: Distinctions of Spiritual Status among the Corinthians," *HTR* 69 (1976) 269–88; and idem, "How Can Some of You Say There Is No Resurrection of the Dead? Spiritual Elitism in Corinth," *NovT* 20 (1978) 203–31.

¹⁰¹ See Josephus, *B.J.* 4.364; 5.219; *A.J.* 2.344; 8.258; 9.80, 127; 5.35.

¹⁰² Murphy-O'Connor, "Baptized for the Dead," 535.

¹⁰³ Robertson and Plummer, *I Corinthians*, 359; also cited in Murphy-O'Connor, "Baptized for the Dead," 536.

¹⁰⁴ Murphy-O'Connor, "Baptized for the Dead," 542.

¹⁰⁵ Ibid., 542–43.

Ordinary Baptism with Ὑπέρ in the Final Sense

In contrast to Jerome Murphy-O'Connor, there are exegetes who believe that 15:29 has everything to do with ordinary baptism. Maria Raeder, Joachim Jeremias, and J. K. Howard are proponents of "baptism by example." They focus on the most disputed word in 15:29: ὑπέρ. Raeder, Jeremias, and Howard read ὑπέρ in its final sense, i.e., "for the purpose of." Each of them considers the baptism referred to in 15:29 to have been ordinary, wherein only the living receive baptism and only for their own sake.

In her brief but oft-cited article, Maria Raeder interprets 15:29 as a reference to ordinary baptism, albeit a baptism sought for a somewhat less than noble motive. While holding 15:29 to refer to an ordinary rite of baptism by example, Raeder seeks to expand upon an idea, briefly proposed earlier by George G. Findlay,[106] that unbaptized persons accepted baptism in the hope of being joined to their deceased loved ones (baptized friends and relatives) at the resurrection.[107] That is, she contends that certain individuals were motivated to undergo the baptismal rite because they desired eternal life, not because of faith in Christ *per se*. Raeder's position quickly gained considerable attention among exegetes, since it was supported and expanded upon by Joachim Jeremias before it actually appeared in print.[108] According to Raeder, the readings of vicarious baptism rest principally upon a misunderstanding of the use of ὑπέρ.[109] She claims that the propensity among exegetes to interpret ὑπέρ in the sense of ἀντί ignores a plethora of other possibilities. Raeder prefers to read ὑπέρ in its final sense.[110] Consequently, she would translate ὑπέρ as "with a view towards," or "for the purpose of."[111]

In considering Paul's use of οἱ νεκροί and the context in which we find 15:29's use, viz., in terms of 1 Cor 15:18 and 23, Raeder holds that οἱ νεκροί

---

[106] G. G. Findlay, *St. Paul's First Epistle to the Corinthians* (EGT; Hodder and Stoughton, 1900) 930–31. Findlay writes: "Paul is referring to a much commoner, indeed normal experience, that the death of Christians leads to the conversion of survivors, who in the first instance 'for the sake of the dead' (their beloved dead) and in the hope of re-union, turn to Christ—e.g., when a dying mother wins her son by the appeal 'Meet me in heaven!' Such appeals, and their frequent salutary effect, give strong and touching evidence of *faith in the resurrection*" (ibid., 931 [emphasis original]). But can faith in the resurrection precede faith in Christ?

[107] Raeder, "Vikariatstaufe?" 258–60. Robertson and Plummer (*I Corinthians*, 360), citing Findlay, consider it a likely possibility.

[108] J. Jeremias, "Flesh and Blood Cannot Inherit the Kingdom of God," (I Cor. XV. 50)," *NTS* 2 (1955–56) 155–56.

[109] Raeder, "Vikariatstaufe?" 259 n. 6. Raeder credits Jeremias for providing the impetus of this idea in a lecture he delivered on 1 Corinthians in the summer of 1953 (ibid.).

[110] "Es liegt sogar näher, das ὑπέρ mit dem Genitiv in finalem Sinn zu deuten, also hier das ὑπέρ der 'Abzweckung' zu sehen" (Raeder, "Vikariatstaufe?" 259). See her extensive footnotes in support of this position (ibid.), and cf. Jeremias, "Flesh and Blood," 156.

[111] Commenting on Raeder's interpretation of ὑπέρ, Barrett (*First Corinthians*, 364) claims that such a use "is not altogether impossible, but this use of the preposition is rare, and it is not easy to see why Paul should express himself in this way."

refers to deceased Christians, not the dead in general. The βαπτιζόμενοι are the heretofore unbaptized relatives and friends of these deceased Christians. These non-Christians undergo the rite of baptism in order to be united with other Christians at the resurrection, not with Christ, because they misunderstand the nature of baptism.[112] Raeder claims that such a misunderstanding grew out of the missionary situation in Corinth, wherein a misplaced practice arose of baptizing solely with a view towards the resurrection, towards unity with deceased loved ones, rather than with a view towards Christ. While Paul may not have approved of baptism for such a motive alone, his inclusion of it in 1 Corinthians 15 most likely seeks only to show the inconsistency of denying the resurrection.[113] So, for Raeder, 15:29 is indicative of a practice of ordinary baptism for an extraordinarily confused motive.

Joachim Jeremias, who follows Raeder's position on ὑπέρ,[114] expands her reading by focusing his attention on the use of νεκρός in 15:29. He notes that throughout 1 Corinthians 15, Paul seems to distinguish consistently between the anarthrous νεκροί and οἱ νεκροί. The former denotes the dead in general (vv. 12, 13, 15, 16, 20, 21, 29b, 32), the latter the Christian dead (vv. 29a, 35, 42, 52). Because Jeremias perceives that non-Christian pagans seek baptism for the purpose of future unity with their beloved dead Christians with whom they hope to share the resurrection, the ὑπέρ cannot indicate a substitutionary sense. Instead, Paul uses ὑπέρ in its final sense in 15:29, just as he uses it in 1 Cor 15:3; 2 Cor 1:6; and Rom 15:8. According to Raeder and Jeremias, this quest for unity, born of an excessive missiology, neither precluded nor demanded faith in Christ himself. Preposterous as such a take on baptism may be to us, Jeremias claims that no other (mis)understanding fits the context of 1 Cor 15:29–32 so well.[115] Commenting on Raeder's and Jeremias' work, Rudolf Schnackenburg says that "it may well be that an exegetical solution has been found which, in a simple and yet convincing way, settles an old *crux interpretum*."[116]

J. K. Howard offers a brief investigation of 15:29,[117] wherein he takes for his outline the three general possibilities of interpretation for 15:29 noted by Robertson and Plummer: ordinary baptism, vicarious baptism, or an unparalleled anomalous circumstance in Corinth.[118] Howard rejects vicarious baptism on the confessional grounds that baptism—vicarious or ordinary—confers absolutely

---

[112] Raeder, "Vikariatstaufe?" 260. In this she cites Findlay, *First Corinthians*, 931 n. 11.

[113] Raeder, "Vikariatstaufe?" 260. Cf. Jeremias, "Flesh and Blood," 156.

[114] Jeremias, "Flesh and Blood," 156. Cf. Beasley-Murray (*Baptism in the New Testament*, 186–87) for a careful refutation of this rendering of ὑπέρ.

[115] Jeremias, "Flesh and Blood," 155–56.

[116] Schnackenburg, *Baptism in the Thought of St. Paul*, 102. In saying this, Schnackenburg adjusts his earlier position that the dead spoken of must have been catechumens or those who died confessing the faith (see idem, *Das Heilsgeschehen bei der Taufe noch dem Apostel Paulus*, 96–98).

[117] J. K. Howard, "Baptism for the Dead: A Study of 1 Corinthians 15:29," *EvQ* 37 (1965) 137–41.

[118] See Robertson and Plummer, *I Corinthians*, 359–60.

nothing, for it is only a sign of a previous conversion of the heart. He accepts Raeder's solution, along with reference to Jeremias' comments, as the correct interpretation of what he considers a Corinthian anomaly. As Howard sees it, some Gentiles converted to Christianity in order to be reunited with deceased loved ones and thereafter were baptized as a seal of their conversion; the desire for eternal life was the catalyst for true conversions to Christ, which were sealed with the sign of baptism. Howard asserts that 15:29 is the fitting end of "Paul's argument concerning the absurdity of denying the resurrection."[119] In a certain sense, we might say that Howard has "baptized" Raeder. Raeder emphasizes the desire for unity as the motivation for the acceptance of baptism, whereas Howard goes one step farther in emphasizing that the desire for unity leads one towards an acceptance of the resurrection of the dead and, therefore, towards Christ, the first fruits of that resurrection, as a motive for conversion and hence for baptism.[120]

Ordinary Baptism with Ὑπέρ in the Causal Sense

Consonant with Maria Raeder, Joachim Jeremias, and J. K. Howard, John D. Reaume and Joel R. White are, *mutatis mutandis*, proponents of baptism by example, except that they take ὑπέρ to mean "on account of," i.e., each independently of one another reads ὑπέρ in its causal rather than final sense. Like Raeder, Jeremias, and Howard, each of them considers the baptism referred to in 15:29 to have been ordinary, but for different reasons.

After a cogent summary of the various readings of 15:29, John D. Reaume begins his exegesis of the verse within the literary context of 1 Corinthians 15. In 1 Corinthians, Paul addresses problems that he perceived within the Corinthian community and concludes his letter with chapter 15, a defense of the resurrection. Reaume notes that Paul divides his argument in chapter 15 into three sections: (1) the resurrection of Christ (vv. 1–11), wherein Christ's resurrection is attested to by witnesses; (2) the resurrection of believers (vv. 12–28), wherein Paul shows the absurdity of denying the resurrection of believers while affirming the resurrection of Christ; and (3) the inconsistency between Christian (and apostolic) behavior and a denial of the resurrection (vv. 29–34), wherein Paul primarily uses rhetorical questions to make his point.[121]

Reaume holds οἱ βαπτιζομενοι to refer to a group of individuals who are accepting baptism in Corinth. The verb βαπτίζω is to be taken literally; he rejects any suggestion that Paul uses βαπτίζω here in a metaphorical or figurative sense, though he acknowledges that βαπτίζω is used figuratively elsewhere in the NT (e.g., Mark 10:38–39) and that it is occasionally used in a "nonstandard"

---

[119] Howard, "Baptism for the Dead," 141.
[120] Ibid., 140–41. Cf. Downey, "I Cor 15:29," 26–30, esp. 26 n. 6.
[121] Reaume, "Another Look at 1 Corinthians 15:29," 466–67.

way by Paul (e.g., 1 Cor 10:2; 12:13; Rom 6:3).[122] Reaume observes that the third person present tense of βαπτίζω in 15:29b (βαπτίζονται)[123] alludes to a contemporaneous activity practiced by a group within the Corinthian community, a group that was most likely known by the community and relatively small. If Paul were referring to all Corinthians, he probably would have used the first or second person plural, as he is wont to do throughout his letter, rather than the third.[124]

Likewise, Reaume reads νεκρός literally. He acknowledges that νεκρός is used literally and figuratively in the NT and in Paul. Reaume admits that there is a nuance to its use in 15:29, but he dismisses any metaphorical connotation. Noticing that νεκρός is used invariably in its literal sense in 1 Corinthians 15 and that the same use is evident in v. 29b, he presumes similar usage in v. 29a. On this basis, Reaume rejects the notion that νεκρός might be used figuratively to refer to either the spiritually dead or to dying bodies as argued by Thompson, O'Neill, and Murphy-O'Connor. Furthermore, Reaume detects a distinction in Paul's use of νεκρός. The articular construction τῶν νεκρῶν denotes a particular designation of dead individuals; the anarthrous noun νεκροί denotes the dead in general. This grammatical distinction is borne out in Paul's usage. "Paul seems to have been distinguishing between the dead in general (vv. 12, 13, 15, 16, 20, 21, 29b) and Christians who have died (vv. 29a, 35, 42, 52)."[125] In claiming that τῶν νεκρῶν refers to Christians, he means that they are baptized. Reaume rejects the suggestion that they were "catechumens"—individuals who desired to be baptized but died before the rite was performed—as anachronistic.[126] In so doing, Reaume appeals to Acts 10:47–48; 16:31–34; 18:8; and 19:5 in which baptism follows immediately upon conversion.[127]

The importance of οἱ βαπτιζόμενοι and τῶν νεκρῶν notwithstanding, "the understanding of the preposition ὑπέρ and the resulting theological implications are the decisive issues of this *crux interpretum*."[128] Reaume notes that ὑπέρ with the genitive, as used by Paul and elsewhere in the NT, may mean "on behalf of"

---

[122] Ibid., 468 n. 49, 469 n. 52.

[123] As regards the use of βαπτίζω, Reaume explicitly follows W. H. Mare, "1 Corinthians," in *The Expositor's Bible Commentary* (ed. F. E. Gaebelein; 12 vols.; Grand Rapids, MI: Zondervan, 1976) 10:287; and Fee, *First Corinthains*, 763 n. 15.

[124] Reaume, "Another Look at 1 Corinthians 15:29," 468–69.

[125] Ibid., 470. Here he follows closely Raeder, "Vikariatstaufe?" 258–59; Jeremias, "Flesh and Blood," 155–56; and BDF §254.

[126] Reaume, "Another Look at 1 Corinthians 15:29," 471. Here Reaume (ibid. 471 n. 64) cites H. L. Goudge (*The First Epistle to the Corinthians with Introduction and Notes* [WC; London: Methuen, 1903] 149–50); Barrett (*First Corinthians*, 364); and Fee (*First Corinthians*, 767). Note that Goudge, Barrett, and Fee offer only the suggestion of a catechuminate; neither Goudge, Barrett, nor Fee postulates a catechuminate or uses the word "catechumen." They only suggest a period of time, however brief, between conversion and baptism.

[127] Reaume, "Another Look at 1 Corinthians 15:29," 471. He also finds support from Beasley-Murray, "Βαπτίζω," 146.

[128] Reaume, "Another Look at 1 Corinthians 15:29," 467.

or "instead of." The former connotes representation, the latter substitution. For the former, Reaume cites Eph 5:2, 25; 1 Thess 5:10; and Titus 2:14; for the latter, John 11:50; 2 Cor 5:14–15; Gal 3:13; and Phlm 13, as well as Rom 5:6, 8; 8:32; and Gal 2:20, wherein persons are the object of ὑπέρ.[129] Aware of the fact that the majority of contemporary exegetes read ὑπέρ as connoting representation or substitution in some sense vis-à-vis vicarious baptism and that such baptism is presumed to have procured some benefit for dead persons, Reaume roundly rejects that position. His rebuff is based on the dearth of evidence for such a practice in the first century and "the theological problem of Paul appealing, without qualification, to a practice that implies that baptism has saving efficacy."[130] Reaume maintains that Paul is using ὑπέρ as "for," "because of," or "on account of," i.e., in a causal sense.[131] Yet, when so used, ὑπέρ rarely has a person as its object. However, Reaume finds four such uses: Acts 9:16; 21:13; Rom 15:9; and Phil 1:29.[132] He dismisses related possibilities, such as "for" in the final sense (as Raeder and Jeremias would have it) or "with reference to" (as

---

[129] See ibid., 471, esp. nn. 65, 66.

[130] Ibid., 472, 475. No one disputes the lack of evidence for vicarious baptism in antiquity. As we saw above with Howard ("Baptism for the Dead," 137–41), it is no surprise to see vicarious baptism denied on confessional grounds—when confessional grounds are stated clearly. But Reaume, in saying that there is no saving efficacy in baptism (a statement that is more confessional than substantial), may go too far. He considers the "disproportionate attention" given to 15:29, a verse that plays but a "minor role" in 1 Corinthians 15, to be the result of those who mistakenly assume that baptism is somehow efficacious (475; see 459 n. 10). Moreover, in denying any saving efficacy to baptism, Reaume cites Fee (*First Corinthians*, 764) for support. This is no little expansion on Fee's position. Fee writes: "It [vicarious baptism] smacks of a 'magical' view of sacramentalism of the worst kind, where a religious rite, performed for someone else, can have saving efficacy" (764–65). Here, Fee does not deny efficacy to baptism *per se* but to baptism performed for someone else. Commenting on 1 Cor 1:10–17, Fee writes: "It seems clear from this passage that Paul does not understand baptism to *effect* salvation. The preaching of the cross does that—when of course it is accompanied by the effectual work of the Spirit. But it would be quite wrong to go on, as some do, and say that baptism is a purely secondary matter. Surely, Paul would not have so understood it. For him baptism comes *after* hearing the gospel, but it does so as the God-ordained mode of faith's response to the gospel" (63–64 [emphasis original]). On the "evangelical flavor" of Fee's commentary, see J. Plevnik's review (*CBQ* 50 [1988] 715–17). For more on Fee's position, which is essentially that of the Pentecostal Church, see G. D. Fee, "Baptism in the Holy Spirit: The Issue of Separability and Subsequence" (chap. 7), in *Gospel and Spirit: Issues in New Testament Hermeneutics* (Peabody, MA: Hendrickson, 1991) 103–199.

[131] Reaume, "Another Look at 1 Corinthians 15:29," 472. Reaume cites BDF §231; "βάπτω," BAGD, 132 (note that 132–33 bears the heading "βάπτω"; Reaume probably intended to cite "ὑπέρ," 838–39); and numerous NT passages including 1 Cor 10:30; 2 Cor 12:8, 10; Rom 15:19; and Phil 1:29. R. F. Collins (*First Corinthians*, 559) expressly rejects Reaume's reading of ὑπέρ as one "that departs from Pauline usage of the preposition."

[132] Reaume, "Another Look at 1 Corinthians 15:29," 473. Note that Reaume attributes Acts 9:16 and 21:13 to Paul rather than to Luke.

some have suggested),[133] because such interpretations presume an ellipsis.[134] Simply stated, Reaume sees 15:29 as a reference to ordinary Christian baptism: people are being baptized on account of the sway of deceased Christians. "No doubt many individuals in the early church were influenced by the testimony of other believers who had recently died or were martyred."[135] Unfortunately on this point, Reaume contradicts his earlier statement that "there is no evidence of persecutions or martyrdoms in the church of Corinth at that time."[136] Insofar as he posits a causal reading of ὑπέρ, this discrepancy hardly dilutes Reaume's very strong argument.[137] But without persecution or martyrdom, how or why would the influence of which he speaks only have come from those who died in the faith?

Joel R. White's reading of 15:29 is similar to Reaume's. White's "'Baptized on account of the Dead': The Meaning of 1 Corinthians 15:29 in Its Context" is the most recent scholarly attempt to grapple specifically with 15:29. In comparable fashion to Reaume, White begins with a critique of the contemporary readings before presenting his own solution to the dilemma. Regrettably, though White gives a detailed exposé of many others' interpretive work, he does not seem to be aware of Reaume's "Another Look at 1 Corinthians 15:29" (published two years prior to his own article). This is a lamentable lacuna, since Reaume and White hold so much in common (especially the causal use of ὑπέρ), and White's appraisal of Reaume's reading would have been noteworthy.

White declines to accept a reading of vicarious baptism on four grounds: (1) the lack of a "contextual mooring" at the end of chapter 15 for such a practice;[138] (2) the "cognitive dissonance" we would have to assume among Paul's interlocutors in Corinth who would deny the resurrection of the dead while performing such a rite on their behalf; (3) the dearth of "any independent historical or biblical parallel" of vicarious baptism; and (4) vicarious baptism's obvious incongruity "with [Paul's] entire theology." Likewise, White does not

---

[133] For example, A. T. Robertson, *A Grammar of the Greek New Testament in Light of Historical Research* (Nashville, TN: Broadman, 1934) 632; and A. Barnes, *Barnes' Notes on the New Testament* (Grand Rapids, MI: Kregel, 1962) 793.

[134] Reaume, "Another Look at 1 Corinthians 15:29," 473. Cf. Robertson and Plummer, *I Corinthians*, 359.

[135] Reaume, "Another Look at 1 Corinthians 15:29," 475.

[136] Ibid., 460; cf. 460 n. 12.

[137] In fact, Thiselton, one of the latest commentators on 1 Corinthians, says, after considerable consideration of the many readings: "We see no reason to reject [Reaume's] view as the least problematic and most convincing of all" (*First Corinthians*, 1249).

[138] J. R. White ("Baptized on account of the Dead," 488 with n. 6, 489, 493) acknowledges Murphy-O'Connor's ("Baptized for the Dead," 532–33) appreciation of 15:29's context as constitutive to his own interpretation. White (493 n. 38) points out that such is an "about-face" on Murphy-O'Connor's part, when compared to Murphy-O'Connor's earlier treatment of the verse in *1 Corinthians* (NTM 10; Wilmington, DL: Glazier, 1979) 144. Murphy-O'Connor incorporated his later thought in the second printing of the book (Collegeville, MN: Liturgical [Glazier] 1991) on the same page.

accept the solution of O'Neill, the use of ὑπέρ preferred by Raeder and Jeremias, or any attempt to render βαπτίζω metaphorically vis-à-vis Murphy-O'Connor, despite White's appreciation for his contextual approach.[139]

White begins with the context. He follows Murphy-O'Connor, who identifies Paul's concern in 15:29 with his apostolic sufferings, inasmuch as 15:29 is situated between Paul's description of Christ's mission (concluded with vv. 20–28) and his own mission (vv. 30–32).[140] White takes βαπτίζω literally, τῶν νεκρῶν metaphorically to refer to "the apostles," νεκροί to refer to the literally dead, and ὅλως as attributively modifying νεκροί rather than ἐγείρονται.[141] But the key to his reading is ὑπέρ in its causal sense. White reads ὑπέρ: (1) in a causal sense describing thanks or praise (Rom 15:9; 1 Cor 10:30; Eph 1:16; 5:20); (2) in a causal sense describing suffering (Phil 1:29); (3) in a seemingly causal sense describing suffering (Acts 5:41; 9:16; 15:26; 21:13; 2 Cor 12:10; Eph 3:13; 2 Thess 1:5); and (4) in a possibly causal sense (Rom 1:5; 15:8; 2 Cor 12:8; Eph 5:20).[142] Thus, he renders his translation: "'Otherwise what will those do who are being baptized on account of the dead (that is, the dead, figuratively speaking; that is the apostles)? For if truly dead persons are not raised, why at all are people being baptized on account of them (that is, the apostles)?'" White maintains that Paul considers himself to be one of "the dead," in his role as an apostle.[143]

Relying on the work of Scott J. Hafemann,[144] White contends that there are at least four instances in which being given over to death should be seen as a metonymy for apostolic suffering, that "either invoke as a controlling metaphor the image of the Roman triumphal procession, which ended in the execution of the prisoners at the end of the procession (1 Cor 4:9; 2 Cor 2:14) or are found within or in direct proximity to 'peristasis catalogues' or 'tribulation lists' (1 Cor 4:9; 2 Cor 4:10–11; 6:9)."[145] For White, 15:29 is the fifth instance. He draws a

---

[139] J. R. White, "Baptized on account of the Dead," 487–92. See Reaume ("Another Look at 1 Corinthians 15:29," 458–66) for a comparable treatment of the same issues.

[140] J. R. White, "Baptized on account of the Dead," 493. See Murphy-O'Connor, "Baptized for the Dead," 534.

[141] J. R. White, "Baptized on account of the Dead," 493 n. 42. Here White follows O'Neill ("1 Corinthians 15:29," 310) and Murphy-O'Connor ("Baptized for the Dead," 540) in reading ὅλος as modifying νεκροί; for its attributive use, he cites BDF §434. White finds four other biblical uses (1 Cor 5:1; 6:7; Matt 5:34; Job 34:8 [LXX variant]) and an extrabiblical usage (P. Oxy. 1676.29–31).

[142] J. R. White, "Baptized on account of the Dead," 497–98. White also cites numerous reference works on this point: "ὑπέρ," BAGD, 838–39; Riesenfeld, "ὑπέρ," 514; J. H. Moulton, A Grammar of New Testament Greek (4 vols.; Edinburgh: T&T Clark) 3:270–71; H. E. Dana and J. R. Mantey, A Manual Grammar of the Greek New Testament (New York, Macmillan, 1927) 111; and LSJ, 1857–58. Cf. Reaume, "Another Look at 1 Corinthians 15:29," 472–73.

[143] J. R. White, "Baptized on account of the Dead," 493–94, quotation 494.

[144] S. J. Hafemann, Suffering and Ministry in the Spirit: Paul's Defense of His Ministry in II Corinthians 2:14–3:3 (Grand Rapids, MI: Eerdmans, 1990) 52–79.

[145] J. R. White, "Baptized on account of the Dead," 495; see 495 n. 52 for the pertinent secondary literature on these themes.

parallel between Christ's sufferings in his redemptive mission (1 Cor 15:12–28; cf. Gal 3:10–14) and Paul's sufferings in his apostolic mission (1 Cor 15:30–32; cf. 2 Cor 4:7–12)—all for naught without the resurrection. Indeed for White, it is Paul's apostolic sufferings that dictate his use of the oath formula νή in 1 Cor 15:31 (found elsewhere in the Bible only in Gen 42:15; cf. Josephus, *C. Ap.* 1.255), wherein Paul boasts (swears) by the Corinthians themselves who are the witnesses to his apostolate (1 Cor 9:1–17).[146] Following Ronald F. Hock, who contends that the sufferings of Paul in 1 Corinthians are voluntary,[147] White holds that v. 31 is Paul's attempt to remind the Corinthians that his daily apostolic death is proven by their very existence as a community of faith (cf. 2 Cor 2:2–3).[148]

The Corinthian community is the same community into which people are being baptized (οἱ βαπτιζόμενοι) through Paul's apostolate. The factionalism among the community (1 Cor 1:13–17) indicates more than a desire to ally themselves with the apostle who baptized them. In light of his reading of 15:29, White maintains that their concern was not to emphasize *by* whom they were baptized but *on account of* whom they were baptized, i.e., under whose influence they were converted. Consequently, White holds that Paul is asking, "If 'truly dead' persons are not raised, what sense does it make for the Corinthians to be baptized on account of those who are 'dying all the time,' namely, the apostles?"[149]

AN ASSESSMENT OF THE CONTEMPORARY READINGS

At this point, the plethora of readings, their disparity, and the lack of consensus in contemporary biblical scholarship are more than evident. An assessment of the contemporary readings is certainly in order, for a careful critique of previous readings will hone our own understanding of the *status quæstionis* and prepare the course for a rereading of 15:29. We assess the contemporary readings with two goals in mind. First, we look back in a scrutiny of the contemporary readings. In so doing, we see that none of them offers a satisfactory reading of 15:29. In addition, we find that the readings we have examined and compared offer invaluable insights for a rereading of 15:29. Their vivacity and complexity reveal that a *tabula rasa* reading of this verse is neither possible nor desirable. We have been given a substantial foundation on which to build by previous scholarship. Second, we look ahead in order to establish precisely the parame-

---

[146] Ibid., 497.

[147] R. F. Hock, *The Social Context of Paul's Ministry* (Philadelphia: Fortress, 1980) 59–62.

[148] J. R. White, "Baptized on account of the Dead," 497. So too, S. J. Hafemann, "'Self-Commendation' and Apostolic Legitimacy in 2 Corinthians: A Pauline Dialectic?" *NTS* 36 (1990) 79.

[149] J. R. White, "Baptized on account of the Dead," 498.

ters of the *status quæstionis* surrounding 15:29. In so doing, we seek to build on that foundation in order to delimit the framework of our own reading.

A Scrutiny of the Readings

Heretofore our examination of the contemporary readings of 15:29 has laid bare some of the weaknesses and strengths inherent in each. A careful scrutiny serves to highlight those aspects to be repudiated and those aspects to be retained in rereading 15:29.

A reading of vicarious baptism, though held by the majority of exegetes, suffers from three formidable difficulties. First, there is a dearth of an exterior or interior historical parallel. Except for the rare patristic secondary references we consider below, nowhere in the history of early Christianity do we find anyone baptizing in such fashion or writing thereof.[150] Nowhere in intertestamental Judaism or the pagan religions of late antiquity is there anything comparable to vicarious baptism.[151]

Second, there is a complete lack of biblical parallel. Such a custom is nowhere alluded to in the Bible. Thus, we must conclude that if such a reading is correct, the verse speaks of something particular and peculiar to Corinth, without parallel, and restricted to a very short space of time. That is, the vicarious baptism spoken of in 15:29 is *sui generis* to Corinth ca. A.D. 50. Preisker's hypo-

---

[150] That is not to say, however, that there are no general parallels in terms of some form of posthumous salvation for the dead, even dead pagans, in Paul, e.g., 1 Cor 5:5 and Rom 11:32; the NT, e.g., 1 Pet 4:6; or the early Church, e.g., when Thecla prays for Falconilla in *Act. Paul. et Thec.* 28–31. For more on these and other examples of posthumous salvation, see Trumbower, *Rescue for the Dead*; and R. Bauckham, *The Fate of the Dead: Studies on the Jewish and Christian Apocalypses* (NovTSup 93; Leiden: Brill, 1998). Nor is it to say that there are no general parallels of sanctification of pagans by believers, e.g., 1 Cor 7:14–16; or that the religious context of early Christianity may not have lent itself to such parallels, e.g., see H.-J. Klauck, *The Religious Context of Early Christianity: A Guide to Graeco-Roman Religions* (trans. B. McNeil; SNTW; Edinburgh: T&T Clark, 2000). But it is to say that there is nothing quite like vicarious baptism.

[151] Of course, that is not to say that Jews or pagans were unconcerned about the fate of the dead, e.g., 1 Sam 28:3–25 (cf. Lev 19:31) and 2 Macc 12:39–45; or Homer, *Od.* XI and Strabo, *Georg.* 16.2.39. Quite the opposite is true. For the Jews, see S. P. Raphael, *Jewish Views of the Afterlife* (Northvale, NJ: Aronson, 1994); Bauckham, *The Fate of the Dead*; and J. Davies, *Death, Burial, and Rebirth in the Religions of Antiquity* (RFCC; London and New York: Routledge, 1999). For the ancient Greeks and Romans, see S. I. Johnston, *Restless Dead: Encounters between the Living and the Dead in Ancient Greece* (Berkeley: University of California Press, 1999); and D. Ogden, *Greek and Roman Necromancy* (Princeton, NJ: Princeton University Press, 2001); see also, G. Luck, *Arcana Mundi: Magic and the Occult in the Greek and Roman Worlds* (Baltimore and London: Johns Hopkins University Press, 1985); F. Graf, *Magic in the Ancient World* (trans. F. Philip; Cambridge, MA: Harvard University Press, 1997); and M. W. Dickie, *Magic and Magicians in the Greco-Roman World* (London and New York: Routledge, 2001); for the sources, see W. Cotter, *Miracles in Greco-Roman Antiquity: A Sourcebook* (London and New York: Routledge, 1999); and D. Ogden, *Magic, Witchcraft, and Ghosts in the Greek and Roman Worlds: A Sourcebook* (Oxford: Oxford University Press, 2002). In all of this, there is nothing quite like vicarious baptism.

thetical eschatological urgency to fill the number of the elect, Moffatt's solidarity and intense faith in the resurrection, and Barrett's overzealous baptismal faith are resourceful enough theories in their expansion of theoretical theological positions deduced from 1 Corinthians, but they are groundless insofar as explaining 15:29.[152] Neither eschatological urgency nor intense, even overzealous, faith in the resurrection or baptism can be shown to have given rise to such a bizarre anomaly as vicarious baptism. By the same token, Rissi's postulation of an existential crisis in the Corinthian community and Martin's kataleptic baptism may be ingenious surmises, but they are arguments from silence. We know of no such external crisis among the Corinthians as Rissi contends. Martin's proleptic/kataleptic distinction is baseless; it seems to grow only out of his own *a priori* understanding of the verse as referring to vicarious baptism. These readings of vicarious baptism are, when the dust settles, little more than educated guesses, conjectures resting upon the presupposition of some theological perversion or historical situation among the Corinthians for which there is no evidence. A reading of 15:29 as an anomalous reaction to some speculative factor simply demonstrates ignorance as to the verse's meaning and cannot be conclusive.

Third, such a reading is a complete rupture within the context of 1 Cor 15:29–34. As Murphy-O'Connor shrewdly observes:

> If we accept that I Cor., XV, 29 refers to vicarious baptism, we are obliged to postulate a complete break between verses 28 and 29, and another between verses 29 and 30–34. In other words, while verse 29 reflects the general theme of this chapter, it has no relation to its immediate context. This consequence has been lost sight of in the discussion of the welter of opinions, but it has a decisive objection to the vicarious baptism interpretation because, according to sound methodology, the probable meaning of a polyvalent phrase is that demanded by its immediate context. By this criterion vicarious baptism is the least likely of the various possibilities of meaning implicit in verse 29. We should rather look for a meaning that integrates the verse into its context.[153]

If not a rupture, we are bound to say that Paul is stringing together loosely related thoughts or that, in one sense or another, the meaning of 15:29 is irrelevant to its immediate context within chapter 15. This is, in fact, claimed by Hans Conzelmann and Jean-Noël Aletti.[154] However, neither Conzelmann nor Aletti

---

[152] Cf. Beasely-Murray, *Baptism in the New Testament*, 188–89.

[153] Murphy-O'Connor, "Baptized for the Dead," 533.

[154] Conzelmann: Paul is simply "stringing different thoughts together" in 1 Cor 15:29–34 and 15:29 is merely an example thereof (*1 Corinthians*, 277). J.-N. Aletti: "... les solutions proposées [for 15:29] ne manquent pas d'ingéniosité, mais comme elles ne modifient pas la logique de l'argumentation paulinienne, qui est claire même si la connotation du v. 29 n'a rien d'évident...." ("L'argumentation de Paul et la position des Corinthiens: 1Co 15,12–34," in *Résurrection du Christ et des chrétiens (1Co 15)* [ed. L. De Lorenzi; SMB 8; Rome: Abbaye de S. Paul h.l.m., 1985] 77–78).

offers any proof for this apparent rupture other than the fact that any other reading would not fit his own interpretation of 1 Corinthians 15.

As we have seen, readings of vicarious baptism are based *solely* upon "the plain and necessary sense of the words."[155] Indeed, all commentators who hold for a reading of vicarious baptism do so in an unfaltering literalism—despite the lack of a comparable historical instance. Yet, if the text were as "plain" and the meanings of the words as "necessary" as so many claim, there scarcely could be such a lack of consensus about them among exegetes, and we would not find so many commentators pleading ignorance as to the verse's meaning. In light of these difficulties, a reading of vicarious baptism seems hopelessly inadequate, even if possible in a strict literal reading of the verse's words.

The weakness of the majority reading is also palpable in the efforts of Downey and DeMaris: both presuppose vicarious baptism and eschew formal exegesis. Each seeks only to explain what seems, *prima facie*, inexplicable. Even were we to grant a reading of vicarious baptism, their theories suffer from other problems. On the one hand, if Downey is correct in saying that the Corinthians thought of baptism as a means of protection from "principalities and powers" in this world and in the next, he simply fails to explain why certain members of the Corinthian community would have foregone such protection in *this* life. Since Downey leans heavily upon the supposed fear among the Corinthians of cosmic powers and struggles, it would seem that were there any means of protection offered against such formidable powers, whatever they might be, anyone would choose to be protected immediately, i.e., to receive baptism as soon as possible.

On the other hand, though DeMaris' detailed information about pagan funerary rites gleaned from archeological digs in Corinth and its environs as well as his illustrations relative to how such a rite as vicarious baptism might have flourished in a culture so earnestly concerned with the fate of its dead are invaluable, he fails to demonstrate that vicarious baptism actually occurred in Corinth (or elsewhere). He just presumes an unequivocal reading of vicarious baptism for 15:29 and takes off from there. What is more, he fails to explain two crucial issues for a reading of vicarious baptism: (1) how such a custom, if it existed at all, managed to slip out of usage without leaving even the hint of its existence anywhere other than in 15:29; and (2) how, if the Corinthian Christians needed to address the local preoccupation regarding the world of the dead, it necessarily follows that they did so by instituting vicarious baptism or, for that matter, by any syncretic adaptation or adoption.[156] DeMaris' theory is further weakened by the fact that we know nothing of the funerary practices of the Corinthian Christians themselves. Although we may adduce that their concern

---

[155] Parry, *First Corinthians*, 228.
[156] On this point, see J. R. White, "Baptized on account of the Dead," 490 n. 15.

for the dead was on par with their pagan contemporaries, Wayne A. Meeks is certainly correct in saying:

> We have no evidence about the funeral practices of Pauline Christians—a silence that in itself would be grounds for doubting a direct identification of the Christian groups with *collegia tenuiorum*—but we can hardly doubt, in the face of the sort of sentiment expressed in, say, 1 Thess 4:13–5:11 or the enigmatic reference to 'baptism for the dead' in 1 Cor 15:29, that these groups made appropriate provision for the burial of deceased Christians.[157]

With their readings of 15:29 wanting, we can only but laud Downey's and DeMaris' attempts to establish the historical locus of 15:29 and, thereby, remind us of the import of 15:29's historical context. Without detailed consideration of the historical situations in which Paul and his early converts found themselves, no sound reading of 15:29 can be mustered.

As we mentioned above, part and parcel of the greater number of readings of vicarious baptism is an allusion to one or more extraordinary second- and third-century Christian texts. Mixed selections from the patristic literature pepper well-nigh every contemporary commentary on 15:29. Though such selections are frequently thought of as relative to the verse's meaning, they are seldom thought of as defining. No doubt this is due to the puissance of the majority reading, for the presumption among so many exegetes is that 15:29, in fact, refers to some form of vicarious baptism or anomalous practice and that a latent strain thereof is discernable in the patristic literature.[158] However, this in itself is somewhat tenuous unless that strain can be traced convincingly—either in theory or in practice—to Paul himself, ancient Corinth, or Corinthian Christianity.

The earliest extant quotation of 15:29 is found in Origen's *In Matt. Hom.* 17.29 (ca. 185–ca. 254), but therein he only mentions the latter half of the verse in support of the resurrection, and his allusion is of little help.[159] The earliest extant interpretation comes with Tertullian (ca. 160–ca. 225). Tertullian (*De res. carn.* 48) claims that Paul is referring to the custom of baptizing a living Christian in the place of another person who died without baptism. As is the case with much of his exegesis, Tertullian lends greater attention to particular biblical passages when he perceives that their meaning is perverted by heresy.[160] Such is the case with 15:29 and the Marcionites.[161] Indeed, it is Tertullian (*Adv. Marc.*

---

[157] Meeks, *First Urban Christians*, 78.

[158] For example, Orr and Walther, *I Corinthians*, 337.

[159] Cf. Foschini, *Baptized for the Dead*, 3; and Thompson, "I Corinthians 15, 29," 652.

[160] See J. H. Waszink, "Tertullian's Principles and Methods of Exegesis," in *Early Christian Literature and the Classical Intellectual Tradition: In Honorem Robert M. Grant* (ed. W. R. Schoedel and R. L. Wilken; ThH 53; Paris: Beauchesne, 1979) 17–31.

[161] For a brief overview of the relevant historical circumstances, see G. Lüdemann, "The Arch-Heretic Marcion and His Time" (chap. 6), in *Heretics: The Other Side of Early Christianity* (trans. J.

1.4) who tells us that the Marcionites practiced a form of vicarious baptism.[162] With his customary vigor, Tertullian refutes the notion that Paul advocated vicarious baptism in 15:29 as ridiculous and heretical (*Adv. Marc.* 5.10). Tertullian believes that 15:29 referred to baptism on behalf of our "dying bodies."[163]

St. John Chrysostom (ca. 315–403) notes the practice of vicarious baptism among the Marcionites (*Hom. in 1 Cor.* 40); still, as we noted earlier, there is no way to be sure of Chrysostom's source. Chrysostom explains in detail his understanding of the Marcionite practice of vicarious baptism:

> When a catechumen died among them, a living person having been hidden underneath the bed of the deceased, they approach the dead person, speak to him and ask him if he would like to receive Baptism. Since he does not answer, the one who is hidden underneath speaks for him, saying that he does wish to be baptized. And so they baptize him for the sake of the one who has just died, just as if he were acting on a stage.[164]

Almost in the same terms as Tertullian, Chrysostom only mentions this because he believes it to be an abomination. Now the Greek Fathers hardly ever read the Latin Fathers, so it is unclear as to how Chrysostom arrived at an explanation which agrees almost to the word with Tertullian's.[165] It certainly seems "probable that either Chrysostom borrowed it from Tertullian, or that both, independently of each other, took it from a more ancient source not known to us."[166]

St. Epiphanius (ca. 315–403) also mentions vicarious baptism in his Πανάριον (or *Against All Heresies*), wherein he catalogues every heresy known to him (eighty in all) since the time of the Lord, and he refutes them one by one. Epiphanius (*Pan.* 28) refers to a practice of vicarious baptism among the Cerinthians,[167] not the Marcionites. He considers it to be heretical and to have arisen out of a misunderstanding of 15:29. According to Epiphanius, when a Cerinthian

---

Bowden; London: SCM, 1996) 148–69. The standard work on the subject is A. von Harnack, *Marcion: Das Evangelium von fremden Gott* (2nd ed.; Leipzig: Henrichs, 1924).

[162] The Marcionite practice is also mentioned very briefly by Didymus the Blind; see K. Staab, ed. *Pauluskommentare aus der griechischen Kirche: Aus Katenenkandschriften gesammelt und herausgegeben* (NTAbh 15; Münster: Aschendorff, 1933) 8.

[163] For an explanation of Tertullian's (as well as Chrysostom's) position, see Thompson, "I Corinthians 15, 29," 654–65; and Trumbower, *Rescue for the Dead*, 37–38.

[164] Chrysostom (*Hom. in 1 Cor.*), as quoted and translated in Foschini, *Baptized for the Dead*, 55.

[165] Foschini, *Baptized for the Dead*, 64 n. 277. For more on the Greek Fathers, see Staab, "1 Kor 15,29 im Lichte der Exegese der griechischen Kirche," 443–50.

[166] Ibid.

[167] Very little is known about the gnostic heretic Cerinthus (fl. ca. 100) and his followers. For more see G. Bardy, "Cérinthe," *RB* 30 (1921) 344–73, and the curious references in Irenaeus (*Adv. haer.* 3.11.1) and Eusebius (*Hist. eccl.* 3.28.6). See also P. Schaff, "Alogians," in *A Dictionary of Early Christian Biography* (ed. H. Wace and W. C. Piercy; 1911, rpt. Peabody, MA: Hendrickson, 1999) 14–15.

catechumen died, a member of the church was baptized in his room so that the deceased might escape the penalties of the unbaptized.

Clearly, Tertullian, Chrysostom, and Epiphanius consider any form of vicarious baptism—whether it be the baptism of the living on behalf of the dead or the baptism of corpses—to be a misinterpretation of 15:29. None of them either claims that the practice originated with Paul or in Corinth. Therefore, although the patristic era may know of aberrant baptismal practices, they are only mentioned in terms of condemnation and heresy. Whether or not such practices arose out of an interpretation of 15:29, or 15:29 was appended to them as a proof-text, remains unknown.[168]

Ambrosiaster is the first to propose vicarious baptism as the exegesis of 15:29 that is necessary to explain an aberration in Corinth.[169] Ambrosiaster (*Com. 1 Cor.*) suggests that vicarious baptism was administered to living Christians on behalf of pagans who died before baptism. However, Ambrosiaster seems to be doing nothing more than opining, since he offers no historical occurrences or sources.[170] Assuredly, there is ample evidence in the early Church of postponing baptism until later in life so as to preclude the possibility of sin thereafter. The pertinent debate concerning this custom focuses on the peril of averting baptism too long (lest one risk damnation, should one die before the baptismal rite) and does not indicate any form of postmortem baptism as an alternative. In any case, the problem of sectarians and heretics baptizing corpses led the Church to condemn the baptism thereof at the Third Council of Carthage in 397.[171] Again, there is no link to Paul or Corinth other than 15:29 itself.

With such a paucity of evidence, we must conclude along with Jeremias that "the gnostic vicarious baptisms, which are mentioned in the patristic literature, are of no help for the understanding of our verse because they evidently have their origin in a misinterpretation of our verse itself."[172] Moreover, even if later practices did not result from a misinterpretation of the verse, the "[p]ractices of heretical Christians in later centuries do not explain the meaning of whatever was being done by some people in the Corinthian church in Paul's time."[173]

---

[168] Foschini agrees: "In the writings of Tertullian, Epiphanius, and Chrysostom, we find nothing at all, or at best, only references that are extremely questionable, in favor of vicarious baptism. Therefore, although this hypothesis is possible philologically, it must be rejected insofar as it is contrary to the Sacred Text itself and to history, or at least because it has no basis therein" (*Baptized for the Dead*, 55).

[169] "Ambrosiaster" is the pseudonym for the unknown author of *Commentaria in xiii Epistolas beati Pauli*, probably written in the late fourth century. See "Ambrosiaster," in *Dictionary of Early Christian Biography*, 15–16.

[170] So too, Preisker, "Die Vikariatstaufe I Cor 15:29," 304 n. 1; and Foschini, *Baptized for the Dead*, 52–53.

[171] Canon 6: "Deinde cavendum est ne mortuos etiam baptizari posse fratrum infirmitas credat."

[172] Jeremias, "Flesh and Blood," 155. So too, Godet, *First Corinthians*, 2:384–85; Raeder, "Vikariatstaufe?" 259; and Foschini, *Baptized for the Dead*, 55.

[173] Orr and Walther, *I Corinthians*, 337.

Therefore, if we are to discover the meaning of 15:29, we need to look much farther back than the patristic literature of later days to Paul and those to whom he preached in first-century Corinth. To be sure, a reading of vicarious baptism cannot be discounted because of the words of 15:29, but despite all the exegetes who hold for that reading, none has presented a solid explanation for the historical circumstances from which vicarious baptism is alleged to have emerged. If not vicarious baptism, then what about ordinary baptism?

Let us begin with the numerous variations and emendations proffered by Dürselen, Foschini, Thompson, O'Neill, and Murphy-O'Connor. At first blush, we find them rather unconvincing; each in some way seems to do violence to the text of 1 Cor 15:29–34. For the most part, they all seem to imply that the text of 15:29, as it stands literally, compels a reading of vicarious baptism. Despite the fact that we will have reason to suggest that Murphy-O'Connor fails to heed his own caution, he perceives the situation clearly: "We are told that an unbiased reading of the verse immediately and naturally suggests such a practice; other opinions would have been proposed only because scholars could not bring themselves (for dogmatic or other reasons) to admit the existence of such a bizarre custom."[174] And in order to evade that incorrect yet so widely accepted reading, they posit enigmatic alternatives in punctuation or verbal definition and modification.

Dürselen, Foschini, and Thompson would alter the punctuation of 15:29. Obviously, there was no punctuation in the original manuscripts of the NT. Since the original Greek text is not punctuated, a debate on the veracity of punctuation is moot, for it can only regress into a denial of the methodology of the best in contemporary textual criticism as it is represented in the N-A^{27} and the *GNT*^{4} vis-à-vis 15:29.[175] Their syntactical alternations seem to be nothing more than lame efforts to have the meaning of the verse change from a reading of vicarious baptism to something more palatable. To accept their readings is to say that without some alteration, 15:29 can be read *only* to indicate the reality of some form of vicarious baptism among the Corinthians. That is certainly not the case. Without apology, we accept the punctuation of the N-A^{27} and the *GNT*^{4} and note that the proposed alternative readings demand a number of, at least implied, ellipses, without which these same readings would scarcely be sensible and for which there is no basis other than creative, albeit educated, guesswork. Still and all, these readings are dubitable on the grounds of their assertions regarding the parameters of investigation and the usage of ὑπέρ and νεκρός.[176]

Dürselen fixes a set of norms that begs the question of a proper reading for 15:29. It is hardly a surprise to discover that his own solution to the question is

---

[174] Murphy-O'Connor, "Baptized for the Dead," 532.

[175] Whereas the N-A^{27} notes one very minor alternate reading, though not related to punctuation (we discuss this below, for now see N-A^{27} *ad loc.*), so elementary is the rendering in the *GNT*^{4} that 15:29 is not even mentioned in the *TCGNT*.

[176] Cf. Reaume, "Another Look at 1 Corinthians 15:29," 466 n. 46.

in complete conformity with his own norms—though only by an altering of the text through the use of the question marks he proposes. Yet, even were we to accept Dürselen's norms, Foschini shows that Dürselen himself has violated them. Foschini reveals Dürselen's oversight:

> [Dürselen's] opinion, we believe, is defective in one respect: it errs in joining the words *hyper auton* with the following phrase *ti kai hemeis kindyneuomen*. For this would be a breach of the very first of the four norms rightly set up by Dürselen himself, namely: the argumentation based on Baptism is parallel to that based on the tribulations of the Apostles. If Dürslen's idea be admitted, there is no parallel between the argumentation in v. 29 and v. 30.[177]

Nevertheless, that is not to say that Foschini's reading is superior to Dürselen's. Oddly enough, it is largely the same. Foschini's rendition hinges on adding question marks different from Dürselen's and reading ὑπέρ as εἰς. The implausibility of the additional punctuation aside, reading ὑπέρ as εἰς is unattested in *Koinē* Greek.[178] Such a desperate attempt to read ὑπέρ as εἰς diminishes Foschini's argument to the point of facile refutation. And Thompson's reading of 15:29 falls for similar reasons. Once again, Thompson amends the punctuation to his own ends on dubious manuscript evidence.[179] More crassly, he translates νεκροί as "dead bodies" as opposed to "dead persons." Such a distinction is unattested and purely speculative, and his appeal to Chrysostom for support is unfounded, as we have already noted. Additionally, there is not a shred of evidence in any part of the Pauline literature for something even resembling such a distinction. Notwithstanding our inability to accept the readings of Dürselen, Foschini, and Thompson, they do point our attention to the need for a very close examination of the literary context of 15:29.

But what of O'Neill and Murphy-O'Connor who also hold for a reading of ordinary baptism with a variance on the text? O'Neill and Murphy-O'Connor bring a sharp focus on the literary context. Holding some things in common, O'Neill and Murphy-O'Connor each argue on two levels. We cannot accept their respective first levels of argumentation, viz., O'Neill's choice of the textual variant from the Leicester codex 69 and Murphy-O'Connor's metaphorical reading of βαπτίζω. The manuscript evidence against O'Neill's position is so formidable as to make his position untenable: it transgresses all the standards of textual criticism.[180] Murphy-O'Connor's metaphorical reading of βαπτίζω is

---

[177] Foschini, *Baptized for the Dead*, 92.

[178] For now, see "ὑπέρ," BAGD, 838. Note that all of the words in 15:29, especially their morphology and syntax, are discussed at length below.

[179] Cf. Conzelmann, *1 Corinthians*, 276 n. 120; and Trumbower, *Rescue for the Dead*, 37 n. 9.

[180] Note that 𝔓⁴⁶, ℵ, A, B, D*, F, G, K, P, Ψ, 075, 0243, 33, 81, 104, 365, 630, 1175, 1241ˢ, 1505, 1739, 1881, 2464, *al*, latt, syh, co, and Epiph end the verse with "αυτων"; this ending is followed by N-A²⁷ and the *GNT*⁴; and D², 𝔐, syᵖ, and boᵐˢ read "των νεκρων." Only codex 69 reads "αυτων των νεκρων." Once again, 15:29 is not mentioned in the *TCGNT*; thus, as regards the textual evidence, no one makes a claim for this variant as the original. The criterion of *lectio difficilior*

also untenable. He himself recognizes its weaknesses, though he maintains it nonetheless, while admitting that Paul uses βαπτίζω elsewhere *exclusively* in reference to the sacrament of baptism.[181] Here we must agree with Barrett—"*Baptized*, without further explanation, can hardly have any other than its normal Pauline meaning"[182]—as well as with Gordon D. Fee and Joel R. White, both of whom consider Murphy-O'Connor's position on βαπτίζω and reject it.[183] With his metaphorical interpretation of βαπτίζω discounted, Murphy-O'Connor's suggestion that 15:29 is a gibe topples precipitously. Therewith, both O'Neill and Murphy-O'Connor's readings may be discounted. Nevertheless, there is much to be said for their common second level of argumentation, viz., that ὅλως modifies νεκροί (15:29b) rather than ἐγείρονται,[184] which is less easily dismissed and is investigated later in our study as we consider 15:29's morphology and syntax.

As we have so often noted, ὑπέρ is the decisive word in 15:29. The readings of the verse which claim it to refer to ordinary baptism by example are best assessed in terms of the translation of ὑπέρ. Raeder and Jeremias read ὑπέρ in its final sense,[185] Reaume and White in its causal sense. All four agree on the normal Pauline usage of βαπτίζω.

Raeder and Jeremias cite other instances of a final ὑπέρ in Paul (1 Cor 15:3; 2 Cor 1:6; Rom 15:8) and translate ὑπέρ τῶν νεκρῶν as "with a view towards the dead [in the resurrection]." Notwithstanding their literal understanding of νεκρός,[186] this translation is roundly refuted by Beasely-Murray: "It demands the insertion of too much that is left unexpressed."[187] We find ourselves tentatively in agreement with him. Such an insertion is barely viable, even if we accept their hypothesis of an extreme missionary zeal on the part of the Corinthians. As we have seen, Raeder and Jeremias maintain that 15:29 refers to pagans who seek baptism for no other reason than to be united with deceased Christians at the resurrection. In other words, though they do not embrace Jesus, they believe that baptism will ensure resurrection. Besides the lack of any bibli-

---

certainly does not apply here given the manuscript evidence. Rissi (*Die Taufe für die Toten*, 53) already dismissed the sort of thing O'Neill proposes. And J. R. White ("Baptized on account of the Dead," 491), who considers O'Neill's position, says that all angles considered, "O'Neill's proposed solution must be deemed unsatisfactory."

[181] Murphy-O'Connor, "Baptized for the Dead," 536.

[182] Barrett, *First Corinthians*, 362.

[183] See Fee, *First Corinthians*, 765 n. 22; and J. R. White, "Baptized on account of the Dead," 492.

[184] Cf. Fee, *First Corinthians*, 765–66.

[185] Recall that above we showed that Howard ("Baptism for the Dead," 137–41), rather than crafting an original reading of 15:29, "baptized" Raeder's reading ("Vikariatstaufe?" 258–60) by suggesting a motive for baptism (union with Christ) less incongruous than the one given by Raeder (union with Christians). Consequently, his reading of the verse is only as strong as Raeder's, upon which it relies, and does not require separate consideration.

[186] See Raeder, "Vikariatstaufe" 269–60; and Jeremias, "Flesh and Blood," 155–56.

[187] Beasely-Murray, *Baptism in the New Testament*, 186.

cal or historical parallel for such action, it seems not only incredible but implausible that persons, who do not accept Christianity, would espouse one of its sacraments as so powerfully efficacious.[188] Furthermore, it seems oddly out of character, from what we know of Paul and the Corinthians, that Corinthian Christians would administer baptism solely for that purpose.[189] Raeder and Jeremias ask us to accept a number of hypothetical ellipses because the ellipses support an historical hypothesis; since Raeder and Jeremias ground their historical hypothesis on the ellipses, theirs seems to be circular reasoning without an historical anchor. In which case, we reckon the readings proposed by Raeder and Jeremias to be unsatisfactory.

Reaume and White read 15:29 in much the same fashion as Raeder and Jeremias but with a different nuance regarding ὑπέρ. Both fittingly follow the lead of Murphy-O'Connor in turning fellow interpreters back to the context. They agree, *mutatis mutandis*, on the translation of ὑπέρ in its causal sense, "because of the influence of" or "on account of." Their respective readings of baptism by example with the causal ὑπέρ seem, at this point in our study, to come the closest to interpreting 15:29 correctly, especially because they do no violence to the text and its literary context. Reaume rejects that the νεκροί are the "dying bodies" vis-à-vis O'Neill, or the "spiritually dead" vis-à-vis Murphy-O'Connor. Instead, he holds that the νεκροί are dead believers. Given the use of νεκρός in 1 Corinthians, this is probably true. Nevertheless, as regards the historical context, Reaume seems to have his wires crossed. Initially, he says—quite correctly—that there is no evidence of persecution or martyrdom in Corinth about the time 1 Corinthians would have been written,[190] then he goes on to say that "many individuals in the early Church were influenced by the testimony of other believers who had recently died or were martyred."[191] Well, on the one hand, we surely agree that many pagans in the early Church were influenced by the testimony of believers—how else could it have been? What is puzzling is how their deaths, if not by persecution or martyrdom for the faith, are significant—how do their presumably natural deaths lead others to baptism? The death of Christians would hardly be out of the ordinary—everyone dies and death was a much more tangible reality in the first century than in our own—but their death *qua* death hardly seems a compelling motive to adopt their religious beliefs. Granted, the witness of those who died in the faith, even if not for the faith, may have been edifying, but why would Paul have spoken of them in terms of their death rather than in terms of their faith? Reaume's explanation of the use of ὑπέρ in the causal sense (and a literal reading of βαπτίζω and νεκρός) is superb,

---

[188] The same holds true for Howard's reading ("Baptized for the Dead," 140–41). Howard offers no grounds for his conjecture that desire for unity leads to an acceptance of resurrection and, therefore, to Christ.

[189] So too, J. R. White, "Baptized on account of the Dead," 491–92, esp. 492 n. 29.

[190] See Reaume, "Another Look at 1 Corinthians 15:29," 460, esp. n. 12.

[191] Ibid., 475.

yet he has left us with a causal without a cause. In the end, we find his reading of 15:29 lacking. For inasmuch as he has accounted for the first half, baptism "on account of," he has failed to account for the second half, "the dead."

Apropos to the dead, White, along the lines of O'Neill and Murphy-O'Connor, propounds a metaphorical reading for τῶν νεκρῶν in 15:29a and claims that ὅλως functions attributively to modify νεκροί in 15:29b. The former "dead" he equates with the apostles; the latter "dead" are the actually dead, i.e., persons who have undergone physical death. This is a somewhat gratuitous claim. Not unlike O'Neill's reading, White contends that the same word is used in the same sentence to mean entirely different things; also not unlike O'Neill's reading, White contends that Paul makes a distinction between two types of "dead." Whereas White spends pages explaining how Paul is identified as an apostle in 2 Corinthians, building a very fine case on that point in conjunction with Hafemann's study,[192] he does not explain—even if we were to grant a metaphorical reading for τῶν νεκρῶν and to accept Murphy-O'Connor's suggestion as to Paul's mindset while composing chapter 15[193]—*how* the dead of 15:29a are to be identified with the apostles. White has reached beyond the pale. On account of this distressing lacuna, White's reading seems less than credible. Again, it is a pity that White seems to have been unaware of Reaume's prior analysis of 15:29 when doing his own explication of 15:29. Barring some difficulties, Reaume's interpretation is preferable to White's. Ultimately, White's reading, jerry-built around a not-so-subtle ellipsis, which identifies some νεκροί with living apostles and some with dead believers, is also untenable. Perhaps, it seems that we are back to square one: so many readings vying for approbation, so little consensus among them, and yet not one of them remains standing after careful critique and comparison. Ever pertinacious, 15:29 still awaits a fiducial interpretation. How do we go about forming it? What is the *status quæstionis* of 15:29?

The *Status Quæstionis*

Our scrutiny of the contemporary readings of 15:29 is profitable in many respects towards establishing the *status quæstionis*. First, in reviewing the numerous contemporary readings, we have garnered a preliminary sense of 15:29 as a *crux interpretum* and the complexities involved in reading the verse. Second, in critiquing the readings, we have found each interpretation to be advantageous towards a rereading of the verse precisely because each reading highlights one or another of the salient issues, even as each reading is deemed insufficient in and of itself. Third, it is now obvious that a rereading of 15:29—

---

[192] Hafemann, *Suffering and Ministry in the Spirit*, 52–79.

[193] "The climax of the discussion in verses 20–28 would have triggered in Paul's mind an association of ideas which induced him to present apostolic labors as the next argument in favor of the resurrection" (Murphy-O'Connor, "Baptized for the Dead," 534).

and a radical one at that—receives its mandate from the fact that the plethora of past efforts has not mitigated confusion about the verse but only expanded the present perplexity. Finally, it has become clear that, if we seek to reread 15:29, we must begin where we find it. Our assessment shows that none of the readings has allotted ample attention to each of the *two* contextual moorings in which we find 15:29: the literary context of 1 Corinthians and the historical context of first-century Corinth. Assuredly, this dearth of suitable contextualization is the vector of failure running through the contemporary readings of 15:29. The *status quæstionis* may be summed up with two questions: How does 15:29 fit in 1 Corinthians? and How does 15:29 fit in first-century Corinth? The key to the interpretation of 15:29 lies in the fusion of these answers. Before we can reread 15:29, we must turn to its contexts, literary and historical, for the *status quæstionis* of our investigation is unavoidably contextual.[194]

First, we must turn to the literary context. All of the contemporary readings, whether they argue for vicarious or ordinary baptism—especially those that prefer emendations and variations of the text—bespeak the acute significance of the literary context. It is to that literary context that we must go with a vengeance. Regarding the literary context, we cannot begin *in medias res* as do so many others. We have to start from scratch, from the beginning. It is clear that 15:29 cannot be read as a "thing apart"; it cannot be read accurately in isolation. In order to establish the literary context of 15:29, we must look to the literary genre and integrity of 1 Corinthians, then to the structure of 1 Corinthians 15, and finally to the morphology and syntax of the words that are 15:29. Such an effort constitutes the second chapter of our study.

Second, we look to the historical context. Downey and DeMaris, with their suggestions of syncretism on the part of Corinthian Christians (and Paul?), have contributed greatly to our study by piquing interest in the religious and cultural milieux of ancient Corinth, in the historical circumstances wherein the Corinthians first heard the "gospel of Paul." In the mid-first century, Paul the Apostle preached in Corinth and won many converts to Jesus Christ. The resulting Corinthian Christianity via Paul is the historical locus of 15:29. As with the literary context, we cannot begin to understand that historical context simply by looking *in medias res*. Once again, we have to start from scratch. Who was this Christian Jew from Tarsus? To whom and in what historical circumstances did he preach in Corinth? And what were his converts supposed to have believed after accepting his proclamation of the Christ? An attempt to answer these three questions, so as to determine the historical context of 15:29, comprises the third chapter of our study.

Once the literary and historical contexts are established, we are primed to get to the heart of the matter: What does 15:29 mean? This represents the subject of our fourth chapter. Culling from all that we have learned through our contex-

---

[194] Cf. Murphy-O'Connor, "Baptized for the Dead," 533–34.

tualizations, we are properly prepared to reread the verse, to offer a new reading of baptism "on account of the dead." That is, once we read 15:29 as we maintain it ought to be read—as an act of faith in the resurrection of Christ and of Christians—then the grave importance of 15:29 for Paul's baptismal theology manifests itself. With this new reading, we are able to venture towards some theological insights into Paul's baptismal thought. Given the paucity of references to baptism in the Pauline literature and the enormous weight placed upon them in contemporary biblical scholarship and theological inquiry, our verse, using the very word βαπτίζω in the letter wherein Paul uses it more than any other of his letters, has much to say about his baptismal theology.

In eking out that baptismal theology, we must take great care. Heretofore, in commentaries and articles too numerous to note, it has become fashionable to turn to Paul's (postulated) baptismal theology in order to inform the meaning of 15:29 rather than to have 15:29 inform our understanding thereof. This is a methodological inversion of sound theological inquiry to be avoided. It is not until the meaning of a verse is assured that it may inform our theology. To apply theological conclusions based on other verses and passages is to abandon the exegetical endeavor. We must seek to know the meaning of our verse, strive to grasp its perspicuity, compare it to similar citations, and query as to its relevance to our understanding of Paul's baptismal theology now and in the future.

In conclusion, though 15:29 is irrefutably concerned with the dead,[195] such a concern is based on the lofty hope of eternal life. A precursory reading of 1 Corinthians 15 indicates that the chapter's matrix is one of resurrection and victory over death. It is with life that 1 Corinthians 15 begins, and it is with life that it ends. The same focus must be ours as we delve into baptism "on account of the dead."

---

[195] "However the philologist reads the language of baptism on behalf of the dead (ὑπὲρ τῶν νεκρῶν), whether one takes ὑπέρ spatially—over, above—or opts for one of its figurative senses—in defense of, in place of, in the name of, for the prosperity of—the practice itself expresses a concern for, an interest in, the dead" (DeMaris, "Demeter in Roman Corinth," 114).

II. Reading 1 Corinthians 15:29 in Literary Context

The goal of this chapter is to read 1 Cor 15:29 as closely as possible in its literary context. In view of the fact that previous readings have proven unsatisfactory, we seek a reading of the verse which flows out of its locus within 1 Corinthians. This demands an overall examination of the genre and integrity of the letter as well as a particular examination of 1 Corinthians 15 and the morphology and syntax of 15:29. If anything became clear in our previous chapter, it is that exegetes have not given sufficient consideration to the vocabulary and syntax of 15:29 within the whole of 1 Corinthians. As we have also seen, most commentators seem all too satisfied to cite the verse as a "mystery" or as representative of an anomalous practice: to claim that 15:29 indicates an incongruity in Paul's (baptismal) thought, in the Corinthians' thought, or both. All in all, any reading must take into account the literal meaning of 15:29, and each contemporary reading is based, in whole or in part, on whether 15:29 speaks of vicarious or ordinary baptism. So in a step towards establishing what 15:29 means, we too must ask what it says. And we must begin at the beginning, first with the letter, then move to the chapter, and finally to the verse itself. The literary genre and compositional integrity of 1 Corinthians are hardly uncontested. The former is the subject of recent and intense scholarly debate; the latter has been debated since the challenge leveled against it by Johannes Weiss.[1] Consensus remains a *desideratum*. Questions of genre and integrity are, of course, interrelated. Because form and content shape and inform one another in any text, we must first address these issues. Then we will be properly prepared to approach 1 Corinthians 15 in general and 15:29 in particular to render precisely the literary context of 15:29.

THE GENRE AND INTEGRITY OF 1 CORINTHIANS

The discernment of genre is crucial in the reading of any text, for genre (form) is inextricably linked to meaning (content). Indeed, the discernment of genre is the initial stage in the reading of texts and integral to the interpretive process. For

---

[1] Weiss, *Der erste Korintherbrief*, xl–xliii.

the most part, though there were countless variations on the theme, 1 Corinthians has been read as a letter alongside the other letters of the NT. Of the twenty-seven books in the NT, twenty-one are letters (or epistles),[2] and thirteen of the twenty-one bear Paul's name. The investigation of their genre has always been of prime importance in NT scholarship. Likewise, their literary integrity is often disputed. The issues of genre and integrity in terms of 1 Corinthians need to be addressed and resolved before we speak of chapter 15 and whet our observations on the particulars of 15:29.

The Genre of 1 Corinthians

Recently, certain scholars have examined NT letters from a rhetorical perspective. In so doing, they have challenged assumptions held for centuries about the bodies of these letters. Here we describe the character of the Hellenistic letter, consider the challenges of rhetorical criticism, and examine the nature of the "letter-essay."

1 Corinthians is a letter—about that there is no dispute. Its overall structure, with the typical opening and closing formulae of a Hellenistic or Greco-Roman letter, ensures its categorization as such. Yet, using the term "letter" (ἐπιστολή) within the milieu of ancient writing denotes a category as wide as the use of the term in our own day. Then, as now, there were many types of letters wherein the body was structured according to the purpose of the letter. It was at the turn of the twentieth century that Adolf Deissmann pioneered the comparative analysis of ancient epistolography by examining hundreds of Hellenistic papyri (mostly from Egypt) which had been continually discovered since 1752.[3] Deissmann drew a sharp distinction between the "letter" and the "epistle." For Deissmann, a letter is a simple, unadorned, non-literary communication between the sender and the addressee(s); an epistle is a carefully crafted literary essay written for a public audience.[4] By his criteria, all of the thirteen letters traditionally attributed to Paul (as well as 2 and 3 John) are letters; Hebrews, 1 and 2 Peter, James, 1

---

[2] There are, of course, twenty-two if we categorize Revelation according to its literary framework. There are also two letters within Acts (15:23–26 and 23:26–30) and seven letters within Revelation (2:1–3:22).

[3] Publication of the papyri began in the series *Ägyptische Urkunden aus den Königlichen Museen zu Berlin: Griechische Urkunden* (Berlin: Weidmann, 1895) and in the first volume of *The Oxyrhynchus Papyri* (ed. B. F. Grenfell and A. S. Hunt; London: Egypt Exploration Fund, 1898).

[4] A. Deissmann, *Bible Studies: Contributions Chiefly from Papyri and Inscriptions to the History of the Language, the Literature, and the Religion of Hellenistic Judaism and Primitive Christianity* (trans. A. Grieve; Edinburgh: T&T Clark, 1901) esp. 9, 48, 58; and idem, *Light from the Ancient East: The New Testament Illustrated by Recently Discovered Texts of the Graeco-Roman World* (trans. L. R. M. Strachan; 2nd ed.; London: Hodder and Stoughton, 1927) esp. 147, 213, 219, 221. For a thorough bibliography of Deissmann's works on epistolary literature, see W. G. Doty, "The Classification of Epistolary Literature," *CBQ* 31 (1969) 183 n. 2.

John, and Jude are epistles.[5] Deissmann's work has not gone without criticism. The objection of W. A. Ramsay, made immediately after the publication of and in reference to Deissmann's *Bible Studies*, that it is impossible "to reduce all the letters of the New Testament to one or other of those categories,"[6] has stood the test of time, for the Greek term itself admits of no such semantic distinctions.[7] Deissmann's particular categorizations of NT letters are fairly draconian,[8] nevertheless his distinction of the prevalent patterns of the "letter" and "epistle" has served as a basis for later scholarly discrimination and is still used, even if with some modification.[9] Rarely does anyone comment on ancient epistolography without mentioning Deissmann. Although we shy away from the extremes of Deissmann's poles, 1 Corinthians surely lies closer to and is best termed a "letter" rather than an "epistle."

1 Corinthians evidences the threefold division of the Hellenistic letter: opening formulae (1:1–9), body (1:10–16:18), and concluding formulae (16:19–24).[10] Paul's opening formulae consist of the standard parts of the Hellenistic letter with only slight modification.[11] In the epistolary prescript, Paul identifies

---

[5] Cf. D. E. Aune, *The New Testament in Its Literary Environment* (LEC 8; Philadelphia: Westminster, 1987) 160.

[6] W. M. Ramsay, *The Letters to the Seven Churches of Asia and Their Place in the Plan of the Apocalypse* (New York: Armstrong, 1905) 24.

[7] M. L. Stirewalt, Jr., *Studies in Ancient Greek Epistolography* (SBLRBS 27; Atlanta: Scholars Press) 87.

[8] For an extensive catalogue of those who agree and disagree with Deissmann, see J. C. Hurd, Jr., *The Origin of 1 Corinthians* (New York: Seabury, 1965) 4 nn. 3–5.

[9] For example, see R. E. Brown (*Introduction to the New Testament* [ABRL; New York: Doubleday, 1997] 410–11 et passim) who variously combines the two, "letter" and "epistle," in categorizing Ephesians, Hebrews, James, 2 Peter, 1 John, and Jude. The discussion of ancient epistolography is, of course, ongoing, especially in the Society of Biblical Literature's Ancient Epistolography Group. See J. L. White ("The Ancient Epistolography Group in Retrospect" *Semeia* 22 [1981] 1–14) for the *raison d'être* of the group's convergence, some of its initial findings, and its aspirations.

[10] General outlines show a divergence of opinion on minor matters. Here we follow, *inter alia*, Robertson and Plummer, *I Corinthians*, xxvii; Fee, *First Corinthians*, 23; Brown, *Introduction to the New Testament*, 512; almost all of the rhetorical analyses; and the various and sundry partition theories too numerous to cite here.

[11] Although Paul follows the customary epistolary practice in the opening formulae of 1 Corinthians (see H. Koskenniemi, *Studien zur Idee und Phraseologie des griechischen Briefs bis 400 n. Chr.* [AASF 102.2; Helsinki: Suomalaisen Tiedeakatemain, 1956] 139–45), he adjusts them to his purposes. On the prayers or thanksgivings, the most thorough examination is given by P. Schubert, *Form and Function of the Pauline Thanksgivings* (BZNW 20; Berlin: Töpelmann, 1939), which was followed up by J. T. Sanders, "The Transition from Opening Epistolary Thanksgiving to Body in the Letters of the Pauline Corpus," *JBL* 81 (1962) 348–62. It is on the basis of these two that J. L. White ("Introductory Formulae in the Body of the Pauline Letter," *JBL* 90 [1971] 91–97) analyzes the variety of introductory formulae Paul used. In response to White's work, which took its beginning with the Pauline letters, T. Y. Mullins ("Formulas in New Testament Epistles," *JBL* 91 [1972] 380–90) prefers to begin the examination of forms outside the Pauline letters, and then see how such

himself and Sosthenes as the senders, the Corinthian church and the saints as the addressees,[12] and offers his wish of "grace and peace" (1:1–3). Here, Paul "baptizes" the Hellenistic prescript by replacing the traditional "greetings" (χάρειν) with "grace" (χάρις),[13] and he "semiticizes" it with his addition of "peace" (εἰρήνη).[14] Then, Paul offers his epistolary thanksgiving or prayer (1:4–9). The concluding formulae (16:19–24) also evidence a slight variation: extensive greetings (ἀσπάζεσθαι) without the standard farewell (ἔρρωσο).[15] The body,

---

forms are appropriated by Paul. Each of these is taken into account by P. Arzt ("The 'Epistolary Introductory Thanksgiving' in the Papyri and in Paul," *NovT* 36 [1994] 29–46), who claims that the scholarly consensus, which holds that Paul uses a more or less common contemporaneous epistolary thanksgiving, is dubious. Arzt's conclusions are in turn challenged by J. T. Reed ("Are Paul's Thanksgivings 'Epistolary'?" *JSNT* 61 [1996] 87–99), who correctly demonstrates that though caution is necessary when speaking of them as "introductory," they are certainly epistolary. Since the introductory formulae often establish mutual concern (a key function in the ancient letter), we are not surprised to find Paul introducing key terms (esp. κοινωνία in 1:9b) after the emphasis on unity in 1:2. The reader is prepared for the message.

[12] M. M. Mitchell (*Paul and the Rhetoric of Reconciliation: An Exegetical Investigation of the Language and Composition of 1 Corinthians* [Louisville: Westminster John Knox, 1991] 193 with nn. 39, 40) points out that this "double" address, i.e., a combined address to the "church" and to the "saints," may be significant. Such a double address is found only in 1 Corinthians. It may indicate Paul's concern with factionalism among the Corinthians, and the textual variants may support this interpretation further. 2 Corinthians, Galatians (though plural in that it is addressed to the "churches" in Galatia), and 1 Thessalonians have only the church address; Romans and Philippians have only the saints' address. We are not surprised, then, to find Paul beginning the body of the letter with a plea against dissention since that is the theme he immediately pursues in 1:10. This places great unity between the prescript and the body. However, as we see below, perhaps Mitchell makes too much of this in order to support her own hypotheses about 1 Corinthians.

[13] Much is often read into this. For example, can we go so far as to say that, combined with ἀπὸ θεοῦ πατρὸς ἡμῶν καὶ κυρίου Ἰησοῦ Χριστοῦ, it is an attempt on Paul's part to rebuke a gnostic Christology present among the Corinthians as W. Grundmann ("χρίω," *TDNT* 9:55-55) would have it?

[14] With Paul's addition of καὶ εἰρήνη to the standard χάρειν/χάρις, many see a strong and significant semiticism (e.g., Robertson and Plummer, *1 Corinthians*, 3; Fee, *First Corinthians*, 34; Conzelmann, *1 Corinthians*, 24 n. 42; and esp. W. Foerster and G. von Rad, "εἰρήνη, εἰρηνεύω, εἰρηνικός, εἰρηνοπιός, εἰρηνοποίεω," *TDNT* 2:402–6), wherein εἰρήνη transposes the שָׁלוֹם—often but not necessarily—found in Hebrew and Aramaic letters as well as the plethora of meanings that שָׁלוֹם signifies. Aune is speculative: "Paul's use of 'peace' probably reflects the Hebrew and Aramaic salutation *šlm*" (*The New Testament in Its Literary Environment*, 184). Cf. "εἰρήνη, ης, ἡ," BAGD, 227–28. On Hebrew and Aramaic epistolography, see J. A. Fitzmyer, "Aramaic Epistolography" and P. E. Dion, "The Aramaic 'Family Letter' and Related Epistolary Forms in Other Oriental Languages and in Hellenistic Greek," *Semeia* 22 (1981) 25–57 and 59–88, respectively; and D. Pardee, "Letters (Hebrew)" and P. E. Dion, "Letters (Aramaic)," *ABD* 4:292–85 and 285–90, respectively.

[15] Other than the fact that Paul omits the farewell—in fact, Paul never expresses a health wish or farewell in his letters—and offers atypical greetings, he shows little deviation from the standard Greco-Roman formulae except, of course, the Christian sentiments. In v. 21b, he adds that they should greet one another "with a holy kiss" (ἐν φιλήματι ἁγίῳ) as he does in Rom 16:16; 2 Cor 13:12; and 1 Thess 5:26 (cf. 1 Pet 5:14: ἐν φιλήματι ἀγάπης). On the significance of this, see W. Klassen, "The Sacred Kiss in the New Testament," *NTS* 39 (1993) 122–35. On the many features

always the greater part of an ancient letter and the most heterogeneous, follows the least rigid formulae (1:10–16:18).[16] As we see below, Paul uses that flexibility to his advantage in 1 Corinthians. That is not to say, however, that Paul does not organize his message. He certainly does. However, the flexibility of epistolary convention allows him much latitude in so doing. As letters of the day go, there is neither anything extraordinary about the opening and closing of the letter nor any indication that what lies between them should be different from any other contemporary Hellenistic letter.

Such was the presumption. 1 Corinthians was generally considered to be a "letter-essay." Most commentators agreed with Robertson and Plummer:

> The *Plan* of the Epistle is very clear. One is seldom in doubt as to where a section begins and ends, or as to what the subject is. There are occasional digressions, or what seem to be such, as the statement of the great Principle of Forbearance (ix. 1–27), or the Hymn in praise of Love (xiii), but their connection with the main argument of the section in which they occur is easily seen."[17]

1 Corinthians, along with the other letters of the NT, was variously debated in terms of content rather than genre. In fact, the epistolary form of the letter-essay, though scrupulously examined, was rarely questioned.[18] Though Deissmann honed our understanding of epistolary literature, even as Weiss opened the floodgates of their compositional integrity, the genre of NT letters, specifically the epistolary genre of the body of the letters, was presumed until seriously called into question, albeit for different reasons, by the rhetorical critics Hans Deiter Betz and Wilhelm Wuellner in the late 1970s.

It is not our task to assess different rhetorical approaches, except as they impinge on 1 Corinthians. And they do. In our venture, rereading 15:29 in context, there seems to be little theoretical or practical justification for attributing

---

which may be encapsulated in the concluding formulae, see Koskenniemi, *Idee und Phraesologie*, 148–51; Doty, *Letters*, 42; S. K. Stowers, *Letter Writing in Greco-Roman Antiquity* (LEC 5; Philadelphia: Westminster, 1986) 22, 61 (esp. the examples from other Greco-Roman letters), 155–56; Aune, *The New Testament in Its Literary Environment*, 164; and cf. Mitchell, *Paul and the Rhetoric of Reconciliation*, 291–94. Noteworthy is the fact that Paul used a secretary as indicated in 16:21; cf. Rom 16:22; Gal 6:11; Col 4:18; and Phlm 19.

[16] J. L. White, "Introductory Formulae," 91 n. 2. On the variety of forms possible in such a letter, see W. G. Doty, "Forms within the New Testament Epistles" (chap. 3), in *Letters in Primitive Christianity* (GBS; Philadelphia: Fortress, 1973) 49–63.

[17] Robertson and Plummer, *I Corinthians*, xxiv (emphasis original).

[18] There is no systematic treatment of ancient epistolary literature in English other than Deissmann's. The two standard, though dated works, are in German: Koskenniemi's *Idee und Phraeseology* deals mostly with the papayri and "non-literary letters," i.e., letters; and K. Thraede's *Grundzüge griechisch-römische Brieftopik* (MKA 48; Munich: Beck, 1970) deals mostly with "literary letters," i.e., epistles. Helpful resources are J. L. White, *Light from Ancient Letters* (FFNT; Philadelphia: Fortress, 1986); and Stowers' *Letter Writing in Greco-Roman Antiquity*.

Greco-Roman rhetorical categories to 1 Corinthians. By "Greco-Roman" or "ancient" rhetorical categories, we follow Aristotle's (*Ars rhet.* 1.3) distinction of the judicial (forensic), deliberative (hortatory), and demonstrative (epideictic). Theoretically, rhetorical categories and epistolography were clearly distinguished by the ancients in form and, for the most part, in function.[19] As Stanley K. Stowers observes, "The classification of letter types according to the three species of rhetoric only partially works. This is because the letter writing tradition was essentially independent of rhetoric."[20] It is not until the fourth century that we see epistolography treated in a rhetorical handbook with Julius Victor's *De epistolis*. Yet, it is hardly surprising that speeches and letters should often have had the same ends (i.e., to persuade, to advise, or to praise or blame). But that does not mean that they used the same techniques to attain them. In fact, as we shall see, "Paul probably did not employ a system of ancient rhetoric to compose his letters."[21] No one in the early Church seems to have noticed such categories in NT epistolography, even though the earlier readers of such epistolography would have been far more equipped and competent to do so because of their locus in or proximity to the Greco-Roman world. In the early and medieval Church, there is no account of anyone discerning an ancient rhetorical genre in Paul. Certainly, someone such as St. Augustine would have noticed one if he saw one. A professor of rhetoric and by any accounting biased in favor of presenting biblical texts in their most favorable light, Augustine (*De doc. chr.* 4) did not discern ancient rhetorical categories in the Pauline literature (or elsewhere in the Bible). Since his efforts were specifically aimed at defending the *eloquentia* of Paul, it seems that Augustine readily would have noticed and lauded classic genres and construction if present.[22] And few noticed them thereafter. Even Philipp Melanchthon, an expert on rhetorical theory and the Pauline literature, who noticed many rhetorical features in the Pauline literature, did not discern ancient rhetorical genres.[23]

---

[19] For an examination of the two standard epistolarly handbooks—Pseudo-Demetrius' Τύποι ἐπιστολικοί and Pseudo-Libanius' Ἐπιστολιμαῖοι χαρακτῆρες—and rhetorical theory, see J. T. Reed, "Using Ancient Rhetorical Categories to Interpret Paul's Letters: A Question of Genre," in *Rhetoric and the New Testament: Essays from the 1992 Heidelberg Conference* (ed. S. E. Porter and T. H. Olbricht; JSNTSup 90; Sheffield: Sheffield Academic Press, 1993) 292–324. (Note that the Ἐπιστολιμαῖοι χαρακτῆρες is often mistakenly attributed to Proclus.)

[20] S. K. Stowers, *Letter Writing in Greco-Roman Antiquity*, 52.

[21] Reed, "Using Ancient Rhetorical Categories to Interpret Paul's Letters," 324.

[22] For more on this, see R. D. Anderson, Jr., *Ancient Rhetorical Theory and Paul* (CBET 18; Kampen, Neth.: Kok Pharos, 1996) 13–14; and G. Bonner, "Appendix A: Augustine's Knowledge of Greek," in *St. Augustine of Hippo: Life and Controversies* (1963; Norwich: Canterbury, 2002) 394–95.

[23] On this, see C. J. Classen, "St. Paul's Epistles and Ancient Greek and Roman Rhetoric," in *Rhetoric and the New Testament*, ed. Porter and Olbricht, 271–78. Cf. Betz, *Galatians*, 14 n. 97. Indeed, as Anderson (*Ancient Rhetorical Theory and Paul*, 15–17) demonstrates, Melanchthon's findings seem to typify German scholarship from his day through C. K. Wilke, C. F. G. Heinrici, and J. Weiss.

That rhetoric was a constitutive element of Greco-Roman education in the first century is a certainty; rhetoric was the marrow of ancient education.[24] Still, that does not tell us to what extent Paul was aware of ancient rhetorical categories and whether or not he consciously used them. Despite all the recent literature on ancient rhetorical categories in Paul, no one has been able to demonstrate the locus of letter writing in its exact setting in (rhetorical) theory or in education.[25] Rhetoric was not part of the ancient handbooks on epistolography.[26] On top of that, we are not even sure where Paul received his classical education;[27] nor are we sure how that education may have differed from place to place.[28] At once Jewish, Greek, and Roman, it is no small task to establish the nature and amplitude of influences on Paul.[29] Raymond E. Brown's remark in this regard is noteworthy: "Caution is indicated about attempts to detect sophisticated rhetorical patterns [in Paul]. There is no way to be sure that Paul would

---

[24] See, e.g., "Education," *OCD*, 369–73; and M. L. Clarke (with D. H. Barry), *Rhetoric at Rome: An Historical Survey* (3rd ed.; London and New York: Routledge, 1996).

[25] A. J. Malhebre, *Ancient Epistolary Theorists* (SBLSBS 19; Atlanta: Scholars Press, 1988) 1–3.

[26] See Malhebre (ibid., 15–68) for a collection of all the pertinent passages from the two standard handbooks by Pseudo-Demetrius and Pseudo-Libanius, as well as many examples from Cicero, Seneca, Pliny, etc.

[27] See E. A. Judge ("Paul's Boasting in Relation to Contemporary Professional Practice," *AusBR* 16 [1968] 37–50) for a careful consideration of the rhetorical knowledge Paul may have had from a rearing either in Tarsus or Jerusalem. Paul tells us nothing of his youth and education. He does not even tell us where he was born. Because we consider the "Tarsus or Jerusalem" question in Chapter III of our study, we will not belabor it here. As regards the biblical witness of things Pauline, we must take Paul's word over Luke's. It is Luke only who tells us that Paul was born in Tarsus but reared and educated in Jerusalem (Acts 9:11, 30; 11:25; 21:39; 22:3; cf. 26:4). That Paul received a Hellenistic education is evident in his use of Greek. Paul never seeks to defend his Hellenistic background. Perhaps it was never challenged? Yet, on more than one occasion, Paul defends his Judaism (Rom 11:1; 2 Cor 11:2; Phil 3:5). Perhaps it was challenged? See J. L. North, "Paul's Protest that He Does Not Lie in the Light of His Cilician Origin," *JTS* 47 (1996) 439–63. The salient issues are discussed in J. Knox, *Chapters in a Life of Paul* (rev. ed.; London: SCM, 1987); as well as in J. Murphy-O'Connor, "Growing Up in Tarsus" (chap. 2) and "A Pharisee in Jerusalem" (chap. 3), in *Paul: A Critical Life* (Oxford: Clarendon, 1996) 32–51 and 52–70, respectively. For further reading, see Murphy-O'Connor's bibliography (372–95).

[28] See T. S. Duncan ("The Style and Language of Saint Paul in His First Letter to the Corinthians," *BSac* 83 [1926] 129–43) for an argument that the form of 1 Corinthians belies a specifically Asianic classical training.

[29] For now, see R. Wallace and W. Williams, *The Three Worlds of Paul of Tarsus* (London and New York: Routledge, 1998); and C. J. den Heyer, *Paul: A Man of Two Worlds* (trans. J. Bowden; Harrisburg, PA: Trinity Press International, 2000). Again, we look at this closely in the third chapter of our study. But for now, we must resist the temptation to partition Paul and his letters into arbitrary, exclusive sectors, e.g., that Paul thinks as a Jew and writes as a Greek. Two books by J. Z. Smith describe the prejudicial perils of doing so with ancient personages and their perceptions: *Map Is Not Territory: Studies in the History of Religions* (SJLA 23; Leiden: Brill, 1978), and *Drudgery Divine: On the Comparison of Early Christianities and the Religions of Late Antiquity* (CSHJ; Chicago: University of Chicago Press, 1990).

have been aware of the classical analyses of rhetoric and/or would have been consciously following them."[30] Here we come to the nucleus of the problem. Since it is impossible for us to determine Paul's knowledge of ancient rhetoric from external criteria, the only criteria we have are his letters. Practically, none of the three categories (judicial, deliberative, and demonstrative) is *ostensible* in reading Paul's letters, including of course 1 Corinthians.[31] After an extensive and exhaustive comparison between ancient rhetorical theory and Paul's letters, especially 1 Corinthians, Galatians, and Romans, R. Dean Anderson, Jr. concludes that Paul probably enjoyed no formal rhetorical training, that Paul's letters come closer to "teaching" than to "argumentation," that Paul wrote reasonable Greek, and that there is an absence of technical rhetorical terminology in Paul's letters.[32] However, the current prevailing preference in the biblical academy to read Paul's letters in terms of classical rhetoric compels us to examine the method and to adjudicate its importance for reading 1 Corinthians.

Hans Deiter Betz's analysis of Galatians as an example of classical rhetoric served as the catalyst for the present predilection to read Paul's letters in terms of ancient rhetoric. In many ways, Betz's *Galatians* was a watershed in NT studies.[33] It marks the advent of the contemporary critical climate in which we find ourselves, an era wherein rhetorical criticism is often heralded as *the* method for reading Paul's letters. In many ways, Betz "initiated a new era in biblical studies or at least in New Testament studies in the United States and, to a lesser degree, elsewhere."[34]

The events that led to Betz's work are difficult to trace. However, it is important to identify but a few. James Muilenberg, in his 1969 Presidential Address to the Society of Biblical Literature, expressed dissatisfaction with the prevalence of form criticism, especially the disintegration it seemed to entail within OT scholarship and called for a new approach to identify the diverse mechanisms by which texts are unified and ordered as wholes. He described this

---

[30] Brown, *Introduction to the New Testament*, 412.

[31] Gratuitous solutions such as that of J. Fairweather ("The Epistle to the Galatians and Classical Rhetoric," *TynBul* 45 [1994] 1–38, 213–44), who maintains that Paul had the ability to write better Greek than he did but chose not to, may be ignored.

[32] Anderson, *Ancient Rhetorical Theory and Paul*, 249–55.

[33] H. D. Betz, *Galatians: A Commentary on Paul's Letter to the Churches in Galatia* (Hermeneia; Philadelphia: Fortress, 1979). An earlier lecture at the 29th General Meeting of the Studiorum Novi Testamenti Societas in August 1974, "The Literary Composition and Function of Paul's Letter to the Galatians" (subsequently enlarged and published under the same title in *NTS* 21 [1974–75] 353–79), was the preview of Betz's full-blown commentary on Galatians as an example of Greco-Roman rhetoric according to the apologetic letter form.

[34] Classen, "St. Paul's Epistles and Ancient Greek and Roman Rhetoric," 265. So formidable was the challenge to the *status quo* in the late 1970s that a planned monograph series on the form and function of the Pauline letters, *qua* letters, by the Society of Biblical Literature never came to fruition.

task as "rhetoric and the methodology as rhetorical criticism."[35] In the same year, *La nouvelle rhétorique: Traité de l'argumentation* by Chaim Perelman and L. Olbrechts-Tyteca, appeared in English for the first time, though it had been written eleven years earlier.[36] Perelman and Olbrechts-Tyteca were concerned with the techniques of argumentation as found in Aristotle's *Ars rhetorica*. Notably, their book is not about rhetorical or literary criticism at all, it is about the philosophy and methods of argumentation in general.[37]

In the early 1970s, a debate was brewing among Pauline scholars over the "paraenetic" section of Romans (12:1–15:13). It came to be known as the "Donfried–Karris" or "Romans" debate. The debate concerned the propriety of certain methodological stances in the investigation of Romans. Grossly oversimplified, Donfried favored a stance that Romans is addressed more to an historical situation ("letter"), while Karris favored emphasis on a theological situation ("epistle").[38] Of course, much more was at stake in Pauline and NT studies than this section of Romans; the debate exemplifies the state of Pauline scholarship at that time.[39] In 1976, Wilhelm Wuellner published a salient article as a response and alternative to that debate: "Paul's Rhetoric of Argumentation in Romans: An Alternative to the Donfried–Karris Debate over Romans."[40] Wuellner states his aim clearly: "My proposal is that a study of the rhetorical nature of Paul's argumentation, or a study of the nature of argumentation in Paul's letters, will help us out of the two impasses created by the fixation with form- and genre-criticism on the one hand, and with specific social or political

---

[35] J. Muilenberg, "Form Criticism and Beyond," *JBL* 88 (1969) 1–18, quotation 8. Hence, the "Muilenberg School."

[36] C. Perelman and L. Olbrechts-Tyteca, *The New Rhetoric: A Treatise on Argumentation* (trans. J. Wilkenson and P. Weaver; Notre Dame, IN: University of Notre Dame Press, 1969). The original French edition is *La nouvelle rhétorique: Traité de l'argumentation* (Paris: Presses Universitaires de France, 1958).

[37] See Anderson (*Ancient Rhetorical Theory and Paul*, 19–23 et passim) for the book's connection to ancient rhetoric.

[38] For the intricacies of this lively debate, see K. P. Donfried, "A Short Note on Romans 16" *JBL* 89 (1970) 441–49; R. J. Karris, "Rom 14:1–15:13 and the Occasion of Romans," *CBQ* 25 (1973) 155–78; K. P. Donfried, "False Presuppositions in the Study of Romans," and R. J. Karris, "The Occasion of Romans: A Response to Professor Donfried" *CBQ* 36 (1974) 332–55 and 356–58, respectively; and K. P. Donfried, ed., *The Romans Debate* (rev. ed; Peabody, MA: Hendrickson, 1991).

[39] Unfortunately and without substantial justification, there has been and continues to be a penchant to cast and discuss issues having to do with Paul's letters almost exclusively under the auspices of Romans. As the latest example, see Dunn, *Theology of Paul*, 25–26. We discuss this further in Chapter IV, especially in terms of Paul's (baptismal) theology and Romans 6.

[40] W. Wuellner, "Paul's Rhetoric of Argumentation in Romans: An Alternative to the Donfried–Karris Debate over Romans," *CBQ* 38 (1976) 330–51. Note that Wuellner's second footnote is to Perelman and Olbrechts-Tyteca's *The New Rhetoric*.

situations on the other hand."[41] He goes on to claim that we should "consider Paul's letters as argumentative . . . [and should] understand argumentation as the use of discourse 'to influence the intensity of an audience's adherence to certain theses.'"[42] According to Wuellner, this study "belongs to traditional or 'new' rhetoric."[43] In other words, Wuellner does not call for an analysis of Paul's letters as ancient Greco-Roman rhetoric (as "letter-speeches") formed by Paul along the lines of Greek rhetors. Not in the least. Rather, Wuellner is building upon the work of Perelman and Olbrechts-Tyteca to inaugurate a study of argumentation in order to assess Paul's utilization thereof.

But that is not all. Wuellner also addresses an article that appeared just before his own, viz., Betz's "The Literary Composition and Function of Paul's Letter to the Galatians," the precursor to his *Galatians*. Fortunately for us, Wuellner clearly states the difference between his own approach and that of Betz to Galatians:

> The difference between my and Betz's procedure is that Betz first states his thesis about the genre and elaborates on the genre. Then he proceeds to derive the evidence for his genre thesis from an analysis of the composition of the Galatian letter. By contrast my procedure is to state first what Betz does later on. I begin with the identification of the epistolary framework. Then, in view of the "interrelations between the epistolary framework and the body," I seek to determine the rhetorical genre by choosing the "best way to approach a piece of argumentation (which is asking) to what sort of judgment it is ultimately directed."[44]

From this, Wuellner goes on to show that Romans is an example of epideictic (demonstrative) rhetoric.[45] Unfortunately, we already find ourselves in a quagmire of confused terminology. That is, the distinction between Greco-Roman or "classical" rhetoric and traditional or "new" rhetoric is often hazy, even where precision of language should be paramount. A perusal of the more recent articles dealing with Paul's rhetoric indicates that many authors (seemingly unaware of the differences) conflate the use of rhetoric with the use of ancient rhetorical

---

[41] Wuellner, "Paul's Rhetoric of Argumentation in Romans," 330. So too, idem, "Greek Rhetoric and Pauline Argumentation," in *Early Christian Literature and the Classical Intellectual Tradition*, ed. Schoedel and Wilken, 188.

[42] Wuellner, "Paul's Rhetoric of Argumentation in Romans," 330. Wuellner takes the internal quotation from Perelman and Olbrechts-Tyteca, *The New Rhetoric*, 14.

[43] Wuellner, "Paul's Rhetoric of Argumentation in Romans," 330.

[44] Ibid., 335. The first internal quotation is taken by Wuellner from W. J. Brandt, *The Rhetoric of Argumentation* (New York: Bobbs-Merrill, 1970) 14; the second is taken from Perelman and Olbrechts-Tyteca, *The New Rhetoric*, 21.

[45] Wuellner, "Paul's Rhetoric of Argumentation in Romans," 335–50.

theory.[46] As of late, there is little consensus in the biblical academy as to the precise meaning of terminology when speaking of rhetorical criticism.[47]

What is clear is this: Betz and Wuellner are after two different things, even "diametrically opposed" in their goals, according to Margaret M. Mitchell.[48] Betz wishes to discern ancient rhetorical genres in letters that demonstrate an author's (e.g., Paul's) dependence on contemporaneous patterns of thought and expression inextricably linked to the formation of this "letter-speech." Wuellner wishes to analyze arguments in texts to discern their effects upon the reader. Wuellner is not so much interested in genre, literary analysis, or even literary theory as he is in the craft of human argumentation that transcends time. He is interested in philosophy. Rhetoric—the art of persuasive speaking or writing and the devices used to that end, or as George A. Kennedy defines the term, "that quality in discourse by which a speaker or writer seeks to accomplish his purposes"[49]—is common to all human communication. The examination of biblical texts for traditional or "new" rhetorical features is not something novel.[50] Yet, acknowledging rhetorical features is not the same thing as endorsing much of the postmodern ideology that often accrues thereto. Betz is concerned with discerning demonstrable patterns in biblical texts, with exegesis. The veracity of Betz's method of rhetorical criticism is easily tested by discerning whether or not the rhetorical patterns he identifies are actually present in a given letter, e.g., Galatians. In other words, does his methodology work?

Wuellner is concerned with extrapolating the philosophical realm of argumentation. Wuellner asks, "Where is rhetorical criticism taking us?"[51] And he answers his own question: "Rhetorical criticism is taking us beyond hermeneu-

---

[46] See S. E. Porter ("The Theoretical Justification for Application of Rhetorical Categories to Pauline Epistolary Literature," in *Rhetoric and the New Testament*, ed. Porter and Olbricht, 100–22) who carefully and concisely discusses the issues involved.

[47] This is not to say that Wuellner, Betz, or anyone else for that matter, does not understand his or others' "rhetorical" terminology or use it consistently. It is only to say that there is no standardized vocabulary for all that falls under the umbrella of "rhetorical criticism." Additionally, there is the problem with the intermingling Greek, Latin, and vernacular nomenclature to describe various rhetorical features and patterns. For a general list, see R. A. Lanham, *A Handlist of Rhetorical Terms* (2nd ed.; Berkeley, CA: University of California Press, 1991). For an extensive glossary of Greek rhetorical terms, see Anderson, *Ancient Rhetorical Theory and Paul*, 300–315; and idem, *Glossary of Greek Rhetorical Terms: Connected to Methods of Argumentation, Figures, and Tropes from Anaximenes to Quintilian* (CBET 24; Leuven: Peeters, 2000).

[48] Mitchell, *Paul and the Rhetoric of Reconciliation*, 6 n. 16. Mitchell's book is an expansion of her doctoral dissertation (written under Betz).

[49] G. A. Kennedy, *New Testament Interpretation through Rhetorical Criticism* (SR; Chapel Hill, NC: University of North Carolina Press, 1984) 3.

[50] See R. Meynet, "Histoire de 'l'analyse rhétorique' en exégèse biblique," *Rhetorica* 8 (1990) 291–320; and B. Standaert, "La rhétorique ancienne dans saint Paul," in *L'apôtre Paul: Personnalité, style et conception du ministère* (ed. A. Vanhoye; BETL 73; Leuven: Leuven Univeristy Press, 1986) 78–92.

[51] W. Wuellner, "Where Is Rhetorical Criticism Taking Us?" *CBQ* 49 (1987) 448–63.

tics and structuralism to poststructuralism and posthermeneutics."[52] Specifically, in terms of biblical studies, Wuellner envisions rhetorical criticism, not as a system or methodology, but as a means to view all literature as social discourse.[53] Rhetorical criticism vis-à-vis Wuellner is more a postmodern philosophical position about the ends of discourse than it is a methodological stance about the use of ancient rhetoric in NT epistolography. His propositions are not methodological, but philosophical. What Wuellner asserts about rhetoric, rhetorical criticism, and the future thereof is founded upon his own acceptance of particular postmodern philosophical positions.[54] Our rejection of those principles on philosophical grounds need not be elaborated here, except to say that we consider philosophical positions and literary theories, which hold that the meaning of texts, especially biblical texts, is discovered more in the interpreter than in the text itself, to be tendentious. Moreover, the force of Wuellner's philosophical convictions pits him at odds with those whose convictions are different from his own, especially orthodox Christians. For example, Wuellner says, "The biblical exegete has joined with other scholars in combating 'uncompromising and irreducible philosophic [and, we may add, dogmatic theological] oppositions presented by all kinds of absolutism [and religious exclusivism].'"[55] That Wuellner should conceive of exegetes (and other scholars) in *combat* with philosophers and theologians, whose thinking or religious convictions are different from his own, demonstrates that his interests are beyond ours in ascertaining 1 Corinthians' literary genre. Perhaps, it is best to take Wuellner at his word: "The verdict is still out on just how successful and profitable the application of rhetorical theory has become in the rebirth of rhetorical criticism in today's practices of biblical interpretation."[56]

The question that remains before us is whether or not Paul utilized a classical rhetorical genre in his letters, particularly in 1 Corinthians. Paul certainly used rhetorical devices, as most writers do, but did he write along the lines of a particular Greco-Roman rhetorical genre? Betz certainly thinks so. As noted, his classification of Galatians as judicial speech in an apologetic letter genre proved

---

[52] Ibid., 449

[53] See ibid., 462–63.

[54] Such philosophical considerations are far afield of our focus here. A careful consideration of Wuellner's "Where Is Rhetorical Criticism Taking Us?" demonstrates the late nineteenth- and early twentieth-century phenomenon of reducing philosophy and, concomitantly, social discourse to politics. Such reductionism was summarily exposed and refuted long ago in Julian Benda's *La trahison des clercs* (Paris: Grasset, 1928). The debate over such reductions is neither surprising nor novel.

[55] W. Wuellner, "Biblical Exegesis in the Light of the History and Historicity of Rhetoric and the Nature of the Rhetoric of Religion," in *Rhetoric and the New Testament*, ed. Porter and Olbricht, 512–13. The internal quotation is taken by Wuellner from Perelman and Olbrechts-Tytecha, *The New Rhetoric*, 510; the asides in square brackets are Wuellner's.

[56] Wuellner, "Biblical Exegesis," 512.

itself a moment in biblical studies.[57] Betz was the first NT scholar to construe an entire NT letter in terms of a "letter-speech."[58] Since his *Galatians*, a plethora of books and articles, which seek to scout out rhetorical patterns in one form or another in the letters of the NT, have appeared.[59] Betz's *Galatians* was praised in many quarters, but not without serious objections against his thesis.[60] While stringent criticism comes as no surprise when a new theory challenges the assumptions of the reigning paradigm, substantial variations on that theory certainly elicit skepticism. Thus, it was no small thing when Joop F. M. Smit examined the same text, Galatians, against the same ancient rhetorical categories as Betz and found it to be a specimen of a deliberative rather than judicial

---

[57] A voice of approval in terms of applying ancient rhetoric to biblical writings was raised by Kennedy, a classicist, in his *New Testament Interpretation through Rhetorical Criticism*. Kennedy applauds the use of Greco-Roman categories in exegetical efforts by NT scholars, but he is concerned with their methodology. In particular, Kennedy (144–52) takes on Betz. For reviews of Kennedy's book, see J. H. Patton, *QJS* 71 (1985) 247–49; V. K. Robbins, *Rhetorica* 3 (1985) 145–49; R. M. Fowler, *JBL* 105 (1986) 328–30. Thus, in the analysis of Paul's letters, some see the need for greater input from classicists, e.g., C. J. Classen, "Paulus und die antike Rhetorik," *ZNW* 82 (1991) 1–33; and Anderson, *Ancient Rhetorical Theory and Paul*, 23–26 et passim.

[58] Rhetorical criticism has subsequently been extended to the whole of the Bible. For a survey, see C. C. Black, II, "Keeping Up with Recent Studies: XVI. Rhetorical Criticism and Biblical Interpretation," *ExpTim* 100 (1989) 252–58; and R. Majercik, T. B. Dozeman, and B. Fiore, "Rhetoric and Rhetorical Criticism," *ABD* 5:710–19.

[59] For example, just to name a few in our chosen bailiwick of 1 Corinthians, see M. Bünker, *Briefformular und rhetorische Disposition im 1. Korintherbrief* (GTA 28; Göttingen: Vandenhoeck and Ruprecht, 1983) 59–72; Aletti, "L'argumentation de Paul et la position des Corinthiens," 63–81; B. Fiore, "'Covert Allusion' in 1 Corinthians 1–4," *CBQ* 47 (1985) 85–102; P. Lampe, "Theological Wisdom and the 'Word about the Cross': The Rhetorical Scheme in 1 Corinthians 1–4," *Int* 44 (1990) 117–3; B. Mack, *Rhetoric and the New Testament* (GBSNTS; Minneapolis: Fortress, 1990) 56–59; Mitchell, *Paul and the Rhetoric of Reconciliation*; J. F. M. Smit, "The Genre of 1 Corinthians 13 in the Light of Classical Rhetoric," *NTS* 33 (1991) 193–216; idem "The Function of First Corinthians 10,23–30: A Rhetorical Anticipation," *Bib* 78 (1997) 377–88; C. B. Puskas, *The Letters of Paul: An Introduction* (GNS 25; Liturgical [Glazier], 1993); D. F. Watson, "Paul's Rhetorical Strategy in 1 Corinthians 15," in *Rhetoric and the New Testament*, ed. Porter and Olbricht, 231–49; J. G. Sigountos, "The Genre of 1 Corinthians 13," *NTS* 40 (1994) 246–60; Witherington, *Conflict and Community in Corinth*; and I. Saw, *Paul's Rhetoric in 1 Corinthians 15: An Analysis Utilizing the Theories of Classical Rhetoric* (Lewiston, NY: Mellen, 1995). A glance at recent volumes of the *CBQ*, *JBL*, *NTS*, *NovT*, *TZ*, and *ZNW* shows the explosion in rhetorical examinations of the epistolary literature of the NT.

[60] In praising the novelty of Betz's *Galatians*, many expressed reservations. See, e.g., the reviews by C. K. Barrett, *Int* 34 (1980) 414–17; J. Swetnam, *Bib* 62 (1981) 594–97; and M. Silva, *WTJ* 45 (1983) 371–85. The trio of extensive reviews by W. D. Davies, P. W. Meyer, and D. E. Aune (*RelSRev* 7 [1981] 310–28) is very helpful in determining the relationship of Betz's analysis to ancient rhetoric. See also H. Hübner, "Der Galaterbrief und das Verhältnis von antiker Rhetorik und Epistolographie," *TZ* 109 (1984) 241–50; and Anderson, *Ancient Rhetorical Theory and Paul*, 106–8.

speech.[61] Here we touch upon the fundamental problem of rhetorical criticism: few espy the same patterns within the same texts, particularly in Paul's letters. Nevertheless, there is a concerted effort within the academy to cast the majority of NT epistolography into terms of Greco-Roman rhetorical categories.[62] If there is a case to be made for 1 Corinthians as an example of Greco-Roman rhetoric, it is made by Mitchell in *Paul and the Rhetoric of Reconciliation: An Exegetical Investigation of the Language and Composition of 1 Corinthians*.[63] Mitchell's goal is crystal clear in the first sentences of her book:

---

[61] J. F. M. Smit, "The Letter of Paul to the Galatians: A Deliberative Speech," *NTS* 35 (1989) 1–26. Note Smit's (4 n. 6) critical remarks about Betz's analysis and the justified implication that Betz bends the (deficient?) genre to fit Paul. Then, note that after stating that the unity of the Galatians is not in dispute and finding that Gal 5:13–6:10 breaks an "unmistakable connection," Smit concludes that the unit is probably a later addition and leaves it out of his rhetorical analysis! Instead of bending the genre, he bends the letter itself. It comes as no surprise that Anderson ("The Letter to the Galatians 1–5.12" [chap. 4], *Ancient Rhetorical Theory and Paul*, 111–167), beginning with a dispassionate survey of the recent scholarship (111–23), offers his own detailed rhetorical analysis (123–65). He concludes that Galatians is not an example of a judicial speech and that Galatians cannot be construed as an example of any of the three rhetorical genres (166–67).

[62] This effort is exemplified in the *ABD* where Betz authors the entry on Galatians ("Galatians, Epistle to the," 2:872–75) and where Betz and Mitchell jointly author the entry on 1 Corinthians ("Corinthians, First Epistle to the," 1:1139–48).

[63] The only other attempt to cast the whole of 1 Corinthians in terms of Greco-Roman rhetoric is Witherington's *Conflict and Community in Corinth: A Socio-Rhetorical Commentary on 1 and 2 Corinthians*. Witherington's work appeared in 1995, four years after Mitchell's *Paul and the Rhetoric of Reconciliation*. In essence, Witherington proffers the same thesis as Mitchell, viz., that 1 Corinthians is an example of deliberative rhetoric (47 n. 140). The strengths of his book are many, not the least of which are the introduction (1–66) and the many excursuses throughout the book which supply bountiful historical and cultural information. Yet, there are weaknesses. First, by attempting such an analysis (1 and 2 Corinthians in one book), Witherington has bitten off more than he can chew. Second, Witherington gives scant attention to Mitchell's work and particularly inappreciable attention to Mitchell's detailed and erudite methodology. His own attempt (52–58) is more bibliographical than methodological. It seems that, methodologically speaking, Witherington's book could not have been written save after Mitchell's. For a contrary opinion, see the review by R. P. Martin, *Bib* 77 (1996) 445–48. Finally, one half of the title, the "socio-," is somewhat lacking; on this, see the review by J. H. Neyrey, *CBQ* 59 (1997) 182–83. Besides numerous articles dealing with portions of 1 Corinthians (many of which we have mentioned above), there are three monographs that deal exclusively with ancient rhetoric and 1 Corinthians, but their shortcoming is that each deals only with 1 Corinthians 1–4 (or portions thereof): S. M. Pogoloff, *Logos and Sophia: The Rhetorical Situation of 1 Corinthians* (SBLDS 134; Atlanta: Scholars Press, 1992); D. Litfin, *St. Paul's Theology of Proclamation: 1 Corinthians 1–4 and Greco-Roman Rhetoric* (SNTSMS 79; Cambridge: Cambridge University Press, 1994); and M. A. Bullmore, *St. Paul's Theology of Rhetorical Style: An Examination of 1 Corinthians 2:1–5 in the Light of First Century Graeco-Roman Rhetorical Culture* (San Francisco: International Scholars Publications, 1995). For a review of Bullmore's work and a summary of the interrelationship (or the lack thereof) among the three, see D. Litfin, *JBL* 116 (1997) 568–70. Additionally, A. Eriksson (*Traditions as Rhetorical Proofs: Pauline Argumentation in 1 Corinthians*; CBNTS 29; Stockholm: Almqvist and Wiksell, 1998) argues that pre-Pauline traditions in 1 Corinthians are used as rhetorical proofs. Unfortunately, he too does not examine the whole of 1 Corinthians.

The subject of this inquiry is the overall genre, function and composition of Paul's first letter to the Corinthians. The thesis which will be propounded, on the basis of an exegetical investigation including a rhetorical analysis of the text, is that 1 Corinthians is a single letter of unitary composition which contains a deliberative argument persuading the Christian community at Corinth to become unified. 1 Corinthians is throughout an argument for ecclesial unity, as centered in the πρόθεσις or thesis statement of the argument, in 1:10.[64]

Does Mitchell succeed? In her careful methodology, she puts forth five "mandates" for the rhetorical examination of NT texts, and she rigorously adheres to them throughout her work:

(1) Rhetorical criticism as employed here is an historical undertaking. (2) Actual speeches from antiquity must be consulted along with the rhetorical handbooks throughout the investigation. (3) The designation of the rhetorical species of a text (as epideictic, deliberative, or forensic) cannot be begged in the analysis. (4) The appropriateness of rhetorical form or genre to content must be demonstrated. (5) The rhetorical unit to be examined should be a compositional unit, which can be further substantiated by successful rhetorical analysis.[65]

These mandates are beyond reproach, and all who would examine texts for ancient rhetorical categories should profit from them.[66]

Then again, there are two fundamental and interrelated problems in her assertion that the whole of 1 Corinthians is a deliberative speech on concord. First, Mitchell redefines the sub-genre of a deliberative rhetorical speech. A deliberative speech is a sustained argument of exhortation aimed at persuading or dissuading a *particular* course of action in the future; the chief appeal is the advantage or benefit (τὸ συμφερόν) to be gained by so doing.[67] A deliberative speech is not a sustained *thematic* argument, an argument that weaves about or draws together a number of matters, even if those matters share a common denominator. Yet in a subtle transformation,[68] Mitchell begins to blend paraenesis and deliberative rhetoric,[69] even as she claims that paraenesis is not deliberative rhetoric.[70] But with her extension of the parameters of deliberative rhetoric, wherein she maintains there may be sections of practical guidance, Mitchell sounds decidedly paraenetic.[71] In commenting on Mitchell's admixture, Ander-

---

[64] Mitchell, *Paul and the Rhetoric of Reconciliation*, 1.
[65] Ibid., 6. They are explained on 6–19.
[66] Yet Classen ("St. Paul's Epistles and Ancient Greek and Roman Rhetoric," 219 n. 78) is a bit skeptical about them.
[67] This is affirmed by Mitchell, *Paul and the Rhetoric of Reconciliation*, 20–32.
[68] Anderson (*Ancient Rhetorical Theory and Paul*, 230–32) explains the change in detail.
[69] Ibid., 50–53.
[70] Ibid., 52–53.
[71] Ibid.

son reminds us that a deliberative speech "is designed to persuade the audience of the proposition, *not* to give them various pieces of concrete advice that will help them to bring the proposition into effect in their lives as a community. And here we have a clear difference in the way examples are used in Paul (generally to support particular advice or exhortation), and in ancient rhetoric (to directly support a proposition)."[72] Mitchell, it would seem, has turned benefit into paraenesis. But there are no examples of such deliberative speeches in antiquity;[73] the examples she claims are, at least, dubious.[74] Furthermore, to translate συμφερόν as "advice" is ambiguous enough,[75] but the suggestion that Paul is using the term in its rhetorical sense seems to be out of the question. Mitchell has violated her third mandate. She has, in effect, begged the designation of the rhetorical species in her analysis.

Second, 1 Cor 1:10 cannot be defended as the πρόθεσις (*propositio*) of all that we find in 1 Corinthians 5–16.[76] However, let us confine ourselves to 1 Corinthians 15. Mitchell claims that it is "especially appropriate" for Paul to end his argument on behalf of concord with reference to the resurrection, because it is the "τέλος" of their unity.[77] She follows the common division of the chapter: vv. 1–11 call the Corinthians to the common *kerygma*; vv. 12–28 show that Christ has been raised as all, dead or alive, will be raised; vv. 29–34 provide human evidence of the resurrection; vv. 35–49 show the eschatological equality to come in the resurrected body; vv. 50–57 are an exhortation of the resurrection all will share in common. Finally, v. 58 is the rhetorical conclusion (εἴλογος), a summation that closes the body of the letter.[78] It is difficult to see how *concord*—thematic or otherwise—even loosely ties this all together. Mitchell's tone becomes pronouncedly homiletic here. Besides ambiguous allusions, we are at a loss to see the link between these (albeit important) Pauline teachings and concord. Certainly, we are at a loss to understand Mitchell's statement:

---

[72] Anderson, *Ancient Rhetorical Theory and Paul*, 232 (emphasis original).

[73] Mitchell "fails to provide a good example of an extant speech that demonstrates her contention that deliberative speeches were often argued by giving concrete advice on various subjects" (Anderson, *Ancient Rhetorical Theory and Paul*, 234).

[74] The examples Mitchell (*Paul and the Rhetoric of Reconciliation*, 200 n. 100) does provide are scrutinized by Anderson (*Ancient Rhetorical Theory and Paul*, 232–34) who claims them to be antithetical to rather than supportive of Mitchell's point.

[75] Mitchell, *Paul and the Rhetoric of Reconciliation*, 35–37 et passim. It is used only three times in 1 Corinthians: 6:12, 10:23, and 12:7. See "συμφέρω," BADG, 780; and cf. 2 Cor 8:10; and 12:1.

[76] It would take far too much space to prove our conviction that 1 Corinthians 1–4, though it resembles deliberative rhetoric, is not an example thereof. In terms of Mitchell's analysis, the fact that no portion of the letter can be construed under the proposed *propositio* weakens her argument. Our own analysis below makes clear how chapters 1–4 fit into the letter as a whole.

[77] Mitchell, *Paul and the Rhetoric of Reconciliation*, 283.

[78] Ibid., 283–90.

The conclusion [v. 58] is short and to the point, and amounts to a restatement of the central argument of the letter: seek the upbuilding of the church in concord, even when it entails sacrificing what appears to be your present advantage, because this is the appropriate Christian behavior of love (τὸ ἔργον τοῦ κυρίου) which will lead to eschatological advantage (οὐκ ἔστιν κενὸς ἐν κυρίῳ).[79]

At best, this is bewildering. If by "central argument" Mitchell is referring to the *propositio* of 1:10, we are again at a loss: Is there any equivocation to be made between 1:10 and 15:58 such as she sees? Quite apparently, no. Thus, despite Mitchell's painstaking investigation, the body of 1 Corinthians is not an example of a deliberative speech. The genre of 1 Corinthians is not that of ancient rhetoric.

What, then, is the genre of 1 Corinthians? It is simply epistolary. In 1 Corinthians, the opening and closing formulae appropriately bespeak their contents. But we are surprised neither to find similarities between letter and speech nor to see the genres confused by commentators. Ancient rhetoric gives insight into the formation of letters, and "albeit in a limited respect, rhetorical theory can still inform our exegesis."[80] David E. Aune observes:

> The overlap between letter and speech suggests two important dimensions for understanding the former. First, oratory was very important in the Greco-Roman world and rhetoric occupied a central role in ancient education. Though primarily connected with oral delivery, rhetoric had a profound effect on all genres including letters. A knowledge of ancient rhetorical theory, therefore, can contribute to understanding letters written by ancients (like Paul and Ignatius) who had more than a basic education. Second, throughout the ancient world there was a high degree of social stratification. Consequently, systems of etiquette prescribed socially appropriate modes of behavior and speech for relating to persons of higher, equal, or lower social status in various situations. In letters, where the sender communicates with a person or group, the social status and relationship of sender and receiver will inevitably influence both *what* is said and *how* it is said.[81]

Although many of the ancient handbooks regard the letter as a one-sided dialogue, it is clear that the ancients distinguished between letter and speech. We should take care in exaggerating the relationship between the letter and the speech.[82] Again, as Aune observes:

> While there are many similarities between written letters and oral communications, there are also significant differences in language, style, and structure. We do not write the way we speak. Neither did the ancients. Oral communication, for example, tends to be *linear* or *sequential*. The immediate context for a

---

[79] Ibid., 290.
[80] Anderson, *Ancient Rhetorical Theory and Paul*, 255.
[81] Aune, *The New Testament in Its Literary Environment*, 158 (emphasis original).
[82] Ibid., 159.

statement is the preceding statement and the "interpretive" paralinguistic features of gesture, tempo, inflection, rhythm, and voice quality. While written texts can also be linear, the reader has the advantage of being able to reread earlier sections of a document not completely understood or fully appreciated on the first reading. Yet since written texts must do without the paralinguistic features of speech, they must be written in a special way to function without an "interpreter" (Plato, *Phaedrus* 275e).[83]

There is no reason to suppose that Paul did not know the difference between the two, nor is there any reason to suppose that his addressees did not know the difference. Correspondingly, there are no grounds to suggest that Paul intended his letters to be read aloud exclusively as if they were speeches. They were read aloud as we see in 1 Thess 5:27 (and Col 4:16) among his addressees on various occasions, most definitely in liturgical settings. They were also read *sub voce* by individuals as letters. Though certainly a highly oral culture, literacy in the first-century Greco-Roman world was not limited to any class or caste; since reading and writing were so necessary in the financial and governmental business of daily life, they spanned societal strata.[84] Paul's letters were most likely read again and again—publicly and privately. Paul's adjuration in 1 Thess 5:27, that his letter be read to all (ἀναγνωσθῆναι τὴν ἐπιστολὴν πᾶσαν τοῖς ἀδελφοῖς; cf. Col 4:16), is not about a method of delivery. Paul simply wants to ensure that "all the members of the community be apprised in public reading of the letter's contents."[85] Moreover, Paul uses the term "letter" (ἐπιστολή) in all internal references to his letters (Rom 16:22; 1 Cor 5:9; 16:3; 2 Cor 7:8; 10:9–11); Paul does not call them speeches. Added to this is the fact that many of Paul's converts were surely able to read his letters on their own or within one forum or another.

To turn to socioeconomics for one moment and the attendant education wealth provided in the first century, we note that Wayne A. Meeks has shown that the extremes of "upper" and "lower" class are not represented in Paul's letters. Paul's converts, for the most part, seem to be of the "middle" class.[86] Many of these people could read. Furthermore, since Paul probably knew the difference between a letter and a speech, we can safely assume that he chose the letter over the speech for a reason.

What sort of letter, then? Which sub-genre? Here 1 Corinthians presents a challenge to the reader. Ancient Greco-Roman letter writing was not as formalized as rhetoric. The rules were few. Stowers observes:

---

[83] Ibid. (emphasis original).

[84] See Alan Millard, "Who Read and Who Wrote" (chap. 6), in *Reading and Writing in the Time of Jesus* (New York: New York University Press, 2000) 154–84.

[85] E. J. Richard, *First and Second Thessalonians* (SacPag 11; Collegeville, MN: Liturgical [Glazier], 1995) 287.

[86] See Meeks, "The Social Level of Pauline Christians" (chap. 2), in *First Urban Christians*, 51–73.

Letter writing remained only on the fringes of formal rhetorical education throughout antiquity. It was never integrated into the rhetorical systems and thus does not appear in the standard handbooks. This means there were never any detailed systematic rules for letters, as there were for standard rhetorical forms. The rules for certain types of speeches, however, were adapted for use in corresponding letter types.[87]

Unlike speeches, the occasions for letters were legion. The two classic epistolary handbooks, Pseudo-Demetrius' Τύποι ἐπιστολικοί and Pseudo-Libanius' Ἐπιστολιμαῖοι χαρακτῆρες, manifest an extraordinary versatility in the composition of letters. The former discusses twenty-one types, the latter forty-one types. A perusal of Cicero's *Epistulae ad familiares* or Seneca's *Epistulae morales* reveals how the Romans adopted the epistolary style of the Greeks. It was from the extensive milieu of Greco-Roman epistolography, too vast to be considered here, that Paul drew in his writing of 1 Corinthians.[88] To be sure, since the letter was such a popular form of communication and because it exhibited the most variety and flexibility, the specific type of letter is difficult to pin down.[89] However, a careful consideration of 1 Corinthians shows it to be a "letter-essay" rather than a "letter-speech."

In his seminal article, Martin Luther Stirewalt, Jr. considers fifteen documents from Epicurus, Dionysius of Halicarnassus, Plutarch, 2 Maccabees, and the *Martyrium Polycarpi* to show that "they agree in form, function, and theory to the extent of constituting a category in themselves."[90] Stirewalt's study is most compelling because his letters are actual and extant, i.e., he is not drawing solely on principles from handbooks' suggestions or samples, but offering examples of documents that are real letters. Particularly striking in Stirewalt's analysis is the triangular relationship within the letter-essay:

> The letter-setting behind the letter-essay is triangular, I-thou-they. The triangle of persons is illustrated in Epicurus, *Letter I to Herodotus*, the introduction of which concludes with the triangular perspective: "Since this method is useful to *all* studying natural science . . . *I* have made an epitome for *you*." The vocative addressing Herodotus follows in the transitional sentence. Thus the writer of the letter-essay holds both the "thou'" and the "they" in mind.[91]

This is the sort of structure we find in 1 Corinthians, especially in 1 Cor 15:29–34. In a number of ways, Paul's use of the letter is best compared to Epicurus'.[92]

---

[87] Stowers, *Letter Writing in Greco-Roman Antiquity*, 34.

[88] Ample explanation of the varied types are found in Stowers, "Types of Letters" (part two, chaps. 6–12), in *Letter Writing in Greco-Roman Antiquity*, 49–173.

[89] Aune, *The New Testament in Its Literary Environment*, 159.

[90] M. L. Stirewalt, Jr., "The Form and Function of the Greek Letter-Essay," in *The Romans Debate*, ed. Donfried, 147–71, quotation 147.

[91] Ibid., 169–70.

[92] Ibid., and Murphy-O'Connor, *Paul the Letter-Writer*, 44.

"[Epicurus] exhorted, encouraged, gave advice, settled disputes, taught his doctrines, and maintained fellowship through his letters. Letters served Epicurus much as they did Paul almost four hundred years later."[93]

As we see below in our examination of 1 Corinthians 15, rhetorical features figure prominently in 1 Corinthians. However, that is not that same as saying that Paul crafted the letter according to any of the forms or norms of ancient rhetoric. When rhetorical elements appear in Paul's letters, they "may be functionally related to, but not formally (and consciously) based upon, the ancient rhetorical practices."[94] Moreover, the latitude of ancient epistolography allows for considerable variation. In fact, "the very flexibility of the epistolary genre allowed for the possibility of rhetorical influence."[95] Therefore, we are on safer ground looking for rhetorical elements in that which is plainly a letter than we are in either claiming that it is something other than what it appears to be or claiming that it is somehow unique. As Jeffrey T. Reed points out, the evidence at our disposal—the ancient epistolary and rhetorical theorists and extant letters—shows that "the rhetorical and epistolary genres may have been betrothed, but they were never wed. Nevertheless, classical and modern theories of rhetoric, when used judiciously and mostly descriptively, may often provide heuristic tools for the analysis and understanding of ancient letters."[96]

To posit 1 Corinthians as a letter-essay is also to admit the suppleness of the letter genre. Losing sight of the pliancy of the ancient letter genre runs the risk of categorizing 1 Corinthians, along with other NT letters, along the lines of arbitrary standards. It would seem that Reed goes a bit too far in stating that "scholars recognize the unique position of Paul's letters within the Graeco-Roman epistolary tradition."[97] Reed is correct in that there are many studies that take this for granted. For example, Raymond F. Collins maintains that "Paul created a new epistolary genre, the ecclesial letter.... His first letter to the Corinthians clearly belongs to this new genre."[98] The categorization of one or more of Paul's letters as "unique," except for that quality which distinguishes individual authorship, is severely problematic. If we were to admit this, then we would be saying that there is a literary genre, even if only a sub-genre, proper to Paul and to Paul alone. By definition, then, there would be nothing to which Paul's letters might be accurately compared (other than themselves). Surely, such uniqueness may be true on an ontological (or theological) level, but there

---

[93] Stowers, *Letter Writing in Greco-Roman Antiquity*, 40.

[94] Reed, "Using Ancient Rhetorical Categories to Interpret Paul's Letters," 324.

[95] J. T. Reed, "The Epistle," in *Handbook of Classical Rhetoric in the Hellenistic Period (330 B.C.–A.D. 400)* (ed. S. E. Porter; Leiden: Brill, 1997) 171.

[96] Reed, "The Epistle," 192.

[97] Reed, "Using Ancient Rhetorical Categories to Interpret Paul's Letters," 223–96, quotation 293.

[98] R. F. Collins, *First Corinthians*, 43. Here Collins is following Thomas H. Olbricht, "An Aristotelian Rhetorical Analysis of 1 Thessalonians," in *Greeks, Romans and Christians*, ed. Balch, Ferguson, and Meeks, 226.

are no grounds for it on an historical (or literary) level.[99] To extrapolate Paul and his letters from their historical surroundings derails literary scrutiny by mooting all issues under the banner of the unique. Inspiration and inerrancy notwithstanding, 1 Corinthians is the product of a first-century Hellenized Jewish-Christian convert who addresses a community of his own converts with whom he is experiencing not a few difficulties. He writes in the elastic letter genre of his era. Much of what he has to say is better understood in the particular and peculiar circumstances that occasioned 1 Corinthians rather than by excising the letter from its historical context. In the meantime, much of what we can say about 1 Corinthians depends on its literary integrity.

The Integrity of 1 Corinthians

As we noted above, the literary integrity of 1 Corinthians has not been considered a given since Weiss' challenge. In terms of our study, the scholarly challenges to 1 Corinthians' integrity need not be summarily affirmed nor denied. On the one hand, the plethora of suggestions beginning with Weiss' indicate that no partition hypothesis has attained a strong consensus. If there were clear evidence of a conflation of sources, this would hardly be the case. On the other hand, an *a priori* dismissal of partitionist claims, especially those arguing a rhetorical structure for the letter, might recklessly brush aside the issue of literary integrity. Indeed, the relatively new tendency to have Paul's letters conform to one or another rhetorical speech pattern seems to be at the root of the facile dismissals of partitionist hypotheses, with little mention of their often strong arguments against the literary integrity of 1 Corinthians. This, of course, is no surprise, since a composite composition of the letter necessitates the abandonment of any overall rhetorical structure (even if rhetorical features or elements may be extrapolated) or, at the very least, the presence of a most extraordinary redactor. Those who claim that a strong epistolary theory imposes an inappropriate linear framework on Paul's often circumlocutional thought are destined to ignore their own advice by imposing a linear rhetorical structure in its place.

Before the question of compositional integrity is addressed, we must consider the pertinent textual criticism of 1 Corinthians. The Chester Beatty Papyrus II ($\mathfrak{P}^{46}$), which dates from about A.D. 200, contains the entirety of the letter with only a few verses missing and a few transposed. The uncial manuscripts ℵ, A, B, D, 06^{abs}, L, Ψ, 056, 0142, 0150, and 0151 have the complete text. So, the Greek text of 1 Corinthians was established within 150 years of its original composition with only the most minute differences. This is extraordinarily early. And

---

[99] For an in depth examination of the nature of comparisons in biblical studies, see J. Z. Smith, "On Comparison" (chap. 2), in *Drudgery Divine*, 36–53.

there is no evidence in the tradition of any variant form of 1 Corinthians.[100] Any redaction of 1 Corinthians would have to have been done either prior to the formation of the *corpus Paulinum* or by the collector of the *corpus*.[101] Walter Schmithals argues that "the existence of the composite epistles in the *corpus Paulinum* is adequately explained only if one sees in the editor also the publisher of the first collection."[102] Schmithals makes this argument (as do many others) on the basis of literary conclusions wherewith he attempts to discern a single hand in the redaction of the *corpus*.[103] The problem, of course, is that there is no textual evidence for this. Arguments for the early composition of a Pauline corpus point to the citations of Paul's letters and Hebrews in *1 Clement* (ca. A.D. 95–96). Of course, there is no doubt that St. Clement knew Hebrews. In the case of Paul's letters, Donald A. Hagner's extensive examination of the Greek text of *1 Clement* reveals that we can say with "certain knowledge" that Clement knew 1 Corinthians and Romans.[104] Whether or not Clement knew of other letters is speculative.[105] Again, since no variant of 1 Corinthians exists, this narrows the window for redaction to within forty or so years of the letter's composition and leaves very little time for interpolations.[106] It also lends support to the probability of an independent circulation of 1 Corinthians. Thus, text criticism lends striking support to the literary integrity of 1 Corinthians. In fact, "if it has to be suspected on the basis of internal evidence that a given letter has been subjected to editorial revision, such revision must have occurred before that letter entered into the stream of textual transmission."[107]

Then again, to claim that no single hand edited the entirety of the *corpus Paulinum* is not to hold that no hand edited 1 Corinthians. To be sure, the narrow window for redaction lends strength to 1 Corinthians' integrity; yet it does not necessarily resolve the apparent internal inconsistencies. Since there are no textual difficulties, Helmut Merklein is certainly correct in noting that the ques-

---

[100] See D. Trobisch, "The Oldest Extant Editions of the Letters of Paul" (chap. 1), in *Paul's Letter Collection: Tracing the Origins* (Minneapolis: Fortress, 1994) 1–27.

[101] H. Y. Gamble, "The Redaction of the Pauline Letters and the Formation of the Pauline Corpus," *JBL* 94 (1975) 404.

[102] W. Schmithals, *Paul and the Gnostics* (trans. J. E. Steely; Nashville: Abingdon, 1972) 272.

[103] See idem, *Gnosticism in Corinth: An Investigation of the Letters to the Corinthians* (trans. J. E. Steely; Nashville: Abingdon, 1971) 87–101.

[104] D. A. Hagner, *The Use of the Old and New Testaments in Clement of Rome* (NovTSup 34; Leiden: Brill, 1973) 237; see Hagner (195–220) for an examination of *1 Clement* with 1 Corinthians and Romans. As to the problems with the Greek texts of Romans, see H. Y. Gamble, *The Textual History of the Letter to the Romans: A Study in Textual and Literary Criticism* (SD 42; Grand Rapids, MI: Eerdmans, 1977).

[105] Hagner, *Use of the Old and New Testaments*, 237; see 220–36 for an examination of other letters. However, Hagner's conclusion (237) that the greater part of the *corpus Paulinum* was known to Clement is a stretch on the basis of his own tentative conclusions regarding texts other than 1 Corinthians, Romans, and Hebrews. On this, see J. Z. Smith, *Drudgery Divine*, 110 n. 44.

[106] J. Murphy-O'Connor, "Interpolations in 1 Corinthians," *CBQ* 48 (1986) 94.

[107] Gamble, "Redaction of the Pauline Letters," 418.

tion of the compositional integrity of 1 Corinthians is a literary question.[108] There is no doubt as to the literary difficulties in 1 Corinthians; however, there is no proof, i.e., no textual evidence, at least, as to anyone being responsible for them except Paul. The ascription of any responsibility to Sosthenes, the co-sender (1 Cor 1:1), or to a secretary, indicated by Paul's greeting in his own hand, is dubious. That Sosthenes had a role in Corinth is supported by Acts 18:17. Co-senders are also acknowledged in 2 Cor 1:1; Gal 1:2; Phil 1:1; Col 1:1; 1 Thess 1:1; 2 Thess 1:1; and Phlm 1. Although the practice of indicating co-senders was rare in Hellenistic epistolography,[109] Cicero (*Att.* 11.5.1) knew of it. The scholarly consensus is that little can be made of them in terms of Paul's authorship and that Paul's occasional slips into the first person plural (or even remaining therein as in 1 and 2 Thessalonians) only emphasize Paul's compositional prerogative. Murphy-O'Connor argues convincingly for significant input from Sosthenes in the composition of 1 Corinthians on the basis of 1 Cor 1:18–31 and 2:6–16 being followed by the emphatic κἀγώ ("I myself") in 1 Cor 2:1 and 3:1,[110] but this only demonstrates Paul's dominance over the letter.[111] In fact, Sosthenes probably had very little to do with 1 Corinthians.[112]

That Paul used a secretary is supported by 1 Cor 16:21. Secretarial help is also apparent in Rom 16:22 (wherein Tertius is identified); Gal 6:11; Col 4:8; 2 Thess 2:17; and Phlm 19. Michael Prior suggests that Sosthenes may have been Paul's secretary,[113] despite the fact that there is no other instance of a secretary's mention in the opening formulae of Hellensitic epistolography and no way to reconcile such a claim about Sosthenes with Tertius' presence in Romans. The lack of research into the role of secretaries in first-century epistolography and the NT letters has been noted.[114] The lacuna was partially filled by E. Randolph Richards' *The Secretary in the Letters of Paul*, wherein Richards notes that, whatever the role of a secretary might have been in a particular letter,[115] the final

---

[108] H. Merklein, "Die Einheitlichkeit des ersten Korinterbriefes," *ZNW* 75 (1984) 157.

[109] E. R. Richards, *The Secretary in the Letters of Paul* (WUNT 2/42; Tübingen: Mohr, 1991) 47.

[110] J. Murphy-O'Connor, "Co-authorship in the Corinthian Correspondence, *RB* 100 (1993) 566–70. However, Murphy-O'Connor does argue for co-authorship of 1 Corinthians (with Sosthenes) and 2 Cor 1–9 (with Timothy), even if the final editorial hand is Paul's.

[111] See Murphy-O'Connor, *Paul the Letter-Writer*, 16–34, esp. 20.

[112] Conzelmann, 20 n. 12; Fee, *First Corinthians*, 31; and R. F. Collins, *First Corinthians*, 42.

[113] M. Prior, *Paul the Letter-Writer and the Second Letter to Timothy* (JSNTSup 23; Sheffield: JSOT Press, 1989) 39–42.

[114] For example, Gamble (*Textual History of the Letter to the Romans*, 76 n. 94) notes in reference thereto that "the question of the possible uses and the types of dictation needs a fresh investigation."

[115] Richards (*Secretary in the Letters of Paul*, passim) argues that the secretary often functioned as a recorder, an editor, a co-author, a composer, or any combination thereof. See also Murphy-O'Connor, *Paul the Letter-Writer*, 8–16.

product was the responsibility of the author.[116] And, although Richards provides criteria for discerning the presence of a secretary,[117] his conclusions are vague and, sometimes, infelicitous.[118] For example, it is on the basis of the use of secretaries in Greco-Roman writing that Gordon J. Bahr detects the inauguration of Paul's greeting at 1 Cor 16:15 rather than 16:21,[119] whereas Richards maintains the widely held position that it begins at 16:21.[120] Yet, Richards takes a different tack when he speculates that the greetings in Rom 16:3–21 might be from Tertius rather than Paul.[121] To what extent Paul used a secretary remains a conundrum. Bahr's counsel is well taken: "In view of the various ways in which he could have used his secretary, and in view of the influence which the secretary could have had on his letters, it would be well to speak with caution on topics such as Pauline terminology or Pauline theology."[122]

Bahr's caution is two-edged. On one side, the caution suggests that we should take great care in pronouncements of Pauline terminology and theology because an editorial hand is as surely present as it is elusive. It might prove laborious to say that this or that belongs to Paul, when, in fact, it may belong to a surreptitious redactor. Here the presumption is that the Pauline authenticity of the text is in question and that such authenticity must be proven. This, no doubt, is the compulsion for caution as Bahr sees it. On the other side, the compulsion for caution, given the evidence Bahr actually presents, may lead us in the opposite direction. That is, if we presume Pauline authenticity, then we must be wary of spying an editorial hand. The evasive editorial hand may exist only to such a small extent as to be negligible. Or, even if it is present now and again, there is no guarantee that its work was not approved by Paul himself. A presumption of Pauline authenticity necessitates care in saying that this or that is non-Pauline. In short, we must ask ourselves where the burden of proof lies in detecting interpolations in Paul's letters, and for our purposes, in 1 Corinthians.

Murphy-O'Connor is speculative about interpolations in 1 Corinthians.[123] Even after an extensive exposé of the seven passages in 1 Corinthians that are often held to be interpolations (1 Cor 2:6–16; 4:6; 6:14; 11:13–16; 14:34–35; 15:31–32; 15:44b–48), Murphy-O'Connor finds only two (1 Cor 4:6; 14:34–35)

---

[116] Richards, *Secretary in the Letters of Paul*, 68 et passim.

[117] Ibid., 68–97.

[118] Evaluations of Richards' book run the gamut from the positive by B. Fiore (*CBQ* 55 [1993] 391–2) to the negative by H. D. Betz (*JTS* 43 [1992] 618–20). For moderate reviews, see R. Penna, *Bib* 73 (1992) 286–88; J. A. D. Weiman, *NovT* 34 (1992) 300–302; and P. Sellew, *JBL* 112 (1993) 536–37. However, Richards (*Secretary in the Letters of Paul*, 2) claims only to write "a *prolegomenon* to the role of a secretary in Paul," by collecting pertinent data. In this, Richards is successful.

[119] G. J. Bahr, "The Subscriptions in the Pauline Letters," *JBL* 87 (1968) 37.

[120] Richards, *Secretary in the Letters of Paul*, 176–77.

[121] Ibid., 171.

[122] G. J. Bahr, "Paul and Letter Writing in the Fifth [*sic*] Century," *CBQ* 28 (1966) 477. Cf. Murphy-O'Connor, *Paul the Letter-Writer*, 34–35.

[123] Murphy-O'Connor, "Interpolations in 1 Corinthians," 94.

to be supported by convincing arguments.[124] Clearly, Murphy-O'Connor is exercising the appropriate caution on behalf of Pauline authenticity and literary unity. Murphy-O'Connor rightly places the burden of proof for interpolations on those who claim to discover them. This caution is not shared by all. In fact, there are those who take Bahr's counsel in favor of multiple interpolations. While it is true that "we do not have access to Paul's letters as he wrote them, but only to the letters as they were incorporated into a collection,"[125] it is a bit much to say as some do that there was substantial editing,[126] or to say that "we can be sure that the editor did not leave the letters just as he found them."[127] Such assertions cannot be substantiated apart from text-critical analyses—analyses which are impossible given the dearth of pertinent sources. Still and all, those who claim to find multiple interpolations consider the burden of proof to be theirs in substantiating them.

Bahr's counsel may be taken to an extreme if the burden of proof is shifted. That is precisely what William O. Walker, Jr. seeks to do. Walker suggests that we shift the burden of proof for interpolations vis-à-vis that presumed by exegetes such as Murphy-O'Connor.[128] Walker maintains that interpolations are to be assumed *a priori*.[129] According to Walker, literary-critical methods are the only important consideration in detecting interpolations, since he believes that each and every Pauline manuscript underwent significant redaction in standardization.[130] Although Walker maintains that text-critical considerations are important,[131] he considers the fact that all manuscripts contain a particular passage to be meaningless because the editing took place before or during the collection.[132] Walker's theory is certainly plausible, but completely unproven. Again, without other manuscripts, nothing can be proven, and Walker's argument is from silence. If we go with what we have, the burden of proof is squarely on the shoulders of anyone who claims this or that pericope of Paul's letters to be non-Pauline.

---

[124] Ibid., 81–94.
[125] L. E. Keck, *Paul and His Letters* (PC; Philadelphia: Fortress, 1979) 15.
[126] L. E. Keck and V. P. Furnish, *The Pauline Letters* (IBT; Nashville: Abingdon, 1985) 50.
[127] Knox, *Chapters in a Life of Paul*, 7.
[128] W. O. Walker, Jr., "The Burden of Proof in Identifying Interpolations in the Pauline Letters," *NTS* 33 (1987) 610–18. See also idem ("1 Corinthians 2.6–16: A Non-Pauline Interpolation? *JSNT* 47 [1992] 75–94), wherein Walker responds to Murphy-O'Connor's "Interpolations in 1 Corinthians" in regard to 1 Cor 2:6–16. For a full exposition, incorporating his earlier articles and engagements with other scholars, see W. O. Walker, Jr., *Interpolations in the Pauline Letters* (JSNTSup 213; Sheffield: Sheffield Academic Press, 2001).
[129] Walker, "The Burden of Proof," 611.
[130] Ibid., 614.
[131] Ibid., 611 et passim.
[132] Ibid., 613.

But there is more. Arguments for the editing and collecting of the *corpus Paulinum* cannot exclude Paul. David Trobisch claims that Paul himself edited the first collection of his letters in an "authorized" recension of Romans, 1 and 2 Corinthians, and Galatians; and he maintains that they form a literary unity.[133] Trobisch argues that the first stage in any selection of letters must have had some assistance—if not some impetus—from the original author.[134] On the basis of manuscript evidence and textual criticism, Trobisch argues for the aforementioned recension in light of two hundred letter collections dating from 300 B.C. to A.D. 400.[135] Contemporaneous letter collections reveal three stages of collection: (1) an authorized recension by the author; (2) an expanded collection after the author's death; and (3) a comprehensive edition that combines all earlier editions.[136] Interestingly, Trobisch does not hold for the original literary unity of 1 Corinthians. He contends that 1 Corinthians is a collection of three separate letters (1 Cor 1:10–4:21; 5:1–6:11; 6:12–16:24),[137] but at the same time, he insists that the uniting hand is the hand of Paul. The textual evidence leaves little room for any other conclusion.

If anything is clear by now, it is that the literary integrity of 1 Corinthians is a ticklish question. Evidence from the extant manuscripts yields few conclusions. Though the *corpus Paulinum* was collected at a very early date, we cannot be sure about the temporal hiatus between original writings and collected works. Evidence from the Greco-Roman practice of the utilization of secretarial help (even if by Sosthenes) in the production of letters admits of such possible variance as to make *a priori* conclusions impossible. So too, with no manuscript evidence, we have seen that the claim for any interpolation is severely weakened when there is no textual evidence to sustain it. Lastly, even if an editorial hand be suspected in 1 Corinthians, we cannot be sure as to whose hand it actually is. All of this leads us to conclude, along with Merklein,[138] that the literary integrity of 1 Corinthians must devolve into a *literary* question. Such a conclusion neither dismisses the textual evidence, wherein one may argue from silence, nor does it create a vacuum, wherein literary criticism is paramount. At this point, we must

---

[133] Trobisch, *Paul's Letter Collection*, 54. Trobisch's *Paul's Letter Collection* summarizes and expands the principal conclusions of his earlier and extensive study *Die Entstehung der Paulusbriefsammlung: Studien zu den Anfängen christlicher Publizistik* (NTOA 10; Göttingen: Vandenhoeck and Ruprecht, 1989).

[134] Trobisch, *Paul's Letter Collection*, 50–51.

[135] In her review, B. E. Bowe (*CBQ* 58 [1996] 172–73) notes that Trobisch has not taken account of alternative scholarly positions. This, perhaps, is Trobisch's greatest strength—sticking to the textual evidence.

[136] Trobisch, "Interpreting the Letters of Paul in the Light of Ancient Letter Collections" (chap. 3) and "Paul's Authorized Recension of the Letter to the Romans, the Two Letters to the Corinthians, and the Letter to the Galatians" (chap. 4), in *Paul's Letter Collection*, 48–54 and 55–96, respectively.

[137] Ibid., 76–80. According to Trobisch, the basis for each original letter is new information received by Paul in three separate stages (76).

[138] Merklein, "Die Einheitlichkeit des ersten Korinterbriefes," 157.

search for the best hypothesis to explain the apparent inconsistencies and redundancies in 1 Corinthians.

That it is a literary question is evident in the analyses of those who hold for integration or partition. As we have seen above, the most recent arguments for the integrity of 1 Corinthians are founded upon classical rhetorical analyses. Mitchell cites Merklein's observation, but she puts a spin on it in her claim that "literary rhetorical analysis [is] the appropriate primary methodology for addressing this question."[139] Unfortunately, this only begs the question of compositional integrity. Can the compositional integrity of 1 Corinthians be proven via rhetorical analysis? Or, is compositional integrity not a prerequisite for rhetorical analysis? According to Mitchell, the latter is the case. As we saw above, she maintains in her fifth "mandate" that "the rhetorical unit to be examined should be a compositional unit, which can be further substantiated by successful rhetorical analysis."[140] This is certainly true: if 1 Corinthians could be proven to be a cohesive deliberative argument, it would defend the compositional integrity of the letter."[141] But it could do no more than defend it, for the assertion of literary integrity is a prerequisite of genre criticism, when the genre is in question. In the case of 1 Corinthians, the overarching epistolary genre is a *fait accompli* in its opening (1:1–9) and closing (16:19–24) formulae and Paul's references to writing (4:14; 5:11; 9:15; 14:37). Apparent difficulties, digressions, and divagations notwithstanding, the burden of proof remains on the part of anyone who would claim that 1 Corinthians is not an ordinary Greco-Roman letter. Because 1 Corinthians is not a cohesive rhetorical argument and, therefore, cannot be defended as an integral whole along the lines of classical rhetorical analysis, literary integrity is not a given. While 1 Corinthians is certainly a letter, the integrity of that letter is another question.

Many exegetes hold for the literary integrity of 1 Corinthians.[142] And they have history on their side. There are no independent manuscripts or manuscript collections with alternatives to the received text of 1 Corinthians. However, the partitionist theories are hardly capricious. 1 Corinthians is a long letter. It treats a mélange of topics. It has apparent inconsistencies, e.g., Timothy's travel plans (1 Cor 4:17 and 16:10), two discussions of idol food (1 Cor 8:1–13 and 10:23–33), and the specious conclusion at the end of chapter 4.[143] Such things cannot

---

[139] Mitchell, *Paul and the Rhetoric of Reconciliation*, 5.

[140] Ibid., 6.

[141] Ibid., 17.

[142] For example, Barrett, *First Corinthians*, 15; Conzelmann, *1 Corinthians*, 3–4; K. E. Bailey, "The Structure of I Corinthians and Paul's Theological Method with Special Reference to 4:17," *NovT* 25 (1983) 152–81; Fee, *First Corinthians*, 15–16; Barbaglio, *La prima lettura ai Corinzi*, 48; and R. F. Collins, *First Corinthians*, 14. See Hurd, ("The Events Which Preceded the Writing of 1 Corinthians" [chap. 2], in *The Origin of 1 Corinthians*, 43–58) for the most sustained argument on behalf of literary integrity.

[143] See Hurd, *The Origin of 1 Corinthians*, 43–47 for a detailed account of the problems.

be ignored. Although it is not uncommon to find commentators who gloss over the objections raised by Weiss and others to the compositional integrity of the letter with little more than a footnote,[144] it is necessary to consider whether or not partitionist hypotheses are viable; otherwise our exegesis of 15:29 would remain non-contextual and, therefore, inadequate.

To be sure, there is a plentitude of partition theories. Since Weiss' original proposal that 1 Corinthians is a composite of two letters,[145] numerous studies have sought to prove that 1 Corinthians is the editorial composite of two or more letters to the Corinthians. Today, partitionist proposals for 1 Corinthians run the gamut from two to as many as five original letters.[146] Each and every partition theory is based upon the fact that 1 Corinthians seems to be somewhat disordered and inconsistent. The arguments for one sort of composite structure or another are somewhat compelling given the fact that 2 Corinthians is generally assumed—though hardly proven—to be a composite of several letters.[147] As we noted above, those exegetes who hold for a rhetorical schema of 1 Corinthians naturally account for apparent inconsistencies or interpolations with a putative rhetorical structure in 1 Corinthians.[148] That 1 Corinthians is, at least in overall structure, a letter with an "argumentative" function is apparent. However, as we have also noted, when an overall rhetorical genre is refuted, the problems remain, but they are somewhat mitigated. The fact of the matter is that the question of 1 Corinthians' literary integrity is raised because of "the absence of any detectable logic in the arrangement of its contents."[149] The viability of partition theories is based on the assumption that such a lack of detectable logic means that something must be awry in the text itself. The assumption is that 1 Corinthians must conform to a presupposed standard of consistency. Given the comparable length of 1 Corinthians and Romans, it is falsely concluded that something must be askew in 1 Corinthians because it lacks the *je ne sais quoi* of Romans. But the *Sitz im Leben* of Romans—a theological treatise addressed to a community that Paul neither founded nor knew—can hardly be paralleled with

---

[144] For example, Kistemaker, *I Corinthians*, 24–25.

[145] Weiss, *Der erste Korintherbrief*, xl–xliii.

[146] The partition theories are far too numerous and complex for elucidation here. For a survey of the partitionist theories, see Hurd, *The Origin of 1 Corinthians*, 43–47; G. Sellin, "Hauptprobleme des ersten Korintherbriefes," *ANRW* 2/24.4:2941–3044; E. de la Serna, "Los orígenes de 1 Corintios," *Bib* 72 (1991) 193–202; and R. F. Collins, *First Corinthians*, 10–14.

[147] Yet there are some who argue for the unity of 2 Corinthians, e.g., A. M. G. Stephenson, *The Authorship and Integrity of the New Testament* (London: SPCK, 1965); W. H. Bates, "The Integrity of II Corinthians," *NTS* (1965–66) 56–69; J. Lambrecht, *Second Corinthians* (SacPag 8; Collegeville, MN: Liturgical [Glazier], 1999) 7–9; and J. D. H. Amador, "Revisiting 2 Corinthians: Rhetoric and the Case for Unity," *NTS* 46 (2000) 92–111. Additionally, W. L. Lane ("Covenant: The Key to Paul's Conflict with Corinth," *TynBul* 33 [1982] 3–29) argues the unity of 2 Corinthians as a *rîb*.

[148] For example, Mitchell, *Paul and the Rhetoric of Reconciliation*, 182–83; Puskas, *Letters of Paul*, 55; Witherington, *Conflict and Community in Corinth*, 71; and, to a certain extent, R. F. Collins, *First Corinthians*, 10–14, 17–20.

[149] Murphy-O'Connor, *Paul: A Critical Life*, 253.

that of 1 Corinthians—a sustained response to an *ad hoc* situation in a community he founded and knew intimately. It would seem that the case of Romans actually supports the unity of 1 Corinthians. Romans has come down to us in two distinct forms, with the most significant variations having to do with chapter 16. None of Paul's other letters are extant in such textual variation. "The case of Romans offers the exception that proves the rule: when textual revisions have taken place they have left their marks in the evidence."[150] And no determinable mark appears in 1 Corinthians.

Romans aside, three other factors militate against the acceptance of any partition theory for 1 Corinthians. First, there is a lack of agreement among partition theories. After almost one hundred years, no partition theory has gained even the semblance of scholarly consensus. Second, given Paul's use of chiastic and parallel structures, "the apparent disorder of [his] thought may at times be a proof not of an interpolation but of the original textual sequence."[151] Third, their complexity demands extraordinary creativity on the part of the redactors. Partitionist claims must be grounded in historical circumstances appropriate to ancient practices of writing and editing.[152] Alistair Stewart-Sykes considers the roles of ancient editors and copyists with reference to the Corinthian correspondence.[153] He demonstrates that most partition theories, especially the highly complex ones, presume composition and scribal practices basically unknown in the ancient world as well as considerable physical dexterity on the part of the redactors.[154] Although Stewart-Sykes does not adjudicate between individual partition theories, he does conclude "that any theory must be capable of explanation with regard to the physical phenomena surrounding the composition and preservation of the epistles, and should thus accord with editorial practice in the first century. In essence this means that simple constructions are more likely to have been made than complex ones, and are therefore to be preferred."[155]

---

[150] Gamble, "Redaction of the Pauline Letters," 418.

[151] J. J. Collins, "Chiasmus, the 'ABA' Pattern and the Text of Paul," in *Studium Paulinorum Congressus Internationalis Catholicus 1961* (2 vols.; AnBib 17–18; Rome: Pontificium Institutum Biblicum, 1963) 2:583.

[152] For a complete treatment of early Christian writing, editing, and publishing, see H. Y. Gamble, *Books and Readers in the Early Church: A History of Early Christian Texts* (New Haven and London: Yale University Press, 1995).

[153] A. Stewart-Sykes, "Ancient Editors and Copyists and Modern Partition Theories: The Case of the Corinthian Correspondence," *JSNT* 61 (1996) 53–64.

[154] Ibid., 54 et passim. See also J. L. White, "New Testament Epistolary Literature in the Framework of Ancient Epistolography," *ANRW* 2/25.2:1730–56.

[155] Ibid., 64. The same basic point, though based on less evidence and prior to most contemporary partition theories of the Corinthian correspondence, is made by O. Roller, *Das Formular der paulinischen Briefe: Ein Beitrag zur Lehre vom antiken Briefe* (BWANT 58; Stuttgart: Kohlhammer, 1933) 42.

There is simply an "embarrassment of riches" for the literary unity of 1 Corinthians.[156] To contend, without any objective or external evidence whatsoever, that Paul could not have written 1 Corinthians as we have it, places an undo onus on Paul as an author (or editor), denigrates a suppositious editor as inept, or observes an unwarranted correlation among Paul's letters. Murphy-O'Connor says it best: "Once the underlying assumptions are brought out clearly, the fundamental flaw of this methodology becomes apparent. It assumes knowledge superior to that of the author by dictating what he should have said. The resultant letters owe more to the aesthetic sense of the scholar than to objective factors."[157] No partition theory meets the burden of proof necessary to show beyond reasonable doubt that 1 Corinthians is a composite.[158] When all is said and done, "the balance of probability will remain with the view that we have [1 Corinthians] substantially as it left the author's hands."[159]

Nonetheless, difficulties remain, especially the rift between 1 Corinthians 1–4 and 5–16.[160] This dilemma has been addressed separately, but in a surprisingly similar way, by Eduardo de la Serna and Martinus C. de Boer.[161] Both de la Serna and de Boer chart a middle course between the integralists and the partitionists. Both argue that 1 Corinthians is the composite of two separate letters, that each of the two was written by Paul himself, and that the cause for the one being appended to the other was the arrival of fresh information from Corinth in the midst of Paul's writing the first half of 1 Corinthians. However, they part ways over which of the two was written first and why. While the notion that Paul combined two letters in 1 Corinthians is not novel,[162] only de la Serna and de Boer present a detailed account thereof and plausible reasons therefor.

De la Serna holds that Paul was in the process of writing a response to the Corinthians' letter (most likely brought to Paul by Stephanas, Fortunatus, and Achaicus [1 Cor 16:17]) when Chloe's people arrived (1 Cor 1:11) with new

---

[156] Hurd, *The Origin of 1 Corinthians*, 50.

[157] Murphy-O'Connor, *Paul: A Critical Life*, 253.

[158] So too, e.g., Hurd, *The Origin of 1 Corinthians*, 74; L. L. Belleville, "Continuity or Discontinuity: A Fresh Look at 1 Corinthians in the Light of First-Century Epistolary Forms and Conventions," *EvQ* 59 (1987) 15–37; and Fee, *First Corinthians*, 15–16.

[159] Barrett, *First Corinthians*, 17.

[160] Note the penchant for rhetorical analyses to concentrate on chapters 1–4, e.g., Fiore, "'Covert Allusion' in 1 Corinthians 1–4"; Lampe, "Theological Wisdom and the 'Word about the Cross': The Rhetorical Scheme in 1 Corinthians 1–4," *Int* 44 (1990) 117–31; Litfin, *St. Paul's Theology of Proclamation: 1 Corinthians 1–4 and Greco-Roman Rhetoric*. See the accounts in Mitchell, *Paul and the Rhetoric of Reconciliation*, 81–183; Puskas, *Letters of Paul*, 61–64; and Witherington, *Conflict and Community in Corinth*, 71–77.

[161] Respectively, De la Serna, "Los orígenes de 1 Corintios," 192–216; and M. C. de Boer, "The Composition of 1 Corinthians," *NTS* 40 (1994) 229–45.

[162] See, e.g., D. Smith, *The Life and Letters of Paul* (New York: Doran, 1919) 259; E. Evans, *The Epistles of Paul the Apostle to the Corinthians* (CB; Oxford: Clarendon, 1930) 20–21; and F. F. Bruce, *I and II Corinthians* (NCBC; Grand Rapids, MI: Eerdmans, 1971) 23–25, 52–53.

information. Paul's original response began with 1 Cor 7:1: "Now concerning (περὶ δέ) the matters about which you wrote." The use of περὶ δέ there and its other uses (7:25; 8:1; 12:1; 16:1, 12) provides the key to the original written response.[163] With that original response near completion, Paul added chapters 1–6; 9:1–10:22; 10:23; 11:1; 11:2–34; 12:31b–14:1a; 15:1–58; and 16:13–24 to highlight his message of unity and love. Thus, de la Serna thinks that our 1 Corinthians is the result of a thorough rewrite by Paul himself, a rewrite necessitated by and in direct reply to the information rendered by Chloe's people and, therefore, the particular local situation of the Corinthian community.[164] So far as de la Serna can see, this is the most likely reason for the inconsistencies and abrupt shifts in subject matter in 1 Corinthians.[165] De la Serna's thesis is compelling in that it seeks to account for divergences in terms of circumstances related in 1 Corinthians itself, viz., at least two separate sources of information: a previous letter from the Corinthians and the arrival of Chloe's people. In 1 Corinthians, Paul is obviously responding to both—of that there is no doubt. But de la Serna's explanation seems a bit too complicated. Why did Paul go to such great editorial gyrations to produce a heterogeneous text? Why did not Paul simply send two letters? Or, why did not he simply attach one set of responses to another under one title?

De Boer, like de la Serna, holds that Paul was in the process of writing a response to the Corinthians when fresh information arrived, but he understands the historical circumstances and Paul's reaction thereto very differently. According to de Boer, Paul first wrote 1 Corinthians 1–4 as a response to the arrival of Chloe's people. Thereafter, Stephanas, Fortunatus, and Achaicus arrived with a letter from the Corinthians. Here de Boer notes that the dual occasion for 1 Corinthians—the response to the information from Chloe's people and the letter from the Corinthians—actually provided a third source of information. De Boer claims:

> That Stephanas and Fortunatus and Achaicus remained mutes as Paul read the letter from Corinth, out loud and in their presence, is historically implausible. It takes no great stretch of historical imagination to suppose that these three men,

---

[163] De la Serna, "Los orígenes de 1 Corintios," 203–7. The use of περὶ δέ has received significant attention from Barrett, *First Corinthians*, 154; Bruce, *I and II Corinthians*, 24, 66; P. Vielhauer, *Geschichte der urchristlichen Literatur* (Berlin: de Gruyter, 1975) 132; Fee, *First Corinthians*, 267; Sellin, "Hauptprobleme," 2941–42; and M. M. Mitchell, "Concerning Περὶ Δέ in 1 Corinthians," *NovT* 31 (1989) 229–56. Hurd (*The Origin of 1 Corinthians*, 64 n. 1) gives an extensive list of those who have noted it from the turn of the century until 1965. Περὶ δέ is found elsewhere in the Pauline literature only in 1 Thess 4:9 and 5:1. This has led to speculation that Paul is responding to a letter there as well. See A. J. Malherbe, "Did the Thessalonians Write to Paul?" in *The Conversation Continues: Studies in Paul and John in Honor of J. Louis Martyn* (ed. R. T. Fortna and B. R. Gaventa; Nashville: Abingdon, 1990) 253–55.

[164] De la Serna, "Los orígenes de 1 Corintios," 209–14.

[165] Ibid., 215–16.

and especially Stephanas, gave Paul a running commentary on the letter from Corinth and that they thus supplied him with further information about the behaviour and the beliefs of Corinthian Christians. Surely Paul must have questioned them closely.[166]

Consequently, Paul is responding under one heading to three disparate sources of information. This historical footing goes a long way in explaining 1 Corinthians.

Incontestably, 1 Cor 1:11 is a sufficient introduction to chapters 1–4. And, as we have seen and as de Boer notes, the phrase περὶ δέ gives ample cohesion to chapters 7–10, 12–14, and 16.[167] It is Paul himself who allows us to conclude that περὶ δέ is related to things in a letter from the Corinthians when he introduces the term in 7:1. But what of chapters 5–6, 11, and 15? Chapters 5–6, with significant thematic links to chapter 7, are most likely the response to things Paul heard from Stephanas, Fortunatus, and Achaicus. Paul responded to these things before he addressed their written concerns.[168] Then, in the process of addressing their written concerns, Paul enumerated (at least) two things that he heard, which are indicated by 1 Cor 11:18 ("I hear that there are divisions among you") and 15:12 ("some of you say").[169] Furthermore, the issues of chapters 5–6 and 15 are linked by 6:14. 1 Cor 6:14 is the first reference to resurrection in the letter and the only one outside chapter 15. De Boer is confident in his theory, but he acknowledges that there are other problems in the letter that cannot be strictly accounted for in a dual letter of sorts.[170] However, the points of continuity in the letter far outweigh the difficulties.

The historical circumspection and the sheer simplicity of de Boer's proposition compel our agreement. 1 Corinthians presents us with a unique situation among Paul's letters by presenting three sources of information: Chloe's people (1:11), a letter (7:1), and Stephanas, Fortunatus, and Achaicus (16:17). No other of Paul's letters is nearly as clear in indicating the precise sources of data to which Paul reacts and retorts. Even if Stephanas, Fortunatus, and Achaicus were not the bearers of the letter,[171] three sources still remain, and each renders a different take on things for Paul. It would be remarkable for Paul to answer each of the three individually, unless we presume that there was no connection between them. It is our contention, following de Boer, that the first half of the letter responds to that which Paul heard from Chloe's people, and that Paul originally intended that his response thereto would constitute a single letter. Upon the arrival of Stephanas, Fortunatus, and Achaicus, Paul responded to the letter they carried, their own commentary thereupon, and their impressions of

---

[166] De Boer, "The Composition of 1 Corinthians," 232.
[167] Ibid., 231–32.
[168] Ibid., 233.
[169] Ibid., 232.
[170] See ibid., 240–42.
[171] Robertson and Plummer (*I Corinthians*, xxiv) say it simply: "We cannot be sure."

the Corinthian community. However, that does not mean that Paul merely abutted one letter to another. No, surely the ideas that were in his mind for the first half remained during his subsequent writing of the second half.

To expect thematic and literary perfection from Paul places far too great a load upon him. On one level, it mixes apples and oranges. Given the critical importance of Paul's letters for Christianity, many are tempted to confuse ontological eminence with literary acumen. Romans proves beyond a shadow of a doubt that Paul is capable of profound theological prose. Yet, there is no reason to assume that Paul was a master of epistolography or rhetoric. In fact, the textual evidence is to the contrary when we consider his other six letters (1 Corinthians notwithstanding). The underlying assumption for partition hypotheses in general is that 1 Corinthians (and more so 2 Corinthians) is, if you will, just too much of a mess to have been composed as it stands. Galatians, Philippians, 1 Thessalonians, and Philemon are spared such scrutiny for their brevity. But the canonical integrity of 1 Corinthians is hardly in question here. When we pause to reflect on 1 Corinthians, we see that Paul is not attempting to write a theological treatise. Instead, we see that Paul writes *ad loc, ad hoc*. Paul's letter is ordered not by his own ruminations but by necessary response to real people and real problems. On another level, Paul's theological acumen is never as sharp as when he exercises his apostolic authority in responding directly and pointedly to the reality of consternation and confusion in a nascent Christian community.

Accordingly, to seek to discern a structure in 1 Corinthians in terms of an intricate pattern—linear, rhetorical, or otherwise—is to impose a rigidity on Paul's letter that is uncalled for and historically ungrounded. It is our claim, from reading and rereading the letter itself, that 1 Corinthians is best seen basically as de Boer describes it: two letters in one, from three fonts. In two basic sections, indicating a consistency of consideration and conviction, Paul addresses the Corinthians. First, in 1:10–4:21, Paul addresses the issue of factionalism, which has been brought to his attention by Chloe's people. Second, in 5:1–15:58 he addresses a host of other problems, which have come to his attention by letter and by Stephanas, Fortunatus, and Achaicus. In this second section, Paul specifically addresses ethical issues (immorality, litigation, marriage, idol food, and worship) in 5:1–11:34 and spiritual issues (gifts, love, glossolalia, and resurrection) in 12:1–15:58.

Our concern with 15:29 puts us at the heart of Paul's concern with the resurrection in chapter 15. It is clear that Paul's discourse on the resurrection is neither novel nor capricious. It is meant to remind the Corinthians of that which Paul has already preached to them (15:1). It is occasioned by Paul's knowledge that some among the Corinthians deny the resurrection of the dead (15:12). To wit, he not only argues that there is a resurrection of the dead (15:12–28), but he also anticipates queries as to how such a resurrection occurs (15:35–58). Right in the middle, we find 15:29–34 and mention of baptism "on account of the dead." Unmistakably, 1 Corinthians 15 is the immediate riposte to an immediate predicament. Unfortunately, we have no external information as to the precise dilemmas and difficulties that existed in the early Corinthian community. We do not know what was reported to Paul by mouth or letter, except insofar as Paul responds thereto. So, we turn first to the structure of chapter 15 and then to specifics of 15:29, in order to render the literary context of baptism "on account of the dead."

THE STRUCTURE OF 1 CORINTHIANS 15

Our prior considerations of the literary integrity of 1 Corinthians have yielded a structure for the whole of the letter. We have determined 1 Corinthians to be seriatim response by Paul to information oral and written. We have concluded that 1 Corinthians 15 is most likely motivated by oral rather than written reports, especially since there is no use of περὶ δέ in the chapter. Finally, in refuting an overall rhetorical or linear structure for the entirety of 1 Corinthians, we see that chapter 15's teaching on the resurrection is neither the conclusion nor the summation of a dominant theme in the letter. And we note that the importance of the resurrection, within the letter itself or in Paul's thinking, is not at all diminished thereby.

1 Corinthians 15

Adjudicating the general sections within 1 Corinthians 15 has not presented a serious problem for biblical scholarship. With few exceptions, the chapter is usually divided into five general units: vv. 1–11, 12–28 (12–19 and 20–28), 29–34, 35–49 (35–44a and 44b–49), and 50–58. The reasons are apparent in the text. First, in vv. 1–11, Paul makes a complete shift in subject matter from 14:40. Chapters 12–14 deal with spiritual gifts. But, 15:1–11 introduces Christ's resurrection (cf. 1 Cor 6:14) and makes a specific statement as to its veracity. Second, in vv. 12–28, Paul expands upon his attestation to the resurrection of Christ by introducing a rhetorical question into the chapter: "Now if Christ is preached as raised from the dead, how can some of you say there is no resurrection of the dead?" Third, in vv. 29–34, Paul introduces another rhetorical question: "Otherwise, what do people mean by being baptized on behalf of the dead?" Fourth, in v. 35, Paul introduces yet another rhetorical question: "But someone will ask, 'How are the dead raised'?" Plainly, this question is parallel to the first question in v. 12. Verses 12–28 are concerned with the fact that Christ has been raised and, therefore, Christians will be raised; vv. 35–49 explain how such resurrection is possible. Finally, in vv. 50–58, "I tell you this, brethren, flesh and blood cannot inherit the kingdom of God, nor does the perishable inherit the imperishable." These verses provide support for the "how" of the resurrection in terms of a "mystery." We proffer an original overall concentric structure of the chapter:

- A   the presentation of Christ's bodily resurrection on the authority of witnesses (vv. 1–11)

- B   an explanation that Christ's resurrection ensures Christians' resurrection (vv. 12–28)

- C   behavior in accord with the resurrection (vv. 29–34)

- B'   an explanation of how bodily resurrection is feasible (vv. 35–49)

- A'   the presentation of bodily resurrection on the authority of "mystery" (vv. 50–58).[172]

Paul's penchant for concentric and parallel structure is well noted. As a Jew, Paul was intimately familiar with this style of writing so prevalent in the OT. So extensive is Paul's use of such structures that Nils W. Lund attempted to couch the whole of 1 Corinthians in a huge concentric structure.[173] Lund's attempt was unsuccessful, but his pioneering work led to serious consideration of concentric and parallel structures in the NT and in Paul.[174] Every earnest examination of Paul's letters takes into account the Hebrew predilection for concentric thought and the ever present A-B-A' pattern, because form informs content and vice versa. Concentric thought, expressed in chiastic or parallel structures, aims to emphasize one thing over another. Strictly speaking, a parallelism emphasizes a notion by repetition, whether that repetition be direct, inverted, or antithetical. Chiasmus is a particular configuration of parallelism, a subspecies that not only repeats for emphasis but repeats around an axial notion. "Authentic chiasmus produces balanced statements, in direct, inverted, or antithetical parallelism, constructed symmetrically about a central idea."[175]

A perusal of chapter 15's structure shows straightway that vv. 29–34 stand in the middle of the chapter. Clearly, as we have indicated, the veracity of Jesus' bodily resurrection (vv. 1–11) parallels the veracity of believers' resurrection (vv. 50–58), but this parallelism also frames another parallelism, viz., two logi-

---

[172] Of course, this overall structure admits of finer distinctions. B (vv. 12–28) is readily seen as comprising two parallel pericopes: b (vv. 12–19) and b' (vv. 20–28). The same holds true for B' (vv. 35–49): b' (vv. 35–44a) and b'' (vv. 44b–49). And C (vv. 29–32), in our opinion, may be divided into a tricolon: a (v. 29), b (vv. 30–32), and a' (vv. 33–34). See below for more.

[173] N. W. Lund, "The First Epistle to the Corinthians" (chap. 7), in *Chiasmus in the New Testament: A Study in the Form and Function of Chiastic Structures* (1942; rpt. Peabody, MA: Henrickson, 1992) 145–96. Cf. J. Breck, *The Shape of Biblical Language: Chiasmus in the Scriptures and Beyond* (Crestwood, NY: St. Vladimir's Seminary Press, 1994) 243–51.

[174] For example, J. Jeremias, "Chiasmus in den Paulusbriefen," *ZNW* 49 (1958) 145–56; J. J. Collins, "Chiasmus, the 'ABA' Pattern and the Text of Paul," 575–83; and Breck, "The Pauline Epistles" (chap. 4), in *The Shape of Biblical Language*, 243–71.

[175] Breck, "Biblical Chiasmus: Exploring Structure for Meaning," *BTB* 17 (1987) 71.

cal explanations pertinent to the resurrection of believers: vv. 12–28, that there is a resurrection of believers because Christ is raised, and vv. 35–49, how that resurrection is possible in terms of a spiritual body. In turn, vv. 12–28 and 35–49 nest another set of verses: 29–34. It certainly follows that these verses support the all-too-obvious theme of resurrection in some way, merely by their locus in the structure of chapter 15, or they simply would not be there. Again, whatever point Paul seeks to make in vv. 29–34 may not be immediately evident, but it is immediately evident that it has something to do with resurrection. That, it would seem, is precisely why the interpretation of 15:29 causes so much consternation.

As we saw in Chapter I of our study, the majority reading of vicarious baptism favors a reading of v. 29 as a radical break from that which precedes it and succeeds it. But this is hardly the case. Whatever it may be saying, v. 29 is not without a very distinctive context. The inability to read the verse coherently within its context has led many to extract it therefrom, because it does not seem to fit, even if found dead center within a chapter that discusses but one theme. That such a notion is prevalent in the contemporary literature seems not so much the result of careful analysis as it is of a "back-reading" from the lack of consensus enveloping the verse. Merely stating that the verse has nothing to do with its context is gratuitous. Furthermore, to suggest that v. 29 is a phrase transitional to an example (as Murphy-O'Connor does while at the same time highlighting the context of the verse)[176] is contextually dismissive insofar as tagging the verse as transitional damns with faint praise any possible significance therein. Finally, DeMaris begs the question completely when he suggests that the "meager context" of 15:29 has been the catalyst for interpretations other than the majority opinion;[177] when, in point of fact, it is his own concurrence with the majority opinion that has led him to determine this meagerness.[178] If vv. 29–34 were considered to be a reference to something, to anything, which is simply seen or ordinarily overt, few would have had a problem reading it. Were this so, our structure might be recognized, and the only question would be how 15:29 relates to resurrection. In other words, any discussion of the structure of chapter 15 would be more or less moot—if v. 29 were easily exegeted.

The following general paradigm, offered by Mitchell is, *mutatis mutandis*, followed by many commentators:

(A) Evidence for the Resurrection of the dead (15:1–34)
    (1) Testimony to Christ's Resurrection (15:1–11)
    (2) Christ's Resurrection involves man's Resurrection (15:12–28)
    (3) Testimony of human conduct to a belief in the Resurrection. Baptisms for the dead. Sufferings of the Apostles (15:29–34)
(B) Difficulty as to the manner of the Resurrection (15:35–49)

---

[176] Murphy-O'Connor, "Baptized for the Dead," 532–34.
[177] DeMaris, "Corinthian Religion and Baptism for the Dead," 674.
[178] Ibid., 671–74.

(C) Triumph of life over death (15:50–58).[179]

This is difficult to fathom because the majority of exegetes also discern a tricolon A-B-A' pattern in other places throughout 1 Corinthians. Even if we were to grant that parts A and C above are not paralleled to one another, how could we grant that parts A.2 and B are not? A careful reading of chapter 15 reveals that the rhetorical questions in vv. 12 and 35 are the lynchpins of the chapter. For this reason, many other commentators stress the parallel of vv. 12–34 and vv. 35–58.[180] Our own understanding of chapter 15's structure follows their lead in paying close attention to this parallel and profits from their detailed attention to each component.[181] However, we depart from their conclusions by factoring out vv. 29–34 and accentuating these verses not only structurally, but thematically. Without doubt, the subject of the chapter is the resurrection of the body. Verse

---

[179] Mitchell, *Paul and the Rhetoric of Reconciliation*, 286. Mitchell bases this paradigm on J. B. Lightfoot, *Notes on the Epistles of St. Paul from Unfinished Commentaries* (London and New York: Macmillan, 1895) 141. With little variation this outline is followed by Godet, *First Corinthians*, 321–450; Weiss, *Der erste Korintherbrief*, 343–80; Robertson and Plummer, *I Corinthians*, 328–81; Allo, *Première épître aux Corinthiens*, 387–454; Conzelmann, *1 Corinthians*, 248–93; Fee, *First Corinthians*, 713–809; and R. F. Collins, *First Corinthians*, 525–84.

[180] For example, on the whole of 1 Corinthians 15, see C. K. Barrett, "The Significance of the Adam–Christ Typology for the Resurrection of the Dead: 1Co 15, 20–22. 45–49," in *Résurrection du Christ et des chrétiens (1Co 15)*, ed. De Lorenzi, 99–102; and J. Holleman, *Resurrection and Parousia: A Traditio-Historical Study of Paul's Eschatology in 1 Corinthians 15* (NovTSup 84; Leiden: Brill, 1996) 40–48; on vv. 12–34, see J. Lambrecht, "Paul's Christological Use of Scripture in 1 Cor. 15.20–28," *NTS* 28 (1982) 502–7; and C. E. Hill, "Paul's Understanding of Christ's Kingdom in I Corinthians 15:20–28," *NovT* 30 (1988) 298–303; and on vv. 35–58, see K. Usami, "'How are the Dead Raised?' (1 Cor 15, 35–58)," *Bib* 57 (1976) 473–78; N. Bonneau, "The Logic of Paul's Argument on the Resurrection Body in 1 Cor 15:35–44a," *ScEs* 45 (1993) 80–92; and S. Brodeur, *The Holy Spirit's Agency in the Resurrection of the Dead: An Exegetico-Theological Study of 1 Corinthians 15,44b–49 and Romans 8,9–13* (TGST 14; Rome: Editrice Pontificia Università Gregoriana, 1996) 17–29.

[181] Because they give scrupulous attention to structure, rhetorical analyses of 1 Corinthians 15 are particularly helpful. For example, on the whole of chapter 15, see S. Cipriani, "La risurrezione di Cristo e la nostra risurrezione nella prospettiva di *1 Cor 15*," *Asprenas* 23 (1976) 116–17; J. N. Vorster, "Resurrection Faith in 1 Corinthians 15," *Neot* 23 (1989) 287–307; Watson, "Paul's Rhetorical Strategy in 1 Corinthians 15," 235–49; and Saw, "A Rhetorical Analysis of 1 Corinthians 15" (chap. 3), in *Paul's Rhetoric in 1 Corinthians 15*, 176–272; on vv. 12–34, see Aletti, "L'argumentation de Paul et la position des Corinthiens," 63–66; and S. M. Lewis, "Structure and Argumentation" (chap. 2), in *"So That God May Be All in All": The Apocalyptic Message of 1 Corinthians 15,12–34* (TGST 42; Rome: Editrice Pontificia Università Gregoriana, 1998) 23–74; and on vv. 35–58, see J.-B. Matand Bulembat, "Le problème principal de Paul dans l'argumentation de 1 Co 15,35–49: L'existence d'un corps 'autre' pour la resurrection" (chap. 2) and "La pointe de la discussion paulinienne dans 1 Co 15,50–58: Nécessité du corps spirituel pour les vivants et victoire éternelle sur la mort" (chap. 3), in *Noyau et enjeux de l'eschatologie paulinienne: De l'apocalyptique juive et de l'eschatologie hellénistique dans quelques argumentations de l'apôtre Paul—Etude rhétorique-exégétique de 1 Co 15,35–58; 2 Co 5,1–10 et Rm 8,18–30* (BZNW 84; Berlin and New York: de Gruyter, 1997) 23–75 and 77–130.

12 begins a series of logical proofs for the resurrection of the body, proofs that are supported on the basis of the preceding fact, that Christ's body has been raised (vv. 1–11). Verse 35 also begins a series of logical proofs about how that resurrection of the body is possible, proofs that are supported on the basis of the succeeding fact, that the dead will be raised (vv. 50–58). The parallelism between vv. 12–28 and 35–49 cannot be missed. And, in point of fact, it is not missed in any commentary on chapter 15; it is missed only in general outlines of structure. Again, if vv. 29–34, and particularly v. 29, were not nested in the middle, few commentators would have a problem with a simple A-B-B'-A' paradigm.

As is apparent in Chapter I of our study, the enigmatic nature of 15:29 has led many commentators to gloss over or simply ignore it altogether and, concomitantly, to place very little weight on vv. 30–34. If for a moment, we were able to put aside the vexing nature of 15:29, if we were to bracket centuries of debate and discussion, if we were to pretend whatever is encased in vv. 29–34 is eminently clear and totally reliable, would not a pentacolon (A-B-C-B'-A') paradigm come immediately to mind in perusing chapter 15? It probably would. It would for two specific reasons. First, A (vv. 1–11) refers to a past event, and A' (vv. 50–58) refers to a future event. B (vv. 12–28) is a series of logical proofs pertinent to A, and B' (vv. 35–49) is a series of logical proofs pertinent to A'. At first glance, C (vv. 29–34) seems out of place. It does not parallel A or B. It is neither a series of proofs nor a reference to past or future. Rather, it refers to ongoing events in the life of the Corinthian community and Paul's own life. Second, B deals with "some of you" (τίνες), and B' deals with "someone" (τίς). The thematic and semantic connections are evident. Again, at first glance, C seems out of place with mention only of another group, "those being baptized" (οἱ βαπτιζόμενοι), and Paul himself. Paul has at least two groups in mind: the "somes" and the "ones." So, C stands outside the parallel but within the pale of A and B, and it also stands between them, literally. Ordinarily, these two reasons would be more than sufficient for the discernment of the A-B-C-B'-A' paradigm within a determined literary unit such as chapter 15.

But 1 Corinthians 15 is no ordinary chapter. As the earliest extant *apologia* for the resurrection, written by the most prolific author of the NT, the theological profundity of chapter 15 is, to say the least, momentous. The exegesis and interpretation of this chapter hies to the very foundations of Christian theology. This, no doubt, explains the consternation over 15:29. Here it stands dead center—physically and structurally—within chapter 15, and its meaning is vigorously debated. It is our suggestion that this is the very reason the majority of exegetes place it off to the side, rather than at the core of the chapter: If 15:29 is merely a minor testimony to the resurrection, a footnote to vv. 1–11, then its exegesis is inconsequential in terms of the interpretation of the chapter. After all, no exegete worth his salt comes to chapter 15 lacking cognizance of the knot that is 15:29. When that knot is discounted as subsidiary, then exegetical inquiry may continue without further ado. So too, when baptism is *a priori* dispatched as relatively unimportant, or "sacramentalism" is pre-posited as a corruption à la Bultmann, then exegetical inquiry is free to ignore it. As we see in Chapters III and IV of our study, a neglect of the historical circumstances surrounding Paul and the Corinthians, as well as of confessional differences among Christians concerning baptism and its theological significance, may have much to do with this. For now, we attend merely to the structure of the chapter as we find it. Without a predisposition against 15:29, i.e., without seeking to diagram the chapter in light of the difficult interpretive history of 15:29 and without any confessional antipathy to baptismal efficacy, 15:29 is hardly disconcerting.

Therefore, we attempt to attend to the structure without preconceptions or prejudices. At first glance, as outlined above, 1 Corinthians 15 seems to manifest a pentacolon chiastic structure, with the central idea in the middle. Nonetheless, we must look a bit more closely for certainty. Perchance tempted to move outward from the middle, it is more appropriate to work from the beginning, just as the chapter has been given to us by Paul. In vv. 1–11, Paul reminds his readers of what he preached and they believed, viz., that Christ has been raised. Paul presents Christ's resurrection as a simple fact. After death, burial, and an hiatus of three days, Christ appeared (ὤφθη) to Cephas, the Twelve, five hundred brethren, James, all the apostles, and Paul. The rationale for this reminder becomes plain only in v. 12. Evidently, Paul has found out that some are denying the resurrection of the dead—tantamount to denying the resurrection of Christ, believing in vain, and ending pitifully (vv. 13–19). However, the fact of Christ's resurrection, the first fruits of redemption (v. 20), is the impetus for the redemption of all things (vv. 21–28). Otherwise (ἐπεί), i.e., if the preceding were not the case, why are people being baptized on account of the dead (v. 29)? Why does Paul risk himself? For a vain hope (vv. 30–32)? Menander's maxim is correct: some have corrupted others and Paul speaks to their mutual shame (vv. 33–34).[182] Then, Paul returns to the question of the resurrection in v. 35. Herewith, the rationale for vv. 29–34 comes to the fore. Paul is not moving on to another theme. Rather, he is couching two forms of active, practical witness to the resurrection—the witness of those who are baptized on account of the dead and his apostolic labors—between two affirmations of the resurrection—the *that* (vv. 12–28) and the *how* (vv. 35–49). Verse 35 commences an explanation of the manner of the resurrection in terms of the transformative potential of the physical (natural) body into a spiritual body (vv. 36–49). But, just as the theorization of resurrection falls short without the fact of Christ's resurrection, so too the theorization of how that resurrection might take place falls short without the verification by Paul in terms of a mystery (vv. 50–

---

[182] Paul's use of Menander's *Thais* is considered below.

58). Thus, we can confirm our initial observations with a more precise rendering of the structure vis-à-vis our second look:

A	Christ is raised, a **fact** attested by the authority of witnesses and by Paul (vv. 1–11)
B	explanation of *that*, there is resurrection of the body, first Christ and then those who belong to him (vv. 12–28)
C	active, practical witnessing to the resurrection (vv. 29–34)
B'	explanation of *how*, the resurrected body is a spiritual body, since a physical (natural) body is raised as a spiritual body (vv. 35–49)
A'	Christians will be raised, a **fact** attested by Paul and the authority of mystery (vv. 50–58).

It should come as no surprise to find the witness of praxis at the center of chapter 15 because 1 Corinthians is the most practical of letters. Paul responds to a plethora of immediate concerns in 1 Corinthians (e.g., immorality, litigation, marriage, idol food, and worship) by means of eminently no-nonsense answers. In fact, Paul stresses imitation of himself at two key junctures in the letter, 4:16 and 11:1. The comparison of groups or positions within the community itself could not possibly take us unawares as we read 1 Corinthians. The very first issue with which Paul deals is, in fact, the factionalism within the community, and, accordingly, its residual arrogance in some of its members (4:18). Thereafter, with each of the problems he addresses, it is plain that he is often speaking to some members of the community rather than to all (e.g., 6:11; 8:2, 7; 10:28). Obviously, if every member of the community were subject to each and every problem Paul mentions in 1 Corinthians, his letter would be very different. As it is, Paul uses the letter not only to instruct the ignorant but also to affirm right faith and morals, and this is especially conspicuous in chapter 15. The very structure of the chapter revolves around some who doubt that there is a resurrection of the dead (15:12)—tantamount to denying the resurrection of Christ for Paul—and someone who doubts how such a thing can come about (15:35)—even if he be only a logical construct in Paul's mind. And, nested within this comparative parallel lies a subtler comparison, viz., vv. 29–34, wherein we encounter the example of those who are baptized on account of the dead, the personal example of Paul, and the "some who have no knowledge of God" (v. 34b)—the ones to whom Paul is speaking specifically, those who question the resurrection in some fashion.

1 Corinthians 15:29–34

Within vv. 29–34, Paul juxtaposes the example of one group of Corinthian Christians against another's, with his own example tethered to boot. While it is not immediately clear as to what those who are spoken of in the third person plural (the ones being baptized on account of the dead) are all about, it is clear from all else that we read in chapter 15 that those to whom Paul is speaking in the second person plural are the ones who doubt the resurrection. Therefore, whatever the former are about, one thing is clear: by being baptized on account of the dead, they are to some degree affirming the resurrection.[183] Moreover, those to whom Paul speaks in the second person must be aware (or at the very least Paul must think them aware) that the practice of baptism on account of the dead is commensurate with faith in the resurrection. Otherwise, the example would make no sense to the Corinthians. Thus, we notice a concentric structure with Paul's invocation of three grammatical persons:

A   3rd p., pl., "they,"
          those on Paul's side, affirming the resurrection (v. 29)

B   1st p., sing., "I,"[184]
          Paul's apostolic example of faith in the resurrection (vv. 30–32)

A'   2nd p., pl., "you,"
          those not on Paul's side, denying the resurrection (vv. 33–34).

Perforce in this structure, A is juxtaposed with A' in an antithetical parallelism. Each pole has two factors: the grammatical person (third or second) and the action (affirmation or denial) proper to each. Surely, the question of v. 29b—"If the dead are not raised at all?"—is the antecedent to Paul's question in v. 30—"Why am I in peril every hour?—and all that follows therewith until the aforementioned shift in v. 35.

In fact, a series of four rhetorical questions in vv. 29–32a fastens the practice of baptism on account of the dead to Paul's own apostolic suffering, a series which has its crescendo in v. 32b: "If the dead are not raised, 'Let us eat and drink, for tomorrow we die.'" In this conditional sentence, the protasis is unmistakably linked to the immediately preceding questions, and the apodosis to the fate of both Paul and Corinthians, should the answers to those questions be somehow invalidating. The apodosis is an exact quotation of Isa 22:13 (LXX);

---

[183] According to Eriksson, "15:29 reconnects with the theme concerning the resurrection of Christ and the Christians. Note the repetition of νεκροὶ ἐγείρονται from 15:20 and 23 in negative form here (οὐκ ἐγείρονται)" (*Traditions as Rhetorical Proof*, 264).

[184] Here we follow the translation of the RSV and favor the first person singular over the first person plural. Verses 30–32a are consistently in the first person singular, except for καὶ ἡμεῖς κινδυνεύομεν (first person plural) in v. 30a. (Verse 32b is the quote from Menander's *Thais*.) Findlay (*First Corinthians*, 931) is correct in noting that Paul may be thinking of himself in terms of the common witness of all the apostles, especially with reference to 1 Cor 15:11. Conzelmann (*1 Corinthians*, 277 n. 124) maintains that "in the principal clause, Paul is thinking of himself"; so too, Fee (*First Corinthians*, 768 n. 36) says that Paul "means 'I myself.'" As R. F. Collins (*First Corinthians*, 559) suggests, Paul is "building up his climax" by moving from the plural to the singular. Paul desires to let his example serve as a lesson. In any case, the issue is the grammatical person, not the number.

Paul's meaning could not be more lucid. Isa 22:1–14, the "Oracle on the Valley of Vision," is the third in a series of catastrophic visions in Isa 21:1–23:18. Isaiah's historical reference is most likely to the end of Sennacherib's seige of Jerusalem in 701 B.C. In that example, the people should have responded to Isaiah as the people of Nineveh had responded to Jonah; instead, they reveled recklessly to their own perdition in God's eyes. The view of life summarized in Isa 22:13 was not an uncommon one in the ancient Near East. And no Corinthian could miss its double entendre in reference to Epicureanism.[185] "Eating and drinking" was synonymous with licentiousness.[186] The homogeneity of protasis and apodosis leads us back to 15:12–19 and, especially, to v. 17: "If Christ has not been raised, your faith is futile and you are still in your sins."[187]

Part and parcel of this affirmation of the resurrection is Paul's personal example of hourly peril, daily dying, and fighting beasts in Ephesus (vv. 30–32a). His (apostolic) labor, bringing him into danger, even danger of death, would be pointless if there were no reward, no resurrection of the dead. Here, Paul does not indicate the precise nature of the peril or spell out what he means by dying daily,[188] except insofar as they are illustrated in his experience at Ephesus. Such an illustration fits perfectly, since 1 Corinthians was most likely written from Ephesus. This reference to fighting with wild beasts presents its own exegetical challenges.[189] It refers to an actual encounter in the arena at Ephesus,[190] or it refers, metaphorically, to Paul's encounter(s) with his opponents in Ephesus.[191] In either case, the point is transparent: earthly struggles on behalf of the faith only make sense in light of the hope of resurrection. Indeed, Paul's apostolic struggles have yielded such fruit in Corinth that the Corinthians are a cause for his boasting in the Lord (v. 31).[192] With the emphatic, "I swear

---

[185] See G. Tomlin, "Christians and Epicureans in 1 Corinthians," *JSNT* 68 (1997) 51–72.

[186] For example, Plutarch, *Mor.* 1098c, 1100d, and 1125d.

[187] In his rhetorical analysis of chapter 15, Eriksson sees the same thing: "Just like the first *refutatio* [15:12–19], the contrary argument in 15:29 is an argument *ad hominem* which indicates that a Corinthian practice, which Paul calls 'baptism for the dead,' contradicts their statement that there is no resurrection of the dead" (*Traditions as Rhetorical Proofs*, 264).

[188] The possibilities are easily gleaned from 2 Cor 11:24–29.

[189] For the issues involved, see R. E. Osborne, "Paul and the Wild Beasts," *JBL* 85 (1966) 225–30. To dodge the issues and suggest that the verse is a scribal interpolation in order to attune it to 2 Tim 4:17, as does D. R. MacDonald ("A Conjectural Emendation of 1 Cor 15:31–32: Or the Case of the Misplaced Lion Fight," *HTR* 73 [1980] 265–76) is groundless and dismissive of all textual evidence. Cf. R. F. Collins, *First Corinthians*, 560.

[190] C. R. Bowen, "I Fought with Beasts at Ephesus," *JBL* 42 (1923) 59–68.

[191] A. J. Malherbe, "The Beasts at Ephesus," *JBL* 87 (1968) 71–80.

[192] On boasting in Paul see, R. F. Collins, *First Corinthians*, 99–101; cf. E. A. Judge, "Paul's Boasting in Relation to Contemporary Professional Practice," *AusBR* 16 (1968) 37–50; C. Forbes, "Comparison, Self-Praise and Irony: Paul's Boasting and the Conventions of Hellenistic Rhetoric," *NTS* 32 (1986) 1–30; and J. R. Wagner, "'Not Beyond the Things Which Are Written': A Call to Boast Only in the Lord (1 Cor 4.6)," *NTS* 44 (1998) 279–87.

by" (νή),[193] Paul increases the poignancy of his argument by associating dire struggles with felicitous consequences. Again the point is transparent: Paul's success at Corinth would be a Pyrrhic victory, if faith in the resurrection were forfeited. Should that be the case, then the pagan response to the vicissitudes of life—"Let us eat and drink for tomorrow we die"—would be the appropriate response.

Paul warns against such beguilement: "Do not be deceived" (Μὴ πλανᾶσθε). In so doing, Paul implies that this is, if you will, "a clear and present danger." The combination of μή with the present imperative of πλανάω insinuates that some Corinthians are already deceived,[194] as is easily culled from the use of the identical phrase in 1 Cor 6:9 and Gal 6:7. It is to this exhortation that Paul ties a quotation from the lost comedy *Thais* by the Athenian dramatist Menander (341/2–292/1 B.C.): "Bad company ruins good morals."[195] That Paul chose to cite a profane author here is strange, since this is the only quotation from a non-biblical source in his letters.[196] However, the oddity is somewhat mitigated by the popularity of Menander, whose plays were very influential in the Greco-Roman world.[197] At this point, it is unnecessary to draw conclusions as to how Paul came to know the phrase,[198] since Menander's writings were well known in Paul's day.[199] Perhaps, Paul saw *Thais* performed? Perhaps, the phrase was a contemporary *bon mot*?[200] In any case, he must have known it would resonate with the Corinthians. This "bad company" is more likely an internal problem of the Corinthian community than an external one. Although it has been suggested that "bad company" refers to pagan seduction against Christianity vis-

---

[193] This is the only occurrence of the affirmative particle νή in the NT (found in the LXX only in Gen 42:15), though it is common enough in contemporaneous diatribes. See BDF §107; and Malherbe, "Beasts at Ephesus," 72. On translation problems with 15:31, see D. S. Deer, "Whose Pride/Rejoicing/Glory(ing) in I Corinthians 15.31?" *BT* 38 (1987) 126–28.

[194] M. Zerwick notes: "Especially in prohibitions it commonly happens that μή with the present imperative is used to forbid the continuation of an act" (*Biblical Greek Illustrated by Examples* [ed. J. Smith; SPIB 114; Rome: Editrice Pontificio Istituto Biblico, 1963] §246).

[195] For more, see "Menander," *OCD*, 669–70.

[196] But cf. Acts 17:28, which quotes Aratus' *Phaenomena*, and Titus 1:12, which quotes an hexameter attributed to Epimenides the Cretan by St. Clement of Alexandria (*Strom.* 1.59.2).

[197] See P. Green, "Theophrastus, Menander, and the Transformation of Attic Comedy" (chap. 5), in *Alexander to Actium: The Historical Evolution of the Hellenistic Age* (HCS 1; Berkeley: University of California Press, 1990) 65–79.

[198] The phrase itself—Φθείρουσιν ἤθη χρηστὰ ὁμιλίαι κακαί—has its own peculiar problems. We might expect an elision between χρηστά and ὁμιλίαι, i.e., χρήσθ' ὁμιλίαι, if it were a reference to a colloquial saying, but Paul does not make it. Instead, he keeps the meter, as was the common literary custom (see BDF §17). Additionally, ἦθος and ὁμιλία are hapax legomena in the NT, while χρηστός is a hapax in 1 Corinthains (cf. Rom 2:4).

[199] Malherbe, "Beasts at Ephesus," 73; and Thiselton, *First Corinthians*, 1254.

[200] So Barrett, *First Corinthians*, 367; and R. F. Collins, *First Corinthians*, 569.

à-vis 1 Corinthians 8–10 (cf. Rom 12:2),[201] it is more likely a reference to "bad company" within the Corinthian community.[202] Context certainly favors the latter opinion. There seems to be very little allowance for the consideration of purely pagan (external) influence in the middle of an extended argument on behalf of the resurrection of Christ and of Christians. Most likely, those to whom Paul alludes are Christians lapsing in faith, perhaps with the aid of friendly pagan inducement, but that does not make them pagans. Moreover, v. 34 certainly points in the direction of an internal problem.

Verse 34 indicates that the ones in sin are the ones who deny the resurrection. Once again Paul speaks in imperatives. He tells them "to sober up" (ἐκνήψατε), i.e., "to come to their senses,"[203] and to do so "properly" (δικαίως).[204] He tells them "to stop sinning" (μὴ ἁμαρτάνετε); this reflects and reaffirms his previous exhortation "to stop being deceived" (μὴ πλανᾶσθε). Paul uses the postpositive γάρ to explain exactly what he means,[205] viz., that "some (τινες) have no knowledge of God." If there be any doubt as to who the "some" are, it is crystal clear in last clause of the verse: "I say this to *your* shame"—πρὸς ἐντροπὴν ὑμῖν λαλῶ—to the same group of people to whom Paul has been speaking all the while: those who deny the resurrection. These words were not written for the evangelization of pagans but for the sake of doctrinal purity within a community.[206] We have come full circle back to the τίνες of 15:12 and we are prepared for the τίς of 15:35.

Like all of chapter 15, vv. 29–34 are an assertion of the resurrection. Given the structure of the chapter and the subunit of vv. 29–34, we can only conclude that, whatever is going on in v. 29, it is certainly an affirmation of the resurrection and an affirmation approved by Paul. Moreover, it must have been something well known to the Corinthians or it would have been fruitless for Paul to have used it as an example. Our task in this study is to determine the nature of this most salient example. In order to do so, we must now turn to the morphology and syntax of 15:29.

---

[201] Robertson and Plummer, *I Corinthians*, 363; Godet, *First Corinthians*, 2.395; and Barrett, *First Corinthians*, 367 (although he is bit unclear on the point).

[202] Conzelmann, *I Corinthians*, 278–79; and Fee, *First Corinthians*, 773. Fee (ibid., n. 62) thinks that the connotations of ὁμιλία (e.g., "companionship" and "conversation") are especially indicative of a difficulty within the Corinthian community.

[203] See "ἐκνήφω," BAGD, 243. Ἐκνήφω is a hapax legomenon in the NT. On the metaphor, cf. Rom 13:11 and 1 Thess 5:6.

[204] See "δικαίως," BAGD, 198.

[205] See Zerwick, *Biblical Greek* §§472, 474.

[206] H. A. Kent, Jr. "A Fresh Look at 1 Corinthians 15:34: An Appeal for Evangelism or a Call to Purity?" *GTJ* 4 (1983) 3–14.

THE MORPHOLOGY AND SYNTAX OF 1 CORINTHIANS 15:29

Thus far, in this second chapter of our study, we have endeavored to set the stage for a new reading of 15:29 by looking to the genre and integrity of 1 Corinthians. In so doing, we have paid scant attention to our first chapter, because the contemporary readings of 15:29 infrequently extend themselves to such issues. Here, it is necessary to return to the issues raised in our first chapter. As we have seen, the words of 15:29 are matters of great contention; most readings of the verse rise and fall by particular and peculiar renditions of 15:29's vocabulary and syntax. For a new reading of 15:29, it is indispensable to examine each of the disputed terms and their various nuances in detail. Our previous examination of the contemporary readings shows the morphology of three words to be paramount in our understanding of the verse: βαπτίζω, νεκρός, and—most especially—ὑπέρ. Because there is far less contention regarding the verse's other vocabulary, it is examined in relation to the aforementioned three and the syntactical structure of 15:29.

The Morphology of 1 Corinthians 15:29

As we saw in Chapter I, the vast majority of the contemporary readings of 15:29 hinge on a precise rendition or combination of renditions of βαπτίζω, νεκρός, or ὑπέρ. Therefore, each of the three must be examined in detail.

The verb βαπτίζω appears seldom in Paul's letters outside 1 Corinthians. Other than its ten occurrences in 1 Corinthians, Paul uses βαπτίζω only in Rom 6:3 (2x) and Gal 3:27. Its cognate βάπτισμα appears only in Rom 6:4.[207] Besides the two uses of βαπτίζω in 15:29, βαπτίζω appears eight other times in 1 Corinthians (1:13, 14, 15, 16 [2x], 17; 10:2; 12:13). Its use in 15:29 notwithstanding, βαπτίζω is always used literally in 1 Corinthians. Since most would agree with T. J. Conant that "the Greek word *baptizein* expresses nothing more than the act of *immersion*, the religious significance of which is derived from the circumstances connected to it,"[208] and also with Barrett that "*baptized*, without further explanation, can hardly have other than its normal Pauline meaning"[209] (i.e., a literal meaning of "to dip," "to immerse"), we too would say the same were it not for the figurative use of βαπτίζω, claimed by scholars such as Murphy-O'Connor and Godet, which compels a thorough examination of βαπτίζω in 15:29.

---

[207] Βάπτισμα also appears in Eph 4:5 and βαπτισμός in Col 2:12.

[208] T. J. Conant, *The Meaning and Use of "Baptizein": Philologically and Historically Investigated for the American Bible Union* (New York: American Bible Union, 1868) 101 (emphasis original).

[209] Barrett, *First Corinthians*, 362 (emphasis original).

In the LXX and the NT, βαπτίζω and βάπτισμα are always used literally,[210] except for their use in Mark 10 and Luke 12. There is no doubt that βαπτίζω and βάπτισμα are used figuratively in Mark 10:38–39 and Luke 12:50. In Mark 10:38–39, the Lord speaks of his own passion as "the baptism that I am to be baptized with" (τὸ βάπτισμα ὃ ἐγὼ βαπτίζομαι βαπτισθῆναι [v. 38] and τὸ βάπτισμα ὃ ἐγὼ βαπτίζομαι βαπτισθήσεσθε [v.39]), after the presumptuous request of James and John to sit at his right and left in glory (Mark 10:37). In Luke 12:50, the Lord also speaks of his passion as a "baptism to be baptized with" (βάπτισμα δὲ ἔχω βαπτισθῆναι) in a series of prophetic sayings calling for conversion (Luke 12:49–59). Such figurative usage as this is closer to βαπτίζω's use in Hellenism, where the sense of "going under" or "perishing" is the predominant usage.[211] Naturally, such a metaphorical use is significant for the understanding of the terms in the NT. However, Mark and Luke (as well as Matthew), in quoting the Lord, also use βάπτισμα literally. When questioned about his authority in Mark 11:29–30 and its parallels (Matt 21:23–7 and Luke 20:1–8), the Lord responds in rabbinical fashion by asking another question, as to whether the baptism of John (τὸ βάπτισμα [τὸ] Ἰωάννου) was from heaven or from men (Mark 11:30; Matt 21:25; Luke 20:4). Thus, there is ample attestation in the NT for a literal or figurative reading of βαπτίζω and βάπτισμα, neither being mutually exclusive,[212] but the balance hangs in favor of a literal reading.

With concern for the use of βαπτίζω in 15:29, we must turn to its other uses in Paul's letters, viz., in Romans and Galatians. In Rom 6:3, the two uses of βαπτίζω are certainly literal: "Do you not know that all of us who have been baptized into Christ Jesus (ἐβαπτίσθημεν εἰς Χριστὸν Ἰησοῦν) were baptized into his death (εἰς τὸν θάνατον αὐτοῦ ἐβαπτίσθημεν)?" So too, in Rom 6:4— "We were buried therefore with him by baptism (διὰ τοῦ βαπτίσματος) into death, so that as Christ was raised from the dead by the glory of the Father, we too might walk in newness of life"—we can only read βάπτισμα literally.[213] And

---

[210] In the LXX, βαπτίζω is used in 2 Kgs 5:14; Isa 21:4; Jdt 12:7; Sir 34:25; βάπτω in Exod 12:22; Lev 4:6, 17; 9:9; 11:32; 14:6, 16, 51; Num 19:18; Deut 33:24; JoshB 3:15; Ruth 2:14; 1 Sam 14:27; 2 Kgs 8:15; Job 9:31; Ps 67:24; DanTh 4:33; 5:21; 2 Macc 1:20; and βαπτός in Ezek 23:15. In the NT, βαπτίζω is used in Matt 3:6, 11 (2x), 13, 14, 16; 28:19; Mark 1:4, 5, 8 (2x), 9; 6:14, 24, 7:4 (2x?); 8:28; 16:16; Luke 3:7, 12, 16 (2x), 21 (2x); 7:29, 30; 11:38; John 1:25, 26, 28, 31, 33 (2x); 3:22, 23 (2x); 26; 4:1, 2; 10:40; Acts 1:5 (2x); 2:38, 41; 8:12, 13, 16, 36, 38; 9:18; 10:47, 48; 11:16 (2x); 16:15, 33; 18:8, 25; 19:3, 4, 5; 22:16; βάπτισμα in Matt 3:7; 21:25; Mark 1:4; 11:30; Luke 3:3; 7:29; 20:4; Acts 1:22; 10:37; 13:24; 18:25; 19:3, 4; 1 Pet 3:21; βαπτισμός in Mark 7:4; Heb 6:2; 9:10; and βάπτω in Luke 16:24; John 13:26 (2x); and Rev 19:13. Additionally, the title βαπτιστής is used twelve times as a reference to John in the synoptics: Matt 3:1; 11:11, 12; 14:2, 8; 16:14; 17:13; Mark 6:25; 8:28; Luke 7:20, 33; and 9:19.

[211] Oepke, "βάπτω," 530.

[212] This is also true outside the NT, e.g., Josephus uses βαπτίζω literally (*B.J.* 3.368, 423) and figuratively (ibid., 3.525; 4.137).

[213] This is likewise true of βάπτισμα in Eph 4:5 and βαπτισμός in Col 2:12. On the lack of any real distinction between the two, see J. Barr, *The Semantics of Biblical Language* (1961; rpt. London: SCM, 1963) 140–44.

the same holds true for Gal 3:27: "For as many of you as were baptized into Christ (εἰς Χριστὸν ἐβαπτίσθητε) have put on Christ." Indeed, in Romans and Galatians, the only other instances of βαπτίζω (and βάπτισμα) outside 1 Corinthians, no figurative reading is plausible. This is especially so given the contexts of Rom 6:1–14, Paul's most extensive discourse on the meaning of baptism, and Gal 3:1–29, Paul's exegesis of the Abraham story in light of Christ.

By far, the most frequent use of βαπτίζω in any of Paul's letters is found in 1 Corinthians. As noted, other than in 15:29, βαπτίζω is used eight times. The first six instances, 1:13, 14, 15, 16 (2x), and 17, are found at the very beginning of the body of the letter. Verse 13b assumes that the Corinthians to whom Paul is writing have been baptized already, and vv. 14–16 remind them that, through no fault of Paul for he baptized few personally, they lack the fraternal unity entailed in baptism. Each instance of βαπτίζω can be read solely literally. The other two instances, 10:2 and 12:13, are found in divergent contexts within the latter part of the letter's body. The former is found within 10:1–13, wherein Paul interprets the meaning of certain Exodus events for Christians; the latter is a key element within 12:12–26, wherein Paul describes the mystical body of Christ. Moreover, 12:12–13 closely parallels Gal 3:26–29 (cf. Eph 2:11–22). Again, the only reading is a literal one. All in all, each and every one of these eight instances of βαπτίζω in 1 Corinthians is to be read literally.

What of the two instances of βαπτίζω in 15:29? Given Paul's other uses of the term, and especially his use thereof in 1 Corinthians, we can read them only in like manner. There is no compelling reason to do otherwise. However, Murphy-O'Connor and Godet reject such a literal reading of βαπτίζω, on the grounds that, with such an understanding of βαπτίζω, the whole of 15:29 must be read exclusively as a reference to vicarious baptism.[214] In other words, the verse cannot mean what it seems to say. And so, they opt for a metaphorical reading, even though both admit that such an understanding of the verb would be rare in the NT, along with Mark 10:38–39 and Luke 12:50, but unique in Paul.[215] Both appeal to the context of 15:29 for their metaphorical understanding of βαπτίζω. That appeal to context might be credible if it were made on the basis of preference for one warranted reading over another. But, as we have seen, that is not their claim. Instead, they assert that the verse can be read in no other sense save to refer to vicarious baptism, which they both consider an absurdity, and such a claim falls to pieces if vicarious baptism is not rejected *a priori* or if 15:29 may be read differently, e.g., as ordinary baptism, when βαπτίζω is taken literally. Consequently, it behooves us to read βαπτίζω as it is read in every

---

[214] Murphy-O'Connor, "Baptized for the Dead," 532–33; and Godet, *First Corinthians*, 384–86.

[215] Murphy-O'Connor, "Baptized for the Dead," 534–35; and Godet, *First Corinthians*, 389–90.

other instance in the Pauline literature (and in all but two locations in the NT), i.e., literally, unless a persuasive argument be made otherwise.

The same holds true for νεκρός, i.e., there is no reason to read it differently in 15:29 from the way it is read throughout Paul's letters, especially in Romans and 1 Corinthians. Νεκρός is a fairly common adjective in the LXX and NT. It appears ninety times in the LXX and 128 times in the NT. Νεκρός is used mostly as a substantive and rarely as a modifier. Νεκρός appears thirty-four times in Paul's letters, with the vast majority in Romans and 1 Corinthians. The appearances of νεκρός are scattered throughout Romans (1:4, 4:17, 24; 6:4, 9, 11, 13; 7:4, 8; 8:10, 11 (2x); 10:7, 9; 11:15; 14:9), but highly concentrated in 1 Corinthians. In 1 Corinthians, we find νεκρός used only in chapter 15. Other than its two instances in 15:29, it is found in vv. 12 (2x), 13, 15, 16, 20, 21, 32, 42, 45, and 52. Elsewhere, Paul only uses the word in 2 Cor 1:9; Gal 1:1; Phil 3:11; 1 Thess 1:10; and 4:16.[216] In the NT, νεκρός is used much more frequently in its literal than figurative sense. When used as a noun, νεκρός simply means "the dead as distinct from the living."[217] The few instances of its figurative sense occur in Matt 8:22 and Luke 9:60, wherein Jesus speaks of letting "the dead bury their dead"; John 5:25, wherein Jesus speaks of the time when "the dead will hear the voice of the Son of God, and those who hear will live";[218] and Eph 5:14, wherein we find an otherwise unknown quotation: "Awake, O sleeper, and arise from the dead, and Christ shall give you light."[219] Sometimes νεκρός is used figuratively as an adjective, e.g., Luke 15:24, 32; Eph 2:1, 5; Col 2:13; Heb 6:1; 9:14; Jam 2:17, 26; and Rev 3:1.

In Paul's letters, νεκρός is always used as a noun in the literal sense. Νεκρός is used recurrently to speak of Christ's resurrection from the dead: Rom 1:4; 4:24; 6:4, 9; 8:11 (2x); 10:7, 9; 1 Cor 15:12a; 15:20; Gal 1:1; Phil 3:11; and 1 Thess 1:10.[220] In turn, it is used to speak of the resurrection of Christians from the dead: Rom 7:4; 11:15; 14:9; 1 Cor 15:12b, 13, 15, 16, 21, 32, 42, 52; 2 Cor 1:9; and 1 Thess 4:16. So too, the other instances, though in varied ways, use νεκρός substantively. Rom 4:17 quotes Gen 17:5. Rom 7:8 speaks of the death of sin apart from the law. And Rom 6:11, 13; and 8:10 articulate the notion of union with Christ's death in baptism, wherein such a "usage in this case is sacramental rather than figurative."[221] Judging, then, from its usage throughout his

---

[216] Νεκρός is also found in the Pauline pseudepigrapha: Eph 1:20; 2:1, 5; 5:14; Col 1:18; 2:12, 13; 2 Tim 2:8; and 4:1.

[217] R. Bultmann, "νεκρός, νεκρόω, νέκρωσις," *TDNT* 4:893.

[218] Eph 2:1, 5 and Col 2:13 show this same sort of usage.

[219] Perhaps a reference to an early Christian (baptismal) hymn, Isa 60:1, or both? For the debate on the background, see R. Schnackenburg, *Ephesians: A Commentary* (trans. H. Heron; Edinburgh: T&T Clark, 1991) 228–29.

[220] It is also used in this fashion in Eph 1:20; Col 1:18; 2:12; 2 Tim 2:8; and 2 Tim 4:1, where Christ is described as "judge of the living and the dead."

[221] Bultmann, "νεκρός," 894. See also, idem "θάνατος, θνῄσκω, ἀποθνῄσκω, συναποθνῄσκω, θανατόω, θνητός, ἀθανασία, (ἀθάνατος)," *TDNT* 3:19.

letters, and especially in 1 Corinthians, Paul is consistent in using νεκρός literally.

But what of its use in 15:29? As we saw above, both O'Neill and Murphy-O'Connor abjure Paul's consistent usage and opt for a figurative reading; and, as with βαπτίζω, it would seem that they opt for such a reading on the supposed intransigence of 15:29. Recall that O'Neill pushes the envelope by using a rare textual variant from the Leicester codex 69, so that νεκρός appears twice in 15:29b (αὐτῶν τῶν νεκρῶν) rather than the simple αὐτῶν in the received text, and he claims an extremely figurative employment of νεκρός in its first and third occurrences, so that νεκρός refers to "corpses," i.e., "their dying bodies," along the lines of *"huper tōn nekrōn sōmatōn."*[222] But, "the dualistic terminology which describes the human σῶμα as νεκρόν (or νεκρός) is not found" in the NT.[223] When Paul does use σῶμα and νεκρόν together in Rom 8:10, νεκρός is clearly a predicate nominative. O'Neill juxtaposes this with his odd rendering of the second occurrence of νεκρός, which he claims is modified by the adverb ὅλως ("actually"), and means "the completely dead."[224] Thus, the first and third occurrences of νεκρός refer to the dying and the second to the dead. Basically, Murphy-O'Connor's reading is the same, though he does not appeal to any textual variant. Murphy-O'Connor also has ὅλως modifying νεκρός in 15:29b, but he opts for a figurative reading of νεκρός in 15:29a.[225] Thus, the dead of 15:29a are the "spiritually dead" and the dead of 15:29b, the ὅλως νεκροί, are the "physically dead."[226] In other words, both O'Neill and Murphy-O'Connor take νεκρός to have two different meanings in 15:29. If we assume for a moment that ὅλως modifies νεκρός vis-à-vis their alternate figurative readings, then ὅλως has transformed the figurative to the literal insofar as "dying bodies" become "dead persons" and the "spiritually dead" become the "physically dead."

But ὅλως does not function that way in Greek. While we have already seen that νεκρός is not used figuratively in Paul's letters, even if it were, ὅλως cannot transform the figurative use of an adjective into a literal use. Rarely used in the NT, ὅλως is often paired with the negatives οὐ and μή, wherewith it is used adverbially, to mean "not at all,"[227] as in Matt 5:34. In fact, save for Matt 5:34, the only other three uses of ὅλως in the NT are found in 1 Cor 5:1; 6:7; and 15:29. In 1 Cor 5:1, ὅλως modifies ἀκούεται ("it is actually reported"); in 1 Cor 6:7, ὅλως modifies ἐστίν ("it is actually"). In 15:29, the same sort of usage is

---

[222] O'Neill, "1 Corinthians 15:29," 310.

[223] Bultmann, "νεκρός," 894. It is found in Ignatius (*Smyrn.* 5.2) and John Chysostom (*Hom. in 1 Cor.* 23). On this, see G. von Rad, G. Bertram, and R. Bultmann, "ζάω, ζωή (βιόω, βίος), ἀναζάω, ζῷον, ζωογονέω, ζωοποιέω," *TDNT* 2:863 n. 267; and Bultmann, "θάνατος," 17 n. 76. See also "νεκρός," BAGD, 534–35.

[224] O'Neill, "1 Corinthians 15:29," 310.

[225] Murphy-O'Connor, "Baptized for the Dead," 536–37.

[226] Ibid., 540.

[227] "ὅλως," BAGD, 565. See ibid. for the various extra-NT references.

obvious in εἰ ὅλως νεκροὶ οὐκ ἐγείρονται—ὅλως is paired with οὐκ to modify ἐγείρονται—hence, "if they (the dead) are not actually raised." In essence, both O'Neill and Murphy-O'Connor claim that νεκρός has two different meanings in 15:29, the first figurative and the second literal. The entreaty for a copula between ὅλως and νεκρός seems little more than a gaff to support an otherwise untenable proposition. Quite simply, as all other contemporary readings of the verse agree, νεκρός refers to dead persons,[228] and ὅλως functions adverbially to modify ἐγείρω. Furthermore, the phrase νεκροὶ οὐκ ἐγείρονται also occurs three other times (vv. 15, 16, 32) in the same section (vv. 12–34) of chapter 15, a section universally read as a singular argument on behalf of the resurrection of the dead. Are we to assume somehow that the dead mentioned therein are not really dead?

The difficulties of βαπτίζω and νεκρός aside, ὑπέρ is the most difficult word in 15:29. As we have seen, ὑπέρ is repeatedly mentioned as the crux of the *crux interpretum* that is 15:29.[229] So much debate over this preposition is somewhat surprising, since it is relatively rare in the NT. Ὑπέρ, a preposition which may take the accusative or the genitive case, appears 150 times in the NT. Since seventy-seven of those appearances are in Paul's letters and twenty-four in the Pauline pseudepigrapha, Paul uses the preposition more frequently than any other NT author. With the accusative, ὑπέρ means "over" or "above."[230] "This use is an extension of the local, physical sense. The general usage is that something (in an undefined way) exceeds another, as if the former were located above or in a superior position to the latter."[231] Thus, Paul uses the preposition nine times with the accusative (1 Cor 4:6; 10:13; 2 Cor 1:8; 12:6, 13; Gal 1:14; Phil 2:9; Phlm 16, 21) and one time as an adverb (2 Cor 11:23).[232]

However, Paul is wont to use ὑπέρ with the genitive,[233] and he does so sixty-seven times in his letters. There are three general ways in which ὑπέρ is used with the genitive. The first way is the most common. Ὑπέρ most often means "on behalf of," "for," or "in the place of" (often to signify substitution).[234] Paul uses ὑπέρ in this sense in Rom 5:6, 7 (2x), 8: 8:31, 32; 9:3; 14:15; 15:30; 16:4; 1 Cor 1:13; 11:24; 12:25; 15:3; 2 Cor 1:6 (2x), 11a; 5:14, 15 (2x),

---

[228] Thompson's claim ("I Corinthians 15, 29," 653–53), on the basis of Origen's *In Matt. Hom.* 17.29 and a distinction between the Jewish and Platonic milieux of resurrection, that νεκρός is used to refer to corpses as opposed to dead persons is gratuitous.

[229] Reaume, "Another Look at 1 Corinthians 15:29," 467.

[230] "ὑπέρ," BAGD, 838.

[231] S. E. Porter, *Idioms of the Greek New Testament* (2nd ed.; BLG 2; Sheffield: Sheffield Academic Press, 1994) 175. Cf. Riesenfeld, "ὑπέρ," 515.

[232] The use of ὑπέρ as an adverb is extremely rare and unknown outside the NT; see "ὑπέρ," BAGD, 839.

[233] For a discussion on the relationship between the genitive, the ablative, and ὑπέρ, see A. T. Robertson, *A Grammar of the Greek New Testament in Light of Historical Research* (London: Hodder and Stoughton, 1914) 629–30.

[234] See Riesenfeld, "ὑπέρ," 507–13; and Porter, *Idioms of the Greek New Testament*, 176–177.

20 (2x), 21; 7:7, 12; 8:16, 23; 9:14; 12:15, 19; Gal 1:4; 2:20; 3:13; Phil 1:4; 2:13; 4:10; 1 Thess 5:10; and Phlm 13.[235] In this sense, ὑπέρ is used in a fashion similar to that of ἀντί.[236] Ὑπέρ and ἀντί often have a similar meaning, but they are not the same and ought not to be confused; such confusion only obfuscates the interpretation of 15:29.[237] For our purposes, there is no need to belabor this usage—whether on behalf of the dead, for the dead, or in place of the dead—in terms of 15:29. If ὑπέρ is to be read in this way in 15:29, "does it make a difference whether these people were being baptized for the benefit or in place of the dead?"[238] The second way, related closely to the first, is rarer, i.e., ὑπέρ in the final sense, as advocated by Raeder and Jeremias. It is "a weaker use of ὑπέρ [than the aforementioned] in the sense of 'in defense or in favor of.'"[239] We find such a use in Rom 1:5; 8:27, 34; 9:27; 10:1; 2 Cor 1:7, 8; 5:12; 7:4, 14; 8:23, 24; 9:2, 3; 12:5 (2x); Phil 1:7; and 1 Thess 3:2. Again, in terms of 15:29, there would be but a modicum of difference in meaning and interpretation whether ὑπέρ is read in the first or second way, since the baptism that is spoken of would be seen as somehow being performed for the benefit, defense, or in favor of the dead. "We thus have a kind of substitution even if, as one may suppose, the candidate was baptized for himself as well as with respect to someone who had died unbaptized."[240]

The third way is the rarest use of ὑπέρ. Here ὑπέρ is used in a causal sense. "Causally ὑπέρ is used to denote the cause or reason: 'on account of,' 'because of.' In the NT, it occurs with verbs and expressions of suffering, the reference being to Christians who endure hardships because of their faith."[241] According to Harald Riesenfeld, there are examples of this usage in Paul's letters,[242] viz., Rom 15:9; 2 Cor 1:11b; 12:8; Phil 1:29; and 2 Thess 1:5.[243] Walter Bauer et al. add 1 Cor 10:30 and 2 Cor 12:10.[244] And we think that a case may be made for the causal reading of Rom 15:8; 1 Cor 4:6; and 2 Cor 13:8. Thus, the two cases of ὑπέρ in 15:29 may be read in the causal sense, as advocated by Reaume and White. The principal stricture against the causal reading of ὑπέρ in 15:29 is that

---

[235] Cf. E. H. Blakeney, "Ὑπέρ with Genitive in N.T.," *ExpTim* 55 (1943–44) 306.

[236] See Zerwick, *Biblical Greek* §91; and A. T. Robertson, "The Use of Ὑπέρ in Business Documents in the Papyri," *Expositor* 8/18 (1919) 321–27.

[237] Zerwick, *Biblical Greek* §94.

[238] Porter, *Idioms of the Greek New Testament*, 177; see also Riesenfeld, "ὑπέρ," 512–13, and Robertson, *Grammar of the Greek New Testament*, 630–31.

[239] Riesenfeld, "ὑπέρ," 513.

[240] Ibid.

[241] Ibid., 514.

[242] For examples of this usage in the NT other than in Paul's letters, see ibid., 514–15.

[243] Ibid., 514–15. However, Riesenfeld (512–13) holds that ὑπέρ in 15:29 is best read in terms of vicarious baptism. Cf. J. R. White, "Baptized on account of the Dead," 497 n. 63.

[244] "ὑπέρ," BAGD, 839.

the causal sense seems to require something other than a person as its object,[245] e.g., Rom 15:8, 9; 1 Cor 10:30; 2 Cor 12:8; 2 Thess 1:5; and even 1 Cor 15:3 show how fine the distinction may be. However, this reflects the prominent usage in Paul's practice; there is no grammatical or syntactical exigency against persons as the objects of ὑπέρ in the causal sense. In fact, there are at least two verses wherein persons are the objects of ὑπέρ and wherewith only a causal reading makes sense: 2 Cor 1:11b and Phil 1:29. In 2 Cor 1:11b, we find ὑπέρ ἡμῶν,[246] "on account of us." In Phil 1:29, we find ὑπέρ Χριστοῦ and ὑπέρ αὐτοῦ, "on account of Christ" and "on account of him." Therefore, there is no reason to preclude a causal reading of ὑπέρ in 15:29. To be sure, the overwhelming preponderance of Paul's usage militates against such a reading: he very seldom employs ὑπέρ in the causal sense and does so nowhere else in 1 Corinthians 15 (1 Cor 4:6 and 10:30 notwithstanding). But, without doubt, a reading of 15:29 with ὑπέρ in the causal sense is plausible and is unquestionably the *lectio difficilior*.

Nonetheless, that is not to say that ὑπέρ must be read in this way, but it is to say that such a reading cannot be brushed aside. At the moment, we have two possibilities for reading ὑπέρ: "for," in the sense of a substitution, and "on account of," in the sense of a reason. This is no surprise, for we saw them spring to the fore through our examination of the contemporary readings in Chapter I. Again, at the moment, there is no sound reason to opt for one possibility over the other. From this point forward, we use both "for" and "on account of," not only to distinguish the two possibilities for the translation of ὑπέρ, but so as not to beg the question between the two until it is definitively answered. Surely, as the title of this study indicates, we favor the "on account of," but we have a ways to go before our point is proven. In the meantime, we must look to the explicit context, i.e., the syntactical structures in which we find ὑπέρ.

The Syntax of 1 Corinthians 15:29

Having considered the principal terms βαπτίζω, νεκρός, and ὑπέρ, we are ready to examine closely the syntax of 15:29. Since 15:29 is comprised of two separate, though closely related, interrogative sentences, it seems best to treat each individually.

Ἐπεὶ τί ποιήσουσιν οἱ βαπτιζόμενοι ὑπὲρ τῶν νεκρῶν; (15:29a) is a simple interrogative sentence. The translation of οἱ βαπτιζόμενοι (pres., pass. or mid., part., nom., masc., pl.) and βαπτίζονται (3rd p., pl., pres., pass. or mid., ind.) poses no real problems when βαπτίζω is read literally. Βαπτιζόμενοι is a simple participle that is paired with an article. The participle, a verbal adjective,

---

[245] M. J. Harris, "Prepositions and Theology in the Greek New Testament," *NIDNTT* 3:1196–97. Cf. Fee, *First Corinthians*, 763–64, esp. 763 n. 11; and Reaume, "Another Look at 1 Corinthians 15:29," 473.

[246] The textual variant, υμων, makes no difference here; see N-A[27] *ad loc.*

is often used substantively with the article, and the use of the article therewith denotes a class or group. "The function of the article is to point out (it was in origin a demonstrative), to determine, to set apart from others, to identify *this* or *these* and not simply 'such.'"[247] Hence, οἱ βαπτιζόμενοι may be translated as "those (the ones) who are baptized," or "those (the ones) who have (get) themselves baptized."[248] In 15:29a, οἱ βαπτιζόμενοι modifies the subject of ποιήσουσιν (3rd p., pl., fut., act., ind.). Ποιέω ("to do," "to make") is a common Greek verb. Apart from 15:29, it appears over five hundred and sixty times in the NT and over fifty times in Paul's letters, twelve of which are in 1 Corinthians (6:15, 18; 7:36, 37, 38 [2x]; 9:23; 10:13, 31 [2x]; 11:24, 25). Ποιήσουσιν is readily translated as "they will do." Within 15:29a, we find ποιήσουσιν οἱ βαπτιζόμενοι immediately after the conjunction ἐπεί and the interrogative pronoun τί (nom., sing., neut.). Here ἐπεί is used in its causal sense ("because," "since," "for," "otherwise").[249] As we noticed in our examination of the structure of 1 Corinthians 15, the two syntactical questions of 15:29 inaugurate a shift in thought from that which precedes them in 1 Cor 15:20–28, and ἐπεί is indicative of a shift rather than a rupture. It is, perhaps, best translated as "otherwise." It is immediately followed by τί, which is best translated as "what." Thus, when we put it all together roughly, we get something like: "Otherwise, what will they do, the ones (those) who are (have or get themselves) baptized." A smoother, simpler, and clear rendering into English, with cognizance of the range of tense, voice, and mood, goes like this: "Otherwise, what are they to do, who have themselves baptized . . . ?"[250]

Bound to that question is the prepositional phrase ὑπὲρ τῶν νεκρῶν. For the moment, we leave aside the relation of ὑπέρ and νεκρός in terms of νεκρός' use with the article in 15:29a (νεκρῶν; gen., pl., masc.; as the object of ὑπέρ), and without the article in 15:29b (νεκροί; nom., pl., masc.; as the subject of ἐγείρονται). Now as we saw above, the adjective νεκρός is used in 15:29 as a substantive and means "a dead person," but its use is nuanced by the presence or absence of the determiner. Again, as we saw with reference to οἱ βαπτιζόμενοι, the article sets one thing or group apart from others.[251] Consequently, the first use of the term, ὑπὲρ τῶν νεκρῶν, is best rendered as "for (on account of) the dead persons (ones)." But the second use is anarthrous. "The omission of the article shows that the speaker regards the person or thing not so much as this or that person or thing, but rather as *such* a person or thing, i.e. regards not the individual but rather its nature or quality."[252] Accordingly, the second use of the

---

[247] Zerwick, *Biblical Greek* §165 (emphasis original); see also §166.
[248] See *GGNT*, 529.
[249] "ἐπεί," BAGD, 284
[250] "ποιέω," BAGD, 681.
[251] Zerwick, *Biblical Greek* §165.
[252] Ibid. §171 (emphasis original).

term νεκροί is best rendered with the collective noun as, "(the) dead." The distinction between the two uses of νεκρός is noteworthy.[253] On the one hand, we see that it is a distinction without a difference: the uses are hardly mutually exclusive because the dead persons of 15:29a are certainly a subspecies of the dead in 15:29b. On the other hand, we see that Paul has two groups in mind: the former, a specific group of dead persons, for or on account of whom some are baptized, and the latter, a generic group, whose resurrection in one way or another grounds motivation for baptism.

Such usage of νεκρός is borne out in the Pauline literature, especially in 1 Corinthians 15. Paul carefully distinguishes between the dead in general and the dead in particular by use of the article. The anarthrous use of νεκρός indicates the dead in general (Rom 1:4; 4:24; 6:4, 9, 11, 13; 7:4, 8:10, 11 [2*x*]; 10:7, 9; 11:15; 14:9; Gal 1:1; Eph 1:20; 2:1, 5; Phil 3:11; Col 2:12, 13; 2 Tim 2:8; 4:1), while the presence of the article seems to indicate a specific group (1 Thess 4:16).[254] Since 1 Corinthians 15 is Paul's most extensive argument on behalf of the resurrection of the dead, it comes as no surprise to find therein the highest concentration of the use of νεκρός in the Pauline literature. Throughout the chapter, the dead are demarcated by the presence or absence of the article: vv. 12 (2*x*), 13, 15, 16, 20, 21, and 32 employ νεκρός anarthrously; vv. 35, 42, and 52 employ νεκρός with the determiner.[255] This usage falls squarely into the principal divisions of the chapter. In vv. 12–28, Paul argues for the *that* (ὅτι) of the resurrection of the dead, an apologetic and logical argument, wherein the resurrection of Christ is assumed to be true; the question is whether or not that same resurrection is operative for others.[256] 1 Cor 15:1–11 spell out that truth definitively. On the basis of the fact of Christ's resurrection, Paul builds a case for the resurrection of others that concludes with the understanding that the resurrection of the dead is the fulfillment of the kingdom of God. In vv. 12, 13, 16, 20, and 21 a general νεκρός is used to advance the argument. In vv. 35–49, as Paul moves from the *that* into the *how* (πῶς), he proceeds from logical argument to explanation of the now established fact: that the dead will be raised. The

---

[253] Indeed, the same argument could be made even if the article were not used in the prepositional phrase ὑπὲρ τῶν νεκρῶν, because there are "three cases in which the absence of the article with a concrete and determinate substantive cannot be insisted upon: proper names, prepositional phrases, and nouns with a following genitive (i.e. where the influence of the Semitic construct state is possible" (Zerwick, *Biblical Greek* §183). The explicit presence of the article only strengthens our point. Cf. Porter, *Idioms of the Greek New Testament*, 106–14.

[254] The use of νεκρός with the article in the various contexts of Rom 4:17; 2 Cor 1:9; and Col 1:18 makes it difficult to determine whether or not a specific group is indicated. Likewise, the unidentified quotation in Eph 5:14 (based on an early Christian hymn and/or Isa 60:1?) and the textual difficulties of 1 Thess 1:10 (see N-A[27] and GNT[4] *ad loc.*) militate against any conclusions therefrom.

[255] Jeremias, "Flesh and Blood," 155–56.

[256] J.-N. Aletti, "La *dispositio* rhétorique dans les épîtres pauliniennes: Propositions de méthode," *NTS* 38 (1992) 396.

νεκροί in vv. 35 and 42 refer to "the dead ones," the specific dead, the ones in whose resurrection there is a lack of faith among some of the Corinthians. So too, in v. 52, following up on the *how*, it is evident that Paul is speaking of a specific group.

Thus in 15:29a, we find νεκρός with the article in reference to a specific group; and in 15:29b, we find νεκρός without the article and thereby intending a general reference. This parallels the usage in 15:32, wherein Paul himself is the specific referent, and the anarthrous νεκροί is the general referent. In other words, "in 1 C[or] 15:15, 16, 29, 32 the article has to be omitted because the concept, not the collective dead, is under discussion (otherwise [v.] 52)."[257] Now without hesitation, we can translate 15:29a as follows: "Otherwise, what are they to do (or doing), who have themselves baptized for (or on account of) the dead?" And we do so with an accurate understanding of dead vis-à-vis ὑπὲρ τῶν νεκρῶν, νεκρός with the definite article. The dead in this short prepositional phrase are a specific group of dead persons, not a generic reference to the collective dead as found with the anarthrous use of νεκρός in 15:29b. For the moment, we leave aside the question of who precisely these dead are, until we look closely at 15:29b, and compare and contrast the dead of 15:29.

Like 15:29a, εἰ ὅλως νεκροὶ οὐκ ἐγείρονται, τί καὶ βαπτίζονται ὑπὲρ αὐτῶν; (15:29b) is an interrogative sentence, but it is also a first class conditional sentence. Occurring over three hundred times in the NT, the simple condition is by no means an anomalous mode of expression,[258] especially for Paul in 1 Corinthians 15 (e.g., vv. 12, 13, 14, 16, 17, 19, 32 [2x], 44).[259] The simple condition is grammatically uncomplicated: εἰ plus indicative (protasis), indicative (apodosis).[260] In 15:29b, we find that exactly. The protasis is introduced by the conditional particle εἰ, which is best rendered as "if," followed by an indicative; then the apodosis follows, also with the indicative: εἰ ... ἐγείρονται (3rd p., pl., pres., pass. or mid., ind. of ἐγείρω), ... βαπτίζονται (3rd p., pl., pres., pass. or mid., ind. of βαπτίζω) .... The simple conditional is often used "in cases where the fulfillment or non-fulfillment of the condition is in fact known or supposed; but this circumstance is to be gathered from the context; the grammatical form is indifferent to it, and means simply what it says, namely 'if ..., then ....'"[261] The construction does not affirm or deny the truth or the reality of the condition described *per se*, i.e., it leaves something to the mind of the reader: "if you hold to the protasis, then you must hold to the apodosis." It is a logical connection rather than a proof statement, i.e., it does not mean: "since

---

[257] BDF §254 (2)
[258] Porter, *Idioms of the Greek New Testament*, 256. For statistical analyses, see J. L. Boyer, "First Class Conditions: What Do They Mean?" *GTJ* 2 (1981) 75–114.
[259] Cf. 1 Cor 15:2; on this, see Porter, *Idioms of the Greek New Testament*, 259.
[260] For more, see "εἰ," BAGD, 219–20; and BDF §372.
[261] Zerwick, *Biblical Greek* §304. See Porter, *Idioms of the Greek New Testament*, 254–56.

the protasis is true, then the apodosis must be true." It is incorrect to translate a simple condition as "since . . ., then . . . ."²⁶² In other words, it simply means that the apodosis follows on the condition of the protasis; it does not mean that the protasis *proves* the apodosis;²⁶³ "εἰ even in a 'real' condition, still means 'if' and not because or the like."²⁶⁴ James L. Boyer sums it up well:

> In summary, what does the first class conditional sentence in NT Greek mean? It means precisely the same as the simple condition in English, "If this . . . then that . . . ." It implies absolutely nothing as to the "relation to reality." It is saying that the result (the apodosis) is as sure as the condition (the protasis). It is a forceful device of language which leaves the judgment and convictions of the hearer with regard to the truthfulness of the supposition to prove or disprove and to enforce the truth of the conclusion.²⁶⁵

In our reading of 15:29, this insight is critical. Without it, we are likely to suppose that Paul is arguing about fact rather than faith. That is, here in 15:29b, Paul is using *belief* in the resurrection of the dead as the protasis, not the reality of the resurrection, not the fact of the resurrection, but the actuality of faith therein. The fact of the resurrection of the dead is not in question; what is in question is the Corinthians' faith therein.

With the theme of resurrection in mind, the use of ἐγείρω in the protasis makes perfect sense. Ἐγείρω, in non-biblical Greek means simply "to awaken."²⁶⁶ Since "the euphemistic description of death as sleep is common among the Greeks,"²⁶⁷ ἐγείρω comes into the NT with the same general meaning, "to wake," "to rouse," including the connotation to wake or be roused from death.²⁶⁸ It is the verb most frequently used by Paul to describe the resurrection.²⁶⁹ He uses it thirty-seven times in his letters; twenty of those uses are in 1 Corinthians, and nineteen of those twenty are in chapter 15 (1 Cor 6:14; 15:4, 12, 13, 14, 15 [3x], 16 [2x], 17, 20, 29, 32, 35, 42, 43 [2x], 44, 52).²⁷⁰ Insofar as 1 Corinthians 15 is Paul's premiere exposition on the resurrection, there is little

---

²⁶² L. W. Ledgerwood III, "What Does the Greek First Class Conditional Imply? Gricean Methodology and the Testimony of the Ancient Greek Grammarians," *GTJ* 12 (1991) 118.

²⁶³ Ibid., 99–118. Porter (*Idioms of the Greek New Testament*, 256–57) is careful to make distinctions. He shows some instances where "since" makes more sense in English (e.g., Mark 4:23 and John 11:12), but he points out how "since" can hardly be used in passages such as Matt 12:27; 26:39, 42; John 10:37; and, so significant for our study, 1 Cor 15:13–14.

²⁶⁴ Zerwick, *Biblical Greek* §308.

²⁶⁵ Boyer, "First Class Conditions," 82.

²⁶⁶ A. Oepke, "ἐγείρω, ἔγερσις, ἐξεγείρω, γρηγορέω, (ἀγρυπνέω)," *TDNT* 2:333.

²⁶⁷ Ibid., 334.

²⁶⁸ See "ἐγείρω," BAGD, 214–15.

²⁶⁹ Thus, Robertson and Plummer (*I Corinthians*, 359) reject any suggestion by the Greek expositors and Evans (and we may presume, Thompson following Evans) that an ellipsis of τῆς ἀναστάσεως would be necessary were Paul speaking about the resurrection.

²⁷⁰ See also Rom 4:24, 25; 6:4, 9; 7:4; 8:11 (2x), 34; 10:9; 13:11; 2 Cor 1:9; 4:14 (2x); 5:15; Gal 1:1; Phil 1:7; and 1 Thess 1:10. Cf. Eph 1:20; 5:14; Col 2:12; and 2 Tim 2:8.

surprise in finding it so often therein. Moreover, in chapter 15 we find a number of instances in which Paul uses ἐγείρω in first class conditional sentences, viz., vv. 12, 13, 14, 16a, 16b, and 17. Likewise, in each of these verses, Paul also uses νεκρός (except in v. 14, where it is easily inferred from the context). Here, with the reiteration of the ἐγείρω/νεκρός combination, the reader is brought back and connected to that key question of 1 Cor 15:12: "Now if Christ is preached as raised from the dead, how can some of you say that there is no resurrection of the dead?"

Besides εἰ and ἐγείρω, the protasis contains two other words that we have already examined closely, viz., ὅλως and νεκρός, as well as the negative particle οὐ, which is paired with the indicative.[271] Previously, we saw that the adverb ὅλως modifies ἐγείρω. Along with εἰ, this reads: "if they are truly raised." But this is negated by οὐ. The use of οὐ in 15:29b intensifies the assumption that the protasis ought to be taken for granted, for the "negative in clauses where the reality of the condition is taken for granted is οὐ."[272] It would seem that Paul wishes to render the condition as plainly as possible in the context. After all he has said earlier in chapter 15, the sharpness of the protasis is evident in this construction.[273] "If the dead are not really raised" is the antithesis of what the Corinthians should believe, the denial of what Paul has preached to them and is currently explaining in chapter 15. No doubt, Paul expects his readers to see in the antithetical nature of this statement, especially if they have been following his argument from the very beginning of the chapter, a striking affirmation of the resurrection of the dead.

The apodosis—τί καὶ βαπτίζονται ὑπὲρ αὐτῶν—follows neatly, not only to complement the protasis, but to link 15:29b back to 15:29a, wherein we also find τί and βαπτίζονται. In looking at the structure of 15:29, we have already seen that the τί ποιήσουσιν οἱ βαπτιζόμενοι of 15:29a parallels the apodosis of 15:29b: τί καὶ βαπτίζονται. In the former, τί functions strictly as an interrogative pronoun, "what"; in the latter case, τί (acc., sing., neut.) functions adverbially, as it frequently does, to mean "why."[274] Here, it is joined with the conjunction καί. The use of καί, coordinating two ideas where one is dependent on the other, lends a "further determination" to the meaning,[275] especially since καί is also used here to introduce a question.[276] Such an ordering suggests a translation of "why at all" or "why still."[277] "Why at all (why still) are they baptized" (βαπτίζονται; 3rd p., pl., pres., pass. or mid., ind. of βαπτίζω) can

---

[271] See "οὐ," BAGD, 590–91.
[272] "εἰ," BAGD, 219.
[273] See Zerwick, *Biblical Greek* §§311, 326.
[274] "τίς, τί," BAGD, 819.
[275] Zerwick, *Biblical Greek* §460.
[276] Ibid. §459.
[277] BDF §442 (14); and *GGNT*, 529.

only refer back to the οἱ βαπτίζομενοι of 15:29a. The final part of 15:29b is ὑπὲρ αὐτῶν, the prepositional phrase that completes the verse and brings us back to the ὑπὲρ τῶν νεκρῶν of 15:29a. As we have indicated, the only textual difficulty in 15:29 lies with αὐτῶν. Significantly, the fact that codex 69 substitutes των νεκρων only serves to indicate that those spoken of as the object of the ὑπέρ in 15:29a are the same ones spoken of in the ὑπέρ of 15:29b. There is no doubt that Paul is speaking about the same group, the dead.

Now all the pieces are in place, and we can render a translation: "Otherwise, what are they to do/doing, who have themselves baptized/are baptized for/or on account of the dead? If the dead are not really raised, why are they baptized for/or on account of them (the dead)?"

THE LITERARY CONTEXT OF 1 CORINTHIANS 15:29

Rendering a translation tells us what 15:29 says, but our task in this study involves more—we want to know what 15:29 means. At this point, it behooves us to summarize what we have learned from the literary context of 15:29 and to see to what extent that literary context is revelatory vis-à-vis the meaning of 15:29. The easiest way to do so is to ask three simple questions. First, what does the genre and the integrity of the letter have to say to us about 1 Corinthians 15? Second, how does 15:29 fit within the structure of chapter 15? Finally, how may we read 15:29 in light of its morphology and syntax? With these questions answered, we are poised to present a new reading.

First, the genre and integrity of 1 Corinthians tell us that chapter 15 is an integral part of 1 Corinthians. In our determination of 1 Corinthians as a letter-essay, along with the knowledge that there is no evidence of textual corruption, we see that chapter 15 addresses but one of a series of difficulties that Paul is aware of among the Corinthians. Paul mentions a number of problems in 1 Corinthians: factionalism (chapter 1), immorality (chapter 5), litigation (chapter 6), marriage (chapter 7), idol food (chapters 8–10), worship (chapter 11), spiritual gifts (chapters 12–14), and finally faith in the resurrection (chapter 15). Evidently, the section concerning faith in the resurrection is neither the conclusion nor the summation of a longer argument because there is no sustained argument throughout the whole of 1 Corinthians. 1 Corinthians is a lengthy, seriatim response of Paul to a number of problems that Paul perceived among the Corinthians. As de Boer has shown, the difficulties are not necessarily mutually exclusive, but they are hardly interdependent. 1 Corinthians 15 is an integral and direct response to one problem: faith in the resurrection of the dead. As 1 Cor 15:12–14 spells out, some among the Corinthians denied the resurrection of the dead. Apparently, they did not deny the resurrection of Christ. Paul presumes that they still believe what he preached and handed down to them, viz., that Christ was raised (1 Cor 15:1–11). That is not the problem. The problem is that some among the Corinthians seem to deny that others will be raised, and so in 1 Cor 15:12–14 Paul uses the resurrection of the Lord as the substantiation for the resurrection of Christ's faithful. Except for a passing remark in 6:14, the resurrection is mentioned nowhere else in 1 Corinthians. Integral though we know it to be to the letter as a whole, chapter 15 is easily read autonomously. Thus, the genre of the letter-essay allows for our looking to it as an independent subunit. And, even if we hold the issue of the letter's integrity in abeyance, no one questions the fact that chapter 15 is Paul's and the fact that he argues logically and systematically on behalf of faith in the resurrection of the dead.

Second, chapter 15 can be taken as a sustained argument in a concentric pentacolon: A, vv: 1–11; B, vv. 12–28, C, vv. 29–34; B' vv. 35–49; A', vv. 50–58. The penchant in the legion of commentaries to relegate 15:29–34 to an aside—and therefore to abrogate its importance—seems to be based on the unwillingness of commentators to deal with 15:29. No commentator questions the intimate relationship between the *that* (vv. 12–28) and the *how* of the resurrection (vv. 35–58). How can vv. 29–34 be extrapolated from that relationship? Moreover, since both the *that* and the *how* begin with rhetorical questions, how can one disunite them from the only other rhetorical questions in chapter 15, viz., vv. 29, 30, and 32 (v. 55 excepted)? Quite simply, to excise vv. 29–34 does violence to the argument of chapter 15 as Paul presents it. All those who denigrate the significance of vv. 29–34 do so with an eye on 15:29, not because of anything found in the literary context as such. To this we may add that there is no reason to suppose that the Corinthians did not clearly understand Paul's references in 1 Cor 15:29–34. One thing is evident in chapter 15: Paul very carefully presents an argument on behalf of the resurrection of the dead with the obvious aim of correcting the infidelity of some members of the Corinthian community. Whatever 15:29 is about, it affirms the resurrection in some way. The Corinthians must have known what Paul was talking about and understood his reference. If there were any doubt about this in Paul's mind, he probably would not have used the example. Most likely, Paul approved of this practice. The vast majority of commentators agree that 15:29 is an affirmation of the resurrection of the dead. It seems foolhardy to presume that Paul would use, in such an important place and on such an important point, an example of a practice that he disapproved. Furthermore, we do not think he would juxtapose the example of his own apostolic labors with it. The claims of Foschini or Murphy-O'Connor that Paul became a bit confused or lost himself in the heat of passion while writing about such an important topic as the resurrection are highly speculative. Of course, such claims are as difficult to prove as they are to disprove. We must assume that Paul chose the words he chose for a reason and that 15:29 is as much a part of his argument as 1 Cor 15:12 and 35, even if we have more difficulty with the former than the latter.

Third, the morphology and syntax of 15:29 *alone* do not lend themselves to a univocal reading of the verse. Were that the case, we would end our study here. A cautious examination of the verse, without jumping to any conclusions, narrows the possibilities but does not determine the meaning. Our scrutiny of the morphology and syntax has solved some but not all questions. Despite the suggestions of Murphy-O'Connor and O'Neill that νεκρός and βαπτίζω may be read figuratively or metaphorically, we have shown that they must be read literally. We have already seen that Paul uses νεκρός with the article to denote deceased Christians and that chapter 15 has the highest concentration of the use of νεκρός in the Pauline literature. So too, in every other instance of its use in 1 Corinthians, βαπτίζω refers to baptism. Consequently, there is no apparent reason to suppose that its use in 15:29 is any different. It is fair to say that were the verse not so difficult, few would have postulated any other reading of βαπτίζω within it. And the use of βαπτίζω with the definite article (οἱ βαπτιζόμενοι) indicates that Paul is referring to a particular group within the larger Corinthian Christian community. Although Robertson and Plummer claim that this use of the article "seems to imply a class of people who practiced something exceptional,"[278] they do so only because of the problematic nature of 15:29. The use of the article denotes a particular group, not necessarily a peculiar group.[279] The οἱ simply indicates that the οἱ βαπτιζόμενοι may be distinguished from the larger group of Corinthians whom Paul addresses; whether or not they are "exceptional" is another matter. But the article's use does heighten Paul's literary identification of three relevant and related groups—the I-thou-they—in the first person, Paul; in the second person, the general audience, who deny the resurrection; and in the third person, the οἱ βατιζόμενοι, who affirm the resurrection of the dead by their acceptance of baptism. The switch to the third person in 15:29, to the first person in 15:30–32, and then to the second person in 15:33–34 poses a dynamic tension. The βαπτιζόμενοι, coterminous with Paul himself, have it right—they, too, are affirming the resurrection; their behavior is laudable. So, who are these βαπτιζόμενοι of 15:29? What sort of baptism are they undergoing?

In the end, it is ὑπέρ which haunts us still. The literary context does not elucidate how ὑπέρ ought to be taken. If ὑπέρ is taken in its most common sense, as substitution, then 15:29 reads that some are baptized *for* the dead, i.e., people are baptized in place of dead persons. This is vicarious baptism, a position held by the vast majority of exegetes. History militates against such a reading, but how then does one argue with the contention that vicarious baptism is an historical anomaly? If ὑπέρ is taken in its final sense, a rarer sense, then 15:29 reads that some are baptized *for* the dead, i.e., people are baptized so that they be united to the dead in the next life. This is ordinary baptism, vis-à-vis Raeder and Jeremias, but the motive is suspect. How does one argue with the contention that some people could believe so strongly in the efficacy of baptism

---

[278] Robertson and Plummer, *I Corinthians*, 329.
[279] Barrett, *First Corinthians*, 362.

without believing in Christ? If ὑπέρ is taken it its causal sense, the rarest of senses, then 15:29 reads that some are baptized *on account of* the dead, i.e., living people are baptized because of a motivation related to the dead. This, too, is ordinary baptism. Reaume claims that some accept baptism because of the influence of dead Christians. But why "dead"? What influence do they have when dead? White also reads ὑπέρ in its causal sense, but his reading falls apart because he reads νεκρός metaphorically. And both Reaume and White deny any efficacy to baptism. So, what about dead Christians motivates people to accept baptism?

There is another way to read 15:29. If we read ὑπέρ in its causal sense, just as Reaume and White do, but look more closely at the literary context, a different reading emerges.

Recall that vv. 29–34 are in the middle of Paul's explanation of the *that* and the *how* of the resurrection and that 15:29 affirms the resurrection. With the acceptance of baptism, one expresses faith in the resurrection. Baptism and resurrection are inextricably linked *by Paul*. Now, the οἱ βαπτιζόμενοι are baptized *on account of* dead Christians. What is their (the βαπτιζόμενοι's) motivation to accept baptism *on account of* dead Christians? We submit that the motivation is faith in the resurrection of the dead: they are baptized because the dead are raised. We submit that some individuals were undergoing the rite of baptism *on account of* their faith in the resurrection of Christ and, therewith, the resurrection of those who had died in Christ. By their acceptance of baptism, they showed their belief that the dead would be raised just as Christ had been raised. Paul finds their reception of baptism commendable and praiseworthy insofar as he compares their action to his own actions (1 Cor 15:30–32) and pits their action against the incredulity of those who deny the resurrection (1 Cor 15:30–34). Between the rhetorical questions that are the start of his expositions concerning the *that* and the *how* of the resurrection, Paul places two additional interrelated rhetorical questions: "Otherwise, (i.e., if there is no resurrection) what are they doing who are baptized on account of the dead? If the dead are not raised, then why are they baptized on account of them?" In other words, Paul lauds baptism as an articulation of faith in the resurrection of the dead. And though this novel reading of 15:29 sees baptism as efficacious, the efficacy of baptism is not evident *per se* in the verse. If taken as a sacrament, the rite of baptism is the means to the resurrection. If taken as a sign and seal of a previous conversion of heart, the rite of baptism is the expression of faith in the resurrection. For the moment, we put aside the exact nature of baptism, so as to focus on the literal reading of the verse. And in fact, the verse can be read as we maintain it ought to be read: as an affirmation on Paul's part of a particular group of individuals who were baptized on account of (faith in the resurrection of) the dead.

But, once again, we remember that there are two ways to read 15:29: as a reference to vicarious or ordinary baptism, all interpretations thereof notwithstanding. We cannot say, solely from the literary context, what 15:29 means. On the one hand, 15:29 could read as a reference to vicarious baptism. On the other hand, 15:29 could read as a reference to ordinary baptism. Yet, we do know that 15:29 must mean one or the other. It cannot mean both. Therefore, we must turn to the historical context of 1 Corinthians—to Paul, Corinth, and Corinthian Christianity. In Chapter III of our study, we look to all three in order to discover more about 15:29 and, most especially, to see if our reading can be supported.

III. Reading 1 Corinthians 15:29 in Historical Context

The importance of the historical context within which we find 15:29 cannot be overemphasized. In Chapter I of our study, after noting the lack of scholarly consensus regarding the reading of 15:29, we concluded that a thorough examination of the verse's literary and historical contexts was in order. In Chapter II of our study, we concluded that an examination of the literary context alone was insufficient to yield a definitive reading of the verse. Because 15:29, when we consider its morphology, syntax, and literary context, may be read either as a reference to ordinary baptism or vicarious baptism, the importance of its historical context is promptly seen as the *sine qua non* for the interpretation of the verse. If we were to read 15:29 as an instance of ordinary baptism, parallels for comparison in Pauline literature and the NT would be readily forthcoming. But if we were to read 15:29 as an instance of vicarious baptism, we have no parallel for comparison in the NT, the early Church, or the first century. On the one hand, this presents no problem, for as we have seen, those who hold for a reading of vicarious baptism among the Corinthians also hold that it was an anomaly. Anomalies by definition are unique and have no parallels. On the other hand, there is a problem in that anomalies do not occur in vacuums. Thus, proponents of vicarious baptism offer a plethora of explanations for its occurrence. They acknowledge that an instance of vicarious baptism among the Corinthian Christians must have its roots somewhere: either in Paul, who brought Christianity to Corinth; in Corinth itself, the historical milieu within which Paul preached; or in a combination of the two, Corinthian Christianity. Thus, it is necessary for us to look at all three. First, we look to Paul, the apostle who brought the gospel to Corinth. Jew, Greek, and Roman, Paul arrived in Corinth with his own cultural conditioning and history. Second, we look to Greco-Roman Corinth, the ancient city with a rich historical background. Corinth was by all accounts a multicultural society wherein a plethora of ancient philosophies and religions flourished. Finally, we look to Corinthian Christianity through the prism of 1 Corinthians. Paul perceived a number of crises of faith among the Corinthians. While the crisis concerning the resurrection of the dead was certainly the most important in Paul's mind (if we are to judge from the attention he devoted to it in 1 Corinthians), there were other problems in the Corinthians' understanding and practice of the faith that Paul preached to them.

In all of this, we are looking for a needle in a haystack—something indicative of vicarious baptism—which is not to say that the needle does not exist, but it is to say that if it exists at all, we should be able to find its traces somewhere.

ST. PAUL THE APOSTLE

Paul defines himself as a Jew (Rom 11:1; 2 Cor 11:22; Gal 1:13–14; 2:15), indeed, a Pharisee (Phil 3:5). But Paul identifies himself as an apostle of Christ Jesus (Rom 1:1, 5; 11:13; 1 Cor 1:1; 4:9; 9:1–5; 15:9; 2 Cor 1:1; 11:5; Gal 1:1, 17; 1 Thess 2:6; cf. 2 Cor 11:13; 12:11–13; Eph 1:1; Col 1:1; 1 Tim 1:1; 2:7; Titus 1:1) and is, no doubt, thought of as such by Luke in Acts, especially in chapters 13–28 (particularly in 13:2–4; 14:4; 15:22–29). Almost everything we know about Paul stems from his letters and Luke's portrayal of Paul in Acts. Of these two principal sources for our knowledge of Paul, the primary is his own letters; the secondary is Acts. Unfortunately, much like the infancy accounts in Matthew and Luke, we all too frequently conflate the data of Paul's letters and Luke's Acts without sufficient reflection and deliberation. Methodologically, it is wiser to keep Paul and Luke separate and distinct. This is markedly so when we consider the momentous weight of Paul's influence on early and contemporary Christianity. Thus, the oft-cited tenet of John Knox in *Chapters in a Life of Paul* is accepted by almost every Pauline scholar today:

> The distinction between primary and secondary sources in this case is of such importance that we can justly say that a fact only suggested in the letters has a status which even the most unequivocal statement of Acts, if not otherwise supported, cannot confer. We may, with proper caution, use Acts to supplement the autobiographical data of the letters, but never to correct them.[1]

In other words, to know Paul we must turn to him first, and thereafter to his eminent biographer, Luke. Even as the vast majority of scholars hold to Paul's letters as the foremost authority on Paul, theories abound as to the person and theology of Paul. To sift through the innumerable studies, even to catalogue them, is an implausible task at this point in time.[2] They run the gamut from those who see Paul as a pious Jew to those who see him as an impious Gentile, from those who accept him as a devoted disciple of Jesus to those who espy in him a religious renegade. What sort of Jew was Paul? What sort of Christian?

To be sure, the dominant portrait in biblical scholarship had been that of Paul's Christianity as a radical departure from a rigid, albeit corrupt, Judaism, the so-called "Reformation Paul." Ferdinand Christian Baur and the Tübingen School posit an abyss between the "binding law" (Judaism) and the "freeing

---

[1] Knox, *Chapters in a Life of Paul*, 19.

[2] J. Ashton, *The Religion of Paul the Apostle* (New Haven and London: Yale University Press, 2000) 3–4 et passim.

gospel" (Christianity) vis-à-vis Martin Luther's dichotomy between the two.[3] Using 1 Cor 1:11–12 as a point of departure, Baur held for a great divide in the early Church between Peter (Jewish, nationalistic, and conditioned by the law) and Paul (Hellenistic, universal, and free of the law).[4] With the onslaught of the *Religionsgeschichtliche*, however, adherence to Baur's paradigm risked finding some form of Greco-Roman paganism or gnosticism as the basis of Paul's Christianity rather than Jesus.[5] Not surprisingly, Baur's view was challenged by Albert Schweitzer, who insisted upon a thoroughly Jewish, though apocalyptic, Paul,[6] and Schweitzer's thinking was revived in a sense by Rudolf Bultmann, who held that Paul abandoned a Jewish mode of thought and expression in favor of a Hellenistic one.[7] This somewhat derogatory view of first-century Judaism began to change a bit with William David Davies,[8] who sought to trace the origin of the lion's share of Paul's thinking to rabbinic Judaism, but things changed significantly with E. P. Sanders.[9]

The "Sanders revolution" was to start with an examination of Palestinian Judaism, and then move on to Paul, instead of starting with Paul as a principal source for Palestinian Judaism.[10] Sanders' extensive investigation reveals that intertestamental Judaism stressed the covenant rather than the law, that "covenantal nomism" was normative, not rigid legalism.[11] In other words, there was nothing "wrong" with Palestinian Judaism; Paul did not consider it flawed *per*

---

[3] For more, see H. Harris, *The Tübingen School: A Historical and Theological Investigation of F. C. Baur* (Grand Rapids, MI: Baker, 1990).

[4] F. C. Baur, "Die Christuspartei in der korinthischen Gemeinde, der Gegensatz des petrinischen und paulinischen Christenthums in der alten Kirche, der Apostel Petrus in Rom," *TZT* 4 (1831) 61–206. Baur's views are further expounded in *Paul, the Apostle of Jesus Christ: His Life and Work, His Epistles and His Doctrine* (ed. and rev. E. Zeller; trans. A. Menzies; 2 vols.; London: Williams and Norgate, 1875–76).

[5] See, e.g., S. J. Hafemann, "Paul and His Interpreters," in *Dictionary of Paul and His Letters* (ed. G. F. Hawthorne; R. P. Martin, and D. G. Reid; Downers Grove, IL and Leicester, Eng.: InterVarsity, 1993) 669. The thesis that Christianity is an extension of paganism continues in contemporary thinking, e.g., see T. Freke and P. Gandy, *The Jesus Mysteries: Was the "Original Jesus" a Pagan God?* (New York: Harmony, 1999).

[6] A. Schweitzer, *Paul and His Interpreters: A Critical Essay* (trans. W. Montgomery; London: A&C Black, 1912).

[7] Bultmann, "The Theology of Paul" (part II), in *Theology of the New Testament*, 1:185–352.

[8] W. D. Davies, *Paul and Rabbinic Judaism: Some Rabbinic Elements in Paul's Theology* (London: SPCK, 1948).

[9] E. P. Sanders, *Paul and Palestinian Judaism: A Comparison of Patterns of Religion* (London: SCM, 1977). The roots of Sanders' argument are found in his "Patterns of Religion in Paul and Rabbinic Judaism: A Holistic Method of Comparison." *HTR* 66 (1973) 455–78. See also idem, *Paul, the Law, and the Jewish People* (Minneapolis: Fortress, 1983); and idem, *Paul* (Oxford: Oxford University Press, 1991).

[10] Thus, E. P. Sanders writes *Paul and Palestinian Judaism* in two parts: first, "Palestinian Judaism," and second, "Paul."

[11] See "Palestinian Judaism 200 BCE–200 CE" (chap. 4), in ibid., 419–28 et passim.

se. Sanders agrees that Paul was dissatisfied with Judaism, but dissatisfied because his own religious understanding had changed with his conversion to Christianity, not because he discovered something wrong within the Judaism he had professed earlier. Sanders says it simply: "In short, *this is what Paul finds wrong with Judaism: it is not Christianity.*"[12] In our study, we follow Sanders' insight and disavow the claim that Paul thought himself to be, or in fact was, an apostate of Judaism because he was an apostle of Christianity. As James D. G. Dunn points out:

> For an apostleship which was indeed a betrayal of Paul's native religion cannot help us appreciate a Christianity which counts the Jewish scriptures as three-quarters of its own canon. Above all, if we rest content with the description of Paul as apostate and apostle, as apostate because apostle, then we condemn Paul to failure and the Christianity of Paul to self-contradiction. For Paul saw his own apostolic work not as a disowning of his heritage, but precisely as its fulfillment—apostle *to the Gentiles*, as apostle *of Israel*.[13]

Insofar as one claims Paul to be a Jew, one stakes a claim as to his religious identity or, at the very least, as to his religious identity as he understood it. It is an understatement to say that he was a radical Jew, as Jewish scholars sometimes describe him;[14] Paul is more than that: he is a Jew, who believes that his Jewishness necessitates his Christianity.

Inextricably linked to the debate about Paul's Judaism is the debate about his Christianity. Recently, a few scholars, picking up on William Wrede's claim that Paul is, when compared to Jesus, "essentially a new phenomenon" and the "second founder of Christianity,"[15] and on Bultmann's claim that "Paul's theology proper, with its theological, anthropological, and soteriological ideas, is not at all a recapitulation of Jesus' own preaching nor a further development of it . . . ,"[16] have sought to drive a wedge between Jesus and Paul. Although only a handful of scholars would accept such statements at face value,[17] the writings of the Jewish scholar Hyam Maccoby,[18] who claims that Paul was not a Jew at all and that he founded his own religion in opposition to Judaism,[19] and those of the

---

[12] Ibid., 552 (emphasis original).

[13] J. D. G. Dunn, "Paul: Apostate or Apostle of Israel?" *ZNW* 89 (1998) 258.

[14] For example, and by far the most interesting, see D. Boyarin, *A Radical Jew: Paul and the Politics of Identity* (CSJLCS 1; Berkeley: University of California Press, 1994).

[15] W. Wrede, *Paul* (trans. E. Lummis; London: Green, 1907) 165, 179–80.

[16] Bultmann, *Theology of the New Testament*, 1:189. See also the first part of Bultmann's *Theology*, wherein he asserts an essential difference between the kerygma of the "earliest Church" and the "Hellenistic Church." Note also that, for Bultmann, "the historical presupposition for Paul's theology is not the kerygma of the oldest Church but that of the Hellenistic Church; it was the latter that mediated the former to Paul" (63).

[17] Cf. Dunn, "Paul: Apostate or Apostle of Israel?" 257–58.

[18] H. Maccoby, *The Mythmaker: Paul and the Invention of Christianity* (New York: Harper and Row, 1986); and idem, *Paul and Hellenism* (London: SCM, 1991).

[19] Maccoby, *Mythmaker*, 183, 113 et passim.

once Christian, now unbelieving, popular biographer A. N. Wilson, who follows a good deal, but not all, of Maccoby's thought,[20] animate discussion about Paul's Christianity.[21] Did Paul found his own religion? That is, is the Christianity Paul preached substantially different from the Christianity of Jesus? David Wenham responds with a resounding "no";[22] John Ashton responds with a resounding "yes."[23] Astoundingly, the question has come back full circle with the recent proposal of Donald Harman Akenson that the key to understanding Jesus is Paul![24] The truth, of course, lies somewhere in the middle. N. T. Wright's point is well taken:

> Jesus believed it was his vocation to bring Israel's history to its climax. Paul believed that Jesus had succeeded in that aim. Paul believed, in consequence of that belief and as part of his own special vocation, that he was himself now called to announce to the whole world that Israel's history had been brought to its climax in that way. *When Paul announced "the gospel" to the Gentile world, therefore, he was deliberately and consciously implementing the achievement of Jesus.* He was, as he himself said, building on the foundation, not laying another one (1 Corinthians 3:11).[25]

Whether or not Paul was entirely successful in his vocation is another matter.

Here, we attempt neither to systematize Paul's theology,[26] nor do we intend to sketch Paul's biography.[27] Instead, we look to Paul for anything that might

---

[20] A. N. Wilson, *Paul: The Mind of the Apostle* (New York and London: Norton, 1997).

[21] For examples, see D. Wenham, *Paul: Follower of Jesus or Founder of Christianity?* (Grand Rapids, MI: Eerdmans, 1995) 2–3.

[22] Ibid., 410 et passim. N. T. Wright (*What Saint Paul Really Said: Was Paul of Tarsus the Real Founder of Christianity?* [Grand Rapids, MI: Eerdmans, 1997] 182) finds himself in complete agreement with Wenham.

[23] Ashton, *Religion of Paul the Apostle*, 3 et passim. Curiously, Maccoby is not mentioned in Ashton's book.

[24] D. H. Akenson, *Saint Saul: A Skeleton Key to the Historical Jesus* (Oxford: Oxford University Press, 2000).

[25] Wright, *What Saint Paul Really Said*, 181 (emphasis original).

[26] Needless to say, the books and articles on Paul's theology are legion. See, e.g., Ridderbos, *Paul*; J. C. Beker, *Paul the Apostle: The Triumph of God in Life and Thought* (Philadelphia: Fortress, 1980); J. A. Fitzmyer, *Paul and His Theology* (2nd ed.; Englewood Cliff, NJ: Prentice Hall, 1989); idem, *According to Paul: Studies in the Theology of the Apostle* (New York/Mahwah, NJ: Paulist, 1993); and J. Becker, *Paul: Apostle to the Gentiles* (trans. O. C. Dean, Jr.; Louisville: Westminster John Knox, 1993). Two recent books are especially notable: J. Louis Martyn, *Theological Issues in the Letters of Paul* (SNTW; Edinburgh: T&T Clark, 1997); and Dunn, *Theology of Paul*.

[27] As with Paul's theology, Paul's biographers are numerous. See R. Jewett, *A Chronology of Paul's Life* (Philadelphia: Fortress, 1979); Murphy-O'Connor, *Paul: A Critical Life*; R. Riesner, *Paul's Early Period: Chronology, Mission Strategy, Theology* (trans. D. Scott; Grand Rapids, MI: Eerdmans, 1998); C. J. Roetzel. *Paul: The Man and the Myth* (SPNT; Columbia, SC: University of South Carolina Press, 1998). For insight as to Paul's thinking, see G. Theissen, *Psychological Aspects of Pauline Theology* (trans. J. P. Galvin; Edinburgh: T&T Clark, 1987); J. H. Neyrey, *Paul, in Other Words: A Cultural Reading of His Letters* (Louisville: Westminster John Knox, 1990); B. J.

disclose something akin to vicarious baptism. In order to do so, it seems best to highlight his conversion as the demarcation of our inquiry. Surely, Paul's background is divergent and complex: a Hellenized Jew turned Christian in the first-century Roman empire. However, Paul's Hellenization and his life in the Roman empire remain constants, while his conversion from Judaism to Christianity is the variable. If there is a hallmark or a dividing line in Paul's life and thought, it is certainly his conversion to Christ. Although there are some scholars who refrain from speaking of Paul as a "convert,"[28] because the term implies that he moves from one thing to another, the experience on the Damascus road was *the* watershed in Paul's life. As long as we consider Paul's conversion to Christianity as a "turning towards" rather than a "turning against," it is fair enough to continue to use terminology so ingrained in common parlance. Jerome Murphy-O'Connor is surely correct in saying of Paul that, "given the radical shift in his perception of God and of the divine plan of salvation implicit in his acceptance of Jesus as the Messiah and the dramatic change in his life-style which ensued, the term is perfectly justified."[29] Accordingly, it is advantageous for us to partition our brief look at Paul along the lines of his pre- and post-conversion settings. Whatever the influences upon him, Paul's encounter with the risen Lord acutely affected his past from Tarsus and Jerusalem and inaugurated his future from persecutor to propagator of Christianity.

Pre-Christian Paul

Of the "pre-Christian" Paul, very little is known. To the great consternation of his innumerable biographers, Paul rarely speaks of his background and early years. When he does recount a biographical tidbit, he does so only to advance an argument for which his personal history is evidentiary. From the *Koinē* Greek of his letters, it is evident that Paul received a good Hellenistic education, but he never mentions how or where. Likewise, in the letters themselves, Paul tells us that he is a Jew: "I myself am an Israelite, a descendant of Abraham, a member of the tribe of Benjamin" (Rom 11:1c); and "Are they Hebrews? So am I. Are they Israelites? So am I. Are they descendants of Abraham? So am I" (2 Cor 11:22). Paul also tells us that he was a specific sort of Jew, a Pharisee: that he was "circumcised on the eighth day, of the people of Israel, of the tribe of Benjamin, a Hebrew born of Hebrews; as to the law a Pharisee, as to zeal a

---

Malina and J. H. Neyrey, *Portraits of Paul: An Archeology of Ancient Personality* (Westminster John Knox, 1996); and T. L. Donaldson, *Paul and the Gentiles: Remapping the Apostle's Convictional Thought World* (Minneapolis: Fortress, 1997).

[28] For example, K. Stendahl, *Paul among Jews and Gentiles* (Philadelphia: Fortress, 1976) 7–23; Betz, *Galatians*, 64; D. Georgi, *Theocracy in Paul's Praxis and Theology* (trans. D. E. Green; Minneapolis: Fortress, 1991) 19; and esp. Ashton, "Paul the Convert" (chap. 3), in *Religion of Paul the Apostle*, 73–104.

[29] Murphy-O'Connor, *Paul: A Critical Life*, 71 n. 2. Cf. Ashton, *Religion of Paul the Apostle*, 76.

persecutor of the church, as to righteousness under the law blameless" (Phil 3:5–6). Rom 11:1c is an integral part of an extended argument in Romans 9–11, wherein Paul defends justification in Christ as consistent with God's promises to his (Jewish) people in the OT, by appealing to his readers with the rhetorical question, "I ask, then, has God rejected his people?" (Rom 11:1a), that he immediately answers: "By no means!" (Rom 11:1b). However, judging from the contexts of 2 Cor 11:1–12:13 and Phil 3:1–4:1, it would seem that Paul speaks of his Jewish background only because his Jewish credentials were questioned in some fashion.[30] But even if these reflect merely a reaffirmation rather than a defense,[31] Paul's point was to assert his Judaism. The revelation of autobiographical particulars is ancillary.

Oddly enough, Paul never defends his Greco-Roman background. In fact, were it not for his facile use of Greek, we might scarcely detect it in his letters, other than to see that he was a well-Hellenized, Diaspora Jew.[32] But Luke tells us in Acts that Paul was born in Tarsus (9:11; 21:39; 22:3; cf. 9:30; 11:25), that he was reared and educated in Jerusalem (22:3; cf. 26:4), that he was a Pharisee (Acts 23:6; 26:5), and that he was a Roman citizen to boot (16:37–38; 22:25–29; 23:27; 25:7–12; 26:32). All of this substantially complicates the person of Paul, for it roots him quite firmly in two, seemingly antithetical, worlds—the Jewish and the Greco-Roman—so much so that he has two names in Acts: Saul and Paul. To complicate matters even further, Luke intimates that Paul's ethnic identity was easily misapprehended even in the first century. In Acts, a Roman tribune, Claudius Lysias, mistakenly thinks Paul to be an Egyptian and is surprised that Paul speaks Greek (21:37–38). And the misidentification occurs in the midst of Paul's having been accused of profaning the Jerusalem temple by Asian Jews (21:27–36) and, then, defending himself before Palestinian Jews (22:1, 3–21), who are pacified by Paul's use of Aramaic (21:40; 22:2), in a speech which turned out to be so ineffective that Paul identifies himself as a Roman citizen to avoid scourging (22:25). Moreover, Paul is more "Roman" than the centurion insofar as the centurion purchased the citizenship that Paul possessed as a birthright (22:28). From here onwards in Acts, Paul remains in imperial custody until Luke concludes his narrative with Paul's imprisonment in Rome.

Again, oddly enough, Luke seems content with a man who is both a Roman of Tarsus and a Pharisee of Jerusalem. Yet early Christian scholars such as

---

[30] So too, Murphy-O'Connor, *Paul: A Critical Life*, 32.

[31] So M. Hengel, *The Pre-Christian Paul* (trans. J. Bowden; London: SCM, 1991) 1.

[32] What of 1 Cor 15:33, wherein Paul quotes Menander's *Thais*? As we saw above, there is little we can say for sure. Thiselton remarks: "Paul may well have heard it cited more than once as a maxim, and we may infer neither knowledge nor ignorance of Greek literature on Paul's part from this quotation" (*First Corinthians*, 1254). Conzelmann, on this point, is blunt: "Conclusions are not to be drawn" (*1 Corinthians*, 278 n. 139).

Origen and St. Jerome wrestled with the obvious problem,[33] as do contemporary scholars:[34] How "Jewish" or "Roman" was Paul? To what extent was he influenced by Hellenistic thought and culture, which overshadowed both Jew and Roman in the first century? No doubt, studies will continue to probe, if not necessarily answer, the "Tarsus or Jerusalem" question—a never-ending "tale of two cities." Given the dearth of solid evidence, it is unlikely that the question will ever be answered adequately, and we do not intend to tackle it here. According to our stated goal in this chapter—to discover some clue relevant to vicarious baptism—taking a stand for or against Tarsus or Jerusalem would not only be foolhardy, it would beg the question. Both cities and their concomitant milieux had a profound effect on Paul;[35] both cities must be factored into any and all facets of things Pauline. To seek to divine a fault line between Tarsus and Jerusalem in Paul's formative influences can only cause an irreparable rupture in his personality that is, in the end, ahistorical. Yet there have been several attempts to do just that. The most notable are those of W. C. van Unnik and Rudolf Bultmann. For Bultmann, Paul is inexorably Cilician;[36] for Unnik, Paul is inexorably Palestinian.[37] Taking one of these stands forces a unwarranted choice between Tarsus and Jerusalem. As Andrie B. du Toit observes:

> For too long the search for the pre-Christian Paul moved within the confines of the Tarsus/Jerusalem dichotomy. Bultmann opted for Tarsus at the cost of Jerusalem, van Unnik for Jerusalem at the cost of Tarsus. This either-or approach should be superseded by a both-and. Tarsus was Paul's main sociological and cultural home, although he also received his first religious impressions there. Jerusalem was his religious and theological home, although he also socialized there. Instead of choosing between Tarsus and Jerusalem, we should let the contribution of each to Paul's development come into its own.[38]

Recognition of the contribution of each allows us to see Paul as a mirror reading of his letters presents him: a Jew from Tarsus who participated in the Hellenistic culture of his day.[39]

---

[33] For the details, see Murphy-O'Connor, *Paul: A Critical Life*, 36–39.

[34] For example, Wallace and Williams, *The Three Worlds of Paul of Tarsus*; Heyer, *Paul: A Man of Two Worlds*; and most recently, A. du Toit, "A Tale of Two Cities: "Tarsus or Jerusalem" Revisited," *NTS* 46 (2000) 375–402.

[35] U. Vanni, "Due città nella formazione di Paolo: Tarso e Gerusalemme," in *Atti del I Simposio di Tarso su S. Paulo Apostolo—Turchia: La Chiesa e la sua storia, V* (ed. L. Padovese; Rome: Pontificio Ateneo Antoniano, 1993) 28–29.

[36] Rudolf Bultmann, "Paulus," in *Religion in Geschichte und Gegenwar: Handworterbch für Theologie und Religionswissenschaft* (2nd ed.; Tübingen: Mohr, 1930) 4: cols. 1020–21; and idem, *Theology of the New Testament*, 1:187–89 et passim.

[37] W. C. van Unnik, *Tarsus or Jerusalem: The City of Paul's Youth* (trans. G. Ogg; London: Epworth, 1962).

[38] Du Toit, "A Tale of Two Cities," 401.

[39] See T. Engberg-Pedersen, "Introduction," in *Paul in His Hellenistic Context* (ed. T. Engberg-Pedersen; T&T Clark, 1994) xv–xx.

Luke straddles the fence in terms of Paul's personal history, not only by placing Paul's birth in Tarsus and his rearing in Jerusalem, but by ascribing to him both a distinctively Roman and a distinctively Jewish name. For according to Luke in Acts, Paul is *Saul* when young (7:58; 8:1), persecuting the Church (9:1), experiencing the Lord (9:4, 8, 11, 17), and in the early stages of his apostolate (9:22, 24; 11:25, 30; 12:25; 13:1). And Paul is *Paul* from 13:9 until the end of the Acts. The penultimate use of *Saul* is Acts 13:2—except for Paul's own reminiscences of his conversion later on in Acts (22:7, 13; 26:14)—wherein the Holy Spirit commands, "Set apart for me Barnabas and Saul for the work to which I have called them." The ultimate use is 13:9, at which point Luke informs us of Paul's other name: "But Saul, who is also called Paul. . . ." Although the original readers of Acts may have known full well from sources outside Acts that Paul was *Paul*, and the neophyte may guess it from 9:11, 30 and 11:25, it is no small thing for this man, previously described as a zealous Jew, to have so thoroughly a Roman name as *Paulus*, the same name as Sergius Paulus, the proconsul mentioned just two verses earlier in Acts 13:7. The name changes from *Saul* to *Paul* at a most auspicious moment in Luke's account—just when Paul is about to become the "Apostle to the Gentiles" in Acts 13–28.

It is likely that at this point in his narrative Luke simply begins to use the name that Paul would have used in non-Jewish contexts, his "public" name.[40] Note how Luke is careful to revert to *Saul* in Acts 22:7, 13 and 26:14, when having Paul recount his conversion experience to Jews. It is not a question of Luke changing Paul's name or of using *Paolos* as a Greek equivalent of *Saulos*.[41] G. A. Harrer demonstrates that Paul, in addition to the *tria nomina* we naturally expect of a Roman citizen, would have also had a *signum* (or *supernomen*).[42] In the Greek East, "it became customary among numbers of provincials and Roman citizens to add informally another name, a name by which a person was called among his acquaintances."[43] Such a name was often given at birth, and numerous first-century inscriptions link the *signum* to a person's name by the use of ὁ καί or *qui et*, just as we find it in Acts 13:9.[44] But 13:9 does not mention Paul's *tria nomina*, so it is difficult to adjudicate the one from the other.[45] After considering all of the possible evidence, Harrer concludes: "We may claim then at least probability in favor of a view that the

---

[40] L. T. Johnson, *The Acts of the Apostles* (SacPag 5; Collegeville, MN: Liturgical [Glazier], 1992) 223.

[41] A. N. Sherwin-White's suggestion of an equivalency between *Paolos* and *Saulos* (*Roman Society and Roman Law in the New Testament* [Oxford: Clarendon, 1963] 153) is shown to be ungrounded by Murphy-O'Connor (*Paul: A Critical Life*, 42–43).

[42] G. A. Harrer, "Saul Who Is Also Called Paul," *HTR* 33 (1940) 19–21.

[43] Ibid., 21.

[44] Ibid., 21–22. See also C. J. Hemer, "The Name of Paul," *TynBul* 36 (1985) 179–83; and Murphy-O'Connor, *Paul: A Critical Life*, 42–43.

[45] See Harrer, "Saul Who Is Also Called Paul," 22–24.

apostle was named *Paul* from birth, with *Saul* as his *signum*."[46] This position is buttressed by that fact that Paul himself never uses the name *Saul*; he always refers to himself as *Paul*. Again, if Paul were a Roman, we would expect to know his full name or *tria nomina*: *praenomen* (given name), *nomen* (ancestral name), and *cognomen* (family name). Yet neither Luke nor Paul provides us with Paul's full name. "It is remarkable that Paul's full name is unknown to us. He must have possessed the characteristic Roman *tria nomina*, but these would not have been used in the Greek and Jewish contexts of his travels, and only as a formal and official Roman designation."[47] This easily explains why Paul may not have used the *tria nomina* in his letters, but it leaves open the question of why Luke did not bother to mention it when Paul confronted Roman authority or demanded his Roman rights.

Although he bore a Roman name, Paul was a devout Jew. Speculation soars, though, as to what cultural milieu dominated his youth—Cilician or Palestinian—or, more precisely, as to where Paul spent his youth and received his early education. The claims of Acts notwithstanding, no one would guess from Paul's letters that he was educated in Jerusalem. Though it is true that Paul does not mention either birth or education in Tarsus (or anywhere else for that matter), the letters point to a solid Hellenistic education.[48] Three predominant factors attest to this. First, there is Paul's facile use of *Koinē* Greek.[49] A familiarity with Greek does not necessitate an education outside Jerusalem,[50] but it certainly favors one.[51] Second, Paul's use of rhetorical devices and Greco-Roman epistolography—as we saw so clearly in Chapter II of our study—manifests an instinctual knowledge of Greek.[52] Third, Paul uses the LXX as his OT text.[53]

---

[46] Ibid., 33.

[47] C. J. Hemer, *The Book of Acts in the Setting of Hellenistic History* (ed. C. H. Gempf; WUNT 49; Tübingen: Mohr [Siebeck], 1989) 128 n. 77.

[48] Thus, the claim by M. Hengel—in many of his works, especially in "Der vorchristliche Paulus" in *Paulus und das antike Judentum* (ed. M. Hengel and U. Heckel; WUNT 58; Tübingen: Mohr [Siebeck], 1991) 177–291; and idem with A. M. Schwemer, *Paul between Damascus and Antioch* (trans. J. Bowden; London: SCM, 1997)—that Paul received his early education in Jerusalem and only inundated himself in Hellenistic culture after his conversion to Christianity, i.e., in the "hidden years," cannot be sustained.

[49] W. C. van Unnik's ("Aramaisms in Paul," *VoxT* 14 [1943] 117–26) speculation that Paul thought in Aramaic and wrote in Greek remains but his own; see du Toit, "A Tale of Two Cities," 392–93.

[50] M. Silva ("Bilingualism and the Character of Palestinian Greek," *Bib* 61 [1980] 198–219) successfully argues that there is no Greek specifically linked either to Palestine or early Christianity such as can be spoken of as distinct from *Koinē*.

[51] So too, e.g., Murphy-O'Connor, *Paul: A Critical Life*, 50–51; and du Toit, "A Tale of Two Cities," 393.

[52] Summed up in du Toit, "A Tale of Two Cities," 385–87. See also, Murphy-O'Connor, *Paul: A Critical Life*, 49–51.

[53] E. E. Ellis (*Paul's Use of the Old Testament* [Edinburgh: Oliver and Boyd, 1957]) demonstrates definitively that Paul relied on the LXX and that, when Paul varies from the LXX, he relies on no extant text, Greek or Hebrew. This is confirmed by the recent study of C. D. Stanley, *Paul and*

"The extent to which Paul reflects the Septuagint, together with his minimal agreement with the Hebrew, raises the question of his knowledge of the Hebrew text and language."[54] All in all, the letters manifest the faculties of a Diaspora-trained Jew, of whose youth we know nothing other than the claims of Luke in Acts 22:3 (cf. 7:58; 23:16), which are difficult to reconcile with Paul's own remarks to the effect that he was somewhat unknown to the churches in Judea (Gal 1:22). "In the absence of any evidence regarding Paul's youth, we must presume the normal, namely, that Paul was already grown up when he left his home in Tarsus."[55] This presumption avoids the pitfalls of a position that would rebuff the importance of either Tarsus or Jerusalem in Paul's formation, e.g., W. M. Ramsay's opinion that Tarsus is the city to be emphasized over Jerusalem,[56] or Martin Hengel's opinion to the contrary.[57] "What is uncertain is not Paul's Tarsian origin, but the length of his original stay there."[58] In short, though Paul may have blossomed in Judea, we cannot discount his roots in Cilicia.

It is Luke who tells us that Paul was born in Tarsus (Acts 9:11; 21:39; 22:3; cf. 9:30; 11:25).[59] Paul is silent on the subject. In addition, Luke tells us that Paul was *born* a Roman citizen (Acts 22:28). And although he does not explicitly link the Roman birthright to Tarsus, Luke's inference is clear: Paul's citizenship is coupled to his birth in Tarsus. On this also, Paul is silent. In the entire Bible, "Tarsus" appears only in the aforementioned verses of Acts and in 2 Maccabees 3:5 and 4:30. Paul never mentions Tarsus. Actually, what Paul does tells us in Rom 11:1; 2 Cor 11:22; Gal 1:13–14; 2:15; and especially Phil 3:5, seems to militate against a birth or rearing at Tarsus. However, Luke has no vested interest in designating Paul as a Diaspora Jew,[60] and he goes to great lengths to specify Paul as a Jerusalem-trained Pharisee (see Acts 22:3; 23:6;

---

the Language of Scripture: Citation Technique in the Pauline Epistles and Contemporary Literature (SNTSMS 74; Cambridge: Cambridge University Press, 1992).

[54] D. M. Smith, "The Pauline Literature," in *It Is Written: Scripture Citing Scripture: Essays in Honour of Barnabas Lindars, SSF* (ed. D. A. Carson and H. G. M. Williamson; Cambridge: Cambridge University Press, 1988) 273. Note that J. Barr ("Paul and the LXX: A Note on Some Recent Work," *JTS* 45 [1994] 593–601) offers some criticism of Ellis, C. D. Stanley, and D. M. Smith's methodologies in terms of their (seeming) reluctance to account for recent text criticism of the LXX, although Barr agrees with their conclusions.

[55] Murphy-O'Connor, *Paul: A Critical Life*, 46.

[56] W. M. Ramsay, "The Tarsian Citizenship of St. Paul," *ExpTim* 16 (1904) 18–21; and idem, *The Cities of St. Paul and Their Influence on His Life and Thought: The Cities of Eastern Asia Minor* (London: Hodder and Stoughton, 1907) 228–35.

[57] Hengel, *Pre-Christian Paul*, 18–39. So too, Unnik, *Tarsus or Jerusalem*, 7; F. F. Bruce, *Paul: Apostle of the Heart Set Free* (1977; rpt. Grand Rapids, MI: Eerdmans, 1996) 43; and W. W. Gasque, "Tarsus," *ABD* 6:334.

[58] Du Toit, "A Tale of Two Cities," 391.

[59] See ibid. for Luke's use of Ταρσεύς in 9:11 and 21:39.

[60] See J. C. Beker, "Luke's Paul as the Legacy of Paul," in *SBLSP 1993* (Atlanta: Scholars Press, 1993) 511–19.

26:4–5),⁶¹ albeit one from Tarsus—even one who returns to Tarsus when in jeopardy (Acts 9:30; cf. 11:25).

To quote Paul in Acts 21:39, Tarsus was "no mean city." Although now a small Turkish city, Tarsus was a leading city in the first century A.D.,⁶² with a rich and varied history. Located on the Cydnus River, Tarsus was the principal city of the eastern plain of Cilicia (or Cilicia Pedias) and a chief trade route from Syria to central Asia Minor.⁶³ With foundations possibly dating to 4000 B.C., Tarsus is known to have existed as a walled city in 2000 B.C. and was part of the Hittite empire until its destruction in 1200 B.C. and later resettlement by the Phoenicians.⁶⁴ Homer (*Il.* IV, 397, 413) mentions the Cilicians as allies of the Trojans. Controlled by the Assyrian empire by the ninth century B.C., then by local kings under both the Assyrians and the Persians in the sixth century B.C., and later by satraps in the fifth century B.C., Cilicia fell into Alexander's control after the battle of Issus in 333 B.C.⁶⁵ After Alexander's death, eastern Cilicia remained under Seleucid control until 67 B.C., when Pompey defeated the pirates in western Cilicia (Cilicia Trachaei) to form one Roman province. However, from about 25 B.C., eastern Cilicia was united with the administration of Rome's Syrian province or the province of Syria-Cilicia, as Paul would have known it and as he referred to it in Gal 1:21.⁶⁶

Similar to its status under the Assyrians and the Persians, Tarsus enjoyed considerable autonomy under the Greeks and Romans. The Seleucids renamed the city "Antioch-on-the-Cydnus," and Tarsus adopted a new constitution and coinage. The city fell under Armenian control, but after the Mithradatic wars and Pompey's victories in the west, it remained a free city under the Romans from 67 B.C. onwards.⁶⁷ From 51–50 B.C., Cicero resided there as the proconsul of Cilicia, even though the proper capital of the province was Antioch; Caesar visited in 47 B.C., wherewith the city honored him by renaming itself "Iuliopolis." After Caesar's assassination and the battle of Philippi in 42 B.C., Tarsus was favored by Marc Antony who controlled the eastern Roman provinces.⁶⁸ Indeed, it was to Tarsus in 41 B.C. that Antony summoned Cleopatra, who obliged by having herself rowed up the Cydnus on her royal barge while dressed as Aphrodite, a scene immortalized by Plutarch (*Ant.* 26) and Shakespeare (*Antony and*

---

⁶¹ See, e.g., M. Enslin, "Once More, Luke and Paul," *ZNW* 61 (1970) 253–71.

⁶² For information on the archeology of the city, see H. Goldman, *Excavations at Gözlü Kule, Tarsus* (vol. 1, *Texts: The Hellenistic and Roman Period*; vol. 2, *Plates: The Hellenistic and Roman Periods*; Princeton, NJ: Princeton University Press, 1950).

⁶³ Gasque, "Tarsus," 333.

⁶⁴ Ibid.

⁶⁵ Bruce, *Paul: Apostle of the Heart Set Free*, 32–33.

⁶⁶ Ibid., 33.

⁶⁷ On the Mithradatic wars, see G. Shipley, *The Greek World after Alexander: 323–30 BC* (RHAW; London and New York: Routledge, 2000) 386–89.

⁶⁸ Bruce, *Paul: Apostle of the Heart Set Free*, 33–34.

Cleopatra, act II, scene 2).[69] Early on in the Roman empire, Tarsus was considered the Roman *metropolis* of Cilicia. After the battle of Actium in 31 B.C., Tarsus shrewdly switched its allegiance from Antony to Augustus who exempted the city from imperial taxation and showed considerable favor to the city throughout his reign.

By all accounts, Tarsus flourished economically and culturally in the first century A.D. In addition to its vigorous trade, Tarsus was famous for its fine flax and the production of *cilicium*, a material woven from the hair of black goats native to the region for protection from moisture (which may shed some light on Paul's work as a tentmaker [σκηνοποιός] in Acts 18:3).[70] Indeed, Tarsus would receive much criticism from Philostratus (*Vit. Apoll.* 1.7; cf. 4.34) and Dio Chrysostom (*Or.* 33–34) for its luxury and immorality.[71] It is Strabo (*Geogr.* 14.5.12, 13) who speaks of the intellectual life of Tarsus as surpassing even that of Athens and Alexandria. Though he points out that few students came from outside the city to its schools, Strabo maintains that Tarsians enjoyed the possibility of an excellent Hellenistic education. The presence of Hellenistic education did not, however, overshadow the eastern roots and character of the city. Dio Chrysostum (*Or.* 33) refers to their dress and music as "Phoenician." Moreover, it was a frontier city, always on the eastern fringe of the Roman empire with an admixture of eastern and western cultures and religions. Pompey, the same general who had brought Roman rule to Cilicia, invaded Palestine in 65 B.C. He besieged Jerusalem for three months, took the city, and entered (but did not destroy) the temple in 63 B.C. A few years later, he installed the governor Gabinius and assigned much of the land won under the Maccabaean rule to the province of Syria. In A.D. 6, the imperial province of Judea was created under Augustus. In A.D. 72, the imperial province of Cilicia was created under Vespasian, with Tarsus as the capital. Just three years earlier, Vespasian had been declared *imperator* after the year of the three emperors (Galba, Otho, and Vitellius) while besieging Jerusalem. On his return to Rome, he left his legions under his son Titus' command. It was Titus who razed the Jerusalem temple in A.D. 70. The only Tarsus and Jerusalem Paul ever knew were long under Roman rule.

Likewise, the only Tarsus Paul knew was inundated with the religious pluralism and syncretism of the Greco-Roman world and showed considerable religious diversity. For example, Tarsus had deep roots in the worship of the god Mithra, a Persian and Hellenistic deity. According to Plutarch (*Pomp.* 24.5), the

---

[69] For the historical details, see Green, *Alexander to Actium*, 670–74.

[70] Even if R. F. Hock (*The Social Context of Paul's Ministry* [Philadelphia: Fortress, 1980] 20–25) is correct in stating that σκηνοποιός is best translated as "leather worker," the coincidence cannot be ignored.

[71] See Murphy-O'Connor, *Paul: A Critical Life*, 34–35; and Bruce, *Paul: Apostle of the Heart Set Free*, 35. Note that these later criticisms may have no bearing on first-century Tarsus.

worship of Mithra was introduced by the pirates in western Cilicia, but it is more likely that it came to Cilicia via the Armenians.[72] In the Greco-Roman period, Mithra became inextricably linked to Mithras, a deity of the Roman mystery religion and military cult whose origins are obscure. How, precisely, they are connected remains uncertain.[73] However, by mid-third century A.D., Tarsus minted coins with the image of Mithras slaying the bull.[74] Zeus-Jupiter, the "sky father," worshiped in one form or another throughout the Greco-Roman world, was venerated in Tarsus as Ba'al-Tarz.[75] So too, the imperial cult flourished in Tarsus. Though Augustus was personally judicious about referring to himself as a god, worship of the Roman emperors burgeoned in the provinces during his reign. "A city which was given official permission to be the center of the provincial [imperial] cult was styled *neokoros* or 'temple-warden' and the cities vied with one another for this title."[76] Tarsus, so steadfast in its allegiance to the emperors in order to maintain favored status, achieved the title twice: once under Hadrian and again under Commodus.[77] Religion remained closely tied to Roman influence in Tarsus well after Paul's death. In the fourth century, Julian the Apostate attempted to lead Rome back to the ancient pagan gods. One god whom Julian promoted in opposition to Christ (the Healer) was Asclepius, the ancient god of healing. Julian insisted that Asclepius' temple in Tarsus be restored, after it had fallen into disuse with the advent of Christianity in Cilicia.[78] Thus, Paul's Tarsian background provided him with a wide exposure to paganism, syncretism, and the politics of religious affiliation.

But Paul tells us that he was a Hebrew and a Pharisee (Rom 11:1; 2 Cor 11:22; Gal 1:13–14; 2:15; Phil 3:5–6). St. Jerome (*Vir. ill.* 5) claims that his family had immigrated to Tarsus from Galilee after the Roman conquest of Palestine, but there is little to support Jerome's claim,[79] even with Luke's testimony that Paul was the son of Pharisees (Acts 23:6). There is ample evidence of the presence of Jews in Tarsus, Cilicia, and throughout Asia Minor. There is no reason to oppose residence in Tarsus with devout (Diaspora) Judaism. Moreover, there is little reason to oppose residence in Tarsus with Pharisaism. Pharisaism was not completely localized in Jerusalem. "It is likely that the Pharisees and their influence extended into Palestine and adjacent areas in Syria

---

[72] M. Clauss, *The Roman Cult of Mithras: The God and His Mysteries* (trans. R. Gordon; London and New York: Routledge, 2000) 4.

[73] Ibid., 7.

[74] Ibid., 4.

[75] J. Ferguson, *The Religions of the Roman Empire* (AGRL; Ithaca, NY: Cornell University Press, 1970) 37.

[76] Ibid., 94.

[77] Ibid., 95.

[78] Ibid., 241.

[79] F. F. Bruce, *New Testament History* (New York: Doubleday, 1969) 236.

and Cilicia."⁸⁰ But it is hardly certain, and many doubt it.⁸¹ Since Josephus and Paul are the only two men who claim to be Pharisees and whose writings are extant, the evidence for Pharisaism in first-century Jerusalem outside the NT and second-century rabbinic Judaism is scant. The evidence for Pharisaism in the Diaspora is almost nonexistent. Anthony J. Saldarini notes:

> In the Diaspora it is unclear what being a Pharisee might have meant. Both Josephus and Paul claimed to be Pharisees and consciously lived in the larger world of the Roman empire. Perhaps they found the Pharisaic view of how to live Judaism a viable response to the intellectual and spiritual challenge of the Hellenistic world view. Though we do not know the teachings of the Pharisees in any detail (despite later rabbinic texts and some New Testament allusions which imply a sect-like way of life), they probably brought Jewish practices into daily life and created a conscious way of life which answered the questions and crises felt by some Jews when confronted with the Greco-Roman world. Neither says how one became a member of the Pharisees nor what kind and intensity of commitment was required. Possibly neither joined a clearly identified group, but rather identified loosely with the Pharisaic way of life because it fitted or could be adapted to fit their needs as Jews living in a largely Greco-Roman world.⁸²

Paul's dedication to Judaism is abundantly evident in his letters and in Acts. It would seem, then, that Paul's self-description as Pharisee can be said to establish little more than that he was a devout Jew.

Paul's identification as a Jew and Pharisee do not preclude other affiliations in the Greco-Roman world. Luke describes Paul as both a citizen (πολίτης) of Tarsus and a citizen of Rome ('Ρωμαῖος, πολιτεία) in Acts 21:39 and 22:25–29. Even if Luke used the term πολίτης loosely to mean resident rather than citizen of Tarsus *per se*,⁸³ the fact remains that local and Roman citizenship was often obtained "on the basis of benefactions or merit, or, in some cases, it could be bought; once gained it would be inherited by successors."⁸⁴ Many Jews enjoyed local and Roman citizenship in the first century A.D. John M. G. Barclay explains:

> Jews are also to be found as Roman citizens, both in Rome itself and in other cities in the empire. Josephus was one but certainly not the only Jew granted Roman citizenship in Rome (*Vita* 423). Many of the Jews who were entitled to the corn-dole in Rome (Philo, *Legatio* 158) probably gained their citizenship on

---

⁸⁰ A. J. Saldarini, *Pharisees, Scribes, and Sadducees in Palestinian Society* (Edinburgh: T&T Clark, 1988) 137.
⁸¹ Murphy-O'Connnor, *Paul: A Critical Life*, 58–59.
⁸² Saldarini, *Pharisees, Scribes, and Sadducees in Palestinian Society*, 138–39.
⁸³ As is suggested by Hengel, *Pre-Christian Paul*, 4–6.
⁸⁴ J. M. G. Barclay, *Jews in the Mediterranean Diaspora: From Alexander to Trajan (323 BCE–117 CE)* (Edinburgh: T&T Clark, 1996) 271–72 n. 32.

manumission. Most of these must have been rather less assimilated than Josephus, who had access to exalted political circles, but they nonetheless took their place in Roman political life, while maintaining the Sabbath and no doubt other Jewish customs. Elsewhere in the Roman empire the legal right of Roman citizenship may not have entailed significant social assimilation, but we may note in this connection such examples as Paul (if we may believe Acts on this matter, Acts 16.37) and those Jews noted in the decrees recorded by Josephus, *A.J.* 14.228–40.[85]

Paul, like so many others of the Diaspora, may have maintained both local and Roman citizenship (and their various benefits) without necessarily compromising himself or his religious identity as a Jew.[86]

Although a protracted examination of Diaspora Judaism is beyond the pale of our study, two things need to be noted about Paul who lived more than half of his life in the Diaspora as both a child and an apostle. First, Diaspora Judaism was not a compromise, but a development, as was Palestinian Judaism. Second, Paul's status as a Diaspora Jew was not anomalous. The invented juxtaposition of and contradistinction between "Hellenism" and "Judaism" in intertestamental studies, which has its roots in Baur and the Tübingen School (and has exercised considerable influence in biblical scholarship ever since), only obfuscates the relationship between Diaspora and Palestinian Judaism by placing them in opposition to one another.[87] By the first century A.D., Hellenism had spread throughout the known world, and Judaism was heavily influenced by it within and without Jerusalem. First-century Judaism was more "like a quite diverse family of ways of adapting the traditions of Israel to the Greco-Roman world" than a family feud.[88] In fact, the most recent evidence clearly shows "that Judea and the Galilee were far from being pure Jewish islands in a sea of Hellenism."[89] As Lee I. Levine lays bare in his book *Judaism and Hellenism in Antiquity: Conflict or Confluence?*,[90] there was far more confluence than conflict. Furthermore, Paul's status as a (Pharisaic) Jew, Tarsian, and Roman citizen cannot be treated as if it were anomalous, although this is often the case in Pauline scholarship. For example, Barclay devotes significant attention to speaking of

---

[85] Ibid., 327–28.

[86] For the options available to Jews as citizens, see P. R. Trebilco, *Jewish Communities in Asia Minor* (SNTSMS 69; Cambridge: Cambridge University Press, 1991) 173–85.

[87] See W. A. Meeks, "Judaism, Hellenism, and the Birth of Christianity," in *Paul beyond the Judaism/Hellenism Divide* (ed. T. Engberg-Pedersen; Louisville: Westminster John Knox, 2001) 17–27.

[88] Ibid., 24.

[89] Ibid., 25.

[90] L. I. Levine, *Judaism and Hellenism in Antiquity: Conflict or Confluence?* (Peabody, MA: Hendrickson, 1998).

Paul as "an anomalous Diaspora Jew,"[91] and sums up his findings in the following paragraph:

> Here, then, we encounter the truly anomalous character of Paul. In his conceptuality Paul is most at home among the particularistic and least accommodated segments of the Diaspora; yet in his utilization of these concepts, and in his social practice, he shatters the ethnic mould in which that ideology was formed. He shows little inclination to form any form of synthesis with his cultural environment, yet he employs the language of a culturally antagonistic Judaism to establish a new social entity which transgresses the boundaries of the Diaspora synagogues. By an extraordinary transference of ideology, Paul deracinates the most culturally conservative forms of Judaism in the Diaspora and uses them in the service of his largely Gentile communities.[92]

It would seem that the basis of Barclay's summation of Paul's anomalous character is founded on placing Diaspora Judaism at odds with Palestinian Judaism. With this he mixes Paul's Christianity. But the only Paul we really know is the Christian Paul, the Apostle to the Gentiles. And the way we know Paul is through his letters. Since there is no doubt that Paul's conversion effected a profound change within him, to say the least, is it not wiser to look to Paul for an explanation in his own words rather than to paint broad strokes about his background? Paul says:

> For though I am free from all men, I have made myself a slave to all, that I might win the more. To the Jews I became as a Jew, in order to win Jews; to those under the law I became as one under the law—though not being myself under the law—that I might win those under the law. To those outside the law I became as one outside the law—not being without law toward God but under the law of Christ—that I might win those outside the law. To the weak I became weak, that I might win the weak. I have become all things to all men, that I might by all means save some. I do it all for the sake of the gospel, that I may share in its blessings (1 Cor 9:19–23; cf. Rom 2:12–16; 11:13–16; 15:1–6; Gal 2:1–10; 5:13–15).

It is methodologically problematic to seek to look diachronically through Paul's Christianity to affirm or to deny the particulars of his upbringing, and it is especially problematic to treat Paul as an anomaly without comparison to other comparable figures.[93] It is better to consider Paul simply as an ordinary Diaspora Jew, and leave the metanoia to the Damascus road and Christianity.

So what can we say about Paul and Tarsus? We can say that Paul was reared as a Diaspora Jew in Tarsus. We can say that most likely it was in Tarsus

---

[91] Barclay, "Paul: An Anomalous Jew" (chap. 13), in *Jews in the Mediterranean Diaspora*, 381–95.

[92] Ibid., 393.

[93] For an extended explanation of the methodology of comparisons related to Paul, see J. Z. Smith, "On Comparisons" (chap. 2), in *Drudgery Divine*, 36–53.

that Paul "learned to speak Greek, grew into the Greek Bible, appropriated the basics of Greek style and rhetoric and acquired a rudimentary knowledge of popular Greek philosophy."[94] Of course, this does not preclude the possibility that Paul expanded his religious education in Jerusalem "at the feet of Gamaliel" (Acts 22:3; 5:34);[95] nor does it preclude an expansion of his Hellenistic education after his conversion,[96] even in his hometown of Tarsus (Acts 9:30). We can say that by the time Paul journeyed to Jerusalem he was well acquainted not only with Greco-Roman language and culture but also with the pagan religions he would invariably have been exposed to in Tarsus. In addition, we can say that he brought no notion of vicarious baptism with him. As we saw above, no one who opts for a reading of vicarious baptism would find it in the early life of Paul. Nor would anyone claim that Paul went up to Jerusalem with any predilection for pagan practices of any kind. We can safely say that he traveled to Jerusalem a pedigreed Jew, albeit a Diaspora Jew, who scarcely knew that he would one day persecute Christians and, then, go on to become one of Christianity's greatest propagators.

We do not know when Paul first came to Jerusalem, and we do not know why. Most likely, he came for religious reasons of one sort or another. Jerusalem was (and is) the spiritual heart of all Judaism. But we also know that there was a Diaspora Cilician community in Jerusalem, and we have reason to suspect that Paul had relatives in Jerusalem (Acts 23:16).

Religious reasons certainly stand out. Jerusalem was the ancient religious and cultural center of Judaism, both Diaspora and Palestinian. As we noted above, it is Paul who tells us that he was a Pharisee (Phil 3:5), and Luke confirms it (Acts 23:6; cf. 22:3). At first glance this may seem to be a startlingly important piece of biographical information, but a closer examination reveals that it is difficult to ascribe much more to it than to say that Paul was a pious and observant Jew. On the one hand, we cannot be sure when and where Paul allied himself to the Pharisaic movement—in Tarsus, Jerusalem, or elsewhere? "Paul never says where he made contact with Pharisaism, in Tarsus, Syria, or Jerusalem. . . . The evidence concerning Pharisaism is so slim that we do not know how Paul came to know about Pharisaism, why he was attracted to it, and what being a Pharisee entailed."[97] While the precise moment Paul became a Pharisee may not be as salient as the piece of information that he was indeed a Pharisee, the fact that we know so little of Pharisaism is regrettable.[98] The advent of a significant body of literature, which denies that deciphering Pharisaism through

---

[94] Du Toit, "A Tale of Two Cities," 401. For an extensive account see Murphy-O'Connor, "Growing Up in Tarsus" (chap. 2), in *Paul: A Critical Life*, 32–51.

[95] Murphy-O'Connor, *Paul: A Critical Life*, 46.

[96] Du Toit, "A Tale of Two Cities," 401.

[97] Saldarini, *Pharisees, Scribes, and Sadducees*, 138.

[98] For a considered examination of the question, see J. Sievers, "Who Were the Pharisees?" in *Hillel and Jesus* (ed. J. H. Charlesworth and L. L. Johns; Minneapolis: Fortress, 1997) 137–55.

the exegesis of second-century rabbinic literature is a fruitful undertaking,[99] shows that there is very little to rely on outside the NT and Josephus,[100] especially since Paul tells us nothing about Pharisaism *per se*. In the most comprehensive review of the Pharisaic movement to date, Roland Deines' *Die Pharisäer: Ihr Verständnis im Spiegel der christlichen und jüdischen Forschung seit Wellhausen und Graetz*,[101] we find an extensive survey of the pertinent scholarship, but little new information because there is little to be had.[102] John P. Meier reviews the book extensively, explaining the scholarly uncertainty about the pre-A.D. 70 Pharisaic movement,[103] and he remarks: "Indeed, one is almost tempted to conclude that the historical Jesus is easier to reconstruct than the historical Pharisee."[104]

The NT and Josephus assure us that the Pharisees played a significant role in first-century Jerusalem society.[105] We can be sure that Paul had a congenial relationship with them as either an old member or a recent convert. And we can be sure that Paul's status as a Diaspora Jew also afforded much congeniality in Jerusalem, for Jerusalem was highly Hellenized. As Levine points out:

> Jerusalem occupied a most unusual position within Jewish Palestine. On the one hand, it was the most Jewish of its cities, given the presence of the Temple, the priesthood, and the leadership of almost every sect and religious group, not to speak of the many religious observances exclusively associated with this city. On the other hand, Jerusalem was also the most Hellenized of Jewish cities, in terms of its population, languages, institutions, and general culture ambiance. Jerusalem's Janus-type posture made it truly remarkable, both for Jewish society and within the larger Roman world.[106]

Acts 2:5–11 attests to the fact that many foreign-born Jews dwelt in Jerusalem (cf. Mark 15:21; Luke 23:26; Acts 11:20). Specifically, according to Acts 6:9 (cf. Acts 24:12) and the Talmudic literature (*T. Meg.* 2:17), there was also a community of Cilician Jews resident in first-century Jerusalem.[107] Given that

---

[99] For the literature, see J. P. Meier, "The Quest for the Historical Pharisee: A Review Essay on Roland Deines, *Die Pharisäer*," *CBQ* 61 (1999) 714 n. 4.

[100] For the most extensive review of Josephus' understanding, see S. Mason, *Flavius Josephus on the Pharisees: A Composition-Critical Study* (StPB 39; Leiden: Brill, 1991).

[101] R. Deines, *Die Pharisäer: Ihr Verständnis im Spiegel der christlichen und jüdischen Forschung seit Wellhausen und Graetz* (WUNT 101; Tübingen: Mohr [Siebeck], 1997).

[102] Note that Deines' is a work in progress, and further volumes are in preparation.

[103] Meier, "The Quest for the Historical Pharisee," 713–22.

[104] Ibid., 714.

[105] See Saldarini, "The Place of the Pharisees in Jewish Society" (chap. 12), in *Pharisees, Scribes, and Sadducees*, 277–97.

[106] Levine, *Judaism and Hellenism in Antiquity*, 94–95.

[107] For references in the Talmudic writings, see J. Jeremias, *Jerusalem in the Time of Jesus: An Investigation into Economic and Social Conditions during the New Testament Period* (trans. F. H. and C. H. Cave; Philadelphia: Fortress, 1969) 66 n. 6.

Cilicians had served in the Hasmonean army of Alexander Jannaeus (Josephus, *B.J.* 1.88), it comes as little surprise to find them there, and this may help to explain the presence of Paul's nephew in the holy city (Acts 23:16—and other relatives?). It would seem these Cilicians were in spiritual concert with other Diaspora Jews living in the city.[108] Archeological and epigraphical evidence suggests that there may have been as many as five Diaspora synagogues in Jerusalem itself.[109] Acts 2:5–11 notwithstanding, Acts 6:9 points to "the institutionalized presence of Diaspora Jews in the city."[110] In other words, the Diaspora Jews retained their particular religious observances in the shadow of the Jerusalem temple. Again, according to Levine:

> We do not know how these synagogues functioned: Were they established on the initiative of those who settled in Jerusalem, or were they sponsored (in whole or in part) by the various Diaspora communities themselves? The latter alternative is quite possible, that these Diaspora communities established synagogues in Jerusalem not only to serve their former residents but also to attend to the needs of those compatriots visiting the city on pilgrimage.[111]

Both the Theodotus inscription and the comments in Acts 6:9 indicate that Diaspora Jews were prominent in first-century Jerusalem. The Theodotus inscription most likely designates a synagogue founded in Jerusalem by Roman Jews,[112] and it may relate to the synagogue of Freedmen in Acts 6:9. Correspondingly, the fact that "some of those who belonged to the synagogue of the Freedmen (as it was called), and of the Cyrenians, and of the Alexandrians, and of those from Cilicia and Asia, arose and disputed with Stephen" (Acts 6:9) illustrates their eminence in the community.

However, prominence in a community is no guarantee of others' acquiescence. A key example of discord among Palestinian Jews, which stands out in the NT, is the debate between the Pharisees and Sadducees over the resurrection, with especial interest to Paul (Acts 23:6–10; cf. 4:1; 5:17; 15:5). To this we might easily add the Essenes, Zealots, Scribes, the Therapeutae and the Qumran community (both of which may have been related to the Essenes), and various other first-century factions localized in Jerusalem.[113] That the attitude of individual Jewish sects varied in distinct stances towards other religions and that

---

[108] Ibid. 65–66.

[109] L. I. Levine, *The Ancient Synagogue: The First Thousand Years* (New Haven and London: Yale University Press, 2000) 53.

[110] Ibid., 54.

[111] Ibid.

[112] See ibid., 54–56, esp. 55 n. 57.

[113] For a look into the rich diversity of first-century Judaism, see E. P. Sanders, *Judaism: Practice and Belief 63 BCE–66 CE* (London: SCM, 1992); and Alan F. Segal, *The Other Judaisms of Late Antiquity* (BJS 127; Atlanta: Scholars Press, 1987).

Hellenism was pervasive in first-century Jerusalem is a given.[114] That there was tension between Palestinian and Diaspora Jews is also a given.[115] But by no means does such tension exclude stress among Diaspora Jews themselves,[116] for Hellenism was hardly homogeneous itself.[117] The aggravation was due more to ethnic than religious dissimilarities. As noted above, it seems that Paul never defends his Diaspora background, although he often defends his Jewish pedigree, but there is some evidence that he may have defended his ethnicity, viz., that Paul's Cilician origins may have been the basis for some to call him a liar and for him to defend himself against the prejudice.[118] Then, of course, there are Paul's frequent self-defenses in Acts. Christianity aside, Paul was acutely aware of struggles for identity in such a complex society. Added to all of this, was the variable posture of Jews to the Roman empire.[119] While a general desire of freedom from foreign rule, especially from the religious point of view, cannot be doubted, "foreign rule was not judged bad by everyone all the time. Some [Jews] preferred foreign rule to that of a despot closer at hand and held that internal Jewish freedom—'autonomy'—was enhanced by the rule of a distant empire."[120] Thus, Paul found himself in complex political and religious situations.[121] Oddly enough, though Paul is so closely identified with the Pharisees in Acts and defends himself as such before his fellow Jews, it is to Rome that he will make his final appeal, not Jerusalem.

Other than in his own letters, the first time we find mention of Paul he is in Jerusalem. He is the young man Saul, a passive participant at the stoning of the protomartyr St. Stephen (Acts 7:58b–8:1a; 22:20) in complete harmony with the law (Deut 17:7). According to Acts, Stephen's murder was not only the inaugu-

---

[114] See R. Goldenberg, *Nations That Know Thee Not: Ancient Jewish Attitudes towards Other Religions* (BSem 52; Sheffield: Sheffield Academic Press, 1997).

[115] See E. Lohse, "Judaism in the Time of the New Testament" (part I), in *The New Testament Environment* (trans. J. E. Steely; London: SCM, 1976) 15–196. And for the scholarly background and history of the question, see D. B. Martin, "Paul and the Judaism/Hellenism Dichotomy: Toward a Social History of the Question," in *Paul beyond the Hellenism/Judaism Divide*, ed. Engberg-Pederson, 29–61.

[116] For extensive citations from Josephus, see M. Goodman with J. Sherwood, "Judaism" (chap. 30), in *The Roman World: 44 BC–AD 180* (RHAW; London and New York: Routledge, 1997) 302–14.

[117] For example, see F. W. Walbank, "The Hellenistic Word: A Homogeneous Culture?" (chap. 4), in *The Hellenistic World* (rev. ed.; Cambridge, MA: Harvard University Press, 1992) 60–78.

[118] J. L. North, "Paul's Protest that He Does Not Lie in the Light of His Cilician Origin," *JTS* 47 (1996) 439–63. The relevant citations are Rom 9:1; 2 Cor 11:31; Gal 1:20; and 1 Tim 2:7; cf. 2 Tim 1:11.

[119] Relatively speaking, though, things were calm during Paul's adulthood; see P. W. Barnett, "'Under Tiberius All Was Quiet,'" *NTS* 21 (1974–75) 564–71.

[120] E. P. Sanders, *Judaism: Practice and Belief*, 41.

[121] For an excellent introduction to the religio-political scene, see A. Wroe, "Governing Judea" (chap. 2), in *Pontius Pilate* (New York: Random House, 1999) 57–115.

ration of persecution—"And on that day a great persecution arose against the church in Jerusalem" (Acts 8:1b)—but also the naissance of Paul's role as a persecutor: "Saul was ravaging the church, and entering house after house, he dragged off men and women and committed them to prison" (Acts 8:3). It would seem that his devotion to Judaism, especially the maintenance of its purity, was paramount for Paul. Zeal for his Father's house consumed him (Ps 69:9).

It is Paul who tells us that he persecuted Christians (1 Cor 15:9; Gal 1:13, 23; Phil 3:6), and Luke confirms it (Acts 8:3; 9:1–2, 21; 22:4–5). But it most difficult to ascertain the nature of this persecution other than to say that it manifests Paul's zeal for Judaism. From the bits and pieces in Paul's letters and Acts, four things are evident: Paul was a zealous Pharisee; Christians were already a discernable subgroup of Judaism in the early 30s; this subgroup had aroused considerable concern within Judaism; and the larger group (in the person of Paul and others) had begun to take action ("persecution") against the subgroup.[122] Luke's rendering of Paul's activities is much stronger than the information we glean from Paul. And this makes perfect sense, as Murphy-O'Connor shows:

> Once it is noticed that the strongest statements concerning Paul's pre-Christian activity always occur as introductions to narratives of his conversion, it becomes obvious that it was in Luke's artistic interest to exaggerate certain negative traits of Paul the persecutor in order to set in great relief the miracle of his conversion and the success of his apostolate. It enhanced the dramatic impact of his book to have the perfect persecutor transformed into the ideal apostle.[123]

Thus, we understand why Paul would have persecuted Christians as aberrant Jews and why Luke would have made much of his harrying activities. Luke's claims seem a bit excessive in terms of bringing prisoners from Damascus and casting votes in the Sanhedrin for death sentences. "Even if the Sanhedrin could pass capital sentences, it is not likely that it or any other Jewish body had authority to put offenders to death for any cause during Paul's lifetime."[124] The Sanhedrin certainly had no authority outside Judea, particularly in a Roman province;[125] and Luke's varying accounts of the source of Paul's authority only confound the problem (see Acts 9:2, 14; 22:5; 26:12). It is well-nigh impossible that Paul went about as a Jewish code enforcer with license to use physical means to secure prisoners.

The question remains, though, as to what is meant when Paul speaks of persecution. Paul makes his strongest statement in Gal 1:13: "I persecuted (ἐδίωκον) the church of God violently (καθ' ὑπερβολήν) and tried to destroy

---

[122] A. J. Hultgren, "Paul's Pre-Christian Persecutions of the Church: Their Purpose, Locale, and Nature," *JBL* 95 (1976) 97.

[123] Murphy-O'Connor, *Paul: A Critical Life*, 65.

[124] Hultgren, "Paul's Pre-Christian Persecutions of the Church," 108 n. 27. See also Murphy-O'Connor, *Paul: A Critical Life*, 65–66.

[125] Murphy-O'Connor, *Paul: A Critical Life*, 66.

(ἐπόρθουν) it." *Prima facie*, this sentence suggests physical attacks (reminiscent of Acts) as strong as torture and death, but when examined closely it refers to Paul's intense commitment rather than his specific actions. Given Paul's use of διώκω elsewhere in terms of the persecutions of Christians (Rom 12:14; Gal 4:29; 6:12) and himself (1 Cor 4:12; 2 Cor 4:9; 12:10; Gal 5:11), persecution is comprised of revilement, slander, and some other undetermined hardships.[126] In other words, Paul went about the environs of Jerusalem denouncing (Jewish) Christians to local authorities, and even if he limited his stalking to Hellenized Jews,[127] he was successful enough to seek to carry his deprecating mission to Damascus. Details such as we find in 2 Cor 4:8–10 and 11:24–25a might indicate the results of Paul's denouncements—flogging and imprisonment—but Paul would not have been empowered to pass sentences and inflict penalties himself.[128] Similarly, καθ' ὑπερβολήν is better translated as "to an extraordinary degree, beyond measure, utterly" without any connotation of physical violence.[129] Again, this emphasizes Paul's zeal in rooting out the new Christian heresy from within Judaism; it does not imply that he himself was physically violent. His goal was to destroy (πορθέω), to put an end to Christianity, but the meaning does not carry over into the personal practice of destroying Christians vis-à-vis violence.[130] Paul worked against Christianity "by refutation and by disciplining its members, under the Jewish system of discipline prevailing at the time, i.e., the judicial flogging and imprisonment, both of which were designed to bring the offender back into line. And he went about this task with incomparable zeal."[131] Actually, it seems to have been the same method employed by the Sanhedrin at Gamaliel's urging in Acts 5:40: "So they took his advice, and when they had called in the apostles, they beat them and charged them not to speak in the name of Jesus and let them go."

While all of this is easy enough to explain along the lines of a Jewish zealot operative in Jerusalem and its environs, the explanation falters a bit in terms of Paul's extending his mission to Damascus. Paul mentions the city only twice: once in terms of his narrow escape from King Aretas (2 Cor 11:32–33) and once in terms of returning to Damascus after a venture into Arabia (Gal 1:17). That Damascus was completely outside Jerusalem's jurisdiction is certain. Although there is some debate as to the extent of local control under Aretas IV and direct control by Rome from A.D. 34 to 62,[132] no dimissorials from Jerusalem would

---

[126] Ibid., 67. So too, Hultgren, "Paul's Pre-Christian Persecutions of the Church," 108–9.

[127] Hengel, *Pre-Christian Paul*, 87.

[128] Murphy-O'Connor, *Paul: A Critical Life*, 68.

[129] "ὑπερβολή, ῆς, ἡ," BAGD, 840. So too, Hultgren, "Paul's Pre-Christian Persecutions of the Church," 109; and Murphy-O'Connor, *Paul: A Critical Life*, 67.

[130] See "πορθέω," BAGD, 693.

[131] Hultgren, "Paul's Pre-Christian Persecutions of the Church," 110.

[132] For more, see J. McRay, "Damascus: The Greco-Roman Period," *ABD* 2:7–8; and D. F. Graf, "Aretas," *ABD* 1:373–76.

have carried much weight there with civil authorities, and it is impossible to know what weight they might have carried in regional Diaspora synagogues.[133] Furthermore, the confusion in Acts 9:2, 14; 22:5; and 26:12 over whose authority Paul carries makes matters worse. So much so that many doubt whether Paul went from Jerusalem to Damascus for the purpose of hounding (Jewish) Christians. Murphy-O'Connor recounts the various scholarly alternatives to Luke's rendering that Paul went to Damascus to persecute Christians,[134] and he concludes: "It is preferable to confess that we do not know why Paul went to Damascus."[135] Perhaps, Murphy-O'Connor goes too far? In the absence of any indication from Paul, other than the fact that he returned to Damascus (Gal 1:17; cf. 1:21), as to why he went to Damascus, is it not better to accept the simplest story line from Acts? Paul tells us that he persecuted Christians (1 Cor 15:9; Gal 1:13, 23; Phil 3:6), but he does not tell us where. Jerusalem is the most likely locale given Gal 1:22 and Luke's account; yet there is no reason to deny that Jerusalem became the point of departure. Undoubtedly, Paul's Diaspora background would have made him an ideal candidate to pursue the Christian heresy outside Jerusalem.[136] That there was a significant population of Jews in Damascus is certain, for Josephus (*B.J.* 2.561) attests to the killing of ten thousand Jews there during the First Jewish Revolt (A.D. 66–70). Given these circumstances—Paul's credentials and a hefty Damascene Jewish population, which may well have had Christian influence—it is no stretch to accept the bottom line from Luke, viz., that Paul set out to extend his harassment of Christians to Damascus. Neither Paul nor Luke tells us why he chose Damascus over any other city. Does it matter? What we do know is that an extremely zealous Jew found more than he ever bargained for on the road to Damascus.

What sort of Jew was Paul? Of this we can be sure: Paul was a Jewish zealot, a man with extensive experience of Judaism and Hellenism within and without Jerusalem, a man with broad knowledge of the workings of the first-century Greco-Roman world, and a man who chose—no doubt with sufficient knowledge of innumerable other options—to be a Pharisee. Not only did Paul make a conscious decision for Judaism, but he made a decision for one of its stricter sects.[137] Not only did this sect have no notion of anything like vicarious baptism; but it also had no notion of ordinary (Christian) baptism *per se*, although it had a penchant for ritual ablutions. While the Pharisaic ritual washings undoubtedly provided a theological and liturgical underpinning for the later

---

[133] The authority known in 1 Macc 15:15–24 had long since ceased. Cf. Josephus, *A.J.* 14.190–95; and idem, *B.J.* 1.474

[134] See Murphy-O'Connor, *Paul: A Critical Life*, 68–70.

[135] Murphy-O'Connor, *Paul: A Critical Life*, 70.

[136] In fact, Hengel (*Pre-Christian Paul*, 87) limits Paul's persecution in Jerusalem to Diaspora synagogues in the city and its immediate vicinity.

[137] For a perspective on the possibilities within Pharisaism, see D. Lührmann, "Paul and the Pharisaic Tradition," *JSNT* 36 (1989) 75–94.

practice of Christian baptism, they had no connotation of initiation. Second-century rabbinic Judaism later developed some form of initiation via ritual bath for Jewish proselytes, but such rituals "cannot be traced with certainty to the first century."[138] Besides, the rabbinic writings use *telibah* in two ways: to describe an ordinary ablution or to describe an immersion during an initiation ceremony.[139] "But there is no evidence that such ablutions, if they occurred, were 'baptisms,' since there is no reliable evidence that they were tied to an initiation rite, administered, or performed in the presence of witnesses."[140] Indeed, by the time Paul finds himself persecuting Christians in Jerusalem and desirous of extending that persecution to Damascus, he is focused on the purity of Judaism, both Palestinian and Diaspora. Paul was the sort of Jew whose zealousness was obsessive and, in a certain sense, regressive. Christianity was an aberration to Paul because it was unfaithful to Jewish tradition. Paul's quest in Damascus was to restore Jews to Judaism, to bring them back literally and figuratively to Jerusalem, to the traditions of their fathers. That zeal excluded any syncretism whatsoever. Plus, that zeal highlights the tremendous transformation of Paul on the road to Damascus.

Christian Paul

On the road to Damascus, Paul of Tarsus became an apostle. Paul is the last person recorded to have seen the risen Lord. The impact of his conversion on his own life, the life of the nascent Church, and the Church throughout the centuries is unparalleled. As we saw above, Paul's influence is so profound that many reckon him to be the second founder of Christianity, and some go so far as to call him the founder of Christianity. As a Diaspora Jew, Paul was particularly well equipped to understand contemporary paganism, the menace of syncretism, and the politics of religious affiliation. His Damascus experience would forever change his understanding of Judaism as well as his own self-definition. As a Pharisee, he had staked his claim within Judaism against all the other possibilities therein. Among the sea of possibilities of religious attachments and movements within first-century Judaism,[141] Paul was rock solid in his Pharisaic convictions. Thus, a look at his conversion experience is essential because "it is impossible to escape the conclusion that much of his theology can be called a universalization of that experience."[142] Paul's conversion leads without delay to his apostolate—the persecutor becomes the propagator.

---

[138] J. E. Taylor, *The Immerser: John the Baptist within Second Temple Judaism* (Grand Rapids, MI: Eerdmans, 1997) 65.

[139] A. Yarbro Collins, "The Origin of Christian Baptism," *StLit* 19 (1989) 32.

[140] Ibid., 34.

[141] See R. A. Horsley, "Popular Prophetic Movements at the Time of Jesus: Their Principal Features and Social Origins," *JSNT* 26 (1986) 3–27.

[142] J. G. Gager, "Some Notes on Paul's Conversion," *NTS* 27 (1980–81) 703.

Despite the fact that the Pharisee Paul may have been predisposed to the notion of resurrection and that the persecutor Paul may have gleaned some knowledge of Christianity as he sought to root it out of Judaism,[143] nothing could have prepared Paul for his encounter with the risen Lord on the Damascus road. It is Luke, in Acts who thrice recounts the appearance of the Lord to Paul on the road to Damascus, but Paul's references to the event are restrained.

According to Acts 9:1–30, the risen Lord appears to Paul—in a theophany comparable to that of Isaiah's (Isa 6:1–9a) and Ezekiel's (Ezek 1:4–3:11)—as he passes along the Damascus road. The Lord hints at a special mission for Paul, Paul is led into the city of Damascus, and he is left blind for three days until Ananias, directed by the Lord, restores Paul's sight and baptizes him. Immediately thereafter, Paul proclaims Jesus as the son of God in Damascus. This preaching stirs up the anger of the Jews in the city, and Paul flees to Jerusalem. Although Barnabas is able to secure the apostles' acceptance of Paul, Paul's preaching angers the Hellenistic Jews in Jerusalem, who also seek Paul's life. Paul flees to Tarsus, and the next time he is mentioned in Acts we find him at Antioch, again with Barnabas (13:1). The story is repeated twice more in Acts, both in speeches by Paul (22:4–16; 26:9–18). The accounts in Acts fill in the blanks of Paul's own reports of an encounter with the Lord, conversion, and call to mission. But the crux of the matter is found in Paul's own words. The restraint he exercises in mentioning his conversion allows us to deduce the essentials. While there are a plethora of possible allusions to his conversion and its aftermath,[144] three references signify the fulcrum of the incident: 1 Cor 9:1; 15:8; and Gal 1:15–17. Each depicts Paul in the process of defending his apostolic authority. It is important to note that in terms of defense, Paul never appeals to anyone or anything other than Jesus for his apostolic authority.

In 1 Cor 9:1, Paul asks: "Am I not free? Am I not an apostle? Have I not seen Jesus our Lord?" (1 Cor 9:1). This question immediately succeeds Paul's first treatment of idol food in 1 Cor 8:1–13 and precedes his second treatment in 1 Cor 10:1–33. In 8:13, Paul concludes his first discourse on idol food on a note of personal example. And Paul links that personal example to 9:1–4; for "grammatically, these verses remain in the first person singular as in 8.13, and in fact, 9.1–4 continue the theme of Paul's personal experience from 8.13."[145] The rest of chapter 9 is a personal defense of Paul's apostolic rights. That is, "the ἀπολογία could not be a defense of his apostolic *office*—at Corinth."[146] Rather,

---

[143] On this, see ibid., 700.

[144] See S. Kim, *The Origin of Paul's Gospel* (2nd ed.; WUNT 2/4; Tübingen: Mohr [Siebeck], 1984) 3–31. Cf. "Paul's Conversion/Call, James D. G. Dunn, and the New Perspective on Paul" (chap. 1), in idem, *Paul and the New Perspective: Second Thoughts on the Origin of Paul's Gospel* (Grand Rapids, MI: Eerdmans, 2002) 1–84.

[145] W. Willis, "An Apostolic Apologia? The Form and Function of 1 Corinthians 9," *JSNT* 24 (1985) 34.

[146] Ibid. (emphasis original).

it is proof of Paul's freedom from the law, as regards dietary restrictions (chapters 8 and 10); and it is the evidence of his apostolic mission, one similar to that of the OT prophets who speak at the Lord's behest,[147] which he describes in the next verse (9:2): "If to others I am not an apostle, at least I am to you; for you are the seal of my apostleship." That is to say, the first two questions are rhetorical; both expect an immediate and resounding "yes." Likewise, the third: Paul has seen (ἑώρακα) the Lord. The use of ὁράω is well attested in the post-resurrection appearances of Jesus (Matt 28:7, 10; Mark 16:7; Luke 24:34; John 20:18, 25, 29; cf. Matt 28:17; Luke 24:37, 39; John 20:14, 20, 27). This appearance of the Lord is surely a reference to his experience on the Damascus road. "Although Paul does not mention this experience by name, only the most biased exegete would deny that this is what Paul is referring to here and in 15:8, and probably in Gal. 1:12–16 as well."[148]

The exact character of Paul's experience has elicited much attention in modern times, along with the other post-resurrection appearances of the Lord, because of advances in the social sciences.[149] Contemporary insights into human psychology and the nature of human understanding have given rise to a series of questions about the post-resurrection appearances of the Lord: Are they objective or subjective? If objective, how so? If subjective, how so? The traditional explanation, that the post-resurrection appearances are the accounts of men and women who saw the risen Jesus in his glorified body, is no longer facilely accepted. Some sixty years ago, Joseph L. Lilly gathered the four reigning hypotheses against the sighting of a glorified body: (1) that the appearances were subjective visions, akin to hallucinations; (2) that the appearances were objective visions of a spirit in such wise as they gave the impression of a corporeal being; (3) that the appearances were subjective manifestations of the subliminal consciousness wherein what was newly believed objectified itself in a vision; and (4) that the appearances were objective psychic phenomena, akin to ghostly appearances.[150] Lilly examines these hypotheses at some length and dismisses all of them as misunderstandings of the nature of Christ's glorified body, which as wholly unique exhibited properties heretofore unknown but foreshadowed in Jesus' earthly life by such incidents as the Transfiguration (Matt 17:2; Mark 9:2–3; Luke 9:29), walking on water (6:19–20), and miraculous escapes from mobs (Luke 4:30; John 7:30, 44; 8:20, 59; 18:6).[151] Close

---

[147] See H. P. Nasuti, "The Woes of the Prophets and the Rights of the Apostle: The Internal Dynamics of 1 Corinthians 9," *CBQ* 50 (1988) 246–64.

[148] Fee, *First Corinthians*, 395 n. 15.

[149] For a summary of the approaches, see J. J. Pilch, "Psychological and Psychoanalytical Approaches to Interpreting the Bible in a Social-Scientific Context," *BTB* (1997) 112–16.

[150] J. L. Lilly, "The Appearances of the Risen Christ: Objective or Subjective?" *CBQ* 4 (1942) 22–23.

[151] Ibid., 36 et passim.

examination of the hypotheses, though, reveals that the question devolves to two choices rather than four: either the appearances were inside the mind, subjective appearances vis-à-vis hypotheses (1) and (3); or the appearances were outside the mind, objective appearances vis-à-vis hypotheses (2) and (4). Variations on the theme of the objective versus the subjective are legion.[152] For example, John J. Pilch concludes that the appearances of the risen Jesus, when taken in terms of their proper cultural context, are really cases of altered states of consciousness;[153] and Stephen T. Davis concludes that the appearances of the risen Jesus, when taken in their proper textual context, are really cases of the objective manifestation of a glorified body.[154]

A thorough examination of the post-resurrection appearances of Jesus and the psychological and cultural variants of the witnesses is beyond the pale of our study.[155] Even so, the relationship between the post-resurrection appearances of Jesus to his disciples in the gospels and to Paul, recounted either in Acts or in his letters, is strained on one count: the disciples knew the risen Lord in his earthly life, but Paul had never seen Jesus. In this sense, Paul's encounter is *sui generis*, and it behooves us to examine closely what Paul said he saw on the Damascus road and what it meant to him. That is, Paul's Damascus experience is just that—Paul's Damascus experience—and the only one who tells us about it, other than Luke, is Paul himself. In 1 Cor 9:1c, the use of ὁράω not only conforms to the disciples' encounter with the Lord, but it also designates the encounter as Paul understands it in the distinction between an appearance (extramental phenomenon) and a vision (intramental phenomenon). The use of the verb ὁράω, one of the most common verbs of "seeing" in the NT, in its basic sense "denotes seeing as sense-perception, hence eye-witnesses ... being there."[156] In its root meaning and common usage in the NT, particularly with respect to the resurrection appearances, there is no way in which ὁράω itself can be taken to refer to anything other than something external to the observer.[157] In Paul's case, this point is even more apparent when compared to his visionary explanation of the "third heaven" in 2 Cor 12:1–4. There Paul shows his own

---

[152] For a cogent introduction to all the issues involved, see G. O'Collins, "The Resurrection: The State of the Questions," in *The Resurrection of Jesus: An Interdisciplinary Symposium on the Resurrection of Jesus* (ed. S. T. Davis, D. Kendall, and G. O'Collins; Oxford: Oxford University Press, 1997) 5–28.

[153] J. J. Pilch, "Appearances of the Risen Jesus in Cultural Context: Experiences of Alternate Reality," *BTB* (1998) 52–60.

[154] S. T. Davis, "'Seeing' the Risen Jesus," in *The Resurrection of Jesus*, ed. Davis, Kendall, and O'Collins, 126–47.

[155] The divergent viewpoints are well represented on the subjective end by G. Lüdemann, *What Really Happened to Jesus: An Historical Approach to the Resurrection* (trans. J. Bowden; Louisville: Westminster John Knox, 1995); and on the objective end by G. O'Collins, *Interpreting the Resurrection: Examining the Major Problems in the Stories of Jesus' Resurrection* (New York/Mahwah, NJ: Paulist, 1988); and idem "The Resurrection Revisited," *Greg* 79 (1998) 169–72.

[156] W. Michaelis, "ὁράω," *TDNT* 5:317.

[157] Ibid., 355–61.

understanding of the distinction between the two, between an appearance and a vision. "Basic here is the observation that in 2 Cor 12:1 Paul does not reckon the Damascus experience among the ὀπτασίαι and ἀποκαλύψεις κυρίου. In 12:2 ff. Paul says nothing about seeing the κύριος in his rapture, and the passages in which he does speak about seeing the Lord always refer to the one experience, i.e., that on the Damascus road."[158] To be sure, Paul demonstrates in the Corinthian letters a distinction with a difference between experiences of the Lord. "To the degree that the rapture of 2 Cor 12:2 ff. was definitely an ecstatic experience, we are forced to conclude, in line with his own judgment as to the special role of the ecstatic element in the pneumatic life, that the Damascus experience could not have for him the characteristics of ecstatic rapture."[159] Insofar as Paul understood things, even if there are a number of contemporary explanations for such things,[160] the experience on the Damascus road was an appearance of the risen Lord.

As we have noted, in 1 Cor 9:1c, Paul uses the verb ὁράω. Paul also uses ὁράω in 1 Cor 15:8: "Last of all, as to one untimely born, he appeared (ὤφθη) also to me." In fact, ὁράω appears three times earlier in the chapter (1 Cor 15:5, 6, 7), wherein Paul recounts the appearance of the Lord to Cephas, to over five hundred brothers, and to James. Gordon D. Fee sums it up:

> Paul is here referring to his having seen the risen Lord on the Damascus road, which he did not consider a visionary experience but an actual resurrection appearance of a kind with the others in this series. The sure evidence of that is (a) his actually including his experience in this enumeration, (b) the repetition of the verb "appeared," and (c) the language he uses to describe his inclusion, that it is "last of all" and "as to one abnormally born."[161]

There is much scholarly discussion as to the rationale of Paul's presentation and arrangement of these appearances of the Lord in 1 Corinthians,[162] but his report clearly demonstrates two things. First, it is proof of the resurrection of Jesus that will bolster, if not provide the foundation for, all that Paul says in 1 Corinthians 15. Second, it manifests Paul's own understanding of his experience on the Damascus road, viz., that the risen Lord appeared to him just as he had appeared to other apostles and Christians. Thus, the criterion of witnesses is twofold and, thereby, doubly important for Paul's following argument on behalf of the resur-

---

[158] Ibid., 357.

[159] Ibid.

[160] See J. L. Lilly, "The Conversion of Saint Paul: The Validity of His Testimony to the Resurrection of Jesus Christ," *CBQ* 6 (1944) 180–204; see also idem, "The Appearances of Christ: Objective or Subjective?"

[161] Fee, *First Corinthians*, 732. See also Fee's comments linking 1 Cor 15:8 to 1 Cor 9:1 and Gal 1:12–16 (ibid., 394–96).

[162] The various points of view are discussed in J. Lambrecht, "Line of Thought in 1 Cor 15,1–11," *Greg* 72 (1991) 655–70.

rection of the dead: there are those to whom the Lord appeared, viz., Cephas, James (whose names must have been familiar to the Corinthians) and hundreds of others; so too, Paul has seen the same Jesus—the separate sightings lend mutual support to themselves.

Moreover, Paul portrays the experience on the Damascus road as an OT theophany and, simultaneously, as the establishment of a mission in Gal 1:15–17: "But when he who had set me apart before I was born, and had called me through his grace, was pleased to reveal his Son to me, in order that I might preach him among the Gentiles, I did not confer with flesh and blood, nor did I go up to Jerusalem to those who were apostles before me, but I went away into Arabia; and again I returned to Damascus." Unpacking Paul's words verse by verse brings much to light. First, v. 15 is reminiscent of Jer 1:5: "Before I formed you in the womb, I knew you and before you were born I consecrated you; I appointed you a prophet to the nations." This imagery also suggests a strong link to 1 Cor 15:8a. "In two very similar texts Paul refers to himself in language associated with birth. . . . This similarity calls attention to yet another parallel between 1 Corinthians 15 and Galatians 1, which further underscores their relationship: both texts make reference to Isaiah 49."[163] Additionally, Gal 1:15 harkens to Acts 13:2, wherein Paul and Barnabas are set apart by the Holy Spirit; Rom 1:1, wherein Paul speaks of himself as being set apart for the gospel, and finally in the themes of separation for service found in the OT (Exod 13:12; 19:12, 23; Lev 13:4, 5; Ezek 45:1, 4).[164] Added to this, Paul puts the onus of revelation squarely on God the Father rather than on Jesus the Son in v. 16a: "[God] was pleased to reveal his Son to me." The revelation of Jesus is the revelation of God. This links v. 16a with v. 12, for "this phrase suggests that 'the revelation of Jesus Christ' in verse 12 is to be interpreted as an objective genitive: God revealed his Son to Paul."[165] Immediately associated with God's revelation is Paul's call to mission. Paul is called in order that (ἵνα) he might preach to the Gentiles; the same word, ἔθνος, is used in Acts 9:15; Isa 49:6; and Jer 1:5. Thus, Paul's call and apostolic mission are one and the same.

To emphasize the divine font of his revelation and gospel, Paul is painstakingly clear about his source; so clear, indeed, that he wishes to highlight it by a *via negativa*. Paul conferred (προσανεθέμην) neither with flesh and blood nor with the apostles in Jerusalem. The force of προσαντίθμι is stronger than just "to confer." It "has the more technical sense of consulting with someone who is recognized as a qualified interpreter about the significance of some sign—a dream, or omen, or portent, or whatever."[166] In other words, Paul uses a word

---

[163] G. W. E. Nickelsburg, "An Ἔκτρωμα, Though Appointed from the Womb: Paul's Apostolic Self-Description in 1 Corinthians 15 and Galatians 1," *HTR* 79 (1986) 202.

[164] F. J. Matera, *Galatians* (SacPag 9; Collegeville, MN: Liturgical [Glazier], 1992) 59.

[165] Ibid.

[166] J. M. G. Dunn, "The Relationship between Paul and Jerusalem according to Galatians 1 and 2," *NTS* 28 (1982) 462.

that conveys the absolute character of his encounter with and consequential mission from the Lord. "Flesh and blood" (cf. 1 Cor 15:50; Eph 6:12; Matt 16:17) is a simple euphemism for humanity.[167] There is no man to whom Paul had to turn for interpretation or authentication of his experience. But Paul goes even further: he does not even have to consult the (other) apostles. The group mentioned in v. 17 is evidently broader than "the Twelve" (see 1 Cor 15:5–7) and rooted in Jerusalem. "Had Paul gone immediately to Jerusalem following his conversion it would have been difficult to contest the claim that his understanding of this revelation had been given him when he consulted with the Jerusalem apostles. But precisely such a consultation is what Paul emphatically denies."[168] The gospel he preaches did not originate with man, and no consultation is necessary, even with others called to be apostles before Paul.[169] Instead of discerning his call, Paul went directly to fulfilling it. The subsequent troubles in Damascus, which Paul recounts in 2 Cor 11:32–33, can only be explained by the fact that Paul set out straightaway to preach the gospel and make converts.[170] F. F. Bruce presents it plainly:

> With no conscious preparation, Paul found himself instantaneously compelled by what he saw and heard to acknowledge that Jesus of Nazareth, the crucified one, was alive after his passion, vindicated and exalted by God, and was now conscripting him into his service. There could be no resistance to this compulsion, no kicking against the goad which was driving him in the opposite direction to that which he had hitherto been pursuing. He capitulated forthwith to the commands of this new master; a conscript he might be, but henceforth also a devoted and lifelong volunteer.[171]

This conforms closely to the same situation we find in Acts 9:18–30. Therein, Paul goes promptly to the synagogues to discourse on the Son of God after his baptism at the hands of Ananias. The experience of the risen Lord is the defining moment in Paul's life and apostolate.[172] It leads Paul to evangelize immediately. Regrettably, as Paul (2 Cor 11:32–33) and Luke (Acts 9:23–25) tell us, the Damascus apostolate came to an abrupt end when Paul had to flee the city for fear of his life.

Paul is by far the foremost of the earliest propagators of Christianity other than the Lord himself. His letters show him to be the most prolific and, perhaps,

---

[167] See Jeremias, "Flesh and Blood," 151–59.

[168] Dunn, "The Relationship between Paul and Jerusalem," 463.

[169] Matera, *Galatians*, 61.

[170] Murphy-O'Connor, *Paul: A Critical Life*, 82. So too, e.g., Bruce, *Paul: Apostle of the Heart Set Free*, 81; Betz, *Galatians*, 74; and Matera, *Galatians*, 61.

[171] Bruce, *Paul: Apostle of the Heart Set Free*, 75.

[172] For more, see B. Corley, "Interpreting Paul's Conversion—Then and Now," in *The Road to Damascus: The Impact of Paul's Conversion on His Life, Thought, and Ministry* (ed. R. N. Longenecker; MNTS; Grand Rapids, MI: Eerdmans, 1997) 1–17.

the most profound author in the NT. Luke's Acts, especially chapters 13–28, show Paul to be the most effective evangelist of the nascent Christian faith in terms of the number of converts made and the expanse of territory covered. According to Paul, there was a seventeen-year hiatus between his conversion in A.D. 33 and what we have come to call the Council of Jerusalem (Gal 2:1–10; Acts 15:4–29) in A.D. 51. Although Luke's account of Paul's First (Acts 13:1–15:3) and Second Missionary Journey (Acts 15:36–18:22) conflates and confuses the chronology of Paul's evangelizing, Luke's general theme is clear, viz., that Paul was "on the job" from the beginning. The principal details are related by Paul in Galatians. Immediately after his conversion and initial evangelization, Paul "went away into Arabia" and again returned to Damascus (Gal 1:17). After three years in Arabia and Damascus, Paul "went up to Jerusalem to visit Cephas, and remained with him fifteen days" (Gal 1:18). Secondary details are related in 2 Cor 11:32–33, wherein we read that Paul fled Damascus due to the wrath of King Aretas.[173] In addition to the details we read in Paul's letters, much of Paul's activities are recounted in Luke's Acts, but there are several omissions in both accounts and several discrepancies between them.

Paul states clearly that he was in Arabia and Damascus for three years before making a return to Jerusalem (Gal 1:17–18). Luke, though he does not state a duration of time, leaves the reader with the impression that Paul's journey to Jerusalem came about shortly after his conversion. On this, we certainly have to follow Paul. But what was Paul doing during that time? The temporal sequence aside, Paul tells us absolutely nothing about what transpired in those three years, except that he went into Arabia and returned to Damascus before journeying to Jerusalem. Luke tells us specifically that the time was passed by preaching in synagogues. There Paul confounded the Jews "by proving that Jesus was the Christ" to the extent that they sought to kill him; therewith he took off from Damascus and went to Jerusalem (Acts 9:20–25). Luke's account seems a bit off keel: Luke admits no knowledge of Arabia, no trouble with anyone other than Jews. According to Paul's own reminiscence, he fled the city for fear of the pagan King Aretas rather than the Jews of Damascus (2 Cor 11:32–33). With such spotty information, we can only assume that Paul began preaching in Damascus, moved his evangelization into the larger surrounding area of the so-called "Arabia of the Nabataeans,"[174] and eventually returned to Damascus. Some scholars speculate that Paul's mission there was primarily to Gentiles, in accord with his conversion experience;[175] others speculate that his mission was directed mostly to Hellenized Jews in the region.[176] For the pur-

---

[173] See D. A. Campbell, "An Anchor for Pauline Chronology: Paul's Flight from 'the Ethnarch of King Aretas' (2 Corinthians 11:32–33)," *JBL* 121 (2002) 279–302.

[174] For the details, see "Arabia and Aretas IV, King of the Nabataeans (9 BCE–40 CE)" (chap. 4), in Hengel and Schwemer, *Paul between Damascus and Antioch*, 106–26.

[175] For example, Murphy-O'Connor, *Paul: A Critical Life*, 85 et passim.

[176] For example, Hengel and Schwemer, *Paul between Damascus and Antioch*, 110 et passim.

poses of our study, it is sufficient to note that Paul's conversion led to an evangelical zeal, no doubt of the caliber he had evidenced as a persecutor of Christianity, that was instantaneously brought to fruition in Damascus. Although Damascus was certainly a thoroughly pagan and Hellenized city, Josephus attests to a considerable Jewish population.[177] With such ample opportunity to preach to both Jew and Gentile, it is safe to say that Paul probably approached either group as situations presented themselves. So too, he probably provoked both the ire of Jew and Gentile to the point of making his position in Damascus and its environs untenable, even life threatening.

Paul and Luke tell us that Paul had set off from Damascus to Jerusalem, but there is some deviation as to Paul's motive and what happened in Jerusalem. Paul claims that he came simply to visit Cephas and stayed fifteen days (Gal 1:18). Luke claims that Paul sought to join the disciples, that his acceptance was only secured by Barnabas' defense, that he preached extensively in Jerusalem at the risk of his life (once more), and that it was necessary to send him back to Tarsus (Acts 9:26–30). Again, we have to follow Paul, especially since Gal 1:16c and the tone of Galatians 2 do not admit of any need on Paul's part for affirmation or confirmation. Paul claims to depart for Syria and Cilicia after the fifteen days, with no mention of apostolic activity in Jerusalem itself. Instead, Paul claims that he was little known in Judea, yet that the news of his previous evangelization had given the disciples cause to glorify God (Gal 1:22–24). Even if Barnabas were the relater of such news, he hardly would have served as a mediator between Paul and anyone in Jerusalem. The crux of the matter, though, is that Paul and Peter met with one another. Speculation soars as to their conversations and conclusions.[178] Except to say that their encounter was a precursor in some fashion to the Council of Jerusalem—either in initial concord or discord as to the mission and conversion of Gentiles that is so richly described both in Galatians 2 and Acts 15—conjecture is futile. Nonetheless, Paul and Luke concur insofar as Paul once more takes his show on the road in the same general direction: Tarsus in Cilicia (Luke) and Syria (Paul).

If the three years between Damascus and Jerusalem are somewhat unexplained, the next fourteen years between Paul's first visit to Jerusalem after his conversion (including his ministry in Syria, Cilicia, Galatia, Macedonia, and Athens) and Corinth remain almost impenetrable at some points. As we have noted, from Jerusalem Paul "went into the regions of Syria and Cilicia" (Gal 1:21), and we are safe in assuming that he visited Antioch on the Orontes (the capital of the Roman province of Syria) and Tarsus in Cilicia in those years. Yet there is an eight- to nine-year lull in Paul's own chronology, until we can estab-

---

[177] At one point, Josephus claims 10,000 (*B.J.* 2.561); at another point, he claims 18,000 (ibid. 7.368).

[178] See Murphy-O'Connor, *Paul: A Critical Life*, 91–95.

lish his presence once again at Antioch in A.D. 46.[179] Clearly, the link established by Luke—that Paul's apostolate in Corinth coincided, at least in part, with Gallio's term of office there (Acts 18:12)—"is the linchpin of Pauline chronology."[180] "The encounter must have taken place between July, when Gallio arrived in Corinth, and September A.D. 51, the last date when he could have sailed to Rome."[181] This ties in quite nicely with Paul's relation in Galatians 1 and 2 to the effect that he spent three years in Damascus/Arabia before his first visit to Jerusalem, plus fourteen years until his second visit, which puts Paul back at Jerusalem in 51. Whereas we cannot be sure of Paul's activities between A.D. 37 and 46, "this gap is to some extent filled by a mission of Paul and Barnabas in Cyprus and southern Asia Minor (Acts 13–14)."[182] That is to say, we cannot be precisely sure of Paul's activities, but the preponderance of evidence suggests that he was preaching the gospel throughout Syria and Cilicia.[183] Working, then, from A.D. 50, Paul was at Antioch in 46, Galatia in 46–48, Macedonia (Philippi and Thessalonica) in 48–50, Corinth in the spring of 50, and Jerusalem in 51.[184] Given the information that we can glean from his letters, Paul founded churches in Galatia, proceeded to found a church in Philippi, and then one in Thessalonica. From Thessalonica, Paul passed through Athens, and then on to Corinth and, later Jerusalem. Paul tells us that his stay in Galatia was accidental, the result of an ailment (Gal 4:13), that he had visited Thessalonica after Philippi (1 Thess 2:2), and that his arrival in Thessalonica was preceded by a mission to Philippi, wherein he had been "shamefully treated" (1 Thess 2:2). In addition, Paul remarks that financial aid had come from Philippi when he was in Thessalonica for which he was immensely grateful (Phil 4:15–20; 2 Cor 11:8–9). Paul also tells us that subsequent to his stay in Thessalonica he had been in Athens (1 Thess 3:1). All of this leaves more than substantial time for Paul to be in Corinth by 50, and all of it squares with Luke's account in Acts 16 and 17. Moreover, Luke has Paul returning to Antioch after the Jerusalem Council (Acts 15:30; 18:22) in accord with Paul's own recounting of the Council and its immediate circumstances in Gal 2:1–14.

The real difficulty is not the dating of the Council vis-à-vis Paul's apostolic work, but the significance of it. According to Paul, the Council occurred after fourteen years of productive ministry, including his ministry in Europe; according to Luke, the European ministry is initiated with the Council. It would seem that Luke's intention is simply to ground Paul's activities as an expansion of the

---

[179] Ibid., 95 and also 26–28.
[180] Ibid., 15.
[181] Ibid., 21.
[182] Ibid., 95.
[183] See J. Murphy-O'Connor, "Pauline Missions before the Jerusalem Conference," *RB* 89 (1982) 71–91.
[184] Murphy-O'Connor, *Paul: A Critical Life*, 28.

missionary efforts begun in Jerusalem rather than in Antioch.[185] In fact, when Paul visited Jerusalem, "he had reached the zenith of his career."[186] From his conversion until his arrival in Corinth and subsequent presence in Jerusalem, Paul was busy about his apostolic work. In Gal 1:11–12, Paul declares to the Galatians that he received the gospel from Christ; in 1 Cor 15:1–2, Paul declares to the Corinthians that he passed on what he had received. As John Knox remarks of Paul:

> He remained in the neighborhood of Damascus for three years or more. After a visit to Jerusalem to become acquainted with Cephas, he returned to Syria (probably to Antioch), then went on (probably soon afterward) to Cilicia. In the course of the next fourteen years he lived and worked in Galatia, Macedonia, Greece and Asia, and possibly elsewhere. He ran into increasing difficulty with conservative Jewish Christians, probably from Judea, and finally went to Jerusalem to talk with the leaders there about the growing rift. This conference ended, as we have seen with their giving him the right hand of fellowship, but with the stipulation of aid for the poor. This aid Paul set about raising. In Romans we see him, the collection completed, ready to embark for Jerusalem to deliver it but apprehensive as to what will happen there.[187]

Paul remains somewhat uneasy because his mandate and ministry do not come from Jerusalem, despite the fact that Luke would have it that way, but from the Lord himself. Then again, we must take care not to posit a false distinction between Palestinian and Hellenistic Christianity,[188] as if Paul's Christianity were somehow deviant; nor may we whitewash the ethnic differences that no doubt arose between Diaspora Jews like Paul and Palestinian Jews like Peter.[189] The long and short of it is that there were dynamic tensions in the early Church, and these tensions were not only recognized among the earliest Christians, but they were resolved in communal fellowship and shared commitment for the poor. Although an exposé of the earliest Christian interrelationships is beyond the pale of our study, we note that both Paul in Galatians and Luke in Acts acknowledge the particular mandate given to Paul, who was "entrusted with the gospel to the uncircumcised" (Gal 2:7). Similarly, we note that Paul's apostolic zeal is part and parcel of a tenure inaugurated directly by Christ.

---

[185] Ibid., 131.
[186] Knox, *Chapters in a Life of Paul*, 40.
[187] Ibid., 41–42.
[188] See H. Marshall, "Palestinian and Hellenistic Christianity: Some Critical Comments," *NTS* 19 (1972–73) 271–87.
[189] On this, see C. D. Stanley, "'Neither Jew nor Greek': Ethnic Conflict in Graeco-Roman Society," *JSNT* 64 (1996) 101–24. For the larger theological perspective, see G. Lüdemann, *Opposition to Paul in Jewish Christianity* (trans. M. E. Boring; Minneapolis: Fortress, 1989).

Paul and Readings of 1 Corinthians 15:29

What sort of Christian was Paul? No doubt, if the *corpus Paulinum* and Acts be taken as any indication, Paul was one of the most important propagators of Christianity in its history. But there is more to the man than his apostolate, for that apostolate is the result of the conviction that Jesus is the Messiah of Israel. The zealousness of Saul the Jew is the zealousness of Paul the Christian. The Pharisaic insight of resurrection is realized in the sight of the resurrected Jesus. The Jew who took on a mission to persecute Christianity on behalf of the Lord is now given a mission to propagate Christianity by the Lord. The lion's share of that mission, as Paul fulfills it, is in preaching the gospel so that Christ might be made known and accepted as the Savior. Throughout, baptism seems to be intimately linked with the acceptance of Christ,[190] no matter what confessional position one holds as to baptism's efficacy. In fact, many hold 1 Cor 1:17 to be an instance of Paul minimizing the importance of baptism in light of his evangelical mission. Even though we dispute this claim, it does recall to our attention that none of those who read 1 Cor 15:29 as a reference to vicarious baptism do so on the basis of such baptism having any foundation in Paul's theology or preaching.

As we noted in Chapter I of our study, many scholars hold the majority reading of vicarious baptism. Yet those same scholars conclude that Paul would have been predisposed against anything resembling vicarious baptism. Arthur Carr, who holds that the Corinthians may have initiated the bizarre custom of vicarious baptism in order to aid friends who would have converted had they been alive in time to hear Paul's preaching, maintains that Paul would have frowned upon such a custom, though he did not condemn it directly.[191] H. V. Martin, the only proponent of the majority reading who maintains that Paul approved of vicarious baptism, reads the verse just as Carr does, except that Martin claims Paul's approval of the practice. Closely read, with his understanding of proleptic baptism,[192] the approval of which Martin speaks is more an affirmation of incorporation into the kingdom than of vicarious baptism *per se*. Herbert Preisker,[193] James Moffatt,[194] Mathis Rissi,[195] and C. K. Barrett,[196] like Carr, also hold that Paul could not have approved of such a practice; yet they are willing to suppose a tacit neutrality on Paul's part—insofar as he offers no strident objection to the practice in 1 Corinthians—because Paul took the practice to be a disordered defense of the resurrection, but did not wish to gainsay any-

---

[190] We consider this closely in Chapter IV of our study below. For now, see Fee, *First Corinthians*, 63–64.

[191] Carr, "Baptism for the Dead," 371–74.

[192] Martin, "Baptism for the Dead," 193.

[193] Preisker, "Die Vikariatstaufe I Cor 15:29," 301–2.

[194] Moffatt, *First Corinthians*, 252–53.

[195] Rissi, "Die Taufe für die Toten," 89.

[196] Barrett, *First Corinthians*, 362.

thing defensive of the resurrection of Christ and his dead. Likewise, all the other commentators cited in Chapter I put a distance between Paul and vicarious baptism, nuance his understanding of the alleged Corinthian practice, and rightly acknowledge that Paul's paramount emphasis in 1 Corinthians 15 is the resurrection of the dead.

As we also saw in Chapter I of our study, James Downey and Richard E. DeMaris read 15:29 as a reference to a vicarious baptism that is the result of syncretism. Downey and DeMaris both contend that vicarious baptism arose from sources outside Paul. However, Downey focuses on the common faith of Paul and the Corinthian Christians, whereas DeMaris (whom we consider again below) posits a gulf between the two on the issue at hand. For Downey, Paul and his followers have fallen victim to fear of cosmic powers and vicarious baptism is the means of protection for those who died unbaptized.[197] Indeed, for Downey, Paul may have sanctioned the practice because he too dreaded powers such as those mentioned in 1 Cor 8:6. Vicarious baptism notwithstanding, Downey's rendition of 15:29 hinges on Paul. Our extensive investigation of Paul indicates that just the opposite is true: Paul's cosmology was hardly so primitive. Moreover, the recent work of Chris Forbes shows that the reigning scholarly opinion of Paul as either drawing such imagery from Jewish apocalypticism or attempting to demythologize the same in passages such as Rom 8:38–39 is ungrounded.[198] Instead, Forbes shows that Paul works "creatively between the angelology and demonology of his Jewish heritage and the world-view of the thoughtful Graeco-Roman philosophical amateur."[199] It would seem that Paul is "in part a product of decades of intelligent engagement with Hellenistic Judaism and Graeco-Roman culture."[200] Intelligent engagement of that nature precludes the primitive spiritualism that Downey sees in Paul and his nascent Christian communities.

Thus, after a somewhat laborious look at Paul, Jewish zealot turned Christian zealot, we find a Christian missionary particularly well suited to preach Christ to the Gentiles because of his background in Diaspora Judaism and because of his unbridled enthusiasm to answer a personal call of the Lord. If the needle of vicarious baptism is to be found anywhere in Paul, Corinth, or Corinthian Christianity, we can safely say that we have eliminated Paul as a possibility. Reiterating the fact that nothing like vicarious baptism is found anywhere else in the NT, early Church, or first century, we also note that nothing like it is found in any of Paul's other letters, insofar as we have them, or in

---

[197] Downey, "1 Cor 15:29," 33–34.

[198] C. Forbes, "Paul's Principalities and Powers: Demythologizing Apocalyptic?" *JSNT* 82 (2001) 61–88.

[199] Idem, "Pauline Demonology and/or Cosmology? Principalities, Powers and the Elements of the World in their Hellenistic Context," *JSNT* 85 (2002) 73.

[200] Ibid.

GRECO-ROMAN CORINTH

By the time Paul arrived there in the early spring of A.D. 50, Corinth had a long and vibrant history of its own. The story of ancient Corinth is easily divided into two periods: the Greek and the Roman. With roots going back to the fifth millennium B.C., the Greek city of Corinth enjoyed considerable political stability and economic success. That stability and success lasted until 146 B.C., when the city was destroyed by the Romans. The city lay more or less fallow for the next hundred years, until it was reestablished as a colony by Julius Caesar in 44 B.C. As a Roman city, Corinth once again flourished. So too, did the Christianity introduced by Paul. But the city suffered two severe earthquakes in A.D. 365 and 375. Classical Corinth eventually came to an end when it was burned to the ground in A.D. 395 by the Visigothic chief Alaric who went on to sack Rome itself in A.D. 410.

The City of Corinth

Not so unlike Paul's own background, then, the story of ancient Corinth is a "tale of two cities." The greatest common denominator between Greek and Roman Corinth is the city's unique location, which poised it for trade. Corinth controlled the Isthmus of Corinth, a narrow stretch of land, between the Saronic and Corinthian Gulfs, which joins central Greece to the Peloponnese, and afforded Corinth two ports: Cenchreae on the Saronic and Lechaeon on the Corinthian. The success of Corinth lay in its ability to serve as a trading center to both. Though the roots of the city may go back as far as the fifth millennium B.C., the city gained prominence with the rise of the Greek city-states. Trade was significantly bolstered by the Corinthian tyrant Periander (625–585 B.C.) who commissioned a roadway across the narrow isthmus for the transportation of light ships. Ships were drawn along on this grooved tract not unlike a railroad. The roadway enabled ships to avoid sailing around the whole of Greece. This was not only convenient, but it was much safer than a voyage around Cape Maleae, a most dangerous trek according to Strabo (*Geogr.* 8.6.20).

As a center of wealth and culture, Corinth was a leading city in the political struggles among Macedonia, the southern city-states of Greece, and eventually the Roman empire. Corinth became a leading city in the Achaean League after the Second Macedonian War, when the Roman general and victor, Titus Quinctius Flamininus, declared the freedom of the Greeks in 196 B.C. at the stadium in Isthmia. However, the relationship between Rome and the League was strained from the start and was uneasy for fifty years as Roman military strength grew. In 146 B.C., the League declared war on Sparta, an act which the Romans considered a declaration of independence and, therefore, an act of subversion against Rome. Rome responded quickly against Corinth. Quintus Caecilius Metellus, the Roman governor of Macedonia, attacked the city by land; he was quickly succeeded by Lucius Mummius Achaicus, a consul and general, who attacked by sea. Mummius' destruction of the city was total: the city was looted and burned to the ground. Thus it lay, with only minimal habitation, until 44 B.C. In that year, the year of his own death, Caesar ordered that Corinth (and Carthage, also destroyed in 146 B.C.) should be refounded as a Roman *colonia*. Caesar recognized the importance of Corinth for trade and defense. In order to secure its fidelity to Rome, the new Colonia Laus Iulia Corintheiensis would be repopulated by Roman freedmen and veterans. As with its Greek predecessor, Roman Corinth began to thrive almost immediately.

Contemporary classical and biblical scholarship have been careful to distinguish Greek Corinth from Roman Corinth. The scholarly consensus is best illustrated by Murphy-O'Connor in *St. Paul's Corinth*: "One of the great commercial centers of the eastern Mediterranean, it was destroyed by the Romans in 146 B.C. and refounded as a colony by Julius Caesar in 44 B.C. Thus, there were in fact two Corinths, one Greek and the other Roman, each with its distinctive institutions and ethos."[201] This consensus was disputed by Wendell Willis in "Corinthusne deletus est?"[202] According to Willis, the small population and sporadic trading activity between 146 and 44 B.C. is indicative of a continuum, albeit a limited one, rather than a total historical rupture.[203] But Willis' challenge was taken up by David W. J. Gill in "Corinth: A Roman Colony in Achaea."[204] Gill acknowledges that there was some continuity, in that some original inhabitants of the city must have returned after its destruction and the departure of Roman troops, but he notes:

> Although there is some evidence for activity at Corinth between the destruction by Mummius and the refoundation, it would be misleading to suggest that there was a civic continuity. It is right for both classical archaeologists and New Testament scholars to stress the Roman nature of the city which was visited by Paul in the first century A.D.[205]

So was the Corinth of Paul's day primarily Greek or Roman? On this issue, it is best to steer a middle course. Such a middle course acknowledges the breakdown of civic life between the destruction of the city and its later reestablishment as a *colonia*, while allowing for the return of some inhabitants

---

[201] J. Murphy-O'Connor, *St. Paul's Corinth: Texts and Archeology* (2nd ed.; GNS 6; Collegeville, MN: Liturgical [Glazier], 1990) 1.
[202] W. Willis, "Corinthusne deletus est? *BZ* 35 (1991) 233–41.
[203] Ibid., 241.
[204] D. W. J. Gill, "Corinth: A Roman Colony in Achaea," *BZ* 37 (1993) 259–64.
[205] Ibid., 264.

immediately after the destruction. "Set in the midst of an immensely fertile area, Corinth had served as the principal market, and probably continued to serve as an exchange center though on a greatly reduced scale."[206] To be sure, Paul encountered an almost thoroughly Roman Corinth, but its Grecian roots are worthy of consideration.

Ancient Greek Corinth enjoyed a particularly handsome reputation. For the most part, the Greek city, like the Roman one later built on its foundations, was a city of commerce. Trade brought great wealth and diversity to the city. Corinth's brisk commercial trade and the frequent passage of ships not only increased income, but also allowed for the quick sale of native Corinthian products, especially ceramics, textiles, and bronze.[207] Combined with their vigorous trade and concomitant skills, the Corinthians were expert craftsmen. Herodotus remarked that the Corinthians loathed artisans less than other Greeks (*Hist.* 2.167); the city was also known for its fine architecture and stonework, hence the "Corinthian" capital.[208] Diversity in population and the exchange of language and ideas though brisk commercial interaction contributed to Corinth's reputation as a city of learning and culture. Although it never achieved the intellectual status of its rival city-state, Athens, Corinth evidenced noteworthy scholarly activity. The reputation for learning and culture in the city was very much alive in the days of Cicero, who visited the ruined city between 79 and 77 B.C., and spoke of it as "the light of all Greece" (*Leg. man.* 5).

Corinth also enjoyed a particularly salacious reputation. Murphy-O'Connor provides a laundry list of citations by ancient authors: "Aristophanes coined the verb *korinthiazesthai*, 'to fornicate' (*Fr.* 354). Philetaerus and Poliochus wrote plays entitled *Korinthiastēs*, 'The Whoremonger' (Athenaeus, *Deipn.* 31c, 559a). Plato used *korinthia korē*, 'a Corinthian girl,' to mean a prostitute (*Resp.* 404d)."[209] Strabo claimed that Corinth hosted 1,000 sacred prostitutes (*Geogr.* 8.6.20). This number seems excessive; yet there is no doubt that temple prostitution was as common as it was in other ancient Greek cities. But it was "Athenian writers that made Corinth the symbol of commercialized love."[210] This was, no doubt, an outgrowth of Corinth's eminence as a wealthy port city. "In reality no better or worse than its contemporaries,"[211] Corinth seems nonetheless to have outshone them in ill repute. For example, it was thought that the city allowed sexual intercourse within its temple precincts, an act of defilement among most Greeks, but the same thing was suspected in Eryx in Sicily and Comana in Asia

---

[206] Murphy-O'Connor, *St. Paul's Corinth*, 48 (see also 44). Cf. Gill, "Corinthusne," 233 n. 2.

[207] See J. Murphy-O'Connor, "Corinthian Bronze," *RB* 90 (1983) 23–26.

[208] On this, see G. Hersey, *The Lost Meaning of Classical Architecture* (Cambridge, MA: MIT Press, 1988) 65–67.

[209] J. Murphy-O'Connor, "Corinth," *ABD* 1:1135–36. See also idem, *St. Paul's Corinth*, 58.

[210] Murphy-O'Connor, "Corinth," 1135.

[211] Ibid., 1136; see also 1338.

Minor.[212] In any case, the profligate characterization of the city continued through Roman times. But, as we shall see, this may have had to do as much with the mores of the city under the Romans themselves as it had to do with their Greek predecessors.

The strikingly alive and boldly attractive city that Paul evangelized, only a hundred or so years after its rebuilding, was Roman Corinth.[213] "In Paul's time, Corinth had eclipsed Athens in political importance and in economic and intellectual life."[214] Corinth's restoration occurred in a remarkably short span of time. Though it is likely that some of its original (Greek) residents remained in the city, the new settlers were mostly freed slaves (Strabo, *Geogr.* 8.6.23). These new settlers were perhaps about three thousand or so, if we assume the same number as those sent to resettle Carthage (Appian, *Hist. rom.* 8.136). They were not necessarily Romans; instead they were slaves who had once been brought to Rome from throughout the empire. From Rome they brought the skills they had learned as slaves. Such skillfulness proved invaluable in restarting an economy. According to Strabo, they found their first capital in robbing graves; they also sold the terra-cotta reliefs and bronze vessels they found at high price (*Geogr.* 8.6).[215] A new economy was quickly born, and a prosperous city arose from far-reaching trade and the ability of its citizens to provide extensive services.

Donald Engels, in *Roman Corinth: An Alternative Model for the Classical City*, remarks: "After Rome, itself, Athens, and Jerusalem, and perhaps Antioch, we know more of human interest that occurred in [Roman Corinth] than for almost any other Roman city. For this, we must thank our sources: Strabo, Plutarch, Pausanias, Apuleius, and, above all, Saint Paul."[216] Engles' chief contribution to Corinthian scholarship has been to establish Roman Corinth as a service city rather than a consumer city. That is, he demonstrates that Corinth did not have the means of production or agricultural strength to support itself, as would a consumer city, a city which produces goods and grows foodstuffs to the point of near self-sufficiency, a city whose trade is incidental to its survival. Instead, Corinth's was a service economy.[217] Engels explains:

---

[212] See P. Green, *Classical Bearings: Interpreting Ancient History and Culture* (Berkeley: University of California Press, 1989) 139, with 286 n. 17.

[213] For a vivid account of the sights Paul would have encountered, see J. Murphy-O'Connor, "The Corinth that Saint Paul Saw," *BA* 47 (1984) 147–59.

[214] S. E. Johnson, *Paul the Apostle and His Cities* (GNS 21; Wilmington, Del.: Glazier, 1987) 97.

[215] For Strabo's texts and a commentary, see Murphy-O'Connor, "Strabo," in *St. Paul's Corinth*, 53–74.

[216] D. Engels, *Roman Corinth: An Alternative Model for the Classical City* (Chicago and London: University of Chicago Press, 1990) 1. These texts are all presented in Murphy-O'Connor's *St. Paul's Corinth*.

[217] See Engels, "The Service Economy" (chap. 3), in *Roman Corinth*, 43–65.

The city of Corinth provided many services which were unavailable in the towns, villas, and villages of the countryside. These services may be divided into two types, primary, or attractive services, and secondary services. Primary services would include religious, educational, cultural, and judicial activities that brought rural residents into the city. While in the city, these individuals would need secondary services such as food, temporary lodging, or the use of a public bath or latrine. Secondary services would not attract the rural resident to the city (few presumably would travel to the city to use a latrine), but would fulfill his needs during his stay. Of course, services offered by the city were also used by city residents, but this activity would only serve to redistribute funds in the city and not earn the city new wealth. It is the services offered to non-residents which earned the city income.[218]

A service economy as prosperous as Corinth's no doubt attracted residents and businessmen from throughout the region. By all accounts, the Corinth of Paul's day was a highly competitive and flourishing town. Strabo (*Geogr.* 8.6.20) and Horace (*Ep.* 1.17.36) both speak of the cutthroat business atmosphere of the city. A century later nothing had changed, for Apuleius (*Metam.* 10.19.25) claimed that the city was full of profiteers who stopped at nothing to outdo their competitors.

Corinth also benefited from Rome's patronage.[219] As a *colonia*, the city most likely had a significant number of veterans who were given land grants and/or large gratuities at the conclusion of their military service. Along with the freedmen, they would be the citizens (*cives*) of the *colonia*, while the previous settlers were considered resident aliens (*incolae*). By the first century A.D., the city probably had 80,000 residents, with 20,000 living in its rural areas.[220] The Roman citizens and their progeny dominated the city through the second century A.D.[221] *Coloniae* followed a particular political structure (with *duoviri* and *aediles*) and adhered to Roman law and customs.[222] Therewith, Corinth was exceptionally well placed to enjoy the security of the *Pax Romana* initiated under Augustus. That Corinth achieved favor in the empire can be seen in its leading role within the province of Achaia. From 27 B.C., Corinth functioned as the capital of the province. And though the provinces of Achaia and Macedonia were joined to the province of Moesia, Claudius restored Achaia as a senatorial province in A.D. 44, with Corinth as its capital (Suetonius, *Claud.* 25). Indeed, Paul's own presence in the city is tied to the proconsulship of Lucius Iunius Gallio (Acts 18:12–17). Paul and Gallio met between July and September in A.D.

---

[218] Ibid., 43.

[219] For an extensive explanation of the relationship between Corinth and Rome, see J. A. Wiseman, "Corinth and Rome I: 228 B.C.–A.D. 267," *ANRW* 2.7.1:438–53.

[220] Engels, *Roman Corinth*, 84.

[221] Ibid., 68.

[222] On Corinth as a *colonia*, see C. S. de Vos, *Church and Community Conflicts: The Relationship of the Thessalonian, Corinthian, and Philippian Churches with Their Wider Civic Communities* (SBLDS 168; Atlanta: Scholars Press, 1997) 110–15.

51.²²³ As the capital of the province, Corinth naturally seems to have taken on an Italianate face. Almost all extant inscriptions from the first century A.D. are in Latin rather than Greek, even though they revert back to Greek after Hadrian.²²⁴ No doubt, the seat of the Roman government prompted the increased use of Latin. Still, the language of the locals—so vigorously engaged in trade throughout the eastern Mediterranean and so anxious to provide services for the entirety of the province—probably remained Greek.²²⁵ The seat of the Roman government contributed to the prosperity of Corinth. Plutarch reports that it was a banking center in the first century (*Mor.* 831a). Provincial government also brought important visitors from Rome itself and other parts of the empire, garrisons of troops, and entrepreneurs of every stripe.

The prosperity of Corinth also brought about the leisure of recreation, even decadence, and the city was a tourist attraction in its own right. The Isthmian Games, one of the three most important religious and athletic festivals in Greece, had been transferred to Sycon during Corinth's desolation; they moved back to Corinth around 40 B.C. The Games, held biennially in honor of Poseidon,²²⁶ attracted a plethora of visitors. The victor of the Games was awarded a crown of celery. That Paul attended the Games in the summer of A.D. 51 is most probable, given his reference to athletic imagery and wreaths (crowns) in 1 Cor 9:24–25. Greek in origin, the Games took on a somewhat Roman character as they grew. "Besides the biennial Isthmian Games, there were also the quadrennial Caesarean Games and the Imperial Contests, the former begun in the reign of Tiberius to honor the imperial family.... The Caesarian and Imperial competitions included contests for the best encomia to reigning emperors and their families, poetry, and singing contests."²²⁷ Nero himself participated in the Games in 67, and proclaimed freedom for the province of Achaia from the stadium in Isthima—just as Flamininus had done 250 years earlier.²²⁸ Corinth also provided some amusements less gallant than summer fêtes. Engels describes the situation:

> Of course, visitors who came to these summer festivals would also be attracted to the other types of entertainment the city offered. Indeed, so important were these attractions to the city that they were advertised on its coins, which may be regarded in part as promotional devices. For example, many Corinthian coin

---

²²³ Murphy-O'Connor, *Paul: A Critical Life*, 21.

²²⁴ J. H. Kent, *Inscriptions 1926–1960: Corinth Results* (vol. 8, pt. 3; Princeton, NJ: Princeton University Press, 1966) 18–19.

²²⁵ See Engels, *Roman Corinth*, 69–71.

²²⁶ On the sanctuary erected there, see E. R. Gebhard, "The Early Sanctuary of Poseidon at Isthmia," *AJA* 91 (1987) 475–76; and for the Roman flair, see Koester, "Melikertes at Isthmia," 395–63.

²²⁷ Engels, *Roman Corinth*, 52.

²²⁸ Ibid., 20.

types depict Aphrodite and her famous temple on the Acrocorinth, reminding the bearer of one kind of entertainment all too freely available in the "City of Aphrodite."[229]

The various Games, and in fact all of the entertainment provided by the city, were intimately linked to the civic and spiritual identity of Corinth's people who hardly thought themselves decadent. Given its mixed ethnicities and cultures, the population of Corinth demonstrated a complex religious diversity. By ancient standards, Corinth was actually a very religious city.

Ancient Religion in Corinth

Roman Corinth was a multicreedal society, a city of expansive religious diversity. Pausanias, in his *Graeciae description*, refers to the cultic practices of Corinth more than to those of any other city in the Peloponnese.[230] This comes as no surprise given the mixture of ethnicity and culture in Corinth. Added to this was the reciprocal relationship between a service city such as Corinth and the festivals and processions attached to its cultic shrines. We catch a glimpse of this in Acts 19:21–41, with the encounter between Paul and Demetrius, the silversmith in Ephesus. Demetrius shows less concern for religious principle than for the damage to the trade industry of statues of Artemis caused by Paul's evangelization. Moreover, if religion is linked to the economic well-being of a city, it is also linked to its political interests. Religious identity in the ancient world was inextricably linked to social identity and political loyalty. With ancient polytheism, there existed a network of flexibilities, but only within a pantheonic paradigm that facilitated a mutuality of deference among the gods and their devotees. For example, a glance at the exchange of letters between Pliny the Younger and Trajan regarding the treatment of Christians reveals more of a political than religious predicament. There the problem is not so much the fact that there are Christians qua Christians in Bythinia, but that they refuse to offer incense to an imperial statue, where such an offering would be sufficient to relieve them of any charge of sedition (see Pliny, *Ep. Tra.* 10.96–97).

Corinth was essentially no different from any other *colonia* in its religious observances. It harbored a plethora of religions: some old and some new, some local and some foreign, and some major and some minor. For our purposes, it is convenient to divide the religions into four groups. First, there were the Greco-Roman cults. These are the cults of the Greek Parthenon and the Roman Pantheon. By the first century A.D., the gods had become so closely identified—the Greek Poseidon and the Roman Neptune, the Greek Aphrodite and the Roman Venus—as to make them almost indistinguishable.[231] Second, there were the

---

[229] Ibid., 52.
[230] See ibid., 43–44.
[231] On the response of Romans to Greek religion, see S. Price, *Religions of the Ancient Greeks* (KTAH; Cambridge: Cambridge University Press, 1999) 143–58.

uniquely Roman cults, especially the imperial cult. Third, there were the Eastern cults of Isis and Serapis. Finally, there was Judaism, a cult whose practice in first-century Corinth is dubious. Thus, we gain insight into the religious currents of the city. But we must keep one thing in mind: "It is difficult to determine which were the most important cults of Roman Corinth, and whether different social groups worshipped different gods. The literary, epigraphic, numismatic, and archaeological evidence often yields seemingly contradictory views concerning the importance of a particular cult."[232] Because the Corinthian Christian community founded by Paul had its own internal social stratification,[233] it is important to examine the socioreligious context of Paul's preaching.

If there is any continuity between the old and the new Corinth, it is in all probability religious. The principal Greek gods and goddesses—Poseidon, Aphrodite, as well as Demeter and Kore—found their sanctuaries rebuilt and their cults flourishing in Roman Corinth. This does not necessarily suggest any historical continuity of religious practice or devotion from 146 through 44 B.C. in the sense of sustained worship at any temples or shrines. Instead, it represents the desire of the new colonists to give due honor to the gods thought to be attached to the city itself.[234] These gods would also have been members of the Roman Pantheon, albeit under different names, and respected among the settlers. Once situated in Corinth and aware of the dedication of former temples and shrines, the settlers rebuilt the sanctuaries to propitiate the gods.[235] Once the city began to thrive again, it was natural for the places of worship and pilgrimage to prosper as well. So too, given the fact that the Greek nature of the city would reestablish itself in the second century A.D., after the dilution of the Roman settlers into a larger and larger Greek population flowing in from the Peloponnese, the same Greek religious habits naturally returned to the city. But in the first century, a Roman flavor was palatable and of little surprise. Romans had come into contact with Greek religion as far back as the sixth century B.C. It was common for Romans to adopt and adapt Greek religious models. Since the Romans believed that their ultimate origins lay in the east, religious continuities were easily established between Greece and Rome.[236] Simply put, the continuity of religions between the original Greeks and the new Roman settlers in Corinth is on one level an antiquarian rivalry and on another, though hardly unrelated

---

[232] Engels, *Roman Corinth*, 95.

[233] G. Theissen, "Social Stratification in the Corinthian Community" (chap. 2), in *The Social Setting of Pauline Christianity: Essays on Corinth* (trans. J. H. Shütz; Philadelphia: Fortress, 1982) 69–119.

[234] Engels, *Roman Corinth*, 94.

[235] Ibid., 95.

[236] Price, *Religions of the Ancient Greeks*, 145–47.

level, an attempt to satisfy the gods who were believed to have great influence over the city.[237]

Poseidon (or Neptune)—god of the sea and earthquakes, brother of Zeus, and one of the twelve Olympians—was honored by the most prominent shrine in Corinth. "Since time immemorial, the Isthmus had been Poseidon's special home. In a city where so many earned their livelihood from the sea, and whose territory was periodically devastated by severe earthquakes, he would be the natural object of particular reverence. It is not surprising that the Roman colonists continued this tradition of reverence for the same reasons."[238] Once the city had been resettled, the Isthmian Games were returned to Corinthian control, after an hiatus of Sikyonian supervision.[239] This was a financial and cultural boon to the city. When Paul arrived in Corinth, he would no doubt have been impressed by Poseidon's sanctuary. "The sanctuary itself consisted of the large Doric temple of Poseidon, a theater, and a stadium where the literary and the athletic contests were held. There were also numerous auxiliary buildings: a bath, stoas, smaller shrines, and a hotel for visiting athletes."[240] Pausanias, who visited Corinth around A.D. 165, devotes the second book of his ten-volume *Graeciae description* to Corinth. Although Corinth had suffered a severe earthquake in A.D. 77 and much of what Pausanias describes would have been somewhat different from the sights encountered by Paul, Pausanias' depiction of the grandeur of Poseidon's sanctuary is astonishing.[241] Moreover, Pausanias also narrates the mythological foundation of Corinth as being a city belonging particularly to Poseidon (*Descr.* 1.7–9).[242]

Although Poseidon's sanctuary was more a cultural than religious center, its religious importance is not to be minimized. Poseidon's cult was respected throughout the Hellenistic world. Unfortunately, no evidence survives of the cultic practices specifically devoted to him or to his worship in Corinth, but two archeological details are noteworthy. First, there is evidence of a *nekuomanteion* cave,[243] i.e., a cave for communication with the dead or ghosts near Poseidon's temple. "Archeology provides no dates for the *nekuomanteion*. The literary sources take Corax there soon after the death of Archilochus, ca. 650 B.C., but the tale is hardly historical. In the second century A.D. Pausanias implied that it was still functioning. Pomponius Mela calls the *nekoumanteion* a 'cave of Neptune,' that is, 'of Poseidon,' confirming the gods direct patronage of the oracle."[244] Again, though the oracle may have been functioning in Paul's day,

---

[237] Engles, *Roman Corinth*, 94.

[238] Ibid., 97.

[239] Ibid., 98.

[240] Ibid., 96.

[241] See Murphy-O'Connor, *St. Paul's Corinth*, 3–8.

[242] See ibid., 9–13.

[243] For the use of the term *nekoumanteion*, see D. Ogden, *Greek and Roman Necromancy* (Princeton, NJ: Princeton University Press, 2001) xviii–xxii.

[244] Ibid., 36. See also Pausanias, *Descr.* 2.33; and Pomponius Mela, *De chor.* 2.51.

we know nothing of it.²⁴⁵ Second, there is some sparse evidence of the cult of Palaimon (Melikertes) in the Roman period.²⁴⁶ Palaimon was a minor sea god, often depicted with the dolphin that saved him from drowning after his mother leapt into the sea. The evidence for this cult in Greek Corinth is, at best, "scanty,"²⁴⁷ but it is more substantial in the second century A.D., even if little may be concluded therefrom. Interestingly, Pausanias mentions that oaths were taken in a cave before the hidden Palaimon (*Descr.* 2.2). Again unfortunately, we know little of the cult. "There can be no doubt about the mystery character of the cult of Melikertes-Palaimon."²⁴⁸ It is most difficult to know whether or not the cult was practiced in the first century A.D. and, if so, to what extent, because of "the community that celebrated this cult, nothing is known."²⁴⁹ Thus, the sanctuary of Poseidon attests to the Greco-Roman religious character of the city, but has left negligible evidence as to the specific religious practices of Paul's day.

After Poseidon, the most important deity was Aphrodite, the goddess of love, sexuality, and reproduction. In some instances, she was honored as the patroness of seafaring. Like Poseidon, Aphrodite was an Olympian, and her cult was Panhellenic. Aphrodite had at least three sanctuaries in Corinth: the one on the Arcocorinth shows her as the Armed Aphrodite, the protectress of Corinth; the one on the western end of the city may have contained a statue by the famous Hermogenes of Cythera; and the third one in the Kraneion district depicts her as Black Aphrodite or *melaina*, referring to her powers over the night.²⁵⁰ Again, Engels explains:

> Aphrodite's prostitutes, who practiced in the Greek city, gave rise to numerous anecdotes and stories. They were temple slaves, over a thousand in number, who had been dedicated to the service of the goddess by both men and women. It was even believed that the city owed much of its wealth in the Greek era to their success in attracting visitors—especially sailors. Indeed, Corinthian prostitutes were the most highly esteemed in the Greek world, and some of the best rose to high social prominence. The tomb of Lais, perhaps the most famous prostitute of all was still an attraction in the Roman era.²⁵¹

However, Aphrodite's presence in the city was hardly restricted to temple prostitution. "The importance of Aphrodite in Roman Corinth reflected the values and needs of its people. The city was a mercantile center where many depended on

---

²⁴⁵ Ogden, *Greek and Roman Necromancy*, 36–37.
²⁴⁶ See H. Koester, "Melikertes at Isthmia: A Roman Mystery Cult," in *Greeks, Romans and Christians*, ed. Balch, Ferguson, and Meeks, 355–66.
²⁴⁷ Ibid., 358.
²⁴⁸ Ibid., 365.
²⁴⁹ Ibid.
²⁵⁰ Engels, *Roman Corinth*, 97–98.
²⁵¹ Ibid., 98.

the sea for their livelihood; a center for entertainment, not only for its local population but for the whole Hellenic world: it is little wonder that Corinth and Aphrodite were identified so closely."[252] Aphrodite (or Venus) also engendered profound ramifications on politics in Corinth. Julius Caesar had claimed descent from Venus. In 46 B.C., Caesar had built a new forum in Rome around a temple dedicated to Venus Genetrix.

The third Olympian, also worshiped in Corinth, was Demeter, the Greek corn goddess. As was the case from the earliest days, she was worshiped alongside her daughter Kore (or Persephone). According to the mythology, Hades (or Pluto) kidnapped the "maiden" Persephone to make her his wife and queen of the underworld. Demeter attempted to rescue her daughter, but unable to rescue her completely, worked out an agreement with Hades that Persephone should spend six months with her and six months with him. Thus, the earth is fruitful when the mother and daughter are untied and fallow when they are separated. From the fifth century B.C., Demeter had been closely identified with the Roman Ceres. In Greek Corinth, the archeological evidence suggests a large and complex sanctuary. The sanctuary was destroyed in 146 B.C., but rebuilt on a smaller scale in Roman Corinth.[253] "The sanctuary was considerably remodeled in Roman times when a new stoa, terrace wall, and several other structures were built. The small shrine was especially popular among the poor, as is shown by the quantities of inexpensive votive offerings found in Roman deposits."[254] Again, though the extensive archeological data reveal the protracted presence of the cult of Demeter and Kore, little is known of its actual practice; and though some studies are illustrative of their cult in other places and of the mysteries that attached to it from Eleusis, that does not necessarily shed light on Corinth.[255] "At Corinth we know very little about the cult since inscriptions are almost wholly lacking and literary sources are meager."[256]

In addition to Poseidon and Palaimon, Aphrodite, and Demeter and Kore, Corinth also honored Athena, Tyche (or Fortuna), and Hermes (or Mercury)—all of whom we might expect to meet in a mercantile city—as well as their local heroes Pegasus and Bellerophon.[257] Athena, the goddess of craftsmen, was closely allied to the story of Pegasus and Bellerophon, a story that was particularly localized in Corinth because of its success in breeding horses. It was

---

[252] Ibid., 98–99.

[253] For an explanation of the archeological evidence, see D. Newton, *Deity and Diet: The Dilemma of Sacrificial Food at Corinth* (JSNTSup 169; Sheffield: Sheffield Academic Press, 1998) 91–96.

[254] Engels, *Roman Corinth*, 101.

[255] For example, L. Alderink, "The Eleusinian Mysteries in Roman Imperial Times," *ANRW* 2/18.2:1457–98; and K. Clinton, "The Eleusinian Mysteries: Roman Initiates and Benefactors, Second Century B.C. to A.D. 267," *ANRW* 2/18.2:1499–1539.

[256] N. Bookidis, "Ritual Dining in the Sanctuary of Demeter and Kore at Corinth," in *Sympotica: A Symposium on the Symposion* (ed. O. Murray; Oxford: Clarendon Press, 1990) 87.

[257] Engels, *Roman Corinth*, 99.

Athena who crafted the golden bridle which Bellerophon used to ride Pegasus; thus, in Corinth she was honored as Athena Chalinitis (or the Bridler).[258] Tyche was the goddess of fortune. Hermes was not only the messenger of the gods, but the patron of merchants and travelers. Along with these gods, Asklepios and Hygeia were honored together at a temple in the north of the city.[259] Much like the aforementioned sanctuaries, little may be gleaned from the archeological evidence.[260] What is certain is that the Asklepieion served as a regional center for medical treatment, especially with extensive bathing, and it probably also served as place of medical training whereat medical students would observe the sick and disabled.[261] "The Corinthian doctor Gaius Vibius Euelpistus was also a priest of Asklepios, and the famous doctor Galen many have used the facility during his stay in the city."[262]

As we have mentioned above, the polytheistic nature of the Hellenistic world allowed a plethora of religions and cults to exist side by side. The Roman settlers had naturally rededicated the former shrines of Greek Corinth with their own Roman emphases, but they also brought distinctively Roman religions to their new *colonia*. We know that the Roman gods Victoria, Concordia, and the Genius of the Colony and Colonists were honored because of inscriptions that survive, but the only extant temple is dedicated to Gens Julia.[263] The number of Latin inscriptions to Jupiter Optimus Maximus, Neptune, Venus, and Apollo demonstrates the syncretistic character of Roman religious practice under Greek influence, yet there is almost no archeological verification of their cults. However, a "striking pattern emerges from references to priesthoods in Roman Corinth. Of the thirty-one extant references, twenty-eight are in Latin and of those twenty are to priests of the imperial cults. Five are to uniquely Roman gods: Jupiter Capiolinus (4), and Janus (1), and the remainder are to Victoria (1), Saturn (1), and the Genius of the colony (1)."[264]

At first glance, this would seem to show an intense religious devotion to the imperial cult. Yet the clear political connection mitigates a quick conclusion. Scholars agree that the imperial cult was prominent in Paul's day at Corinth, but the details of its cultic practices are few.[265] This is especially true since the Isthmian and Imperial Games were amalgamated in Paul's day, and inscriptions are difficult to distinguish in terms of actual cultic practice vis-à-vis political honors. Engels correctly notes:

---

[258] Ibid.
[259] Ibid., 100.
[260] For a summary of the evidence, see Newton, *Deity and Diet*, 99.
[261] Engels, *Roman Corinth*, 100.
[262] Ibid., 101.
[263] Ibid.
[264] Ibid., 102.
[265] Newton, *Deity and Diet*, 105.

Many of these inscriptions were set up by the colonists or the descendants of the colonists who were sent by Julius Caesar in 44 B.C. to refound the city, and who thus owed their high social position to the imperial house. Moreover, many of the duovirs and other magistrates, or their families, owed their freedom or citizenship to the imperial house, as can be seen from their names. As did may colonial elites, the Corinthian aristocracy wished to retain the heritage and religious traditions of their homeland to distinguish themselves from the Greek majority by worshiping the gods of the Roman state. In general, the Latin-speaking aristocracy seems to have paid particular devotion to the gods of Rome, and after them, to the traditional gods of the Greco-Roman pantheon; they seem to have paid little attention to the Oriental and mystery religions. Since Corinth was the capital of the province of Achaea, it is obvious that special attention would be paid to the imperial cult. It was a wider projection of the old civic religion that expressed loyalty to the city's gods and hence, would gain the city favor in their sight. Therefore, provincial capitals would want to be seen as especially zealous towards the emperor; it was through such capitals and their governors that the divine emperors came most clearly in contact with the governed.[266]

Now, that is not to denigrate the sincerity of religious belief accorded to the cult or to dismiss its significance, but it does demonstrate that religious motives were mixed with political ones. While it is true that all of this would change in the second and third centuries A.D., when the language of Corinth reverted to Greek because of the overarching Greek cultural milieu of the Peloponnese and the Roman settlers intermarried heavily with their surrounding Greek neighbors,[267] Paul's Corinth was definitively Roman in government and official religion.

Two eastern religions are known to have been practiced in Corinth: the cult of Isis and Serapis and the cult of Cybele. Of the latter, there is no evidence whatsoever, except for a reference to her temple on the Arcocorinth by Pausanias (*Descr.* 2.4). Isis and Serapis were Egyptian gods. Archeological evidence for them is also sparse in Corinth,[268] and only the most general conclusions may be drawn. According to the mythology, Isis was the wife of Osiris and the mother of Horus. She was reckoned the goddess of the Mediterranean. Serapis, a god of healing, was given divinity by Osiris. Isis and Serapis came to be closely identified because of the similarity of their rites, including incubation, the interpretation of dreams, and healing powers. Both cults were widespread in the Hellenistic period, but Isis tended to overshadow Serapis among the Romans. Lucius Apuleius' *Metamorphoses* is the only source of knowledge for the cult in Corinth. Apuleius claims to have been converted to Isis there and gives detailed descriptions of her rites (*Metam.* 2 and 11). The archeological evidence reveals that Isis had her own temple in Cenchreae and two in Corinth proper,

---

[266] Engels, *Roman Corinth*, 102.

[267] Ibid., 106.

[268] All of the relevant archeological data are compiled in D. E. Smith, "The Egyptian Cults at Corinth," *HTR* 70 (1977) 201–31.

both of which were adjoining temples of Serapis.²⁶⁹ It also reveals that the cult was in vogue in the first century A.D.²⁷⁰ Paul may have witnessed some of the ceremonies of the cult while he was in Corinth, and it has been argued that the cult may shed light on 1 Cor 7:1–5.²⁷¹ Like the Asklepieia, the Serapia may also have served as medical centers.²⁷² Oddly enough, Luke reports that at Cenchreae Paul cut his hair, for he had taken a vow (Acts 18:18; cf. 21:24). While this is consistently thought to be in reference to the Nazirite custom of Num 6:1–21, followers of Isis often cut their hair in devotional practices.²⁷³ The eastern religions, much like the relatively minor cult of Demeter and Kore, did not occupy a strong hold in the city, even if by happenstance we might know a bit more about them.²⁷⁴ The Latin speaking elite favored the traditional Greco-Roman pantheon in the gods of Poseidon and Aphrodite and the Roman imperial cult, but the numerous votive offerings to Demeter and Kore and the inclusive processions of Isis and Serapis described by Apuleius indicate some popularity among the poor.²⁷⁵ However, their standing within Roman Corinthian society is most difficult to adjudicate.

Aside from Acts 18, the evidence for Jews in Corinth is minimal. In fact, there is less literary and physical evidence for the presence of Jews in first-century A.D. Corinth than for any of the aforementioned religions. The literary evidence comes from two sources: Strabo and Philo. As we saw above, Strabo (*Geogr.* 8.6.23) claims that a number of freedmen came from Rome as part of the Roman colonization of Corinth by Julius Caesar in 44 B.C. While this group may have included Jews, since it was representative of the diverse ethnic backgrounds of slaves in Rome, it is by no means certain that any substantial number of Jews were included. Philo (*Legat.* 36.281) says that Jewish colonists were sent to Corinth (and across the Aegean coast) as a result of the pogrom of Jews in Alexandria by Caligula in A.D. 38. However, the actual historical circumstances—whether this pogrom was Caligula's or Flaccus' doing and whether anyone was exiled and to where—remain dubious.²⁷⁶ To Philo's account, we may add Acts 18:2, which recounts that Aquilla and Priscilla had found themselves in Corinth as a result of Claudius' expulsion of Jews from Rome. The Jews suffered from Claudius, who in his first regnal year (A.D. 41), had limited their meetings (Dio Cassius, *Hist. roma.* 60.6.6). Some Jews may have left

---

²⁶⁹ Engels, *Roman Corinth*, 103.
²⁷⁰ Newton, *Deity and Diet*, 99–100.
²⁷¹ R. Oster, "Use, Misuse, and Neglect of Archeological Evidence in Some Modern Works on 1 Corinthians (1 Cor. 7.15; 8.10; 11.2–16; 12.14–26)," *ZNW* 83 (1992) 61.
²⁷² Engels, *Roman Corinth*, 105.
²⁷³ Ibid.
²⁷⁴ Ibid., 105.
²⁷⁵ Ibid.
²⁷⁶ See E. S. Gruen, *Diaspora: Jews amidst Greeks and Romans* (Cambridge, MA: Harvard University Press, 2002) 51–62.

Rome in fear of later reprisals.[277] Suetonius (*Claud.* 25.4) mentions an expulsion of the Jews by Claudius, though without a date. The date is fixed at 49 according to Orosius (*Hist. adv. pag.* 7.6.15). "The dating of this event evades absolute precision. We know that Paul, not long thereafter, came before the tribunal of Gallio, the Roman governor of Achaea. And Gallio's proconsulship can be dated to 50/51 or 51/52. This is close enough. It is hard to escape the conclusion that Acts and Suetonius refer to the same event."[278] Therefore, though there is sufficient warrant to assume the presence of some Jews in Corinth, it is disappointing that there is neither any literary evidence of their presence nor any extant writings of first-century Jews in Corinth.

Disappointing, as well, is the dearth of archeological evidence. There are but two epigraphic fragments that attest to the presence of Jews in Roman Corinth.[279] Regrettably, neither can be dated any earlier than the fourth century A.D.[280] The first is a marble cornice most likely used as the lintel above the door of a synagogue. It contains the letters: ΓШΓΗ ΘΒΡ; these are reconstructed to read: (Συνα)γωγὴ Ἐβρ(αίων) or "Synagogue of the Hebrews."[281] The second is a marble impost, probably from the same synagogue, which is decorated with menorahs, palm branches, and citrons.[282] Other than these two pieces there is nothing extant of Jews in Corinth, unless we add one Christian gravestone from the many in Corinth dating to the late fourth century. "The name on one of these, 'Noumenis' (a shortened from of 'Noumenios,' a name that may be of Jewish origin), could be that of a Jewish Christian,"[283] but this is tenuous.

According to Acts 18, there was nothing less than a sizeable Jewish community in Corinth. But the very text of Acts 18 is problematic, and its account of Paul's stay in Corinth "cannot be accepted at face value."[284] It is beyond the pale of our study to look closely into the text; yet we do note that it seems to be a conflation of two textual traditions, the Western and the Alexandrian.[285] Murphy-O'Connor describes essentials of the text:

> The most primitive story (vv. 1, 4a, 5b, 6, 9, 10, 12–14a, 15b, 16–18) narrated only an abortive attempt to convert Jews, after which Paul was consoled by a vision of Christ, whose efficacious protection was immediately demonstrated by the refusal of Gallio to hear the charge laid against Paul by the Jews. I see no reason to refuse the historicity of the events narrated in this document. Manifestly, however, it is not a complete account of Paul's founding visit to

---

[277] See ibid., 36–41.

[278] Ibid. 38.

[279] For a complete exposition of the archeological findings at Corinth, see of V. P. Furnish, "Corinth in Paul's Time: What Can Archeology Tell Us?" *BAR* 15 (May/June 1988) 15–27.

[280] Ibid., 26.

[281] Ibid.

[282] Ibid.

[283] Ibid.

[284] Murphy-O'Connor, *Paul: A Critical Life*, 259.

[285] For the details, see the *TCGNT*, 406–12.

Corinth. That much has been omitted is indicated by the fact that Paul stayed a considerable time and made many converts.[286]

So too, there is no reason to refuse the more basic historicity of the text, viz., that there were Jews in Corinth and an established synagogue when Paul arrived, even if the literary archeological findings are shaky.[287] In fact, there are only five other locations in the Mediterranean (Egypt, Cyrenaica, the province of Asia, the province of Syria, and Rome) about which there are extant references describing Diaspora life in any depth, and even these have large gaps.[288] Building on the data we have, we can assume that Paul came upon a Diaspora community in Corinth not so different from his own in Tarsus, with rich ethnic diversity and the enormous challenge of maintaining their ancient faith in a thoroughly pagan atmosphere.

Ancient Corinth and Readings of 1 Corinthians 15:29

In a much broader sense than even our contemporary usage, "diversity" was a hallmark of the first-century Greco-Roman world. It was especially so in Corinth, with its assorted historical background and rich cross-cultural foreground. Staking a claim about the relationships among the various religious groups in Corinth is an exceedingly delicate matter. The religious pluralism of the ancient world in general and of Corinth in particular allow not only insight into how diverse religious adherences coexisted but also into how they defined themselves in contrast to one another. With more cultic practices in Corinth than any other city in the Peloponnese—Greco-Roman, Roman, and Eastern religions, as well as Judaism—flourishing in the city, Paul faced a colossal challenge in founding a Christian community. As a Diaspora Jew, this challenge was mitigated, at least in a small way, by Paul's own familiarity with maintaining the ancient faith in divergent circumstances. To be sure, the broad stance of pagan religions in the Greco-Roman world was assimilation and accommodation. Syncretism was neither a problematic program nor a knotty affair from a polytheistic standpoint. One of the most salient examples is found in Acts 17:16–33. At the Areopagus, Paul uses the expansive inclusiveness of Greco-Roman religious thinking to speak of a "god unknown." And with this, the men of Athens seemed to have little difficulty; their objection arose when Paul began to speak of the resurrection. Conversely, the Jewish stance—Palestinian and Diaspora—was narrow. Judaism stresses its exclusivity in matters religious. Paul's own opposition to syncretism was no doubt rooted in his heritage, and his apprehensions about syncretism are evident in 1 Corinthians 8 and 10. But Paul was the

---

[286] Murphy-O'Connor, *Paul: A Critical Life*, 259.
[287] Oster, "Use, Misuse, and Neglect of Archeological Evidence in Some Modern Works on 1 Corinthians," 57.
[288] Barclay, *Jews in the Mediterranean Diaspora*, 10.

"Apostle to the Gentiles," which meant that he had to find a way to incorporate both Jews and Gentiles into his missionary apostolate. According to E. P. Sanders, Paul included both seemingly irreconcilable groups:

> Paul found a broad middle. He forged a Christianity that was Jewish to the degree that it forbade idolatry and extra-marital sex and was Gentile to the degree that it forbade circumcision, Sabbath, and dietary laws. It was both and neither. Eventually, of course, Christianity lost its appeal for Jews, but that had not happened in Paul's day and happened, when it did happen, for factors other than Paul's theology, not the least of which were the Jewish wars with Rome. Paul himself was Jewish, and his position appealed, at the least, to Barnabas and was acceptable to Barnabas and even to Peter until James enforced a boundary for Jewish Christianity. A century after Paul, Justin provides evidence of Christianity's continuing appeal to both Jews and Gentiles. Paul was in large part responsible for that success. Paul found the right boundaries for the success of Christianity, and for that reason we still regard him as the Great Apostle.[289]

To the extent that Paul was able to form a *tertium quid* in his Christian community, he necessarily formed a group—with members who did not come from a vacuum but from the multicreedal Corinth in which Paul preached, and who did not live their newly found faith in a vacuum—which now identified itself as unified and distinct.

As we saw in Chapter I of our study, Richard E. DeMaris speculates that vicarious baptism arose in Corinth due to a particular baptismal enthusiasm among the Corinthian Christians and a general preoccupation with the dead in the Roman era, well beyond the scope of Christianity.[290] For DeMaris, 15:29 is a clear reference to vicarious baptism. Without any firsthand knowledge of the burial practices of Corinthian Christians,[291] DeMaris turns to the broader context of Greco-Roman religion. Of course, DeMaris' presentation of the milieu,[292] the importance of ritual,[293] and the feasible resemblances to pagan practices is a major contribution,[294] but the leap to find a base in the supposed practice is too much a stretch for two reasons: first, there is no vicarious baptism among the pagans, and second, our knowledge of the pagan practices themselves is sketchy at best. That DeMaris reads 15:29 to be nothing other than a reference to vicarious baptism is the cause of his search for a root in Corinth's historical context. Finding nothing resembling vicarious baptism *per se*, DeMaris' emphasis on a general preoccupation with the realm of the dead among all the citizens of Corinth is well taken, but there is a missing link. That is, without some piece of evidence to link the two, a cause and effect relationship cannot be established.

---

[289] E. P. Sanders, "Paul between Jews and Gentiles in Corinth," *JSNT* 65 (1997) 83.

[290] DeMaris, "Corinthian Religion and Baptism for the Dead," 662, 672.

[291] See Meeks, *First Urban Christians*, 78.

[292] DeMaris, "Demeter in Roman Corinth," 105–17.

[293] DeMaris, "Funerals and Baptisms," 23–34.

[294] DeMaris, "Corinthian Religion and Baptism for the Dead," 661–82.

Granted that concern for the fate of the dead may have been as acute within Christianity as it was within paganism, that does not necessarily link the practices of one community with the other *a priori*. Vicarious baptism among Christians would have to be established as such before a comparison could be made with contemporaneous practices, Christian or not. What is more, our grasp of Greco-Roman funeral rites in Corinth in the first century A.D. and beyond is inexact.[295] The move from the early Roman practice of cremation to the Greek practice of inhumation in the first century B.C., which DeMaris holds as a factor in the heightening concern for the dead and a cause for "anxiety" as it played out in Corinth,[296] is multifaceted; such a move cannot be limited to any single factor. In fact, Arthur D. Nock presents an extensive examination of this development and concludes that religious reasons were most likely the least important reason for the change.[297] Whether in burning or burial, the respect for the remains of the dead stays about the same, e.g., libation tubes are found in both.[298] Nock deduces that the change was likely nothing more than one of "fashion."[299] "By fashion we mean the habits of the rich, which gradually permeated the classes below them,"[300] but any specifically religious orientation for the change remains unknown. Thus, we must conclude that DeMaris' finding of similarities between a supposed vicarious baptism and Corinthian burial customs is weak. Because the existence or nonexistence of the practice of vicarious baptism itself is the question at hand, something that might have borne some resemblance to it cannot substantiate its existence.

Moreover, as we have seen, the melding of Greek and Roman customs, whatever they may be, must admit of some adaptation, however slight, in the prism of Corinthian Christianity. Our wide-ranging examination of the diversity of religious belief in Corinth yields nothing resembling vicarious baptism. That is not to say that the absence of any resemblance in the larger historical context within which Paul founded a Christian community precludes its incidence. But it is to say that if such a practice arose, it did not arise out of some prior ritual or observance that is traceable to Greco-Roman religion. In short, the needle of vicarious baptism is not found in the haystack of the multicreedal ancient Corinthian religious environment. Conscious that many scholars suggest the roots of vicarious baptism to be found in some contingency particular and peculiar to

---

[295] For an extensive look at the varieties of practices, rites, cemeteries, and tombs (including their accoutrements), see J. M. C. Toynbee, *Death and Burial in the Roman World* (Baltimore and London: Johns Hopkins University Press, 1971).
[296] DeMaris, "Corinthian Religion and Baptism for the Dead," 671, 673.
[297] A. D. Nock, "Cremation and Burial in the Roman Empire," *HTR* 25 (1932) 321–59.
[298] Ibid., 332.
[299] Ibid., 357.
[300] Ibid., 358.

Corinthian Christianity, we now turn our attention specifically to Christian Corinth.

CORINTHIAN CHRISTIANITY AND ITS EARLY CRISES

Thus far in this third chapter of our study, we have considered Paul, the devout Jew who became a leading apostle of Christ, and Greco-Roman Corinth, the site of Paul's evangelical efforts in A.D. 50. Now we turn our attention to the fruit of his preaching in Corinth: Corinthian Christianity. Because the focus of our study, 1 Cor 15:29, is an important element in 1 Corinthians 15, which is Paul's strongest defense of the resurrection and an indication of a crisis of faith among Corinthian Christians about the resurrection, it behooves us to take into account all of the crises of faith that can be gleaned from 1 Corinthians. In searching for the needle of vicarious baptism—part and parcel of a crisis in faith by everyone's account—in the haystack comprised of Paul, Corinth, and Corinthian Christianity, a careful focus on the difficulties Paul addresses in 1 Corinthians is in order. Before we turn to the crisis of faith in the resurrection of the dead, we look to factionalism (chapters 1–4), ethical issues (chapters 5–11), and spiritual issues (chapters 12–14), in the hope that an examination of these crises will shed light on the crisis of faith in the resurrection of the dead. Then, we turn our attention to the resurrection in chapter 15.

There are as many vantage points from which to approach Corinthian Christianity as there are commentators on 1 and 2 Corinthians. The long and short of it is that we do not know as much about Corinthian Christianity as we do about what Paul thought it ought to be. As C. K. Barrett remarks:

> If Romans gives us the most systematic presentation of Paul's theology, it is nevertheless from the Corinthian epistles that we gain the most complete and many-sided picture of how Paul believed that his theological convictions should be expressed in the life of a Church. To say this is not to claim that the Corinthian Church was a paragon of all Churches; there was often wide divergence between what happened in Corinth and what Paul thought ought to happen. But both pictures—the actual and the ideal—contribute to our understanding of Pauline Christianity in its practical expression, and we learn much of what Paul thought right from what the Corinthians got wrong. In the Corinthian epistles Paul deals with an exceptionally large number of practical problems, always on the basis of a theological grasp of the situation, so that there is in fact no more important source for Paul's conception of the Christian way of life.[301]

Barrett's point is well taken in that 1 Corinthians presents us with a picture of the actual and the ideal. On the one hand, 1 Corinthians presents us with a laundry list of actual crises; on the other hand, in conjunction with those crises, Paul

---

[301] C. K. Barrett, "Christianity at Corinth," *BJRL* 46 (1964) 269.

presents the ideals from which the Corinthians have departed and to which he begs them to return. In essence, 1 Corinthians is the simultaneous exposition of two phenomena—crises and solutions—in one fell swoop.

Teasing out the crises from their solutions, or the actual from the ideal, has been and continues to be a major challenge in Pauline scholarship.[302] Why? Because we do not have any other source to discriminate the actual situation in Corinth other than Paul's own understanding thereof in 1 Corinthians. Acts 18, even if taken at face value, tells us very little about Corinthian Christianity. 2 Corinthians presents us with the same problems as 1 Corinthians, perhaps to higher degree. And 1 Corinthians seems almost to taunt us with the lost information it mentions: gossip from Chloe's people (1:11), Paul's previous letter (5:9), a letter to which Paul responds (7:1), and whatever Stephanus and company may have told Paul (16:17). Providentially, we have Paul's six other authentic letters (and even the Pauline pseudepigrapha), insight into the Diaspora Jew-turned-Christian apostle Paul, and knowledge of Roman Corinth.[303] But there is not a word about Corinthian Christianity other than from Paul. Now this does not place tension between Paul and the Corinthians. It is not as if we know what they said and know what Paul said in such wise that we can contrast the former and the latter. Yet it does place an onus upon us to read carefully what Paul says in regard to the crises he identifies in 1 Corinthians. These crises as identified in 1 Corinthians do not lend themselves to neat categorization.

Moreover, there are many opinions as to the reasons for the crises.[304] None has gained scholarly consensus. J. C. Hurd, Jr. lays the blame on Paul's shoulders. Hurd maintains that Paul changed his teaching and thereby caused confusion among the Corinthians.[305] The difficulty is to draw the line between the old and new teachings, something that Hurd fails to do adequately, even with a carefully constructed table.[306] For a while, Walter Schmithals' claim of Gnosticism among the Corinthians held sway,[307] yet it is rarely held today, though

---

[302] For an introduction to the problem from the historical point of view, to the effect that we cannot know the outcome of crises from Paul's letters because the letters are part of the crises themselves, see C. K. Barrett, "Pauline Controversies in the Post-Pauline Period," *NTS* 20 (1973–74) 229–45.

[303] *1 Clement* is of no help to us here, except to prove that Paul's attempts to resolve discord were not ultimately successful. The letter, written sometime between A.D. 80 and 140, but most likely in A.D. 95 or 96, was written to quell conflict between Corinthian Christians.

[304] See B. W. Winter, *After Paul Left Corinth: The Influence of Secular Ethics and Social Change* (Grand Rapids, MI: Eerdmans, 2001) 25–28.

[305] See Hurd, "Paul's First Preaching in Corinth" (chap. 8) and "Retrospect and Prospect" (chap. 9), in *The Origin of 1 Corinthians*, 273–88 and 289–96.

[306] Ibid., 290–93. As regards eschatology, Hurd's thesis is augmented by C. L. Mearns, "Early Eschatological Development in Paul: The Evidence of 1 Corinthians," *JSNT* 22 (1984) 19–35.

[307] W. Schmithals, *Gnosticism in Corinth: An Investigation of the Letters to the Corinthians* (trans. J. E. Steely; Nashville: Abingdon, 1971); see also idem, *Paul and the Gnostics* (trans. J. E. Steely. Nashville: Abingdon, 1972); idem, "The Pre-Pauline Tradition in 1 Corinthians 15:20–28,"

some would see a nascent Christian Gnosticism in Corinth.[308] Later, Anthony C. Thiselton's assertion of an "over-realized eschatology" among the Corinthians,[309] one that places undue emphasis on an immanent eschaton, rather than the "realized eschatology" of Paul's own teaching,[310] attracted much attention. However, Thiselton's theory seems a bit stretched when we consider the ethical issues Paul addresses in 1 Corinthians 5–11, all of which have to do with practicalities only tangentially related to the eschaton.[311] As we noted above, Margaret M. Mitchell argues in favor of factionalism as the basis for the whole of 1 Corinthians,[312] but this is entirely dependent upon her reading of 1 Corinthians as an example of deliberative discourse. Recently, David Wenham proposed that the Corinthians were arguing the traditions of Jesus against those of Paul."[313] The proposal draws heavily from Wenham's earlier book;[314] but the same difficulty that plagues the book is present in his proposal: Can we really contrast Jesus and Paul, especially in terms of 1 Corinthians? Most recently, Bruce W. Winter has performed the valuable service of locating the problems in the *Sitz-im-Leben* at Corinth, wherein problems "arose partly because the Christians were 'cosmopolitans,' i.e., citizens of the world and, in particular, citizens or residents of Roman Corinth. They had grown up in, and imbibed that culture before they became Christians."[315] And Winter claims that some other problems were the result of particular events in the city.[316] Winter's theory seems closest to the mark because he takes into account the fact that the persons to whom Paul wrote in 1 Corinthians were all inexperienced converts, persons who were in a process of conversion and therefore in need of further explanation as the vicissitudes of life in first-century Corinth impacted upon their new and untested status as Christians.

All of the aforementioned explanations are valuable and informative. The reason that none has gained consensus is that each seems insufficient to account

---

(trans. C. N. Jefford) *PRSt* 20 (1993) 356–80; and idem, *The Theology of First Corinthians* (trans. O. C. Dean, Jr.; Louisville: Westminster John Knox, 1997).

[308] For example, R. McL. Wilson, "How Gnostic Were the Corinthians?" *NTS* 19 (1972–73) 65–74; and G. E. Sterling, "'Wisdom among the Perfect': Creation Traditions in Alexandrian Judaism and Corinthian Christianity," *NovT* 37 (1995) 355–84.

[309] A. C. Thiselton, "Realized Eschatology at Corinth," *NTS* 24 (1977–78) 510–26; see also idem, *The First Epistle to the Corinthians* (NIGTC; Grand Rapids, MI: Eerdmans, 2000) 357–65.

[310] For the various explanations of an over-realized eschatology, see Thiselton, "Realized Eschatology at Corinth," 510–11. Cf., e.g., Barrett, *First Corinthians*, 109.

[311] Cf. R. B. Hays ("The Conversion of the Imagination: Scripture and Eschatology in 1 Corinthians," *NTS* 45 [1999] 391–412) who argues for too little rather than too much eschatological awareness among the Corinthians.

[312] Mitchell, *Paul and the Rhetoric of Reconciliation*, 1 et passim. Cf. Thiselton, *First Corinthians*, 41–52.

[313] D. Wenham, "Whatever Went Wrong in Corinth?" *ExpTim* 108 (1997) 137–41.

[314] Idem, *Paul: Follower of Jesus or Founder of Christianity?*

[315] Winter, *After Paul Left Corinth*, 27.

[316] Ibid., 27–28.

for *all* of the crises and persons addressed by Paul in 1 Corinthians. And that is the key. Does there need to be a *single* explanation for the problems at Corinth? Perhaps not. The presumption of a single, overarching cause for the Corinthian crises is unfounded. The varied sources of Paul's information regarding the situation in Corinth, the multifaceted issues he seeks to redress, and the assorted persons to whom he speaks (e.g., the married and the unmarried in chapter 7) militate against any singular concern on Paul's part other than to correct a plethora of erroneous notions among the Corinthians. Only with somewhat contrived rationalizations can we detect a macro-root error to link the question of *porneia* in chapter 5 to that of the resurrection in chapter 15, or the question of civil adjudication in chapter 6 to that of worship in chapter 14. Indeed, as we saw above, it is the apparent lack of unity and the diversity of issues addressed in 1 Corinthians that has led to so many partition theories. The bottom line is that at least some of the Corinthians were in error according to the information at Paul's disposal; 1 Corinthians is Paul's attempt to reiterate what he had already taught them or to render further elucidation of prior teaching in terms of Paul's perception of their errors. For the purposes of our study, we turn first to an overview of the crises and their solutions in general as an aid to establish the background of chapter 15. Our purpose is neither to establish a lone origin for each of them nor to examine the crises in detail. Instead, we attempt to discern a pattern of response in Paul that is illustrative of his stance towards the tribulations in Corinth.

That there were a number of crises in Corinthian Christianity between Paul's departure from Corinth and his authoring of 1 Corinthians is a given. The categorizing of the crises in Corinthian Christianity is closely linked to one's overall understanding of 1 Corinthians' literary integrity and structure. As commentators differ in their understanding of these matters, so their understanding of the interrelationships of the crises varies. This is readily seen in commentaries' tables of contents. Earlier in our study, we agreed with Martinus C. de Boer's insight as to the arrangement of 1 Corinthians.[317] De Boer's understanding of 1 Corinthians as a letter in two parts—the first dealing with factionalism (1:10–4:21) and the second dealing with a host of other problems (5:1–15:58), with chapter 16 serving as the conclusion of the whole—lends itself to a simple categorization of the letter. Thus, we take a brief look at the factionalism represented in the first part. We divide the second part into two sections: ethical issues (5:1–11:34) and spiritual issues (12:1–14:40). And we leave chapter 15 for a separate treatment thereafter.

---

[317] De Boer, "The Composition of 1 Corinthians," 229–45.

Factionalism (1 Corinthians 1–4)

The first major crisis that Paul speaks of in 1 Corinthians is factionalism (σχίσματα). Although Paul will deal with the ramifications of factionalism in 1 Corinthians 1–4, he presents the crisis and the solution in 1 Cor 1:10–11. The problem is stated clearly in v. 11, viz., that there is quarreling among them; and the solution precedes it in v. 10, viz., "that all of you agree and that there be no dissentions among you, but that you be united in the same mind (νοῦς) and in the same judgment (γνώμη)." On the surface, Paul's argument is simple: he renders an explanation of the problem of discord in terms of leadership in the community (1:12–17); he speaks of σοφία and its proper discernment (1:18–3:4); he returns to leadership in the community (3:5–23); and, particularly to his own leadership (4:1–13).[318] Paul concludes in 4:14–21 that he writes not to shame them,[319] but to admonish them, especially the arrogant; to ask their imitation of himself; to explain that he is their father in Christ; to mention that he sends Timothy as a guide; and to remind them that he himself will come to sort things out, even if he has to do so "with a rod" (4:21). There is no doubt that Paul is distraught by the factionalism in Corinth.[320] And there is no doubt about his solution to the problem: "He wants his converts to stand firm, not only in the Lord, but also in their loyalty to him."[321]

As we indicated above in our discussion of 1 Corinthians' literary genre, scholars are unanimous in holding chapters 1–4 as a distinct subunit in 1 Corinthians.[322] Within that subunit, scholars are also unanimous in distinguishing the smaller segments (1:10–17, 18–25, 26–31; 2:1–5, 6–16; 3:1–4, 5–17, 18–23; 4:1–5, 6–13, 14–21),[323] but consensus soon disintegrates over their arrangement

---

[318] So too, with minor variations, N. A. Dahl, "Paul and the Church at Corinth according to 1 Corinthians 1:10–4:21," in *Christian History and Interpretation: Studies Presented to John Knox* (ed. W. R. Farmer, C. F. D. Moule, and R. R. Niebuhr; Cambridge: Cambridge University Press, 1967) 320–21; Fee, *First Corinthians*, 50–51; and Horsley, *1 Corinthians*, 42–43.

[319] On the subject of honor/shame in the Corinthian letters, see D. A. deSilva, "'Let the One Who Claims Honor Establish That Claim in the Lord': Honor Discourse in the Corinthian Correspondence," *BTB* 28 (1998) 61–74.

[320] R. Bieringer writes: "In all of Paul's authentic letters the immediacy of the apostle-community relationship can be felt" ("Paul's Divine Jealousy: The Apostle and His Communities in Relationship," *LS* 17 [1992] 229). It is the immediacy of Paul's relationship with the Corinthians that intensifies Paul's distress at any quarreling among them.

[321] Knox, *Chapters in a Life of Paul*, 80. E. Schüssler Fiorenza's argument ("Rhetorical Situation and Historical Reconstruction in 1 Corinthians," *NTS* 33 [1987] 386–403) that Paul appeals only to those of elevated social status, like himself, to make decisions over those of low social status (especially women) seems to push loyalty too far. Recall that Paul never supports the "Paul party."

[322] So too, J. F. M. Smit, "'What Is Apollos? What Is Paul?' In Search for the Coherence of First Corinthians 1:10–4:21," *NovT* 154 (2002) 231. Again, as we noted above, this is especially true of rhetorical criticisms, e.g., Pogoloff, *Logos and Sophia*; Litfin, *Paul's Theology of Proclamation*; and Bullmore, *St. Paul's Theology of Rhetorical Style*.

[323] So too, Smit, "'What Is Apollos? What Is Paul?'" 232; see ibid., n. 2 for citations.

and interrelationship.[324] Our purpose here is neither to attempt to referee divergent opinions on the minute structure of chapters 1–4 nor to delineate the finer theological points of Paul's argumentation. Thirty-five years ago, Nils A. Dahl referred to the surfeit of such attempts as "a chaos which is already bad enough."[325] Dahl correctly insists that we must stick closely to "the perspective under which Paul envisages the situation at Corinth" and that any background reconstruction "must be based upon information contained within the section itself."[326] Our purpose, then, is to find the simple nature of the crisis and Paul's response thereto. For this reason, we adopt an uncomplicated structure for our examination. Peter F. Ellis proposes a simple tricolon structure: A (1:10–2:5), the source of the problem, the cross, and wisdom; B (2:6–16), a mature understanding of the cross and wisdom; and A' (3:1–4:21), advice about teachers.[327] Thus, Paul "gets his point across clearly and at the same time spares the feelings of the troublesome Corinthian teachers and their overenthusiastic followers. In this particular case, Paul's chiastic format constitutes a powerful argument for the unity of everything he says in 1:10–4:21."[328]

In the first part (A; 1:10–2:5), Paul's initial ruminations are clear. There is factionalism among the community in that some claim allegiance to Paul, Apollos, Cephas, or Christ. Paul does not wish to admonish those who claim allegiance to anyone other than himself or to chide anyone who would put a teacher over Christ, but to distance himself from the very notion that the factions are the result of any divisive teaching on Paul's or anyone else's part. Paul asks (v. 13), "Is Christ divided? Was Paul crucified for you? Or were you baptized in the name of Paul?" On a practical level, Paul distances himself by reminding them that he baptized few among them (vv. 14–16). Since the "existence of a 'Paul-group' itself implies opposition to Paul in Corinth,"[329] Paul is careful to disassociate himself, rather than to argue on behalf of one group or another, and to move the argument away from personal loyalty to nothing other than Jesus Christ and him crucified. Likewise, there is no indictment of Apollos or Cephas, but only of the Corinthians themselves.[330] Both Apollos and Cephas are evidently known to the Corinthians. Apollos appears prominently in 1 Corinthians

---

[324] Ibid., 232–35. Smit renders his own understanding of the chapters' small segments and their connections to show a unity of syntax, semantics, and pragmatics (235–51).

[325] Dahl, "Paul and the Church at Corinth," 317.

[326] Ibid. Like ourselves, Dahl presumes the integrity of 1 Corinthians, eschews the incorporation of outside texts (even other Pauline letters) until the internal evidence has been established, and realizes that total reconstruction is impossible (317–18).

[327] P. F. Ellis, *Seven Pauline Letters* (Collegeville, MN: Liturgical, 1982) 45–58.

[328] Ibid., 47.

[329] Barrett, *First Corinthians*, 43.

[330] "There is no reason to think that either Apollos or Cephas was in any way responsible for the use that was made of their names by people at Corinth who claimed to be independent of Paul" (Dahl, "Paul and the Church at Corinth," 323).

(3:4–6, 22; 3:22; 4:6; 16:12) and elsewhere (Acts 18:24; 19:1; Titus 3:13); Cephas, too, is prominent in 1 Corinthians as an apostle (3:22; 9:5) and an early witness of the risen Lord (15:5), as well as in Galatians (1:18; 2:7–9, 11, 14). The problem lies not with Apollos or Cephas. The problem lies in the fact that there is an unwarranted dissension among them that is most likely doctrinal in nature, i.e., they disagree on some points and invoke an authority to support their positions. Paul does not articulate their opinions. The details of their disagreements remain unknown,[331] and their full extent eludes us. Although it is argued that their factionalism is rooted in politics or personality,[332] Paul's invocation of the cross as the *spes unica* speaks otherwise. It is the wisdom of speech (σοφία λόγου) versus the cross of Christ (σταυρὸς τοῦ Χριστοῦ).

Paul says, "the cross is folly to those who are perishing" (v. 18). By invoking Isa 29:14 and Jer 9:23–24, Paul intends to refute the notion that the cross is a new form of wisdom.[333] The citations from Isaiah and Jeremiah rail against the idea that the salvation promised by God in the OT may be considered along the lines of a philosophy. God is not known through wisdom, but through revelation. "The cross, then, constitutes the point at which, and/or the means through which, God's presence and promise become *operative* as that which *actualizes* and *transforms*. It differs from human weakness and folly not in degree but in kind."[334] Paul is able to say that the cross is, at first glance, unacceptable to Jews and Greeks alike; their individual modes of resistance—seeking signs or seeking wisdom—are not the issue (1:22–24). The issue is that God's foolishness bests man's wisdom.[335] While Paul has made an effort to indicate the paradox of God's power over human wisdom in general, he also specifies the particular Corinthian context. Verses 26–28 speak directly to his converts. Paul notes that they are not all of the same strength, whether it be socially or personally, but their individual strengths, like human wisdom, are overshadowed by the cross. If there is any boasting (καυχᾶσθαι) to be done, it is boasting in the Lord.[336] Paul's reference to boasting is not merely an insight that both Jews and Greeks

---

[331] Fee, *First Corinthians*, 55–56.

[332] L. L. Welborn ("On the Discord in Corinth: 1 Corinthians 1–4 and Ancient Politics," *JBL* 106 [1987] 85–111) argues strongly for political dissention on the basis of Corinthian history and the ancient politics of a *polis*. While there is much to sustain his findings vis-à-vis antiquity, there is little to tie them specifically to v. 12. On this point, see Mitchell, *Paul and the Rhetoric of Reconciliation*, 83–86. Mitchell (84) also shows the tenuousness of personal identifications. Cf. Thiselton, *First Corinthians*, 121–22. On the question of gnosticism, see J.-M. Sevrin, "La gnose à Corinthe: Questions de méthode et observations sur 1 Co 1,17–3,3," in *The Corinthian Correspondence* (ed. R. Bieringer; BETL 125; Leuven: Leuven University Press, 1996) 121–39.

[333] On Paul's use of the OT here, see R. F. Collins, *First Corinthians*, 94–96.

[334] Thiselton, *First Corinthians*, 156 (emphasis original).

[335] See J. M. Reese, "Paul Proclaims the Wisdom of the Cross: Scandal and Foolishness," *BTB* 9 (1979) 147–53.

[336] On Paul's use of καυχᾶθαι, καύχημα, and καύχησις, especially coupled with the use of Jer 9:23–24 (LXX), see C. K. Barrett, "Boasting (καυχᾶσθαι, κτλ.) in the Pauline Epistles," in *L'apôtre Paul*, ed. Vanhoye, 363–68.

would have been hard pressed to come to know on their own, viz., that pride goes before a fall, it is a principle of his apostolate: "For what we preach is not ourselves, but Jesus Christ as Lord, with ourselves as your servants for Jesus' sake" (2 Cor 4:5).[337] It is not Paul's intention to enter into their arguments over wisdom; rather "he insists to the Corinthians that for them to live in their language of *sophia* and *sophia logou* is divisive and inappropriate."[338]

In denouncing their invocation of human wisdom, Paul invites the Corinthians to recall how he came to them with nothing other than the mystery (μυστήριον),[339] not with lofty words or wisdom, but with nothing other than "Jesus Christ and him crucified" (1 Cor 2:1–2). Therewith, Paul reminds them that he was neither personally self-assured nor particularly eloquent in handing on the faith to them. Paul presented not himself, but demonstrations of the "Spirit and of power" (cf. Gal 3:5); their faith was to rest not in the wisdom of men—even of Paul—but in the "power of God" (1 Cor 2:3–5). Paul's "settled resolve was that he would do only what served the gospel of Christ crucified, regardless of people's expectations or seductive shortcuts to success, most of all the seduction of self-advertisement."[340] Just as the strength of the gospel does not rest on Paul, so the Corinthians should not argue among themselves in terms of human personalities or wisdom.[341] Fee paraphrases:

> Thus [Paul] says in effect, "So you think the gospel is a form of *sophia*? How foolish can you get? Look at its *message*; it is based on the story of a crucified Messiah. Who in the name of wisdom would have dreamed that up? Only God is so wise as to be foolish" (1:18–25); "Furthermore, look at its *recipients*. Yourselves! Who in the name of wisdom would have chosen you to be the new people of God?" (1:26–31); "Finally, remember my own *preaching*. Who in the

---

[337] Ibid., 368.

[338] R. A. Horsley, "Wisdom of the Word and Words of Wisdom in Corinth," *CBQ* 39 (1977) 224–39.

[339] The RSV prefers the variant reading of "testimony" (μαρτύριον), but the N-A^{27} and the *GNT*^{4} favor "mystery" (μυστήριον). "The reading μαρτύριον seems to be a recollection of 1.6, whereas μυστήριον here prepares for its usage in ver. 7" (*TCGNT*, 480). The undertone of Greco-Roman mystery religions has kept this verse a *crux interpretum*. Conzelmann (*1 Corinthians*, 53 n. 6) says: "It is impossible to decide." Barrett (*First Corinthians*, 62–63) favors testimony, but R. F. Collins (*First Corinthians*, 188) and Thiselton (*First Corinthians*, 207–8) favor mystery. For now, we note that there is sufficient evidence to support a Semitic understanding of μυστήριον, as shown by R. E. Brown, "The Pre-Christian Semitic Concept of 'Mystery,'" *CBQ* 20 (1958) 417–43; idem, "The Semitic Background of the New Testament *Mysterion* (I)," *Bib* 39 (1958) 426–48; idem, "The Semitic Background of the New Testament *Mysterion* (II)," *Bib* 40 (1959) 70–87; and idem, *The Semitic Background of the Term "Mystery" in the New Testament* (BS 21; Philadelphia: Fortress [Facet], 1968).

[340] Thiselton, *First Corinthians*, 212.

[341] Ibid.

name of wisdom would have come in such weakness? Yet look at the results" (2:1–5)."[342]

This first part of Paul's argument aims to change the Corinthians' perspective. Paul desires that they abandon any concept of human leadership and wisdom; instead, they ought to look to the cross. Paul came to Corinth in order to proclaim Christ and Christ crucified. Along the lines of 1 Cor 15:1–11, Paul has imparted only what he received—Christ and Christ crucified—nothing of his own.

In the second part (B; 2:6–16), Paul elucidates a mature understanding of the cross and wisdom. Paul does this by essentially equating the two, inasmuch as he now uses σοφία in a different sense. He has pushed human wisdom to the side in order to replace it with a divine wisdom, "which God decreed before the ages for our glorification" (v. 7). Paul did, indeed, come to impart wisdom, a wisdom not of this world, but of God. Thus, wisdom is used positively by Paul to denote both God's salvific plan in Christ and the substance of that plan, viz., salvation; it is used negatively to denote human argumentation and the substance of such argumentation, viz., standards different from Christ's.[343] The quotation in v. 9 is most likely a version of Isa 64:4 (64:3 [LXX]; *1 Clem.* 34:8 repeats Paul's rendition),[344] but the exact source is unknown. Even if there is some uncertainty about the source of Paul's citation, the function of the text is clear. "First, Scripture supports the fact that people in the present age do not understand what God accomplished in Christ: God's ways (his 'wisdom') are not even conceivable by the merely human mind. Second, what they are ignorant of is the salvation that God 'has prepared for those who love him.'"[345] It is only with the Spirit that spiritual gifts are understood.[346] With v. 13, Paul hones in on his point: "And we impart this in words not taught by human wisdom but taught by the Spirit, interpreting spiritual truths to those who possess the Spirit."[347] Paul, by his own example, shows that he must mete out the explanations of spiritual truths, even to those who already enjoy the Spirit, according to their ability to

---

[342] Fee, *First Corinthians*, 67.

[343] Barrett, *First Corinthians*, 67–68.

[344] On Paul's use of Isa 64:4, see R. F. Collins, *First Corinthians*, 131–32; and cf. Thiselton, *First Corinthians*, 248–52.

[345] Fee, *First Corinthians*, 107.

[346] "To know God completely is the privilege of God's *Pneuma*. If a man wants to know God, to get a profound insight into God's wisdom, he must have a share in the same *Pneuma* in accordance with the principle 'like by like,' and as a consequence of this Paul writes 'we have not received the *pneuma* of the world, but the *Pneuma* which is from God that we might know what God has given us,' τὰ ὑπὸ τοῦ θεοῦ χαρισθέντα ὑμῖν, v. 12. The *Pneuma* must be man's property, if he wants to be a σοφός" (B. E. Gärtner, "The Pauline and Johannine Idea of 'To Know God' against the Hellenistic Background: The Greek Philosophical Principle 'Like by Like' in Paul and John," *NTS* 14 [1967–68] 218).

[347] For an explanation of the difficulties in translating this verse, see Barrett, *First Corinthians*, 75–76; and Thiselton, *First Corinthians*, 264–66.

assimilate them. It would seem, then, that factionalism and discord are not the result of a lack of the Spirit, but of an unwillingness to yield to further instruction and enlightenment.

If misunderstandings are in some fashion the province of the spiritual man (πνευματικός), then what are we to say of the unspiritual man (ψυχικός)? Paul makes a very sharp distinction: "the unspiritual man does not receive the gifts of the Spirit of God, for they are folly to him, and he is not able to understand them because they are spiritually discerned" (v. 14); whereas, "the spiritual man judges all things, but is himself to be judged by no one" (v. 15). Paul's distinction is between those who are of the Spirit and those who are not.[348] This is a great solace to the Corinthians, and at the same time, a warning, for they may easily infer that both πνευματικοί and ψυχικοί are among them. Aside from its use here, πνευματικός is found frequently in 1 Corinthians (3:1; 9:11; 10:3, 4 [2x]; 12:1; 14:1, 37; 15:44 [2x], 46 [2x]) and the Pauline literature (Rom 1:1; 7:14; 15:27; Gal 6:1; Eph 1:3; 5:19; 6:12; Col 1:9; 3:16; cf. 1 Pet 2:5 [2x]). By contrast, ψυχικός is rare: it appears elsewhere only in 1 Corinthians (15:44 (2x), 46; cf. *4 Macc* 1:32; Jam 3:15; Jude 19). The juxtaposition of the two terms appears only here and in 15:44 and 46.[349] However, πνευματικός is paired with σάρκινος in 3:1 (cf. its only other uses in the NT: Rom 7:14; 2 Cor 3:3; Heb 7:16) and helps to refine our understanding of ψυχικός. Here as in 3:1 and 15:44–46, the ψυχικός is at best "a babe in Christ," but more precisely an unbeliever—one to whom *no* wisdom has been accorded. Paul is addressing the Corinthians as πνευματικοί, spiritual men, that which they are (or ought to be) by having accepted Paul's preaching; but by their slipping into factionalism, they risk reversion to their prior state as ψυχικοί, merely human, unspiritual men. Verse 15 drives Paul's point home: the spiritual man judges everything, but the unspiritual man dare not think to judge the spiritual.[350] Paul's invocation of Isa 40:13, wherewith he equates the mind of the Lord (i.e., YHWH; νοῦν κυρίου) with the mind of Christ (νοῦν Χριστοῦ),[351] harkens back to what the spiritual men of Corinth should have known all along, viz., the mind of Christ, "a constellation of thoughts and beliefs that provide the criteria for judgment and

---

[348] See R. A. Horsley, "*Pneumatikos* vs. *Psychikos*: Distinctions of Spiritual Status among the Corinthians," *HTR* 69 (1976) 269–88.

[349] See below for our discussion of these verses in 1 Corinthians 15. For now, see the discussion in Horsley ("*Pneumatikos* vs. *Psychikos*," 274–88) for the background of the distinction.

[350] "Having received the Spirit who searches everything (*panta*, 2:10), the spiritual person is capable of testing all things—and all persons (cf. 14:24). On the other hand the spiritual person, to whom Paul draws attention be means of an untranslated *autos*, 'that one' can be properly judged by no human being" (R. F. Collins, *First Corinthians*, 137).

[351] See Thiselton (*First Corinthains*, 271–76) for a discussion of textual issues in vv. 15–16, as well as comments on Paul's use of Isa 40:13.

action."³⁵² It would seem as if the argument has come around to its beginnings. As Fee observes:

> Paul began by insisting that his message was in fact an expression of wisdom—God's own wisdom, revealed as such by the Spirit. He at least—in contrast to the merely *psychikos* person, the mere human being without the Spirit—understands the mind of Christ. As those who possess the Spirit the Corinthians also potentially possess that same mind. However, as he will point out, their behavior betrays them. They do, but they don't. The concern from here on will be to force them to acknowledge the folly of their "wisdom," which is expressing itself in quarrels and thereby destroying the very church for which Christ died.³⁵³

For this reason, Paul begins the final stage of his argument in 1 Corinthians 1–4 by waning back to where he had begun in 1:10, with their strife and their pseudo-identification with teachers in the community.

In the third part (A'; 3:1–4:21), then, we return to the issue at hand. In 3:1–9, Paul recounts how he first fed the Corinthians with milk, since they were not ready for solid food—they were still in the flesh, still σαρκικοί. Likewise, claims Paul, if there is jealousy and strife among them, or if some say that they belong to Paul or Apollos, then they are still σαρκικοί. Paul and Apollos are merely servants (διάκονοι) and coworkers (συνεργοί),³⁵⁴ one in their contributions to aiding God's growth. Paul speaks of the community as a building for which he, as a wise (σοφός) builder, laid the foundation, "which is Jesus Christ" (v. 11). Here Paul borrows the structure and vocabulary of pagan temple construction contracts,³⁵⁵ with which the Corinthians were no doubt familiar, in order to relate the importance of a foundation. Ancient contracts stipulated that if anyone did damage to a foundation or construction project, the builder would do harm to him.³⁵⁶ "In the spiritual realm, Paul simply states that if any man does harm to God's temple, God will do harm to him."³⁵⁷ For it is to God's building that Paul and Apollos have collaborated their efforts. With that in mind, Paul asks them whether or not they are aware of what they are called to be. In so doing, Paul advances the construction metaphor by speaking of them not only as God's building (οἰκοδομή) but also as God's sanctuary (ναός). The stage is now set for Paul's admonition in v. 18: "Let no one deceive himself." The world's wisdom cannot see the holiness of God's sanctuary. We are immediately re-

---

³⁵² R. F. Collins, *First Corinthians*, 138.

³⁵³ Fee, *First Corinthians*, 120.

³⁵⁴ On translating 1 Cor 3:9, see V. P. Furnish, "Fellow Workers in God's Service," *JBL* 80 (1961) 364–70.

³⁵⁵ J. Shanor ("Paul as Master Builder: Construction Terms in First Corinthians," *NTS* 34 [1988]) 461–71) demonstrates the similarity of Paul's building metaphors to the language found in contemporaneous building contracts, especially a rather lengthy inscription found in Arcadia.

³⁵⁶ Ibid., 462, 471.

³⁵⁷ Ibid., 471.

minded of 1:18–25 and 3:16–17. The Corinthians must become fools so that they might become wise. Raymond F. Collins explains:

> If this seems paradoxical, and it is, then Paul offers an explanation (the first *gar*, v. 19a). The wisdom of this age is foolishness in the sight of God. In support of this contention (the second *gar*, v. 19b), Paul offers an argument from authority. His argument is based on two scriptural passages treated as one. The two passages are taken from the Jewish wisdom tradition: Job 5:13 and Ps 93:11 [LXX]. They speak of the futility of human wisdom. Paul has modified the two passages in such a way that they are to be interpreted in the light of one another. The scriptural citations evoke the biblical context from which they are drawn and substantiate Paul's affirmation that in the eyes of God human wisdom is foolish.[358]

The wisdom of the world is naught in God's plan for them; nor is the contentiousness of the wise and the crafty permissible in their dealings with one another, particularly when it comes to the things of God. Having been built on the foundation of Christ, the Corinthians are God's sanctuary. Paul's own words sum it up best: "So let no one boast of men. For all things are yours, whether Paul or Apollos or Cephas or the world or life or death or the present or the future, all are yours; and you are Christ's; and Christ is God's" (vv. 21–23).

But how ought the Corinthians to think of Paul, Apollos, or Cephas? Paul stresses that the Corinthians should regard Paul and Apollos as attendants of Christ (ὑπηρέτας Χριστοῦ) and stewards of the mysteries of God (οἰκονόμους μυστηρίων θεοῦ).[359] This ties Paul's instruction back to 2:1, wherein Paul spoke of his coming to preach the mystery of "Jesus Christ and him crucified." Paul has told them what he delivered to them, and now he asks for their trust. Because Paul has already spoken to the Corinthians about their theological misapprehensions as well as the apposite deference owed to their teachers, there is only one reason for Paul to go on: part and parcel of the problem in Corinth is the stance of many towards Paul himself.[360] These people are not simply *for* Apollos or Peter; they are decidedly *anti*-Paul. They are rejecting both his teaching *and* his authority."[361] Paul's riposte is decisive in 4:1–5. In verses pregnant with forensic terminology, Paul speaks as if in a courtroom.[362] He will be judged by no one—not by the Corinthians, not by any human court, not even by himself—but by the Lord, when he comes. Verse 6, "that you may learn by us not to go beyond what is written," which advances Paul's argument to the level of the personal example of Paul and Apollos, is a notorious *crux interpretum*. "Unfortunately, from the point of view of most modern interpreters, these words have

---
[358] R. F. Collins, *First Corinthians*, 163–64.
[359] On the importance of stewardship in the Greco-Roman milieu, see ibid., 168–69.
[360] Fee, *First Corinthians*, 156.
[361] Ibid. (emphasis original).
[362] R. F. Collins, *First Corinthians*, 169.

tended to conceal more than they reveal."³⁶³ Nonetheless, the gist of the verse is clear, viz., that they are neither to go beyond the example they were shown in Paul and Apollos,³⁶⁴ nor are they to dispute among themselves. Paul and Apollos are examples to be followed,³⁶⁵ as there is no contention between them so there should be none among the Corinthians. It is v. 7 (with its γάρ) that provides the rationale. Their arrogance and factionalism are indications of ingratitude. In point of fact, the Corinthians have nothing that they did not receive from Paul, and what they received was a gift. "'Boasting' is an affront to the Giver, representing as one's own achievement something which was rather the result of God's generosity."³⁶⁶

Constitutive of their misconstruing Paul's gift, the gift of the Spirit, is that the Corinthians do not realize that they are "already filled" (v. 8). Starting with v. 8 and continuing through v. 13, Paul aims to reprove the Corinthians. As Paul himself states, "I do not write this to make you ashamed but to admonish you as my beloved children" (v. 14). Paul portrays their success in contrast to his hardship.³⁶⁷ Whether or not Paul is referring to spiritual achievement vis-à-vis a realized eschatology,³⁶⁸ or to worldly achievement vis-à-vis social status,³⁶⁹ one thing is clear, i.e., "they have misconceived the very nature of salvation, in the present *and* in the future."³⁷⁰ They have neglected Paul's teaching that salvation is God's gift;³⁷¹ no one has it on his own. Yet many have taken security in salvation as if it were their proper possession. Peter Marshall has gone to the heart of the matter by showing that the problem lies in hubris.³⁷² Members of the com-

---

³⁶³ J. R. Wagner, "'Not Beyond the Things Which Are Written,'" 279. Conzelmann (*1 Corinthians*, 86) considers parts of it "unintelligible." See Thiselton (*First Corinthians*, 348–56) for the most expansive explanation. Interestingly, M. D. Hooker ("Beyond the Things That are Written? St Paul's Use of Scripture," *NTS* 27 [1980–81] 295–309) claims that Paul is saying that "you must not start trying to add philosophical notions to the basic Christian Gospel" (296). Cf. idem, "'Beyond the Things Which are Written': An Examination of I Cor VI.6," *NTS* 10 (1963–64) 127–32.

³⁶⁴ R. Tyler ("First Corinthians 4:6 and Hellenistic Pedagogy," *CBQ* 60 [1998] 97–103) argues persuasively that Paul's expression "not to go beyond what is written" is a pedagogical conception that the Corinthians would recognize from their elementary education, wherewith they would learn to write by following closely the teacher's example.

³⁶⁵ Cf. B. Fiore, "'Covert Allusion' in 1 Corinthians 1–4," *CBQ* 47 (1985) 94.

³⁶⁶ De Silva, "'Let One Who Claims Honor Establish That Claim in the Lord,'" 67.

³⁶⁷ On the *peristalsis* catalogues, see J. T. Fitzgerald, *Cracks in an Earthen Vessel: An Examination of the Catalogue of Hardships in the Corinthian Correspondence* (SBLDS 99; Atlanta: Scholars Press, 1988) 117–48.

³⁶⁸ Barrett, *First Corinthians*, 109; Thiselton, "Realized Eschatology at Corinth," 510–26; and idem, *First Corinthians*, 359–65.

³⁶⁹ Fitzgerald, *Cracks in an Earthen Vessel*, 134–43; and R. F. Collins, *First Corinthians*, 182–91.

³⁷⁰ D. J. Doughty, "The Presence and Future of Salvation in Corinth," *ZNW* 66 (1975) 63 (emphasis original).

³⁷¹ Ibid., 90.

³⁷² See P. Marshall, *Enmity in Corinth: Social Conventions in Paul's Relations with the Corinthians* (WUNT 2/23; Tübingen: Mohr [Siebeck], 1987) 194–218. Well aware of the fact that the

munity "consider themselves to be superior both to their fellow Christians and Paul and are behaving in a hubristic manner towards them."[373] Paul is careful to avoid the same pitfall in his reminder that they "have many guides in Christ," none of whom Paul wishes to discount, but only one father, Paul, who is father solely on account of the gospel. Therefore, Paul can securely urge them to become imitators of himself—μιμηταί μου γίνεσθε.[374] Inquiry into this phrase, found here in 4:16 and in 11:1 (cf. Eph 5:1; 1 Thess 1:6; 2:14; cf. also Phil 3:17; 2 Thess 3:7, 9), yields the following results, according to D. M. Stanley:

> (1) Paul urges this "imitation" of himself only to those communities which he has founded. (2) It is the necessary result of having accepted "his" gospel, which creates a special relationship between himself and the churches he founded. While Paul insists that his kerygma is essentially the same as that preached by other apostles, he is also aware that, as his personal testimony to Christ, his preaching and way of life have their own characteristic modalities, determined chiefly by his conviction that he carries on the role of Christ as the suffering servant of God. (3) Thus the *imitatio Christi* which Paul proposes to his communities is a mediated imitation. It springs both from Paul's apostolic authority as an authentic representative of Christian tradition, and from the recognized need of those he has fathered in the faith to have an objective, concrete norm against which they can "test" (δοκιμάζειν) the influence of the Spirit.[375]

Though Paul has initiated this section with a reminder that the Corinthians are his beloved (4:14; and will refer to them later in the same way in 10:14; 15:58) and though he will send Timothy to remind them of his ways in Christ (4:17),[376] Paul does not defer mentioning that there are those who are still arrogant, as though he were not coming (v. 18). But Paul is coming with power (δύναμις) rather than talk (λόγος). Colloquially, Paul speaks plainly in 4:21 to tell them that there is an easy way, in a spirit of love and gentleness, or a hard way, with a rod[377]—the choice belongs to them.[378]

---

word ὕβρις does not appear in the pericope, Marshall shows that the concept is certainly there because "some of the more important vocabulary and ideas associated with it in Greek authors are clearly present" (194–95).

[373] Ibid., 217–18.

[374] If there were in fact any question in the early Church about the creditable example of Paul, the answer is surely in the affirmative; see Bondi, R. A. "Become Such as I Am: St. Paul in the Acts of the Apostles," *BTB* 27 (1997) 164–76.

[375] D. M. Stanley, "'Become Imitators of Me': The Pauline Conception of Apostolic Tradition," *Bib* 40 (1959) 877.

[376] Bailey ("The Structure of I Corinthians," 151–81) suggests that 4:17 is key to understanding the whole of 4:17–7:40, but this seems to overrate the importance of Timothy's visit here and in 16:10.

[377] Here ῥάβδος, a *hapax legomenon* in Paul (though common enough in the LXX and NT), is allied to the correction we saw earlier in 4:6; cf. Prov 13:24.

[378] So too, R. F. Collins, *First Corinthians*, 202.

Yet in a sense, they have no choice. Paul wants the Corinthians to resolve their factionalism. Clearly, Paul tells them that their discord is based on a misunderstanding of the gospel message that he preached. Thus, the overarching path to concord is to return to Paul's, i.e., Christ's, original gospel. The issue is not that they distorted his teachings or someone else came preaching something different from what Paul had originally said. On the one hand, "we cannot assume that when Corinthian practices differed from Paul's wishes the differences were merely distortions of Paul's teachings. His converts may not have been forgetting his lessons, but learning from others'."[379] On the other hand, there is no reason to presuppose that others—Apollos, Cephas, or anyone else for that matter—brought anything to Corinth worthy of disputation.[380] Were that the case, Paul would have devoted perforce much more attention to the problematic teachings, rather than to the supposed debate and resultant discord. By and large, though, the source of the misunderstandings is not the *cause célèbre*, but factionalism resultant upon the misunderstandings, which may only be repaired by concord in truth. What truth? The gospel as Paul understands it to be. Nothing short of that will do. Paul wishes his converts to stand firm in the gospel he preached, which is the equivalent of standing firm not only in the Lord but in loyalty to Paul.[381] Our exposition of 1 Corinthians 1–4 portrays Paul, the founder of Corinthian Christianity, urging that his flock be "united in the same mind and in the same judgment" (1:10). Paul evinces this unity in three foci: (1) Paul taught nothing other than Jesus Christ and him crucified (2:2); (2) only the spiritual man understands spiritual things (2:11); and (3) Paul's testimony of Jesus and the Spirit is trustworthy (4:1–2). Factionalism, then, is healed only by Jesus, the Spirit, and the truth, i.e., the gospel preached by Paul.

As we proposed earlier in our study, the report from Chloe's people seems to have been the impetus behind 1 Corinthians 1–4. "For these chapters only a single item of information need be presupposed. Thus the single mention of a report by Chloe's people in 1:11 fully provides the occasion for these four chapters."[382] Chapters 5 and 6 (along with some other parts, e.g., 11:8; 15:12) are the response to the report of Stephanas, Fortunatus, and Achaicus, who carried a letter from the Corinthians, which occasioned the lion's share of chapters 7–16—"now concerning the matters about which you wrote" (7:1).[383] So, chapters 1–4 are the response to one specific informational item, factionalism, and chap-

---

[379] M. Smith, "Paul's Arguments as Evidence of the Christianity from Which He Diverged," *HTR* 79 (1986) 254.

[380] Even if, as M. Smith (ibid., 260 et passim) suggests, Cephas or others may have brought earlier teachings, i.e., things that Paul may not have known because of his lack of knowledge of Jesus' earthly ministry, hence making some Corinthians the first "back to Jesus" Christians, it seems unlikely that Paul would have brooked any opposition on those grounds.

[381] Knox, *Chapters in a Life of Paul*, 80.

[382] Hurd, *The Origin of 1 Corinthians*, 77.

[383] De Boer, "The Composition of 1 Corinthians," 232–33.

ters 5–16 are the response to a slew of items.³⁸⁴ The result of both oral and written information, the "laundry list" of chapters 5–16 does not lend itself to precise organization along the lines of a clear-cut structure. However, it is facile to catch sight of two general issues: the ethical (5:1–11:34) and the spiritual (12:1–14:40). For that reason, we trace the ethical and spiritual issues in chapters 5 through 14, and then consider the last issue, viz., the resurrection of the dead. Less facile it is to appreciate the extent to which any or all of the Corinthians' problems may have been stimuli for Paul's theological reflection. The Corinthians have provided—unawares—situations for deliberation that might never have come to Paul's attention otherwise.³⁸⁵ And as any reader of 1 Corinthians knows, the Corinthians caught Paul's attention with their poor behavior.

Ethical Issues (1 Corinthians 5–11)

That Paul's attention was fixed on what he learned from Stephanas and company, by mouth or by letter, is evidenced in the consideration he gives to their problems. In no other letter by Paul, and indeed in no other biblical book, does an author deal with so many practical problems. Principally noteworthy is Paul's proximity both to the people themselves and to their particular problems. Paul addresses a community (one he founded and with which he lived), living in a city (wherein he resided, much like the city of his birth), about issues (with which he is personally familiar as a Diaspora Jew and a well-traveled Christian), and over which he exercises authority, albeit the authority of Christ and the gospel. To be sure, Paul is neither naïve about the people to whom he preached and the circumstances in which he preached, nor is he timid when it comes to using his authority, even with a (metaphorical) rod. For this reason, the secondary literature pertaining to 1 Corinthians 5–11 is vast. Christians past and present are deeply interested in Paul's ethics, i.e., in the practical teaching he offered in response to ethical dilemmas in Corinth.

Speaking of 1 Corinthians in general, Victor P. Furnish remarks:

> Perhaps surprisingly, there seem to be few points where the moral instruction has been shaped or supported to any significant extent by citations from Scripture, by teachings attributed to the Lord, or by insights ascribed to the Spirit's leading. Instead, the pattern of Paul's argumentation suggests that his ethical reflection and judgments have been informed primarily by the truth of the gospel, as he understands that.³⁸⁶

---

³⁸⁴ See de la Serna, "Los orígenes de 1 Corintios," 202–16.

³⁸⁵ See S. Cipriani, "La communità di Corinto come 'stimolo' alla riflessione teologica di S. Paolo," *Lateranum* 50 (1984) 86–100.

³⁸⁶ V. P. Furnish, "Belonging to Christ: A Paradigm for Ethics in First Corinthians," *Int* 44 (1990) 157. Furnish goes on to say: "Were it possible to expand this study to include chapter 5–7, it could be shown how this paradigm also operates there (note, esp., 5:6–8; 6:11, 19–20; 7:22–24) and

That is not to say that Paul does not take the Scriptures, the Lord, or the Spirit as supreme authorities, but it does suggest the vitality of Paul's apostleship. As Paul asserts in 1:17, Christ sent him to preach the gospel and anything short of that would lessen the power of the cross. Crucial to that preaching is Paul's apostolic leadership. His job is not merely to enunciate general principles; his job is to communicate to the Corinthians what is expected of them as they abide in the gospel he handed on to them. Were he to do less than that, he would shirk his responsibility. Paul evangelized and established a church in Corinth on the foundation of Christ. In order for the building (i.e., the community of believers) to stand firm, there is a need for guidance. Paul is desirous to offer it to them, so that they might be "guiltless on the day of our Lord Jesus Christ" (1:9). So too, our own desire for guiltlessness piques our curiosity in Paul's ethical reflection and judgment. Paul's application of the truth of the gospel to specific situations is invaluable.

It has been reported to Paul that there is immorality (πορνεία) among the Corinthians, an immorality that is offensive even to pagans, for a man is living with his father's wife (5:1). It is a situation that calls for community mourning; it is a situation that demands the removal of the offender from the community forthwith (5:2, 13). "Paul's argument moves from a condemnation of a specific vice to a denunciation of a general one, the vice of 'sexual immorality.'"[387] This leaves Paul some latitude to address the general issue of avoiding immorality of any kind about which he had written earlier (5:9). The matter is particularly pressing, though. Paul does not limit himself to vice, particular or general. He goes further and expresses dismay about the community's mistaken tolerance, for the immorality is among them (ἐν ὑμῖν πορνεία). Paul treats the problem of the personal morality of the man in question as one problem, and the community's forbearance as another problem.[388] Thus, chapter 5 is a matter not only of immorality, but also of church discipline. Paul calls upon the community to act against this immorality, along the lines of Deut 17:2–7, which Paul evokes in 5:13.

The immorality is that of ὥστε γυναῖκά τινα τοῦ πατρὸς ἔχειν, a man is living with his father's wife. Given the similarity to Lev 18:8, the woman is most likely his stepmother. But there are a number of possibilities afoot. She might have been his father's divorced wife or concubine, legitimate or not.[389] The motive for union may have been monetary or political.[390] Although we do

---

how it is related to the apostle's eschatological expectations (e.g., 5:5; 6:2, 9–11; 7:29–32) and his view of Christ's resurrection. (Apart from chap. 15, the latter is mentioned explicitly only in 6:14.)" (157 n. 18).

[387] P. S. Zaas, "'Cast Out the Evil Man from Your Midst' (1 Cor 5:13b)," *JBL* 103 (1984) 259.

[388] G. Harris, "The Beginnings of Church Discipline: 1 Corinthians 5," *NTS* 37 (1991) 5.

[389] R. F. Collins, *First Corinthians*, 209. Barrett (*First Corinthians*, 122) thinks legitimate; Conzelmann (*1 Corinthians*, 96) thinks illegitimate. But there is no way to tell for certain.

[390] J. K. Chow, *Patronage and Power: A Study of Social Networks in Corinth* (JSNTSup 75; Sheffield: JSOT Press, 1992) 132–39. Chow also notes that were money or politics involved the

not know why these two were together, in "any of these possibilities the relationship would have been considered incestuous and in violation of social norms."[391] Neither Jewish (Lev 18:7–29; Deut 22:30; 27:20) nor Roman law (Gaius, *Inst.* 1.6) would have sanctioned anything of the sort. To add insult to injury, the problem is current. By using ἔχειν, Paul indicates that the problem is ongoing—not something that has happened just once or so.[392] Additionally, it would seem that the woman is not a Christian, otherwise she would have been subject to the same fate as the fellow. "Given the full mutuality of men and women in the marital issues addressed in chapter 7, it is nearly impossible that she could have been a member of the community and not in v. 5 have been brought under the same judgment as her lover."[393] And the judgment in v. 5 is severe: "delivered over to Satan for the destruction of the flesh, that his spirit may be saved in the day of the Lord Jesus."[394] Yet, it is also medicinal for the individual and for the community. While it may be argued that this man is to act as the scapegoat for the community (vis-à-vis the atonement texts of Leviticus 16) and for his own healing as well,[395] since the time of Origen (*Fr. 1 Cor.* 24.93.12–13) the verse has been taken to mean that the punishment is remedial, a means to purify the sinful man so that he may one day return to the community.[396] If he were to be permitted to remain in the community, the community would be at risk.[397]

In the meantime, the Corinthians must fulfill their proper role: to act as a community in addressing the problem and redressing the risk.[398] Again, whether or not the remedy will prove effective to the sinner—and "Paul offers no guarantee that expulsion will have the desired effect"[399]—the community's moment

---

woman may have been the same age as the man; in fact, she may have been younger than he. See also Winter, "Criminal Law and Christian Partiality (1 Corinthians 15)" (chap. 3), in *After Paul Left Corinth*, 44–57. Winter explains how Roman law favored those with high social status.

[391] R. F. Collins, *First Corinthians*, 209.

[392] Fee, *First Corinthians*, 200.

[393] Ibid., 201.

[394] As J. T. South remarks: "It is impossible to delineate all that being delivered to Satan might have been expected to include, but the evidence points away from the curse/death interpretation.... Anyone with a sense of identity as a member of the 'body of Christ,' redeemed from sin, and living in fellowship with God and other redeemed people could not help feeling the effects of being formally, visibly, and completely excluded from that community. The sense of loss would of necessity be overwhelming" ("A Critique of the 'Curse/Death' Interpretation of 1 Corinthians 5.1–8," *NTS* 39 [1993] 61).

[395] V. G. Shillington, "Atonement Texture in 1 Corinthians 5.5," *JSNT* 71 (1998) 29–50. See pp. 30–32 for Shillington's understanding of Tertullian's reading of 1 Cor 5:5.

[396] See J. Cambier, "La chair et l'esprit en I Cor. V. 5," *NTS* 15 (1968–69) 221–32.

[397] On this point, see M. Pascuzzi, *Ethics, Ecclesiology and Church Discipline: A Rhetorical Analysis of 1 Corinthians 5* (TGST 32; Rome: Editrice Pontificia Università Gregoriana, 1997) 155–64.

[398] Harris, "Beginnings of Church Discipline," 5.

[399] South, "A Critique of the 'Curse/Death' Interpretation of 1 Corinthians 5.1–8," 559.

of action is already late in coming.[400] Paul is upset that the Corinthians had misunderstood his prior written proscription about associating with immoral men. And now they must take action, for without action the community imperils its holiness. Paul expects that the community show itself to be one "whose Spirit-guided behavior would give concrete expression to its status."[401] In fact, the toleration "of an impenitent offender would indicate a false and presumptuous sense of security and would lead to moral contamination."[402] Paul is not as interested in ordering the Corinthians to obey him as he is in trying to make them see what is at stake in their indolence. Essentially, the situation becomes a didactic moment for Paul. We ought not to look upon chapter 5 as an attempt on Paul's part to (re)establish his authority, "thereby turning a religious-moral issue into a politics-of-authority issue."[403] Rather, "when we consider the offense and the discipline in light of Paul's ecclesial ideas, we can observe that the discipline clearly fits the offense."[404] Furthermore, the stakes are high. The Corinthian community is hardly ready for "solid food" (3:2), but there is a need for the community to begin to exercise its responsibilities on its own. For this reason, we are not surprised to see Paul catalogue some particularly knotty vices in vv. 10–11.[405] Since they are called to be united and holy, they must act in unison for the good. Indeed, their judgment has been at fault and is in need of enlightenment, so Paul urges them to do what they ought to have done already: to drive out the wicked person from among them.[406]

The Corinthians' deficiency in union and holiness is also evident in their civil litigiousness, so prominent in 1 Corinthians 6.[407] 1 Corinthians 5 and 6 are closely related both in theme and in 1 Corinthians' literary structure.[408] Again, the issue is one of the proper behavior of a Christian community. Disputes are being taken from their rightful place within the community and brought to outsiders. This is the reverse of what is expected, since "the saints will judge the world" (6:2; cf. Dan 7:22). Paul's experience in the Diaspora had equipped him

---

[400] Harris, "Beginnings of Church Discipline," 5.

[401] Pascuzzi, *Ethics, Ecclesiology and Church Discipline*, 163.

[402] G. W. H. Lampe, "Church Discipline and the Interpretation of the Epistles to the Corinthians," in *Christian History and Interpretation*, ed. Farmer, Moule, and Niebuhr, 355.

[403] Pascuzzi, *Ethics, Ecclesiology and Church Discipline*, 165.

[404] Ibid.

[405] Although some commentators (e.g., Conzelmann, *1 Corinthians*, 100–101) maintain that the vice catalogues of 5:10–11 and 6:9–10 are not based on the immediate *Sitz-im-Leben* of Corinth but are the recasting of traditional material not related *per se* to the Corinthians, there is no reason to presume that the vices mentioned in chapters 5 and 6 were not real ills among early Corinthian Christians, especially since their placement seems to conform to Paul's epistolary style. See P. S. Zaas, "Catalogues and Context: 1 Corinthians 5 and 6," *NTS* 34 (1988) 622–29.

[406] For the textual issues in v. 13, see R. F. Collins, *First Corinthians*, 223–24.

[407] See A. C. Mitchell, "Rich and Poor in the Courts of Corinth: Litigiousness and Status in 1 Corinthians 6.1–11," *NTS* 39 (1993) 562–86.

[408] Zaas, "Catalogues and Context," 629. For more, see W. Deming, "The Unity of 1 Corinthians 5–6," *JBL* 115 (1996) 289–312.

well to appreciate the delicate position of a community of believers within a larger pagan context.[409] Moreover, Greco-Roman civil society allowed for at least three other methods of conflict resolution besides formal civil adjudication, i.e., arbitration, conciliation, and compromise.[410] Paul's experience had also given him an insight into the often corrupt practices of Roman litigation (much more the province of the elite than of the ordinary person).[411] Corruption or favoritism notwithstanding, "the unrighteous will not inherit the kingdom of God" (v. 9a); likewise, Paul explains that all sorts of sinners are also excluded (v. 9b–10). "The vices that Paul adds to the catalogue in 6.9f point to the connection between idolatry and sexual vice and point as well to the importance of the Decalogue in Paul's Torah."[412] In other words, Paul is expanding the original list from "those who bear the name of brother" (5:11) to those with whom the Corinthian Christians are engaging in civil litigation. "The boasting which Paul confronts in 1 Corinthians 1–5 also appears to have split over the issue of the successful litigant scoring a victory. It does not seem that the Corinthian Christians felt a sense of disgust over the way in which the local legal system operated. On the contrary, they endorsed it by taking cases to it."[413] But in 6:11–12, Paul tells them that this is the very route they should have left behind. It is within the community that they were washed, sanctified, and justified in Christ and the Spirit. And it is within the community that they must resolve their disputes, for anything less is a denunciation of Christ and the Spirit.

1 Cor 6:12–20 seems to be fraught with slogans,[414] which Paul uses to advance his argument that Corinthians must separate themselves from the sinful practices of the *polis* in which they live.[415] While the origin of the slogan "all things are lawful for me" (6:12; cf. 10:23) remains obscure, its meaning is clear: "do whatever you wish."[416] All in all, it is a mandate for self-indulgence. This goes to show that they have failed to integrate the Spirit individually (as they failed collectively in regard to community purity). Paul, on the contrary, would not have them be enslaved by food (v. 13) or sexual licentiousness (v. 15), because both are sins against the body. The first-century Romans enjoyed great laxity in terms of gluttony, drunkenness, and sexual liberty. It was common for

---

[409] Yet we must be careful not to make too facile an identification between sects (in qualified conflict with broader society) and associations (in relative unanimity with broader society). For a wide range of possibilities, see P. A Harland, "Honouring the Emperor or Assailing the Beast: Participation in Civic Life among Associations (Jewish, Christian and Other) in Asia Minor and the Apocalypse of John," *JSNT* 77 (2000) 99–121.

[410] J. D. M. Derrett, "Judgment and 1 Corinthians 6," *NTS* 37 (1991) 24–26.

[411] On this, see Winter, *After Paul Left Corinth*, 58–68.

[412] Zaas, "Catalogues and Context," 629.

[413] Winter, *After Paul Left Corinth*, 69–70.

[414] Murphy-O'Connor, "Corinthian Slogans in 1 Cor 6:12–20," 391–96.

[415] See B. J. Dodd, "Paul's Paradigmatic 'I' and 1 Corinthians 6.12," *JSNT* 59 (1995) 39–58.

[416] Winter, *After Paul Left Corinth*, 81–82.

them to gather, especially at civic festivals and dinners, to engage therein. "The East of the empire had a long history of the unholy trinity of eating, drinking, and immorality at dinners."[417] (This point will not be lost in 11:17–34 or 15:32.) While it is true that, of the three, eating is necessary for life, Paul dismisses an analogy between the stomach for eating and the body for fornication,[418] which the Corinthians seem to have used in order to justify their dalliance with prostitution,[419] especially temple prostitution.[420] This is crystallized in his citation of Gen 2:24 (cf. Eph 5:31) and his emphasis in fleeing fornication.[421] The sexual union is not to be treated lightly or to be regarded as something merely perfunctory. Therefore, Paul asks, "Do you not know that your body is a temple of the Holy Spirit within you, which you have from God?" (v. 19). Then, by reminding them that they "were bought with a price" (v. 20a), Paul brings them back to what he had said in v. 11. The price, though dear, is not the issue here (cf. 7:23); what is at stake is "that the transaction has been duly carried out and completed,"[422] i.e., their pagan ways and excuses are in the past. Personal integration of the Spirit forswears enslavement of the body for freedom of the body, wherein God may be glorified (cf. 15:44b–49 and Rom 8:9–13).[423]

Paul's move from speaking of the body at the end of chapter 6 to a discussion of marriage in chapter 7 does not *necessarily* link the two thematically or sequentially. In 7:1, Paul is obviously switching from what he knows by hearsay—from Chloe's people or Stephanas and company or both—to that which the Corinthians wrote to him: "Now concerning the matters about which you wrote" (Περὶ δὲ ἐγράψατε).[424] It would seem, though, that the discussions of chapters 5 and 6 may have been written by Paul in anticipation of his response to their (written) questions about marriage or, at least, placed appropriately within 1 Corinthians in order to provide a backdrop to marital issues.[425] Chapter 7 is the response to the Corinthians' questions about marriage. Evidently, Paul is more interested in giving his own opinions rather than commands from the Lord (vv. 6–7, 10, 12, 17, 25, 40). Paul's considered opinion, formed in his understanding of eschatological urgency,[426] is best seen in v. 26: "I think that in view of the

---

[417] Ibid., 85.

[418] Barrett, *First Corinthians*, 147–48.

[419] Winter, *After Paul Left Corinth*, 87–88, rightly warns against ascribing this unilaterally to the Corinthians—Christian or not—without close attention to first-century Corinth's sociopolitical context(s).

[420] See B. S. Rosner, "Temple Prostitution in 1 Corinthians 6:12–20," *NovT* 40 (1998) 336–51.

[421] Cf. B. Byrne, "Sinning against One's Own Body: Paul's Understanding of the Sexual Relationship in 1 Corinthians 6:18," *CBQ* 45 (1983) 613.

[422] Barrett, *First Corinthians*, 152.

[423] For more, see Brodeur, *The Holy Spirit's Agency in the Resurrection of the Dead*, 157–62, 236–43.

[424] Mitchell, "Concerning Περὶ Δέ in 1 Corinthians," 229–56.

[425] So too, Byrne, "Sinning against One's Own Body," 615.

[426] See Fee, *First Corinthians*, 267–70.

present distress it is well for a person to remain as he is." Given that Paul's opinions are the response to questions in the previous letter from the Corinthians—questions not at our disposal—we ought to take note that this "does not necessarily represent Paul's total theology of marriage,"[427] but a series of viable options. As with chapters 1–4, a simple tricolon structure is discernable in chapter 7: A (7:1–16), some general instructions about marriage; B (7:17–24), some general recommendations about stability; and A' (7:25–40), some general advice about celibacy.[428]

In the first part (A; 7:1–16), Paul acknowledges that celibacy is a viable option,[429] even as he recognizes marriage as the norm.[430] Likewise, conjugal rights are the norm in marriage "except perhaps by agreement for a season, that you may devote yourselves to prayer" (v. 5). And although Paul expresses the ease of the celibate state in his own life, he does not fail to concede that each person has a special gift from God, including those who married. Not unlike 1 Thess 4:3–8, wherein Paul speaks of the holiness and honor implicit in marriage, "God's will is the sanctification of his people and that sanctification is to be found within a conjugal life lived in accordance with the will of God."[431] Nonetheless, though Paul does advocate celibacy, he understands human passion along with concupiscence. While v. 9 might seem to say that marriage is a cure-all for lust, the context of the passage reveals that Paul seeks only to enliven introspection so that each individual may know the status to which God has called him. "In this case, then, Paul is not so much offering marriage as the remedy for the sexual desire of 'enflamed youth,' which is the most common way of viewing the text, but as the proper alternative for those who are already consumed by that desire and are sinning."[432] That is, those who are not called to celibacy will find it well-nigh impossible to live that way. Verses 12–16 are the lynchpin to Paul's positive assessment of marriage in that the spouses are mutually consecrated. An unbelieving spouse may be the cause of separation, but a

---

[427] Byrne, "Sinning against One's Own Body," 615. See Fee (*First Corinthians*, 268 n. 3) for further reading on Paul's understanding of marriage in light of chapter 7.

[428] P. F. Ellis, *Seven Pauline Letters*, 67–68.

[429] Hurd (*The Origin of 1 Corinthians*, 62–63) rightfully maintains that 7:1 is a reference to something the Corinthians had written to Paul. For the background, i.e., what might have occasioned this phrase among the Corinthians, see D. L. Balch, "Backgrounds of I Cor. VII: Sayings of the Lord in Q; Moses as an Ascetic Θεῖος 'Ἀνήρ in II Cor. III," *NTS* 18 (1971–72) 351–64; and cf. F. Neirynck, "The Sayings of Jesus in 1 Corinthians," in *The Corinthian Correspondence*, ed. Bieringer, 141–76.

[430] On the possible motives for celibacy, see W. Deming, "The Motivation for Celibacy in 1 Corinthians 7: A Review of Scholarly Opinion" (chap. 1), in *Paul on Marriage and Celibacy: The Hellenistic Background of 1 Corinthians 7* (SNTSMS 83; Cambridge: Cambridge University Press, 1995) 5–49.

[431] R. F. Collins, "The Unity of Paul's Paraenesis in 1 Thess. 4.3–8 and 1 Cor. 7.1–7: A Significant Parallel," *NTS* 29 (1983) 423.

[432] Fee, *First Corinthians*, 289.

believer should never be such. The goal is peace, peace in the Lord. "Wife, how do you know whether you will save your husband? Husband, how do you know whether you will save your wife?" (v. 16).

The second part (B; 7:17–24), a general rule about stability, reinforces the notion that Paul is more concerned with a settled constancy, which may extend beyond the boundaries of marriage and celibacy, than with an exposition on the value of the married or celibate state *per se*. Within the broader context of marriage and celibacy, Paul uses circumcision and slavery in order to illustrate his point, viz., "that no state of life is incompatible with the Christian calling;"[433] or, "that one should remain in the state in which he is called" (v. 20; cf. v. 24). In fact, "what Paul says about circumcision and slavery is ethical advice which could stand on its own, outside the argumentation in 1 Corinthians 7."[434] The advice is the same, but the two examples are not exactly parallel. In the first instance (vv. 17–19), circumcision itself is immaterial: whether or not one is circumcised is inconsequential. The only thing important is keeping the commandments of God. One is not given any option in terms of circumcision; one is simply to remain as he is. However, in the second instance (vv. 21–24), slavery is also seen as inconsequential, but mutable. That is, one's status in society is negligible in terms of one's status in the kingdom of God. One's status as a freedman in the Lord is immutable as compared to one's social status, but "if you can gain your freedom [vis-à-vis your social status], avail yourself of the opportunity" (v. 21b).[435] Again, what is important is that one sees his life in the Lord as paramount.[436]

Finally, Paul moves on to the third part (A'; 7:25–40), wherein he addresses the unmarried. He suggests celibacy, while at the same time stating plainly that there is nothing wrong with marriage.[437] According to Paul, the "appointed time has grown very short" (v.29a), and he wants the Corinthians "to be free from anxieties" (v. 32). Paul understands the responsibilities of the married state (vv. 33–35). His understanding manifests his belief that marriage is a good ordained by God, but that it comes with burdens. These burdens, it would seem, Paul

---

[433] G. W. Dawes, "'But If You Can Gain Your Freedom' (1 Corinthians 7:17–24)," *CBQ* 52 (1990) 697.

[434] Ibid., 686.

[435] See ibid., 691. For more, see W. Deming, "A Diatribe Pattern in 1 Cor. 7:21–22: A New Perspective on Paul's Directions to Slaves," *NovT* 37 (1995) 130–37.

[436] Of particular interest in the interpretation of chapter 7 is B. R. Braxton, *The Tyranny of Resolution: 1 Corinthians 7:17–24* (SBLDS 181; Atlanta: Society of Biblical Literature, 2000). Braxton points out that while the example of circumcision may be one well chosen by Paul, the example of slavery is too easily misread in our contemporary situation. Braxton demonstrates clearly, particularly through a jaunt of ideological criticism, that Paul had no intention of advocating complacency—never mind slavery—in sociopolitical situations. The key phrase for Braxton, is in v. 21: "if you can gain your freedom, avail yourself of the opportunity."

[437] See Deming, "The Stoic–Cynic Marriage Debate" (chap. 2), in *Paul on Marriage and Celibacy*, 50–107.

wishes to spare them as they prepare for the coming of Christ and the inauguration of the kingdom wherein marriage will pass away (cf. Matt 22:30; Mark 12:25; Luke 20:35). But Paul is a "realist" when it comes to human relations; an eschatological urgency may provoke a healthy tension between this world and the next (as in 1 Thess 5:1–11), but the vicissitudes of life are not to be ignored.[438] It is no sin to marry, and it is no sin not to marry. Although Paul is more than willing to offer his opinion advocating celibacy to them, he is careful not to lay any restraint upon them, for his interest is in good order and devotion to the Lord (v. 35). Here, "we catch a glimpse of an understanding of holiness according to which [renunciation] is practiced in order to reach a higher stage in the relation to God."[439] Paul sees detachment from things of the world, even if they are good, as a freedom for deeper devotion. Along the lines of the Lord's response in terms of divorce in Matt 19:3–12, Paul is more interested in having the Corinthians live up to their individual callings than he is in dispensing advice about marriage. Yet since they have asked, he renders his opinion and uses himself as an example. Recognizing that his is not the last word on the matter, Paul can conclude with "I think that I have the Spirit of God." In other words, he has proffered sound advice, but freedom remains theirs in terms of marriage and celibacy.

From the περὶ δέ in 8:1, it is palpable that Paul is moving on to another point raised by the Corinthians' letter. Quickly enough we see that marriage and celibacy were not the only issues related to freedom about which the Corinthians were concerned. One of the more pressing problems for nascent Christian communities in the Greco-Roman world was the extent of their participation in the broader sociopolitical and cultural milieux in which they found themselves. That problem seems to have come to particular notice in the question of eating food offered to idols (εἰδωλόθυτα).[440] The Corinthians were unsure of the proper Christian stance towards idol food, i.e., there was some disagreement among them in this matter about which they turned to Paul for resolution.[441] In similar fashion to his response to their questions regarding marriage and celibacy, Paul is not as interested in spelling out precise rules as he is in presenting principles and examples based on one's freedom in Christ and one's responsibilities towards fellow believers. The problem of idol food will constitute 1 Corinthians 8, 9, and 10.[442] A close reading reveals once again a tricolon structure. First, Paul

---

[438] R. F. Collins, *First Corinthians*, 290–91.

[439] Conzelmann, *1 Corinthians*, 134.

[440] On the precise meaning of εἰδωλόθυτα in this context, see G. D. Fee, "Εἰδωλόθυτα Once Again: An Interpretation of 1 Corinthians 8–10," *Bib* 61 (1980) 181–87.

[441] D. G. Horrell, "Theological Principle or Christological Praxis? Pauline Ethics in 1 Corinthians 8.1–11.1," *JSNT* 67 (1997) 84–85.

[442] The literary integrity of these chapters has been challenged; see Hurd (*The Origin of 1 Corinthians*, 115) for the most prominent partition theories. However, A. T. Cheung (*Idol Food in Corinth: Jewish Background and Pauline Legacy* [JSNTSup 176; Sheffield: Sheffield Academic

introduces the problem (A; 8:1–13); second, Paul presents principles relative to the problem (B; 9:1–10:22); and third, Paul offers a practical solution (A'; 10:23–11:1).[443] In essence, Paul demonstrates the reciprocal relationship between liberty in Christ and liability in the Christian community.

In his introduction to the problem (A; 8:1–13), Paul begins with the principle that encapsulates his argument, viz., that this is a problem more related to love than to knowledge (vv. 1–3).[444] However, Paul must introduce one relevant piece of knowledge, knowledge they presumably should have possessed already. Reminiscent of the *Šĕmaʿ* (Deut 6:4; 11:13–21; Num 15:37–41), Paul confirms that idols have no real existence, for there is only one God. Verse 5 acknowledges that others may call on "gods" and "lords,"[445] but their nonexistence is a foregone conclusion in light of the one God and the particular confession of faith in v. 6. The high Christology expressed in v. 6 is an emphatic refutation of idols. It is "likely that v. 6 comprises an already established creedal formula, but even so it is surely one with which Paul is in wholehearted agreement."[446] Perhaps, Paul specifically uses it to remind them of what they already know? Perhaps, it had been quoted to Paul in the Corinthians' letter? In any case, v. 7, with the robust adversative ἀλλά states clearly that some do not possess this piece of knowledge. Some are partaking of idol food in the same way as they did in the former, non-Christian days, as if the idols had real existence, because their faith in Christ is weak. Like the idols themselves, idol food means nothing (v. 8), and so Paul seems to have no problem with those eating it, unless the liberty becomes "a stumbling block for the weak" (vv. 9–10). While most commentators on vv. 7–13 conclude that the weak are upset by those who eat idol food because the weak think such an act to be contrary to faith (vis-à-vis Romans 14–15),[447] "it is better to understand the sin into which the 'weak' are being led as that sin of idolatry which is so forcefully condemned in chapter 10."[448] That is, if the weak believe in the existence of idols—not through the fault of those Christians who eat the idol food in clear conscience of the nonexistence of idols and therefore with indifference to idol food as such—it is better to avoid idol food than to lead others into sin. Their liberty must be tempered by liability.

But Paul does not ask them to curtail their liberty without some explanation, particularly without mention of his own liberty. Thus in the second part (B; 9:1–10:22), Paul presents principles relative to the problem in order to expose the

---

Press, 1999] 83–85 et passim) shows that the complexity of the interrelationship of the chapters demands their integrity.

[443] P. F. Ellis, *Seven Pauline Letters*, 76.

[444] So too, Horrell, "Theological Principle or Christological Praxis?" 86–87. See Thiselton (*First Corinthians*, 626–27) on love (ἀγάπη) and knowledge (γνῶσις).

[445] R. F. Collins, *First Corinthians*, 319.

[446] Horrell, "Theological Principle or Christological Praxis?" 88.

[447] See G. W. Dawes ("The Danger of Idolatry: First Corinthians 8:7–13," *CBQ* 58 [1996] 82–91) who lays out the majority opinion on 8:7–13.

[448] Ibid., 98.

temperance he advocates with four examples: his rights as an apostle (9:1–23), the danger of taking salvation for granted (9:24–27), the Hebrews in the desert (10:1–13), and the table of the Lord (10:14–22).[449] Paul's use of himself as a model is arresting. From v. 1 through v. 14, Paul describes all that he is entitled to because of his apostolic status, only to say that he "has made no use of any right" (v. 15). Rather, he became all things to all men (v. 22) in order to save them.[450] Paul has given up everything for the good of others. "He and his co-workers, more than any others (οὐ μᾶλλον ἡμεῖς), have a right, an ἐξουσία, which is surely unquestionable. However, strikingly, it is a right that they choose not to invoke, so as not to place any stumbling block in the way of the gospel (v. 12)."[451] Then, Paul moves on to an example that is close to home in Corinth. Verses 24–27 are, no doubt, a reference to the Isthmian Games, which Paul probably witnessed in 51. Winners of the various games were crowned with perishable crowns of celery and pine branches.[452] Athletes competed for a prize, after preparing themselves by self-discipline. So too, Paul would have the Corinthians discipline themselves, just as he does for the sake of the gospel, as an expression of true freedom.[453] In yet another example, Paul appeals to the experience of the Hebrews in the desert. By use of typology, Paul explains that they were cleansed, as in their passing through the Red Sea, fed by God, as in manna, and given life, as in the Rock (Exod 17:6; Num 20:11; Wis 11:4–8).[454] Despite all they were given, the Hebrews still managed to displease God, and they suffered for it (1 Cor 10:5–10).[455] The "passage is a warning against complacency: the Israelites all partook in the rituals of community membership just as much as the Corinthians, yet this was no guarantee of salvation."[456] Finally, in 10:14–24, Paul extends his example to the Eucharist. Simply stated, the partaking of the Lord's meal and the meal of demons is incompatible—there is no sharing of the Lord's cup and cup of demons (v. 21)—the two are absolutely and mutually exclusive. Fellowship (κοινωνία) at the one table precludes fellowship at the other.

---

[449] P. F. Ellis, *Seven Pauline Letters*, 76.

[450] "Paul's example may conceivably inspire a Christian discipleship which seeks to be Christ-like, yet which recognizes that this may involve difficult judgments about which words of Christ (or of other scriptural witnesses) are appropriate to particular and changing circumstances" (D. G. Horrell, "'The Lord Commanded... But I Have Not Used...': Exegetical and Hermeneutical Reflections on 1 Cor 9.14–15," *NTS* 43 [1997] 603).

[451] Horrell, "Theological Principle or Christological Praxis?" 93.

[452] See Newton, *Deity and Diet*, 323–24.

[453] Nasuti, "The Woes of the Prophets and the Rights of the Apostle," 263.

[454] On the "Rock," see Fee, *First Corinthians*, 447–49.

[455] See W. A. Meeks, "'And Rose Up to Play: Midrash and Paraenesis in 1 Corinthians 10:1–22," *JSNT* 16 (1982) 64–78.

[456] Horrell, "Theological Principle or Christological Praxis?" 96.

Now, with the principles and examples noted, Paul attempts to offer a practical solution (A'; 10:23–11:1) to the problem. Although some commentators attempt to distinguish between the eating of idol food at temples and at home,[457] such solutions fail to capture the nuances of Paul's teaching on this matter. In vv. 23–26 Paul lays down some simple facts: all is lawful, but all is not beneficial; one seeks the good of the other, rather than himself; and anything sold in the marketplace is good, for "the earth is the Lord's and everything in it" (Ps 24:1; 50:15; cf. Peter's vision in Acts 10). Ergo, there is nothing wrong with eating idol food. But then he returns to the question he introduced in chapter 8, viz., what happens if it were to cause scandal? If so, then the circumstances warrant one to refrain from the idol food, not because there is anything wrong with it *per se*, but because of the other's weak conscience (10:28–29). After a series of rhetorical questions to which Paul expects the Corinthians to give a proper answer,[458] Paul concludes that all must be done to the glory of God (v. 31), without offence to Jew or Greek, or to anyone. The practical solution, then, is for each to fulfill his responsibility towards the other in κοινωνία. Even though the weak need to come to know the nonexistence of idols, the strong must act in cognizance of their brothers' failing in that regard.[459] And Paul concludes in 11:1 by bringing the example back to himself. In 8:13, Paul says, "I will never eat meat, lest I cause my brother to fall;" and in 11:1, he says, "Be imitators of me as I am of Christ." Paul's imitation is founded on love. "Love can require temporary and partial restraint in the practice of justified freedom out of respect for another person's conscience, even if this conscience is erring. Love can limit freedom, if not in principle, at least in practice."[460]

1 Cor 11:2–34 speaks of two specific practices having to do with worship and order. Although the switch from the topic of idol food and freedom is rather abrupt and may seem out of place,[461] there is a certain logic to Paul's turning from the general scale of worship and order in terms of relations between Christians and pagans to the specifics of Christian worship and order among the Corinthians.[462] As with other issues that Paul addresses in 1 Corinthians, the particular source of his knowledge of the practices in his absence remains somewhat obscure. It is difficult to discern whether Paul is responding to what he has

---

[457] For the details of these arguments, see ibid., 98–101.

[458] On Paul's use of rhetorical questions in 10:27–30, see J. F. M. Smit, "The Function of First Corinthians 10,23–30: A Rhetorical Application," *Bib* 78 (1997) 377–88.

[459] See P. Borgen, "'Yes,' 'No,' 'How Far?': The Participation of Jew and Christians in Pagan Cults," in *Paul in His Hellenistic Context*, ed. Engberg-Pederson, 48–54.

[460] J. Delobel, "Coherence and Relevance of 1 Cor 8–10," in *The Corinthian Correspondence*, ed. Bieringer, 189. Note how keen Paul is on this point in Gal 2:11–21. Peter had acted according to Paul's way of thinking (by eating with Gentiles) until some Jews arrived; then, Peter reverted to Jewish dietary practices. Knowing that this would offend the conscience of the Gentiles (who were the "weak" in this case), Paul upbraids him.

[461] See Conzelmann, *1 Corinthians*, 182.

[462] See Fee, *First Corinthians*, 471–72.

heard or read, but Paul's use of σχίσματα in v. 18, the only use of the word in 1 Corinthians other than in 1:10, indicates that the quarreling among the Corinthians extends even into their commemorations of the Lord's Supper. Not only does this tie chapter 11 with chapter 1, but it also ties those two chapters with chapter 12 (which begins with the classic περὶ δέ and seemingly denotes a response to the Corinthians' letter), wherein Paul warns against any discord (σχίσμα) in the body of Christ (12:25). And much like his rejoinder in 4:21b, Paul promises to give further instructions upon his return (11:34b). As far as Paul is concerned, the Corinthians are simultaneously worthy of commendation (11:2) and condemnation (11:17) in their worship and order. The commendation (vv. 2–16) is the verification of a practice that is upheld by the Corinthians, handed down by Paul, and followed by the other churches. The condemnation (vv. 17–34) is more an explanation that is descriptive of a practice, also handed down, which the Corinthians have mismanaged, so much so that Paul recalls its foundation with the Lord Jesus' words verbatim as the model for the Corinthians to emulate.

Verses 2–16 render a particular and peculiar insight into Corinthian worship and order. The subsection discusses the propriety of head coverings or veiling for men and women at prayer. According to Paul, men ought to pray with their heads uncovered and women with their heads covered. This is a conventional practice of worship grounded by Paul in tradition, theology, Scripture, and common usage, though its precise meaning is obscure. In v. 2, Paul appeals to tradition, to what was handed down by him, using παράδιδωμι and παραλαμβάνω, which link his introduction to v. 23 and 15:1–3 (cf. 5:5; 13:3; 15:24). In v. 3, Paul appeals to theology for an analogy, viz., that just as God is the head of Christ, so the husband is the head of his wife. The use of κεφαλή here for "head" is curious, for the OT and LXX would suggest εἰκών or δόξα, as are found in v. 7[463]—τὴν κεφαλὴν εἰκὼν καὶ δόξα.[464] Nonetheless, the statement is consistent with Paul's understanding of the relationship between the Father and Son (see 3:21–23; 15:25–28; cf. Col 1:18–20) and marriage (7:4; 14:35; Eph 5:22–23; Col 3:18). Men should be unveiled as women should be veiled, according to vv. 4–6, but whether the veiling refers to hair (i.e., long hair) or a head covering (i.e., a hat) is not apparent. Evidence from the socioreligious situation of Corinth and Paul's letters is scarce and lends itself to mixed results. For example, Murphy-O'Connor argues for long hair rather than a hat,[465] while Richard Oster agues the opposite;[466] Antoinette Clark Wire argues these verses

---

[463] Conzelmann, *1 Corinthians*, 183.

[464] For a detailed discussion of the multiple meanings of κεφαλή, see Thiselton, *First Corinthians*, 812–26.

[465] J. Murphy-O'Connor, "Sex and Logic in 1 Corinthians 11:2–16," *CBQ* 42 (1980) 482–500.

[466] R. Oster, "When Men Wore Veils to Worship: The Historical Context of 1 Corinthians 11.4," *NTS* 34 (1988) 481–505.

to be an affirmation of women's role in worship,[467] while Joël Delobel argues that Paul is concerned with restraining women in worship.[468] In any case, Paul goes on to appeal to creation in vv. 7–12 as a foundation for vv. 4–6. Paul's allusions to Gen 1:26–27 (establishing man in the image of God) and to Genesis 2 (establishing the fact that man precedes woman) culminate in the implicit understanding of Gen 3:16, viz., that man rules over woman. However, this is tempered by v. 12, which reminds the Corinthians that man is now born from woman.[469] Thus, the conclusion does not appear to be one of superiority of man over woman as much as it is an indication of right ordering, of each knowing his or her place. All of this is supposed to lead the Corinthians to a foregone conclusion as they judge for themselves (vv. 13–15); but if they are unable to grasp Paul's conclusion, they need only look to the similar practice among the other churches (v. 16). Paul's final argument rests on the common practice of the churches in this respect (as in 4:17 and 7:17) and, as he does later in 14:34 regarding glossolalia, he considers anyone who would disregard the established norm to be contentious. "Paul ends by falling back on his apostolic authority and virtually ordering the Corinthians how to behave. The idea, in brief, would be this: Christians are not contentious—so *you* must not be contentious."[470]

That authority carries over into the further instructions in vv. 17–34. If vv. 2–16 deal with a matter that seems relatively in control, vv. 17–34 deal with a matter that is out of control. Their gathering together (in worship) is for the worse. "The style of this section, together with Paul's redescription of what he understands to be taking place at the Lord's Supper, indicates that he is not responding to a question first raised by the addressees, but initiates the raising of an urgent matter for censure and re-education."[471] As noted above, the division and quarreling referred to in chapter 1 is evidenced in their worship. Censured in chapter 1 for their divisiveness, the Corinthians are censured again for their individualism. While there is a surfeit of possibilities to explain their conduct—enjoying the physical meal over the spiritual meal,[472] one starting before another,[473] or some having more than others[474]—the problem is the same: "When

---

[467] Wire, "Women in the Image and Glory of God: 1 Corinthians 11:2–6" (chap. 6), in *Corinthian Woman Prophets*, 116–34.

[468] J. Delobel, "1 Cor 11,2–16: Towards a Coherent Interpretation," in *L'apôtre Paul*, ed. Vanhoye, 369–89. Note that Delobel's article motivated J. Murphy-O'Connor ("1 Corinthians 11:2–16 Once Again," *CBQ* 50 [1988] 265–74) to refine his earlier article ("Sex and Logic in 1 Corinthians 11:2–16").

[469] As to the question of the angels in v. 10, cf. 1 Tim 5:21; and see Fee, *First Corinthians*, 518–222.

[470] T. Engberg-Pederson, "1 Corinthians and the Character of Pauline Exhortation," *JBL* 110 (1991) 685 (emphasis original).

[471] Thiselton, *First Corinthians*, 849.

[472] Conzelmann, *1 Corinthians*, 194.

[473] Murphy-O'Connor, *St. Paul's Corinth*, 160–61.

[474] Thiselton, *First Corinthians*, 859. For an extended treatment of the socioeconomic implications, see G. Theissen, "Social Integration and Sacramental Activity: An Analysis of 1 Cor. 11:17–

you meet together, it is not the Lord's Supper that you eat" (v. 20).[475] In other words, the Corinthians have it wrong.[476] This compels Paul to reeducate by recounting Jesus' actions (vv. 23–24) and explaining their significance (vv. 27–32). Again, as we saw above, Paul begins v. 23 with an emphasis on the fact that he is only handing on what had been given to him by the Lord. Thus, Paul gives his own rendition of the institution narrative, emphasizing the Lord's action on their behalf and their need to remember,[477] with the added note of the Lord's Supper as the proclamation of the Lord's death until he comes (v. 26). The "until he comes" is meant to strike a chord in their consciousness to the effect that the Lord himself has set the parameters to be followed until the eschaton. Failure to observe those parameters has serious consequences: profanation of the Lord's body and blood (v. 27), condemnation (v. 28–29), and sickness and death (v. 30). Verses 31–32 recall Paul's appeal to their own judgment as in vv. 13–15. Thus it behooves them to remember that there will be a divine judgment, which they may escape, if they judge rightly and avoid the condemnation the world earns at the eschaton. Verse 33, with its ὥστε and ἀδελφοί μου, harkens back to the ὥστε of v. 27, evoking an intimacy between Paul and the Corinthians,[478] which serves as a gentle summary that they ought to attend to one another. It is followed (v. 34) by a subtle cue from Paul that he will have more to say later. In the meantime, Paul turns his attention to issues affiliated with worship and order—spiritual issues.

Spiritual Issues (1 Corinthians 12–14)

Paul's move, from worship and order to "gifts of the Spirit" (πνευματικά),[479] is a natural progression. Most likely, spiritual issues made themselves manifest in community prayer, as we see in 14:26. Paul's use of περὶ δέ to introduce this

---

34" (chap. 4), in *The Social Setting of Pauline Christianity: Essays on Corinth* (trans. J. H. Schütz; Philadelphia: Fortress, 1982) 145–74.

[475] See S. C. Barton, "Paul's Sense of Place: An Anthropological Approach to Community Formation in Corinth," *NTS* 32 (1986) 225–46.

[476] Apparently, they were not the first or the last to misconstrue the Lord's Supper. For example, see Jude 12 and the textual variants of 2 Pet 2:13.

[477] Note the different word order of the institution narrative in v. 24—τοῦτό μού ἐστιν σῶμα—from that in the Matt 26:26; Mark 14:22; and Luke 22:19—τοῦτό ἐστιν τὸ σῶμά μου. Winter (*After Paul Left Corinth*, 153–54) suggests that the μου may be shifted to give greater emphasis to the Lord's action on their behalf. Added to this is the dual remembrance (vv. 24–25), which is not found in the synoptics.

[478] R. F. Collins, *First Corinthians*, 440.

[479] Conzelmann (*1 Corinthians*, 204) points out that τῶν πνευματικῶν should be taken as neuter rather than masculine in light of its comparison to χαρίσματα (14:1), but as Barrett (*First Corinthians*, 278) remarks: "It seems impossible to find objective ground for a decision between the two possibilities, and little difference in sense is involved—spiritual persons are those who have spiritual gifts."

section indicates that he is probably answering a query raised by the Corinthians' letter (cf. 5:9; 7:1).[480] However, as we saw with ethical issues, Paul's answer does not necessarily clarify the local situation in Corinth. "In the whole of Paul's discussion of the gifts in chapters 12–14, one major problem stands out: What was the situation in the Corinthian community that prompted the Corinthians to ask Paul the question 'concerning spiritual gifts' (12:1)?"[481] Reading through chapters 12–14, the circumstances point to a problem related to glossolalia. Since the focus of chapter 12 is a unity of gifts (all interrelated in the community), that of chapter 13 is love (as more important than speaking in tongues), and that of chapter 14 is practical counsel for speaking in tongues, we are bereft of other prospects. To be sure, Paul has no problem with glossolalia *per se*, for he speaks in tongues more than the Corinthians do (14:18); "the problem is almost certainly an *abuse* of the gift of tongues."[482] While the thematic relationship of chapters 12–14 is evident,[483] the structural relationship is debated. Joop F. M. Smit presents the best argument for a rhetorical structure,[484] but the tricolon structure offered by Peter F. Ellis is more consistent with the overarching structure of 1 Corinthians.[485] Ellis notes a parallel, easily seen in chapters 12–14, regarding spiritual issues that, conveniently, follows the chapters' sequence. The first part, chapter 12 (A), concerns the gifts of the Spirit in general; the second part, chapter 13 (B), notes the preeminence of love; and the third part, chapter 14 (A'), treats glossolalia.[486]

In the first part (A; 12:1–31), Paul begins sternly. In v. 2, he recalls issues with which he already dealt in chapters 8 and 10 by reminding the Corinthians that they are no longer "heathen," no longer to be led by "dumb idols" (cf. Hab 2:18; Ps 113:15; 3 Macc 4:16). And in v. 3, he seeks neither to adjudicate glossolalia as a religious form nor to establish its proper use (that will come in chapter 14); instead, he is intent upon the content: the Holy Spirit always affirms that "Jesus is Lord"—anything else is anathema.[487] When we connect v. 3 with

---

[480] This is Paul's antepenultimate use of περὶ δέ, previously seen in 7:1, 25; 8:1, and used later only in 16:1, 12. See Hurd, *The Origin of First Corinthians*, 62 et passim; and Mitchell, "Concerning Περὶ Δέ in 1 Corinthians," 229–56.

[481] P. F. Ellis, *Seven Pauline Letters*, 92.

[482] Fee, *First Corinthians*, 571 (emphasis original).

[483] So Hurd: "The crux of the problem is the extent to which these chapters share a unity of purpose" (*The Origin of 1 Corinthians*, 188).

[484] J. F. M. Smit, "Argument and Genre of 1 Corinthians 12–14," in *Rhetoric and the New Testament*, ed. Porter and Olbricht, 211–30.

[485] This is especially so given Smit's unusual understanding of 1 Corinthians 13 as a rhetorical encomium, as prerequisite of his understanding of chapters 12–14; see idem, "The Genre of 1 Corinthians 13 in the Light of Classical Rhetoric," *NovT* 33 (1991) 193–216.

[486] P. F. Ellis, *Seven Pauline Letters*, 91–92.

[487] Winter ("Religious Curses and Christian Vindictiveness [1 Corinthians 12–14]" [chap. 8], in *After Paul Left Corinth*, 164–83) maintains that Paul is responding here specifically in a way the Corinthians would understand. "A reading of 12:3a in its immediate context and that of 1 Corinthians as a whole can help us see how some Christians acted in a thoroughly 'Corinthian

14:37–38, Paul's message is loud and clear: "Whoever rejects him rejects Jesus; whoever recognizes him recognizes the Lord."[488] Once he has laid the groundwork, indicated the seriousness of the matter, and established his authority in vv. 1–3, Paul is free to discuss the spiritual gifts.[489] The first thing he says is that there are a variety of *gifts*, i.e., they are not inherent in individuals. "With this emphasis, Paul puts the hybrists, those who consider themselves to be people of the Spirit (cf. 14:37) in their place. Anyone within the community who disdains the gifts given to any member disdains the work of the Spirit."[490] It is the Spirit, the Lord, and God who are responsible for this. Here, "the Trinitarian formula is the more impressive because it seems to be artless and unconscious."[491] The Trinitarian invocation of unity is emblematic of the unity Paul champions for the community, to whom each gift has been given "for the common good" (v. 8). Whether it be wisdom, knowledge, faith, healing, miracles, prophecy, the discernment of spirits, tongues, or the interpretation thereof, all gifts "are inspired by one and the same Spirit, who apportions to each one individually as he wills" (v. 11). Early on, Paul introduced the topic of glossolalia, but before treating it specifically, he imparts his generic understanding of the Spirit at work in the Corinthian community, which "consists of many persons very variously endowed, and the gifts bestowed upon individuals benefit the whole."[492]

To paint a picture of unity, Paul compares the community to the human body as a model for the body of Christ. The use of the body as a metaphor for unity is hardly unique to Paul.[493] What is unique to Paul is the collective root, viz., the Spirit. Members of the body of Christ are unified by the Spirit in baptism.[494] Jew or Greek, slave or free (cf. Gal 3:28), "all were made to drink (ἐποτίσθημεν) of one Spirit" (v. 13).[495] Obviously, the Corinthian unity is not one of race, class, or former religion. Paul then goes on to detail his analogy in vv. 14–26. Paul argues that the many parts make one body (v. 20), but thereafter he qualifies his argument to show that there is a hierarchy of dependence among the parts. By this Paul does not admit of any superiority; in fact, he aims to reconcile their divisiveness by pleading for the interdependence. "He argues that

---

way' when it came to handling conflicts, division, and retaliation against adversaries within their religious mind-set" (183).

[488] Smit, "Argument and Genre of 1 Corinthians 12–14," 214.
[489] Barrett, *First Corinthians*, 281.
[490] R. F. Collins, *First Corinthians*, 450.
[491] Barrett, *First Corinthians*, 284.
[492] Robertson and Plummer, *I Corinthians*, 269.
[493] See R. F. Collins (*First Corinthians*, 458–60) for examples from ancient literature.
[494] See Schnackenburg, *Baptism in the Thought of St. Paul*, 83–85; and cf. Fee, *First Corinthians*, 603–6.
[495] C. J. Cuming ("Ἐποτίσθημεν [I Corinthians 12.13]," *NTS* 27 [1980–81] 283–85) opts for a translation of ἐποτίσθημεν along the lines of being "watered" rather than being "imbibed" to the effect that the affusion at baptism is the source of the Spirit's indwelling.

the apparently weaker, the internal organs, are the more necessary, and that the apparently less seemly, the sexual organs are accorded the higher honor (of clothing being implied)."[496] This moves the argument along on the note of "unity and mutual concern, with a decided emphasis on God's own care for the one who lacks."[497] All suffer together; all rejoice together (v. 26). That having been said, Paul asserts himself plainly to the Corinthians: "Now you are the body of Christ and individually members of it" (v. 27). In vv. 28–30, Paul proffers his own hierarchical list. In his inventory of offices and ministries, at least as Paul understood them (see Eph 4:11 for a similar list), Paul is quite careful. With apostles first and glossolalia last, Paul has decidedly "pulled rank."[498] Last is not least, however. Rather, Paul places glossolalia last because it is a bone of contention in the Corinthian community. Paul does not admonish them because they are desirous of gifts, among which tongues and their interpretation are certainly included in chapter 14, but for their lack of love. Paul says: "Zealously strive for the greatest gifts. Yes, an even still more excellent way I show you."[499] That is the way of love.

In the second part (B; 13:1–13),[500] Paul begins by stating his point clearly.[501] Without love (ἀγάπη), the gift of tongues rings hollow.[502] Likewise, the understanding of prophecies and mysteries,[503] the faith to move mountains, the renunciation of all temporal goods, and even the sacrifice of the body to burning,[504] are naught without love. Again, Paul's point is crystal clear: there is

---

[496] Fee, *First Corinthians*, 609.

[497] Ibid.

[498] Horsley, *1 Corinthians*, 173.

[499] Translation: J. F. M. Smit, "Two Puzzles: 1 Corinthians 12.31 and 13.3: A Rhetorical Solution," *NTS* 39 (1993) 248.

[500] Hypotheses that chapter 13 is not original to 1 Corinthians are as numerous as they are diverse. Is it a hymn with existence prior to 1 Corinthians? A later interpolation? In fact, no matter how it came to be where it is, it is perfectly fitted to its place in 1 Corinthians, especially with its evident links to chapters 12 and 14. For more, see Fee, *First Corinthians*, 626. J. T. Sanders' opinion that chapter 13 is a later redaction and somehow misplaced seems implausible ("First Corinthians 13: Its Interpretation since the First World War," *Int* 20 [1966] 183–87).

[501] Questions of the genre of 1 Corinthians 13 are legion; see J. G. Sigountos, "The Genre of 1 Corinthians 13," *NTS* 40 (1994) 246–47. Sigountos agrees with Smit ("The Genre of 1 Corinthians 13 in the Light of Classical Rhetoric," 193–216) that chapter 13 is an encomium (albeit for different reasons). Building on their work, C. Focant ("1 Corinthiens 13: Anyalyse rhétorique et analyse de structures," in *The Corinthian Correspondence*, ed. Bieringer, 199–245) posits a rhetorical structure. But his mixing of ancient and modern rhetoric with contemporary structuralism—an approach he admits is eclectic (215)—leaves us with a theory peculiar to one chapter.

[502] On the metaphor of angelic speech and cymbals, see R. F. Collins, *First Corinthians*, 471–74. See also T. K. Sanders, "A New Approach to 1 Corinthians 13:1," *NTS* 36 (1990) 614–18.

[503] Both of these Paul considers to be significant for the community. On prophecy, see 1 Cor 14:1–25 and 1 Thess 5:19–20. On mystery, see 1 Cor 2:1, 7; 4:1; 14:2; and 15:51.

[504] Smit ("The Genre of 1 Corinthians 13," 257–58) is one of the few who argues for the textual variant ἵνα καυχήσωμαι (that I may boast) over ἵνα καυθήσομαι (that I should be burned), but we follow the common usage of καυθήσομαι, as explained in the *TCGNT*, 497–98.

no gain without love, no matter what gifts one has been given. Paul's description of love in vv. 4–6 is eminently practical and certainly addressed to the Corinthian situation. It is a measured response to the immaturity in faith of which Paul spoke earlier in 3:1–4 and to which Paul will compare his own maturity in 13:11–12 (cf. 14:20). Paul's purpose, then, is not so much to criticize whatever mischief has been wrought in the community by a misuse of glossolalia as to show them the hallmarks of the "excellent way" of love. In so doing, Paul asks them to put their hope in love rather than in spiritual gifts *per se*. Verse 7, wherein Paul explains that love is the foundation of faith and the staying power that allows for hope,[505] leads right into his assertion that prophecy, tongues, and knowledge—the very issues about which there is so much contention in the community—are fleeting. With this said, Paul can speak of his own growth in the faith. Paul has given up childish ways, so too should the Corinthians, for the behavior they evidence is that of children. Specifically, as we see in chapter 14, they must stop the squabbling about glossolalia. 1 Corinthians 13, "although it mentions speaking in tongues only obliquely (13.1, 8, 11), shares with 1 Cor. 14 the purpose which becomes explicit in the latter chapter—Paul's desire to curtail speaking in tongues at Corinth."[506] It is not Paul's intention to terminate the spiritual gift involved with speaking in tongues, but to harness a gift gone awry and to demonstrate its place in the hierarchy of gifts bestowed by the Spirit, whose bestowal of gifts is intended for bolstering and uniting them rather than causing dissention and division. By using the dual image of a mirror through which we see dimly only one day to see clearly (v. 12a) and partial knowledge only to be fully known later (v. 12b), Paul brings his point home. The metaphor of a mirror was common in the first century A.D. and Corinth was renowned for its bronze mirrors.[507] "The two halves of the verse are parallel. Face-to-face vision and full knowledge correspond to one another."[508] That is a point they cannot miss. Yet Paul reasserts his position to recap the abiding character of faith, hope, and love, a troika he often uses (cf. Rom 5:1–5; Phil 1:9–10; Col 1:4–5; 1 Thess 1:3; 5:8; 2 Thess 1:3–4). Now, with the gifts of the Spirit exposed and the preeminence of love emphasized, Paul turns his attention to the particulars of glossolalia.

The third part (A'; 14:1–40) is Paul's treatment of glossolalia.[509] Verse 1 signals a tie back to chapter 13 and to 12:31, without which chapter 14 would be

---

[505] See E. Wong, "1 Corinthians 13:7 and Christian Hope," *LS* 17 (1992) 232–42.

[506] Hurd, *The Origin of 1 Corinthians*, 189–90.

[507] See R. F. Collins, *First Corinthians*, 486–87.

[508] J. Lambrecht, "The Most Eminent Way: A Study of 1 Corinthians 13," in *Pauline Studies* (BETL 125; Leuven: Leuven University Press, 1994) 94.

[509] Here we presume the miraculous nature of glossolalia, as do almost all commentators, as being consonant with Paul's rendition of it in 1 Corinthians. Bob Zerhusen ("The Problem of Tongues in 1 Cor 14: A Reexamination," *BTB* 27 [1997] 139–52) argues that the trouble was merely one of misunderstanding of foreign languages in a polyglot society. Zerhusen contends that prophecy was

rather anemic. Thiselton notes that "the key to an accurate understanding of Paul's arguments and declarations in this chapter depends on a full appreciation of two factors initially: (a) vv. 1–25 relate integrally to what Paul has said about *love* in 13:1–13; (b) vv. 26–40 reflect concerns about *differentiation and ordering* which Paul has expounded in 12:4–31."[510] Consequently, we examine the chapter according to these parameters. Verses 1–25 are principally concerned with the needs of others, while vv. 26–40 are concerned with peaceful organization.[511]

In short, vv. 1–19 are based on the notion that the gift of tongues is laudable, even if it is also the least important gift and the one most prone to abuse and mishandling (at least in Corinth).[512] "To make these points, Paul compares the gift of tongues with the gift of prophecy and bears down hard on the contrast between the two in relation to the basic criterion for the evaluation of gifts—their potential for the building up of the community."[513] Verses 20–25 continue that theme by emphasizing the Christian community's responsibility to edify the larger society in which it finds itself, along the lines of the individual's responsibility to edify his fellow believers. Paul accomplishes this by commending the language of tongues as a mode of communication with God and the Spirit (v. 2) and at the same time insisting that prophecy is more commendable because it builds up the Church (v. 3),[514] previously identified as the body of Christ (13:27). Paul's preferences in vv. 4–5 underscore his heartfelt commitment to the unity of the community.[515] He uses himself as an example: If he brought nothing but (unintelligible) tongues, how would it benefit them (vv. 6–9)? And the same may be said for them. This leads Paul directly to demand of them prayer for the power of interpretation (v. 13). "As before, the Corinthians' practice of uninterpreted tongues is what is being challenged, not tongues as such. This is further confirmed by vv. 27–28, which again disallow uninterpreted tongues, but otherwise *regulate* the expression of the gift *when there is interpretation.*"[516] Indeed, Paul claims to speak in tongues more than they (v. 18; cf. v. 6), but prophecy is preferable because it instructs others, while the meaning of tongues too often remains only in the mind. Moreover, offering a *midrash pesher* of Isa 28:11–12, Paul reminds them of their responsibilities to unbelievers and outsiders (cf. Gen 2:7 and 1 Cor 15:45). Although vv. 22–25 are

---

miraculous, but tongues were just misconstrued native languages (152 et passim). While Zerhusen's argument is well put, he fails to account for Paul's constant juxtaposing of tongues and prophecy as gifts of the Spirit. How can we say one is supernatural and the other natural?

[510] Thiselton, *First Corinthians*, 1074 (emphasis original).
[511] Ibid.
[512] P. F. Ellis, *Seven Pauline Letters*, 101.
[513] Ibid.
[514] On prophecy in 1 Corinthians 14, see Thiselton, *First Corinthians*, 1087–98.
[515] See W. E. Ward, "Theological Issues Raised in First Corinthians," *RevExp* 57 (1960) 432.
[516] Fee, *First Corinthians*, 669 (emphasis original).

somewhat obscure[517]—how are tongues for believers and prophecy for unbelievers?[518]—Paul is powerful in maintaining that tongues may give the impression of madness whereas prophecy may lead to conversion (vv. 23, 25);[519] indeed, v. 25 quotes Isa 45:14 (cf. Zech 8:23) with all the implications thereof. Surely, tongues, at least uninterpreted tongues, have been put in their place.

But there is more. Paul's intention is to curtail tongues, not to eradicate a legitimate, perhaps overindulged, gift of the Spirit. Verses 26–40 are concerned with answering directly the question the Corinthians themselves seem to have put before him in their letter, viz., how to establish order in their worship and prayer. Thus Paul tells them what to do when they come together. He tells them that hymns, lessons, revelations, tongues, and interpretations are acceptable as long as "all things be done for edification" (v. 26). Speaking in tongues and the interpretation of tongues are to be limited, but tongues are to be hushed if there is no one to interpret them (vv. 27–28); prophecy is also limited and orderly and is to be weighed (vv. 29–32). Their orderliness is to reflect the God of peace (v. 33a). As in 4:17; 7:17; and 11:6, Paul appeals to the practice of the other churches for his injunction that women be silent.[520] This has led many to see that the problem in the Corinthian community may have been caused more by women than by men.[521] Given the chapter's context, it may be that Paul is speaking hyperbolically to effect order in the assembly (11:2–16 notwithstanding). However, a similar injunction found in 1 Tim 2:11–15, where the teaching is substantially the same and grounded in Genesis 3, indicates at the very least that the proscription was not exclusively instigated by Corinthian disorderliness. In any case, Paul is also anxious to salve wounds of divisiveness by enjoining the Corinthians to behave as other communities, to whom the Word of God has also come (v. 36). Then Paul brings down the boom in vv. 37–38 to cement his authority: "If anyone thinks that he is a prophet, or spiritual, he should acknowledge that what I am writing to you is a command of the Lord. If anyone does not recognize this, he is not recognized." This is harsh, to say the least. Yet it is explicable, given the extent to which Paul has gone to make his point: "What is

---

[517] The positions of various commentators are laid out in Thiselton, *First Corinthians*, 1122–30.

[518] K. O. Sandnes offers the best answer: "Paul is arguing from the consequence of the spiritual gifts upon the outsiders with a constant view to convincing and persuading the believers about which gift to give priority to" ("Prophecy—A Sign for Believers [1 Cor 14, 20–25]," *Bib* 77 [1996] 14).

[519] Surely, prophecy had its own proper place and respect among Jews and Greco-Romans; see T. Callan, "Prophecy and Ecstasy in Greco-Roman Religion and 1 Corinthians," *NovT* 28 (1985) 125–40.

[520] Verses 33b–36 present a number of textual difficulties; on this see Wire, *The Corinthian Women Prophets*, 149–52. Conzelmann's position (*1 Corinthians*, 246), that vv. 33b–36 are an interpolation, has not gained any consensus. This is especially true in light of 1 Tim 2:11–12.

[521] See Thiselton (*First Corinthians*, 1150–61) for a variety of explanations of the type of silence Paul suggests.

imperative is that when the community comes together for worship, the order in the assembly should reflect the order that exists in the body of Christ. Everything is to be done with propriety and in order."[522]

The Resurrection of the Dead (1 Corinthians 15)

1 Corinthians 15 is Paul's most extensive treatment of the resurrection and the heart of the matter of our investigation of 15:29. In Chapter II of our study, we concluded that chapter 15 is most likely a response to oral reports (hence the absence of περὶ δέ) and that vv. 29–34 are central to the chapter according to the outline we presented. Chapter II also looked to the structure of chapter 15 as well as to the morphology and syntax of 15:29, especially βαπτίζω, νεκρός, and ὑπέρ. Here our concern is primarily with the historical context of Paul's writing to the Corinthians about the resurrection. Building on our prior considerations, we examine chapter 15 in terms of the outline presented earlier (in Chapter II):

A   Christ is raised, a **fact** attested by the authority of witnesses and by Paul (vv. 1–11)

B   explanation of *that*, there is resurrection of the body, first Christ and then those who belong to him (vv. 12–28)

C   active, practical witnessing to the resurrection (vv. 29–34)

B'   explanation of *how*, the resurrected body is a spiritual body, since a physical (natural) body is raised as a spiritual body (vv. 35–49)

A'   Christians will be raised, a **fact** attested by Paul and the authority of mystery (vv. 50–58).

We noticed that Paul's criteria substantiating the fact of Christ's resurrection (A) parallel his criteria for the fact of the resurrection of Christians (A'). Between that parallelism is another, viz., Paul's explanation of the resurrection of the body, *that* there is a resurrection (B), parallels his explanation of the spiritual body, *how* there is a resurrection (B'). And nested between this parallelism is Paul's attestation of active, practical witnessing to the resurrection (C). This innermost core evidences all three grammatical persons: the third person in v. 29, the first person in vv. 30–32, and the second person in vv. 33–34. There is no doubt that this core is concerned with advancing Paul's argument on behalf of the resurrection in the whole of 1 Corinthians 15, but there is broad speculation as to the precise way in which it does so. For the moment then, since the purpose of this chapter of our study is to shed light on vv. 29–34 and particularly on v. 29, we postpone treatment of these verses until we have looked at the rest of chapter 15 in its historical context. Although it is not immediately palpable what some of the Corinthians believed as an alternative to Paul's understanding

---

[522] R. F. Collins, *First Corinthians*, 517.

of the resurrection,[523] we need to probe the Corinthians' denial of the resurrection of Christ and of Christians through the prism of Paul's responses thereto in chapter 15. Now we turn to Paul's most rigorous defense of the resurrection in the hope of shedding light on the setting in which baptism on account of the dead affirms the resurrection in 15:29.

The first section of 1 Corinthians 15 (A; vv. 1–11) is concerned with verifying the reality of the resurrection vis-à-vis the testimony of witnesses. Paul begins the section by reminding the Corinthians of the good news that he once preached to them and they accepted as their salvation, unless they have come to believe in vain (vv. 1–2; cf. vv. 12, 58). "There is, nonetheless, a proviso. Those to whom the gospel is preached are saved under the condition that they hold fast to what they have heard."[524] Paul does not countenance any improvisation on his gospel as a viable alternative (cf. 1 Thess 2:2, 13). Paul goes on to say that "I handed on to you as of first importance what I had received" (v. 3a). In so saying, Paul notes that the Corinthians should be no different from him on the matters to follow. His use of παραδίδωμι (cf. 1 Cor 5:15; 11:2; 11:23; 13:3; 15:24) indicates that the Corinthians ought to receive what is handed on by Paul, just as he received what was handed on to him. Here Paul refers "to a continuity of handing on and receiving which constitutes, in effect, an early creed which declares the absolute fundamentals of Christian faith and on which Christian identity (and the experience of salvation) is built."[525] This early creed, most often referred to as the *kerygma*,[526] seems primary in the hierarchy of early Christian beliefs. Verses 1–3a are a salient proem highlighting the significance of what he is about to propound, one that could not have been lost on his Corinthian readers.

What is of first importance? The resurrection of Christ—"that Christ died for our sins in accordance with the scriptures, that he was buried, that he was raised on the third day in accordance with the scriptures, and that he appeared to Cephas, then to the twelve" (vv. 3b–6). It would seem that vv. 3b–5, the *kerygma*, is pre-Pauline. "The creed in vv. 3–5 was received by Paul as a unity."[527] There is much speculation as to whether or not v. 6 and what follows is part of the original *kerygma*. Such a consideration need not distract us here.[528] For even if it is an addition, Paul added it "in order to show that the resurrection could be verified."[529] Thus, vv. 3b–6 have a very simple message to proclaim.

---

[523] J. H. Wilson, "The Corinthians Who Say There Is No Resurrection of the Dead," 91.

[524] R. F. Collins, *First Corinthians*, 533.

[525] Thiselton, *First Corinthians*, 1186. For a list of studies on Paul and tradition, see ibid., 1186–87.

[526] For a concise presentation, which focuses on the work of C. H. Dodd, see W. Baird, "What is the Kerygma? A Study of I Cor 15:3–8 and Gal 1:11–17," *JBL* 76 (1957) 181–91.

[527] J. Murphy-O'Connor, "Tradition and Redaction in 1 Cor 15:3–7," *CBQ* 43 (1981) 589.

[528] For more on this, see Fee, *First Corinthians*, 729–31.

[529] Murphy-O'Connor, "Tradition and Redaction," 589.

This message was proclaimed earlier in Corinth by Paul, and in chapter 15 it is reproclaimed because it is either denied, or at least, misunderstood. Christ died on account of our sins. Because he was really dead, he was buried. Moreover, he was raised from the dead. All of this happened in accordance with the scriptures. And after he was raised, he appeared to Cephas, to the twelve, and to hundreds. There is no ambivalence on Paul's part. There is no hint that he speaks of anything less than a bodily resurrection of Jesus that is eminently verifiable because others saw Jesus alive after he was dead and buried.[530] This assertion would have come as no surprise to the Corinthians, especially in 1 Corinthians, for Paul claimed earlier in the letter (9:1) that he had seen the Lord in connection to his apostolic status. The use of ὁράω in 9:1 and 15:5, 6, 7, and 8 leaves little other choice. This is unmistakable considering Paul's understanding of the difference between an appearance, as he speaks of here, and a vision, as he speaks of in 2 Cor 12:1. Furthermore, Paul's deliberations in 1 Cor 15:35–49, about the nature of a resurrected body akin to Jesus', leaves little doubt that Paul understood Jesus' resurrection to be bodily and expected the same understanding on the part of the Corinthians. Presumably, there were hundreds to whom they could go for verification.

But there is no need to go to anyone other than Paul. Verse 7 not only extends the list of appearances but also serves as a transition towards Paul's own experience.[531] Christ appeared to James, obviously known to Paul in Gal 1:19, and to all the apostles. Then Christ appeared to Paul, "as to one untimely born (ἔκτρωμα)" (v. 8). But as Paul would have it, Christ appeared to him last and definitely least. In conjunction with himself as the last to see the Lord, Paul is self-effacing in claiming that he is unfit to be an apostle because he persecuted the Church (vv. 9–10). Paul's description of himself as an ἔκτρωμα is difficult to grasp. His is the only use of the word in the NT (cf. its three uses in the LXX: Num 12:12; Job 3:16; Eccl 6:3). On the one hand, it may refer to his initial persecution of the Church. In Gal 1:13–15, Paul describes himself as a persecutor, even though he had been set apart before he was born, and he uses the word to describe his late start.[532] On the other hand, it may be descriptive of his personal insufficiency. "Paul wanted his readers to know that his apostolate had its origin in an act of God's grace: he did not deserve it, nor did he ask for it, for in his own eyes he was no more than a 'miscarriage.'"[533] Nevertheless, the thrust of Paul's assertion is the fact that he has seen the Lord. That is, he not only proclaimed to them what had been handed down to him, but he also attested to what he himself saw. In accord with the defense of his apostleship in chapter 9, Paul

---

[530] R. J. Sider, "St. Paul's Understanding of the Nature and Significance of the Resurrection in I Corinthians XV:1–19," *NovT* 19 (1977) 140–41.

[531] Cf. Murphy-O'Connor, "Tradition and Redaction," 589.

[532] Nickelsburg, "An Ἔκτρωμα, Though Appointed from the Womb," 198–205.

[533] H. W. Hollander and G. E. van der Hout, "The Apostle Paul Calling Himself an Abortion: 1 Cor. 15:8 within the Context of 1 Cor. 15:8–10," *NovT* 38 (1996) 236.

buttresses his proclamation of the gospel, particularly that matter of "first importance," by his own personal witness of the resurrected Lord. Therewith, Paul can conclude this section with v. 11: "Whether it was I or they, so we preach and so you believed."

Thus for Paul, the resurrection of Christ is a simple fact, indeed, a fact that is well substantiated by numerous eyewitnesses including himself. While it may be claimed that Paul is not interested in proving the resurrection of the dead but only in laying groundwork for the explanation of the resurrection in what follows in chapter 15,[534] "the very fact that Paul placed a lengthy list of eyewitnesses of the appearances of the risen Jesus at the very beginning of the whole discussion is most easily explained by the suggestion that the apostle feared some of his addressees entertained doubts on this matter."[535] Because of this, Paul desires to be as clear as possible. As Jan Lambrecht points out:

> Not only do the appearances mentioned by Paul refer not to pre-paschal experiences but to insight *and* sight which occurred after the Easter event, not only does their mention possess a confirmatory function with regard to the reality of Jesus' resurrection without which believers' hope of their own resurrection could not be maintained, but that mention is also very much needed, it would seem, because these appearances must still "prove" Jesus' resurrection, about which some in the Corinthian community most probably had their doubts.[536]

The nature of their doubts remains elusive to us.[537] Did they deny the bodily resurrection of Christ? Did they accept the bodily resurrection of Christ and deny the bodily resurrection of believers? The variations on the theme of their misconstrual of Paul's earlier preaching are legion.[538] "Most writers concede that we have insufficient evidence to specify one solution in such a way as to decisively exclude others. Most commentators believe that few if any denied the resurrection of *Christ*; but some failed to follow through the eschatological and ethical entailments of what it meant to share in Christ's resurrection, not least corporately as his body."[539] This leads us to focus on the Corinthians' denial of the resurrection of believers, similar to the concern addressed by Paul in 1 Thess 4:13–18. This is borne out in the argumentation made by Paul in the whole of chapter 15. For Paul, the lynchpin of faith in the resurrection of believers is faith in the resurrection of Christ. Denial of the one is tantamount to denial of the

---

[534] Fee, *First Corinthians*, 718.
[535] Sider, "St. Paul's Understanding of the Nature and Significance of the Resurrection," 132.
[536] Lambrecht, "Line of Thought in 1 Cor 15, 1–11," 670 (emphasis original).
[537] On the general question of resurrection, see J. Lambrecht, "To Meet the Lord: Scripture about Life after Death," in *Pauline Studies* (BETL 125; Leuven: Leuven University Press, 1994) 411–41; and for the particular question in terms of Paul, see ibid., 423–32.
[538] For the plentitude of theories, see Thiselton, *First Corinthians*, 1172–76; and M. D. Goulder, *Paul and the Competing Mission in Corinth* (LPS; Peabody, MA: Hendrickson, 2001) 182–85.
[539] Thiselton, *First Cornthians*, 1176 (emphasis original).

other. Since the bodily resurrection of Christ is already accomplished and the bodily resurrection of believers is yet to come, it is natural for Paul to start with what is already seen and believed, viz., Christ's resurrection, and then to move on to what ought to be believed even if not yet seen, viz., the resurrection of believers.

The second section of 1 Corinthians 15 (B; vv. 12–28) is concerned with linking the resurrection of Christ to the resurrection of Christians. The resurrection is an established fact according to the preceding section (vv. 1–11). Any doubt as to the veracity of Christ's resurrection is settled. Paul introduces the second section with a logical question: "Now if Christ is preached as raised from the dead, how can some of you say there is no resurrection of the dead?" That is, with the fact established that Christ is raised, then resurrection from the dead is possible. With the use of this first class conditional sentence in interrogative form, Paul does not begin with a denial, but with an affirmation. Jan Lambrecht reconstructs Paul's reasoning:

> If Christ is risen (protasis), there is, of course, a resurrection of the dead (apodosis). This implication, consisting of an antecedent and a consequent, functions as the "maior" of Paul's argumentation, which is left uncompleted but can easily be completed since the content of the protasis, the resurrection of Christ, has been substantiated in vv. 1–11. So, we are allowed to supply Paul's reasoning with the "minor": Indeed, Christ is risen. The conclusion can now be drawn: Thus, there is a resurrection of the dead. Already in vv. 12–19, as in 20–22, Paul sees Christ's resurrection as the basis for that of Christians. His argumentation does not start with a formal rule of logic: if there is no resurrection of the dead, then Christ is not risen.[540]

There is no need for any argumentation that would abjure what is already forsworn. That is, the problem is not whether or not Christ has been raised, or whether or not Christians are to be raised, the problem is that this truth is lost on some of the Corinthians—"some (τίνες) among you (ἐν ὑμῖν)." The specific nature of their denial remains somewhat obscure,[541] but Paul is more interested in supporting the resurrection at this point than explaining how it comes about (which he saves for vv. 35–49). Verse 12 is a rhetorical question indicative of the problem in Corinth about faith in the resurrection of the dead, not in the resurrection of Christ.[542] "The issue is the denial that Christians will be raised from the dead. Paul does not set out to prove that Jesus has been raised from the dead. That Jesus has been raised is the basis on which he builds his argu-

---

[540] Lambrecht, "Paul's Christological Use of Scripture in 1 Cor. 15.20–28," 503.

[541] "A complete and certain retrieval of the original intent and meaning of the statements of the Corinthians is not possible; however, some interpretations are more or less likely than others. Verses 12–34 should not be looked upon as a detailed counterargument of all the beliefs of the Corinthians; Paul merely takes one statement—that there is no resurrection—and presents the radical consequences flowing from it" (Lewis, *"So That God May Be All in All,"* 38).

[542] Aletti, "La *dispositio* rhétorique dans les épîtres pauliniennes," 396.

ment."[543] In such wise, v. 13, another first class conditional sentence, continues to drive home Paul's reasoning: "If there is no resurrection of the dead, then Christ has not been raised." Therewith, Paul turns the incredulity that some of them hold about the resurrection of believers into incredulity about the resurrection of Christ. Paul's turns their thinking on its head by identifying it with a denial of the *kerygma*, the very substance of Christian faith.

What are the implications of the thinking of some Corinthians? Following vv. 12–13, we find five more conditional sentences in vv. 15–19 (with v. 15 and v. 18 inverted); they momentarily allow for some Corinthians' (mistaken) hypothesis.[544] These verses speak rather plainly for themselves: if Christ is not raised, then Paul's preaching and the Corinthians' faith is in vain (v. 14); if the dead are not raised, Paul misrepresented God by proclaiming Christ raised (v. 15); if Christ has not been raised, the Corinthians' faith is futile, they are still in their sins, and those who have fallen asleep have perished (vv. 16–18). The stakes do not get any higher. Walter Schmithals says it well:

> Thus, as Paul argues in v. 13 and again in vv. 15b–16, if there is no resurrection of the dead, then Christ also was not raised. And in vv. 14, 17–19, he alludes to the disastrous consequences of this false assertion. Though Paul does not openly outline the idea, a certain logic stands behind the arguments of vv. 12–19, namely, that the raising of the dead and the raising of Christ are inextricably connected, with the result that the one stands or falls with the other and that the raising of Jesus consequently assures the raising of Christians.[545]

In point of fact, Paul is telling them that a denial of the resurrection of believers is a denial of everything he has preached to them and everything they have believed. Without faith in the resurrection of believers there is no faith in anything that Paul has proclaimed to them, there is no forgiveness of sins, and there is no hope for the living or for the dead. Spelling this out again and again, almost to the point of redundancy, is no accident. Paul is pointedly and poignantly attempting to forestall an existent crisis, a crisis of faith in the resurrection of the dead, a crisis of faith imperiling the underpinnings of his apostolic witness. "Paul is not arguing in timeless theoretical terms, without regard to the *real* situation, but is challenging the Corinthians in light of their faith."[546] The gravity of the real situation is encompassed in Paul's declaration in v. 19 that without the resurrection of the dead and all entailed therein, "we are of all men most to be pitied."

---

[543] R. F. Collins, *First Corinthians*, 543.

[544] Fee, *First Corinthians*, 741.

[545] W. Schmithals, "The Pre-Pauline Tradition in 1 Corinthians 15:20–28," trans. C. N. Jefford, *PRSt* 20 (1993) 358–59.

[546] Conzelmann, *1 Corinthians*, 267 (emphasis original).

But there is no need for pity because Christ has been raised. Having demonstrated the preposterousness of a denial of the resurrection, Paul goes on in vv. 20–28 to support the connection between Christ's resurrection and that of believers (cf. 1 Thess 4:13–18). Christ has already been raised, and he is "the first fruits (ἀπαρχή) of those who have fallen asleep." "His reasoning is almost syllogistic as he articulates an explanation (with the explanatory *gar*) in v. 21 and clarifies his explanation (with an additional *gar*) in vv. 22–23."[547] For as one man brought death, so one man brings resurrection (v. 21); for as in Adam all die, so in Christ all live (v. 22). According to C. K. Barrett:

> The most important thing to observe in relation to v. 21, with its twofold invocation of an ἄνθρωπος, is the connection between sin and death, righteousness and life. Death arises not from some natural mortality, the fact that human organs after a time wear out; it comes from sin. It is because man sinned that the whole race is subject to death. If the process is to be reversed it must be reversed as a whole, and sin must be replaced by righteousness. But if righteousness is to be more than an abstraction it must be expressed in the righteous act, the δικαίωμα, of a man; only a man can offer to God an obedience to neutralize the disobedience of the man Adam. Thus Paul's argument builds up.[548]

And thus the horror, if men were still in their sins, that Paul spoke of in v. 17. With this point established, Paul sharpens his explanation. There is an ordering (τάγμα) to resurrection:[549] Christ first and then, at his coming (παρουσία),[550] those who belong to him (v. 23), those who belong to him by having been baptized in his name (cf. 1:13; 3:23).[551]

And then comes the end (τὸ τέλος). At the end, Christ will destroy every rule, authority, and power (cf. Rom 8:38) prior to handing over the kingdom to his Father. Christ will reign until this is accomplished, until he puts all enemies under his feet (Ps 110:1; cf. Matt 22:44; Mark 12:36; Luke 20:42–43; Acts 2:34–35; Heb 1:3, 13). There is an enormous amount of protracted exegetical debate about 1 Cor 15:24–28, and much of it not need concern us here.[552] But we note that in v. 27 Paul speaks of death as the last enemy. "By separating it and drawing special attention to it, emphasis is placed on the fact that the reign of Christ is not complete until death is conquered; everything is still in process."[553] In other words, Paul is reassuring those Corinthians who deny the

---

[547] R. F. Collins, *First Corinthians*, 547.
[548] Barrett, "The Significance of the Adam–Christ Typology for the Resurrection of the Dead," 106.
[549] See Robertson and Plummer (*I Corinthians*, 354) on τάγμα.
[550] See Thiselton (*First Corinthians*, 1229–30) on παρουσία.
[551] R. F. Collins, *First Corinthians*, 552.
[552] For a recent discussion, see Aletti, "L'argumentation de Paul et la position des Corinthiens," 82–97.
[553] Lewis, *"So That God May Be All in All,"* 58.

resurrection that death's end is near; "Paul's focus of interest is on what Jesus Christ *did* and *does* and *will do*."[554] One thing Christ will do is destroy death. In v. 27a, Paul quotes Ps 8:6: "For God has put all things into subjection under his feet" (cf. Phil 3:21). Moreover, Paul interprets the quotation in v. 27b: "But when it says, 'All things are put in subjection under him,' it is plain that he is excepted who put all things under him." Another thing Christ will do is prepare everything for the Father. "On the one hand, death itself will thereby finally have been subjected to Christ (v. 24c); on the other hand, with that final subduing of death the time of Christ's reign comes to its end, so that he may hand over the 'rule' to the Father (v. 24b), who thus becomes 'all in all' (v. 28)."[555] This lays great stress on the Corinthians—and all Christians—as participants in a divine drama inaugurated by the Father in his sending of the Son, unfolding in the resurrection of Christ and those who belong to him, and culminating in the return of the Son and his servants to the Father.[556] "And yet, though Christ himself has indeed been raised from the dead, the resurrection of the dead does not occur; it remains, for the time being, a promise, even if its realization is on the horizon."[557] For it is through the ministrations of the Son and the Spirit that Christians are brought to the Father, and the penultimate moment of resurrection is the last thing to occur before the final restoration. "For Paul the resurrection of the dead is in function of the fulfillment of the kingdom of God."[558] And for all intents and purposes, this entire section ought to have convinced those doubting Corinthians *that* "Christ has been raised from the dead, the first fruits of those who have fallen asleep" (v. 20).

The fourth section of 1 Corinthians 15 (B'; vv. 35–49) is concerned with forestalling the objections of an imaginary interlocutor (τίς, "someone") about the nature of the resurrection of the body. Since we have put the third section (C; vv. 29–34) on the back-burner, we may immediately address the question Paul anticipates from the Corinthians: "How are the dead raised? With what kind of body do they come?" (v. 35).[559] To be sure, what follows in vv. 36–49 is Paul's attempt to answer the question. Paul does so in two distinct arguments. The first is an argument from analogy (vv. 36–44a); the second is one from Scripture,

---

[554] J. F. Jansen, "I Cor. 15.24–28 and the Future of Jesus Christ," *SJT* 40 (1987) 546 (emphasis original).

[555] Fee, *First Corinthians*, 759. On the parallel structure of vv. 24 and 28, see J. Lambrecht, "Structure and Line of Thought in 1 Cor. 15:23–28," *NovT* 32 (1990) 143–51.

[556] On the theological implications, see G. B. Caird, "Everything to Everyone: The Theology of the Corinthian Epistles," *Int* 13 (1959) 387–99.

[557] M. C. de Boer, "Paul's Use of a Resurrection Tradition in 1 Cor 15,20–28," in *The Corinthian Correspondence*, ed. Bieringer, 651.

[558] R. F. Collins, *First Corinthians*, 555.

[559] See B. Schneider, "The Corporate Meaning and Background of 1 Cor. 15,45b—ὁ ἔσχατος Ἀδὰμ εἰσ πνεῦμα ζῳοποιοῦν," *CBQ* 29 (1967) 450–67.

specifically Genesis (vv. 44b–49).[560] Once Paul has set up his question in v. 35, the argument which follows in vv. 36–44a "contains three illustrations, related to one another by the word *sōma* ('body') and by the related word *sarx* ('flesh'), but differing in nature and intention."[561] This foundation allows Paul to proceed to his second argument about Gen 2:7 and the relationship between Adam and Christ. "The 'principle of resurrection' forged in vv. 35–44a provides the parameters within which he can then discuss how the resurrection applies to Christ, and through Christ, to those who believe."[562] It would seem that some Corinthians have not only denied the resurrection of the body on the grounds that it did not happen with Christ (hence vv. 1–11) and thus it will not happen with Christians (hence vv. 12–28), but have implied that it cannot happen at all on account of the nature of the body itself.[563] So in this section, Paul is anxious to show that a theory dismissive of the possibility of bodily resurrection is mistaken.[564]

Paul begins his argument from analogy with an invective. He addresses his invented interlocutor as a "fool" in the vocative case (ἄφρων), which is intensified by the σύ ("you"). Paul's first example is with a simple seed (vv. 36–38), something anyone would understand (cf. John 12:24). "What you sow does not come to life unless it dies" (v. 36). "The phrase of Paul in v. 36, according to the natural sense of the words, insists on the fact that the seed has to die: the seed 'you' sow. The life-giving power is not a power of the sower."[565] Rather, what is sown is not the body (σῶμα) that is to be (γενησόμενον),[566] but merely a seed (v. 37). It is God who gives the body (σῶμα) life and to each of the seeds its own body (σῶμα).[567] Why? Because not all flesh (σάρξ) is alike. Here Paul moves into his second example of higher things (vv. 39–40), an example that raises the threshold. By moving from σῶμα to σάρξ, Paul seeks to describe the diverse nature of God's creation.[568] There is different flesh for different parts of God's creation: humans, animals, birds, and fish (cf. Gen 1:20, 24; 8:17).[569] Verses 40–

---

[560] See Bonneau, "The Logic of Paul's Argument on the Resurrection," 79–82.

[561] Dawes, "1 Corinthians 7:17–24," 687.

[562] Bonneau, "The Logic of Paul's Argument on the Resurrection Body," 90.

[563] Robertson and Plummer say it best: "Granted that historical testimony and natural fitness are in favour of believing that Christ rose again as an earnest that we shall be raised, is our bodily resurrection possible? Can we conceive such as thing? We cannot be expected to believe what is impossible and inconceivable" (*1 Corinthians*, 368).

[564] D. B. Martin, *The Corinthian Body*, 125.

[565] Usami, "How are the Dead Raised?" 479.

[566] The use of ἔρχονται could hardly be expected in terms of germination. Barrett (*First Corinthians*, 370) explains it: "Paul is probably thinking of a real *coming*—out of graves, with Christ" (emphasis original).

[567] For an extensive treatment, see E. E. Ellis, "*Sōma* in First Corinthians," *Int* 44 (1990) 132–44.

[568] Usami, "How are the Dead Raised?" 481.

[569] For a detailed summary of the pertinent understandings of the contemporaneous Greek science, see Brodeur, *The Holy Spirit's Agency in the Resurrection of the Dead*, 34–80.

41 continue on to state that there are earthly bodies and heavenly bodies (σώματα), each with its own proper glory (δόξα). Because the stars encapsulate the beauty of the heavens (Sir 43:9), Paul's reference to them bridges the depths of the earth and the heights of heaven and everything in-between. "What is important to note is that each has its own kind of 'glory,' so that in this argument, even though the earthly body must die, it is not without its own glory."[570] In both examples, Paul emphasizes God's creative role: he raises life from death in the earth, and he generates the radiance of heaven.[571]

Now Paul is poised to make the analogy in v. 42a: "So it is with the resurrection of the dead (ἀνάστασις τῶν νεκρῶν)." In vv. 42b–44a, there follows a sequence of comparisons, each one using σπείρεται and ἐγείρεται. As Fee notes:

> With a series of four staccato clauses, each repeating the verbs "it is sown, it is raised," he applies the first analogy of the seed (the first three clauses, vv. 42b–43) and then the analogy of the differing kinds of bodies (v. 44a). In so doing, he keeps alive the metaphor of the seed through the first verb ("it is sown"), but expresses the language of resurrection with the second ("it is raised"). The clauses have no expressed subject; "body" is more likely intended as the subject for *both* verbs in each set, thus implying genuine continuity between the present body and its future expression.[572]

The exact type of continuity notwithstanding,[573] Paul's implication of bodily continuity grounds the resurrection of the dead in the resurrection of Christ, the first fruits (v. 20), whose body was buried and is already raised. It leaves little doubt in the minds of Paul's readers about the reality of resurrection from the dead.[574] Paul's analogy concludes, then, with v. 44a: "It is sown as a physical [natural] body (σῶμα ψυχικόν), it is raised as a spiritual body (σῶμα πνευματικόν)." Because of Paul's relatively rare use of ψυχικός (2:14; 15:44 [2x], 46; cf. the only other NT uses in Jas 3:15 and Jude 1:19) and the frequent use of πνευματικός (in chapters 1–4, 8–10, 12–14, and 15) with only one other instance binding them together (1 Cor 2:14), there is much discussion about the

---

[570] Fee, *First Corinthians*, 783.

[571] "The full import of vv. 36–41 lies in the merging of the main point of the two examples—the time axis of the first example and the space axis of the second example—to form a new implied question: Can God transform (before/after) an earthly body into a heavenly body (below/above)? Only this question can adequately lead to discovering the particular configuration of the resurrection body" (Bonneau, "The Logic of Paul's Argument on the Resurrection Body," 86).

[572] Fee, *First Corinthians*, 784 (emphasis original).

[573] For discussion on continuity as agricultural, organic, or by divine intervention and Paul's understandings thereof, see R. J. Sider, "The Pauline Conception of the Resurrection Body in 1 Corinthians XV. 35–54," *NTS* 21 (1974–75) 430–32.

[574] One of the best studies on understandings of the bodily resurrection is M. E. Dahl, *The Resurrection of the Body: A Study of 1 Corinthians 15* (SBT 36; Naperville, IL: Allenson, 1962). Cf. the earlier J. A. T. Robinson, *The Body: A Study in Pauline Theology* (SBT; Chicago: Regney, 1952).

distinction between them.[575] In terms of 2:14, it most likely indicates the distinction between a spiritual elite and their inferiors,[576] and that sheds some light on its meaning here to indicate a qualitative difference. The natural body is to be raised as an inspirited body; the continuity is in the body, and the body is changed into another type of body.[577] This new body cannot be thought of as anything less than a body. Nor is this body a "noncorporeal" body. "The impossibility of the concept [of a nonbody body] is clear when one tries to translate such language back into Greek and imagine how Paul could have conceived, in Greek, of a 'nonbody body.'"[578] Thus Paul has answered the question "with what kind of body do they come—a spiritual, an inspirited body.[579]

This sets the ground for Paul's argument from Genesis in vv. 44b–49.[580] Paul begins with a first class conditional sentence that links his prior analogy to his present argument: "If there is a physical [natural] body, there is also a spiritual one" (v. 44b). With that, Paul presents a *midrash pesher* of Gen 2:7 (LXX; cf. Isa 28:11–12; 1 Cor 14:21),[581] in which he adds πρῶτος.[582] Paul writes, "'The first man Adam became a living being (ψυχὴν ζῶσαν)'; the last Adam became a life-giving spirit (πνεῦμα ζῳοποιοῦν)" (v. 45).[583] The parallel with vv. 20–22 is obvious (cf. Rom 5:12–19). Through Adam came sin, and through Christ came resurrection; though one man, the first, became alive, the last Adam (Christ) became life-giving (the first fruits of resurrection). "The seed analogy shows

---

[575] See Horsley, "*Pneumatikos* vs. *Psychikos*," 269–73.

[576] Ibid., 288. But Horsley (ibid.) is clear in stating that "no adequate comparative material has been found from which to establish the precise origin and significance of this unusual terminology."

[577] There is much debate about whether Paul is specifically "anti-gnostic" here, as Schmithals claims (*Gnosticism in Corinth*, 156–285). Such a claim may unnecessarily limit Paul's terminology by suggesting that it can be read only in one way. For more, see E. H. Pagels, "'The Mystery of the Resurrection': A Gnostic Reading of 1 Corinthians 15," *JBL* 93 (1974) 276–88.

[578] D. B. Martin, *The Corinthian Body*, 128.

[579] Cf. R. F. Collins, *First Corinthians*, 547. On theories of the nature of the resurrection body, see Thiselton, *First Corinthians*, 1276–80.

[580] For a detailed rendering of this subsection see Brodeur, "A Close Reading of 1 Cor 15,44b–49" (chap. 2), in *The Holy Spirit's Agency in the Resurrection of the Dead*, 89–143.

[581] The LXX reads: ἐγένετο ὁ ἄνθρωπος εἰς ψυχὴν ζῶσαν. Paul's version reads: ἐγένετο ὁ πρῶτος ἄνθρωπος Ἀδὰμ εἰς ψυχὴν ζῶσαν.

[582] According to C. D. Stanley, "Nothing in either Greek or Hebrew textual tradition offers any reason to think that Paul might have used the word πρῶτος in his *Vorlage* of Gen 2:7" (*Paul and the Language of Scripture: Citation Technique in the Pauline Epistles and Contemporary Literature* [SNTSMS 74; Cambridge: Cambridge University Press, 1992], 208). Stanley also offers evidence to show that "Paul may not have added the proper name Ἀδάμ," since it is found in Theodotion and Symmachus (209).

[583] For more on v. 45b, see B. Schneider, "The Corporate Meaning and Background of 1 Cor. 15,45b," 450–67. See also Philo, *Opif.* 47.136–41 and *Abr.* 56; and on Philo, see R. A. Horsley, "'How Can Some of You Say that There Is No Resurrection of the Dead?' Spiritual Elitism in Corinth," *NovT* 20 (1978) 216–23. For another perspective from the contemporary literature, see L. Painchaud, "Le sommaire anthropogonique de *L'Écrit sans Titre* (NH II, 117:27–118:2) à la lumière de 1 *Co* 15:45–47," *VC* 44 (1990) 382–93.

that these adjectives refer to two forms of the body."[584] The theme of creation is continued in v. 46, wherein Paul says that the natural body precedes the spiritual. In other words, there is an ordering vis-à-vis God's intervention in Genesis and with Jesus. "The first man was from the earth (ἐκ γῆς), a man of dust (χοϊκός); the second man is from heaven (ἐξ οὐρανοῦ)" (v. 47). Then Paul can bring the argument to a close in v. 48: "As was the man of dust, so are those who are of the dust; and as is the man of heaven, so are those who are of heaven." The Corinthians are surely men of dust who await the resurrection until they become men of heaven, until they become alive in Christ, the first fruits. They share in the dust of the first Adam—suffering all of the ordinary effects of life and death as human beings—until the resurrection—when they shall share in the life of the second Adam (cf. Rom 8:9–13).[585] That is, "all share the likeness of the earthly man; salvation, without which resurrection is unthinkable, with which resurrection is certain, means that we come to share also in the image of the heavenly man."[586] All of this makes perfect sense with Paul's application in v. 49: "Just as we have borne the image of the man of dust, we shall also bear (φορέσομεν) the image of the man of heaven."[587] For all intents and purposes, this entire section ought to show doubting Christians *how* their resurrection will take place. Paul's purpose is not to dictate exactly the state of the resurrected body in its precise natural or pneumatological characteristics but to demonstrate the feasibility, indeed the reality, of a bodily continuum from earthly to heavenly existence at the parousia.[588]

The fifth and final section of 1 Corinthians 15 (A'; vv. 50–58) is concerned with explaining the transformation of men of dust to heavenly men. Speaking directly in the first person singular, Paul tells the Corinthians that "flesh and blood cannot inherit the kingdom of God, nor does the perishable inherit the imperishable" (v. 50). The Semitic pairing of σάρξ and αἷμα "denotes the natural man as a frail creature in opposition to God."[589] Humanity alone cannot

---

[584] Goulder, *Paul and the Competing Mission in Corinth*, 193.

[585] A thorough exposition is found in C. K. Barrett, *From First Adam to Last: A Study in Pauline Theology* (New York: Scribner, 1962). But for now, see A. J. M. Wedderburn, "The Body of Christ and Related Concepts in 1 Corinthians," *SJT* 24 (1971) 74–96. On Rom 8:9–13, see Brodeur "A Close Reading of Rom 8,9–13" (chap. 5), in *The Holy Spirit's Agency in the Resurrection of the Dead*, 177–232.

[586] Barrett, "The Significance of the Adam–Christ Typology for the Resurrection of the Dead," 121.

[587] Here we favor a reading of φορέσομεν (future indicative) over φορέσωμεν (hortatory subjunctive), as indicated in the *TCGNT*, 502 . For a contrary opinion, see Fee, *First Corinthians* 794–95.

[588] The agency is, of course, that of the Holy Spirit. On this, see Brodeur, "Theological Reflections on 1Cor 15,44b–49" (chap. 3), in *The Holy Spirit's Agency in the Resurrection of the Dead*, 145–62.

[589] Jeremias, "Flesh and Blood," 152. A similar use of σάρξ καὶ αἷμα is found in Gal 1:16. Cf. its use in Sir 14:18; 17:31; Eph 6:12; and Heb 2:14.

accede to the kingdom, nor can the perishable alone accede to imperishability. Joachim Jeremias' summary is noteworthy:

> Τὸ σὰρξ καὶ αἷμα is opposed in the second line of v. 50 ἡ φθορά, an *abstractum pro concreto*, meaning (as the context shows in v. 42 and 52 and the use of διαφθορά in Acts ii. 27, 31; xiii. 34–7) corpses in decomposition. That means: the two lines of v. 50 are contrasting men of flesh and blood on the one hand and corpses in decomposition on the other. In other words, the first line refers to those who are alive at the parousia, the second line to those who died before the parousia. The parallelism is thus not synonymous, but synthetic and the meaning of v. 50 is: neither the living nor the dead can take part in the Kingdom of God—as they are.[590]

Something has to change for the living and the dead.[591] What is to change is a mystery (μυστήριον; cf. 1 Cor 2:7; 4:1; 13:2; 14:2; Rom 11:25; 16:25) presented to the Corinthians as an indisputable fact: "All will be changed" (v. 51b; cf. Gal 4:20; Rom 1:23). "In the Pauline corpus the term μυστήριον is firmly connected with the *kerygma* of Christ."[592] That is, the mystery of which Paul speaks was predestined from of old (cf. 1 Cor 2:7; Rom 16:25); it is the very thing which Paul announces (cf. 1 Cor 2:1; Rom 11:25) and of which the servants of Christ are the stewards (cf. 1 Cor 4:1). Clearly, the announcement that "all will be changed" is a profundity of God's salvific plan. This change will occur instantly, at the last trumpet:[593] the dead will be raised and the living will be changed (v. 52). No group, i.e., neither the living nor the dead, is favored over the other in terms of the transformation. Paul's account here is very similar to 1 Thess 4:13–18 and Phil 3:21. It is not merely didactic; it is meant to supply hope (1 Thess 3:13b).

When this occurs (v. 54a–b), then will come to pass all that is written. In vv. 54c–55, Paul invokes the authority of the OT once again with a combination of Isa 25:8 and Hos 13:14.[594] Both quotations are variations of the LXX.[595] With

---

[590] Jeremias, "Flesh and Blood," 152. For an argument in favor of synonymous parallelism and an interpretation of σὰρξ καὶ αἷμα as a reference to humanity (living and dead), see J. Gillman, "Transformation in 1 Cor 15,50–53," *ETL* 58 (1982) 309–33, esp. 313, 316.

[591] "By σὰρξ καὶ αἷμα is meant our present mortal nature, not our evil propensities, which would be σὰρξ without αἷμα (Rom viii. 12, 13). The expression here refers to those who are still living, whereas ἡ φθορά refers to those who have died. If living flesh cannot inherit, how much less dead and corrupted flesh. Our present bodies, whether living or dead, are absolutely unfitted for the kingdom: *there must be a transformation*" (Robertson and Plummer, *I Corinthians*, 376 [emphasis added]).

[592] G. Bornkamm, "μυστήριον, μυεώ," *TDNT* 4:819.

[593] The trumpet (σάλπιγξ) is laden with meaning (see G. Friedrich, "σάλπιγξ," *TDNT* 7:71–88). It is a common eschatological symbol (see 2 Esdr. 6:23), which Paul also uses in 1 Thess 4:16 (cf. Matt 24:31; Heb 12:19; Rev 8:2).

[594] Isa 25:8 (LXX): Κατπιεν ὁ θάνατος ἰσχύσας. Hos 13:14 (LXX): Ποῦ ἡ δίκη σου, θάνατε; Ποῦ τὸ κέντρον σου, ᾅδη; [?]

[595] There is much contention about the text of 1 Cor 15:54–55 itself; for the textual variations, see the *TCGNT*, 502–3.

Isa 25:8, Paul uses νῖκος ("victory") instead of ἰσχύσας ("strength") to render the verse as "Death has been swallowed up in victory."[596] "In doing so he is reflecting a common LXX idiom for the translation of the Hebrew 'forever.'"[597] With Hos 13:14, Paul's variation is more complex. In v. 55a, νῖκος is used instead of δίκη. "The fact that Paul puts νῖκος, 'victory' in place of δίκη 'penalty' is manifestly due to the Isaiah passage."[598] And the substitution of ᾅδε with θάνατε in v. 55b (along with the movement of σου to the first position, closer to the vocative) intensifies that victory—over death. "Where, O death, is your victory? Where, O death, is your sting?" (v. 55). Verse 56, questioned as a possible gloss,[599] introduces two pillars of Paul's theology: sin and the law.[600] In fact, v. 56 introduces them in terms of death. "By connecting death with sin and sin with the law, Paul described humanity with the help of concepts which he shared with many of his Hellenistic contemporaries and which we suppose were well-known to his addressees in Corinth too."[601] By expanding the notion of death in terms of sin and the law, other obstacles to resurrection, Paul also expands the victory he so ardently spoke of in vv. 54–55 with v. 57: "But thanks be to God, who gives us the victory (νῖκος) through our Lord Jesus Christ." Thus, we can identify the theme of vv. 50–58: "bodily transformation resulting in a definitive victory over death."[602] And we can see the final verse of chapter 15 as exhortative. The Corinthians are to be "steadfast, immovable, always abounding in the work of the Lord"; their "labor is not in vain" (v. 58), which brings us neatly back to vv. 2 and 14. Their labor is not in vain because of the promise of resurrection. Whether living or dead at the parousia,[603] each member of the Corinthian community is assured of change, transformation, and heavenly

---

[596] There is some precedent for Paul's usage in Aquila's LXX; see Conzelmann, *1 Corinthians*, 292.

[597] Fee, *First Corinthians*, 803. Cf. MT: בִּלַּע הַמָּוֶת לָנֶצַח rendered in the RSV as "He will swallow up death forever."

[598] Ibid.

[599] Here we follow Robertson and Plummer (*I Corinthians*, 379), who maintain that "there is no need to suspect that it is a gloss." Barrett (*First Corinthians*, 384) believes that it fits well in its context and is original. Conzelmann (*1 Corinthians*, 384) claims: "This verse interrupts the train of thought; it looks like a gloss. Yet it can be explained in the context as an exegetical remark." For more, see F. W. Horn, "1 Korinther 15,56—ein exegetischer Stachel," *ZNW* 82 (1991) 88–105; and T. Söding, "'Die Kraft der Sünde ist das Gesetz' (1Kor 15, 56): Anmerkungen zum Hintergrund und zur Pointe einer gestzeskritischen Sentenz des Apostels Paulus," *ZNW* 83 (1992) 74–84.

[600] H. W. Hollander and J. Holleman ("The Relationship of Death, Sin, and Law in 1 Cor 15:56," *NovT* 35 [1993] 270–91) offer an extensive treatment of v. 56, which—gloss or not—is still puzzling at this juncture in 1 Corinthians 15.

[601] Ibid., 291.

[602] J. Gillman, "A Thematic Comparison: 1 Cor 15:50–57 and 2 Cor 5:1–5)," *JBL* 107 (1988) 451.

[603] On whether or not Paul expected to see the parousia in his lifetime, see A. C. Perriman, "Paul and the Parousia: 1 Corinthinas 15. 50–57 and 2 Corinthians 5. 1–5," *NTS* 35 (1989) 512–21.

existence along with Christ. The whole of 1 Corinthians 15, and in particular Paul's closing remarks, could not end on a higher note of hope.

Christian Corinth and Readings of 1 Corinthians 15:29

Writing much later to the Romans, Paul says "since we are justified by faith, we have peace with God through our Lord Jesus Christ. Through him we have obtained access to this grace in which we stand, and we rejoice in our hope of sharing the glory of God. More than that, we rejoice in our sufferings, knowing that suffering produces endurance, and endurance produces character, and character produces hope, and hope does not disappoint us, because God's love has been poured into our hearts through the Holy Spirit which has been given to us" (Rom 5:1–5). It is, no doubt, Paul's hope that 1 Corinthians will allay the many crises of faith among the nascent Christians in Corinth. As we noted above, there is a plethora of theories to explain the reasons for the crises, but none has gained scholarly consensus. Our own examination of the disparate crises reveals that there is probably no single factor at root. If there is a general theme to be found, it is that Paul is dissatisfied with the information he has received about Corinth. And he is dissatisfied on a number of levels: the Corinthians are divided among themselves in factions; there are ethical problems inconsistent with Christianity, as they relate to outsiders and as they relate to themselves; there are spiritual problems; and there is skepticism about Paul's salient teaching regarding the resurrection of Christ and the dead. "For [Paul] the truth of his gospel is finally tested in its ability to work its way out in the exigencies of everyday life in some very ticklish situations."[604] Paul dealt head-on with crises in Corinth. If there were a crisis in connection with baptism, we should know of it in 1 Corinthians.

But there is no baptismal crisis in 1 Corinthians. "There are four places in 1 Corinthians where Paul mentions baptism (1:13–17; 10:1–2; 12:13; 15:29), more than in any of his other letters, yet baptism itself is never his principal topic."[605] In 1:13–15, baptism is only mentioned tangentially. Paul is insistent that no one was baptized in his name and that he himself performed few baptisms in Corinth. In 1:16–17, the fact that Paul did perform some baptisms seems more an afterthought, and Paul insists that his preaching of the gospel is prior to his baptizing. The next mention of baptism is not until 10:2, wherein baptism is a metaphor; after that baptism is mentioned in 12:13, somewhat metaphorically, as a source of unity; and the last mention of baptism in 1 Corinthians is 15:29. Now in chapter 15, and especially in 15:29, it is clear that the primary issue at hand is the resurrection of the dead, not baptism. As all the commentators agree, the inclusion of baptism "on account of the dead"—whether or not Paul approved

---

[604] Fee, *First Corinthians*, 16.
[605] V. P. Furnish, *The Theology of the First Letter to the Corinthians* (NTT; Cambridge: Cambridge University Press, 1999) 91.

thereof and no matter how one might read the phrase—is marginal in contrast to the point at hand (resurrection), even if it is crucial to our study. Paul is using 15:29 to buttress his defense of the resurrection. So baptism *per se* figures only on the periphery of 1 Corinthians. Of course, baptism's ontological significance is immense for Christians early and late, but its historical significance as plumbed in 1 Corinthians and Paul's concern therein is not a center of attention. Even a perusal of 1 Corinthians reveals that Paul speaks, and speaks forcefully, to prominent issues, at least to the issues that were prominent in his own mind vis-à-vis the Corinthian situation, and such a perusal cannot leave the reader unenlightened as to Paul's own thinking on these matters. Yet at the same time, a perusal discloses very little about baptism among the Corinthians or Paul's reckoning with it, except inasmuch as it is a reality on the sidelines.

However, as we have seen above, a closer look at 1 Corinthians reveals a letter that pays strident attention to the problems Paul discerned in Corinthian Christianity. "First Corinthians is anything but a work of systematic theology. It is a practical letter addressed to a single, though complex situation, aimed at telling its readers not so much what they ought to think as what they ought to do—or ought not to do."[606] We have taken great care to show what it is that Paul asked them to do and not to do in the fifteen chapters of instruction in 1 Corinthians. Paul's response to the factionalism within the Corinthian community is thorough and pointed. He gives his appeal early on to the Corinthians: "that all of you agree and that there be no dissension among you, but that you be united in the same mind and the same judgment" (1 Cor 1:10). In four eloquent chapters, wherein Paul denies his own eloquence in favor of the cross of Christ, Paul goes so far as to threaten to come to them with a rod (4:21), if they do not settle their differences and adhere to the gospel Paul proclaimed to them. Paul referred to all the ethical and spiritual problems he discerned from the information available to him. The ethical issues in chapters 5–11—immorality and church discipline, litigation and integration, marriage and celibacy, idol food and freedom, worship and order—are a veritable inventory of the difficulties faced by a budding Christian community in Greco-Romanism. In the same vein, chapters 12–14 treat the spiritual issues—how to deal with the gifts of the Holy Spirit, the meaning of a love of God unknown outside Christian revelation, and the mature restraint of the ecstatic gift of tongues—we might expect to find among those still up-and-coming in their life in the Spirit. In terms of the resurrection of the dead in chapter 15, Paul's elucidation is "the close and crown of the whole epistle,"[607] and an extensive instruction to those among the Corinthians who deny, doubt, or question the resurrection of the dead. These were the crises in Corinthian Christianity. Providentially, "Paul did not have ready-made theologi-

---

[606] Barrett, *First Corinthians*, 17.
[607] K. Barth, *The Resurrection of the Dead* (trans. H. J. Stenning; New York: Revell, 1933) 11.

cal bandages to apply to Corinthian wounds."[608] Instead, 1 Corinthians is Paul's application of the theological principles of his gospel to the exigencies in Corinth. As Furnish writes:

> Even as Romans is generally considered the most theological of Paul's letters, so I Corinthians is commonly regarded as one of his most practical. Yet the apostle himself seems to have discerned that the pastoral problems with which he was faced in Corinth were but symptoms of an underlying misunderstanding of his gospel. Therefore, in dealing with those problems he repeatedly calls on his hearers to consider what the gospel has accomplished among them, and how, when it is faithfully received, the gospel wholly redefines and reshapes believers' lives. It is in this connection that we meet Paul the theologian even in I Corinthians—identifying what he understands to constitute the gospel, explicating its truth, and commenting on what it entails.[609]

The key, of course, is that Paul intertwines the theological and the practical in terms of the immediate situation of faith and practice in the Corinthian community. The *raison d'être* for 1 Corinthians is the Corinthian situation, the situation that calls for Paul's immediate and straightforward application of the gospel to the state of affairs that is Corinthian Christianity.

That immediate and straightforward application of the gospel does not extend to baptism in 1 Corinthians. Moreover, it does not extend to any theological or practical exigency begetting vicarious baptism. In Chapter I of our study, we delineated the various renderings of the majority reading to the effect that some existential necessity or pressure triggered the anomaly of vicarious baptism. On the one hand, Arthur Carr holds for a theological feebleness among the Corinthians, which developed out of a weak theological understanding of baptism, wherewith the Corinthians thought that they could save those who died before Paul came to Corinth.[610] Herbert Preisker likewise sees a theological misunderstanding: the Corinthians sought to hasten the parousia by increasing the number of the elect through vicarious baptism of the dead.[611] James Moffatt, crediting the Corinthians with more theological acumen than Carr or Preisker, considers vicarious baptism to be the ritual reaction ensuring salvation for catechumens who died before baptism.[612] All of these commentators agree that once theological equilibrium was achieved, vicarious baptism just faded away. On the other hand, Mathis Rissi and C. K. Barrett (following Rissi) judge vicarious baptism to have resulted from an existential dilemma. For Rissi, the dilemma is an epidemic or accident, which occurred just once and precipitated some vicarious baptisms;[613] for Barrett, many were dying without baptism and such deaths

---

[608] Furnish, *Theology of First Corinthians*, 27.
[609] Ibid., 18.
[610] Carr, "Baptism for the Dead," 371–74.
[611] Preisker, "Die Vikariatstaufe I Cor 15:29," 299–304.
[612] Moffatt, *First Corinthians*, 252–53.
[613] Rissi, "Die Taufe für die Toten," 89.

inspired vicarious baptism as a means of proclamation.[614] Our predicament, if we were to accept either theological or practical exigencies, would be to explain why Paul never mentioned them in 1 Corinthians. Without doubt, 1 Corinthians gives much more tribute to the Corinthians' theological insight than Carr, Preisker, or Moffatt seem to admit. Yes, Paul went to great lengths of explanation. Therefore, it seems that such a blatant misunderstanding of baptism would have provoked Paul's attention, if not his ire, were it present among the Corinthians. So too, Rissi and Barrett fail to connect the dots between death (expected or unexpected) and vicarious baptism. It is true, as we saw in Chapter II of our study, that 15:29 may be read literally this way, but there is no practical exigency that we know of in Corinthian Christianity that grounds such a reading. Theirs is educated guesswork, but it is guesswork nonetheless. All in all, there are simply no grounds for vicarious baptism in Corinthian Christianity.

Much of the same may be said about certain readings of 15:29 that refer to ordinary baptism. That is, some readings consider a theological innovation or distortion as the root cause of an ordinary baptism, which was performed for extraordinary reasons, that Paul disapproved. As we noted in Chapter I, Maria Raeder,[615] followed by Joachim Jeremias,[616] proffers ordinary baptism administered for those who wanted to join loved ones in the resurrection but who did not believe in Jesus as Lord. Somehow, some non-Christian Corinthians accepted baptism as a means to eternal life, but did not accept Jesus as Lord. These individuals focused solely on the resurrection, with little emphasis on Jesus, but a misplaced and impassioned missionary zeal on the part of the Corinthian Christians allowed such ordinary baptism. This seems highly unlikely after a close reading of 1 Corinthians. Missionary work does not figure into the letter, nor does the letter evidence inclusion in the community as the result of anything other than faith in Christ. J. K. Howard's understanding, built of the foundation of Raeder and Jeremias, seems to bring things a little closer to (a Corinthian) home. Howard maintains that a desire for unity in the resurrection becomes the impetus for many individuals to accept Christ, the source of the eternal life in which they have come to believe.[617] In one sense, we may say that Howard "baptizes" Raeder and Jeremias and makes their reading more palatable; in another, we may say that Howard has also put "the cart before the horse" insofar as he postulates the acceptance of so fundamental a truth about Christ before accepting Christ. How could that be possible? Nothing in 1 Corinthians indicates such theological primitivism among the Corinthians. Much closer to the mark come John D. Reaume and Joel R. White. Reaume opts for ordinary baptism on

---

[614] Barrett, *First Corinthians*, 363.

[615] Raeder, "Vikariatstaufe?" 258–60. So too, Findlay, *First Corinthians*, 930–31.

[616] Jeremias, "Flesh and Blood," 155–56. So too, Schnakenburg, *Baptism in the Thought of St. Paul*, 102.

[617] Howard, "Baptism for the Dead," 141.

account of the influence that dead Christians, especially martyred Christians, exerted to the effect that many were converted to Christianity.[618] White—reading 15:29's τῶν νεκρῶν metaphorically to refer to the apostles and Paul, who are "dead" in terms of their suffering for the faith—sees the positive influence of the apostles' endurance as the impetus for conversion.[619] Still, with the absence of any specific persecutions and martyrdom in the early 50s, Reaume's thesis is difficult to ground. And again as we saw above, there is no reason to assume a metaphorical reading of νεκρός, which leaves White's reading unacceptable.

All of the above leads to the conclusion that the exigencies used to support a reading of vicarious baptism (or even an oddly-motivated ordinary baptism) involve, without exception, arguments from silence. None of them have any foundation in Corinthian Christianity; all have been speculated in order to make sense of particular readings of 15:29, in order to find some means to justify what seems to be so unjustifiable. Our portrait of Corinthian Christianity discloses nothing remotely akin to any crises (theological, existential, or otherwise) that would merit any seemingly twisted innovation on the part of Corinthian Christians to substantiate vicarious baptism. Vicarious baptism is not the result of any misunderstanding on the part of the Corinthians. The needle of vicarious baptism—or of even some of the factors used to rationalize readings of unusual ordinary baptism—is nowhere to be found in the haystack of Corinthian Christianity, at least as far as we know it from 1 Corinthians.

THE HISTORICAL CONTEX OF 1 CORINTHIANS 15:29

The historical context of 15:29 lends great insight into the circumstances of the verse. The purpose of our investigation has been to cast a discerning eye on the whole of 1 Corinthians with the intent of distinguishing between a reading of ordinary or vicarious baptism. In Chapter II, we concluded that a finely tuned reading of 15:29 from a literary perspective is inconclusive in that regard. Strictly speaking, the words of 15:29 could be absolutely interpreted in themselves as a reference to either ordinary or vicarious baptism. Having passed through the crucible of the historical context, we now can see that a reading of vicarious baptism is ungrounded. We searched diligently for the needle of vicarious baptism in the haystack of 1 Corinthians, but we did not find it because it is not there. In a close scrutiny of Paul, Greco-Roman Corinth, and Corinthian Christianity, we explored far and wide to no avail. At this point in our study, it is necessary to sum up our findings and look forward towards a new reading of 15:29.

---

[618] Reaume, "Another Look at 1 Corinthians 15:29," 475.
[619] J. R. White, "Baptized on account of the Dead," 497.

For our purposes, summing up an extensive undertaking into three different, though mutually inclusive areas—Paul, Greco-Roman Corinth, and Corinthian Christianity—is neither a task of melding the three into a composite portrait nor of *proving* anything vis-à-vis 15:29. Instead, it is a task of investigation in the hopes of finding any vestige that would support a reading of vicarious baptism. As we stated above, readings of vicarious baptism—all of which we have addressed—explain it away as an anomaly; and as anomalies are by definition unique and without parallel, they cannot be directly tackled or compared with anything else. Were it the case that the very words of 15:29 could not be read in any other way than as a reference to vicarious baptism, we would have to conclude that the verse does refer to vicarious baptism. From our extensive examination of the verse's background, we might pause here with the medial conclusion that 15:29 is indeed representative of a vicarious baptism variance, unknown in any other quarter, but we would also have to conclude that the various and sundry explanations of this aberration are not satisfactorily rendered by any of those who hold for such a reading. That is, if Reginald St. John Parry and the many others who insist that anything other than a reading of vicarious baptism does violence to "the plain and necessary sense of the words" of 15:29,[620] then we would have nowhere to turn, except to proffer yet another audacious, though educated and reasoned, guess as to an historical circumstance, which may have given rise to such an unusual and brief custom as vicarious baptism and disappeared from sight almost immediately upon its incidence.

But as we saw in Chapters I and II, the "plain and necessary sense" of 15:29 is hardly plain or necessary. Numerous scholars are willing to read 15:29 as a reference to ordinary baptism, no matter how extraordinary that reference might be. We are not at all hopelessly adrift when we find that vicarious baptism fails to materialize itself in the Corinthian milieux. Quite to the contrary, ordinary baptism stands as a viable option. In fact, our analyses of the literary and historical contexts, taken together, indicate that ordinary baptism is the only viable option. At first glance, this would seem to be a moment of relief, for until this point vicarious baptism seems to have been the impenetrable and irrefutable *lectio difficilior*. Close inspection, however, reveals that it is seemingly impenetrable only because it springs out of an argument from silence. There is no other instance of vicarious baptism and nothing that comes remotely close to it. Likewise, it is seemingly irrefutable because another plain and necessary sense of the words, viz., that some are being baptized "on account of the dead," is almost beyond our comprehension. What could this mean? What is Paul speaking of in 15:29? Yet when the cacophony of readings from silence is itself silenced and a reading of vicarious baptism is found to be not only refutable but also unworkable, a reading of ordinary baptism presents itself as the *lectio difficilior*.

---

[620] Parry, *First Corinthians*, 228.

Without appeal to rites otherwise unknown and without recourse to historical circumstances otherwise unattested, how do we read 15:29? In other words, when we read 15:29 at face value, we have an astounding and stirring insight into the earliest baptismal awareness in Christianity. Baptism and death are inextricably joined in the immediate context of 15:29 and within the larger context of 1 Corinthians 15—a chapter dealing almost exclusively with the resurrection. To seek to understand the momentous insight of these few lines within the whole of 1 Corinthians is certainly more difficult than writing it off as an anomaly. The issues that swirl around this verse are the issues that swirled around in Paul's mind in such wise as he appreciated the conceptions of the Corinthian community. Delving deeply into 15:29, without disassociating it from its literary and historical contexts, insofar as we know them, and endeavoring to comprehend this inimitable verse is, without question, the *lectio difficilior*. What, precisely, is Paul driving at when he links ordinary baptism and the dead under the aegis of the resurrection?

This brings us to the third section of 1 Corinthians 15 (C; vv. 29–34), which we left for consideration until now. Verses 29–34 are a series of three affirmations of the resurrection in the form of three separate assertions. The first two indicate an active, practical witness to the resurrection: some seem to be accepting baptism on its behalf and some seem to be undergoing danger on its behalf. And the third indicates Paul's ire towards those who would deny the resurrection, a denial he considers sinful and shameful. As we indicated in Chapter II of our study, a practicable understanding of the section is seen through the distinction of grammatical persons in a concentric structure of antithetical parallelism:

A   3rd p., pl., "they,"
         those on Paul's side, affirming the resurrection (v. 29)

B   1st p., sing., "I"
         Paul's apostolic example of faith in the resurrection (vv. 30–32)

A'   2nd p., pl., "you,"
         those not on Paul's side, denying the resurrection (vv. 33–34).

In the first instance (A), Paul distances βαπτιζόμενοι from the general audience of 1 Corinthians. In the second instance (B), Paul refers to his own apostolic endeavors as without benefit, if there were no resurrection of the dead. And in the third instance (A'), Paul reverts to the general audience by warning against those whose bad company would ruin others' morals. Here we do not wish to repeat all we said in Chapter II, but only to focus on the historical situation. We have already examined the morphology and syntax of 15:29 in Chapter II to the effect that there is one group pitted against another in Paul's prose. It is the "they" against the "you." This comes as no surprise since the rampant factionalism within the community is a major concern of Paul's throughout 1 Corinthians. Whatever "baptism on account of the dead" is, it is an affirmation of the resurrection, and that affirmation is directed to those who need to hear it.

"Paul's reference to the Corinthian practice of baptism of the dead in his argument against the Corinthians' denial of the resurrection gives the impression that the Corinthians were being inconsistent in their practice and belief, that is, in rejection of life after death (cf. 1 Cor 15:19, 32). Yet those who were baptized might not have seen it that way."[621] If 1 Corinthians 1–4 indicates anything, it indicates that there were divisions within the community and that those divisions did not exclude theological heterogeneity; if 1 Corinthians 5–15 indicates anything, it indicates that Paul desired them to amend their beliefs and practices according to his understanding of the gospel. It comes as no surprise to find that Paul should juxtapose one group against another in terms of individuated belief and practice. T. Engberg-Pederson, concluding an article on social practice and 1 Corinthians in general, remarks:

> I have argued that according to Paul the gospel is directly *about* social practice, moreover that Paul takes this so seriously that he lets it govern his own practice in relation to the Corinthians. . . . I have been concerned to present a certain view of the exact content of the gospel and a connected view of the character of Pauline theology. The gospel is one of love, of giving up oneself for others and of willing that and willing it alone. Therefore "believing" the gospel ("subscribing" to it) is a matter of *living* in a certain way. Paul's thought is centered on this idea of living, on his own living in such a way that he exemplifies the gospel, and on his addressees' living in the same way. The basic feature of Paul's thought informs his *paraenesis*, but it is also one that makes *paraenesis the form* of Pauline thought. Here the general (or theological), the particular (or practical), and the personal are fused into a single concern, which is the one of how Paul himself lives and should live (as a Christian) and how his addressees live and should live (as Christians). It is an astonishing fact about human thought that although Paul's letters are sharply focused on this highly specific question, these letters also make a universal claim.[622]

In relatively few words, vv. 29–34 amalgamate this specific tripartite relationship of the general (theological), what the Corinthians ought to believe; the particular (practical), what the Corinthians ought to do in terms of their belief; and the personal, Paul's own example. For Paul, belief and practice are meant to be one indivisible reality. Therefore, 15:29 "must be allowed to stand as *Paul's* question addressed to the Corinthians who say there is no resurrection *from the dead*, asking them how they can say so in the place of their own practice."[623]

Verse 29's "they"—the βαπτιζόμενοι, a group spoken of in the third person plural—are undergoing the rite of baptism so as to affirm the resurrection in

---

[621] Chow, *Patronage and Power*, 164–65.

[622] T. Engberg-Pedersen, "The Gospel and Social Practice according to 1 Corinthians," *NTS* 33 (1987) 582–83 (emphasis original).

[623] J. H. Schütz, "Apostolic Authority and the Control of Tradition: I Cor XV," *NTS* 15 (1968–69) 444 (emphasis original).

some way.[624] Their particular practice is concomitant with the theological truth that Paul has been at pains to demonstrate in the whole of 1 Corinthians 15, viz., the resurrection of Christ and of Christians. This group is designated with reference to another group in vv. 33–34. The imperatives of vv. 33–34—the "you" (τίνες) in the second person plural—parallel the "some of you" (τίνες) and the "someone" (τίς) among the "you" in vv. 12 and 35. Thus "baptism on account of the dead" puts faith into practice. The "you" are not told that they ought to baptize on account of the dead. The practice is mentioned to highlight their theological ineptitude, i.e., lack of faith in the resurrection. As we noted in Chapter II, Paul's use of Isa 22:13 (LXX) in reference to eating and drinking prior to an inevitable death and his quotation from Menander's *Thais* to the effect that bad company ruins morals, serve to drive that point home: all would be lost without resurrection. And in the center is the personal: Paul's perils, his daily dying, and his fighting with beasts at Ephesus are nothing, "if the dead are not raised" (vv. 30–32). Again, as we noted in Chapter II, Paul does not specify the nature of his perils or daily dying,[625] nor is his allusion to wild beasts at Ephesus abundantly clear to us,[626] but his meaning is easily gleaned to the effect that his apostolic struggles (or anyone's apostolic struggles for that matter) are futile without the resurrection. What is abundantly clear is that the βαπτιζόμενοι and Paul are both in the process of some practical activity that is affirmative of the resurrection. What remains somewhat vague is the nature of the disagreement between some Corinthians and others vis-à-vis baptism and resurrection. Our move towards a new reading of the verse must perforce explore the relationship between this most extraordinary of ordinary baptisms and the resurrection.

The necessity of rejecting a reading of vicarious baptism and accepting one of ordinary baptism is only one piece of the puzzle that is 15:29. A reading of vicarious baptism is not rejected because it is too hard, but because it is too easy. It is far too easy to bracket 15:29 as a thing apart in 1 Corinthians 15, as something outside the pale of the chapter. It is much harder to return again and again to this apparently opaque verse, to compare baptismal practice and resurrection belief to one another among the Corinthians, and to demand that we, as well, reconcile our rites and faith. As we noted in Chapter I and fundamentally agreed

---

[624] "Such a practice is ridiculous if the dead are not raised. The practice probably shows the importance accorded to baptism in Corinthian belief, without baptism, no resurrection, and perhaps even resurrection as a direct consequence of baptism" (Eriksson, *Traditions as Rhetorical Proofs*, 264–65).

[625] See 2 Cor 11:24–29 for some of the possibilities.

[626] As noted above, Bowen ("I Fought with Wild Beasts," 59–68) opts for an actual, physical encounter in the arena, while Malherbe ("The Beasts at Ephesus," 71–80) opts for a figurative reading in terms of Paul's theological opponents at Ephesus. For our purposes the question is moot. But recall that MacDonald ("A Conjectural Emendation of 1 Cor 15:31–32," 265–76), who thinks almost the whole of vv. 31–32 to be an interpolation, would still leave us Paul's reference to the raising of the dead as part of the original text; cf. R. F. Collins, *First Corinthians*, 560.

with in Chapter II of our study, there are already a number of scholars who opt for a reading of ordinary baptism, albeit in different senses, because a reading of ordinary baptism is, in fact, viable. As we have seen in this chapter, with vicarious baptism abandoned as a solid foundation for interpreting 15:29, a reading of ordinary baptism for the verse is not only viable but vital. However, taking 15:29 as a reference to ordinary baptism requires a bona-fide explanation and interpretation. Thus far, we have fleshed out the contemporary readings of 15:29 (Chapter I), investigated 15:29's literary context (Chapter II), and explored 15:29's historical context (Chapter III), but there is much more to be done. We must explain and interpret 15:29 on the basis of these analyses.

What must we do, then, to reread 15:29? First, we must remember that the multiplicity of contemporary readings is cause enough for a rereading. The plethora of theories and lack of agreement among scholars is sufficient to justify such an endeavor. Though we have narrowed the viable readings down to ordinary baptism, we know that there are significant deviations of opinion among scholars who hold for such a reading to merit a rereading of the verse in terms of ordinary baptism. Second, the literary context of the verse suggests that there is a split within the Corinthian community over the resurrection. 1 Corinthians 15 makes it apparent that some among the Corinthians do not accept the resurrection of the dead. Such a denial is, for Paul, a denial of the resurrection of Christ. Without doubt, Paul's purpose in 1 Corinthians 15 is to affirm the resurrection of Christ and of Christians, to correct the erroneous understanding of those who would deny it, and to strengthen the resolve of those who accept it. A broad examination of Paul's own background and the city of Corinth in which he preached the gospel reveals that Paul was eminently prepared to argue his message among the Corinthians. 1 Corinthians shows clearly that he addressed a number of crises in his newly-found community and that he "pulled no punches" to settle them. But *baptism* was not a crisis in Corinth. Except for 15:29, the few references to baptism in 1 Corinthians (1:13–17; 10:2; 12:13; baptism is not mentioned in 2 Corinthians) are negligible.[627] Throughout 1 Corinthians, we see that factionalism is a problem, ethical and spiritual issues are knotty, and faith in the resurrection of the dead is critical. And baptism? Baptism only comes up in chapter 15 in terms of resurrection. It is safe to say that had there not been a crisis of faith regarding the resurrection, there would be no mention of baptism "on account of the dead" in 1 Corinthians.

Yet the mention of baptism "on account of the dead" in 15:29 is our concern. In order to reread the verse, we need a change of venue. Instead of starting from a point of view that focuses on 15:29 under the auspices of baptism, we need to focus on 15:29—a illustration of baptism—under the auspices of the

---

[627] See Schnakenburg (*Baptism in the Thought of St. Paul*, 78–82) for a brief discussion about whether or not every passage in the Pauline literature that speaks of dying and rising should be considered "baptismal."

resurrection, 15:29's literary and historical locus in 1 Corinthians 15. Once that focus is achieved, we need to look closely at other illustrations of baptism in the Pauline literature. Because references to baptism in the Pauline literature are somewhat scarce, especially references that offer analytical insight into Paul's understanding thereof, we need to compare and contrast 15:29 with them. Lastly, as it is a salient reference to baptism, 15:29 has something to say about Paul's baptismal theology. When cogently explained and properly interpreted, 15:29 will inform and expand our knowledge of Paul's baptismal thought. Our fourth and final chapter is an attempt to do just that.

IV. Rereading 1 Corinthians 15:29

Our examination of 1 Cor 15:29's literary and historical contexts has prepared us to read 15:29 anew as well as to explore its insights and implications. In this our fourth and final chapter, we endeavor to interpret 15:29 by building upon the findings of our investigations thus far. First, we explicate our understanding of the verse. We look to 15:29 against its background in 1 Corinthians. We pay special attention to the circumstances in which we find the verse, viz., 1 Corinthians 15 and Paul's defense of the resurrection of Christ and of Christians. Second, we delve into Paul's baptismal theology. Although references to baptism are rare in the Pauline literature, there are more mentions of baptism in 1 Corinthians than in any other letter. Paul certainly has something to say about baptism in 1 Corinthians, something that surely merits our concerted attention. But just as we cannot read anything within 1 Corinthians outside its context of 1 Corinthians, so too we cannot hope to glean an understanding of a theological truth mentioned in 1 Corinthians—in our case baptism—without consideration of that same truth within the larger context of the *corpus Paulinum*. Again, though references to baptism are few, they are pertinent, if not paramount, to an understanding of Paul's baptismal theology. Particularly significant is Paul's reference to baptism in Rom 6:1–14 (the oft-cited *locus classicus* of baptism in Paul) and in Gal 3:26–29. Last in this chapter, we offer a summary of our study.

A NEW READING OF 1 CORINTHIANS 15:29

At this point in our study, a new reading of 15:29 entails a recapitulation of our previous conclusions. That 15:29 is a *crux interpretum* is without doubt. Our investigation into the literary context makes that point as strongly as possible, for we have seen that 1 Corinthians 15 is an integral whole. That is, 15:29–34 is part of Paul's logical and systematic defense of the resurrection of the dead in 1 Corinthians 15. In fact, we have argued that 15:29–34 is not only part of Paul's defense but also the center of a concentric pentacolon. All readings of 1 Corinthians 15 that relegate 15:29–34 and especially 15:29 to the sidelines do so on the presumption that the verses are an aberration of one type or another, either an historical or a literary anomaly. Again, as we have seen, there is a perfectly legitimate way to read 15:29 as a reference to ordinary baptism. While it is true that the literary context does not necessitate such a reading of ordinary baptism any more than it necessitates the majority reading of vicarious baptism, the literary context does not, in fact, demand a reading one way or the other. By leaving the reading open until the historical context was taken into consideration, we allowed vast insight into Paul, Greco-Roman Corinth, and Corinthian Christianity, insight that precluded 15:29 as a reference to vicarious baptism. Thus, 15:29 is a reference to ordinary baptism, albeit an extraordinary one, because of its crucial connection to Paul's defense of the resurrection of the dead.

Reading 1 Corinthians 15:29 Anew

Reading 15:29 anew begins with the words of the verse themselves: Ἐπεὶ τί ποιήσουσιν οἱ βαπτιζόμενοι ὑπὲρ τῶν νεκρῶν; εἰ ὅλως νεκροὶ οὐκ ἐγείρονται, τί καὶ βαπτίζονται ὑπὲρ αὐτῶν; [?] We noted that only three words caused exegetical problems: βαπτίζω, νεκρός, and ὑπέρ. Given its use in Rom 6:3 (and βάπτισμα in 6:4); 1 Cor 1:13, 14, 15, 16, 17; 10:2; 12:13; and Gal 3:27, we concluded that βαπτίζω must be read in its literal sense, "I baptize." Here Paul refers to a sacrament that is attendant to the Christian life. We also found that νεκρός ought to be taken in its literal sense, that νεκρός is used as a substantive, and that it simply means "the dead as distinct from the living."[1] The dead of whom Paul speaks in 15:29 are dead persons. From the context of 1 Corinthians 15, it is clear that they are dead Christians, the dearly departed of the Corinthian community. No doubt their deaths, which seemed indistinguishable from those of any other (pagan) persons, occasioned qualms and uncertainties among the Corinthians akin to those which Paul addressed among the Thessalonians (1 Thess 4:13–5:11); no doubt, 1 Corinthians 15 is Paul's response to such Corinthian qualms and uncertainties as he appreciated them. Far more difficult for our reading than βαπτίζω and νεκρός is ὑπέρ, the crux of this *crux interpretum*.[2] Relatively rare in the NT, Paul uses ὑπέρ more than any other NT writer. As we saw, there are many ways in which ὑπέρ may be read with the genitive. The rarest way is in the causal sense. "Causally ὑπέρ is used to denote the cause or reason: 'on account of,' 'because of.' In the NT it occurs with verbs and expressions of suffering, the reference being to Christians who endure hardships because of their faith."[3] In choosing this rare usage, we found ourselves in agreement with John D. Reame and Joel R. White.[4] With all of this in mind, we rendered our own translation of 15:29: "Otherwise what are they to do, who

---

[1] Bultmann, "νεκρός," 893.
[2] See Reaume, "Another Look at 1 Corinthians 15:29," 467.
[3] Riesenfeld, "ὑπέρ," 513.
[4] Reaume, "Another Look at 1 Corinthians 15:29," 471–72; and J. R. White, "Baptized on account of the Dead," 497–98.

have themselves baptized on account of the dead? If the dead are not really raised, why are they baptized on account of them?"

In essence, then, 15:29 is two closely related rhetorical questions, which Paul puts to the Corinthians. They are similar to, but different from, the rhetorical questions Paul poses in 15:12 and 35. These questions are asked in terms of the grammatical second person, but 15:29 is posed in the third person. In vv. 12 and 35, the questions presume a denial of the resurrection of the dead. The rhetorical question in v. 12 shows that the denial of the resurrection of the dead by some Corinthians is considered by Paul to be tantamount to a denial of the resurrection of Christ, "the first fruits of those who have fallen asleep" (v. 20). The rhetorical question in v. 35 contends that some Corinthians deny the resurrection of the dead because they do not accept the resurrection of the body. For Paul, such a denial evidences ignorance; what is sown "does not come to life unless it dies" (v. 36). The questions of both vv. 12 and 35 are posed so that Paul can remind the Corinthians of what he preached to them (vv. 1–11) and provide clarification in terms of their qualms and uncertainties vis-à-vis vv. 12 and 35. All of it is meant for those Corinthians who deny the resurrection. But what of 15:29? The ones "who have themselves baptized on account of the dead" are obviously not part of the larger group Paul is addressing in chapter 15. In fact, "if the dead are not really raised," it would seem that they should stop doing whatever it is they are doing—accepting baptism on account of the dead, i.e., on account of dead Christians—because it would be futile. On the contrary, Paul is not reproving the βαπτιζόμενοι; he is reproving the Corinthians who deny the resurrection of the dead. Paul is not asking the βαπτιζόμενοι to alter their actions; he is asking the other Corinthians to alter theirs in terms of accepting what Paul preached to them, unless they believed in vain (v. 14). Apparently, "they" (the third person, βαπτιζόμενοι) are being offered as an example to the "you" (the second person, τίνες and τίς).

That the one group is being held up as a laudable example to the other is more evident in Paul's association of the βαπτιζόμενοι with himself. For immediately after 15:29, Paul asks another rhetorical question: "Why am I in peril every hour?" (v. 30). Paul then speaks of "daily dying" and fighting "beasts at Ephesus" (vv. 31–32). Whether Paul's reference here is to actual physical suffering or metaphorical suffering is immaterial. The point is that any such suffering is worthless if there is no hope of resurrection from the dead. As Paul says so eloquently in v. 32, "If the dead are not raised, 'Let us eat and drink for tomorrow we die.'" This citation of Isa 22:13 (LXX) not only refers to recklessness in God's eyes, but also to Epicureanism. Failing to hope in the resurrection of the dead leads one outside God's promises and back into the hopeless licentiousness of the past. The Corinthians could not have missed this point. Paul also tells them to avoid deception, quoting Menander's *Thais* to the effect that they ought to break away from any company that leads to faithlessness in morals

(v. 33), to come to their right mind and avoid sin (v. 34a), and finally to recognize that their lack of knowledge of God is shameful (v. 34b). Hence, we still find one group under Paul's admonition. Conversely, those who are undergoing baptism on account of the dead affirm the resurrection by their actions. Just so, Paul affirms the resurrection by his actions. But the group of Corinthians whom he addresses directly does not. The message is clear: the resurrection of the dead rightly motivates the βαπτιζόμενοι and Paul. The juxtaposing of the βαπτιζόμενοι and the Corinthians in general highlights the contrast within the entire Corinthian community.

As is evident in 1 Corinthians 1–4, the Corinthian community was splintered by factionalism. Paul begins 1 Corinthians by appealing for agreement, an end of dissention, and union "in the same mind and the same judgment" (1:10). Paul is not creating the factions; they are already there, and some of the Corinthians are arrogant (4:18). We noted earlier that there is a plethora of suggestions accounting for the problems in Corinth but none has gained consensus and each seems insufficient to explain the varied and sundry topics Paul addresses in 1 Corinthians. We will never know exactly what went wrong in Corinth because it was not a single thing that went wrong and because the things that went wrong were hardly homogeneous. William Baird points out that Paul was not fighting on a single front, that the disagreements in Corinth arose from numerous situations, that no single methodology can explain all of the problems Paul addresses, that Paul orders 1 Corinthians according to problems as he understood them and not according to the factions themselves, that the factions cannot be limited to any particular problem, and that some, though few, patterns may emerge.[5] According to Baird, "the most common feature of the Corinthian character, however, is pride. Although Paul says 'some are arrogant' (4:18), he indicates that many Corinthians are proud of everything from a case of incest (5:2) to possession of knowledge (8:1). This pride has fostered the factionalism that plagues the congregation."[6] No doubt, the pride that permeates the community is a cause for Paul's frequent warnings in 1 Corinthians to boast only in the Lord (1:31 [2x]; 3:21; 4:7; 5:6; 9:15, 16; 13:4). For Paul, the theme of boasting "is fundamentally theological" and linked to trust, "with the question of where a man is ultimately to place his confidence, in himself or in God."[7] The whole of 1 Corinthians 15 is Paul's response to the Corinthians' lack of trust in God's promise of resurrection for believers and to their lack of confidence in the gospel he preached to them. By arguing logically and proffering the personal example of the βαπτιζόμενοι and himself, Paul takes advantage of the factional-

---

[5] W. Baird, "'One against the Other': Intra-Church Conflict in 1 Corinthians," in *The Conversation Continues*, ed. Fortna and Gaventa, 130–31.

[6] Ibid., 131.

[7] Barrett, "Boasting (καυχᾶθαι, κτλ.) in the Pauline Epistles," in *L'apôtre Paul*, ed. Vanhoye, 368.

ism in order to attempt to heal discord with evidentiary truth and works so as to bring all the Corinthians back to the same mind and judgment.

The positioning of one group as an example to another is not a matter of Paul exonerating one group of *persons* and condemning another. Paul wants to deal with the problem of faith in the resurrection of the dead. Earlier on in 4:16 and 11:1 (cf. 4:6), Paul called for imitation of himself as he does here in 15:30–32. But it is always a specific type of imitation: imitation of Paul as a "father in Christ Jesus through the gospel" (4:16), imitation of Paul as Paul himself is an imitator "of Christ" (11:1), or imitation of Paul as he struggles on in the hope of his resurrection (15:30–32). Likewise, 15:29 can be seen as the praising of the βαπτιζόμενοι because they are affirming the resurrection of the dead in accepting baptism; theirs is an act of faith that opposes the lack of faith Paul perceives among so many Corinthians. Paul's tribute is not to any group or faction. Paul's tribute is to an act of faith that is exemplary. In like manner, Paul's teachings on ethical and spiritual issues are not meant to take sides, but to remind them of the gospel he preached in Corinth. Indeed, Paul reels at the notion that some might claim to belong to him rather than Christ (1:12–17). Paul is especially interested in distancing himself from the pride he condemns. As is his wont throughout his letters, Paul is calling the Corinthians back to the gospel and Christ. It is no accident that he begins with baptism in 1 Corinthians 1. Baptism should have been the source of the Corinthians' unity in the Lord and concord with one another. Baptism is the antithesis of factionalism. For that reason, Paul says that he is thankful to have baptized but few of them. "Paul certainly did not baptize people in his own name, but he wanted the people to look to Christ who redeemed them and not to the preacher who baptized them."[8] Pride and factionalism are indications of the relinquishing of their baptismal character, and Paul wants nothing to do with that. "It would be a mistake and also anachronistic to suppose that Paul draws a contrast between a sacramental ministry and a preaching ministry as such."[9] The contrast is between hearing and accepting the gospel. Christ sent Paul to preach the gospel; it is up to the Corinthians to accept it and remain faithful in it. Hearing the gospel is perforce prior to accepting it. And one cannot be baptized without hearing and accepting. For Paul, baptism is "not only a preparatory sacrament—as for John the Baptist—but a sacrament of fulfillment."[10] Paul's preaching ministry precedes his sacramental ministry, but the two are inseparable. Baptism is *the* ultimate act of faith in the gospel, in Christ's resurrection, and in his promise of eternal life to believers. Thus, Paul applauds the βαπτιζόμενοι for what they are doing, for accepting baptism and all that goes with it, for affirming the resurrection of the dead.

---

[8] Kistemaker, *I Corinthians*, 50.
[9] Thiselton, *First Corinthians*, 142.
[10] Ridderbos, *Paul*, 399.

By any measure, the Corinthian community was a young one at the time of 1 Corinthians, "babes in Christ" (3:1). But the more recent converts are even younger, the βαπτιζόμενοι are the youngest in the faith. Again, Paul does not intend to exacerbate the community's pride or factionalism by using them as a model. Instead, Paul desires that the Corinthians harken back to their original baptismal innocence. Wrapping up the first major section of 1 Corinthians in 4:17 with an emphasis on imitation in 4:16, Paul explains his rationale for sending Timothy: "Therefore I sent to you Timothy, my beloved and faithful child in the Lord, to remind you of my ways in Christ." Inaugurating the last major section of 1 Corinthians in 15:1–2, Paul explains that he is not going to say anything he has not said before: "Now I would remind you, brethren, in what terms I preached to you the gospel, which you received, in which you stand, by which you are saved, if you hold fast—unless you believed in vain." Much of 1 Corinthians, especially chapters 5–14, is about clarification as the Corinthian community matures in theological reflection and existential experience. But much is also about jogging the collective Corinthian memory. Paul's utilization of the βαπτιζόμενοι's example is meant to teach, even to repeat a lesson that all should have learned and inculcated. Commending the newly baptized is not condemning those older in the faith. And speaking well of the βαπτιζόμενοι is not meant to solve every problem or conflict in Corinth, if so there would be no need for 1 Corinthians 1–14; but Paul is comforted by their act of faith and willing to use it as an ideal for the edification of the entire Corinthian community. Particularly, Paul specifies union between baptism and the *kerygma*. Paul handed on to the Corinthians what was handed on to him, viz., Christ was buried, that he was raised, and that he appeared to many believers including Paul (15:3–8).[11] In other words, Christ is raised from the dead—there is no doubt about it—"Christ the first fruits, then at his coming those who belong to Christ" (15:23). The βαπτιζόμενοι are exemplars. In their acceptance of baptism, they eagerly receive all that Paul has to hand on to them. What more could Paul ask of them?

Indeed, Paul asks nothing more of them. But he does present them to their fellow Corinthians for appreciation. It is to the βαπτιζόμενοι's fellow Corinthians that Paul poses the rhetorical questions of 15:29: "Otherwise what are they to do, who have themselves baptized on account of the dead? If the dead are not really raised, why are they baptized on account of them?" A rhetorical question does not so much expect an answer as it makes a statement. After the whole of 15:12–28, Paul's statement in 15:29 is unambiguous. Without a hope of resurrection, those who have themselves baptized on account of the dead are wasting their time. If the dead are not raised, there is no reason to be baptized on account of them. There is no resurrection of the dead. "But if there is no resur-

---

[11] For more on Paul's sources in 1 Cor 15:3–7, see Murphy-O'Connor, "Tradition and Redaction in 1 Cor 15:3–7," 582–89.

rection of the dead, then Christ has not been raised; if Christ has not been raised, then our preaching is in vain and your faith is in vain" (15:13–14). To put it another way, baptism is futile and fruitless. Without faith in the resurrection of Christ and of Christians there is no reason to be baptized. As Paul puts it to them, baptism without resurrection is for naught. This bond between baptism and resurrection is no accident in 1 Corinthians 15. Paul could have placed an affirmation of baptism anywhere in the letter—baptism is certainly relevant to each and every aspect of the Christian life—but he chose to place it in reference to the resurrection. For example, his affirmation of baptism might have fit well in chapters 1–4 as a catalyst for unity; it might have proved valuable as the underpinning to a life in Christ as the solution for every ethical dilemma in chapters 5–11; and it certainly would have provided a solid basis for the inspiration of the Holy Spirit in chapters 12–14; but it is to resurrection that Paul ties baptism.

Summing up our reading of 15:29 is uncomplicated. In 15:29 Paul presents the ongoing acceptance of baptism by one group within the Corinthian community as a praiseworthy example for the whole community. Baptism is the act of faith whereby they profess conviction in what Paul preached in Corinth, viz., Christ is raised and the dead in Christ are destined for resurrection.[12] With the reception of baptism, the βαπτιζόμενοι shame the proud Corinthians who have come to doubt the truth Paul preached about Christ and the resurrection of the dead. The product of their pride is ignorance of God. Once more, Paul does not offer the βαπτιζόμενοι's example to lord one group of persons over another. Rather, he presents their good example because it is one that each and every Corinthian Christian demonstrated on the occasion of baptism. By reminding all the Corinthians of the faith in the resurrection they once celebrated, Paul seeks to bring them back to the innocence of belief once virile among them. 15:29 is, if you will, an *aide memoire*. One can almost hear Paul bellowing: "Look at those eager baptismal candidates. Look at their faith. It was once yours. They believe all that I preached about Jesus. They do not doubt that many persons including myself have seen him alive after death. They do not doubt that those among us who have fallen asleep will rise on the last day. As a matter of fact, it is their firm faith in the resurrection of Christ and of his dead that moves them to baptism. That is what they believe. That is what you once believed. Come back to your senses!"

---

[12] It is too far afield of our study to discuss the state of the soul between death and resurrection or to argue the consistency of the time of reception of the resurrected body vis-à-vis 1 Corinthians 15 and 2 Corinthians 5. On the former, see B. P. Prusak, "Bodily Resurrection in Catholic Perspectives," *TS* 61 (2000) 64–105; and Cipriani, "La risurrezione di Cristo e la nostra risurrezione nella prospettiva di *1 Cor* 15," 112–35. On the latter, see P. Woodbridge, "Time of Receipt of the Resurrection Body—A Pauline Inconsistency?" in *Paul and the Corinthians: Studies on a Community in Conflict* (ed. T. J. Burke and J. K. Elliot; NovTSup 109; Leiden: Brill, 2003) 241–58.

1 Corinthians 15:29 and the Resurrection of the Dead

As uncomplicated as our reading of 15:29 is, its full import becomes clear only when we realize the gravity of the crisis of faith in the resurrection of the dead. All of the other crises of faith discussed by Paul in 1 Corinthians—factionalism, issues ethical and spiritual—pale in comparison to the crisis of faith in the resurrection of the dead. The crises of 1 Corinthians 1–14 concern the proper living of the Christian life. The confusions manifested by the Corinthians and the counsel Paul offers them are no great surprise. Young, eager, and inexperienced in the ways of Christ, the Corinthian community was a pilgrim people in the very earliest stages of life in Christ. The crisis of faith in 1 Corinthians 15 is different. At its root, it does not concern the proper living of the Christian life— it concerns whether or not there is a Christian life at all. That is, baptism is incorporation into Christ in this life, an incorporation that follows into the next life. And it does so in an inimitable fashion: Christ died, was buried, and was raised as the first fruits of the resurrection; so too, the baptized die, are buried, and will rise.[13] As some Corinthian Christians die and are buried, the community's faith in the resurrection is tested because the resurrection of their bodies is a future event. But not just *a* future event; it is *the* future event—the parousia. Baptism is the act of faith that incorporates one into Christ and, therefore, into his resurrection. Baptism simultaneously incorporates one into Christ here and hereafter. If the baptized do not believe that their departed Christian brothers and sisters are destined for life eternal, they have *de facto* renounced Christ and the baptism that incorporated them into him. "For if the dead are not raised, then Christ has not been raised. If Christ has not been raised, your faith is futile and you are still in your sins. Then those who have fallen asleep in Christ have perished. If for this life only we have hoped in Christ, we are of all men most to be pitied" (15:16–19). With 15:29, Paul is telling the Corinthians that faith in the resurrection of the body is a *sine qua non* of Christianity. The resurrection of Christ and believers is one. Christians, walking in the newness of life by virtue of baptism, are already ordained to the resurrection of the body. Paul sees "'the resurrection of the dead' as a single theological event, but it takes place in two phases: first the Messiah, then at his coming all his people."[14]

"Now faith is the assurance of things hoped for, the conviction of things not seen" (Heb 11:1). Baptism is the act of faith that expresses conviction in the resurrection now seen in Christ (1 Cor 15:3–11) but not yet seen in his faithful. Doubt in the resurrection of the body has plagued Christianity from its beginning. Providentially, the earliest extant work of Christian literature—Paul's 1

---

[13] N. R. Petersen ("Pauline Baptism and 'Secondary Burial,'" *HTR* 79 [1986] 217–26) presents an out-of-the-ordinary theory about the believer being buried in baptism and then again in death along the lines of one's remains being buried and then reburied after a transferal.

[14] N. T. Wright, "Jesus' Resurrection and Christian Origins," *Greg* 83 (2002) 622.

Thessalonians—anticipates the difficulty.[15] "But we would not have you ignorant, brethren, concerning those who have fallen asleep, that you may not grieve as others do who have no hope" (1 Thess 4:13).[16] According to John's gospel, St. Thomas refused to accept the testimony of the apostles when they told him they had seen the Lord. And when Thomas made his confession of faith, he was admonished by the Lord: "Jesus said to him, 'Have you believed because you have seen me? Blessed are those who have not seen and yet believe'" (John 20:29). At the simple and crucial juncture in the Acts of the Apostles when Paul preached at the Areopagus, Luke tells us that the majority of Paul's listeners were moved to mockery when "they heard of the resurrection of the dead" (Acts 17:32; cf. 17:18). Even with the widespread acceptance of Christianity over the next four hundred years in the Roman empire, St. Augustine could say, "No doctrine of the Christian faith is so vehemently and so obstinately opposed as the doctrine of the resurrection of the flesh" (*En. in Ps.*, Ps. 88, ser. 2, par. 5). Two thousand years later the same problem confronts Christianity. Consequently, Paul's prescience is astute in bringing together baptism and resurrection in 1 Corinthians 15. Baptism without belief in the resurrection of the body is not an option for Christians according to Paul. Paul preached a specific *kerygma* in Corinth, one that had been handed on to him and that he handed on to the Corinthians, part and parcel of which was the bodily resurrection of Christ and the divine promise that those incorporated into Christ would one day enjoy the same resurrection. At the parousia, "the trumpet will sound, and the dead will be raised imperishable, and we shall be changed" (1 Cor 15:52). "And the dead in Christ will rise first; then we who are alive, who are left, shall be caught up together with them in the clouds to meet the Lord in the air; and so we shall always be with the Lord" (1 Thess 4:16b–18). "This is the world of heaven, eternal life with Christ in the presence of God."[17]

Aside from the references to baptism in 1 Corinthians 1 and 15, two other remarks about baptism in 1 Corinthians, both with motifs of resurrection, are found in 10:2–12 and 12:12–13. In 10:1–5, Paul equates the Exodus of the Hebrews through the Red Sea to a baptism (πάντες εἰς τὸν Μωϋσῆν

---

[15] Interestingly, the same problem arises between two distinct groups of nascent Christians. See J. M. G. Barclay, "Thessalonica and Corinth: Social Contrasts in Pauline Christianity," *JSNT* 47 (1992) 49–74.

[16] On the question of development in Paul's mind, see J. Plevnik, "The Taking Up of the Faithful and the Resurrection of the Dead in 1 Thessalonians 4:13–18," *CBQ* 46 (1984) 274–83; and B. F. Meyer, "Did Paul's View of the Resurrection of the Dead Undergo Development?" *TS* 47 (1986) 363–87. See also B. F. Meyer's later comments on Plevnik's article in "Paul and the Resurrection of the Dead," *TS* 48 (1987) 157–58. Note that the history of scholarship regarding such development is chronicled in R. N. Longenecker, "Is There Development in Paul's Resurrection Thought?" in *Life in the Face of Death: The Resurrection Message of the New Testament* (ed. R. N. Longenecker; MNTS; Grand Rapids, MI: Eerdmans, 1998) 171–202.

[17] Plevnik, "The Taking Up of the Faithful and the Resurrection," 282.

ἐβαπτίσθησαν). Here the baptism is the fulfillment of God's promises to Abraham: the inauguration of a new life in a new land and eternal prosperity as God's chosen people. G. R. Beasley-Murray, even though he does not press the point, says:

> The most plausible lesson that I have noted from this association of Christian baptism with the Exodus is based on the dual recognition that in both instances the people of God experience deliverance, yet the real counterpart to the Exodus is *the Christ event* of cross and resurrection; it could be maintained therefore that we have hinted here yet again *the unity of baptism and the redemptive action of Christ* that we perceived to lie at the root of Rom. 6.1 ff. etc.[18]

While this lesson of association is full of hope, it carries a warning about self-righteousness. 1 Cor 10:2–12 relays a message about "complacency" and a reminder that initiation into God's favor is "no guarantee of salvation,"[19] i.e., God's favor, though once embraced as the Hebrews accepted it, may be disowned. Insofar as baptism and resurrection are so closely allied, Paul's reference to baptism in v. 2 implies, at the very least, that a sharing in baptism is a sharing in Christ's cross and resurrection—his salvific work as typified in God's salvific favor to the Hebrews. It is no coincidence that this reference to baptism is so closely connected to Gal 3:26–29, a vital citation regarding baptism.[20] The new life initiated by baptism is a new life in this world and in the next, or it is no life at all.[21]

Similarly, in 12:12–13, Paul reminds the Corinthians that by one Spirit they are all baptized into one body (ἐν ἑνὶ πνεύματι ἡμεῖς πάντες εἰς ἓν σῶμα ἐβαπτίσθημεν) and are all members of the body of Christ (12:27). "As a metaphor for a social or a political group the body was a classic topos in ancient literature. It was, in fact, the most common topos for unity."[22] But in Paul, the usual metaphor is transformed by the unusual bond of unity, the Spirit. This Spirit "is not a 'sphere' or a (symbolically conceived) 'element,' into which the baptized is 'immersed,' rather He is the power that builds up and quickens the Body of Christ."[23] The Spirit's agency makes all the baptized alive in Christ. "In that all the baptized receive the [Spirit] that flows through all, [and] they all become one 'body' through this power."[24] Let us recall that the Spirit is also the

---

[18] Beasley-Murray, *Baptism in the New Testament*, 185 (emphasis original). We discuss Rom 6:1–14 at length below.

[19] Horrell, "Theological Principle or Theological Praxis?" 96.

[20] We discuss Gal 3:26–29 at length below.

[21] See G. W. Hansen, "Resurrection and the Christian Life in Paul's Letters," in *Life in the Face of Death*, ed. Longenecker, 203–24.

[22] R. F. Collins, *First Corinthians*, 458; for other uses of the metaphor of the body, see ibid., 458–61.

[23] Schnackenburg, *Baptism in the Thought of St. Paul*, 29.

[24] Ibid.

agent of the resurrection,[25] and baptism effects the indwelling of the Spirit.[26] As Paul says, "If the Spirit of him who raised Jesus from the dead dwells in you, he who raised Christ Jesus from the dead will give life to your mortal bodies also through his Spirit which dwells in you" (Rom 8:11). So too, we read in 1 Cor 15:45: "Thus it is written, 'The first man Adam became a living being'; the last Adam became a life-giving spirit" (see Gen 2:7). Remarking on Rom 8:11, James D. G. Dunn makes a crucial observation:

> On the one hand, Paul implies that the risen Christ is now experienced in and through the Spirit, indeed as the Spirit of God, the Spirit of creation and of prophecy. It is not that 'Christ' and 'Spirit' are synonymous, but 'Spirit *indwelling*,' 'Christ *in you*.' Christ's effective lordship over his own is coterminous with the Spirit's activity in their lives. On the other hand, Paul implies that the Spirit of God is now to be characterized and identified with the Spirit of Christ, as that power which determined Christ in his ministry and in so doing provided a pattern of life in the Spirit. The life-giving Spirit is not independent of the risen Christ (cf. 1 Cor 15:45).[27]

The Spirit, then, is not only the agent of baptism and resurrection, but also the animating principle of Christ's body and the members thereof. Like the "already and not yet" inauguration of the kingdom of God at the Incarnation, the baptized potentially participate in the resurrection of Christ. They are members of the living body of Christ in the Spirit.[28]

Surely, there is little need to qualify "resurrection" vis-à-vis 15:29. Yet as Murray J. Harris points out:

> If the term "resurrection" is to be qualified at all, Paul prefers to qualify it by the phrase "of the dead" (*tōn nekrōn*). This qualification has the effect of juxtaposing two virtual opposites—namely, "raising to life" and "the dead." Thus it draws attention to God's magnificent victory over death by means of resurrection. More than that, however, the phrase "of the dead" is personal in reference and plural in form (unlike the formulas "of the body" or "of the flesh"), and so

---

[25] For a summary of the Holy Spirit's agency in the resurrection, see Brodeur, "The Holy Spirit, God's Agent in the Resurrection" (chap. 7), in *The Holy Spirit's Agency in the Resurrection of the Dead*, 259–70.

[26] For a discussion of the various interpretations of 1 Cor 12:13, see A. R. Cross, "Spirit- and Water-Baptism in 1 Corinthians 12.13," in *Dimensions of Baptism: Biblical and Theological Studies* (ed. S. E. Porter and A. R. Cross; JSNTSup 234; Sheffield: Sheffield Academic Press, 2002) 120–48.

[27] J. D. G. Dunn, *Romans 1–8* (WBC 38A; Dallas: Word Books, 1988) 446 (emphasis original).

[28] Indeed, salvation in Christ is inextricably linked to life in the Spirit. See D. G. Powers, *Salvation through Participation: An Examination of the Notion of Participation of the Believers' Corporate Unity with Christ in Early Christian Soteriology* (CBET 29; Leuven: Peeters, 2001).

it aptly highlights the communal and interpersonal nature of the resurrection state.²⁹

The highlighting of the communal and interpersonal nature of the resurrection in 15:29 could not have been lost upon the Corinthians. Aware of the factions that had developed among them, cognizant of the fact that their infidelities had reached Paul through Chloe's people, desirous of Paul's guidance by writing to him and sending emissaries, the Corinthians were well poised to receive Paul's message in 1 Corinthians. How many Corinthians came to their senses after 1 Corinthians is not ours to know.

BAPTISM IN THE THEOLOGY OF ST. PAUL

Baptism in the theology of Paul is an elusive presence. Two difficulties immediately confront us: first, the expansive nature of any general theology of Paul and second, the dearth of any exposition of baptism in Paul's letters. The first difficulty is somewhat mollified by the recent publication of Dunn's *The Theology of Paul the Apostle* (1998). Combined treatments of Paul's life and thought notwithstanding, Dunn's is the first expansive treatment since D. E. H. Whiteley's *The Theology of Paul* (1964) and Herman Ridderbos' *Paul: An Outline of His Theology* (1966).³⁰ A perusal of Dunn's magisterial work of eight hundred pages immediately shows the depth and complexity characteristic of any attempt to speak extensively about Paul's theology.³¹ In addressing a specific stratum of Paul's theology, i.e., his baptismal theology, we are grappling with an essential aspect, but not the whole, of Paul's theological enterprise. The second difficulty is, perhaps, more confounding. Try as we might to struggle with Paul's baptismal theology, there is no place in the Pauline literature wherein baptism is treated *per se*. Lars Hartman observes:

> It is worthy of notice that in the texts he left behind we never encounter a passage over which could be put the title 'On Baptism,' and in which Paul explicitly presents a few fundamental features of his theology of baptism. Instead, in the cases where he comments on baptism, he is actually discussing something else, and he adduces baptism to use elements of his and/or others' thinking thereon as arguments in the treatment of the problem which is being discussed in the occasional epistolary context.³²

---

[29] M. J. Harris, "Resurrection and Immortality in the Pauline Corpus," in *Life in the Face of Death*, ed. Longenecker, 150.

[30] D. E. H. Whiteley, *The Theology of Paul* (Philadelphia: Fortress, 1964); Ridderbos' book was originally published in Dutch and appeared in English translation in 1975. For more on the history of Pauline theological scholarship, see Dunn, *Theology of Paul*, 2–6.

[31] See also J. D. G. Dunn, "Prolegomena to a Theology of Paul," *NTS* 40 (1994) 407–32.

[32] Hartman, *"Into the Name of the Lord Jesus,"* 52.

An attempt to detail the theology of Paul, even an attempt to detail his baptismal theology (which would necessarily involve the whole of Paul's theology), is beyond the pale of this study. Our study is intended as a contribution to Paul's baptismal theology, not a restatement thereof. Moreover, an attempt to find more source material outside the Pauline literature is, obviously, out of the question. Thus, with reference to our reading of 15:29, we do four things here. First, we look to Rom 6:1–14, which is spoken of by many as the *locus classicus* of baptism in Paul. Second, we look to Gal 3:26–29. Third, we look to other references to baptism in the Pauline literature and review our findings. Finally, we seek to integrate our reading of 15:29 within the larger context of Paul's baptismal theology.

Romans 6:1–14

Rom 6:1–14 is often spoken of as the *locus classicus* of Paul's understanding of baptism, yet in many ways this is a misnomer. Rom 6:1–14 is certainly the pericope most frequently referenced in terms of Paul's baptismal theology and the most heavily weighed against other references thereto, but Rom 6:1–14 is mostly not about baptism. As Hendrikus Boers notes, the pericope is about "the new dominion of life in Christ, after death to sin."[33] Nonetheless, in the history of the pericope's interpretation "a structure determined by the theme of death to sin and life in Christ became submerged, even if not drowned out, in a restructuring in which the focus shifted to baptism as the center of discussion, even though baptism is mentioned explicitly only in vv. 3–4."[34] Furthermore, a strong emphasis has also been placed on the theme of justification by faith (or righteousness) in relation to baptism, "even though the passage contains no hint whatsoever of this doctrine."[35] Baptism and justification, constitutive of and concomitant with death to sin and life in Christ, are not the heart of the matter. That is not to say that Rom 6:1–14 does not have much to tell us about baptism, but it is to say that the passage is more a *locus classicus* in Pauline scholarship than in Paul's baptismal theology. Likewise, much stress has been placed on the similarity between the "dying and rising" motif in Rom 6:1–14, as well as in Gal 2:19–20 and Col 2:11–12, and Hellenistic mystery religions.[36] After our

---

[33] H. Boers, "The Structure and Meaning of Romans 6:1–14," *CBQ* 63 (2001) 664.

[34] Ibid., 665.

[35] Ibid.

[36] G. Wagner (*Das religionsgeschichtliche Problem von Römer 6,1–11* (ATANT 39; Zurich: Zwingli, 1962) is most thorough in analyzing the various mystery religions said to have influenced Paul. However, Wagner's conclusions are stark insofar as he sees absolutely no influence whatsoever. A. J. M. Wedderburn (*Baptism and Resurrection: Studies in Pauline Theology against Its Greco-Roman Background* (WUNT 44; Tübingen: Mohr [Siebeck], 1987) is more nuanced. Wedderburn concludes that Paul used language not unlike that of the Hellenistic mystery religions out of sensitivity to his readers, but that the ideas are separate and distinct. For the opposite opinion, see

previous investigation of Paul's background, we presume that Paul was careful to use terminology familiar to his addressees.[37] The only choice he had in order to speak to Greco-Romans, Corinthians, or anyone else in the Hellenistic world was the religious *lingua franca* common to human religious experience. Because all religious societies deal with issues such as initiation, earthly struggles, and new life in one form or another, Paul's message would have risked ambiguity and uncertainty, if he ignored the idiom of the day.[38] On a similar note, though, Rom 6:1–14 is not focused on the Lord's dying and rising,[39] or even on the believer's dying and rising *per se*; it is focused on death to sin and life in Christ.[40]

The death to sin and life in Christ spoken of in Romans 6 dovetails with the conclusion of the first part of Romans on the salvific power of the gospel,[41] especially with Romans 5 and 7. Joseph A. Fitzmyer observes:

> The assurance and hope of salvation, of which chap. 5 spoke, meant that Christian life and conduct not only involve the fulfilling of duties, but even demand it. The new life brought by Christ entails a reshaping of human beings. Through baptism, they are identified with Christ's death and resurrection, and their very being or "self" is transformed. So the outlook of newly justified persons has been freed of sin and selfishness and is such as to exclude sinful conduct from their ken. Chapter 7 will carry the description of this freedom still farther (freedom from the law).[42]

The believer is supposed to have died to sin (6:1–2) through his identification with Christ. Identification with Christ has brought about a new life that has

---

J. Z. Smith "On Comparing Stories" (chap. 4), in *Drudgery Divine*, 85–115. The most comprehensive introduction to the problem is found in Agersnap, "Preparatory Studies of the Historical Background" (part 1) in *Baptism and New Life*, 52–198. For a theological exposition, see R. C. Tannehill, *Dying and Rising with Christ: A Study in Pauline Theology* (BZNW 32; Berlin: Töpelmann, 1967). Moving outside the area of biblical scholarship, see T. M. Finn, *From Death to Rebirth: Ritual and Conversion in Antiquity* (New York/Mahwah, NJ: Paulist, 1997).

[37] Cf. Wedderburn, *Baptism and Resurrection*, 345.

[38] Cf. Agersnap, *Baptism and New Life*, 98.

[39] For a summary of Hellenistic figures compared to Christ vis-à-vis Rom 6:1–14, see H. D. Betz, "Transferring a Ritual: Paul's Interpretation of Baptism in Romans 6," in *Paul in His Hellenistic Context*, ed. Engberg-Pedersen, 84–118.

[40] Thus, sin's dominion is ceded for Christ's. "According to the argument of Romans 6, baptism into Christ's death means incorporation into a particular system of control, a system with which Paul is also compelled to exhort his readers to comply. Sin shall no longer exercise its control. Instead, submit to the control of 'righteousness,' 'obedience,' 'grace,' and 'God.' If you do, pleads Paul, life shall be yours" (J. W. Aageson, "'Control' in Pauline Language and Culture: A Study of Romans 6," *NTS* 42 [1996] 88).

[41] Here we follow B. Byrne, *Romans* (SacPag 6; Collegeville, MN: Liturgical [Glazier], 1996) 27–28. Byrne divides Romans between the gospel's saving power (1:18–11:36) and the summons to live according to the gospel (12:1–15:13). Dunn's outline is similar (*Romans 1–8*, vii–xi). Cf. J. A. Fitzmyer, *Romans* (AB 33; New York: Doubleday, 1993) vii–xii. For an outline of Rom 6:1–14, we follow Boers, "The Structure and Meaning of Romans 6:1–14," 676 et passim.

[42] Fitzmyer, *Romans*, 429.

transformed the believer. This new life brings with it a radical freedom. In this life, it is a freedom from the Mosaic law in order to live in love. Dying to the self and dying to sin are analogous to Christ's own death; death with Christ is life anew. Baptism into Christ is baptism into his death; just as he was raised, the believer will be raised (6:3–4). Everything that Paul speaks of in vv. 5–11 in one way or another centers on an aspect of the transformation wrought in the believer by baptism, a transformation in Christ that is constitutive of identification not only with Christ's ministry but with his very person. In baptism, the believer's old life is buried, buried with the crucified Christ, "and the meaning and purpose of this costly act is that a new life of obedience should follow, made possible by the indwelling Spirit of that same Christ."[43] Verses 12–14 exhort the believer to live according to what he has become. Sin may not reign, nor passion, nor the law, because the believer has been brought from death to life.[44]

Although Rom 6:1–14 traces themes far too subtle for expansive clarification here, "the argument rests upon the believer's baptismal union with Christ."[45] This is not a static union with Christ; it is a participation in Christ. In v. 3, Paul says that the believer is baptized into Christ's death. "The rite of Christian initiation introduces human beings into a union with Christ suffering and dying. Paul's phrase is bold; he wants to bring out that the Christian is not merely identified with the 'dying Christ,' who has won victory over sin, but is introduced into the very act by which that victory is won."[46] It is the participation in baptism that effects participation in the dying and rising of Christ. The believer's life in the here-and-now is comparable to the death and resurrection of Christ. The believer has not yet (physically) died, and therefore the believer has not yet been resurrected from death, as Christ is; but the believer has died to sin and therefore the believer is "able to walk in newness of life" (v. 4) in this world. Col 2:12 and 3:1 ("raised with him into newness of life") equate the effect of baptism with resurrection directly.[47] In Romans, however, there is a fine distinction, perhaps without a difference, viz., the indwelling of the Spirit begins with baptism and carries through until resurrection, but the believer is not resurrected at baptism. Adela Yarbro Collins notes:

> One of the distinctive features of Romans 6 is that Paul avoids saying 'we have risen' with Christ; rather he speaks of 'newness of life.' The implication of Paul's restraint is that the transformation is not complete. There is still an

---

[43] A. Campbell, "Dying with Christ: The Origin of a Metaphor?" in *Baptism, the New Testament, and the Church: Historical and Contemporary Studies in Honour of R. E. O. White* (ed. S. E. Porter and A. R. Cross; JSNTSup 171; Sheffield: Sheffield Academic Press, 1999) 285.

[44] See Byrne, *Romans*, 193–95. Cf. D. Hellholm, "Enthymemic Argumentation in Paul: The Case of Romans 6," in *Paul in His Hellenistic Context*, ed. Engberg-Pedersen, 119–79.

[45] Byrne, *Romans*, 188.

[46] Fitzmyer, *Romans*, 433.

[47] See Dunn (*Romans 1–8*, 330) for a more extensive explanation.

apocalyptic expectation of a future, fuller transformation into a heavenly form of life. This expectation fits with Paul's use throughout the passage of the imperative alongside the indicative. 'Newness of life' is a real present possibility, both spiritually and ethically, but the actualizing of that possibility requires decision and commitment as well as grace.[48]

Simply stated: the present and future reality of the believer are radically changed at baptism.[49] The believer's resurrection is in the future, but his life in Christ has begun in baptism. Baptism induces a new life that is as real in this world as it will be in the next. Clearly, Paul's accent here is not on death but on life. Death has been conquered by Christ, a given in Paul's letters and specifically in Romans. "Participation in Christ's death is the basis upon which this new life is made possible, but Christ's death is not in the forefront in this part of Paul's reasoning."[50] With baptism there is "life to God in Christ Jesus" (Rom 6:11).[51]

Galatians 3:26–29

Paul speaks of baptismal life in Rom 6:3–4 by invoking the image of the believer placing himself in Christ, by a baptism into Christ that is a baptism into Christ's death, and by coupling baptism into death with rising to newness of life. But in Gal 3:27, he says, "For (γάρ) as many of you as were baptized into Christ (εἰς Χριστόν) have put on Christ (Χριστὸν ἐνεδύσασθε)."[52] This image is more evocative of the believer taking on a mantle than of entering into death and resurrection; yet the heart of the matter is the same. Baptism into Christ is baptism into his death and resurrection as well as clothing oneself with Christ—two sides of the one coin of transformation in Christ via baptism. In Gal 3:2, Paul asks the Galatians, "Did you receive the Spirit by works of the law, or by hearing with faith?"[53] Galatians 3 is Paul's answer to this question. With a careful interpretation of the Abraham story, Paul shows that righteousness comes by faith, to both Abraham and Israel. Likewise, the promise of Abraham is extended to the Gentiles by Christ. The law may have served as a temporary custodian until the coming of Christ, but now with faith in Christ there is no need of a custodian. The promise made to Abraham and fulfilled in Christ is

---

[48] Yarbro Collins, "The Origin of Christian Baptism," 42.

[49] Cf. Carlson, "The Role of Baptism in Paul's Thought," 261–63.

[50] Boers, "The Structure and Meaning of Romans 6:1–14," 677–78.

[51] The dogmatic theology pertinent to Romans 6 and baptism is expertly presented in L. Bergin, *O Prophecticum Lavacrum: Baptism as Symbolic Act of Eschatological Salvation* (AnGreg 277; Rome: Editrice Pontificia Università Gregoriana, 1999).

[52] For more on the baptismal phrases in Paul, see A. J. M. Wedderburn, "Some Observations on Paul's Use of the Phrases 'in Christ' and 'with Christ,'" *JSNT* 25 (1985) 83–97; B. B. Colijn, "Paul's Use of the 'in Christ' Formula," *ATJ* 23 (1991) 9–26; and Hartman, "'Into the Name of the Lord Jesus,'" (chap. 3), in *"Into the Name of the Lord Jesus,"* 37–50.

[53] Given the overall polemical tenor of Galatians, the question unmistakably represents Paul's impression of the Galatians' confusion on this point. See J. M. G. Barclay, "Mirror-Reading a Polemical Letter: Galatians as a Test Case," *JSNT* 31 (1987) 73–93.

coextensive with faith, not works of the law; the law passes away with the fulfillment of the promise. Obviously, the Galatians have been perturbed about the relationship of law and righteousness since Paul's presence among them.[54] Because Paul wishes to emphasize the role of faith in Christ for the believer, it is fitting that he begins his conclusion to Galatians 3 with v. 26: "For (γάρ) in Christ Jesus you are all sons of God, through faith."[55] This identifies election in Christ with the election of Israel (Exod 4:22; Deut 14:1–12; Jer 31:9; *Jub.* 1:24–25; cf. Gal 4:6–7; Rom 8:14). And with this, any distinction between Jew and Greek is obliterated, the promise to Abraham is underscored as a promise to all the nations, and faith (in Christ) is seen as the fulcrum of righteousness.

The second use of γάρ in v. 27 confirms a tight integration with v. 26. The Galatians are not under the law because they are "sons of God through faith" and because they have been "baptized into Christ" and have "put on Christ."[56] While we might be contented with "baptized into Christ" as the source of the status of sons of God, Paul goes farther and adds "putting on Christ" as a corresponding referent to baptism, thereby adding a new dimension. The use of ἐνδύω ("to dress," "to clothe")[57] is a masterstroke on Paul's part. On the one hand, it is a representation that appeals to both Jew and Greco-Roman. The LXX employs ἐνδύω to speak of being clothed with salvation (2 Chr 6:41), righteousness (Job 29:14; Ps 131:9; Isa 59:17), and even shame (Ps 34:26).[58] Many mystery religions utilized a symbolic bath or reclothing as a means of initiation,[59] and Paul's language is also strongly reminiscent of the Roman *toga virilis* ceremony.[60] The Galatians, whether Jews or Greco-Romans, had within their diverse religious backgrounds some ready vocabulary and imagery applicable to Christian baptism. On the other hand, insofar as we know the history of the baptismal rite,[61] Paul may be invoking a common baptismal practice among the Galatians (as well as other early Christians). "The new robe, put on as one comes out of the water, signifies Christ himself. For he is the 'place' in which the baptized now find their corporate life."[62] Moreover, Paul uses ἐνδύω in Rom

---

[54] See R. Jewett, "The Agitators and the Galatian Congregation," *NTS* 17 (1970–71) 198–212.

[55] See Matera (*Galatians*, 144) for an outline of γάρ's use in Gal 3:26–29.

[56] Ibid.

[57] See "ἐνδύω," BAGD, 264.

[58] Matera, *Galatians*, 142.

[59] A complete description of the possibilities is found in S. Angus, *The Mystery-Religions: A Study in the Religious Background of Early Christianity* (1928; rpt. New York: Dover, 1975) 91–143.

[60] See J. A. Harrill, "Coming of Age and Putting on Christ: The *Toga Virilis* Ceremony, Its Paraenesis, and Paul's Interpretation of Baptism in Galatians," *NovT* 44 (2002) 252–77. Cf. Oster, "When Men Wore Veils to Worship," 488–505.

[61] On Gal 3:27–28 as a formula from a prior baptismal rite, see R. N. Longenecker, *Galatians* (WBC 41; Dallas: Word Books, 1990) 154–55.

[62] J. L. Martyn, *Galatians* (AB 33A; New York: Doubleday, 1997) 375–76.

13:12–14 and 1 Thess 5:8, and ἐνδύω is also found in Eph 4:24; 6:11, 14; and Col 3:10, 12. But significant for our study is Paul's four-fold employment of ἐνδύω in 1 Cor 15:53–54 to describe being clothed with the resurrection body.

The final γάρ at the end of v. 28 bespeaks the radical baptismal equality among the Galatians because by baptism and putting on Christ they are "all one in Christ Jesus." As Paul would have the Galatians understand, baptism nullifies any distinction among them as "Jew or Greek," "slave or free," and "male or female" (cf. Rom 10:12; 1 Cor 12:12–13; Col 3:11). Paul draws these antitheses from the language of the Abrahamic covenant of circumcision in order to show that the stipulations for righteousness have changed in Christ.[63] "According to Gal 3:28, the distinctions represented by these antitheses are irrelevant in Christian baptism, which is open to all those who believe in Christ Jesus without distinction."[64] Because the Galatians are one in Christ via baptism, "all members of the Christian community live baptized as full members of the community."[65] This leads to the conclusion in v. 29: "If you are Christ's, then you are Abraham's offspring, heirs according to promise" (cf. Rom 8:17; Titus 3:5–7). In other words, Abraham was justified by faith (in God) and Christians are justified by faith (in Christ), a theme found at length in Romans 4 and, of course, right here in Galatians 3. Naturally, on one level, this faith is to be taken with the utmost seriousness in and of itself; but, on another level, we cannot neglect its essential link with baptism in Romans and Galatians. "In this passage [Gal 3:26–29] the exegetes frequently either exalt baptism at the expense of faith or faith at the expense of baptism."[66] Neither one of these is a viable option, as Frank J. Matera explains:

> Contemporary authors caution against viewing baptism in isolation from faith, thereby turning it into a sacral act which works independently of faith. While this caution is well taken, it owes more to Catholic–Protestant debates over the nature of the sacraments than it does to Paul's own thought. If the Apostle does not envision a sacrament that works independently of faith, neither does he envision a personal faith which effects its own salvation. Faith is made possible by the faith of Jesus Christ so that believers are saved by what Christ has done. Baptism is the means by which believers associate themselves with Christ's faith, thereby becoming incorporated into Christ.[67]

Instead, we need to call attention to the unity of faith and baptism. For Paul, baptism certainly comes after the hearing of the gospel as a faith-full response,

---

[63] For parallels in pagan antiquity, see F. F. Bruce, *The Epistle to the Galatians: A Commentary on the Greek Text* (NIGTC; Grand Rapids, MI: Eerdmans, 1982) 187–91.

[64] T. W. Martin, "The Covenant of Circumcision (Genesis 17:9–14) and the Situational Antitheses in Galatians 3:28," *JBL* 122 (2003) 125.

[65] Ibid.

[66] Beasley-Murray, *Baptism in the New Testament*, 151.

[67] Matera, *Galatians*, 145–46.

but it does so as the divinely established form of that faith-full response to Christ Jesus.[68]

Baptism in the Pauline Literature

Other than the references to baptism in Romans, 1 Corinthians, and Galatians, the other texts in the Pauline literature that mention baptism explicitly are Eph 4:5 and Col 2:12. In Eph 4:5, we read that there is "one Lord, one faith, one baptism (βάπτισμα), one God and Father of us all." The verse, which appears to be an early baptismal formula,[69] is strongly reminiscent of 1 Cor 8:6, except for the mention of baptism. The accent is on the unity of the Christian faith. It stresses "the dignity and importance accorded to baptism in virtue of its inclusion in this enumeration of the great 'unities' of our faith."[70] No doubt, baptism is linked to faith for the purpose of highlighting the interrelationship of the two. The Lord comes preaching the gospel, to which the believer gives his assent of faith in the sacrament of baptism, and thereby becomes a child of God the Father in like manner to the baptismal teaching of Gal 3:26–29. In Eph 4:4–6, baptism is a *fait accompli* and is mentioned to challenge the Ephesians' unity with one another.[71] There are five allusions to the effects of baptism in Ephesians, but they are all peripheral. In Eph 1:13, we read that believers are "sealed (ἐσφραγίσθητε) with the promised Holy Spirit"; in whom they "were sealed (ἐσφραγίσθητε) for the day of redemption" (Eph 4:30; cf. 2 Cor 1:22). Eph 2:4–6 speaks of believers being "made alive," "raised up with him," and sitting "in heavenly places" (cf. Col 2:13). "If we (in baptism) have really attained life 'with Christ,' we also have a part in the triumph of the Risen Lord and in his heavenly ascent to the throne."[72] Eph 4:22–24, with strong parallels to 1 Cor 15:35–57 and Gal 3:26–29, has believers "putting on (ἐνδύσασθαι) a new nature, created after the likeness of God in true righteousness and holiness." Finally, Eph 5:22–27, which makes an analogy between Christ's love for the Church and spousal love, alludes to baptism as a sanctification and cleansing, as a moment of sacrifice (cf. 1 Cor 7:14). Here baptism is "the visible and effective sign which made Christ's death relevant to the one baptized."[73]

Col 2:11–13 also articulates baptism as a visible and effective sign analogous to circumcision. According to 2:12, believers "are buried with him in

---

[68] See Fee, *First Corinthians*, 63–64.

[69] See M. Y. MacDonald, *Colossians and Ephesians* (SacPag 17; Collegeville, MN: Liturgical [Glazier], 2000) 287–88.

[70] Beasley-Murray, *Baptism in the New Testament*, 199.

[71] As such, Eph 4:4–6 presents the same challenge of concord to Christians today. See A. R. Cross, "'One Baptism' (Ephesians 4:5): A Challenge to the Church," in *Baptism, the New Testament, and the Church*, ed. Porter and Cross, 173–209.

[72] Schanckenburg, *Baptism in the Thought of St. Paul*, 75.

[73] Hartman, *"Into the Name of the Lord Jesus,"* 105.

baptism (συνταηέντε αὐτῷ ἐν τῷ βαπτισμῷ)" and "raised with him through faith in the working of God, who raised him from the dead." Though very much like Rom 6:3–4, Col 2:12 identifies more closely with the Lord's baptism and resurrection than the believer's. The consequences of baptism are expressed later in Col 3:1–4, much as they are in Eph 2:4–6. In Col 3:1–4, the believer is reminded that he shares in the resurrected life of Christ and therefore ought to set his mind on higher things, because believers have died with Christ and will one day appear with him in glory (cf. 1 Tim 6:12; Titus 3:5–7). The concern is "not on the means but on the effect; those who formerly were 'dead' have now become the 'living.'"[74] And much like Gal 3:26–29, Col 3:10–11 refers to having shed the old nature (self) and "having put on a new nature (self)" (ἐνδυσάμενοι τὸν νέον) in baptism. "The contrast between the old self and the new self makes it clear that the new self refers to the transformation of the believer in the first instance and not to Christ himself. But there are strong notions here of close identification with Christ in baptism."[75] And just like Gal 3:28, the effect of baptism is a unity: "Here there cannot be Greek and Jew, circumcised and uncircumcised, barbarian, Scythian, slave, freeman, but Christ is all, and in all" (Rom 10:12; Col 3:11; cf. 1 Cor 12:12–13; 15:28).

The remnants of an early baptismal hymn found in 2 Tim 2:11–13 (and also in Polycarp, *Ep. Phil.* 5),[76] lay strong emphasis on baptismal life in Christ:

> If we have died with him, we shall also live with him;
> if we endure, we shall also reign with him;
> if we deny him, he also will deny us;
> if we are faithless, he remains faithful—for he cannot deny himself.

To be sure, these lines from 2 Timothy encapsulate the hallmarks of baptism in Paul. Baptism brings us into Christ's death and resurrection; it raises us to newness of life here and hereafter; it neither annihilates our freedom nor compels our behavior; but it ensures that the promise made to Abraham is fulfilled in Christ Jesus, who with the Father and the Spirit, is ever faithful to us.

What, then, do we glean as Paul's baptismal theology? Perhaps, it is best to speak in terms of three traditional baptismal themes: justification by faith, participation in Christ's life, and the gift of the Holy Spirit.[77] Although "there is a danger that we subdivide into distinct and discrete elements what Paul simply saw as the same event with differing emphases in differing cases,"[78] the danger is mitigated by our need to tease out the various components of the singular baptismal event. Evidently, each of the three is inextricably linked with the other

---

[74] Schanckenburg, *Baptism in the Thought of St. Paul*, 69.

[75] MacDonald, *Colossians and Ephesians*, 137–38.

[76] See Beasley-Murray, *Baptism in the New Testament*, 207–9.

[77] This tripartite division, both in its history and *raison d'être*, is elucidated in Dunn, *Theology of Paul*, 442–59 et passim.

[78] Ibid., 455.

to the extent that it is impossible to speak of one without the other two. At the same time, given the enormity of God's revelation involved in baptism, separating one from the other is useful for our studied examination.

Justification (δικαίωσις) by faith (πίστις), the total acceptance of the *kerygma*,[79] is the effect of sacramental baptism. As Paul says to the Corinthians: "You were washed, you were justified in the name of the Lord Jesus Christ and in the Spirit of our God" (1 Cor 6:11; cf. Eph 5:25–27). This washing is the removal of the stain of original and personal sin. It is the restoration of the believer to a state of innocence before God. Yet it is something that was bought at a price, and such a price demands life in conformity to the innocence that is restored in baptism (1 Cor 6:20; 7:23). The believer becomes justified through the sanctifying grace of baptism while at the same time beginning a participation in Christ's life through the Spirit. Baptism is not only the means of the forgiveness of sins (Col 1:13–14), but the fortification to avoid sin in the future, "for he who died has freed us from sin" (Rom 6:7). Thus, justification is not an end in itself; it is not as if faith has procured salvation. Rather, justification by faith is the inauguration of a life "that is pure and blameless for the day of Christ" (Phil 1:10; cf. 1 Thess 5:23; Phil 2:15; Eph 1:4; Col 1:22). In imitation of the Lord, "whose death he died to sin and whose life he lives in God," the believer must consider himself "dead to sin and alive to God in Christ Jesus" (Rom 6:10–11). The resultant justification of the believer in baptism is the foundation of life in Christ. In such wise, the believer bears the responsibility that Paul has borne: to imitate Christ. "Be imitators of me, as I am of Christ" (1 Cor 11:1; cf. 1 Cor 4:16; Thess 1:6; 2 Thess 3:7–9; Eph 5:1).

Participation in Christ's life through baptism is an identification with the Lord's sacrificial death, burial, and resurrection (Rom 6:3–4; cf. Col 2:11–12). It effects a unity among God's elect heretofore unknown, though foreshadowed in the corporate identity of Israel, which Paul claims "was baptized (ἐβαπτίσθησαν) in the cloud and in the sea" (1 Cor 10:2). "For just as the body is one and has many members, and all the members of the body, though many, are one body, so it is with Christ. For by one Spirit we were all baptized into one body" (1 Cor 12:12–13). The mystical body of Christ, of which Christ is the head, is formed by the many members through baptism, by which each of the members has been incorporated therein. Within this body, there is no worldly distinction among the baptized; they are all "one in Christ Jesus," Abraham's offspring, heirs according to promise (Gal 3:27–28; cf. Romans 4; 1 Cor 12:12–13; Col 3:11). The unity effected by incorporation into Christ and with one another means that "there is one body and one Spirit," as well as only "one Lord, one

---

[79] Here, we eschew any discussion of Catholic–Protestant debate on justification by faith. Writing in the Catholic tradition, we presume the Catholic understanding that "faith, by itself, if it has no works, is dead" (Jas 2:17). For more see, H. G. Anderson, T. A. Murphy, and J. A. Burgess, eds., *Justification by Faith* (LCD 7; Minneapolis: Augsburg, 1985).

faith, one baptism" (Eph 4:5). The baptized have "put on Christ" (Gal 3:27) and thereby have become alive in the Spirit. Participation in Christ's life on earth is a foretaste of participation in his heavenly life. Putting on Christ in this life is also analogous to the transformation of the body at the parousia (1 Cor 15:53–54).

But baptism, besides effecting justification and participation, is also the moment of the gift of the Holy Spirit to the believer. In baptism, Christ "has put his seal upon us and given us his Spirit in our hearts as a guarantee" (2 Cor 1:22; cf. Eph 4:30). Indeed, as we saw in our examination of 1 Corinthians 12–14, the gifts of the Spirit were evident and vibrant in Corinth. Traditionally, we speak of the gifts of the Holy Spirit as wisdom, understanding, counsel, fortitude, knowledge, piety, and fear of the Lord (see Isa 11:1–2) and the fruits of the Holy Spirit as charity, joy, peace, patience, kindness, goodness, generosity, gentleness, faithfulness, modesty, self-control, and chastity (cf. Gal 5:22–23). Even a cursory reading of the *corpus Paulinum* reveals that such gifts and fruits were operative in the communities which Paul founded and encouraged in his writing. That is not to say that Paul takes these gifts and fruits for granted in any sense; instead, Paul sees them as signs of transformation in Christ wrought by baptism. "The connection between baptism and the Spirit does not consist specifically in an incidental outpouring of unusual gifts of the Spirit, but in the transition of the baptized into the new life that has been brought to light by Christ, in which not only are the guilt and uncleanness of sin washed away, but in which, positively, the new government of the Holy Spirit prevails."[80] This is well expressed in Titus 3:5: "He saved us, not because of deeds done by us in righteousness, but in virtue of his own mercy by the washing of regeneration and renewal in the Holy Spirit." The washing of regeneration in baptism is the restoration of innocence and the renewal of the believer in the Spirit. There are far too many references and allusions to the Spirit in the Pauline literature (over one hundred) to expose here. Gal 5:5 sums it all up: "For through the Spirit, by faith, we wait for the hope of righteousness."

1 Corinthians 15:29 and Baptism in St. Paul

What does our new reading of 1 Cor 15:29 have to add to Paul's theology of baptism? The three traditional baptismal themes—justification by faith, participation in Christ's life, and the gift of the Holy Spirit—help us to form the answer. Recall that we rendered 15:29 thus: "Otherwise what are they to do, who have themselves baptized on account of the dead? If the dead are not really raised, why are they baptized on account of them?" We said that Paul holds up the βαπτιζόμενοι as a laudable example for the Corinthians because the βαπτιζόμενοι's motivation for undergoing the rite of baptism is their steadfast faith in the resurrection of Christ and of Christians. They believe that Christ has been

---

[80] Ridderbos, *Paul*, 398–99.

raised and that the νεκροί are destined for life. Therefore, they undergo the rite of baptism "on account of the dead"—on account of the fact that "if there is no resurrection of the dead, then Christ has not been raised" (1 Cor 15:13). So what does our reading of 15:29 add? It adds three things: first, 15:29 as another principal baptismal text in addition to Rom 6:1–14 and Gal 3:26–29; second, 15:29 as the strongest fastening of baptism and resurrection in the Pauline literature; and third, 15:29's unmistakable accent on the importance of the sacramental rite of baptism.

As we noted above, biblical scholarship has long held Rom 6:1–14 to be the principal baptismal text in the Pauline literature. Following closely behind as a second principal text is Gal 3:26–29; and, in the lion's share of contemporary Pauline scholarship, the baptismal references in 1 Corinthians trail third. Following upon all we have said thus far in our study, this ordering is methodologically questionable; still, a close examination reveals the reasons for such an ordering, even if it does not validate them. Ever since the Protestant Reformation and the writings of Martin Luther and Philipp Melanchton, Romans has been taken as a key text in the NT and the primary text in Paul, and this exaltation of Romans continues into our own day.[81] Because in Paul's letters the only references to baptism *per se* are in Romans, 1 Corinthians, and Galatians—among which Romans is continually considered the *primus inter pares*—1 Corinthians and Galatians vie for "second place." Now, in terms of baptismal references, it is no wonder that Gal 3:26–29 is taken as more important than 1 Corinthians. Although baptism is frequently mentioned in 1 Cor 1:13–17, it is certainly not the focus of Paul's attention in chapter 1, and many biblicists take vv. 14–17 as a denigration of the importance of baptism. Likewise, the metaphorical baptismal topos in 1 Cor 10:2 sheds little light on first-century baptismal practice; and 1 Cor 12:13 focuses on the one Spirit and the one body, with baptism as an *a priori* and without explication. Furthermore, as we saw extensively in Chapter I of our study, 15:29—so hotly contested and taken as a reference to a baptismal aberration, whether one of vicarious baptism or misbegotten ordinary baptism, performed for one or more mistaken reasons—is left out in the cold. When 15:29 is considered an aberration of some sort, it is not considered relevant, except in passing, to Paul's baptismal theology; as such, it is unimportant, or it is benignly disregarded. At most, it is taken, as a stepchild-type affirmation of

---

[81] For example, in one of the most recent and important works on Paul's theology, Dunn writes: "How to write a theology of Paul then? Paul's letter to the Christians in Rome is the nearest thing we have to Paul's own answer to that question. Which is also to say that Romans provides us with an example of the way Paul himself chose to order the sequence of themes of his theology. If, therefore, we wish to grasp at and dialogue with the mature theology of Paul we cannot do better than take Romans as a kind of template on which to construct our own statement of Paul's theology, a dominant chord by which to tune our own lesser instruments. A theology of Paul which sets out to describe and discuss the theology of Paul at the time he wrote Romans and by constant reference to Romans as prompter and plumb line is surely headed in the right direction" (*Theology of Paul*, 26).

the resurrection, i.e., Paul is not interested in approving or disapproving the Corinthian practice; he is only interested in affirming the resurrection of the dead.

But what if 15:29 is taken as we interpret it? If 15:29 is read as we think it ought to be read—as an instance of ordinary baptism, undergone for all the right reasons and praised by Paul, who mentions it specifically to highlight the good example of the βαπτιζόμενοι—then 15:29 certainly becomes the principal reference to baptism in 1 Corinthians. If 15:29 is read as we read it, then it is perfectly reasonable to place it alongside Rom 6:1–14 and Gal 3:26–29 as a principal baptismal text in Paul. Moreover, it is also reasonable to reconsider any adjudication of priority in Paul's principal baptismal references. Specifically, we might challenge the presumption of precedence for Rom 6:1–14 before 1 Cor 15:29. Insofar as Paul's baptismal theology is concerned, Rom 6:1–14 is frequently taken to hold priority for two reasons: Romans is presupposed to be a more mature expression of Paul's thought than 1 Corinthians in general; and, in particular, Rom 6:1–14 is presumed far more significant than 1 Cor 15:29, given the contemporary readings of 15:29, as we noted earlier. As to the priority of Romans over 1 Corinthians, the jury is still out. Any prioritization of Paul's letters remains a matter of scholarly debate, for Paul gives no prioritization to his letters. As to the priority of Rom 6:1–14 over 1 Cor 15:29, assuming for the moment that we grant Romans and 1 Corinthians equal status, there is no reason to rank one ahead of the other in any sense, if our interpretation of 15:29 is adopted. Therefore, 15:29 should take its rightful place as a principal text alongside Rom 6:1–14 and Gal 3:26–29. Perhaps 15:29 is not the new *locus classicus* of baptismal theology in Paul, but it is surely a contender for more careful consideration in future studies of Paul's baptismal theology.

As we noted above, there is no single instance in the Pauline literature of Paul speaking directly about baptism. This holds true for 15:29: 1 Corinthians 15 is about the resurrection, not baptism *per se*. Likewise, in Rom 6:1–14 Paul is not speaking about baptism in and of itself; he is speaking about the new dominion of life in Christ, after death to sin. Without doubt, the passage has strong overtones related to the theme of justification by faith and to the resurrection in terms of walking in the newness of life. The same holds true for Gal 3:26–29. Paul's main point is not about baptism, but about its effects. Baptism is the precursor to clothing oneself with Christ, being incorporated into him, and thus becoming a legatee to God's promise to Abraham fulfilled in Christ Jesus. No matter what one's take on Rom 6:1–14 or Gal 3:26–29 and regardless of the valuable baptismal insights contained in both, neither of the two is expressly a discourse on baptism. However, given the paucity of references to baptism in Paul's letters, these two pericopes are central to flushing out Paul's baptismal theology. And the same holds true for 15:29. No matter what one's take on 15:29, its contextual mooring in 1 Corinthians 15 precludes any consideration of the verse outside the dominant topic of resurrection. The contexts of Romans 6,

1 Corinthians 15, and Galatians 3 cannot be overemphasized; there are innumerable places wherein Paul might have mentioned baptism in his letters, but these are his chosen ones. Assuming our reading of 15:29 for the moment, Rom 6:1–14; Gal 3:26–29; and 1 Cor 15:29 stand on equal footing in terms of their inclusion of baptism as consequential to and not determinative of the overriding concern of their larger contexts. This point is most pertinent to Paul's baptismal theology: If no one citation of baptism in Paul's letters is claimed as directly focused on baptism, but only germane thereto, then extraordinary dexterity is necessitated in estimating the extent of any one citation's relevance, especially when that relevance must be weighed concomitantly with the other citations.

But what if 15:29 were taken as we interpret it? What is the issue at hand to which Paul ties baptism? The answer, of course, is the resurrection of Christ's dead. Taken as we interpret it, 15:29 fastens baptism and resurrection more closely than any other citation. In Rom 6:1–14, even though the death and resurrection of the Lord are mentioned in terms of newness of life for believers and the death to sin that enables them to share in Christ's resurrection, the accent is on Christ's resurrection rather than the believer's. Whereas in 15:29, the accent is on the resurrection of the faithful. Incontestably, the two accents are mutually inclusive rather than exclusive, but the difference draws attention to subtleties. In Romans 6, Paul is discussing neither baptism nor the resurrection *per se*; in a certain sense, then, baptism and resurrection are removed from one another and only fixed to one another inasmuch as they relate to the dominion of life in Christ after death to sin. But in 15:29, Paul directly relates baptism and resurrection to one another as the heart of the matter. So too, in Galatians 3 (as in Romans 6), resurrection is not an overt theme. Relating baptism to the baptized being sons of God, all one in Christ, and Abraham's offspring is apposite to resurrection, though hardly confined to it. Yet in 1 Corinthians 15 no one questions the overarching theme of resurrection. Here Paul chose unequivocally to include baptism under the aegis of resurrection, particularly the resurrection of the dead in 1 Cor 15:12–58. Not only that, but the inclusion of 1 Cor 15:44b–49 describes the Holy Spirit's agency in the resurrection, thereby enabling us to see connections between baptism and the Spirit not evident in Galatians or even Rom 8:9–13. If 15:29 is interpreted as we read it, there is now a vital and vibrant link between baptism and the resurrection, which is exemplified by the βαπτιζόμενοι in their acceptance of baptism "on account of the (resurrection of the) dead." Reading 15:29 anew will enable future considerations of Paul's baptismal theology, as well as considerations of his resurrection theology, to become richer.[82]

---

[82] For example, N. T. Wright's *The Resurrection of the Son of God* (Minneapolis: Fortress, 2003), one of the most important and up-to-date books on the resurrection, devotes one part (out of five) to the resurrection in Paul and two chapters to the resurrection in the Corinthian correspondence. However, Wright claims that there is "no agreement" on 15:29 and therefore considers it only

As we noted above, 15:29 places an unmistakable accent on the importance of the sacramental rite of baptism. It is clear from 15:29 that the sacrament is the means by which the βαπτιζόμενοι come to share in the resurrection of Christ and of Christians. Baptism is the effective sign wherein faith in the *kerygma* is made manifest. In 15:31–32, Paul parallels his own apostolic witness with the witness given by the βαπτιζόμενοι in the reception of sacramental baptism. While Rom 6:1–14 and Gal 3:26–29 highlight essential aspects of baptism—dominion of life in Christ, death to sin, newness of life, unity, and full participation in God's promises—15:29 highlights the reception of the sacrament itself: "Otherwise what are they to do, who have themselves baptized on account of the dead? If the dead are not really raised, why are they baptized on account of them?" In other words, baptism makes no sense without faith in the resurrection of the dead, just as Paul's sufferings make no sense without it. Yet Paul does not ask, "Otherwise what are they to do, who have *faith* in the resurrection? If the dead are not raised, why do they *believe* on account of them?" The reasons for this entail no degradation of faith's significance, or justification by faith. Instead, the focus here is sharpened on faith leading to action, to the moment of grace and sanctification, communicated to the believer by God, that is baptism. Now, it is not our desire to argue here the Catholic versus the Protestant conception of baptismal efficacy (effective sacrament versus sign of a previous effect) or to discuss confessional tenets which lie outside the Bible, but we must say that 15:29 shifts the weight from faith to rite as the moment of the infusion of grace.[83] It is undeniable that the βαπτιζόμενοι have faith, yet Paul points to ritual as the means to effect participation in God's promise, incorporation into Christ, incorporation into the Church, and eventual resurrection from the dead.

What if 15:29 is taken as we interpret it? Then, there is new support for the sacramental rite of baptism as the normative means of public witness and profession of faith, as the instant of incorporation into Christ and his Church. What is more, 15:29 demonstrates a unity of believers inasmuch as the βαπτιζόμενοι are baptized "on account of the dead." In this instance, the dead persons, whom the βαπτιζόμενοι believe destined for resurrection, are not strangers. Given the relatively small size of the Christian community in Corinth at the time of 1 Corinthians, the dead are the saints and the sinners with whom the βαπτιζόμενοι were associated. The acceptance of baptism in 15:29 expresses the βαπτιζόμενοι's trust in Paul's gospel: not only is Christ raised, but departed brothers and sisters are truly destined to share in resurrected glory. Furthermore,

---

as an indistinct affirmation of the resurrection (ibid., 338–39). How different would Wright's understanding of 1 Corinthians 15 and Paul's teaching on resurrection be if he adopted our interpretation of 15:29?

[83] The notion that sacraments are perforce later developments in early Christianity is refuted in D. E. Aune, "The Phenomenon of Early Christian 'Anti-Sacramentalism,'" in *Studies in the New Testament and Early Christian Literature* (ed. D. E. Aune; NovTSup 33; Leiden: Brill, 1972) 194–214.

15:29 might shed some light on 1 Cor 1:14–17. Too often taken to be a slight of baptism by Paul in favor of preaching the gospel, 1:14–17 may be instead a reference to Paul's conception of baptism as an acceptance of the gospel on the part of believers. Paul did in fact come to preach, not to baptize. Baptism is something that occurs only after an acceptance of the gospel in faith. If so many of the Corinthians are in error, or at least, confusion as 1 Corinthians 1 makes so clear, Paul may be thankful that he baptized but a few of them because he wishes to distance himself, albeit rhetorically, from their corruption of the sacrament. Keeping 15:29 as the center of our attention, we are brought closer to a sense of the awesome nature and consequences of baptism. Baptism is incorporation into Christ, the Christian faithful—living and dead—and participation in the divine life here and hereafter. In an age when Christians casually speak of their own salvation and even universal salvation as presumed facts, a look back to the early days of Paul in Corinth is well worth the effort. Some two thousand years ago, the Apostle to the Gentiles preached Jesus as Messiah and Lord—once dead and now raised by the power of the Holy Spirit. Paul preached "Christ crucified, a stumbling block to Jews and a folly to Gentiles" (1 Cor 1:23). Paul begged and exhorted his listeners to respond in faith to the gospel. One such act of faith was baptism "on account of the dead."

BAPTISM AND RESURRECTION

We began this study with a quotation from the Catholic baptismal rite: "'What do you ask of God's Church?' 'Eternal life.'" Therein, contemporary Christian liturgy illustrates the inextricable link between baptism and resurrection. The bond between the two is a constant theme in Paul, the NT, and the early Church. We asserted that 1 Cor 15:29 is an example of that same theme. In our translation and interpretation of 15:29—"Otherwise what are they to do, who have themselves baptized on account of the dead? If the dead are not really raised, why are they baptized on account of them?"—we found a matchless unity of baptism and resurrection based on faith in the gospel of Jesus Christ that Paul preached in Corinth.

In order to prove this, we proceeded in four simple steps that constitute the four chapters of our study. First, we examined the variety of interpretations of 15:29 in contemporary biblical scholarship, beginning with the readings of 15:29 as an instance of vicarious baptism and continuing through the readings of the verse as a form of ordinary baptism, and we provided an assessment of these readings. We concluded that there was a need to delve more deeply into the literary and historical milieux of 15:29. Second, we explored the literary context. We looked to the genre and integrity of 1 Corinthians, the structure of 1 Corinthians 15, and the morphology and syntax of 15:29. We found that the literary context alone is insufficient for an interpretation of the verse. Read solely in its literary context, 15:29 may be interpreted as a reference to ordinary or vicarious baptism. We concluded that a thorough exposition of the three historical contexts pertinent to 15:29—Paul, Greco-Roman Corinth, and Corinthian Christianity—was in order. Third, we delved into the extraordinarily complex areas of 15:29's overall historical context. Because the words themselves of 15:29 admit of a reading of ordinary or vicarious baptism and because a reading of vicarious baptism proved to make difficult historical claims (while a reading of ordinary baptism complements 1 Corinthians and the Pauline literature), we made a concerted effort to find some semblance of a custom to ground a reading of vicarious baptism. We closely examined the pre-Christian and Christian Paul, we searched Greco-Roman Corinth and its ancient religions, and we analyzed Corinthian Christianity through the lens of the crises discussed by Paul in 1 Corinthians. But something like vicarious baptism was nowhere to be found. We concluded that without any historical foundation whatsoever, vicarious baptism was not a viable interpretation of 15:29 and, concomitantly, that the historical claims made by previously examined interpretations of ordinary baptism were also historically unsubstantiated. Finally, we were left with the opportunity to read 15:29 anew. We interpreted 15:29 to be an extraordinary reference to ordinary baptism with a distinctive connection to the resurrection of Christ and of Christians. 15:29 is a dual rhetorical question in which Paul lauds one group of persons, who accept baptism on account of their faith in the resurrection of Christ and his faithful, as a praiseworthy example to those who would deny the resurrection of the dead. The unique confluence of baptism and resurrection in 15:29 presents a select insight into Paul's baptismal theology. After inquiry into Paul's baptismal theology in Rom 6:1–14, Gal 3:26–29, and the Pauline literature in general, we concluded that 15:29 should be considered as a principal baptismal text in the Pauline literature, that its amalgamation of baptism and resurrection is unique among the principal baptismal references in Paul, and that 15:29 places a strong accent on the sacramental rite of baptism.

To conclude, we recall the controversy and confusion attending 15:29. We are aware that our reading of 15:29 is but one more attempt to interpret this somewhat vexing verse. However, we are convinced that our reading is viable and that if 15:29 is interpreted as we claim it ought to be, a small advance has been made in Pauline scholarship, particularly in Paul's theology of baptism. Baptism "on account of the dead" is a legacy of faith in the sacrament of baptism as the sign and seal of Christ's promise and Paul's preaching of life everlasting.

Bibliography

PRIMARY SOURCES AND PRINCIPAL REFERENCE WORKS

Aland, B., K. Aland, M. Black, J. Karavidopoulos, C. M. Martini, and B. M. Metzger, eds. *The Greek New Testament.* 4th rev. ed. Stuttgart: Deutsche Bibelgesellschaft, 1993.

Aland, K. *Vollständige Konkordanz zum griechischen Neuen Testament unter Zugrundlegung aller modernen kritischen Textausgaben und des Textus Receptus.* 2 vols. in 3. ANTF IV, 1,1. Berlin: de Gruyter, 1983.

Aland, K., and B. Aland. *The Text of the New Testament: An Introduction to the Critical Editions and to the Theory and Practice of Modern Textual Criticism.* Trans. E. F. Rhodes. 2nd ed. Grand Rapids, MI: Eerdmans, 1989.

Balz, H., and G. Schneider, eds. *Exegetical Dictionary of the New Testament.* Trans. V. P. Howard, J. W. Medendorp, and J. W. Thompson. 3 vols. Grand Rapids, MI: Eerdmans, 1990.

Bauer, W., W. F. Arndt, F. W. Gingrich, and F. W. Danker. *A Greek-English Lexicon of the New Testament and Other Early Christian Literature.* 2nd ed. Chicago and London: University of Chicago Press, 1979.

Bible de Jérusalem, 1966.

Blass, F., and A. Debrunner. *A Greek Grammar of the New Testament and Other Early Christian Literature.* Trans. and rev. R. W. Funk. Chicago and London: University of Chicago Press, 1961.

The Book of Doctrine and Covenants. Ed. Joseph Smith et al. 1835; rpt. Independence, MO: The Board of Publication of the Reorganized Church of Jesus Christ of Latter Day Saints, 1970.

The Book of Mormon: Another Testament of Jesus Christ. (Trans. ?) Joseph Smith. 1930; rpt. Salt Lake City: The Church of Jesus Christ of Latter-Day Saints, 1981.

Botterweck, G. J., and H. Ringgren, eds. *Theological Dictionary of the Old Testament.* Trans. J. T. Willis, G. W. Bromiley, and D. E. Greene. Grand Rapids, MI: Eerdmans, 1974–.

Bratcher, R. G. *Old Testament Quotations in the New Testament.* 3rd ed. New York: United Bible Societies, 1987.

Brown, C., ed. *New International Dictionary of New Testament Theology.* 4 vols. Grand Rapids, MI: Zondervan, 1975–85.

Brown, R. E., J. A. Fitzmyer, and R. E. Murphy, eds. *The Jerome Biblical Commentary.* Englewood Cliffs, NJ: Prentice Hall, 1968.

———. *The New Jerome Biblical Commentary*. Englewood Cliffs, NJ: Prentice Hall, 1990.

Buttrick, G. A., ed. *The Interpreter's Dictionary of the Bible*. 4 vols. Nashville: Abingdon, 1962. *Supplementary Volume*. Ed. K. R. Crim. Nashville: Abingdon, 1976.

Catechism of the Catholic Church. 2nd ed. Rome: Libreria Editrice Vaticana, 1997.

Dana, H. E., and J. R. Mantey. *A Manual Grammar of the Greek New Testament*. New York, Macmillan, 1927.

Denzinger, H., and A. Schönmetzer. *Enchiridion symbolorum: Definitionum et declarationum de rebus fidei et morum*. 36th ed. Freiburg: Herder, 1976.

Ellingworth, P., and H. Hatton. *A Translator's Handbook on Paul's First Letter to the Corinthians*. Helps for Translators. Stuttgart: United Bible Societies, 1985.

Elliott, J. K. *A Survey of Manuscripts Used in Editions of the Greek New Testament*. NovTSup 57. Leiden: Brill, 1987.

Evans, C. A., and S. E. Porter. *Dictionary of New Testament Background*. Downers Grove, IL and Leicester, Eng.: InterVarsity, 2000.

Freedman, D. N., ed. *The Anchor Bible Dictionary*. 6 vols. New York: Doubleday, 1992.

Goldman, H. *Excavations at Gözlü Kule, Tarsus*. Vol. 1, *Texts: The Hellenistic and Roman Periods*. Vol. 2, *Plates: The Hellenistic and Roman Periods*. Princeton, NJ: Princeton University Press, 1950.

Hammond, N. G. L., and H. H. Scullard, eds. *The Oxford Classical Dictionary*. 2nd ed. Oxford: Clarendon, 1970.

Hawthorne, G. F., R. P. Martin, and D. G. Reid, eds. *Dictionary of Paul and His Letters*. Downers Grove, IL and Leicester, Eng.: InterVarsity, 1993.

Kittel, G., and G. Friedrich, eds. *Theological Dictionary of the New Testament*. Trans. and ed. G. W. Bromiley. 10 vols. Grand Rapids, MI: Eerdmans, 1964–76.

Louw, J. P., and E. A. Nida, eds. *The Greek-English Lexicon of the New Testament: Based on Semantic Domains*. 2nd ed. 2 vols. New York: United Bible Societies, 1989.

Ludlow, D. H., ed. *Encyclopedia of Mormonism*. 5 vols. New York: Macmillan, 1992.

Lust, J., E. Eynikel, and K. Hauspie. *A Greek–English Lexicon of the Septuagint*. Part I, Α–Ι (with the collaboration of G. Chamberlain). Stuttgart: Deutsche Bibelgesellschaft, 1992. Part II, Κ–Ω. Stuttgart: Deutsche Bibelgesellschaft, 1996.

Metzger, B. M. *A Textual Commentary on the Greek New Testament*. 2nd ed. Stuttgart: Deutsche Bibelgesellschaft, 1994.

Miller, M., trans. and ed. *Menander: Plays and Fragments*. London: Penguin, 1987.

Moule, C. F. D. *An Idiom Book of New Testament Greek*. 2nd ed. Cambridge: Cambridge University Press, 1959.

Moulton, J. H. *A Grammar of New Testament Greek*. 4 vols. Edinburgh: T&T Clark, 1908–1976. Vol. 1, *Prolegomena* by J. H. Moulton (3rd ed.; 1908); vol. 2, *Accidence and Word-Formation with an Appendix on Semitisms in the New Testament* by J. H. Moulton and W. F. Howard (1928); vol. 3, *Syntax* by N. Turner (1963); vol. 4, *Style* by N. Turner (1976).

Murray, P., and T. S. Dorsch, trans. and ed. *Classical Literary Criticism*. Rev. ed. London: Penguin, 2000.

Nestle, E., B. and K. Aland, J. Karavidopoulos, C. M. Martini, and B. M. Metzger, eds. *Novum Testamentum Graece*. 27th ed. Stuttgart: Deutsche Bibelgesellschaft, 1993.

The New American Bible (with revised New Testament), 1987.

The New Revised Standard Version of the Bible, 1990.
Porter, S. E. *Idioms of the Greek New Testament*. BLG 2. 2nd ed. Sheffield: Sheffield Academic Press, 1994.
Rahlfs, A., ed. *Septuaginta: Id est Vetus Testamentum graece iuxta LXX interpretes*. 2 vols. in 1. Stuttgart: Deutsche Bibelgesellschaft, 1979.
The Revised Standard Version of the Bible, 1973.
Robertson, A. T. *A Grammar of the Greek New Testament in the Light of Historical Research*. London: Hodder and Stoughton, 1914.
Rüger, H. M., ed. *Biblia Hebraica Stuttgartensia*. 4th cor. ed. Stuttgart: Deutsche Bibelgesellschaft, 1990.
La sacra Bibbia della Conferenza Episcopale Italiana, 1971.
Spicq, C. *Theological Lexicon of the New Testament*. Trans. and ed. J. D. Ernest. 3 vols. Peabody, MA: Hendrickson, 1994.
Wace, H., and W. C. Piercy, eds. *A Dictionary of Early Christian Biography*. 1911; rpt. Peabody, MA: Hendrickson, 1999.
Zerwick, M. *Analysis Philologica Novi Testamenti Graeci*. 4th ed. SPIB 107. Rome: Editrice Pontificio Istituto Biblico, 1966.
―――. *Biblical Greek Illustrated by Examples*. English edition adapted from the fourth Latin edition by Joseph Smith. SPIB 114. Rome: Editrice Pontificio Istituto Biblico, 1963.
Zerwick, M., and M. Grosvenor. *A Grammatical Analysis of the Greek New Testament*. 4th rev. ed. Rome: Editrice Pontificio Istituto Biblico, 1993.

SECONDARY LITERATURE CONSULTED

Aageson, J. W. "'Control' in Pauline Language and Culture: A Study of Rom 6." *NTS* 42 (1996) 75–89.

———. *Written Also for Our Sake: Paul and the Art of Biblical Interpretation.* Louisville: Westminster John Knox, 1993.

Aasgaard, R. "Brotherhood in Plutarch and Paul: Its Role and Character." In *Constructing Early Christian Families*, ed. Moxnes, 166–82.

Agersnap, S. *Baptism and the New Life: A Study of Romans 6.1–14.* Trans. C. and F. Crowley. Aarhus, Den.: Aarhus University Press, 1999.

Akenson, D. H. *Saint Saul: A Skeleton Key to the Historical Jesus.* Oxford: Oxford University Press, 2000.

Alderink, L. "The Eleusinian Mysteries in Roman Imperial Times." *ANRW* 2/18.2:1457–98.

Aletti, J.-N. "L'argumentation de Paul et la position des Corinthiens: 1Co 15,12–34." In *Résurrection du Christ et des chrétiens (1Co 15)*, ed. De Lorenzi, 63–81.

———. "L'autorité apostolique de Paul: Théorie et pratique." In *L'apôtre Paul*, ed. Vanhoye, 229–46.

———. "La *dispositio* rhétorique dans les épîtres pauliniennes: Propositions de méthode." *NTS* 38 (1992) 385–401.

———. "La présence d'un modèle rhétorique en Romains: Son rôle et son importance." *Bib* 71 (1990) 1–24.

Alexander, L. "Hellenistic Letter-Forms and the Structure of Philippians." *JSNT* 37 (1989) 87–101.

———. "Paul and the Hellenistic Schools: The Evidence of Galen." In *Paul in His Hellenistic Context*, ed. Engberg-Pedersen, 60–83.

Allison, D. C., Jr. *The End of the Ages Has Come: An Early Interpretation of the Passion and Resurrection of Jesus.* SNTW. Edinburgh: T&T Clark, 1987.

———. "Jesus and the Covenant: A Response to E. P. Sanders." *JSNT* 37 (1989) 87–101.

Allo, E.-B. *Première épître aux Corinthiens.* EBib. Paris: Gabalda, 1935.

Amador, J. D. H. "Revisiting 2 Corinthians: Rhetoric and the Case for Unity." *NTS* 46 (2000) 92–111.

Anatolios, K. "Christ, Scripture, and the Christian Story of Meaning in Origen." *Greg* 78 (1997) 55–77.

Anderson, H. G., T. A. Murphy, and J. A. Burgess, eds. *Justification by Faith.* LCD 7. Minneapolis: Augsburg, 1985.

Anderson, R. D., Jr. *Ancient Rhetorical Theory and Paul.* CBET 18. Kampen, Neth.: Kok Pharos, 1996.

———. *Glossary of Greek Rhetorical Terms: Connected to Methods of Argumentation, Figures, and Tropes from Anaximenes to Quintilian.* CBET 24. Leuven: Peeters, 2000.

Angus, S. *The Mystery-Religions: A Study in the Religious Background of Early Christianity.* 1928; rpt. New York: Dover, 1975.

Annas, J. E. *Hellenistic Philosophy of Mind.* HCS 8. Berkeley: University of California Press, 1992.

Arnold, C. E. "Power." In *Dictionary of Paul and His Letters*, ed. Hawthorne, Martin, and Reid, 723–25.
Arzt, P. "The 'Epistolary Introductory Thanksgiving' in the Papyri and in Paul." *NovT* 36 (1994) 29–46.
Ascough, R. S. *What are They Saying about the Formation of the Pauline Churches?* New York/ Mahwah, NJ: Paulist, 1998.
Ashley, B. M. *Living the Truth in Love: A Biblical Introduction to Moral Theology.* Staten Island, NY: Alba House, 1996.
Ashton, J. *The Religion of Paul the Apostle.* New Haven and London: Yale University Press, 2000.
Atkinson, K. "On Further Defining the First-Century CE Synagogue: Fact or Fiction—? A Rejoinder to H. C. Kee." *NTS* 43 (1997) 491–502.
Aune, D. E. "Expansion and Recruitment among Hellenistic Religions: The Case of Mithraism." In *Recruitment, Conquest, and Conflict*, ed. Borgen, Robbins, and Gowler, 39–56.
———. "Human Nature and Ethics in Hellenistic Philosophical Traditions and Paul: Some Issues and Problems." In *Paul in His Hellenistic Context*, ed. Engberg-Pedersen, 291–312.
———. *The New Testament in Its Literary Environment.* LEC 8. Philadelphia: Westminster, 1987.
———. "The Phenomenon of Early Christian 'Anti-Sacramentalism.'" In *Studies in the New Testament and Early Christian Literature*, ed. Aune, 194–214.
———. Review of H. D. Betz, *Galatians: A Commentary on Paul's Letter to the Churches in Galatia. RelSRev* 7 (1981) 323–28.
———, ed. *Studies in the New Testament and Early Christian Literature: Essays in Honor of Allen P. Wikgren.* NovTSup 33. Leiden: Brill, 1972.
Badcock, F. J. "Baptism for the Dead." *ExpTim* 54 (1942–43) 330.
Bahr, G. J. "Paul and Letter Writing in the Fifth [*sic*] Century." *CBQ* 28 (1966) 465–77.
———. "The Subscriptions in the Pauline Letters." *JBL* 87 (1986) 27–41.
Bailey, K. E. "The Structure of I Corinthians and Paul's Theological Method with Special Reference to 4:17." *NovT* 25 (1983) 152–81.
Baird, W. *The Corinthian Church—A Biblical Approach to Urban Culture.* New York and Nashville: Abingdon, 1964.
———."'One against the Other': Intra-Church Conflict in 1 Corinthians." In *The Conversation Continues*, ed. Fortna and Gaventa, 116–36.
———."Pauline Eschatology in Hermeneutical Perspective." *NTS* 17 (1970–71) 314–27.
———. "What is the Kerygma? A Study of I Cor 15:3–8 and Gal 1:11–17." *JBL* 76 (1957) 181–91.
Balch, D. L. "Backgrounds of I Cor. VII: Sayings of the Lord in Q; Moses as an Ascetic Θεῖος 'Ανήρ in II Cor. III." *NTS* 18 (1971–72) 351–64.
Balch, D. L., E. Ferguson, and W. A. Meeks, eds. *Greeks, Romans and Christians: Essays in Honor of Abraham J. Malherbe.* Minneapolis: Fortress, 1990.
Bammel, E. "Rechtsfindung in Korinth." *ETL* 73 (1997) 107–13.
Barbaglio, G. *La prima lettera ai Corinzi: Introduzione, versione, commento.* SOC 16. Bologna: Dehoniane, 1995.

Barclay, J. M. G. "Deviance and Apostasy: Some Applications of Deviance Theory to First-Century Judaism and Christianity." In *Modelling Early Christianity*, ed. Esler, 114–27.

———. "The Family as the Bearer of Religion in Judaism and Early Christianity." In *Constructing Early Christian Families*, ed. Moxnes, 66–80.

———. *Jews in the Mediterranean Diaspora: From Alexander to Trajan (323 BCE–117 CE)*. Edinburgh: T&T Clark, 1996.

———. "Mirror-Reading a Polemical Letter: Galatians as a Test Case." *JSNT* 31 (1987) 73–93.

———. "Thessalonica and Corinth: Social Contrasts in Pauline Christianity." *JSNT* 47 (1992) 49–74.

Barclay, W. "Hellenistic Thought in New Testament Times—Epicurians: The Way of Tranquility." *ExpTim* 72 (1960–61) 78–81, 101–4, 146–49.

Bardy, G. "Cérinthe." *RB* 30 (1921) 344–73.

Barlow, P. L. *Mormons and the Bible: The Place of the Latter-Day Saints in American Religion*. Oxford: Oxford University Press, 1991.

Barnett, P. W. "Opposition in Corinth." *JSNT* 22 (1984) 3–17.

———. "'Under Tiberius All Was Quiet.'" *NTS* 21 (1974–75) 564–71.

Barr, J. *The Concept of Biblical Theology: An Old Testament Perspective*. Minneapolis: Fortress, 1999.

———. "Paul and the LXX: A Note on Some Recent Work." *JTS* 45 (1994) 593–601.

———. *The Semantics of Biblical Language*. 1961; rpt. London: SCM, 1963.

Barré, M. L. "Qumran and the 'Weakness' of Paul." *CBQ* 42 (1980) 216–27.

Barrett, C. K. "Boasting (καυχᾶθαι, κτλ.) in the Pauline Epistles." In *L'apôtre Paul*, ed. Vanhoye, 363–68.

———. "Christianity at Corinth." *BJRL* 46 (1964) 269–97.

———. *A Commentary on the First Epistle to the Corinthians*. BNTC. 2nd ed. London: A&C Black, 1971.

———. *From First Adam to Last*. New York: Scribner, 1962.

———. *Paul: An Introduction to His Thought*. OCT. London: Chapman, 1994.

———. "Paul's Opponents in II Corinthians." *NTS* 17 (1970–71) 233–54.

———. "Pauline Controversies in the Post-Pauline Period." *NTS* 20 (1973–74) 229–45.

———. Review of M. Hengel and A. M. Schwemer, *Paul between Damascus and Antioch: The Unknown Years*. *JTS* 49 (1998) 242–45.

———. "The Significance of the Adam-Christ Typology for the Resurrection of the Dead: 1Co 15, 20–22. 45–49." In *Résurrection du Christ et des chrétiens (1Co 15)*, ed. De Lorenzi, 99–122.

Bartchy, S. S. "Undermining Ancient Patriarchy: The Apostle Paul's Vision of a Society of Siblings." *BTB* 29 (1999) 68–78.

Barth, K. *The Resurrection of the Dead*. Trans. H. J. Stenning. New York: Revell, 1933.

Bartley, P. *Mormonism: The Prophet, the Book and the Cult*. Dublin: Veritas, 1989.

Barton, J. *The Spirit and the Letter: Studies in the Biblical Canon*. London: SPCK, 1997.

Barton, S. C. "Paul's Sense of Place: An Anthropological Approach to Community Formation in Corinth." *NTS* 32 (1986) 225–46.

———. "The Relativisation of Family Ties in the Jewish and Graeco-Roman Traditions." In *Constructing Early Christian Families*, ed. Moxnes, 81–100.

Bates, W. H. "The Integrity of II Corinthians." *NTS* 12 (1965–66) 56–69.

Batey, R. "The Μία Σάρξ Union of Christ and His Church." *NTS* 13 (1966–67) 270–81.
Bauckham, R. *The Fate of the Dead: Studies on the Jewish and Christian Apocalypses.* NovTSup 93. Leiden: Brill, 1998.
———. "Life, Death, and the Afterlife in Second Temple Judaism." In *Life in the Face of Death*, ed. Longenecker, 80–95.
Baur, F. C. "Die Christuspartei in der korinthischen Gemeinde, der Gegensatz des petrinischen und paulinischen Christenthums in der alten Kirche, der Apostel Petrus in Rom." *TZT* 4 (1831) 61–206.
———. *Paul, the Apostle of Jesus Christ: His Life and Work, His Epistles and His Doctrine.* Ed. and rev. E. Zeller. Trans. A Menzies. 2 vols. London: Williams and Norgate, 1875–76.
Beard, M., J. North, and S. Price. *Religions of Rome.* 2 vols. Vol. 1, *A History.* Vol. 2, *A Sourcebook.* Cambridge: Cambridge University Press, 1998.
Beardslee, W. A. *First Corinthians: A Commentary for Today.* St. Louis, MO: Chalice, 1994.
Beasley-Murray, G. R. "Baptism." In *Dictionary of Paul and His Letters*, ed. Hawthorne, Martin, Reid, 60–66.
———. *Baptism in the New Testament.* Grand Rapids, MI: Eerdmans, 1962.
Beatty, B. "Inspirational Literature: The Heresy of Historicism." *DRev* 115 (1997) 282–99.
Becker, J. *Paul: Apostle to the Gentiles.* Trans. O. C. Dean, Jr. Louisville: Westminster John Knox, 1993.
Behm, J. "αἷμα, αἱματεκχυσία." *TDNT* 1:172–77.
Beker, J. C. "The Faithfulness of God and the Priority of Israel in Paul's Letter to the Romans." *HTR* 79 (1986) 10–16.
———. "Luke's Paul as the Legacy of Paul." In *SBLSP 1993.* Atlanta: Scholars Press, 1993.
———. *Paul the Apostle: The Triumph of God in Life and Thought.* Philadelphia: Fortress, 1980.
———. "Paul's Theology: Consistent or Inconsistent?" *NTS* 34 (1988) 364–77.
Belleville, L. L. "Continuity or Discontinuity: A Fresh Look at 1 Corinthians in the Light of First-Century Epistolary Forms and Conventions." *EvQ* 59 (1987) 15–37.
———. "'Imitate Me, Just as I Imitate Christ': Discipleship in the Corinthian Correspondence." *Patterns of Discipleship in the New Testament.* Ed. R. N. Longenecker. Grand Rapids, MI: Eerdmans, 1996.
Benda, J. *La trahison des clercs.* Paris: Grasset, 1928.
Benoit, P. "Pauline Angelology and Demonology: Reflexions on the Designations of the Heavenly Powers and on the Origin of Angelic Evil According to Paul." *RSB* 3 (1983) 1–18.
Benoît, P., and R. Murphy, eds. *Immortality and Resurrection.* Con 60. New York: Herder and Herder, 1970.
Bentoglio, G. *Apertura e disponibilità: L'accoglienza nell'Epistolario Paolino.* TGST 2. Rome: Pontificia Università Gregoriana, 1995.
Benzi, G. *Paolo e il suo vangelo.* IBO. Brescia: Queriniana, 2001.
Berger, K. "Rhetorical Criticism, New Form Criticism, and New Testament Hermeneutics." In *Rhetoric and the New Testament*, ed. Porter and Olbricht, 390–96.

Bergin, L. *O Prophecticum Lavacrum: Baptism as Symbolic Act of Eschatological Salvation*. AnGreg 277. Rome: Editrice Pontificia Università Gregoriana, 1999.
Best, E. "Dead in Trespasses and Sins (Eph. 2.1)." *JNST* 13 (1981) 9–25.
———. *Paul and His Converts: The Sprunt Lectures 1985*. Edinburgh: T&T Clark, 1988.
———. "Paul's Apostolic Authority—?" *JSNT* 27 (1986) 3–25.
———. "Who Used Whom? The Relationship of Ephesians and Colossians." *NTS* 43 (1997) 72–96.
Betz, H. D. "Antiquity and Christianity." *JBL* 117 (1998) 3–22.
———. *Galatians: A Commentary on Paul's Letter to the Churches in Galatia*. Hermeneia. Philadelphia: Fortress, 1979.
———. "Paul." *ABD* 5:198–201.
———. "The Problem of Rhetoric and Theology according to the Apostle Paul." In *L'apôtre Paul*, ed. Vanhoye, 16–48.
———. "Transferring a Ritual: Paul's Interpretation of Baptism in Romans 6." In *Paul in His Hellenistic Context*, ed. Engberg-Pedersen, 84–118.
———. Review of E. R. Richards, *The Secretary in the Letters of Paul*. *JTS* 43 (1992) 618–20.
Betz, H. D., and M. M. Mitchell. "First Epistle to the Corinthians." *ABD* 1:1139–48.
Bieringer, R. "The Corinthian Correspondence: Colloquium Biblicum Lovaniense XLIII (1994)." *ETL* 71 (1995) 266–76.
———. "Paul's Divine Jealousy: The Apostle and His Communities in Relationship." *LS* 17 (1992) 197–231.
———, ed. *The Corinthian Correspondence*. BETL 125. Leuven: Leuven University Press, 1996.
Billows, R. A. *Antigonos the One-Eyed and the Creation of the Hellenistic State*. HCS 4. Berkeley: University of California Press, 1990.
Black, C. C., II. "Keeping up with Recent Studies: XVI. Rhetorical Criticism and Biblical Interpretation." *ExpTim* 100 (1989) 252–58.
Blakeney, E. H. "Ὑπέρ with Genitive in N.T." *ExpTim* 55 (1943–44) 306.
Bockmuehl, M. *Revelation and Mystery in Ancient Judaism and Pauline Christianity*. 1990; rpt. Grand Rapids, MI: Eerdmans, 1997.
Boer, M. C. de. "The Composition of 1 Corinthians." *NTS* 40 (1994) 229–45.
———. *The Defeat of Death: Apocalyptic Eschatology in 1 Corinthians 15 and Romans 5*. JSNTSup 22: Sheffield: Academic Press, 1988.
———. "Images of Paul in the Post-Apostolic Period." *CBQ* 42 (1980) 359–80.
———. "Paul's Use of a Resurrection Tradition in 1 Cor 15,20–28." In *The Corinthian Correspondence*, ed. Bieringer, 639–51.
Boers, H. "Apocalyptic Eschatology in I Corinthians 15: An Essay in Contemporary Interpretation." *Int* 21 (1967) 50–65.
———. "The Form Critical Study of Paul's Letters: I Thessalonians as a Case Study." *NTS* 22 (1975–76) 140–58.
———. "The Structure and Meaning of Romans 6:1–14." *CBQ* 63 (2001) 664–82.
Bolt, P. G. "Life, Death, and the Afterlife in the Greco-Roman World." In *Life in the Face of Death*, ed. Longenecker, 51–79.
Bondi, R. A. "Become Such as I Am: St. Paul in the Acts of the Apostles." *BTB* 27 (1997) 164–76.

Bonneau, N. "The Logic of Paul's Argument on the Resurrection Body in 1 Cor 15:35–44a." *ScEs* 45 (1993) 79–92.
Bonner, G. *St. Augustine of Hippo: Life and Controversies.* 1963; rpt. Norwich: Canterbury, 2002.
Bonsor, J. A. *Athens and Jerusalem: The Role of Philosophy in Theology.* New York/Mahwah, NJ: Paulist, 1993.
Bookidis, N. "Ritual Dining in the Sanctuary of Demeter and Kore at Corinth." In *Sympotica: A Symposium on the Symposion.* Ed. O. Murray. Oxford: Clarendon Press, 1990. 86–94.
Borchert, G. L. "The Resurrection: 1 Corinthians 15." *RevExp* 80 (1983) 401–15.
Borgen, P. *Early Christianity and Hellenistic Judaism.* Edinburgh: T&T Clark, 1996.
———. "'Yes,' 'No,' 'How Far?': The Participation of Jews and Christians in Pagan Cults." In *Paul in His Hellenistic Context,* ed. Engberg-Pedersen, 30–59.
Borgen, P., V. K. Robbins, and D. B. Gowler, eds. *Recruitment, Conquest, and Conflict: Strategies in Judaism, Early Christianity, and the Greco-Roman World.* ESEC. Atlanta: Scholars Press, 1998.
Boring, M. E. "The 'Third Quest' and the Apostolic Faith." *Int* 50 (1996) 341–54.
Bornkamm, G. "μυστήριον, μυεώ." *TDNT* 4:802–28.
Botha, P. "The Verbal Art of the Pauline Letters: Rhetoric, Performance and Presence." In *Rhetoric and the New Testament,* ed. Porter and Olbricht, 409–28.
Bowe, B. E. Review of D. Trobisch, *Paul's Letter Collection: Tracing the Origins. CBQ* 58 (1996) 172–73.
Bowen, C. R. "I Fought with Beasts at Ephesus." *JBL* 42 (1923) 59–68.
Bowers, P. "Paul and Religious Propoganda in the First Century." *NovT* 22 (1980) 316–23.
Bowers, W. P. "Jewish Communities in Spain in the Time of Paul the Apostle." *JTS* 26 (1975) 395–402.
Boyarin, D. *A Radical Jew: Paul and the Politics of Identity.* CSJLCS 1. Berkeley: University of California Press, 1997.
Boyer, J. L. "First Class Conditions: What Do They Mean?" *GTJ* 2 (1981) 75–114.
Bradley, D. G. "The *Topos* as a Form in the Pauline Paraenesis." *JBL* 72 (1953) 238–46.
Brandt, W. J. *The Rhetoric of Argumentation.* New York: Bobbs-Merrill, 1970.
Branick, V. P. "Apocalyptic Paul?" *CBQ* 47 (1985) 664–75.
———. "The Sinful Flesh of the Son of God (Rom 8:3): A Key Image of Pauline Theology." *CBQ* 47 (1985) 246–62.
Brankin, P. M. "Are Mormons Christians?" *Extension* 82 (March-April 1988) 19–20.
Braxton, B. R. *The Tyranny of Resolution: I Corinthians 7:17–24.* SBLDS 181. Atlanta: Society of Biblical Literature, 2000.
Breck, J. "Biblical Chiasmus: Exploring Structure for Meaning." *BTB* 17 (1987) 70–74.
———. *The Shape of Biblical Language: Chiasmus in the Scriptures and Beyond.* Crestwood, NY: St. Vladimir's Seminary Press, 1994.
Brent, A. "Luke-Acts and the Imperial Cult in Asia Minor." *JTS* 48 (1997) 411–38.
Brodeur, S. *The Holy Spirit's Agency in the Resurrection of the Dead: An Exegetico-Theological Study of 1 Corinthians 15,44b–49 and Romans 8,9–13.* TGST 14. Rome: Editrice Pontificia Università Gregoriana, 1996.

Brodie, T. L. "The Systematic Use of the Pentateuch in 1 Corinthians." In *The Corinthian Correspondence*, ed. Bieringer, 441–57.
Broneer, O. T. "Paul and the Pagan Cults at Isthmia." *HTR* 64 (1971) 169–187.
Brown, R. E. *An Introduction to the New Testament*. ABRL. New York: Doubleday, 1997.
———. "The Pre-Christian Semitic Concept of 'Mystery.'" *CBQ* 20 (1958) 417–43.
———. "The Semitic Background of the New Testament *Mysterion* (I)." *Bib* 39 (1958) 426–48.
———. "The Semitic Background of the New Testament *Mysterion* (II)." *Bib* 40 (1959) 70–87.
———. *The Semitic Background of the Term "Mystery" in the New Testament*. BS 21. Philadelphia: Fortress (Facet), 1968.
Brown, R. E., J. R. Donahue, D. Senior, and A. Yarbro Collins. "Aspects of New Testament Thought." *NJBC* §81, 1354–81.
Brown, S. *The Origins of Christianity: A Historical Introduction to the New Testament*. Rev. ed. OBS. Oxford: Oxford University Press, 1993.
Bruce, F. F. *The Epistle to the Galatians: A Commentary on the Greek Text*. NIGTC. Grand Rapids, MI: Eerdmans, 1982.
———. *I and II Corinthians*. NCBC. Grand Rapids, MI: Eerdmans, 1971.
———. *New Testament History*. New York: Doubleday, 1969.
———. *Paul: Apostle of the Heart Set Free*. 1977; rpt. Grand Rapids, MI: Eerdmans, 1996.
———. "Paul on Immortality." *SJT* 24 (1971) 457–72.
Brunt, J. C. "More on the *Topos* as a New Testament Form." *JBL* 104 (1985) 495–500.
———. "The New Testament and Classical Studies." *NTS* 22 (1975–76) 229–42.
Buchanan, G. W. "Worship, Feasts and Ceremonies in the Early Christian-Jewish Church." *NTS* 26 (1979–80) 279–97.
Büchsel, F. "ἀλλάσσω, ἀντάλλαγμα, ἀπ-, δι-, καταλλάσσω, καταλλαγή, ἀποκατ-, μεταλλάσσω." *TDNT* 1:251–59.
———. "γίνομαι, γένεσις, γένος, γένημα, ἀπογίνομαι, παλιγγενεσία." *TDNT* 1:681–89.
———. "δίδωμι, δῶρον, δωρέομαι, δώρημα, δωρεά, δωρεάν, ἀπω-, ἀνταποδίδωμι, ἀνταπόδοσις, ἀνταπόδομα, παραδίωμι, παράδοσις." *TDNT* 2:166–73.
Buck, C. H. "Early Order in the Pauline Corpus." *JBL* 68 (1949) 351–57.
Buckley, J. J. "A Cult-Mystery in the *Gospel of Philip*." *JBL* 99 (1980) 569–81.
Bullmore, M. A. *St. Paul's Theology of Rhetorical Style: An Examination of 1 Corinthians 2:1–5 in the Light of First Century Graeco-Roman Rhetorical Culture*. San Francisco: International Scholar Publications, 1995.
Bultmann, R. "θάνατος, θνήσκω, ἀποθνήσκω, συναποθνήσκω, θανατόω, θνητός, ἀθανασία (ἀθάνατος)." *TDNT* 3:7–25.
———. "νεκρός, νεκρόω, νέκρωσις." *TDNT* 4:892–95.
———. "Paulus," in *Religion in Geschichte und Gegenwart: Handwörterbuch für Theologie und Religionswissenschaft*. 2nd ed. Tübingen: Mohr, 1930.
———. *Theology of the New Testament*. Trans. K. Grobel. 2 vols. London: SCM, 1952 (vol. 1); 1955 (vol. 2).
Bünker, M. *Briefformular und rhetorische Disposition im 1. Korintherbrief*. GTA 28. Göttingen: Vandenhoeck and Ruprecht, 1983.

Burke, T. J., and J. K. Elliott. *Paul and the Corinthians: Studies on a Community in Conflict.* NovTSup 109. Leiden: Brill, 2003.
Burtchaell, J. T. *From Synagogue to Church: Public Services and Offices in the Earliest Christian Communities.* Cambridge: Cambridge University Press, 1992.
Bynum, C. W. *The Resurrection of the Body in Western Christianity, 200–1336.* ACLSLHR 15. New York: Columbia University Press, 1995.
Byrne, B. "Christ's Pre-Existence in Pauline Soteriology." *TS* 58 (1997) 308–30.
———. "Eschatologies of Resurrection and Destruction: The Ethical Significance of Paul's Dispute with the Corinthians." *DRev* 104 (1986) 288–98.
———. *Romans.* SacPag 6. Collegeville, MN: Liturgical (Glazier), 1996.
———. "Sinning against One's Own Body: Paul's Understanding of the Sexual Relationship in 1 Corinthians 6:18." *CBQ* 45 (1983) 608–16.
Caird, G. B. *The Language and Imagery of the Bible.* London: Duckworth, 1980.
———. "Everything to Everyone: The Theology of the Corinthian Epistles." *Int* 13 (1959) 387–99.
Calame, C. *The Craft of Poetic Speech in Ancient Greece.* Trans. J. Orion. Ithica, NY and London: Cornell University Press, 1995.
Callan, T. "Prophecy and Ecstasy in Greco-Roman Religion and in 1 Corinthians." *NovT* 27 (1985) 125–40.
Cambier, J. "La chair et l'esprit en I Cor. V. 5." *NTS* 15 (1968–69) 221–32.
Campbell, A. "Dying and Rising with Christ: The Origin of a Metaphor?" In *Baptism, the New Testament, and the Church*, ed. Porter and Cross, 273–93.
Campbell, D. A. "An Anchor for Pauline Chronology: Paul's Flight from 'the Ethnarch of King Aretas' (2 Corinthians 11:32–33)." *JBL* 121 (2002) 279–302.
Campbell, R. A. *The Elders: Seniority within Earliest Christianity.* SNTW. Edinburgh: T&T Clark, 1994.
Carlson, R. P. "The Role of Baptism in Paul's Thought." *Int* 47 (1993) 255–66.
Carmignac, J. "Les dangers de l'eschatologie." *NTS* 17 (1970–71) 365–90.
Carr, A. "Baptism for the Dead (1 Corinthians XV. 19 [sic])." *Expositor* 9 (1901) 371–78.
Carrez, M. "With What Body Do the Dead Rise Again?" Trans. R. Ockenden. In *Immortality and Resurrection*, ed. Benoît and Murphy, 92–102.
Carter, T. L. "'Big Men' in Corinth." *JSNT* 66 (1997) 45–71.
———. *Paul and the Power of Sin: Redefining "Beyond the Pale."* SNTSMS 115. Cambridge: Cambridge University Press, 2002.
Cheung, A. T. *Idol Food in Corinth: Jewish Background and Pauline Legacy.* JSNTSup 176. Sheffield: Sheffield Academic Press, 1999.
Chevallier, M.-A. "L'apologie du baptême d'eau à la fin du premier siècle: Introduction secondaire de l'étiologie dans les récits du baptême de Jésus." *NTS* 32 (1986) 582–43.
Chow, J. K. *Patronage and Power: A Study of Social Networks in Corinth.* JSNTSup 75. Sheffield: JSOT Press, 1992.
Church, F. F. "Rhetorical Structure and Design in Paul's Letter to Philemon." *HTR* 71 (1978) 17–33.
Cipriani, S. "La communità di Corinto come 'stimolo' alla riflessione teologica di S. Paolo." *Lateranum* 50 (1984) 86–100.

———. "La risurrezione di Cristo e la nostra risurrezione nella prospettiva di *1 Cor* 15." *Asprenas* 23 (1976) 112–35.
Clarke, M. L. (with D. H. Berry) *Rhetoric at Rome: A Historical Survey*. 3rd ed. London and New York: Routledge, 1996.
Classen, C. J. "St. Paul's Epistles and Ancient Greek and Roman Rhetoric." In *Rhetoric and the New Testament*, ed. Porter and Olbricht, 265–91.
———. "Paulus und die antike Rhetorik." *ZNW* 82 (1991) 1–33.
Clauss, M. *The Roman Cult of Mithras: The God and His Mysteries*. Trans. R. Gordon. London and New York: Routledge, 2000.
Clinton, K. "The Eleusinian Mysteries: Roman Initiates and Benefactors, Second Century B.C. to B.C. 267." *ANRW* 2/18.2:1499–1539.
Cohen, S. J. D. *From the Maccabees to the Mishnah*. LEC 7. Philadelphia: Westminster, 1987.
Cohn-Sherbok, D. M. "Jesus' Defense of the Resurrection of the Dead." *JSNT* 11 (1981) 64–73.
Colijn, B. B. "Paul's Use of the 'in Christ' Formula." *ATJ* 23 (1991) 9–26.
Collins, J. J. "Chiasmus, the 'ABA' Pattern and the Text of Paul." In *Studiorum Paulinorum Congressus Internationalis Catholicus 1961*. AnBib 17–18. Rome: Pontificium Institutum Biblicum, 1963. 2:575–83.
———. "Natural Theology and Biblical Tradition: The Case of Hellenistic Judaism." *CBQ* 60 (1998) 1–15.
———. *Jewish Wisdom in the Hellenistic Age*. Edinburgh: T&T Clark, 1997.
Collins, R. F. *First Corinthians*. SacPag 7. Collegeville, MN: Liturgical (Glazier), 1999.
———. *Letters That Paul Did Not Write: The Epistle to the Hebrews and the Pauline Pseudepigrapha*. GNS 28. Wilmington, DE: Glazier, 1988.
———. "Reflections on 1 Corinthians as a Hellenistic Letter." In *The Corinthian Correspondence*, ed. Bieringer, 39–61.
———. "The Unity of Paul's Paraenesis in 1 Thess. 4.3–8 and 1 Cor. 7.1–7: A Significant Parallel." *NTS* 29 (1983) 420–29.
Conant, T. J. *The Meaning and Use of "Baptizein": Philologically and Historically Investigated for the American Bible Union*. New York: American Bible Union, 1868.
Conzelmann, H. *1 Corinthians: A Commentary on the First Epistle to the Corinthians*. Trans. J. W. Leitch. Hermeneia. Philadelphia: Fortress, 1975.
Corley, B. "Interpreting Paul's Conversion—Then and Now." In *The Road from Damascus*, ed. Longenecker, 1–17.
Corsani, B. "'Εκ Πίστεως in the Letters of Paul." In *The New Testament Age: Essays in Honor of Bo Reicke*. Ed. W. C. Weinrich. 2 vols. Macon, GA: Mercer University Press, 1984. 1:87–93.
Cotter, W. *Miracles in Greco-Roman Antiquity: A Sourcebook*. London and New York: Routledge, 1999.
Cousar, C. B. *The Letters of Paul*. IBT. Nashville: Abingdon, 1996.
Craddock, F. B. "Preaching to Corinthians." *Int* 44 (1990) 158–68.
Craffert, P. F. Review of B. Witherington III, *Paul's Narrative Thought World: The Tapestry of Tragedy and Triumph*. *CBQ* 58 (1996) 176–77.
Craig, W. L. "The Historicity of the Empty Tomb of Jesus." *NTS* 31 (1985) 39–67.
Crook, Z. A. "Paul's Riposte and Praise of the Thessalonians." *BTB* 27 (1997) 153–63.

Cross, A. R. "Spirit- and Water-Baptism in 1 Corinthians 12.13." In *Dimensions of Baptism*, ed. Porter and Cross, 120–48.

———. "'One Baptism' (Ephesians 4.5): A Challenge to the Church." In *Baptism, the New Testament, and the Church*, ed. Porter and Cross, 173–209.

Cuming, C. J. "Επoτίσθημεν" (I Corinthians 12. 13)." *NTS* 27 (1980–81) 283–85.

Cummings, O. F. "Is Mormon Baptism Valid?" *Worship* 71 (1997) 146–53.

Cummings, S. A. *Paul and the Crucified Christ in Antioch: Maccabean Martyrdom and Galatians 1 and 2.* SNTSMS 114. Cambridge: Cambridge University Press, 2001.

Dahl, M. E. *The Resurrection of the Body: A Study of I Corinthians 15.* SBT 36. Naperville, IL: Allenson, 1962.

Dahl, N. A. "Letter." In *IDBSup*, 538–41.

———."Paul and the Church at Corinth according to 1 Corinthians 1:10–4:21." In *Christian History and Interpretation*, ed. Farmer, Moule, and Niebuhr, 313–35.

Daniel-Rops, H. *Daily Life in Palestine at the Time of Christ.* Trans. P. O'Brian. London: Phoenix, 1962.

Das, A. A. *Paul, the Law, and the Covenant.* Peabody, MA: Hendrickson, 2001.

Davies, D. J. *Death, Ritual and Belief: The Rhetoric of Funerary Rites.* London and Washington, D.C.: Cassell, 1997.

Davies, J. *Death, Burial, and Rebirth in the Religions of Antiquity.* RFCC. London and New York: Routledge, 1999.

Davies, W. D. "Paul and the People of Israel." *NTS* 24 (1977–78) 4–39.

———. *Paul and Rabbinic Judaism: Some Rabbinic Elements in Paul's Theology.* London: SPCK, 1948.

———. *Paul and Rabbinic Judaism: Some Rabbinic Elements in Pauline Theology.* Rev. ed. New York: Harper and Row, 1955.

———. "Reflections on the Mormon 'Canon.'" *HTR* 79 (1986) 44–66.

———. Review of H. D. Betz, *Galatians: A Commentary on Paul's Letters to the Churches in Galatia. RelSRev* 7 (1981) 310–18.

Davis, C. A. *The Structure of Paul's Theology: "The Truth Which Is the Gospel."* Lewiston, NY: Mellen, 1995.

Davis, S. T. "'Seeing' the Risen Jesus." In *The Resurrection*, ed. Davis, Kendall, and O'Collins, 126–47.

Davis, S. T., D. Kendall, and G. O'Collins, eds. *The Resurrection: An Interdisciplinary Symposium on the Resurrection of Jesus.* Oxford: Oxford University Press, 1998.

Dawes, G. W. "But If You Can Gain Your Freedom (1 Corinthians 7:17–24)." *CBQ* 52 (1990) 681–97.

———. "The Danger of Idolatry: First Corinthians 8:7–13." *CBQ* 58 (1996) 82–98.

Deer, D. S. "Whose Pride/Rejoicing/Glory(ing) in I Corinthians 15.31?" *BT* 38 (1987) 126–28.

Deines, R. *Die Pharisäer: Ihr Verständnis im Spiegel der christlichen und jüdischen Forschung seit Wellhausen und Graetz.* WUNT 101. Tübingen: Mohr (Siebeck), 1997.

Deissmann, A. *Light from the Ancient Near East: The New Testament Illustrated by Recently Discovered Texts of the Graeco-Roman World.* Trans. L. R. M. Strachan. 2nd ed. London: Hodder and Stoughton, 1927.

———. *Paul: A Study in Social and Religious History*. Trans. W. E. Wilson. 2nd ed.; 1927; rpt. New York: Harper, 1957.
Delobel, J. "Coherence and Relevance of 1 Cor 8–10." In *The Corinthian Correspondence*, ed. Bieringer, 177–90.
———. "1 Cor 11,2–16: Towards a Coherent Interpretation." In *L'apôtre Paul*, ed. Vanhoye, 369–89.
De Lorenzi, L., ed. *Résurrection du Christ et des chrétiens (1Co 15)*. SMB 8. Rome: Abbaye de S. Paul h.l.m., 1985.
DeMaris, R. E. "Corinthian Religion and Baptism for the Dead (1 Corinthians 15:29): Insights from Archeology and Anthropology." *JBL* 114 (1995) 661–82.
———. "Demeter in Roman Corinth: Local Development in a Mediterranean Religion." *Numen* 42 (1995) 105–17.
———. "Funerals and Baptisms, Ordinary and Otherwise: Ritual Criticism and Corinthian Rites." *BTB* 29 (1999) 23–34.
Deming, W. "A Diatribe Pattern in 1 Cor. 7:21–22: A New Perspective on Paul's Directions to Slaves." *NovT* 37 (1995) 130–37.
———. *Paul on Marriage and Celibacy: The Hellenistic Background of 1 Corinthians 7*. SNTSMS 83. Cambridge: Cambridge University Press, 1995.
———. "The Unity of 1 Corinthians 5–6." *JBL* 115 (1996) 289–312.
Derrett, J. D. M. "Judgment and 1 Corinthians 6." *NTS* 37 (1991) 22–36.
deSilva, D. A. "'Let the One Who Claims Honor Establish That Claim in the Lord': Honor Discourse in the Corinthian Correspondence." *BTB* 28 (1998) 61–74.
Dewey, J. "Textuality in an Oral Culture: A Survey of the Pauline Traditions." *Semeia* 65 (1994) 37–65.
Dicharry, W. *Human Authors of the New Testament, Volume 2: Paul and John*. Maynooth, Ire.: St. Paul Publications, 1992.
Dickie, M. W. *Magic and Magicians in the Greco-Roman World*. London and New York: Routledge, 2001.
Di Marco, A.-S. "Rhetoric and Hermeneutic—on a Rhetorical Pattern: Chiasmus and Circularity." In *Rhetoric and the New Testament*, ed. Porter and Olbricht, 479–91.
Dion, P. E. "The Aramaic 'Family Letter' and Related Epistolary Forms in Other Oriental Languages and in Hellenistic Greek." *Semeia* 22 (1981) 59–88.
———. "Letters (Aramaic)." *ABD* 4:285–90.
Dodd, B. J. "Paul's Paradigmatic 'I' and 1 Corinthians 6.12." *JSNT* 59 (1995) 39–58.
Dodd, C. H. "The Mind of Paul: Change and Development." *BJRL* 18 (1934) 69–110.
Donaldson, T. L. *Paul and the Gentiles: Remapping the Apostle's Convictional World*. Minneapolis: Fortress, 1997.
Donfried, K. P., ed. *The Romans Debate*. Rev. ed. Peabody, MA: Hendrickson, 1991.
Doohan, H. *The Corinthian Correspondence: Ministering in the Best and Worst of Times*. SWE. San Jose, CA: Resource Publications, 1996.
Doty, W. G. "The Classification of Epistolary Literature." *CBQ* 31 (1969) 183–99.
———. *Letters in Primitive Christianity*. GBS. Philadelphia: Fortress, 1973.
Doughty, D. J. "The Presence and Future of Salvation in Corinth." *ZNW* 66 (1975) 61–90.
Downey, J. "Der Christus der jüdischen Christen: Ein pluralistisches Modell für afrikanische Theologie." *ZM* 1 (1975) 197–214.
———. "1 Cor 15:29 and the Theology of Baptism." *ED* 38 (1985) 23–35.

Duggan, M. W. "The Spirit in the Body in First Corinthians." *TBT* 18 (1980) 388–93.
Dulles, A. *The Assurance of Things Hoped For: A Theology of Christian Faith*. Oxford: Oxford University Press, 1994.
Duncan, T. S. "The Style and Language of Saint Paul in His First Letter to the Corinthians." *BSac* 83 (1926) 129–43.
Dunn, J. D. G. *1 Corinthians*. NTG. Sheffield: Sheffield Academic Press, 1995.
———. "Paul: Apostate or Apostle of Israel? *ZNW* 89 (1998) 256–71.
———. "Prolegomena to a Theology of Paul." *NTS* 40 (1994) 407–32.
———. "The Relationship between Paul and Jerusalem according to Galatians 1 and 2." *NTS* 28 (1982) 461–78.
———. *Romans 1–8*. WBC 38A. Dallas: Word Books, 1988.
———. *Romans 9–16*. WBC 38B. Dallas: Word Books, 1988.
———. *The Theology of Paul the Apostle*. Edinburgh: T&T Clark, 1998.
———. *Unity and Diversity in the New Testament: An Inquiry into the Character of Earliest Christianity*. 2nd ed. Harrisburg, PA: Trinity Press International, 1990.
Dürselen, P. "'Die Taufe für die Toten': I Kor. 15,29." *TSK* [no vol.] (1903) 291–308.
Edersheim, A. *Sketches of Jewish Social Life*. Rev. ed. Peabody, MA: Hendrickson, 1994.
Ehrman, B. D. *The New Testament: A Historical Introduction to the Early Christian Writings*. Oxford: Oxford University Press, 1997.
———. *The Orthodox Corruption of Scripture: The Effect of Early Christological Controversies on the Text of the New Testament*. Oxford: Oxford University Press, 1993.
Elliott, J. H. "A Catholic Gospel: Reflections on 'Early Catholicism' in the New Testament." *CBQ* 31 (1969) 213–23.
———. "The Jewish Messianic Movement: From Faction to Sect." In *Modelling Early Christianity*, ed. Esler, 75–95.
Elliott, J. K., ed. *The Apocryphal Jesus: Legends of the Early Church*. Oxford: Oxford University Press, 1996.
Elliott, N. *Liberating Paul: The Justice of God and the Politics of the Apostle*. Sheffield: Sheffield Academic Press, 1995.
Ellis, E. E. "Paul and His Co-Workers." *NTS* 17 (1970–71) 437–52.
———. *Paul's Use of the Old Testament*. Edinburgh: Oliver and Boyd, 1957.
———. *Pauline Theology: Ministry and Society*. Grand Rapids, MI: Eerdmans, 1989.
———. "*Sōma* in First Corinthians." *Int* 44 (1990) 132–34.
———. "Traditions in 1 Corinthians." *NTS* 32 (1986) 481–502.
Ellis, P. F. *Seven Pauline Letters*. Collegeville, MN: Liturgical, 1982.
Engberg-Pederson, T. "1 Corinthians 11:16 and the Character of Pauline Exhortation." *JBL* 110 (1991) 679–89.
———."The Gospel and Social Practice according to 1 Corinthians." *NTS* 33 (1987) 577–84.
———. "Introduction." In *Paul in His Hellenistic Context*, ed. Engberg-Pedersen, xv–xxvi.
———. *Paul and the Stoics*. Louisville: Westminster John Knox, 2000.
———, ed. *Paul beyond the Judaism/Hellenistic Divide*. Louisville: Westminster John Knox, 2001.
———, ed. *Paul in His Hellenistic Context*. SNTW. Edinburgh: T&T Clark, 1994.

Engels, D. *Roman Corinth: An Alternative Model for the Classical City*. Chicago and London: University of Chicago Press, 1990.
Enslin, M. "Once More, Luke and Paul." *ZNW* 61 (1970) 253–71.
Eriksson, A. *Traditions as Rhetorical Proofs: Pauline Argumentation in 1 Corinthians*. CBNTS 29. Stockholm: Almqvist and Wiksell, 1998.
Esler, P. F. *The First Christians in Their Social Worlds: Social-Scientific Approaches to New Testament Interpretation*. London and New York: Routledge, 1994.
———. Review of D. G. Horrell, *The Social Ethos of the Corinthian Correspondence: Interests and Ideology from 1 Corinthians to 1 Clement*. *JTS* 49 (1998) 253–60.
———, ed. *Modelling Early Christianity: Social-Scientific Studies of the New Testament in Its Context*. London and New York: Routledge, 1995.
Evans, C. A. *Noncanonical Writings and New Testament Interpretation*. Peabody, MA: Hendrickson, 1992.
———. "Source, Form and Redaction Criticism: The 'Traditional' Methods of Synoptic Interpretation." In *Approaches to New Testament Study*, ed. Porter and Tombs, 17–45.
Evans, E. *The Epistles of Paul the Apostle to the Corinthians*. CB. Oxford: Clarendon, 1930.
Fairweather, J. "The Epistle to the Galatians and Classical Rhetoric." *TynBul* 45 (1994) 1–38, 213–44.
Fape, M. O. *Paul's Concept of Baptism and Its Present Implications for Believers: Walking in the Newness of Life*. TST 78. Lewiston, NY: Mellen, 1999.
Farmer, W. R., C. F. D. Moule, and R. R. Niebuhr, eds. *Christian History and Interpretation: Studies Presented to John Knox*. Cambridge: Cambridge University Press, 1967.
Fatum, L. "Brotherhood in Christ: A Gender Hermeneutical Reading of 1 Thessalonians." In *Constructing Early Christian Families*, ed. Moxnes, 183–97.
Faw, C. E. "Death and Resurrection in Paul's Letters." *JBR* 27 (1959) 291–98.
Fee, G. D. "Bibliographies: 1 Corinthians." In *Pauline Theology, Volume II: 1 and Corithians*, ed. Hay, 255–70.
———. "Χάρις in II Corinthians I.15: Apostolic Parousia and Paul—Corinth Chronology." *NTS* 24 (1977–78) 533–38.
———. Εἰδωλόθυτα Once Again: An Interpretation of 1 Corinthians 8–10." *Bib* 61 (1980) 172–97.
———. *The First Epistle to the Corinthians*. NICNT. Grand Rapids, MI: Eerdmans, 1987.
———. *Gospel and Spirit: Issues in New Testament Hermeneutics*. Peabody, MA: Hendrickson, 1991.
———. "Toward a Theology of 1 Corinthians." In *Pauline Theology, Volume II: 1 and 2 Corinthians*, ed. Hay, 37–58.
Feeney, D. *Literature and Religion at Rome: Cultures, Contexts, and Beliefs*. RLC. Cambridge: Cambridge University Press, 1998.
Felman, L. H., and M. Reinhold, eds. *Jewish Life and Thought among the Greeks and Romans: Primary Readings*. Edinburgh: T&T Clark, 1996.
Ferguson, E. "Inscriptions and the Origin of Infant Baptism." *JTS* 30 (1979) 37–46.
Ferguson, J. *The Religions of the Roman Empire*. AGRL. Ithaca, NY: Cornell University Press, 1970.

Feuillet, A. "La coupe et le baptême de la Passion (*Mc* X,35–40; cf. *Mt* XX,20–33; *Lc* XII,50)." *RB* 74 (1967) 356–91.
Findlay, G. G. *St. Paul's First Epistle to the Corinthians*. EGT. London: Hodder and Stoughton, 1900.
Finn, T. M. *From Death to Rebirth: Ritual and Conversion in Antiquity*. New York/Mahwah, NJ: Paulist, 1997.
———. "The God-Fearers Reconsidered." *CBQ* 47 (1985) 75–84.
Fiore, B. "'Covert Allusion' in 1 Corinthians 1–4." *CBQ* 47 (1985) 85–102.
———. Review of E. R. Richards, *The Secretary in the Letters of Paul*. *CBQ* 55 (1993) 391–92.
———. Review of D. Litfin, *St. Paul's Theology of Proclamation: 1 Corinthians 1–4 and Greco-Roman Rhetoric*. *CBQ* 58 (1996) 160–62.
Fish, S. E. *Is There a Text in This Class? The Authority of Interpretive Communities*. Cambridge, MA: Harvard University Press, 1980.
Fitzgerald, J. T. *Cracks in an Earthen Vessel: An Examination of the Catalogue of Hardships in the Corinthian Correspondence*. SBLDS 99. Atlanta: Scholars Press, 1988.
Fitzmyer, J. A. *According to Paul: Studies in the Theology of the Apostle*. New York/Mahwah, NJ: Paulist, 1993.
———. "Aramaic Epistolography." *Semeia* 22 (1981) 25–57.
———. "Paul." *NJBC* §79, 1329–37.
———. "Pauline Theology." *NJBC* §82, 1383–416.
———. *Romans*. AB 33. New York: Doubleday, 1993.
Flanagan, N. *Friend Paul: Letters, Theology, Humanity*. London: G. Chapman, 1986.
Focant, C. "1 Corinthiens 13: Anyalyse rhétorique et analyse de structures." In *The Corinthian Correspondence*, ed. Bieringer, 199–245.
Foerster, W., and J. Herrmann. "κλῆρος, κληρόω, προσκληρόω, ὁλόκληρος, ὁλοκληρία, κληρονόμος, συγκληρονόμος, κληρονομέω, κατακληρονομέω, κληρρονομία." *TDNT* 3:758–85.
Foerster, W., and G. von Rad. "εἰρήνη, εἰηνεύω, εἰρηνικός, εἰρηνοποιός, εἰηνοποίεω." *TDNT* 2:400–420.
Forbes, C. "Comparison, Self-Praise and Irony: Paul's Boasting and the Conventions of Hellenistic Rhetoric." *NTS* 32 (1986) 1–30.
———. "Paul's Principalities and Powers: Demythologizing Apocalyptic?" *JSNT* 82 (2001) 61–88.
———. Pauline Demonology and/or Cosmology? Principalities, Powers and the Elements of the World in their Hellenistic Context." *JSNT* 85 (2002) 51–73.
Fortna, R. T., and B. R. Gaventa, eds. *The Conversation Continues: Studies in Paul and John in Honor of J. Louis Martyn*. Nashville: Abingdon, 1990.
Foschini, B. M. "'Those Who Are Baptized for the Dead' I Cor. 15:29: An Exegetical Historical Dissertation." S.T.D. diss., Pontificium Anthenaeum Antonianum, 1948.
———. "'Those Who Are Baptized for the Dead' I Cor. 15:29: An Exegetical Historical Dissertation." *CBQ* 12 (1950) 260–76, 379–88; 13 (1951) 46–78, 172–98, 276–83.
———. *"Those Who Are Baptized for the Dead" I Cor. 15:29: An Exegetical Historical Dissertation*. Worcester, MA: Heffernan, 1951.
Fowler, R. M. Review of G. A. Kennedy, *New Testament Interpretation through Rhetorical Criticism*. *JBL* 105 (1986) 328–30.

Freed, E. D. *The Apostle Paul, Christian Jew: Faithfulness and Law.* New York: University of America Press, 1994.
Freke, T., and P. Gandy. *The Jesus Mysteries: Was the "Original Jesus" a Pagan God?* New York: Harmony, 1999.
Friedrich, G. "σάλπιγξ." *TDNT* 7:71–88.
Furgusson, D. "Interpreting the Resurrection." *SJT* 38 (1985) 287–305.
Furnish, V. P. "Belonging to Christ: A Paradigm for Ethics in 1 Corinthians." *Int* 44 (1990) 145–57.
———. "Corinth in Paul's Time: What Can Archeology Tell Us?" *BAR* 15 (May/June 1988) 15–27.
———."Fellow Workers in God's Service." *JBL* 80 (1961) 364–70.
———. "Theology in 1 Corinthians." In *Pauline Theology, Volume II: 1 and 2 Corinthians*, ed. Hay, 59–89.
———. *The Theology of the First Letter to the Corinthians.* NTT. Cambridge: Cambridge University Press, 1999.
Gager, J. G. *Reinventing Paul.* Oxford: Oxford University Press, 2000.
———. "Some Notes on Paul's Conversion." *NTS* 27 (1980–81) 697–704.
Galot, J. Review of L. De Lorenzi, ed., *Résurrection du Christ et des Chrétiens (1 Co 15). Greg* 68 (1987) 395–96.
Galinsky, K. *Augustan Culture: An Interpretive Introduction.* Princeton, NJ: Princeton University Press, 1996.
Galvin, J. P. "'I Believe . . . in Jesus Christ, His Only Son, Our Lord': The Earthly Jesus and the Christ of Faith." *Int* 50 (1996) 373–82.
Gamble, H. Y. *Books and Readers in the Early Church: A History of Early Christian Texts.* New Haven and London: Yale University Press, 1995.
———. "The Redaction of the Pauline Letters and the Formation of the Pauline Corpus." *JBL* 94 (1975) 403–18.
———. *The Textual History of the Letter to the Romans: A Study in Textual and Literary Criticism.* SD 42; Grand Rapids, MI: Eerdmans, 1977.
Gärtner, B. E. "The Pauline and Johannine Idea of 'To Know God' against the Hellenistic Background: The Greek Philosophical Principle 'Like by Like' in Paul and John." *NTS* 14 (1967–68) 209–31.
Gasque, W. W. "Tarsus." *ABD* 6:333–34.
Gaventa, B. R. Review of M. C. de Boer, *The Defeat of Death: Apocalyptic Eschatology in 1 Corinthians 15 and Romans 5. CBQ* 52 (1990) 741–42.
Gebhard, E. R. "The Early Sanctuary of Poseidon at Isthmia." *AJA* 91 (1987) 475–76.
Genest, O. "L'interprétation de la mort de Jésus en situation discursive. Un cas-type: L'articulation des figures de cette mort en 1–2 Corinthiens." *NTS* 34 (1988) 506–35.
Georgi, D. *The Opponents of Paul in Second Corinthians.* Ed. J. Riches. SNTW. Edinburgh: T&T Clark, 1987.
———. *Theocracy in Paul's Praxis and Theology.* Trans. D. E. Green. Minneapolis: Fortress, 1991.
Giardino, T. F. Review of R. P. Martin, *The Spirit and the Congregation: Studies in 1 Corinthians 12–15. SpT* 37 (1985) 367–68.
Gilhus, I. S. "Family Structures in Gnostic Religion." In *Constructing Early Christian Families*, ed. Moxnes, 235–49.
Gill, D. W. J. "Corinth: A Roman Colony in Achaea." *BZ* 37 (1993) 259–64.

Gillespie, T. W. *The First Theologians: A Study in Early Christian Prophecy*. Grand Rapids, MI: Eerdmans, 1994.

———. "A Pattern of Prophetic Speech in 1 Corinthians." *JBL* 97 (1978) 74–95.

Gillman, J. "A Thematic Comparison: 1 Cor 15:50–57 and 2 Cor 5:1–5." *JBL* 107 (1988) 439–54.

———. "Transformation in 1 Cor 15,50–53." *ETL* 58 (1982) 309–33.

Glancy, J. A. "Obstacles to Slaves' Participation in the Corinthian Church." *JBL* 117 (1998) 481–501.

Godet, F. *Commentary on St. Paul's First Epistle to the Corinthians*. Trans. A. Cusin. 2 vols. CFTL 30. Edinburgh: T&T Clark, 1898.

Goldenberg, R. *Nations That Know Thee Not: Ancient Jewish Attitudes towards Other Religions*. BSem 52. Sheffield: Sheffield Academic Press, 1997.

Goodman, M., with J. Sherwood. *The Roman World: 44 BC–AD 180*. RHAW. London and New York: Routledge, 1997.

Goudge, H. L. *The First Epistle to the Corinthians with Introduction and Notes*. WC. London: Methuen, 1903.

Goulder, M. D. *Paul and the Competing Mission in Corinth*. LPS. Peabody, MA: Hendrickson, 2001.

Grabbe, L. L. *An Introduction to First Century Judaism: Jewish Religion and History in the Second Temple Period*. Edinburgh: T&T Clark, 1996.

Graf, D. F. "Aretas," *ABD* 1:373–76.

Graf, F. *Magic in the Ancient World*. Trans. F. Philip. Cambridge, MA: Harvard University Press, 1997.

Grant, R. M. "Literary Criticism and the New Testament Canon." *JSNT* 16 (1982) 24–44.

———. *Paul in the Roman World: The Conflict at Corinth*. Louisville: Westminster John Knox, 2001.

Green, H. A. *The Economic and Social Origins of Gnosticism*. SBLDS 77. Atlanta: Scholars Press, 1985.

Green, J. B. "Death of Christ." In *Dictionary of Paul and His Letters*, ed. Hawthorne, Martin, and Reid, 201–9.

Green, P. *Alexander to Actium: The Historical Evolution of the Hellenistic Age*. HCS 1. Berkeley: University of California Press, 1990.

———. *Classical Bearings: Interpreting Ancient History and Culture*. Berkeley: University of California Press, 1989.

Grosheide, F. W. *Commentary on the First Epistle to the Corinthians*. NICNT. Grand Rapids, MI: Eerdmans, 1953.

Gruen, E. S. *Diaspora: Jews amidst Greeks and Romans*. Cambridge, MA: Harvard University Press, 2002.

———. *The Hellenistic World and the Coming of Rome*. 1984; rpt. 2 vols. in 1. University of California Press, 1986.

Grundmann, W. "δύναμαι, δυνατός, δυνατέω, ἀδύνατος, ἀδινατέω, δύναμις, δυνάστης, δυναμόω, ἐνδυναμόω." *TDNT* 2:284–317.

———. "χρίω." *TDNT* 9:527–80.

Guerra, A. J. *Romans and Apologetic Tradition: The Purpose, Genre, and Audience of Paul's Letter*. SNTSMS 81. Cambridge: Cambridge University Press, 1995.

Gundry, R. H. "The Hellenization of Dominical Tradition and Christianization of Jewish Tradition in the Eschatology of 1–2 Thessalonians." *NTS* 33 (1987) 161–78.
Guyot, G. H. "The Chronology of St. Paul." *CBQ* 6 (1944) 28–36.
Hafemann, S. "'Self-Commendation' and Apostolic Legitimacy in 2 Corinthians: A Pauline Dialectic?" *NTS* 36 (1990) 66–88.
———. *Suffering and Ministry in the Spirit: Paul's Defense of His Ministry in II Corinthians 2:14–3:3*. Grand Rapids, MI: Eerdmans, 1987.
Hagner, D. A. *The Use of the Old and New Testaments in Clement of Rome*. NovTSup 34. Leiden: Brill, 1973.
Hallote, R. S. *Death, Burial, and Afterlife in the Biblical World: How the Israelites and Their Neighbors Treated the Dead*. Chicago: Dee, 2001.
Hanhart, K. "Paul's Hope in the Face of Death." *JBL* 88 (1969) 445–57.
Hansen, G. W. "Resurrection and the Christian Life in Paul's Letters." In *Life in the Face of Death*, ed. Longenecker, 203–24.
Hanson, A. T. *Studies in Paul's Technique and Theology*. London: SPCK, 1974.
Harder, G. "φθείρω, φθορά, φθαρτός, ἄφθαρτος, ἀφθαρσία, αφθορία, διαφθείρω, διαφθορά, καταφθείρω." *TDNT* 9:93–106.
Harland, P. A. "Honouring the Emperor or Assailing the Beast: Participation in Civic Life among Associations (Jewish, Christian and Other) in Asia Minor and the Apocalypse of John." *JSNT* 77 (2000) 99–121.
Harnack, A. von. *Marcion: Das Evangelium von fremden Gott*. 2nd ed. Leipzig: Henrichs, 1924.
Harrer, G. A. "Saul Who Also Is Called Paul." *HTR* 33 (1940) 19–33.
Harrill, J. A. "Coming of Age and Putting on Christ: The *Toga Virilis* Ceremony, Its Paraenesis, and Paul's Interpretation of Baptism in Galatians." *NovT* 44 (2002) 252–77.
Harris, H. *The Tübingen School: A Historical and Theological Investigation of F. C. Baur*. Grand Rapids, MI: Baker, 1990.
Harris, M. J. "Resurrection and Immortality in the Pauline Corpus." In *Life in the Face of Death*, ed. Longenecker, 147–70.
Harris, G. "The Beginnings of Church Discipline: 1 Corinthians 5." *NTS* 37 (1991) 1–21.
Harrisville, R. A. *I Corinthians*. ACNT. Minneapolis: Augsburg, 1987.
Hartman, L. "Baptism." *ABD* 1:583–94.
———. *"Into the Name of the Lord Jesus": Baptism in the Early Church*. SNTW. Edinburgh: T&T Clark, 1997.
Hatina, T. R. "Jewish Religious Backgrounds of the New Testament: Pharisees and Sadducees as Case Studies." In *Approaches to New Testament Study*, ed. Porter and Tombs, 46–76.
Hauck, F. "περισσεύω, ὑπερπερισσεύω, περισσός, ὑπερεκπερισσοῦ, ὑπερεκπερισσῶς, περισσεία, περίσσευμα." *TDNT* 6:58–63.
Hawthorne, G. F. "Christian Baptism and the Contribution of Melito of Sardis Reconsidered." In *Studies in the New Testament and Early Christian Literature*, ed. Aune, 241–51.
Hay, D. M., ed. *Pauline Theology, Volume II: 1 and 2 Corinthians*. Minneapolis: Fortress, 1993.
Hays, R. B. *The Moral Vision of the New Testament: A Contemporary Introduction to New Testament Ethics*. Edinburgh: T&T Clark, 1996.

———. "The Conversion of the Imagination: Scripture and Eschatology in 1 Corinthians." *NTS* 45 (1999) 391–412.
Heawood, P. J. "Baptism for the Dead." *ExpTim* 55 (1943–44) 278.
Heil, J. P. "Those Now 'Asleep' (Not Dead) Must Be 'Awakened' for the Day of the Lord in I Thess 5.9–10." *NTS* 46 (2000) 464–71.
Hellholm, D. "Enthymemic Argumentation in Paul: The Case of Romans 6." In *Paul in His Hellenistic Context*, ed. Engberg-Pedersen, 119–79.
Hemer, C. J. *The Book of Acts in the Setting of Hellenistic History*. Ed. C. H. Gempf. WUNT 49. Tübingen: Mohr (Siebeck), 1989.
———. *The Letters to the Seven Churches of Asia in Their Local Setting*. JSNTSup 11. Sheffield: Sheffield Academic Press, 1986.
———. "The Name of Paul." *TynBul* 36 (1985) 179–83.
Hengel, M. *Between Jesus and Paul: Studies in the Earliest History of Christianity*. 1983; rpt. Surrey: XPress Reprints, 1997.
———. "Der vorchristliche Paulus." In *Paulus und das antike Judentum*. Ed. M. Hengel and U. Heckel. WUNT 58. Tübingen: Mohr (Siebeck), 1991. 177–291.
———. *Judaism and Hellenism: Studies in Their Encounter in Palestine during the Hellenistic Period*. Trans. J. Bowden. Vol. 1, Text. Vol. 2, Notes and Bibliography. Philadelphia: Fortress, 1974.
———. *The Pre-Christian Paul*. Trans. J. Bowden. London: SCM, 1991.
Hengel, M., and A. M. Schwemer. *Paul between Damascus and Antioch: The Unknown Years*. Trans. J. Bowden. London: SCM, 1997.
Hensell, E. Review of D. Wenham, *Paul: Follower of Christ or Founder of Christianity?* (Grand Rapids, MI: Eerdmans, 1995). *CBQ* 59 (1997) 180–81.
Henry, W. "Le baptême des morts." *DACL*, vol. 2.1, cols. 380–82.
Héring, J. *The First Epistle of Saint Paul to the Corinthians*. Trans. A. W. Heathcote and P. J. Allcock. London: Epworth, 1962.
Hersey, G. *The Lost Meaning of Classical Architecture*. Cambridge, MA: MIT Press, 1988.
Heyer, C. J. den. *Paul: A Man of Two Worlds*. Trans. J. Bowden. Harrisburg, PA: Trinity Press International, 2000.
Hickling, C. J. A. Review of G. Barbaglio, *La prima lettera ai Corinizi*. *JTS* 48 (1997) 602–4.
Hill, C. E. "Paul's Understanding of Christ's Kingdom in I Corinthians 15:20–28." *NovT* 30 (1988) 297–320.
Hock, R. F. *The Social Context of Paul's Ministry*. Philadelphia: Fortress, 1980.
Hodge, C. *1 Corinthians*. CCC. Wheaton, IL: Good News (Crossway), 1995.
Hollander, H. W., and G. E. van der Hout. "The Apostle Paul Calling Himself an Abortion: 1 Cor 15:8 within the Context of 1 Cor 15:8–10." *NovT* 38 (1996) 224–36.
Hollander, H. W., and J. Holleman, "The Relationship of Death, Sin, and the Law in 1 Cor 15:56." *NovT* 35 (1993) 271–91.
Holleman, J. "Jesus' Resurrection as the Beginning of the Eschatological Resurrection (1 Cor 15,20)." In *The Corinthian Correspondence*, ed. Bieringer, 653–65.
———. *Resurrection and Parousia: A Traditio-Historical Study of Paul's Eschatology in 1 Corinthians 15*. NovTSup 84. Leiden: Brill, 1996.

Hooker, M. D. "Beyond the Things That are Written? St Paul's Use of Scripture." *NTS* 27 (1980–81) 295–309.

———. "'Beyond the Things Which are Written': An Examination of I Cor VI.6." *NTS* 10 (1963–64) 127–32.

Hoppe, L. J. *The Synagogues and Churches of Ancient Palestine*. Collegeville, MN: Liturgical (Glazier), 1994.

Horn, F. W. "1 Korinther 15,56—ein exegetischer Stachel." *ZNW* 82 (1991) 88–105.

Horrell, D. G. "The Development of Theological Ideology in Pauline Christianity: A Structuration Theory Perspective." In *Modelling Early Christianity*, ed. Esler, 224–36.

———. "'The Lord Commanded . . . But I Have Not Used . . .': Exegetical and Hermeneutical Reflections on 1 Cor 9.14–15." *NTS* 43 (1997) 587–603.

———. Review of R. Bieringer, ed. *The Corinthian Correspondence*. *JST* 49 (1998) 248–53.

———. *The Social Ethos of the Corinthian Correspondence: Interests and Ideology from 1 Corinthians to 1 Clement*. SNTW. Edinburgh: T&T Clark, 1996.

———. "Theological Principle or Christological Praxis?: Pauline Ethics in 1 Corinthians 8.1–11.1." *JSNT* 67 (1997) 83–114.

Horsley, R. A. "'How Can Some of You Say That There is No Resurrection of the Dead?' Spiritual Elitism in Corinth." *NovT* 20 (1978) 203–31.

———. "The Law of Nature in Philo and Cicero." *HTR* 71 (1978) 35–59.

———. "*Pneumatikos* vs. *Psychikos*: Distinctions of Spiritual Status among the Corinthians." *HTR* 69 (1976) 269–88.

———. "Popular Prophetic Movements at the Time of Jesus: Their Principal Features and Social Origins." *JSNT* 26 (1986) 3–27.

———. "Wisdom of Word and Words of Wisdom in Corinth." *CBQ* 39 (1977) 224–39.

———, ed. *Paul and Politics: Ekklesia, Israel, Imperium, Interpretation. Essays in Honor of Krister Stendahl*. Harrisburg, PA: Trinity Press International, 2000.

Howard, J. K. "Baptism for the Dead: A Study of 1 Corinthians 15:29." *EvQ* 37 (1965) 137–41.

Hübner, H. "Der Galaterbrief und das Verhältnis von antiker Rhetorik und Epistolographie," *TZ* 109 (1984) 241–50.

Hultgren, A. J. "Paul's Pre-Christian Persecutions of the Church: Their Purpose, Locale, and Nature." *JBL* 95 (1976) 97–111.

Hurd, J. C., Jr. *The Origin of 1 Corinthians*. New York: Seabury, 1965.

Hurtado, L. W. "First-Century Jewish Monotheism." *JSNT* 71 (1998) 3–26.

———. "What Do We Mean by 'First-Century Jewish Monotheism'?" In *SBLSP 1993*. Atlanta: Scholars Press, 1993. 348–67.

Hyldahl, N. "Die Frage nach des literarischen Einheit des Zweiten Korintherbriefes." *ZNW* 64 (1973) 289–306.

"I mormoni chi sono? In che cosa credono?" Editorial. *CivC* 3 (July 16, 1994) 107–20.

Ingraffia, B. D. *Postmodern Theory and Biblical Theology: Vanquishing God's Shadow*. Cambridge: Cambridge University Press, 1995.

Jaffee, M. S. *Torah in the Mouth: Writing and Oral Tradition in Palestinian Judaism 200 BCE–400 CE*. Oxford: Oxford University Press, 2001.

Jansen, J. F. "I Cor. 15.24–28 and the Future of Jesus Christ." *SJT* 40 (1987) 543–70.

Jaquette, J. L. Review of A. R. Brown, *The Cross and Human Transformation: Paul's Apocalyptic Word in 1 Corinthians*. *CBQ* 59 (1997) 150–52.
Jeffers, J. S. *The Greco-Roman World of the New Testament Era: Exploring the Background of Early Christianity*. Downers Grove, IL: InterVarsity, 1999.
Jeremias, J. "Chiasmus in den Paulusbriefen." *ZNW* 49 (1958) 145–56.
———. "Flesh and Blood Cannot Inherit the Kingdom of God." *NTS* 2 (1955–56) 151–59.
———. *Jerusalem in the Time of Jesus: An Investigation into Economic and Social Conditions during the New Testament Period*. Trans. F. H. and C. H. Cave. Philadelphia: Fortress, 1969.
Jewett, R. "The Agitators and the Galatian Congregation." *NTS* 17 (1970–71) 198–212.
———. "The Redaction of I Corinthians and the Trajectory of the Pauline School." *JAARSup* 44 (1978) 389–444.
———. "Romans as an Ambassadorial Letter." *Int* 36 (1982) 5–20.
Johnson, K. "The Pauline Letters from Caesarea." *ExpTim* 68 (1956–57) 24–26.
Johnson, L. T. "The New Testament's Anti-Jewish Slander and the Conventions of Ancient Polemic." *JBL* 108 (1989) 419–41.
———. *Religious Experience in Earliest Christianity: A Missing Dimension in New Testament Studies*. Minneapolis: Fortress, 1998.
Johnson, S. E. *Paul the Apostle and His Cities*. GNS 21. Wilmington, DL: Glazier, 1987.
———. "Unsolved Questions about Early Christianity in Anatolia." In *Studies in the New Testament and Early Christian Literature*, ed. Aune, 181–93.
Johnston, S. I. *Restless Dead: Encounters between the Living and the Dead in Ancient Greece*. Berkeley: University of California Press, 1999.
Joubert, S. J. "Managing the Household: Paul as *Paterfamilias* of the Christian Household Group in Corinth." In *Modelling Early Christianity*, ed. Esler, 213–235.
Joyce, J. D. "Baptism on Behalf of the Dead: An Interpretation of I Corinthians 15:29–34." *Encounter* 26 (1965) 269–77.
Judge, E. A. "The Early Christians as a Scholastic Community." *JRH* 1 (1960–61) 4–15.
———. "The Early Christians as a Scholastic Community: Part II." *JRH* 1 (1960–61) 125–37.
———. "Paul's Boasting in Relation to Contemporary Professional Practice." *AusBR* 16 (1968) 37–50.
Karris, R. J. "The Occasion of Romans: A Response to Professor Donfried" *CBQ* 36 (1974) 356–58.
———. "Rom 14:1–15:13 and the Occasion of Romans," *CBQ* 25 (1973) 155–78.
Kariuki Njiru, P. *Charisms and the Holy Spirit's Activity in the Body of Christ*. TGST 86. Rome: Editrice Pontificia Università Gregoriana, 2002.
Käsemann, E. *Commentary on Romans*. Ed. and trans. G. W. Bromiley. Grand Rapids, MI: Eerdmans, 1980.
———. *Perspectives on Paul*. Trans. M. Kohl. Philadelphia: Fortress, 1971.
Keck, L. E. *Paul and His Letters*. PC. Philadelphia: Fortress, 1979.
Kee, H. C. "Defining the First-Century CE Synagogue: Problems and Progress." *NTS* 41 (1995) 481–500.
Kelly, J. F. *The World of the Early Christians*. MFC 1. Collegeville, MN: Liturgical (Glazier), 1997.

Kennedy, G. A. *Classical Rhetoric and Its Christian and Secular Tradition from Ancient to Modern Times.* Chapel Hill, NC: University of North Carolina Press, 1980.

———. *A New History of Classical Rhetoric: An Extensive Revision and Abridgment of "The Art of Persuasion in Greece," "The Art of Rhetoric in the Roman World," and "Greek Rhetoric under the Christian Emperors" with Additional Discussion of Late Latin Rhetoric.* Princeton, NJ: Princeton University Press, 1994.

———. *New Testament Interpretation through Rhetorical Criticism.* SR. Chapel Hill, NC: University of North Carolina Press, 1984.

Kenny, A. *A Stylometric Study of the New Testament.* Oxford: Clarendon, 1986.

Kent, H. A., Jr. "A Fresh Look at 1 Corinthians 15:34: An Appeal for Evangelism or a Call to Purity?" *GTJ* 4 (1983) 3–14.

Kent, J. H. *Inscriptions 1926–1960: Corinth Results.* Vol. 8, pt. 3. Princeton, NJ: Princeton University Press, 1966.

Kim, C.-H. "The Papyrus Invitation." *JBL* 94 (1975) 391–402.

Kim, S. *The Origin of Paul's Gospel.* 2nd ed. WUNT 2/4. Tübingen: Mohr (Siebeck), 1984.

———. *Paul and the New Perspective: Second Thoughts on the Origin of Paul's Gospel.* Grand Rapids, MI: Eerdmans, 2002.

Kirby, J. T. "The Syntax of Romans 5.12: A Rhetorical Approach." *NTS* 33 (1987) 283–86.

Kistemaker, S. J. *I Corinthians.* NTC. Grand Rapids, MI: Baker, 1993.

Kittredge, C. B. *Community and Authority: The Rhetoric of Obedience in the Pauline Tradition.* HTS 45. Harrisburg, PA: Trinity Press International, 1998.

Klassen, W. "The Sacred Kiss in the New Testament." *NTS* 39 (1993) 122–35.

Klauck, H.-J. *Magic and Paganism in Early Christianity: The World of the Acts of the Apostles.* Trans. B. McNeil. Edinburgh: T&T Clark, 2000.

———. *The Religious Context of Early Christianity: A Guide to Graeco-Roman Religions.* Trans. B. McNeil. SNTW. Edinburgh: T&T Clark, 2000.

Kleinknect, H., and W. Gutbrod. "νόμος, ἀνομία, ἄνομος, ἔννομος, νομικός, νόμιμος, νομοθέτης, νομοθεσία, νομοθετέω, παρανομία, παρανομέω." *TDNT* 4:1022–91.

Kloppenborg, J. S. "Φιλαδελφία, Θεοδίδακτος and the Dioscuri: Rhetorical Engagement in 1 Thessalonians 4.9–12." *NTS* 39 (1993) 265–89.

Knox, J. *Chapters in a Life of Paul.* Rev. ed. London: SCM, 1987.

Koester, H. *Ancient Christian Gospels: Their History and Development.* Harrisburg, PA: Trinity Press International, 1990.

———. "Melikertes at Isthmia: A Roman Mystery Cult." In *Greeks, Romans, and Christians,* ed. Balch, Ferguson, and Meeks, 355–66.

Koskenniemi, H. *Studien zur Idee und Phraseologie des griechischen Briefes bis 400 n. Chr.* AASF 102.2. Helsinki: Suomalaisen Tiedeakatemain, 1956.

Kraabel, A. T. "The Disappearance of the God-Fearers." *Numen* 28 (1981) 113–26.

Kreitzer, L. J. "'Crude Language' and 'Shameful Things Done in Secret' (Ephesians 5.4, 12): Allusions to the Cult of Demeter/Cybele in Hierapolis." *JSNT* 71 (1998) 51–77.

———. "Eschatology." In *Dictionary of Paul and His Letters,* ed. Hawthorne, Martin, and Reid, 253–69.

———. "Resurrection." In *Dictionary of Paul and His Letters,* ed. Hawthorne, Martin, and Reid, 805–12.

Kremer, J. "Paul: The Resurrection of Jesus, the Cause and Exemplar of our Resurrection." Trans. D. Bourke. In *Immortality and Resurrection*, ed. Benoît and Murphy, 78–91.
Kruse, C. G. *Paul, the Law, and Justification*. Peabody, MA: Hendrickson, 1996.
Kuck, D. W. *Judgment and Community Conflict: Paul's Use of Apocalyptic Judgment Language in 1 Corinthians 3:5–4:5*. NovTSup 66. Leiden: Brill, 1992.
Kugel, J. L., and R. A. Greer. *Early Biblical Interpretation*. LEC 3. Philadelphia: Westminster, 1986.
Kurz, W. S. "Hellenistic Rhetoric in the Christological Proof of Luke-Acts." *CBQ* 42 (1980) 171–95.
Lambrecht, J. "Line of Thought in 1 Cor 15,1–11." *Greg* 72 (1991) 655–70.
———. "Paul's Christological Use of Scripture." *NTS* 28 (1982) 502–27.
———. *Pauline Studies*. BETL 125. Leuven: Leuven University Press, 1994.
———. "Structure and Line of Thought in 1 Cor. 15:23–28." *NovT* 32 (1990) 143–51.
Lampe, G. W. H. "Church Discipline and the Interpretation of the Epistles to the Corinthians." In *Christian History and Interpretation*, ed. Farmer, Moule, and Niebuhr, 337–61.
Lampe, P. "Theological Wisdom and the 'Word about the Cross': The Rhetorical Scheme in I Corinthians 1–4." *Int* 44 (1990) 117–31.
Lane, W. L. "Covenant: The Key to Paul's Conflict with Corinth." *TynBul* 33 (1982) 3–29.
Lane Fox, R. J. Review of H. Y. Gamble, *Books and Readers in the Early Church: A History of Early Christian Texts*. *JBL* 116 (1997) 552–53.
Lategan, B. "Textual Space as Rhetorical Device." In *Rhetoric and the New Testament*, ed. Porter and Olbricht, 397–408.
Lanham, R. A. *A Handlist of Rhetorical Terms*. 2nd ed. Berkeley: University of California Press, 1991.
Lassen, E. M. "The Roman Family: Ideal and Metaphor." In *Constructing Early Christian Families*, ed. Moxnes, 103–20.
Ledgerwood, L. W., III. "What Does the Greek First Class Conditional Imply? Gricean Methodology and the Testimony of the Ancient Greek Grammarians." *GTJ* 12 (1991) 99–118.
Légasse, S. Review of J. Murphy-O'Connor, *Paul: A Critical Life*. *Bib* 78 (1997) 586–89.
Levenson, J. D. *The Death and Resurrection of the Beloved Son: The Transformation of Child Sacrifice in Judaism and Christianity*. New Haven and London: Yale University Press, 1993.
Levine, L. I. *Judaism and Hellenism in Antiquity: Conflict or Confluence?* Peabody, MA: Hendrickson, 1998.
———. "The Nature and Origin of the Palestinian Synagogue Reconsidered." *JBL* 115 (1996) 425–48.
———. *The Ancient Synagogue: The First Thousand Years*. New Haven and London: Yale University Press, 2000.
Lewis, S. M. *"So That God May Be All in All": The Apocalyptic Message of 1 Corinthians 15,12–34*. TGST 42. Rome: Editrice Pontificia Università Gregoriana, 1998.
Liebert, D. H. "The 'Apostolic Form of Writing': Group Letters Before and After 1 Corinthians." In *The Corinthian Correspondence*, ed. Bieringer, 433–40.

Lietaert Peerbolte, L. J. *The Antecedents of Christ: A Traditio-Historical Study of the Earliest Christian Views on Eschatological Opponents.* JSJSup 49. Leiden: Brill, 1996.
Lieu, J. M. *Image and Reality: The Jews in the World of the Christians in the Second Century.* Edinburgh: T&T Clark, 1996.
Lightfoot, J. B. *Notes on the Epistles of St. Paul from Unfinished Commentaries.* London and New York: Macmillan, 1895.
Lilly, J. L. "The Appearances of the Risen Christ: Objective or Subjective?" *CBQ* 4 (1942) 22–36.
———. "The Conversion of Saint Paul: The Validity of His Testimony to the Resurrection of Jesus Christ." *CBQ* 6 (1944) 180–204.
Lincoln, A. T. *Paradise Now and Not Yet: Studies in the Role of the Heavenly Dimension in Paul's Thought with Special Reference to His Eschatology.* SNTSMS 43. Cambridge: Cambridge University Press, 1981.
Lindars, B. "Jesus Risen: Bodily Resurrection but No Empty Tomb." *Theology* 89 (1986) 90–96.
———. "The Place of the Old Testament in the Formation of New Testament Theology." *NTS* 23 (1976–77) 59–66.
———. "The Sound of the Trumpet: Paul and Eschatology." *BJRL* 67 (1984–85) 766–82.
Lindemann, A. "Paulus und die Korinthische Eschatologie: Zur These von einer 'Entwicklung' im paulinischen Denken." *NTS* 37 (1991) 373–99.
Litfin, D. Review of M. A. Bullmore, *St. Paul's Theology of Rhetorical Style: An Examination of 1 Corinthians 2:1–5 in the Light of First Century Graeco-Roman Rhetorical Culture.* *JBL* 116 (1997) 568–70.
———. *St. Paul's Theology of Proclamation: 1 Corinthians 1–4 and Greco-Roman Rhetoric.* SNTSMS 79. Cambridge: Cambridge University Press, 1994.
Loader, W. R. G. "Christ at the Right Hand—Ps. CX.1 in the New Testament." *NTS* 24 (1977–78) 199–217.
Logan, A. H. B. *Gnostic Truth and Christian Heresy: A Study in the History of Gnosticism.* Edinburgh: T&T Clark, 1996.
Lohse, E. "St. Peter's Apostleship in the Judgment of St. Paul, Apostle to the Gentiles." *Greg* 72 (1991) 419–35.
———. *The New Testament Environment.* Trans. J. E. Steely. London: SCM, 1976.
Longenecker, R. N. *Biblical Exegesis in the Apostolic Period.* 2nd ed. Grand Rapids, MI: Eerdmans, 1997.
———. *Galatians.* WBC 41. Dallas: Word Books, 1990.
———. "Is There Development in Paul's Resurrection Thought?" In *Life in the Face of Death*, ed. Longenecker, 171–202.
———, ed. *Life in the Face of Death: The Resurrection Message of the New Testament.* MNTS. Grand Rapids, MI: Eerdmans, 1998.
———, ed. *The Road from Damascus: The Impact of Paul's Conversion on His Life, Thought, and Ministry.* MNTS. Grand Rapids, MI: Eerdmans, 1997.
Lubomirski, M. "Per un metodo in esegesi: Gerd Theissen, *Pyschologische Aspekte paulinischer Theologie.*" *Greg* 72 (1991) 419–35.
Luck, G. *Arcana Mundi: Magic and the Occult in the Greek and Roman Worlds.* Baltimore and London: Johns Hopkins University Press, 1985.

Lüdemann, G. *Heretics: The Other Side of Early Christianity*. Trans. J. Bowden. London: SCM, 1996.
———. *Opposition to Paul in Jewish Christianity*. Trans. M. E. Boring. Minneapolis: Fortress, 1989.
———. *What Really Happened to Jesus: A Historical Approach to the Resurrection*. Trans. J. Bowden. Louisville: Westminster John Knox, 1995.
Lührmann, D. "Paul and the Pharisaic Tradition." *JSNT* 36 (1989) 75–94.
Luibhéid, C. *A Scholarly Reconstruction of St. Paul and His Times: The Historical Evidence*. StCl 18. Lewiston, NY: Mellen, 2002.
Lund, N. W. *Chiasmus in the New Testament: A Study in the Form and Function of Chiastic Structures*. 1942; rpt. Peabody, MA: Hendrickson, 1992.
Maccoby, H. *The Mythmaker: Paul and the Invention of Christianity*. New York: Harper and Row, 1986.
———. *Paul and Hellenism*. London: SCM, 1991.
MacDonald, D. R. "A Conjectural Emendation of 1 Cor 15:31–32: Or the Case of the Misplaced Lion Fight." *HTR* 73 (1980) 265–76.
MacDonald, M. Y. *Colossians and Ephesians*. SacPag 17. Collegeville, MN: Liturgical (Glazier), 2000.
———. *The Pauline Churches: A Socio-Historical Study of Institutionalization in the Pauline and Deutero-Pauline Writings*. SNTSMS 60. Cambridge: Cambridge University Press, 1988.
Mack, B. *Rhetoric and the New Testament*. GBSNTS. Minneapolis: Fortress, 1990.
MacMullen, R. *Paganism in the Roman Empire*. New Haven and London: Yale University Press, 1981.
Malherbe, A. J. *Ancient Epistolary Theorists*. SBLSBS 19. Atlanta: Scholars Press, 1988. Also published under the same title in the *JRelS* 5 (1977) 3–77.
———. "The Beasts at Ephesus." *JBL* 87 (1968) 71–80.
———. "Determinism and Free Will in Paul: The Argument of 1 Corinthians 8 and 9." In *Paul in His Hellenistic Context*, ed. Engberg-Pedersen, 231–55.
———. "Did the Thessalonians Write to Paul?" In *The Conversation Continues*, ed. Fortna and Gaventa, 246–57.
———. *Moral Exhortation, A Greco-Roman Sourcebook*. LEC 4. Philadelphia: Westminster, 1986.
Malina, B. J. "Early Christian Groups: Using Small Group Formation Theory to Explain Christian Organizations." In *Modelling Early Christianity*, ed. Esler, 96–113.
———. *The Social World of Jesus and the Gospels*. London and New York: Routledge, 1996.
Malina, B. J., and J. H. Neyrey. *Portraits of Paul: An Archaeology of Ancient Personality*. Louisville: Westminster John Knox, 1996.
Marcus, J. "'Under the Law': The Background of a Pauline Expression." *CBQ* 63 (2001) 72–83.
Marshall, H. "Palestinian and Hellenistic Christianity: Some Critical Comments." *NTS* 19 (1972–73) 271–87.
Marshall, I. H. "A New Understanding of the Present and the Future." In *The Road from Damascus*, ed. Longenecker, 43–61.

Marshall, P. *Enmity in Corinth: Social Conventions in Paul's Relations with the Corinthians.* WUNT 2/23. Tübingen: Mohr (Siebeck), 1987.
Martin, D. B. *The Corinthian Body.* New Haven and London: Yale University Press, 1995.
Martin, H. V. "Baptism for the Dead." *ExpTim* 54 (1942–43) 192–93.
———. "The Messianic Age." *ExpTim* 52 (1940–41) 270–75.
———. "Proleptic Eschatology." *ExpTim* 51 (1939–40) 88–90.
Martin, J. P. "Toward a Post-Critical Paradigm." *NTS* 33 (1987) 370–85.
Martin, L. H. *Hellenistic Religions: An Introduction.* Oxford: Oxford University Press, 1987.
Martin, R. P. *Reconciliation: A Study of Paul's Theology.* NFTL. Atlanta: John Knox, 1981.
———. Review of B. Witherington III, *Conflict and Community in Corinth: A Socio-Rhetorical Commentary on 1 and 2 Corinthians. Bib* 77 (1996) 445–48.
Martin, T. W. "The Covenant of Circumcision (Genesis 17:9–14) and the Situational Antitheses in Galatians 3:28." *JBL* 122 (2003) 111–25.
Martyn, J. L. *Galatians.* AB 33A. New York: Doubleday, 1997.
———. *Theological Issues in the Letters of Paul.* SNTW. Edinburgh: T&T Clark, 1997.
Marx, J. "Théologie de la gloire et matérialisme chrétien." *PHC* 9 (1980) 15–29.
Masalles, V. *La profecia en la asamblea cristiana.* TGST 74. Rome: Editrice Pontificia Università Gregoriana, 2001.
Mason, J. P. *The Resurrection according to Paul.* Lewiston, NY: Mellen, 1992.
Mason, S. *Flavius Josephus on the Pharisees: A Composition-Critical Study.* StPB 39. Leinden: Brill, 1991.
Massingberd Ford, J. "The First Epistle to the Corinthians or the First Epistle to the Hebrews?" *CBQ* 26 (1988) 402–16.
Matand Bulembat, J.-B. *Noyau et enjeux de l'eschatologie paulinienne: De l'apocalyptique juive et de l'eschatologie hellénistique dans quelques argumentations de l'apôtre Paul—Etude rhétorique-exégétique de 1 Co 15,35–58; 2 Co 5,1–10 et Rm 8,18–30.* BZNW 84. Berlin and New York: de Gruyter, 1997.
Matera, F. J. *Galatians.* SacPag 9. Collegeville, MN: Liturgical (Glazier), 1992.
Matthews, V. H. *Manners and Customs in the Bible: An Illustrated Guide to Life in Biblical Times.* Rev. ed. Peabody, MA: Hendrickson, 1991.
McCant, J. W. "Paul's Thorn of Rejected Apostleship." *NTS* 34 (1988) 550–72.
McKenzie, L. *Pagan Resurrection Myths and the Resurrection of Jesus.* SAE. Charlottesville, VA: Bookwrights, 1997.
McMurrin, S. M. *The Theological Foundations of the Mormon Religion.* 1965; rpt. Salt Lake City: University of Utah Press, 1977.
McNamara, M. Review of E. P. Sanders, *Paul and Palestinian Judaism: A Comparison of Patterns of Religion. JSNT* 5 (1979) 67–73.
McRay, J. "Damascus: The Greco-Roman Period," *ABD* 2:7–8.
Mearns, C. L. "Early Eschatological Development in Paul: The Evidence of 1 Corinthians." *JSNT* 22 (1984) 19–35.
Meeks, W. A. "'And Rose Up to Play': Midrash and Paraenesis in 1 Corinthians 10:1–22." *JSNT* 16 (1982) 64–78.
———. *The First Urban Christians: The Social World of the Apostle Paul.* New Haven and London: Yale University Press, 1983.

———. "A Hermeneutics of Social Embodiment." *HTR* 79 (1986) 176–86.
———. *The Moral World of the First Christians*. London: SPCK, 1987.
———. *The Origins of Christian Morality: The First Two Centuries*. New Haven and London: Yale University Press, 1993.
———. "The Social Context of Pauline Theology." *Int* 36 (1992) 266–77.
———, ed. *The Writings of St. Paul: Annotated Text and Criticism*. Norton Critical Editions. New York: Norton, 1972.
Meggitt, J. J. Review of B. J. Malina, *The Social World of Jesus and the Gospels*. *JTS* 49 (1998) 215–19.
———. *Paul, Poverty, and Survival*. SNTW. Edinburgh: T&T Clark, 1998.
Meier, J. P. "The Quest for the Historical Pharisee: A Review Essay on Roland Deines, *Die Pharisäer*." *CBQ* 61 (1999) 713–22.
Merklein, H. "Der Theologe als Prophet: Zur Funktion prophetischen Redens im theologischen Diskurs des Paulus." *NTS* (1992) 402–29.
Meyer, B. F. "Did Paul's View of the Resurrection of the Dead Undergo Development?" *TS* 47 (1986) 363–87.
———. "Paul and the Resurrection of the Dead." *TS* 48 (1987) 157–58.
Meyer, M. W. "Mystery Religions." *ABD* 4:941–45.
Meyer, P. W. "The Holy Spirit in the Pauline Letters: A Contextual Exploration." *Int* 33 (1979) 3–18.
———. Review of H. D. Betz, *Galatians: A Commentary on Paul's Letter to the Churches in Galatia*. *RelSRev* 7 (1981) 318–23.
Meynet, R. "Histoire de 'l'analyse rhétorique' en exégèse biblique," *Rhetorica* 8 (1990) 291–320.
Michaelis, W. "ὁράω." *TDNT* 5:315–82.
Millard, Alan. *Reading and Writing in the Time of Jesus*. New York: New York University Press, 2000.
Mitchell, A. C. Review of M. M. Mitchell, *Paul and the Rhetoric of Reconciliation: An Exegetical Investigation of the Language and Composition of 1 Corinthians*. *TS* 54 (1993) 163–65.
———. "Rich and Poor in the Courts of Corinth: Litigiousness and Status in 1 Corinthians 6.1–11." *NTS* 39 (1993) 562–86.
Mitchell, M. M. "Concerning Περὶ Δέ in 1 Corinthians." *NovT* 31 (1989) 229–56.
———. *Paul and the Rhetoric of Reconciliation: An Exegetical Investigation of the Language and Composition of 1 Corinthians*. Louisville: Westminster John Knox, 1991.
Moffatt, J. *The First Epistle to the Corinthians*. MNTC. London: Hodder and Stoughton, 1938.
Moiser, J. "1 Corinthians 15." *IBS* 14 (1992) 10–30.
Morris, L. *The First Epistle of Paul to the Corinthians: An Introduction and Commentary*. 2nd ed. TNTC. Leicester: InterVarsity, 1985.
Morton, H. V. *In the Steps of the Master*. 1964; rpt. Cambridge: Da Capo, 2002.
———. *In the Steps of St. Paul*. 1964; rpt. Cambridge: Da Capo, 2002.
Moule, C. F. D. "The Influence of Circumstances on the Use of Eschatological Terms." *JTS* 15 (1964) 1–15.

———. "St. Paul and Dualism: The Pauline Conception of Resurrection." *NTS* 13 (1965–66) 106–23.

Mounce, R. H. "Continuity of the Primitive Tradition: Some Pre-Pauline Elements in I Corinthians 15." *Int* (1959) 417–24.

Mowery, R. L. "The Articular Prepositional Attributes in the Pauline Corpus." *Bib* 71 (1990) 85–92.

Moxnes, H. "The Historical Jesus: From Master Narrative to Cultural Context." *BTB* 28 (1998) 135–49.

———. "What is a Family? Problems in Constructing Early Christian Families." In *Constructing Early Christian Families*, ed. Moxnes, 13–41.

———, ed. *Constructing Early Christian Families: Family as Social Reality and Metaphor*. London and New York: Routledge, 1997.

Muilenburg, J. "Form Criticism and Beyond." *JBL* 88 (1969) 1–18.

Mullins, T. Y. "Formulas in the New Testament Epistles." *JBL* 91 (1972) 380–90.

———. "Topos as a New Testament Form." *JBL* 99 (1980) 541–47.

———. "Paul's Thorn in the Flesh." *JBL* 76 (1957) 299–303.

Murphy, J. J. "Early Christianity as a 'Persuasive Campaign': Evidence from the Acts of the Apostles and the Letters of Paul." In *Rhetoric and the New Testament*, ed. Porter and Olbricht, 90–99.

Murphy-O'Connor, J. "'Baptized for the Dead' (I Cor., XV, 29): A Corinthian Slogan?" *RB* 88 (1981) 532–43.

———. "Co-authorship in the Corinthian Correspondence." *RB* 100 (1993) 562–79.

———. "Corinth." *ABD* 1:1134–39.

———. "Corinthian Bronze." *RB* 90 (1983) 23–26.

———. "The Corinth That Saint Paul Saw." *BA* 47 (1984) 147–59.

———. "Corinthian Slogans in 1 Cor 6:12–20." *CBQ* 40 (1978) 391–96.

———. "Does St. Paul Find Meaning in Suffering?" *PP* 8 (1994) 99–102.

———. *I Corinthians*. NTM 10. Dublin: Veritas, 1979.

———. "1 Corinthians 11:2–16 Once Again." *CBQ* 50 (1988) 265–74.

———. "The First Letter to the Corinthians." *NJBC* §49, 798–815.

———. "Interpolations in 1 Corinthians." *CBQ* 48 (1986) 81–94.

———. *Paul: A Critical Life*. Oxford: Clarendon, 1996.

———. *Paul the Letter-Writer: His World, His Options, His Skills*. GNS 41. Collegeville, MN: Liturgical (Glazier), 1995.

———. "Pauline Missions before the Jerusalem Conference." *RB* 89 (1982) 71–91.

———. "Sex and Logic in 1 Corinthians 11:2–16." *CBQ* 42 (1980) 482–500.

———. *St. Paul's Corinth: Texts and Archaeology*. 2nd ed. Collegeville, MN: Liturgical [Glazier], 1990.

———. "Tradition and Redaction in 1 Cor 15:3–7." *CBQ* 43 (1981) 582–89.

Murrow, S. B. *Paul, His Letters and His Theology: An Introduction to the Pauline Epistles*. New York/Mahwah, NJ: Paulist, 1986.

Mussies, G. "Greek as the Vehicle of Early Christianity." *NTS* 29 (1983) 356–69.

Nardoni, E. "The Concept of Charism in Paul." *CBQ* 55 (1993) 68–80.

Nasuti, H. P. "The Woes of the Prophets and the Rights of the Apostle: The Internal Dynamics of 1 Corinthians 9." *CBQ* 50 (1988) 246–64.

Neirynck, F. "The Sayings of Jesus in 1 Corinthians." In *The Corinthian Correspondence*, ed. Bieringer, 141–76.

———. Review of D. Wenham, *Paul: Follower of Christ or Founder of Christianity? ETL* 73 (1997) 181–82.
Neumann, K. J. *The Authenticity of the Pauline Epistles in the Light of Stylostatistical Analysis.* SBLDS 120. Atlanta: Scholars Press, 1990.
Newton, D. *Deity and Diet: The Dilemma of Sacrificial Food at Corinth.* JSNTSup 169. Sheffield: Sheffield Academic Press, 1998.
Neyrey, J. H. "Body Language in 1 Corinthians: The Use of Anthropological Models for Understanding Paul and His Opponents." *Semeia* 35 (1986) 129–70.
———. *Paul, In Other Words: A Cultural Reading of His Letters.* Louisville: Westminster John Knox, 1990.
———. Review of B. Witherington III, *Conflict and Community in Corinth: A Socio-Rhetorical Commentary on 1 and 2 Corinthians. CBQ* 59 (1997) 182–83.
Nibley, H. W. "Baptism for the Dead in Ancient Times." *IE* 51 (1948) 786–88, 836–38, and 52 (1949) 24–26, 60, 109–10, 112, 146–48, 180–83.
Nickelsburg, G. W. E. "An Ἔκτρωμα, Though Appointed from the Womb: Paul's Apostolic Self-Description in 1 Corinthians 15 and Galatians 1." *HTR* 79 (1986) 198–205.
Nock, A. D. "Cremation and Burial in the Roman Empire." *HTR* 25 (1932) 321–59.
Noegel, S., J. Walker, and B. Wheeler, eds. *Prayer, Magic, and the Stars in the Ancient and Late Antique World.* MH. University Park, PA: Pennsylvania State University Press, 2003.
North, J. L., "Paul's Protest That He Does Not Lie in the Light of His Cilician Origin." *JTS* 47 (1996) 439–63.
———. Review of J. Murphy-O'Connor, *Paul: A Critical Life. JST* 49 (1998) 245–48.
Oakes, P. Review of P. F. Esler, ed., *Modelling Early Christianity: Social-Scientific Studies of the New Testament in Its Context. JST* 49 (1998) 281–84.
O'Brien, J. M. "I Corinthians 15:19–26." *Int* 49 (1995) 182–85.
O'Collins, G. *Interpreting the Resurrection: Examining the Major Problems in the Stories of Jesus' Resurrection.* New York/Mahwah, NJ: Paulist, 1988.
———. "The Resurrection Revisited." *Greg* 79 (1998) 169–72.
———. "The Resurrection: The State of the Questions." In *The Resurrection*, ed. Davis, Kendall, and O'Collins, 5–28.
O'Collins, G., and D. Kendall. *The Bible for Theology: Ten Principles for the Theological Use of Scripture.* New York/Mahwah, NJ: Paulist, 1997.
Oepke, A. " βάπτω, βαπτίζω, βαπτισμός, βάπτισμα, βαπτιστής." *TDNT* 1:529–46.
———. "δύω, ἐκδύω, ἀπεκδύω, ἐνδύω, ἐπενδύω, ἀπέκδυσις." *TDNT* 2:318–21.
———. "ἐγείρω, ἔγερσις, ἐξεγείρω, γρηγορέω (ἀγρυπέω)." *TDNT* 2:333–39.
Ogden, D. *Greek and Roman Necromancy.* Princeton, NJ: Princeton University Press, 2001.
———. *Magic, Witchcraft, and Ghosts in the Greek and Roman Worlds: A Sourcebook.* Oxford: Oxford University Press, 2002.
Olbricht, T. H. "An Aristotelian Rhetorical Analysis of 1 Thessalonians." In *Greeks, Romans and Christians*, ed. Balch, Ferguson, and Meeks, 216–36.
Olson, S. N. "Pauline Expressions of Confidence in His Addressees." *CBQ* 47 (1985) 282–95.
O'Mahony, K. "Roman Corinth and Christian Corinthians." *ScrC* 27 (1997) 115–24.

O'Neill, J. C. "The Conflict between Baptism and the Gift of the Spirit in Acts." *JSNT* 63 (1996) 87–103.
———. "1 Corinthians 7,14 and Infant Baptism." In *L'apôtre Paul*, ed. Vanhoye, 357–61.
———. "1 Corinthians 15:29." *ExpTim* 91 (1979) 310–11.
Orr, W. F., and J. A. Walther. *I Corinthians*. AB 32. Garden City, NY: Doubleday, 1976.
Osborne, R. E. "Paul and the Wild Beasts." *JBL* 85 (1966) 225–30.
Osei-Bonsu, J. "Anthropological Dualism in the New Testament." *SJT* 40 (1987) 571–90.
Osiek, C. "The Family in Early Christianity: 'Family Values' Revisited." *CBQ* 58 (1996) 1–24.
———. Review of J. L. Hoppe, *The Synagogues and Churches of Ancient Palestine* (Collegeville, MN: Liturgical [Glazier], 1994). *CBQ* 58 (1996) 155.
———. *What Are They Saying about the Social Setting of the New Testament?* Rev. ed. New York; Mahwah, NJ: Paulist, 1992.
Osiek, C., and D. L. Balch. *Families in the New Testament World: Households and House Churches*. FRC. Louisville: Westminster John Knox, 1997.
Oster, R. "Use, Misuse, and Neglect of Archeological Evidence in Some Modern Works on 1 Corinthians (1 Cor. 7.15; 8.10; 11.2–16; 12.14–26)." *ZNW* 83 (1992) 52–73.
———. "When Men Wore Veils to Worship: The Historical Context of 1 Corinthians 11.4." *NTS* 34 (1988) 481–505.
Otto, R. E. "'If Possible I May Attain the Resurrection from the Dead' (Philippians 3:11)." *CBQ* 57 (1995) 324–40.
Overman, J. A. "The God-Fearers: Some Neglected Features." *JSNT* 32 (1988) 17–26.
Pagels, E. H. *The Gnostic Paul: Gnostic Exegesis of the Pauline Letters*. 1975; rpt. Philadelphia: Trinity Press International, 1992.
———. "'The Mystery of the Resurrection': A Gnostic Reading of 1 Corinthians 15." *JBL* 93 (1974) 276–88.
Painchaud, L. "Le sommaire anthropogonique de *L'Écrit sans Titre* (NH II, 117:27–118:2) à la lumiere de 1 Co 15:45–47." *VC* 44 (1990) 382–93.
Pardee, D. "Letters (Hebrew)." *ABD* 4:282–85.
Parratt, J. K. "The Holy Spirit and Baptism: Part I. The Gospels and the Acts of the Apostles." *ExpTim* 82 (1970–71) 231–35.
———. "The Holy Spirit and Baptism: Part II. The Pauline Evidence." *ExpTim* 82 (1970–71) 266–71.
Parry, R. St. J. *The First Epistle of Paul the Apostle to the Corinthians*. 2nd ed. CGTSC. Cambridge: Cambridge University Press, 1926.
Pascuzzi, M. *Ethics, Ecclesiology and Church Discipline: A Rhetorical Analysis of 1 Corinthians 5*. TGST 32. Rome: Editrice Pontificia Università Gregoriana, 1997.
Patrick, D., and A. Scult. *Rhetoric and Biblical Interpretation*. BL 26. Decatur, GA: Almond, 1990.
Patton, J. H. Review of G. A. Kennedy, *New Testament Interpretation through Rhetorical Criticism*. *QJS* 71 (1985) 247–49.
Pearson, B. A. "Christians and Jews in First-Century Alexandria." *HTR* 79 (1986) 206–16.
———. *The Emergence of the Christian Religion: Essays on Early Christianity*. Harrisburg, PA: Trinity Press International, 1997.

———. *The* Pneumatikos–Psychikos *Terminology in 1 Corinthians*. SBLDS 12. Missoula, MT: Society of Biblical Literature, 1973.
Peel, M. L. *The Epistle to Rheginos: A Valentinian Letter on Resurrection.* NTL. London: SCM, 1969.
Penna, A. *Saint Paul the Apostle.* Trans. K. C. Thompson. London: St. Paul Publications, 1960.
Penna, R. *Paul the Apostle: A Theological and Exegetical Study.* Trans. T. P. Wahl. 2 vols. Vol. 1, *Jew and Greek Alike.* Vol. 2, *Wisdom and Folly of the Cross.* Liturgical (Glazier): Collegeville, MN, 1996.
———. Review of E. R. Richards, *The Secretary in the Letters of Paul. Bib* 73 (1992) 286–88.
Perelman, C., and L. Olbrechts-Tyteca. *The New Rhetoric: A Treatise on Argumentation.* Trans. J. Wilkinson and P. Weaver. Notre Dame, IN: University of Notre Dame Press, 1969.
Perkins, J. *The Suffering Self: Pain and Narrative Representation in Early Christian Art.* London and New York: Routledge, 1995.
Perkins, P. "Gnostic Christologies and the New Testament." *CBQ* 43 (1981) 590–606.
Perriman, A. C. "Paul and the Parousia: 1 Corinthians 15.50–57 and 2 Corinthians 5.1–5." *NTS* 35 (1989) 512–21.
Petersen, N. R. "Pauline Baptism and 'Secondary Burial.'" *HTR* 79 (1986) 217–26.
Peterson, B. K. *Eloquence and the Proclamation of the Gospel in Corinth.* SBLDS 163. Atlanta: Scholars Press, 1998.
Pilch, J. J. "Appearances of the Risen Jesus in Cultural Context: Experiences of Alternate Reality." *BTB* 28 (1998) 52–60.
———. "Psychological and Psychoanalytical Approaches to Interpreting the Bible in Social-Scientific Context." *BTB* 27 (1997) 112–16.
Plevnik, J. Review of G. D. Fee, *The First Epistle to the Corinthians. CBQ* 50 (1988) 715–17.
———. *What Are They Saying about Paul?* New York/Mahwah, NJ: Paulist, 1986.
Pogoloff, S. M. *Logos and Sophia: The Rhetorical Situation of 1 Corinthians.* SBLDS 134. Atlanta: Scholars Press, 1992.
Pokorný, P. "Christologie et baptême à l'époque du christianisme primitif." *NTS* 27 (1980–81) 368–80.
Pomeroy, S. B. *Families in Classical and Hellenistic Greece: Representations and Realities.* Oxford: Clarendon, 1997.
Porter, S. E. "Literary Approaches to the New Testament: From Formalism to Deconstruction and Back." In *Approaches to New Testament Study*, ed. Porter and Tombs, 77–128.
———. *Paul in Acts.* LPS. Peabody, MA: Hendrickson, 2001.
———. "Paul of Tarsus and His Letters." In *Handbook of Classical Rhetoric*, ed. Porter, 533–85.
———. "The Pauline Concept of Original Sin, in Light of Rabbinic Background." *TynBul* 41 (1990) 3–30.
———. "The Theoretical Justification for Application of Rhetorical Categories to Pauline Epistolary Literature." In *Rhetoric and the New Testament*, ed. Porter and Olbricht, 100–22.

———, ed. *Handbook of Classical Rhetoric in the Hellenistic Perod (330 B.C.–A.D. 400)*. Leiden: Brill, 1997.

Porter, S. E., and A. R. Cross, eds. *Baptism, the New Testament, and the Church: Historical and Contemporary Studies in Honour of R. E. O. White*. JSNTSup 171. Sheffield: Sheffield Academic Press, 1999.

———. *Dimensions of Baptism: Biblical and Theological Studies*. JSNTSup 234. Sheffield: Sheffield Academic Press, 2002.

Porter, S. E., and T. H. Olbricht, eds. *Rhetoric and the New Testament: Essays from the 1992 Heildelberg Conference*. JSNTSup 90. Sheffield: Sheffield Academic Press, 1993.

Porter, S. E., and J. T. Reed, "Philippians as a Macro-Chiasm and Its Exegetical Significance." *NTS* 44 (1998) 213–231.

Porter, S. E., and D. Tombs, eds. *Approaches to New Testament Study*. JSNTSup 120. Sheffield: Sheffield Academic Press, 1995. 17–45.

Powers, D. G. *Salvation through Participation: An Examination of the Notion of Participation of the Believers' Corporate Unity with Christ in Early Christian Soteriology*. CBET 29. Leuven: Peeters, 2001.

Pratt, F. *The Theology of Saint Paul*. Trans. J. L. Stoddard. 2 vols. Westminster, MD: Newman Bookshop, 1927.

Preisker, H. "Die Vikariatstaufe I Cor 15:29—ein eschatologischer, nicht sakramentaler Brauch." *ZNW* 23 (1924) 298–304.

Price, S. *Religions of the Ancient Greeks*. KTAH. Cambridge: Cambridge University Press, 1999.

Prior, D. *The Message of First Corinthians: Life in the Local Church*. TBST. Downers Grove, IL and Leicester, Eng.: InterVarsity, 1985.

Prior, M. *Paul the Letter-Writer and the Second Letter to Timothy*. JSNTSup 23. Sheffield: JSOT Press, 1989.

Prusak, B. P. "Bodily Resurrection in Catholic Prespectives." *TS* 61 (2000) 64–105.

Puskas, C. B. *The Letters of Paul: An Introduction*. GNS 25. Collegeville, MN: Liturgical (Glazier), 1993.

Quast, K. *Reading the Corinthian Correspondence: An Introduction*. New York/Mahwah, NJ: Paulist, 1994.

Quell, G. et al. "ἁμαρτάνω, ἁμάρτημα, ἁμαρτία." *TDNT* 1:267–316.

Quinn, J. J. "Resurrection at Death? Law of Prayer–Law of Belief." *DunRev* 22 (1999) 83–87.

Rad, G. von, G. Bertram, and R. Bultmann. "ζάω, ζωή (βιόω, βίος), ἀναζάω, ζῷον, ζωογονέω, ζωοποιεηω." *TDNT* 3:863

Raeder, M. "Vikariatstaufe in 1 Cor 15:29." *ZNW* 46 (1955) 258–60.

Rahner, H. "The Christian Mystery and the Pagan Mysteries." In *The Mysteries: Papers from the Eranos Yearbooks*. Ed. J. Campbell. Trans. R. Manheim. BolS 30. New York: Pantheon, 1955. 337–401.

Räisänen, H. *Paul and the Law*. Philadelphia: Fortress, 1983.

Ramsaran, R. A. "More Than an Opinion: Paul's Rhetorical Maxim in First Corinthians 7:25–26." *CBQ* 57 (1995) 531–41.

Ramsay, W. M. *The Cities of St. Paul and Their Influence on His Life and Thought: The Cities of Eastern Asia Minor*. London: Hodder and Stoughton, 1907.

———. *St. Paul the Traveler and Roman Citizen.* 1925. Ed. and rev. M. Wilson. London: Kregel, 2001.
———. *The Letters to the Seven Churches of Asia and Their Place in the Plan of the Apocalypse.* New York: Armstrong, 1905.
———. "The Tarsian Citizenship of St. Paul." ExpTim 16 (1904) 18–21.
Raphael, S. P. *Jewish Views of the Afterlife.* Northvale, NJ: Aronson, 1994.
Reaume, J. D. "Another Look at 1 Corinthians 15:29, 'Baptized for the Dead.'" *BSac* 152 (1995) 457–75.
Reed, J. T. "Are Paul's Thanksgivings 'Epistolary'?" *JSNT* 61 (1996) 87–99.
———. "The Epistle." In *Handbook of Classical Rhetoric*, ed. Porter, 171–93.
———. "Modern Linguistics and the New Testament: A Basic Guide to Theory, Terminology, and Literature." In *Approaches to New Testament Study*, ed. Porter and Tombs, 222–265.
———. "Using Ancient Rhetorical Categories to Interpret Paul's Letters: A Question of Genre." In *Rhetoric and the New Testament*, ed. Porter and Olbricht, 292–324.
Reese, J. M. "Paul Proclaims the Wisdom of the Cross: Scandal and Foolishness." *BTB* 9 (1979) 147–53.
Reid, J. B. *Jesus, God's Emptiness, God's Fullness: The Christology of St. Paul.* New York/Mahwah, NJ: Paulist, 1990.
Reitzenstein, R. *Hellenistic Mystery-Religions: Their Basic Ideas and Significance.* Trans. J. E. Steely. PTMS 15. Pittsburgh: Pickwick, 1978.
Ricciotti, G. *Paolo Apostolo: Biografia con introduzione critica e illustrazione.* Rome: Poliglotta Vaticana, 1946.
Richard, E. J. *First and Second Thessalonians.* SacPag 11. Collegeville, MN: Liturgical (Glazier), 1995.
Richards, E. R. *The Secretary in the Letters of Paul.* WUNT 2/42. Tübingen: Mohr (Siebeck), 1991.
Riches, J. K. "The Social World of Jesus." *Int* 50 (1996) 383–93.
Richter, P. "Social-Scientific Criticism of the New Testament: An Appraisal and Extended Example." In *Approaches to New Testament Study*, ed. Porter and Tombs, 266–309.
Ridderbos, H. *Paul: An Outline of His Theology.* Trans. J. R. de Witt. Grand Rapids, MI: Eerdmans, 1975.
Riesenfeld, H. "ὑπέρ." *TDNT* 8:507–16.
Riesner, R. *Paul's Early Period: Chronology, Mission Strategy, Theology.* Trans. D. Scott. Grand Rapids, MI: Eerdmans, 1998.
Ring, G. C. "Christ's Resurrection and the Dying and Rising Gods." *CBQ* 6 (1944) 216–29.
Rissi, M. *Die Taufe für die Toten: Ein Beitrag zur paulinschen Tauflehre.* ATANT 42. Zurich: Zwigli, 1962.
Rivkin, E. *What Crucified Jesus? Messianism, Pharisaism, and the Development of Christianity.* New York: UAHC Press, 1997.
Robbins, C. J. "Rhetorical Structure of Philippians 2:6–11." *CBQ* 42 (1980) 73–82.
Robbins, V. K. "Narrative in Ancient Rhetoric and Rhetoric in Ancient Narrative." In *SBLSP 1996.* Atlanta: Scholars Press, 1996.

———. "Rhetoric and Culture: Exploring Types of Cultural Rhetoric in a Text." In *Rhetoric and the New Testament*, ed. Porter and Olbricht, 443–63.
———. "Social-Scientific Criticism and Literary Studies: Prospects for Cooperation in Biblical Interpretation." In *Modelling Early Christianity*, ed. Esler, 274–89.
———. *The Tapestry of Early Christian Discourse: Rhetoric, Society and Ideology*. London and New York: Routledge, 1996.
———. Review of G. A. Kennedy, *New Testament Interpretation through Rhetorical Criticism*. *Rhetorica* 3 (1985) 145–49.
Robertson, A., and A. Plummer. *A Critical and Exegetical Commentary on the First Epistle of St. Paul to the Corinthians*. 2nd ed. ICC. Edinburgh: T&T Clark, 1914.
Robertson, A. T. "The Use of Ὑπέρ in Business Documents in the Papyri." *Expositor* 8/18 (1919) 321–27.
Robinson, J. A. T. *The Body: A Study in Pauline Theology*. SBT. Chicago: Regnery, 1952.
Robinson, W. C. "The Bodily Resurrection." *CToday* 10 (1966) 351–52.
Roetzel, C. J. *Judgment in the Community: A Study in the Relationship between Eschatology and Ecclesiology in Paul*. Leiden: Brill, 1972.
———. *Paul: The Man and the Myth*. SPNT. Columbia, SC: University of South Carolina Press, 1998.
Rogerson, J. W. "The Hebrew Conception of Corporate Personality: A Re-Examination." *JTS* 21 (1970) 1–16.
Rohrbaugh, R. L. "'Social Location of Thought' as a Heuristic Construct in New Testament Study." *JSNT* 30 (1987) 103–19.
Rolland, P. "La structure littéraire de la Deuxième Epître aux Corinthiens." *Bib* 71 (1990) 73–84.
Roller, O. *Das Formular der paulinischen Briefe: Ein Beitrag zur Lehre vom antiken Briefe*. BWANT 58. Stuttgart: Kohlhammer, 1933.
Rosner, B. S. "Temple Prostitution in 1 Corinthians 6:12–20." *NovT* 40 (1998) 336–51.
Saldarini, A. J. *Pharisees, Scribes, and Sadducees in Palestinian Society*. Edinburgh: T&T Clark, 1988.
Sanders, E. P. *Judaism: Practice and Belief 63 BCE–66 CE*. London: SCM, 1992.
———. *Paul*. Oxford: Oxford University Press, 1991.
———. *Paul, the Law, and the Jewish People*. Minneapolis: Fortress, 1983.
———. *Paul and Palestinian Judaism: A Comparison of Patterns of Religion*. London: SCM, 1977.
———. "Patterns of Religion in Paul and Rabbinic Judaism: A Holistic Method of Comparison." *HTR* 66 (1973) 455–78.
Sanders, J. T. "First Corinthians 13: Its Interpretation since the First World War." *Int* 20 (1966) 159–87.
———. "The Transition from Opening Epistolary Thanksgiving to Body in the Letters of the Pauline Corpus." *JBL* 81 (1962) 348–62.
———. "Paul between Jews and Gentiles in Corinth." *JSNT* 65 (1997) 67–83.
Sanders, T. K. "A New Approach to 1 Corinthians 13.1." *NTS* 36 (1990) 614–18.
Sandmel, S. *Judaism and Christian Beginnings*. Oxford: Oxford University Press, 1978.
Sandnes, K. O. "Prophecy—A Sign for Believers (1 Cor 14,20–25)." *Bib* 77 (1996) 1–15.
Saw, I. *Paul's Rhetoric in 1 Corinthians 15: An Analysis Utilizing the Theories of Classical Rhetoric*. Lewiston, NY: Mellen, 1995.

Schaff, P. "Alogians." In *Dictionary of Early Christian Biography*, ed. Wace and Piercy, 14–15.
Schenk, W. "Der 1. Korintherbrief als Briefsammlung." *ZNW* 60 (1969) 219–43.
Schmid, L. "κέντρον." *TDNT* 3:663–68.
Schmidt, T. E. "Mark 15.16–32: The Crucifixion Narrative and the Roman Triumphal Procession." *NTS* 41 (1995) 1–18.
Schmithals, W. *Gnosticism in Corinth: An Investigation of the Letters to the Corinthians*. Trans. J. E. Steely. Nashville: Abingdon, 1971.
———. *Paul and the Gnostics*. Trans. J. E. Steely. Nashville: Abingdon, 1972.
———. "The Pre-Pauline Tradition in 1 Corinthians 15:20–28." Trans. C. N. Jefford. *PRSt* 20 (1993) 356–80.
———. *The Theology of First Corinthians*. Trans. O. C. Dean, Jr. Louisville: Westminster John Knox, 1997.
Schmitz, P. C. "The Grammar of Resurrection in Isaiah 26:19a–c." *JBL* 122 (2003) 145–49.
Schnackenburg, R. *Baptism in the Thought of St. Paul: A Study in Pauline Theology*. Trans. G. R. Beasley-Murray. Oxford: Basil Blackwell, 1964.
———. *Das Heilsgeschehen bei der Taufe noch dem Apostel Paulus: Eine Studie zur paulinischen Theologie*. MTS 1. Munich: Zink, 1950.
———. *Ephesians: A Commentary*. Trans. H. Heron. Edinburgh: T&T Clark, 1991.
Schneider, B. "The Corporate Meaning and Background of 1 Cor. 15,45b—ὁ ἔσξατος Ἀδὰμ εἰσ πνεῦμα ζῳοποιοῦν." *CBQ* 29 (1967) 450–67.
Schneider, C. "κινέω, μετακινέω." *TDNT* 3:718–20.
Schoedel, W. R., and R. L. Wilken, eds. *Early Christian Literature and the Classical Intellectual Tradition: In Honorem Robert M. Grant*. ThH 53. Paris: Beauchesne, 1979. 17–31.
Scholla, R. W. "Into the Image of God: Pauline Eschatology and the Transformation of Believers." *Greg* 78 (1997) 33–54.
Schubert, P. *Form and Function of the Pauline Thanksgivings*. BZNW 20. Berlin: Töpelmann, 1939.
Schüssler Fiorenza, E. "Rhetorical Situation and Historical Reconstruction in 1 Corinthians." *NTS* 33 (1987) 386–403.
Schütz, J. H. "Apostolic Authority and the Control of Tradition: I Cor. XV." *NTS* 15 (1968–69) 439–57.
Schwartz, D. R. *Studies in the Jewish Background of Christianity*. WUNT 60. Tübingen: Mohr (Siebeck), 1992.
Schweitzer, A. *Die Mystik des Apostels Paulus*. Tübingen: Mohr (Siebeck), 1930.
———. *Paul and His Interpreters: A Critical Essay*. Trans. W. Montgomery. London: A&C Black, 1912.
Schweizer, E. and R. Meyer. "σάρξ, σαρκικός, σάρκινος." *TDNT* 7:98–151.
Scott, J. M. "The Triumph of God in 2 Cor 2.14: Additional Evidence of Merkabah Mysticism in Paul." *NTS* 42 (1996) 260–81.
Seesemann, H. "οἶδα." *TDNT* 5:116–19.
Segal, A. F. *Paul the Convert: The Apostolate and Apostasy of Saul the Pharisee*. New Haven and London: Yale University Press, 1990.

———. "Paul's Thinking about Resurrection in Its Jewish Context." *NTS* 44 (1998) 400–419.

———. "Some Observations about Mysticism and the Spread of Notions of Life after Death in Hebrew Thought." In *SBLSP 1996*. Atlanta: Scholars Press, 1996.

———. *The Other Judaisms of Late Antiquity*. BJS 127. Atlanta: Scholars Press, 1987.

———. "Universalism in Judaism and Christianity." In *Paul in His Hellenistic Context*, ed. Engberg-Pedersen, 1–29.

Sellew, P. Review of E. R. Richards, *The Secretary in the Letters of Paul*. *JBL* 112 (1993) 536–37.

Sellin, G. "Hauptprobleme des ersten Korintherbriefes." *ANRW* 2/24.4:2941–3044.

———. *Der Streit um die Auferstehung der Toten: Eine religionsgeschichtliche und exegetische Untersuchung von 1. Korinther 15*. FRLANT 138. Göttingen: Vandenhoeck and Ruprecht, 1986.

Sencourt, R. *Saint Paul: Envoy of Grace*. Sheed and Ward, 1948.

Senft, C. *La première épître de saint-Paul aux Corinthiens*. CNT 7. Neuchâtel/Paris: Delachaux and Niestlé, 1979.

Serna, E. de la. "Los orígenes de 1 Corintios." *Bib* 72 (1991) 192–216.

Setzer, C. "Resurrection of the Dead as Symbol and Strategy." *JAAR* 69 (2001) 65–101.

Sevrin, J.-M. "La gnose à Corinthe: Questions de méthode et observations sur 1 Co 1,17–3,3." In *The Corinthian Correspondence*, ed. Bieringer, 121–39.

Shanor, J. "Paul as Master Builder: Construction Terms in First Corinthians." *NTS* 34 (1988) 461–71.

Sharpe, J. L., III. "The Second Adam in the *Apocalypse of Moses*." *CBQ* 35 (1973) 35–46.

Sherwin-White, A. N. *Roman Society and Roman Law in the New Testament*. Oxford: Clarendon, 1963.

Shillington, V. G. "Atonement Texture in 1 Corinthians 5.5." *JSNT* 71 (1998) 29–50.

Shipley, G. *The Greek World after Alexander: 323–30 BC*. RHAW. London and New York: Routledge, 2000.

Shipps, J. *Mormonism: The Story of a New Religious Tradition*. Urbana and Chicago: University of Illinois Press, 1985.

Sider, R. J. "The Pauline Conception of the Resurrection Body in I Corinthians XV.35–54." *NTS* 21 (1974–75) 428–39.

———. "St. Paul's Understanding of the Nature and Significance of the Resurrection in I Corinthians XV 1–19." *NovT* 19 (1977) 124–41.

Siegert, F. "Homily and Panegyrical Sermon." In *Handbook of Classical Rhetoric*, ed. Porter, 421–43.

Sievers, J. "Who Were the Pharisees?" In *Hillel and Jesus*. Ed. J. H. Charlesworth and L. L. Johns. Minneapolis: Fortress, 1997. 137–55.

Sigountos, J. G. "The Genre of 1 Corinthians 13." *NTS* 40 (1994) 246–60.

Silva, M. "Bilingualism and the Character of Palestinian Greek." *Bib* 61 (1980) 198–219.

Simon, W. G. *The First Epistle to the Corinthians*. London: SCM, 1959.

Smalley, S. S. "The Delay of the Parousia." *JBL* 83 (1964) 41–54.

Smit, J. F. M. *"About the Idol Offerings": Rhetoric, Social Context and Theology of Paul's Discourse in First Corinthians 8:1–11:1*. Leuven: Peeters, 2000.

———. "Argument and Genre of 1 Corinthians 12–14." In *Rhetoric and the New Testament*, ed. Porter and Olbricht, 211–30.

―――. "The Function of 1 Corinthians 10,23–30: A Rhetorical Anticipation." *Bib* 78 (1997) 377–88.

―――. "The Genre of 1 Corinthians 13 in the Light of Classical Rhetoric." *NovT* 33 (1991) 193–216.

―――. "The Rhetorical Disposition of First Corinthians 8:7–14:4." *CBQ* 59 (1997) 476–91.

―――. "Two Puzzles: 1 Corinthians 12.31 and 13.3: A Rhetorical Solution." *NTS* 39 (1993) 246–64.

―――. "'What Is Apollos? What Is Paul?' In Search for the Coherence of First Corinthians 1:10–4:21." *NovT* 154 (2002) 231–51.

Smith, D. *The Life and Letters of Paul*. New York: Doran, 1919.

Smith, D. E. "The Egyptian Cults at Corinth." *HTR* 70 (1977) 201–31.

Smith, D. M. "The Pauline Literature." In *It Is Written: Scripture Citing Scripture. Essays in Honour of Barnabas Lindars, SSF*. Ed. D. A. Carson and H. G. M. Williamson. Cambridge: Cambridge University Press, 1988. 265–91.

Smith, J. Z. *Drudgery Divine: On the Comparison of Early Christianities and the Religions of Late Antiquity*. CSHJ. Chicago: University of Chicago Press, 1990.

―――. *Imagining Religion: From Babylon to Jonestown*. CSHJ. Chicago and London: University of Chicago Press, 1982.

―――. *To Take Place: Toward Theory in Ritual*. CSHJ. Chicago and London: University of Chicago Press, 1987.

Smith, M. "Paul's Arguments as Evidence of the Christianity from Which He Diverged." *HTR* 79 (1986) 254–60.

Söding, T. "'Die Kraft der Sünde ist das Gesetz' (1 Kor 15,56) Anmerkungen zum Hintergrund und zur Pointe einer gesetzeskritischen Sentenz des Apostels Paulus." *ZNW* 83 (1992) 74–84.

South, J. T. "A Critique of the 'Curse/Death' Interpretation of 1 Corinthians 5.1–8." *NTS* 39 (1993) 539–61.

Spencer, F. S. "Paul's Odyssey in Acts: Status Struggles and Island Adventures." *BTB* 28 (1998) 150–59.

Staab, K. "1 Kor 15,29 im Lichte der Exegese der griechischen Kirche." *Studiorum Paulinorum Congressus Internationalis Catholicus 1961*. AnBib 17–18. 2 vols. Rome: Pontificium Institutum Biblicum, 1963. 1.442–50.

―――, ed. *Pauluskommentare aus der griechischen Kirche: Aus Katenenkandschriften gesammelt und herausgegeben*. NTAbh 15. Münster: Aschendorff, 1933.

Stamps, D. L. "Rethinking the Rhetorical Stiuation: The Extextualization of the Situation in the New Testament Epistles." In *Rhetoric and the New Testament*, ed. Porter and Olbricht, 193–209.

―――. "Rhetorical Criticism of the New Testament: Ancient and Modern Evaluations of Argumentation." In *Approaches to New Testament Study*, ed. Porter and Tombs, 129–169.

Standaert, B. "La rhétorique ancienne dans saint Paul." In *L'apôtre Paul*, ed. Vanhoye, 78–92.

Stanley, C. D. *Paul and the Language of Scripture: Citation Technique in the Pauline Epistles and Contemporary Literature*. SNTSMS 74. Cambridge: Cambridge University Press, 1992.

Stanley, D. M. "'Become Imitators of Me': The Pauline Conception of Apostolic Tradition." *Bib* 40 (1959) 859–77.

———. *Christ's Resurrection in Pauline Soteriology*. AnBib 13. Rome: Editrice Pontificio Istituto Biblico, 1961.

Stasiak, K. *Return to Grace: A Theology for Infant Baptism*. Collegeville, MN: Liturgical (Pueblo), 1996.

Stauffer, E. "ἑδραῖος, ἑδραίωμα." *TDNT* 2:362–64.

Stendahl, K. "The Apostle Paul and the Introspective Conscience of the West." *HTR* 56 (1963) 199–215.

———. *Paul among Jews and Gentiles*. Philadelphia: Fortress, 1976.

Stephenson, A. M. G. *The Authorship and Integrity of the New Testament*. London: SPCK, 1965.

Sterling, G. E. "'Wisdom among the Perfect': Creation Traditions in Alexandrian Judaism and Corinthian Christianity." *NovT* 37 (1995) 355–84.

Stewart-Sykes, A. "Ancient Editors and Copyists and Modern Partition Theories: The Case of the Corinthian Correspondence." *JSNT* 61 (1996) 53–64.

Stirewalt, M. L., Jr. "The Form and Function of the Greek Letter-Essay." In *The Romans Debate*, ed. Donfried, 145–71.

———. *Studies in Ancient Greek Epistolography*. SBLRBS 27. Atlanta: Scholars Press, 1993.

Stowers, S. K. *Letter Writing in Greco-Roman Antiquity*. LEC 5. Philadelphia: Westminster, 1986.

———. "Letters (Greek and Latin)." *ABD* 4:290–93.

Sundberg, A. C., Jr. "Enabling Language in Paul." *HTR* 79 (1986) 270–77.

Surgy, P. de and M. Carrez. *Les épîtres de Paul—I Corinthiens: Commentaire pastoral*. EV. Paris: Bayard, 1996.

Swindoll, P. *Paul: A Man of Grace and Grit*. Nashville: The W Publishing Group, 2002.

Talbert, C. H. "The Concept of Immortals in Mediterranean Antiquity." *JBL* 94 (1975) 419–36.

———. "Paul, Judaism, and the Revisionists." *CBQ* 63 (2001) 1–22.

Tambasco, A. J. *In the Days of Paul: The Social World and Teaching of the Apostle*. New York/Mahwah, NJ: Paulist, 1991.

Tannehill, R. C. *Dying and Rising with Christ: A Study in Pauline Theology*. BZNW 32. Berlin: Töpelmann, 1967.

Taylor, J. *Where Did Christianity Come From?* Collegeville, MN: Liturgical (Glazier), 2001.

Taylor, J. E. *The Immerser: John the Baptist within Second Temple Judaism*. Grand Rapids, MI: Eerdmans, 1997.

Taylor, M. J. *Paul: His Letters, Message and Heritage—A Reflective Commentary*. Staten Island, NY: Alba House, 1997.

Taylor, N. H. "The Social Nature of Conversion in the Early Christian World." In *Modelling Early Christianity*, ed. Esler, 128–36.

Teeple, H. M. "The Historical Beginnings of the Resurrection Faith." In *Studies in the New Testament and Early Christian Literature*, ed. Aune, 107–20.

Theissen, G. "Legitimation und Lebensunterhalt: Ein Beitrag zur Soziologie urchristlicher Missionare." *NTS* 21 (1974–75) 192–221.

———. *Psychological Aspects of Pauline Theology*. Trans. J. P. Gavin. Edinburgh: T&T Clark, 1987.
———. *Social Reality and the Early Christians: Theology, Ethics, and the World of the New Testament*. Trans. M. Kohl. Edinburgh: T&T Clark, 1993.
———. *The Social Setting of Pauline Christianity: Essays on Corinth*. Trans. J. H. Shütz. Philadelphia: Fortress, 1982.
Thielman, F. "The Coherence of Paul's View of the Law: The Evidence of First Corinthians." *NTS* 38 (1992) 235–53.
Thiering, B. E. "Inner and Outer Cleansing at Qumran as a Background to New Testament Baptism." *NTS* 26 (1979–80) 266–77.
———. "Qumran Initiation and New Testament Baptism." *NTS* 27 (1980–81) 615–31.
Thiselton, A. C. *The First Epistle to the Corinthians*. NIGTC. Grand Rapids, MI: Eerdmans, 2000.
———. "Realized Eschatology at Corinth." *NTS* 24 (1977–78) 510–26.
Thomas, C. *Reading the Letters of Saint Paul: Study, Reflection, and Prayer*. New York/Mahwah, NJ: Paulist, 2002.
Thompson, I. H. *Chiasmus in the Pauline Letters*. JSNTSup 111. Sheffield: Sheffield Academic Press, 1995.
Thompson, K. C. "I Corinthians 15, 29 and Baptism for the Dead." In *Studia Evangelica*. Vol. 2, Part 1. Ed. F. L. Cross. TU 87. Berlin: Akademie Verlag, 1964. 647–59.
Thurén, L. "On Studying Ethical Argumentation and Persuasion in the New Testament." In *Rhetoric and the New Testament*, ed. Porter and Olbricht, 464–78.
Toit, A. du. "Primitive Christian Belief in the Resurrection of Jesus in Light of the Pauline Resurrection and Appearance Terminology." *Neot* 23 (1989) 309–30.
———. "A Tale of Two Cities: 'Tarsus or Jerusalem' Revisited." *NTS* 46 (2000) 375–402.
———. "Vilification as a Pragmatic Device in Early Christian Epistolography." *Bib* 75 (1994) 403–12.
Tomlin, G. "Christians and Epicureans in 1 Corinthians." *JSNT* 68 (1997) 51–72.
Tomson, P. J. "La première épître aux Corinthiens comme document de la tradition apostolique de halakha." In *The Corinthian Correspondence*, ed. Bieringer, 459–70.
Towner, P. H. "Gnosis and Realized Eschatology in Ephesus (of the Pastoral Epistles) and the Corinthian Enthusiasm." *JSNT* 31 (1987) 95–124.
Toynbee, J. M. C. *Death and Burial in the Roman World*. Baltimore and London: Johns Hopkins University Press, 1971.
Thraede, K. *Grundzüge griechisch-römische Brieftopik*. MKA 48. Munich: Beck, 1970.
Trebilco, P. R. *Jewish Communities in Asia Minor*. SNTSMS 69. Cambridge: Cambridge University Press, 1991.
Trobisch, D. *Die Entstehung der Paulusbriefsammlung: Studien zu den Anfängen christlicher Publizistik*. NTOA 10. Göttingen: Vandenhoeck and Ruprecht, 1989.
———. *Paul's Letter Collection: Tracing the Origins*. Minneapolis: Fortress, 1994.
Trumbower, J. A. *Rescue for the Dead: The Posthumous Salvation of Non-Christians in Early Christianity*. OSHT. Oxford: Oxford University Press, 2001.
Tuckett, C. M. "The Corinthians Who Say 'There Is No Resurrection of the Dead' (1 Cor 5,12)." In *The Corinthian Correspondence*, ed. Bieringer, 247–75.

Turcan, R. *The Cults of the Roman Empire.* Trans. A. Nevill. AW. Oxford and Cambridge, MA: Blackwell, 1996.

Tyler, R. L. "First Corinthians 4:6 and Hellensitic Pedagogy." *CBQ* 60 (1998) 97–103.

Unnik, W. C. van. "Aramaisms in Paul." *VoxT* 14 (1943) 117–26.

———. *Tarsus or Jerusalem: The City of Paul's Youth.* Trans. G. Ogg. London: Epworth, 1962.

Usami, K. "'How Are the Dead Raised?' (1 Cor 15,35–58)." *Bib* 57 (1976) 468–93.

Vanhoozer, K. J. *Is There a Meaning in This Text? The Bible, the Reader, and the Morality of Literary Knowledge.* Grand Rapids, MI: Zondervan, 1998.

Vanhoye, A. "Personnalité de Paul et exégèse paulinienne." In *L'apôtre Paul*, ed. Vanhoye, 3–15.

———, ed. *L'apôtre Paul: Personnalité, style, et conception du ministère.* BETL 73. Leuven: Leuven University Press, 1986.

Vanni, U. "Due città nella formazione di Paolo: Tarso e Gerusalemme." In *Atti del I Simposio di Tarso su S. Paulo Apostolo—Turchia: La Chiesa e la sua storia, V.* Ed. L. Padovese. Rome: Pontificio Ateneo Antoniano, 1993. 17–29.

Verhoef, E. "The Senders of the Letters to the Corinthians and the Use of 'I' and 'We.'" In *The Corinthian Correspondence*, ed. Bieringer, 417–25.

Verner, D. C. *The Household of God: The Social World of the Pastoral Epistles.* SBLDS 71. Chico, CA: Scholars Press, 1981.

Veyne, P. *Did the Greeks Believe in Their Myths? An Essay on the Constitutive Imagination.* Trans. P. Wissing. Chicago and London: University of Chicago Press, 1988.

Vielhauer, P. *Geschichte der urchristlichen Literatur.* Berlin: de Gruyter, 1975.

Vorster, J. N. "Resurrection Faith in 1 Corinthians 15. *Neot* 23 (1989) 287–307.

———. "Toward the Interactional Model for the Analysis of Letters." *Neot* 24 (1990) 107–30.

———."Why Opt for a Rhetorical Approach?" *Neot* 29 (1995) 393–418.

Vos, C. S. de. *Church and Community Conflicts: The Relationship of the Thessalonian, Corinthian, and Philippian Churches with Their Wider Civic Communities.* SBLDS 168. Atlanta: Scholars Press, 1999.

Wagner, G. *Das religionsgeschichtliche Problem von Römer 6,1–11.* ATANT 39. Zurich: Zwingli, 1962.

Wagner, J. R. "'Not Beyond the Things Which Are Written': A Call to Boast Only in the Lord (1 Cor 4.6)." *NTS* 44 (1998) 279–87.

Walbank, F. W. *The Hellenistic World.* Rev. ed. Cambridge, MA: Harvard University Press, 1992

Walker, W. O., Jr. "Acts and the Pauline Corpus Reconsidered." *JSNT* 24 (1985) 3–23.

———. "The Burden of Proof in Identifying Interpolations in the Pauline Letters." *NTS* 33 (1987) 610–18.

———. "1 Corinthians 2.6–16: A Non-Pauline Interpolation." *JSNT* 47 (1992) 75–94.

———. *Interpolations in the Pauline Letters.* JSNTSup 213. Sheffield: Sheffield Academic Press, 2001.

———. "Translation and Interpretation of Ἐὰν Μή in Galatians 2:16." *JBL* 116 (1997) 515–20.

Wallace, R. and W. Williams. *The Three Worlds of Paul of Tarsus.* London and New York: Routledge, 1998.

Walter, E. *The First Epistle to the Corinthians*. Trans. S. and E. Young. NTSR 13. Sheed and Ward, 1968.
Ward, R. F. "Pauline Voice and Presence as Strategic Communication." *Semeia* 65 (1994) 95–107.
Ward, W. E. "Theological Issues Raised in First Corinthians." *RevExp* 57 (1960) 422–37.
Waszink, J. H. "Tertullian's Principles and Methods of Exegesis." In *Early Christian Literature and the Classical Intellectual Tradition*, ed. Schoedel and Wilken, 17–31.
Watson, D. F. "Paul's Rhetorical Strategy in 1 Corinthians 15." In *Rhetoric and the New Testament*, ed. Porter and Olbricht, 231–49.
———. Review of D. Litfin, *St. Paul's Theology of Proclamation: 1 Corinthians 1–4 and Greco-Roman Rhetoric*. *Bib* 77 (1996) 128–31.
———. "A Rhetorical Analysis of Philippians and Its Implications for the Unity Question." *NovT* 30 (1988) 57–88.
Watson, F. *Paul, Judaism and the Gentiles: A Sociological Approach*. SNTSMS 56. Cambridge: Cambridge University Press, 1986.
Watson, N. *First Epistle to the Corinthians*. EC. London: Epworth, 1992.
Wedderburn, A. J. M. *Baptism and Resurrection: Studies in Pauline Theology against Its Greco-Roman Background*. WUNT 44. Tübingen: Mohr (Siebeck), 1987.
———. *Beyond Resurrection*. Peabody, MA: Hendrickson, 1999.
———. "The Body of Christ and Related Concepts in 1 Corinthians." *SJT* 24 (1971) 74–96.
———. "Hellenistic Christian Traditions in Romans 6?" *NTS* 29 (1983) 337–55.
———. "The Problem of the Denial of the Resurrection in I Corinthians XV." *NovT* 23 (1981) 229–41.
———. *The Reasons for Romans*. Edinburgh: T&T Clark, 1991.
———. "Some Observations on Paul's Use of the Phrases 'in Christ' and 'with Christ.'" *JSNT* 25 (1985) 83–97.
———. "The Soteriology of the Mysteries and Pauline Baptismal Theology." *NovT* 29 (1987) 53–72.
Weiman, J. A. D. Review of E. R. Richards, *The Secretary in the Letters of Paul*. *NovT* 34 (1992) 300–302.
Weiss, J. *Der erste Korintherbrief*. MeyerK 5. Göttingen: Vandenhoeck and Ruprecht, 1910.
Welborn, L. L. "The Identification of 2 Corinthians 10–13 with the 'Letter of Tears.'" *NovT* 29 (1987) 53–72.
———. "On the Discord in Corinth: 1 Corinthians 1–4 and Ancient Politics." *JBL* 106 (1987) 85–111.
———. *Politics and Rhetoric in the Corinthian Epistles*. Macon, GA: Mercer University Press, 1997.
Wenham, D. *Paul: Follower of Jesus or Founder of Christianity?* Grand Rapids, MI: Eerdmans, 1995.
———. "Whatever Went Wrong in Corinth?" *ExpTim* 108 (1997) 137–41.
Westcott, B. F. "Ambrosiaster." In *Dictionary of Early Christian Biography*, ed. Wace and Piercy, 15–16.
Westerholm, S. *Preface to the Study of Paul*. Grand Rapids, MI: 1997.
White, J. L. "The Ancient Epistolography Group in Retrospect." *Semeia* 22 (1981) 1–14.

———. "Introductory Formulae in the Body of the Pauline Letter." *JBL* 90 (1971) 91–97.

———. *Light from Ancient Letters*. FFNT. Philadelphia: Fortress, 1986.

———. "New Testament Epistolary Literature in the Framework of Ancient Epistolography." *ANRW* 2/25.2:1730–56.

———. "Saint Paul and the Apostolic Letter Tradition." *CBQ* 45 (1983) 433–44.

White, J. R. "'Baptized on account of the Dead': The Meaning of 1 Corinthians 15:29 in Its Context." *JBL* 116 (1997) 487–99.

White, L. M., and O. L. Yarbrough, eds. *The Social World of the First Christians: Essays in Honor of Wayne A. Meeks*. Philadelphia: Fortress, 1995.

Whiteley, D. E. H. *The Theology of Paul*. Philadelphia: Fortress, 1964.

Wilckens, U. "Zur Entwicklung des Paulinischen Gesetzesverständnisses." *NTS* 28 (1982) 154–90.

Wiles, M. F. *The Divine Apostle: The Interpretation of St. Paul's Epistles in the Early Church*. Cambridge: Cambridge University Press, 1967.

Wiles, V. *Making Sense of Paul: A Basic Introduction to Pauline Theology*. Peabody, MA: Hendrickson, 2000.

Williams, M. A. *Rethinking "Gnosticism": An Argument for Dismantling a Dubious Category*. Princeton, NJ: Princeton University Press, 1996.

Willis, W. "An Apostolic Apologia? The Form and Function of 1 Corinthians 9." *JSNT* 24 (1985) 33–48.

———. "Corinthusne deletus est?" *BZ* 35 (1991) 233–41.

———. *Idol Meat at Corinth: The Pauline Argument in 1 Corinthians 8 and 10*. SBLDS 68. Chico, CA: Scholars Press, 1985.

Wills, L. "The Form of the Sermon in Hellenistic Judaism and Early Christianity." *HTR* 77 (1984) 277–99.

Wilson, A. "The Pragmatics of Politeness and Pauline Epistolography: A Case Study of the Letter to Philemon." *JSNT* 48 (1992) 107–19.

Wilson, A. N. *Paul: The Mind of the Apostle*. New York and London: Norton, 1997.

Wilson, J. H. "The Corinthians Who Say There Is No Resurrection of the Dead." *ZNW* 59 (1968) 90–107.

Wilson, R. McL. *The Gnostic Problem: A Study of the Relations between Hellenistic Judaism and the Gnostic Heresy*. London: Mowbray, 1958.

———. "How Gnostic Were the Corinthians?" *NTS* 19 (1972–73) 65–74.

———. "Of Words and Meanings." *JSNT* 37 (1989) 9–15.

Winger, M. *By What Law? The Meaning of Νόμος in the Letters of Paul*. SBLDS 128. Atlanta: Scholars Press, 1982.

Winter, B. W. *After Paul Left Corinth: The Influence of Secular Ethics and Social Change*. Grand Rapids, MI: Eerdmans, 2001.

———. *Philo and Paul among the Sophists*. SNTSMS 96. Cambridge: Cambridge University Press, 1997.

Wire, A. C. *The Corinthian Women Prophets: A Reconstruction through Paul's Rhetoric*. Minneapolis: Fortress, 1990.

Wiseman, J. A. "Corinth and Rome I: 228 B.C.–A.D. 267." *ANRW* 2.7.1:438–53.

Witherington, B., III. *Conflict and Community in Corinth: A Socio-Rhetorical Commentary on 1 and 2 Corinthians*. Grand Rapids, MI: Eerdmans, 1995.

———. *Jesus, Paul and the End of the World: A Comparative Study in New Testament Eschatology*. Downers Grove, IL: InterVarsity, 1992.
———. *The Paul Quest: The Renewed Search for the Jew of Tarsus*. Downers Grove, IL and Leicester, Eng.: InterVarsity, 1998.
———. *Paul's Narrative Thought World: The Tapestry of Tragedy and Triumph*. Louisville: Westminster John Knox, 1994.
Wong, E. "1 Corinthians 13:7 and Christian Hope." *LS* 17 (1992) 232–42.
Woodbridge, P. "Time of Receipt of the Resurrection Body—A Pauline Inconsistency?" In *Paul and the Corinthians*, ed. Burke and Elliott, 241–58.
Wrede, W. *Paul*. Trans. E. Lummis. London: Green, 1907.
Wright, N. T. "Jesus' Resurrection and Christian Origins." *Greg* 83 (2002) 615–35.
———. *The Resurrection of the Son of God*. Minneapolis: Fortress, 2003.
Wrightman, P. *Paul's Later Letters: From Promise to Fulfillment*. Staten Island, NY: Alba House, 1984.
Wroe, A. *Pontius Pilate*. New York: Random House, 1999.
Wuellner, W. "Biblical Exegesis in the Light of the History and the Historicity of Rhetoric and the Nature of the Rhetoric of Religion." In *Rhetoric and the New Testament*, ed. Porter and Olbricht, 492–513.
———. "Greek Rhetoric and Pauline Argumentation." In *Early Christian Literature and the Classical Intellectual Tradition*, ed. Schoedel and Wilken, 177–88.
———"Paul as Pastor: The Function of Rhetorical Questions in First Corinthians." *L'apôtre Paul*, ed. Vanhoye, 49–77.
———. "Paul's Rhetoric of Argumentation in Romans: An Alternative to the Donfried–Karris Debate over Romans. *CBQ* 38 (1976) 330–51.
———. "Where Is Rhetorical Criticism Taking Us?" *CBQ* 49 (1987) 448–63.
Yamauchi, E. M. "Life, Death, and the Afterlife in the Ancient Near East." In *Life in the Face of Death*, ed. Longenecker, 21–50.
———. *Pre-Christian Gnosticism: A Survey of the Proposed Evidences*. Grand Rapids, MI: Eerdmans, 1973.
Yarbro Collins, A. "The Origin of Christian Baptism." *StLit* 19 (1989) 28–44.
Yeats, R. "Colossians and Gnosis." *JSNT* 27 (1986) 49–68.
Young, B. H. *Paul the Jewish Theologian: A Pharisee among Christians, Jews, and Gentiles*. Peabody, MA: Hendrickson, 1997.
Young, F. "The Pastoral Epistles and the Ethics of Reading." *JSNT* 45 (1992) 105–20.
Zaas, P. S. "'Cast Out the Evil Man from Your Midst' (1 Cor 5:13b)." *JBL* 103 (1984) 259–61.
———. "Catalogues and Context: 1 Corinthians 5 and 6." *NTS* 34 (1988) 622–29.
Zerhusen, B. "The Problem Tongues in 1 Cor 14: A Reexamination." *BTB* 27 (1997) 139–52.
Ziesler, J. A. *The Meaning of Righteousness in Paul: A Linguistic and Theological Inquiry*. Cambridge: Cambridge University Press, 1972.
———. *Pauline Christianity*. Rev. ed. OBS. Oxford: Oxford University Press, 1990.
Zodhiates, S. *Conquering the Fear of Death in View of the Empty Tomb: An Exposition of I Corinthians 15 Based upon the Original Greek Text*. Grand Rapids, MI: Eerdmans, 1970.

Index of Biblical Literature

Genesis
- 3 — 203
- 1:26–27 — 196
- 2:7 — 212, 214 n. 582, 239
- 2:24 — 188
- 3:16 — 196
- 17:5 — 98
- 42:15 — 36

Leviticus
- 18:8 — 184
- 19:31 — 37 n. 151

Numbers
- 6:1–21 — 163
- 15:37–41 — 192

Deuteronomy
- 6:4 — 192
- 11:13–21 — 192
- 17:2–7 — 184

1 Samuel
- 28:3–25 — 37 n. 151

2 Chronicles
- 6:41 — 245

Job
- 5:13 — 179
- 29:14 — 245

Psalms
- 8:6 — 211
- 93:11 — 179
- 34:26 — 245
- 131:9 — 245

Isaiah
- 49 — 142
- 6:1–9a — 138
- 21:1–23:18 — 92
- 22:1–14 — 92
- 22:13 — 91–92, 226, 231
- 25:8 — 216–17
- 28:11–12 — 202
- 29:14 — 174
- 40:13 — 177
- 45:14 — 203
- 49:6 — 142
- 59:17 — 245
- 64:4 — 176

Jeremiah
- 1:5 — 142
- 9:23–24 — 174

Ezekiel
- 1:4–3:11 — 138

Hosea
- 13:14 — 216–17

2 Maccabees
- 3:5 — 123
- 4:30 — 123
- 12:39–45 — 14, 37 n. 151

Matthew		9:18–30	143
5:34	28, 99	9:30	121
8:22	98	10:47–48	32
12:27	106 n. 263	11:25	121
19:3–12	191	13:2	121, 142
21:23–27	96	13:7	121
26:39	106 n. 263	13:9	121
26:42	106 n. 263	16:12	136
28:7	139	16:31–34	32
		17:16–33	165
Mark		17:28	93 n. 196
7:6	26	18:2	163
10:38	27	18:8	32
10:38–39	31, 96, 97	18:17	73
11:29–30	96	18:23–28	13
16:7	139	19:5	32
		19:21–41	156
Luke		21:13	33
9:60	98	21:39	124, 127
12:50	27, 96, 97	22:3	123
15:24	98	22:5	136
15:32	98	22:7	121
20:1–8	96	22:13	121
24:34	139	22:25–29	127
		26:14	121
John			
5:25	98	Romans	
10:37	106	5	242
11:50	33	6	242, 243, 252–53
20:18	139	7	242
20:25	139	9–11	119
20:29	139	1:1	142
		1:4	98
Acts of the Apostles		1:5	101
13–14	146	3:27	24
15	145	4:17	98
16	146	4:24	98
17	146	5:6	33, 100
18	164–65, 169	5:7	100
2:5–11	131, 132	5:8	33, 100
6:9	131, 132	6:1ff.	238
9:1–30	138	6:1–14	97, 229, 241–44,
9:2	136		251, 252–54, 256
9:11	121	6:3	32, 95–96, 230, 243
9:14	136	6:3–4	241, 244, 248
9:15	142	6:4	96, 98, 230
9:16	33	6:5–11	243

INDEX OF BIBLICAL LITERATURE

6:9	98		219, 235
6:11	98	5–14	183, 234
6:12–14	243	5–15	225
6:13	98	5–16	66, 80, 183–84
7:4	98	6	108, 171, 182, 186, 188
7:8	98		
8:9–13	253	7	108, 185, 188–90
8:10	98, 99	7–10	82
8:11	98, 239	7–16	182
8:27	101	8	165, 191
8:31	100	8–10	94, 108
8:32	33, 100	9	191, 206
8:34	101	10	165, 191, 192
8:38–39	149	11	108, 195
9:3	100	12	195, 198
9:27	101	12–14	82, 84, 108, 168, 171, 197–204, 219, 235, 250
10:1	101		
10:7	98		
10:9	98	13	198, 200–201, 202
11:1	119, 123	14	171, 198, 200, 201–202
11:15	98		
11:32	37 n. 151	15	9, 31, 38, 49, 66, 81, 82, 84–90, 98, 106–9, 141, 142, 149, 204–18, 219, 224, 226, 227, 229, 230–32, 235, 236–37, 252, 253
12:1–15:13	59–60		
13:12–14	246		
14:9	98		
14:15	100		
15:8	30, 45, 101, 102		
15:9	33, 101, 102		
15:30	100	16	82, 171
16:3–21	74	1:1–9	53–54, 77
16:4	100	1:1–11	176
16:22	73	1:10	65–67, 178, 195
		1:10–11	172
1 Corinthians		1:10–2:5	173
1	108, 196, 233, 236, 237, 251, 255	1:10–4:21	76, 83, 171, 173
		1:10–16:18	53–55
1–4	66 n. 76, 80–82, 168, 172–83, 189, 219, 225, 232, 235	1:11	82, 182
		1:11–12	115
		1:13	97, 100, 230
1–5	187	1:13–17	218, 227, 251
1–6	81	1:13b	97
1–14	234, 236	1:14	97, 230
5	108, 171, 182, 184, 186, 188	1:14–16	97
		1:14–17	15, 255
5–6	82	1:15	97, 230
5–11	168, 170, 183–97,	1:16	97, 230

1 Corinthians (cont.)		6:14	82, 109
1:16–17	218	6:16	16
1:17	97, 148, 184, 230	7:1	81, 82, 188
1:18–25	179	7:1–5	163
1:18–31	73	7:1–16	189
1:26–28	174	7:9	189
2:1	73, 179	7:12–16	189
2:6–16	73, 173, 176	7:14	14, 16
2:9	176	7:14–16	37 n. 151
2:12	176 n. 346	7:17–19	190
2:13	176	7:17–24	190
2:14	213–14	7:21–24	190
2:15	177	7:25–40	190
3:1	73, 177	7:26	188
3:1–4	201	8:1	191
3:1–9	178	8:1–13	77, 138, 192
3:1–4:21	173, 178	8:5	192
3:16–17	179	8:6	18, 149, 192, 247
3:18	178	8:7	192
3:19	179	8:7–13	192
4:1–5	179	8:13	138
4:6	74–75, 101, 102, 179	9:1	138, 206
		9:1c	140, 141
4:7	180	9:1–4	138
4:8–13	180	9:1–14	193
4:9	35	9:1–17	36
4:14	77	9:1–23	193
4:14–21	172	9:1–10:22	81, 192
4:16	90, 181, 233, 234	9:2	139
4:17	77, 181, 234	9:15	77
4:17–7:40	181 n. 376	9:24–25	19 n. 50, 155
4:18	90	9:24–27	193
4:21	181	10:1–13	19
4:21b	195	10:1–33	138
5:1	28, 99	10:2	32, 97, 218, 227, 230, 238, 251
5:1–11:34	83, 171, 183		
5:1–15:58	83, 171	10:2–12	238
5:1–6:11	76	10:14–22	193
5:5	37 n. 151, 185	10:23	81
5:10–11	186	10:23–26	194
5:11	77	10:23–33	77
5:13	184	10:23–11:1	192, 194
6:7	36, 28, 99	10:30	101, 102
6:9	93, 187	11:1	81, 90, 181, 194, 233
6:11–12	187		
6:12–20	187	11:2	195
6:12–16:24	76	11:2–16	195, 196

INDEX OF BIBLICAL LITERATURE 307

11:2–34	81, 194	15:1–3	195
11:4–6	195, 196	15:1–3a	205
11:7	195	15:1–11	31, 66, 84–86, 88–90, 104, 108, 109, 204, 205, 208
11:7–12	196		
11:12	196		
11:13–15	197	15:1–34	86
11:17–34	195, 196	15:1–58	81
11:18	195	15:2	217
11:23	195, 197	15:3	30, 45, 100, 103
11:24	100, 197 n. 477	15:3b–5	205
11:27	197	15:3b–6	205–6
11:31–32	197	15:5	206
11:33	197	15:6	205, 206
12:1–3	198	15:7	206
12:1–14:40	171, 183	15:8	138, 139, 141, 206
12:1–15:58	83	15:8a	142
12:2	198	15:11	91 n. 184, 207
12:3	198	15:12	13, 22, 84, 87–89, 94, 98, 104, 107, 109, 208, 226, 231
12:4–31	202		
12:12–13	238		
12:13	32, 97, 218, 227, 230, 251	15:12a	98
		15:12b	98
12:14–26	199	15:12–14	108–9
12:25	100	15:12–19	16, 92, 208, 209
12:28–30	200	15:12–28	31, 36, 66, 83, 84–86, 88–90, 104, 109, 204, 208, 234
12:31	201		
12:31b–14a	81		
13:4–6	201	15:12–34	87, 100
13:7	201	15:12–58	253
13:11–12	201	15:13	98, 104, 107, 209
14:1	201	15:13–14	106 n. 263
14:1–19	202	15:14	28, 107, 209, 217
14:1–25	202	15:15	98, 105
14:4–5	202	15:15–19	209
14:20–25	202	15:15b–16	209
14:22–25	202–3	15:16	98, 104, 105
14:25	203	15:16a	107
14:26	197	15:16b	107
14:26–40	202, 203	15:17	92, 107, 210
14:27–28	202	15:17–19	209
14:34	196	15:18	29
14:34–35	74–75	15:19	209
14:37	77	15:20	98, 104
14:37–38	199, 203	15:20–22	208, 214
14:40	84	15:20–28	27, 84, 103, 210
15:1–2	147, 234	15:21	98, 104, 210

1 Corinthians (cont.)		15:50	216
15:22–23	210	15:50–57	66
15:23	29	15:50–58	84–90, 109, 204, 215, 217
15:24–28	18, 210		
15:27	210	15:52	98, 105
15:27a	211	15:53–54	246
15:27b	211	15:54c–55	216
15:28	38	15:55a	217
15:29–32	30, 91	15:55b	217
15:29–34	31, 38, 66, 69, 83, 84–94, 109, 111, 204, 224, 225, 229	15:56	217
		15:57	217
		15:58	66–67, 217
15:30	22–23, 44, 91, 109	16:10	77, 181 n. 376
15:30–32	36, 91, 92, 110, 111, 204, 224	16:13–24	81
		16:15	74
15:30–34	38, 88, 111	16:19–24	53–54, 77
15:31	36, 92, 93	16:21	73–74
15:31–32	27, 254		
15:32	98, 105, 109	2 Corinthians	
15:32b	91	1:1	73
15:33–34	91, 110, 204, 224, 226	1:6	30, 45, 100
		1:7	101
15:34	94	1:8	101
15:35	84, 87–89, 91, 94, 105, 109, 212, 226, 231	1:9	98
		1:11a	100
		1:11b	101, 102
15:35–44a	84	2:2–3	36
15:35–58	87	2:14	35
15:35–49	66, 84–86, 88–90, 104, 109. 204, 206, 211	4:8–10	135
		4:10–11	35
		5:12	101
15:35–57	247	5:14	100
15:35–58	83	5:14–15	33
15:36	212	5:15	100
15:36–44a	212	5:20	100–101
15:36–49	211–12	5:21	101
15:40–41	212–13	6:9	35
15:42	105	7:4	101
15:42a	98, 213	7:7	101
15:42b–44a	213	7:12	101
15:44	177	7:14	101
15:44a	213	8:16	101
15:44b–49	84, 214, 253	8:23	101
15:45	98, 239	8:24	101
15:46	177, 215	9:2	101
15:48	215	9:3	101
15:49	215	9:14	101

11:22	123	5:5	250
11:24–25a	135	5:13–6:10	64 n. 61
11:32–33	143	6:7	93
12:1	141, 206	6:11	73
12:1–4	140		
12:2ff.	141	Ephesians	
12:5	101	1:13	247
12:8	101, 102	1:20	98 n. 220
12:10	101	2:1	98
12:15	101	2:4–6	247, 248
12:19	101	2:5	98
13:8	101	4:4–6	247
		4:5	95 n. 207, 247
Galatians		4:22–24	247
1	142, 146	4:24	246
2	145, 146	5:2	33
3	244, 246, 253	5:14	98
1:1	98	5:22–27	247
1:2	73	5:25	33
1:4	101	6:11	246
1:11–12	147	6:14	246
1:12	142		
1:12–16	139	Philippians	
1:13	134	1:1	73
1:13–14	123	1:4	101
1:13–15	206	1:7	101
1:15	142	1:29	33, 101, 102
1:15–17	138, 142	2:13	101
1:16a	142	3:5	123
1:17	143	3:11	98
1:21	124	3:21	216
2:1–14	146	4:10	101
2:15	123		
2:19–20	241	Colossians	
2:20	33, 101	1:1	73
3:1–29	97	1:18	98 n. 220
3:2	244	2:10–15	18
3:13	33, 101	2:11–12	241
3:26	245	2:11–13	247
3:26–29	97, 229, 238, 241, 244–47, 248, 251, 252–54, 256	2:12	95 n. 207, 98 n. 220, 243, 247–48
		2:13	98
3:27	95, 97, 230, 244, 245	3:1	243
		3:1–4	248
3:28	246, 248	3:10	246
3:29	246	3:10–11	248

Colossians (cont.)
    3:12   246
    4:8   73
    6:14   68

1 Thessalonians
    1:1   73
    1:10   98
    3:2   101
    4:3–8   189
    4:13–18   207, 216
    4:13–5:11   40
    4:16   98
    5:8   246
    5:10   33, 101
    5:27   68

2 Thessalonians
    1:1   73
    1:5   101, 102
    2:17   73

1 Timothy
    2:11–15   203

2 Timothy
    2:8   98 n. 220
    2:11–13   248

    4:1   98 n. 220

Titus
    1:12   93 n. 196
    2:14   33
    3:5   250

Philemon
    1   73
    13   33, 101
    19   73

Hebrews
    6:1   98
    9:14   98

James
    2:17   98
    2:26   98

1 Peter
    3:19–22   18
    4:6   37 n. 151

Revelation
    3:1   98
    7:4   13

Index of Ancient Literature and Apocrypha

Acta Johannis
114   20

Acta Pauli et Theclae
28–31   37 n. 150

Apocalypsis Pauli
13–14   20

Appian
Historia romana
8.136   153

Apuleius
Metamorphoses
2   162
10.19.25   154
11   162

Aristophanes
Fragmenta
354   152

Aristotle
Ars rhetorica
1.3   56

Athenaeus
Deipnnosophistae
31c, 559a 152

Augustine
De doctrina christiana
4   56

Enarrationes in Psalmos
Ps. 88,
ser. 2, par. 5   237

Cicero
Epistulae ad Atticum
11.5.1   73

*Pro Lege manilia
(De imperio Cn. Pompeii)*
5   152

Clement of Alexandria
Stromata
1.52.9   93 n. 196

Clement of Rome
1 Clement
34.8   176

Dio Cassius
Historia romana
60.6.6   163

Dio Chrysostom
Orationes
33   125
33–34   125

1 Enoch
47:5   13

Epiphanius
*Panarion
(Adversus haereses)*
28   41

2 Esdras
   4:35   13

Eusebius
  Historia ecclesiastica
   3.28.6   41 n. 167
   6.44.2–6   20

Gaius
  Institutiones
   1.6   185

Herodotus
  Historiae
   2.167   152

Homer
  Ilias
   IV, 397, 413   124

  Odyssea
   XI   37 n. 151

Horace
  Epistulae
   1.17.36   154

Ignatius of Antioch
  Epistula ad Smyrnaeos
   5.2   99 n. 223

Irenaeus
  Adversus haereses
   3.11.1   41 n. 167

Jerome
  De viris illustribus
   5   126

John Chrysostom
  Homiliae in 1 ad Corinthios
   23   99 n. 223
   40   25, 41

Josephus
  Antiquities judaicae
   2.344   28 n. 101
   5.35   28 n. 101
   8.258   28 n. 101
   9.80, 127   28 n. 101
   14.190–95 136 n. 133
   14.228–40 128

  Bellum judaicum
   1.47   136 n. 133
   1.88   132
   2.561   136, 145 n. 177
   3.368, 423 96 n. 212
   3.525   96 n. 212
   4.137   96 n. 212
   4.364   28 n. 101
   5.219   28 n. 101
   7.368   145 n. 177

  Contra Apionem
   1.255   36

Marcus Aurelius
  Meditationes
   12.33   26

Origen
  Fragmenta ex commentaries in epistulam I ad Corinthios
   24.93.12–13   185

  Homiliae in Matthaeum
   17.27   24, 40, 100 n. 228

Orosius
  Historiae adversum paganos
   7.6.15   164

Oxyrhynchus Papyri
   1676.29–31   35 n. 141

Passio Perpetuae et Felicitatis
   4   20

Pausanias
  Graeciae description
   1.7–9   158
   2.2   159

2.33	158 n. 244	*Pompeius*	
2.4	162	24.5	125

Philo
De Abrahamo
56   214 n. 583

De opificio mundi
47.136–141   214 n. 583

Legatio ad Gaium
36.281   163
158   127

Philostratus
Vita Apollonii
1.7   125
4.34   125

Plato
Phaedrus
275e   68

Respublica
404d   152

Pliny the Younger
Epistulae ad Trajanum
10.96–97   156

Plutarch
Antonius
26   124

Moralia
773d   26
831a   155
1098c   92 n. 186
1100d   92 n. 186
1125d   92 n. 186

Pomponius Mela
De chorographia
2.51   158 n. 244

Polycarp
Epistola ad Phillippenses
5   248

Shepherd of Hermas
Similtudes
6.5–6   13
9.16.5–6   20

Strabo
Geographica
8.6   153
8.6.20   150, 152, 154
8.6.23   153, 163
14.5.12,13   125
16.2.39   37 n. 151

Suetonius
Divus Claudius
25   154
25.4   164

Tertullian
Adversus Marcionem
1.4   40–41
5.10   25, 41

De resurrectione carnis
48   40
48.11   25

Tosefta Megillah
2:17   131

Index of Modern Authors

Aageson, J. W., 242 n. 40
Agersnap, S., 10, 11 n. 14, 12 n. 19, 242 n. 36, 242 n. 38
Akenson, D. H., 117
Aland, K., 22 n. 64
Alderink, L., 160 n. 255
Aletti, J.-N., 38, 63 n. 59, 87 n. 181, 104 n. 256, 208 n. 542, 210 n. 552
Allo, E.-B., 11 n. 14, 87 n. 179
Amador, J. D. H., 78 n. 147
Anderson, H. G., 249 n. 79
Anderson, R. D., Jr., 56 n. 22, 56 n. 23, 58, 59 n. 37, 61 n. 47, 63 n. 57, 63 n. 60, 64 n. 61, 65 n. 68, 65–67
Angus, S., 245 n. 59
Arzt, P., 54 n. 11
Ashton, J., 114 n. 2, 117, 118 nn. 28–29,
Aune, D. E., 53 n. 5, 54 n. 14, 55 n. 14, 63 n. 60, 67–68, 69 n. 89, 254 n. 83
Bahr, G. J., 74–75
Bailey, K. E., 77 n. 142, 181 n. 376
Baird, W., 205 n. 526, 232
Balch, D. L., 189 n. 429
Barbaglio, G., 11 n. 14, 17, 77 n. 142
Barclay, J. M. G, 127–29, 165 n. 288, 237 n. 15, 244 n. 53
Bardy, G., 41 n. 167
Barlow, P. L., 2 n. 3
Barnes, A., 34 n. 133
Barnett, P. W., 133 n. 119
Barr, J., 96 n. 213, 123 n. 54
Barrett, C. K., 11 n. 14, 15, 26 n. 88, 29 n. 111, 32 n. 126, 38, 45, 63 n. 60, 77 n. 142, 80 n. 159, 81 n. 163, 87 n. 180, 93 n. 200, 95, 110 n. 279, 148, 168, 169 n. 302, 170 n. 310, 173 n. 329, 174 n. 336, 175 n. 337, 175 n. 339, 176 n. 343, 176 n. 347, 180 n. 368, 184 n. 389, 188 n. 418, 188 n. 422, 197 n. 479, 199 n. 489, 199 n. 491, 210, 212 n. 566, 215 nn. 585–86, 217 n. 599, 219 n. 606, 220–21, 232 n. 7
Barry, D. H., 57 n. 24
Barth, K., 219 n. 607
Barton, S. C., 197 n. 475
Bates, W. H., 78 n. 147
Bauckham, R., 37 nn. 150–51
Baur, F. C., 114–15, 128
Beasley-Murray, G. R., 10, 19 n. 49, 32 n. 127, 38 n. 152, 45, 238, 246 n. 66, 247 n. 70, 248 n. 76
Becker, J., 117 n. 26
Beker, J. C., 117 n. 26, 123 n. 60
Belleville, L. L., 80 n. 158
Benda, J., 62 n. 54
Bergin, L., 244 n. 51
Bertram, G., 99 n. 223
Betz, H. D., 55, 56 n. 23, 58, 60–63, 64 n. 62, 74 n. 118, 242 n. 39
Bieringer, R., 172 n. 320
Black, C. C., II, 63 n. 58
Blakeney, E. H., 101 n. 235
Boer, M. C. de, 80–82, 171, 182 n. 383, 211 n. 557
Boers, H., 241, 242 n. 41, 244 n. 50
Bondi, R. A., 181 n. 374
Bonneau, N., 87 n. 180, 212 n. 560, 212 n. 562, 213 n. 571
Bonner, G., 56 n. 22

Bookidis, N., 160 n. 256
Borchert, G. L., 11 n. 14
Borgen, P., 194 n. 459
Bornkamm, G., 216 n. 592
Bowe, B. E., 76 n. 135
Bowen, C. R., 92 n. 190, 226 n. 626
Boyarin, D., 116 n. 14
Boyer, J. L., 106
Brandt, W. J. 60 n. 44
Brankin, P. M., 2 n. 4
Braxton, B. R., 190 n. 436
Breck, J., 85 nn. 173–75
Brodeur, S., 87 n. 180, 188 n. 423, 212 n. 569, 214 n. 580, 215 n. 585, 215 n. 588, 239 n. 25
Broneer, O. T., 19 n. 50
Brown, R. E., 53 nn. 9–10, 57, 58 n. 30, 175 n. 339
Bruce, F. F., 80 n. 162, 81 n. 163, 123 n. 57, 124 nn. 65–66, 124 n. 68, 125 n. 71, 126 n. 79, 143, 246 n. 63
Bullmore, M. A., 64 n. 63, 172 n. 322
Bultmann, R., 11 n. 14, 19 n. 49, 98 n. 217, 98 n. 221, 99 n. 223, 115–16, 120, 230
Bünker, M., 63 n. 59
Burgess, J. A., 249 n. 79
Byrne, B., 188 n. 421, 188 n. 425, 189 n. 427, 242 n. 41, 243 nn. 44–45
Caird, G. B., 211 n. 556
Callan, T., 203 n. 519
Cambier, J., 185 n. 396
Campbell, A., 243 n. 43
Campbell, D. A., 144 n. 173
Carlson, R. P., 8 n. 6, 244 n. 49
Carr, A., 11 n. 14, 13, 16, 148, 220–21
Carrez, M., 11 n. 14
Cheung, A. T., 191 n. 442
Chow, J. K., 184 n. 390, 225 n. 621
Cipriani, S., 87 n. 181, 183 n. 385, 235 n. 12
Clarke, M. L., 57 n. 24
Classen, C. J., 56 n. 23, 58 n. 34, 63 n. 57, 65 n. 66
Clauss, M., 126 nn. 72–74
Clinton, K., 160 n. 255

Colijn, B. B., 244 n. 52
Collins, J. J., 79 n. 151
Collins, R. F., 11 n. 14, 70, 77 n. 142, 78 n. 146, 78 n. 148, 87 n. 179, 91 n. 184, 92 n. 189, 92 n. 192, 93 n. 200, 174 n. 333, 175 n. 339, 176 n. 344, 177 n. 350, 178 n. 352, 179, 180 n. 369, 181 n. 378, 184 n. 389, 185 n. 391, 186 n. 406, 189 n. 431, 191 n. 438, 192 n. 445, 197 n. 478, 199 n. 490, 199 n. 493, 200 n. 502, 201 n. 507, 204 n. 522, 205 n. 524, 209 n. 543, 210 n. 547, 210 n. 551, 211 n. 558, 214 n. 579, 226 n. 626, 238 n. 22
Conant, T. J., 95
Conzelmann, H., 8 n. 5, 11 n. 14, 15 n. 33, 38, 44 n. 179, 73 n. 112, 77 n. 142, 87 n. 179, 91 n. 184, 94 n. 202, 119 n. 32, 180 n. 363, 184 n. 389, 186 n. 405, 191 n. 439, 194 n. 461, 195 n. 463, 196 n. 472, 197 n. 479, 203 n. 520, 209 n. 546, 217 n. 596, 217 n. 599
Corley, B., 143 n. 172
Cotter, W., 37 n. 151
Cross, A. R., 239 n. 26, 247 n. 71
Cuming, C. J., 199 n. 495
Cummings, O. F., 2 n. 4
Dahl, M. E., 213 n. 574
Dahl, N. A., 172 n. 318, 173
Dana, H. E., 35 n. 142
Davies, D. J., 37 n. 151
Davies, W. D., 63 n. 60, 115
Davis, S. T., 140
Dawes, G. W., 190 nn. 433–35, 192 nn. 447–48, 212 n. 561
Deer, D. S., 93 n. 193
Deines, R., 131
Deissmann, A., 52–53, 55
Delobel, J., 194 n. 460, 196
De Lorenzi, L., 87 n. 180
DeMaris, R. E., 9, 11 n. 14, 17, 19–21, 39–40, 48, 49 n. 195, 86, 149, 166–67
Deming, W., 189 n. 430, 190 n. 435, 190 n. 437

Derrett, J. D. M., 187 n. 410
deSilva, D. A., 172 n. 319, 180 n. 366
Dickie, M. W., 37 n. 151
Dion, P. E., 54 n. 14
Dodd, B. J., 187 n. 415
Dodd, C. H., 205 n. 526
Donaldson, T. L., 118 n. 27
Donfried, K. P., 59
Doty, W. G., 52 n. 4, 55 nn. 15–16
Doughty, D. J., 180 nn. 370–71
Downey, J., 11 n. 14, 17–19, 31 n. 120, 39–40, 48, 149
Dozeman, T. B., 63 n. 58
Duncan, T. S., 57 n. 28
Dunn, J. D. G., 11 n. 14, 19 n. 49, 59 n. 39, 116, 117 n. 26, 138 n. 144, 142 n. 166, 143 n. 168, 239–40, 242 n. 41, 243 n. 47, 248 nn. 77–78, 251 n. 81
Dürselen, P., 10 n. 12, 21–22, 43–44
Ellis, E. E., 122 n. 53, 123 n. 54, 212 n. 567
Ellis, P. F., 173, 189 n. 428, 192 n. 443, 193 n. 449, 198, 202 nn. 512–13
Engberg-Pederson, T., 120 n. 39, 196 n. 470, 225
Engels, D., 153–56, 157 n. 232, 157 nn. 234–35, 158 nn. 237–40, 159, 160 n. 252, 160 n. 254, 160 n. 257, 161–63, 164 nn. 277–78
Enslin, M., 124 n. 61
Eriksson, A., 64 n. 63, 91 n. 183, 92 n. 187, 226 n. 624
Evans, E., 23–24, 80 n. 162, 106 n. 269
Fairweather, J., 58 n. 31
Fee, G. D., 8 n. 6, 32 n. 123, 32 n. 126, 33 n. 130, 45, 54 n. 14, 77 n. 142, 80 n. 158, 81 n. 163, 91 n. 184, 94 n. 202, 102 n. 245, 139 n. 148, 141, 148, 172 n. 318, 174 n. 331, 175–76, 178, 179 n. 360, 185 nn. 392–93, 188 n. 426, 189 n. 427, 189 n. 432, 191 n. 440, 193 n. 454, 194 n. 462, 196 n. 469, 198 n. 482, 199 n. 494, 200 nn. 496–97, 200 n. 500, 202 n. 516, 205 n. 527, 207 n. 534, 209 n. 544, 211 n. 555, 213, 215 n. 587, 217 nn. 597–98, 218 n. 604, 247 n. 68
Ferguson, J., 126 nn. 75–78
Findlay, G. G., 29 n. 106, 91 n. 184
Finn, T. M., 13 n. 23, 242 n. 36
Fiore, B., 63 nn. 58–59, 74 n. 118, 80 n. 160, 180 n. 365
Fitzgerald, J. T., 180 n. 367, 180 n. 369
Fitzmyer, J. A., 54 n. 14, 117 n. 26, 242, 243 n. 46
Focant, C., 200 n. 501
Foerster, W., 54 n. 14
Forbes, C., 92 n. 192, 149
Foschini, B. M., 8, 9, 11 n. 15, 21–23, 40 n. 159, 41 nn. 164–65, 42 n. 168, 42 n. 170, 42 n. 172, 43–44
Fowler, R. M., 63 n. 57
Freke, T., 115 n. 5
Friedrich, G., 216 n. 593
Furnish, V. P., 164 nn. 279–83, 178 n. 344, 183, 218 n. 605, 220
Gager, J. G., 137 n. 142, 138 n. 143
Gamble, H. Y., 72 n. 101, 72 n. 104, 72 n. 107, 73 n. 114, 79 n. 150, 79 n. 152
Gandy, P., 115 n. 5
Gärtner, B. E., 176 n. 346
Gasque, W. W., 123 n. 57, 124 nn. 63–64
Gebhard, E. R., 155 n. 226
Georgi, D., 118 n. 28
Gill, D. W. J., 151
Gillman, J., 216 n. 590, 217 n. 602
Godet, F., 27, 87 n. 179, 95, 97
Goldenberg, R., 133 n. 114
Goldman, H., 124 n. 62
Goodman, M., 133 n. 116
Goudge, H. L., 32 n. 126
Goulder, M. D., 207 n. 538, 215 n. 584
Graf, D. F., 135 n. 132
Graf, F., 37 n. 151
Green, P., 93 n. 197, 125 n. 69, 153 n. 212
Grosheide, F. W., 11 n. 16, 12 n. 17
Gruen, E. S., 163 n. 276

Grundmann, W., 54 n. 13
Hafemann, S., 35, 36 n. 148, 47, 115 n. 5
Hagner, D. A., 72
Hansen, G. W., 238 nn. 21–22
Harland, P. A., 187 n. 409
Harnack, A. von, 41 n. 161
Harrer, G. A., 121 nn. 42–45, 122 n. 46
Harrill, J. A., 245 n. 60
Harris, H., 115 n. 3
Harris, M. J., 102 n. 245, 239–40
Harris, G., 184 n. 388, 185 n. 398, 186 n. 400
Harrisville, R. A., 11 n. 14
Hartman, L., 11 n. 14, 240, 244 n. 52, 247 n. 73
Hays, R. B., 170 n. 311
Heinrici, C. F. G., 56 n. 23
Hellholm, D., 243 n. 44
Hemer, C. J., 121 n. 44, 122 n. 47
Hengel, M., 119 n. 31, 122 n. 48, 123, 127 n. 83, 135 n. 127, 136 n. 136, 144 n. 174, 144 n. 176
Hersey, G., 152 n. 208
Heydenreich, A. L. C., 24 n. 71
Heyer, C. J. den, 57 n. 29
Hill, C. E., 87 n. 180
Hock, R. F., 36, 125 n. 70
Hodge, C., 8 n. 6
Hollander, H. W., 206 n. 533, 217 nn. 600–601
Holleman, J., 87 n. 180, 217 nn. 600–601
Hooker, M. D., 180 n. 363
Horn, F. W., 217 n. 599
Horrell, D. G., 191 n. 441, 192 n. 444, 192 n. 446, 193 nn. 450–51, 193 n. 456, 194 n. 457, 238 n. 19
Horsley, R. A., 28, 137 n. 141, 172 n. 318, 175 n. 338, 177 nn. 348–49, 200 n. 498, 214 nn. 575–76, 214 n. 583
Hout, G. E. van der, 206 n. 533
Howard, J. K., 29–31, 33 n. 130, 45 n. 185, 46 n. 188, 221
Hübner, H., 63 n. 60

Hultgren, A. J., 134 n. 122, 134 n. 124, 135 n. 126, 135 n. 129, 135 n. 131
Hurd, J. C., Jr., 53 n. 8, 77 nn. 142–43, 78 n. 146, 80 n. 156, 80 n. 158, 81 n. 163, 169, 169 nn. 305–6, 182 n. 382, 189 n. 429, 191 n. 442, 198 n. 480, 198 n. 483, 201 n. 506
Jansen, J. F., 211 n. 554
Jeremias, J., 29–30, 32 n. 125, 33, 35, 42 n. 172, 45–46, 85 n. 174, 101, 104 n. 255, 110, 131 n. 107, 132 n. 108, 143 n. 167, 215 n. 589, 216, 221
Jewett, R., 117 n. 27, 245 n. 54
Johnson, L. T., 121 n. 40
Johnson, S. E., 153 n. 214
Johnston, S. I., 37 n. 151
Joyce, J. D., 9, 11 n. 14, 16
Judge, E. A., 57 n. 27, 92 n. 192
Karris, R. J., 59
Keck, L. E., 75 nn. 125–26
Kennedy, G. A., 61, 63 n. 57
Kent, H. A., Jr., 94 n. 206
Kent, J. H., 155 n. 224
Kim, S., 138 n. 144
Kistemaker, S. J., 8 n. 6, 11 n. 15, 78 n. 144, 233 n. 8
Klauck, H.-J., 37 n. 150
Klassen, W., 54 n. 15
Knox, J., 57 n. 27, 75 n. 127, 114, 147, 172 n. 321, 182 n. 381
Koester, H., 19 n. 50, 155 n. 226, 159 nn. 246–49
Koskenniemi, H., 53 n. 11, 55 n. 15, 55 n. 18
Lambrecht, J., 78 n. 147, 87 n. 180, 141 n. 162, 201 n. 508, 207–8, 211 n. 555
Lampe, G. W. H., 14 n. 27, 186 n. 402
Lampe, P., 63 n. 59, 80 n. 160
Lane, W. L., 78 n. 147
Lanham, R. A., 61 n. 47
Ledgerwood, L. W., III, 106 nn. 262–63
Levine, L. I., 128, 131–32
Lewis, S. M., 87 n. 181, 208 n. 541, 210 n. 553

INDEX OF MODERN AUTHORS

Lightfoot, J. B., 87 n. 179
Lilly, J. L., 139, 141 n. 160
Litfin, D., 64 n. 63, 80 n. 160, 172 n. 322
Lohse, E., 133 n. 115
Longenecker, R. N., 237 n. 16, 238 n. 21, 245 n. 61
Luck, G., 37 n. 151
Lüdemann, G., 40 n. 161, 140 n. 155, 147 n. 189
Ludlow, D. H., 2 n. 2
Lührmann, D., 136 n. 137
Lund, N. W., 85
Maccoby, H., 116–17
MacDonald, D. R., 92 n. 189
MacDonald, M. Y., 226 n. 626, 247 n. 69, 248 n. 75
Mack, B., 63 n. 59
Majercik, R., 63 n. 58
Malherbe, A. J., 57 nn. 25–26, 81 n. 163, 92 n. 191, 93 n. 193, 93 n. 199, 226 n. 626
Malina, B. J., 118 n. 27
Mantey, J. R., 35 n. 142
Mare, W. H., 32 n. 123
Marshall, H., 147 n. 188
Marshall, P., 180, 181 n. 373
Martin, D. B., 133 n. 115, 212 n. 564, 214 n. 578
Martin, H. V., 11 n. 14, 12, 16–18, 38, 148
Martin, R. P., 64 n. 63
Martin, T. W., 246 nn. 64–65
Martyn, J. L., 117 n. 26, 245 n. 62
Mason, S., 131 n. 100
Matand Bulembat, J.-B., 87 n. 181
Matera, F. J., 142 nn. 164–65, 143 nn. 169–70, 245 nn. 55–56, 245 n. 58, 246
McMurrin, S. M., 2 n. 2
McRay, J., 135 n. 132
Mearns, C. L., 169 n. 306
Meeks, W. A., 8 n. 6, 40, 68, 128 nn. 87–89, 166 n. 291, 193 n. 455
Meier, J. P., 131
Merklein, H., 72–73, 76–77

Meyer, B. F., 237 n. 16
Meyer, P. W., 63 n. 60
Meynet, R., 61 n. 50
Michaelis, W., 140 nn. 156–57, 141 nn. 158–59
Millard, Alan., 68 n. 84
Mitchell, A. C., 186 n. 407
Mitchell, M. M., 54 n. 12, 55 n. 15, 61, 63 n. 59, 64–67, 77, 78 n. 148, 80 n. 160, 81 n. 163, 86–87, 170, 174 n. 332, 188 n. 424
Moffatt, J., 11 n. 14, 14, 38, 148, 220–21
Moiser, J., 27 n. 91
Moulton, J. H., 35 n. 142
Muilenburg, J., 58–59
Mullins, T. Y., 53 n. 11
Murphy, T. A., 249 n. 79
Murphy-O'Connor, J., 11 n. 15, 26 n. 89, 27–29, 32, 34 n. 138, 35, 38, 43–45, 47, 57 n. 27, 69 n. 92, 72 n. 106, 73–75, 78 n. 149, 80, 86, 95, 97, 99–100, 110, 117 n. 27, 118, 119 n. 30, 120 n. 33, 121 n. 41, 122 nn. 51–52, 123 n. 55, 125 n. 71, 127 n. 81, 130 n. 95, 134–36, 143 n. 170, 144 n. 175, 145 n. 178, 145 nn. 178–84, 147 n. 185, 151–52, 153 n. 213, 153 n. 215, 155 n. 223, 158 nn. 241–42, 164, 165 n. 286, 187 n. 414, 195, 196 n. 468, 196 n. 473, 205 n. 527, 205 n. 529, 206 n. 531, 234 n. 11
Nasuti, H. P., 139 n. 147, 193 n. 453
Neirynck, F., 189 n. 429
Nestle, E., 22 n. 64
Newton, D., 160 n. 253, 161 n. 260, 161 n. 265, 163 n. 270, 193 n. 452
Neyrey, J. H., 64 n. 63, 117 n. 27, 118 n. 27
Nickelsburg, G. W. E., 142 n. 163, 206 n. 532
Nock, A. D., 167
North, J. L., 57 n. 27, 133 n. 118
O'Collins, G., 140 n. 152, 140 n. 155

Oepke, A., 12, 96 n. 211, 106 n. 266–67
Ogden, D., 37 n. 151, 158 nn. 243–44, 159 n. 245
Olbrechts-Tyteca, L., 59–60, 62 n. 55
Olbricht, T. H., 62 n. 55, 70
O'Neill, J. C., 21, 25–27, 32, 35, 43–47, 99–100, 110
Orr, W. F., 11 n. 14, 17, 40 n. 158, 42 n. 173
Osborne, R. E., 92 n. 189
Oster, R., 163 n. 271, 165 n. 287, 195, 245 n. 60
Pagels, E. H., 214 n. 577
Painchaud, L., 214 n. 583
Pardee, D., 54 n. 14
Parry, R. St. J., 11 n. 14, 12 n. 18, 16, 39, 223
Pascuzzi, M., 185 n. 397, 186 n. 401, 186 nn. 403–4
Patton, J. H., 63 n. 57
Penna, R., 74 n. 118
Perelman, C., 59–60, 62 n. 55
Perriman, A. C., 217 n. 603
Petersen, N. R., 236 n. 13
Pilch, J. J., 139 n. 149, 140
Plevnik, J., 33 n. 130, 237 n. 16, 237 n. 17
Plummer, A., 16, 28, 30, 53 n. 10, 54 n. 14, 55, 82 n. 171, 87 n. 179, 94 n. 201, 106 n. 269, 110, 199 n. 492, 210 n. 549, 212 n. 563, 216 n. 59, 217 n. 599
Pogoloff, S. M., 64 n. 63, 172 n. 322
Porter, S. E., 61 n. 46, 62 n. 55, 100 n. 231, 100 n. 234, 101 n. 238, 104 n. 253, 105 nn. 258–59, 106 n. 263
Powers, D. G., 239 n. 28
Pratt, F., 11 n. 14
Preisker, H., 11 n. 14, 13–14, 37, 42 n. 170, 148, 220–21
Price, S., 156 n. 231, 157 n. 236
Prior, M., 73
Prusak, B. P., 235 n. 12
Puskas, C. B., 63 n. 59, 78 n. 148, 80 n. 160
Rad, G. von, 54 n. 14

Raeder, M., 11 n.15, 29–30, 33, 35, 42 n. 172, 45–46, 101, 110, 221
Ramsay, W. M., 53, 123
Raphael, S. P., 37 n. 151
Reaume, J. D., 9 n. 9, 11 n. 15, 26 n. 87, 31–34, 35 n. 142, 43 n. 176, 45–47, 100 n. 229, 102 n. 245, 111, 221–22, 230
Reed, J. T., 56 n. 19, 56 n. 21, 70
Reese. J. M., 174 n. 335
Richard, E. J., 68
Richards, E. R., 73–74
Ridderbos, H., 11 n. 14, 117 n. 26, 233 n. 10, 240, 250 n. 80
Riesenfeld, H., 10 n. 13, 35 n. 142, 100 n. 231, 100 n. 234, 101 n. 238–43, 230 n. 3
Riesner, R., 117 n. 27
Rissi, M., 8–9, 10, 14–15, 38, 45 n. 180, 148, 220–21
Robbins, V. K., 63 n. 57
Robertson, A., 16, 28, 30, 53 n. 10, 54 n. 14, 55, 82 n. 171, 87 n. 179, 94 n. 201, 106 n. 269, 110, 199 n. 492, 210 n. 549, 212 n. 563, 217 n. 599
Robertson, A. T., 34 n. 133, 100 n. 233, 101 n. 236, 216 n. 591
Robinson, J. A. T., 213 n. 574
Roetzel, C. J., 117 n. 27
Roller, O., 79 n. 155
Rosner, B. S., 188 n. 420
Saldarini, A. J., 127, 130 n. 96, 131 n. 105
Sanders, E. P., 115–16, 132 n. 113, 133 n. 120, 166
Sanders, J. T., 53 n. 11, 200 n. 500
Sanders, T. K., 200 n. 502
Sandnes, K. O., 203 n. 518
Saw, I., 63 n. 59, 87 n. 181
Schaff, P., 41 n. 167
Schmithals, W., 72, 169, 209, 214 n. 577
Schnackenburg, R., 11 nn. 14–15, 30, 98 n. 219, 199 n. 494, 227 n. 627, 238 nn. 23–24, 247 n. 72, 248 n. 74

Schneider, B., 211 n. 559, 214 n. 583
Schubert, P., 53 n. 11
Schüssler Fiorenza, E., 172 n. 321
Schütz, J. H., 225 n. 623
Schweitzer, A., 14 n. 27, 115
Schwemer, A. M., 122 n. 48, 144 n. 174, 144 n. 176
Segal, A. F., 132 n. 113
Sellew, P., 74 n. 118
Sellin, G., 11 n. 14, 78 n. 146, 81 n. 163
Semler, J. S., 24 n. 71
Senft, C., 11 n. 14
Serna, E. de la, 78 n. 146, 80–81, 183 n. 384
Sevrin, J.-M., 174 n. 332
Shanor, J., 178 nn. 355–57
Sherwin-White, A. N., 121 n. 41
Sherwood, J., 133 n. 116
Shillington, V. G., 185 n. 395
Shipley, G., 124 n. 67
Ships, J., 2 n. 2
Sider, R. J., 206 n. 530, 207 n. 535, 213 n. 573
Sievers, J., 130 n. 98
Sigountos, J. G., 63 n. 59, 200 n. 501
Silva, M., 63 n. 60, 122 n. 50
Simon, W. H., 8 n. 6
Smit, J. F. M., 63–64, 172 n. 322, 172 n. 323, 173 n. 324, 194 n. 458, 198–99, 200 n. 499, 200 n. 504
Smith, D., 80 n. 162
Smith, D. E., 162 n. 268
Smith, D. M., 123 n. 54
Smith, J. Z., 57 n. 29, 71 n. 99, 72 n. 105, 129 n. 93, 242 n. 36
Smith, M., 182 nn. 379–80
Söding, T., 217 n. 599
South, J. T., 185 n. 394, 185 n. 399
Staab, K., 26 n. 86, 41 n. 162, 41 n. 165
Standaert, B., 61 n. 50
Stanley, C. D., 122 n. 53, 123 n. 54, 147 n. 189, 214 n. 582
Stanley, D. M., 181
Stendahl, K., 118 n. 28
Stephenson, A. M. G., 78 n. 147

Sterling, G. E., 170 n. 308
Stewart-Sykes, A., 79
Stirewalt, M. L., Jr., 53 n. 7, 69
Stowers, S. K., 55 n. 15, 55 n. 18, 56, 68–70
Sundberg, A. C., Jr.
Surgy, P. de, 11 n. 14
Swetnam, J., 63 n. 60
Tannehill, R. C., 242 n. 36
Taylor, J. E., 137 n. 138
Theissen, G., 117 n. 27, 157 n. 233, 196 n. 474
Thiselton, A. C., 11 n. 15, 34 n. 137, 93 n. 199, 119 n. 32, 170, 174 n. 334, 175 n. 339, 175 nn. 340–41, 176 n. 344, 176 n. 347, 177 n. 351, 180 n. 363, 180 n. 368, 192 n. 444, 195 n. 464, 196 n. 471, 196 n. 474, 202 nn. 510–11, 202 n. 514, 203 n. 517, 203 n. 521, 205 n. 525, 207 nn. 538–39, 210 n. 550, 214 n. 579, 233 n. 9
Thompson, K. C., 8 n. 5, 21, 22 n. 64, 23–25, 32, 40 n. 159, 41 n. 163, 43–44, 100 n. 228, 106 n. 269
Thraede, K., 55 n. 18
Toit, A. du, 120, 122 n. 49, 122 nn. 51–52, 123 nn. 58–59, 130 n. 94, 130 n. 96
Tomlin, G., 92 n. 185
Toynbee, J. M. C., 167 n. 295
Trebilco, P. R., 128 n. 86
Trobisch, D., 72 n. 100, 76
Trumbower, J. A., 14 n. 30, 15 n. 33, 37 n. 150, 44 n. 179
Tyler, R. L., 180 n. 364
Unnik, W. C. van, 120, 122 n. 49, 123 n. 57
Usami, K., 87 n. 180, 212 n. 565, 212 n. 568
Vanni, U., 120 n. 35
Vielhauer, P., 81 n. 163
Vorster, J. N., 87 n. 181
Vos, C. S. de, 154 n. 222
Wagner, G., 11 n. 14, 241 n. 36
Wagner, J. R., 92 n. 192, 180 n. 363

Walbank, F. W., 133 n. 117
Walker, W. O., Jr., 75
Wallace, R., 57 n. 29, 120 n. 34
Walther, J. A., 11 n. 14, 17, 40 n. 158, 42 n. 173
Ward, W. E., 202 n. 515
Waszink, J. H., 40 n. 160
Watson, D. F., 63 n. 59, 87 n. 181
Wedderburn, A. J. M., 215 n. 585, 241 n. 36, 242 n. 37, 244 n. 52
Weiman, J. A. D., 74 n. 118
Weiss, J., 11 n. 14, 51, 56 n. 23, 71, 78, 87 n. 179
Welborn, L. L., 174 n. 332
Wenham, D., 117, 170
White, J. L., 53 n. 9, 53 n. 11, 55 n. 16, 55 n. 18, 79 n. 154
White, J. R., 9 n. 9, 17 n. 43, 34–36, 39 n. 156, 45–47, 101 n. 243, 111, 221–22, 230
Whiteley, D. E. H., 240
Wilke, C. K., 56 n. 23
Williams, W., 57 n. 29, 120 n. 34
Willis, W., 138 nn. 145–46, 151
Wilson, A. N., 117
Wilson, J. H., 205 n. 523
Wilson, R. McL., 170 n. 308
Winter, B. W., 169 n. 304, 170, 185 n. 390, 187 n. 411, 187 n. 413, 187 n. 416, 188 n. 417, 188 n. 419, 197 n. 477, 198 n. 487
Wire, A. C., 195–96, 203 n. 520
Wiseman, J. A., 154 n. 219
Witherington, B., III, 11 n. 14, 63 n. 59, 64 n. 63, 78 n. 148, 80 n. 160
Wong, E., 201 n. 505
Woodbridge, P., 235 n. 12
Wrede, W., 116
Wright, N. T., 117, 236 n. 14, 253 n. 82
Wroe, A., 133 n. 121
Wuellner, W., 55, 59–62
Yarbro Collins, A., 137 nn. 139–40, 243–44
Zaas, P. S., 184 n. 387, 186 n. 405, 186 n. 408, 187 n. 412
Zerhusen, B., 201 n. 509
Zerwick, M., 93 n. 194, 94 n. 205, 101 nn. 236–37, 103 n. 247, 103 nn. 251–52, 104 n. 253, 105 n. 261, 106 n. 264, 107 n. 273, 107 nn. 275–76

Index of Subjects

Ambrosiaster, 42
Apollos, 173–74, 178–80, 182
apostolic suffering, 35–36, 47, 222
    beasts of Ephesus and, 92, 226, 231
    resurrection and, 91–93
appearances, post-resurrection, 89, 206–7
    objective vs. subjective nature of, 139–41
    Paul's conversion and, 139–43
Apuleius, 153, 163
Aristotle, rhetoric and, 56, 59
Augustine, rhetoric and, 56

baptism
    as antithesis of factionalism, 233
    Catholic, 1, 2, 7
    into Christ's death, 243–44
    death and, 224
    of desire, 7 n. 3, 14
    efficacy of, 14–16, 17–18, 33, 89, 110–11, 247, 249, 254
    effects of, 247–50
    eternal life and, 1, 5–6, 233, 255, 256
    Exodus and, 237–38
    faith and, 245–47
    faith in the resurrection and, 5, 15, 17, 91, 110, 111, 224, 225–26, 232–37, 250–51, 253, 254
    Holy Spirit and, 238–39, 243, 248, 250
    incorporation into Christ and, 236, 244–45, 249, 252, 254, 255
    John the Baptist's, 16, 19, 233
    justification and, 249–50, 252, 254
    kataleptic, 16, 38
    kerygma and, 234, 237, 249, 254
    Mormon, 1–3
    ordinary, 1, 4, 5, 21–31, 110–11, 113, 136, 223, 226–27, 230, 256
        15:29 with punctuation emendations and, 21–25, 43–44; variant readings of 15:29 supporting, 25–28, 44–45
    proleptic, 16, 38
    protection from cosmic powers and, 17–18, 39
    Protestant, 2, 7
    "putting on Christ" and, 245–46, 250
    resurrection and, 14, 111, 226, 233–35, 243–44, 253–56
    sacramentalism and, 13–15, 18, 89
    sacrament of, 7, 45, 111, 230, 251, 254, 256
    theology of, Paul's (*see* baptismal theology of Paul)
    vicarious, 1–4, 10–20, 34, 113, 118, 130, 136, 148–49, 166, 230
        Cerinthian practice of, 41–

42; difficulties with interpreting 15:29 as, 37–39, 86, 166; lack of evidence for, 33 n. 130, 37–38, 167, 221–23, 256; Marcionite practice of, 40–41; syncretism and, 17–20.
See also *baptizō*
baptismal theology of Paul, 5, 12, 20, 49, 228, 229
   1 Corinthians 15:29 and, 250–56
   Galatians and, 244–47
   Pauline literature and, 247–50
   resurrection theology and, 253
   Romans and, 241–44
boasting, 92, 174, 180, 232
body, 212
   sins against the, 187–88
   as temple of the Holy Spirit, 178–79, 188
body of Christ, 195, 238, 249
baptizō, 3, 14, 15, 22–25, 27, 30, 31–32, 35, 36, 44–45, 95–98, 102–103, 107–8, 110, 224, 225, 226, 230–35, 248, 250, 252, 253, 254
Book of Mormon, 2 n. 2,
Book of Doctrine and Covenants, 2 n. 2

catechumens, 12, 14, 32
celibacy, Paul's view of, 189–91
Cephas, 173–74, 206
Cicero, 69, 124, 152
circumcision, 190
Clement of Rome (*1 Clement*), 72, 169 n. 103
conversion, Paul's. *See under* Paul
1 Corinthians
   crises of faith and (*see* Corinthian Christianity)
   as letter, 52–55, 67–69, 77, 83
   as letter-essay, 55, 69–71, 108–9
   literary unity of, 71–81
   partition theories and, 77–83

   as practical letter, 220
   redaction and, 71–76
   rhetoric and, 55–58, 62, 64–67, 70, 77, 78, 87 n. 181 (*see also under* rhetorical categories; rhetorical criticism)
   structure of, 84–90
2 Corinthians
   crises of faith and, 169
   partition theories and, 78
Corinth
   baptismal practice in, 2, 13–17
   belief in cosmic powers in, 17–18, 39
   Greek, 150–52, 157, 159–61
   historical context of, 17–19, 40
   history of, 150–51
   Imperial Games in, 155–56, 161
   Isthmian Games in, 155–56, 161, 193
   religion in, 156–65
      Eastern, 162–63; Greco-Roman, 156–61; Judaism, 157, 163–65; Roman, 161–62
   Roman, 150–51, 153–57, 159–62
   as trading center, 150, 152, 155
Corinthian Christianity
   absence of baptismal crisis in, 218, 227
   crises in, 168–70, 219, 236
   denial of resurrection in, 89–91 *passim*, 94, 106, 108–9, 168, 204–12, 217, 225, 226, 227, 231, 232–33, 236
   ethical issues in, 183–84
   factionalism in, 90, 172–83, 224–25, 232
   gifts of the Spirit and, 180, 197–204
   glossolalia and, 198–203
   idol food and, 191–94

INDEX OF SUBJECTS

immorality in, 184–86
litigiousness in, 186–87
sexual immorality in, 184–88
women in, 195–96
worship and order in, 194–96
Council of Jerusalem, 145, 146
cross, wisdom of the, 174–76

dead, the, 254
  as metaphor of apostolic suffering, 35–36, 47, 222, 231
  treatment of in Corinth, 19–20, 39–40, 167.
  See also *nekros*
death
  baptism and, 224
  Christ as destroyer of, 211
  as last enemy, 210
  to sin, 242–43, 252
  victory over, 217
Diaspora Judaism. *See under* Judaism and Paul
Dionysius of Halicarnassus, 69

egeirō, 106–7
Ephesus, 92, 226, 231
Epicureanism, 92, 231
Epicurus, 69–70
Epiphanius, 41–42
eschatology, 18, 170, 180
eschaton, 170, 197
ethical issues in Corinth. *See under* Corinthian Christianity
Eucharist (Lord's Supper), 193, 195, 196–97

factionalism. *See* Corinthian Christianity

Gaius, 161
Galatians
  baptismal text in, 244–47
  classical rhetoric and, 58, 62–63
glossolalia, 198–203

gnosticism, 18, 169–70

holōs, 21, 26–28, 35, 45, 47, 99–100, 107
Holy Spirit
  agency in resurrection, 239, 243, 253
  and baptism, 238–39, 243, 248, 250
  gifts of the, 180, 197–204
  and spiritual man, 177
  wisdom and the, 176–78,
huper, 4, 22–23, 28, 43–44, 95, 100–102, 103, 108, 110–11, 230
  causal sense, 31–36, 45–47, 101–2, 111
  final sense, 29–31, 45–46, 101, 110

idol food, 138–39, 191–94
imitation, 181, 194, 233
Imperial Games. *See under* Corinth
Isthmian Games. *See under* Corinth

Jerome, 120
John Chrysostom, 24–25, 26 n. 86, 41, 42
Josephus, 28, 127, 131, 133 n. 116, 136, 145
Judaism and Paul
  Cilician, 131–32
  in Corinth, 157
  Diaspora, 119, 123, 126–33, 136, 137, 149, 165
  Palestinian, 115, 128, 129, 130, 132–33, 165
  Pharisaism, 118, 119, 126–27
Julius Caesar, 124, 150–51, 160, 161
justification, 249–50, 252, 254

kerygma, 66, 116 n. 16, 181, 205, 209, 216, 234, 237, 249, 254

letter, literary form of
   1 Corinthians and, 67–71
   rhetoric and, 69, 70
   speech and, 67–69
Lord's Supper. *See* Eucharist
love
   as foundation of imitation, 194
   and gifts of the Spirit, 200–201
   preeminence of, 201
Luke, as source of knowledge about Paul, 114
Luther, Martin, 115, 251

marriage, Paul's view of, 188–91, 195
Melanchthon, Phillip, 56, 251
Menander, 89
   Thais, 93, 119 n. 32, 226, 231
miscarriage, Paul as a, 206
Mithra, 125–26
mystery, 175, 179, 200
   resurrection as, 85, 89–90, 204, 214 n. 577, 216
nekros, 3, 21, 24–28, 29–30, 32, 35, 43, 47, 95, 98–100, 103–5, 110, 111, 230, 239, 251

ordinary baptism. *See under* baptism
Origen, 24, 120

papyri
   Chester Beatty, 71
   Hellenistic, 54
   Oxyrhynchus, 52 n. 3
parousia, 13–14, 18, 215–16, 217, 220, 236, 237, 250
partition theories, 77–83
patristic references to 15:29, 24, 40–42
Paul
   conversion experience of, 118, 137–43, 145
   Hellenistic influences on, 120, 122, 128, 130, 133, 149
   in Jerusalem, 133, 136
   Judaism of, 115–16, 118–23, 126–37 (*see also* Judaism and Paul)
   as a miscarriage, 206
   missionary activity of, 143–47
   as persecutor of Christians, 134–37, 206
   pre-Christian, 118–20, 134
   as Roman, 119–23, 127
Pausanias, 153, 156, 158–59
Pharisee(s)
   Paul as a (*see* Judaism and Paul: Pharisaism)
   resurrection and, 132, 148
Philo, 28, 163, 214 n. 583
Pliny the Younger, 57 n. 26
Plutarch, 69, 153
Pompey, 124, 125
Pseudo-Demetrius, 69
Pseudo-Libanius, 69

redaction and 1 Corinthians, 71–76
religion. *See* Corinth: religion in; Judaism and Paul
resurrected body
   nature of, 211–15
   as sown, 212–13, 214
   as spiritual body, 86, 89, 204, 213
resurrection
   baptism and, 9, 224, 235, 253–56
   communal nature of, 238–39
   Holy Spirit and, 239, 243, 253
   as mystery, 85, 89–90, 204, 214 n. 577, 216
resurrection appearances, 89, 139–42, 206–7
resurrection of believers, 88, 207–8, 253
   as bodily, 213–14
   Corinthian denial of (*see under* Corinthian Christianity)
   first Adam and, 214–15, 239
   second Adam and, 214–15, 239

resurrection of Christ, 205–6
   as bodily, 206–7, 213
   as fact, 85, 88, 89, 204–5, 207
   relation to resurrection of believers, 208–10, 236 (*see also* Corinthian Christianity: denial of resurrection in)
   witness to, 89, 90
   witnesses to, 85, 207
resurrection theology of Paul, 253
rhetorical categories, 56
   absence of in Paul, 56–58, 67
   and 1 Corinthians, 55–56, 58, 62, 64–67, 70 (*see also* 1 Corinthians: rhetoric; rhetorical criticism)
   distinction from epistolography, 56–57
rhetorical criticism, 58–62, 64, 65, 67
   1 Corinthians and, 55–56, 64–67, 77 (*see also* 1 Corinthians: rhetoric; rhetorical categories)
   Galatians and, 58, 61
   postmodern philosophy and, 61–62
   Romans and, 59–60
Romans
   as emphasizing Christ's resurrection, 253
   primary baptismal text and, 241–44, 251
   rhetoric and, 59–60
   textual revisions and, 78–79

Sadducees and resurrection, 24, 132
Seneca, 69
sexual immorality in Corinth, 184–88
Shakespeare, Tarsus in, 124
slavery, 190
Smith, Joseph, 2–3
Sosthenes, 54, 73, 76

Spirit. *See* Holy Spirit
spiritual man vs. unspiritual man, 177
Strabo, 125, 163
Suetonius, 164
syncretism
   in Corinth, 17, 165–66
   Paul and, 165–66
   vicarious baptism and, 17–20, 149

Tarsus
   Caesar and, 124
   of Paul, 124–26, 129–30
   religion in, 125–26
telibah, 137
temple, body as God's, 178–79
Tertullian, 2, 24–25, 40–41, 42
Thais (Menander), 93, 119 n. 32, 226, 231
Titus, 125
toga virilis ceremony, 245

veiling of women, 195
vicarious baptism. *See under* baptism
victory over death, 217, 243

wisdom (divine), 176, 178
   of the cross, 174–76
   spiritual man and, 177
wisdom, human, 174–76, 179
women, role in worship of, 195–96

www.ingramcontent.com/pod-product-compliance
Lightning Source LLC
Chambersburg PA
CBHW021818300426
44114CB00009BA/226